Compliments
of
Southern California
Savings

# Paul Wallach's
# Guide to the Restaurants
# of Southern California

"A witty and wonderful adventure in
more than 1,000 restaurants from hot dogs to haute cuisine."
Including Las Vegas

First Printing

ISBN: 0-932948-030

**American Guide Publications**
P.O. Box 1000
Glendale, California 91209

**AMERICAN GUIDE PUBLICATIONS**
Richard Firth
Vice President-Publications

**Editor:**
Barbara Roisman Cooper

**Associate Editor:**
Adrienne Denny

**Assistants:**
Danna Sigal, Alexandra Buchanan

**Cover Design:**
W. G. Barry

**Typesetting:**
Dynatype, Glendale CA

# ACKNOWLEDGEMENTS

At the risk of making these acknowledgements appear similar to Greer Garson's marathon Academy acceptance speech, there are people I feel I *must* acknowledge. The preparation of this guidebook involved many who gave generously of their time and expertise. My first advisory board helped set the standards. They included:

Melvin Belli
Epicure, attorney

Joe Cerrell
Cerrell and Associates

Hernando Courtright
Proprietor
Beverly Wilshire Hotel

Hon. James E. Cunningham, Sr.
California Superior Court
Member of Chefs de Cuisine

Leland Garrison, M.D.
Oakville Winery

Henri Lewin
Sr. Vice President
Hilton Corp.

Cyril Magnin
Chief of Protocol
City of San Francisco

Neil Morgan
Columnist for San Diego Tribune

Robert Mondavi
Mondavi Vineyards

James Nassikas
President
Stanford Court

Harry G. Serlis
President Emeritus
Wine Institute

Now in its seventh edition, we are grateful for the contributions, direct and indirect, of a great number of people whom I will attempt to list here. Obviously, when so many are involved there will be a few inadvertent omissions.

Herb Baus, Fred Beaton, Norman Bogner, Judith Child, Craig Claiborne, Geoff Edwards, Burt Hixson, Jackie Joseph, Alexis Lichine, Jackie Olden, Sgt. Ted Oglesby LAPD, Ardison Phillips, Ronnie Schell, Peter Sichel.

ABOUT MERRILL SHINDLER...

The reviews bylined "MS" have been written by Merrill Shindler, a fine restaurant critic whose work appears on a regular basis in the Los Angeles *Herald Examiner*, *Los Angeles Magazine* and other major publications.

If there is an art to restaurant reviewing—and I believe there is—it is to write subjectively and objectively at the same time, an apparent improbability. But I have learned that readers of this Guide want to know *who* is speaking to them, little insights that reveal the critic's personal reactions to restaurants and food. The objectivity comes into play when the critic writes about restaurants he may not personally enjoy—but must describe in fairness to those who may be interested in just that type of food, decor and more.

Shindler describes himself as a "big, old, hungry boy" whose test of any restaurant is whether or not you have licked your plate clean. This is an uncharacteristically modest statement. Shindler knows more about restaurants—particularly Oriental and Mid-Eastern, than most writers I know. He visits restaurants anonymously and insists on paying for his meals.

With this issue we are delighted to present the restaurant reviews of Merrill Shindler who brings balance, wit and incisive reporting to this Guide.

Special acknowledgement to Hugh Carpenter, our advisor on Chinese food and restaurants. Mr. Carpenter was a student of Chinese history at Dartmouth College and a graduate student at the University of Michigan. A lecturer and instructor, Mr. Carpenter's major work, *Chinese Cooking for Everyone*, is in the finishing stages.

Mr. Shinobu Ishizuka, our advisor on Japanese restaurants, is the author and publisher of *Guide to Japanese Food and Restaurants in Southern California*.

# CONTENTS

Mr. Paul Wallach, President
Paul Wallach Enterprises, Inc.
The Biltmore Hotel
515 South Olive, Suite 1317
Los Angeles, California 90013

Dear Paul:

As Mayor of Los Angeles, I have the honor to receive guests from all over the world. It has given me the greatest pleasure, during my term of office, to accept from the city a growing number of compliments on its outstanding cuisine. You, of all people, appreciate the vast variety of restaurants here, offering visitors something they can't get everywhere: adventure in dining.

But, in order to fully enjoy what these restaurants have to offer, visitors—and natives alike—need some kind of intelligent guide to the region's culinary riches. Your *Guide to the Restaurants of Southern California* fills the bill. In providing for the discriminating diner the information he or she needs to satisfy palate and pocketbook, it does the City of Los Angeles and its important restaurant industry a very valuable service.

Congratulations on the new restaurant guide, and keep up the good work.

Sincerely,

*Tom Bradley*

TOM BRADLEY
MAYOR

TB: bfm

# FOREWORD

## by Ralph Story

In the beginning, they say, someone tilted our continent and gently shook it. Everything loose, everyone who didn't fit the prim and proper pattern of East and Midwest, came tumbling to the West Coast where they are still milling about smartly. These Yanquis were superimposed (and it was an imposition) on the elegant and easy-living Californios who had struggled north from New Spain to rescue this dusty Eden from the exploring Russians and Englishmen. The original Pobladores simply moved in on the placid, berry-picking, basket-weaving Shoshone Indians and introduced them to Christianity, alcohol and disease. Recent evidence indicates the Shoshones may have displaced some tall, blonde predecessors, but that only proves that history repeats. These great migrations, so legendary in story and so picturesque on film, were really just a lot of misfits looking for more scheming space. Each new wave of migrants took advantage of the people already here and then sold some of it to everyone who followed. And one of them was the author of this book.

Paul Wallach has asked me to explain Southern California in a few brief paragraphs on the premise that some transient, wondering where to eat and picking up this prestigious tome, might also be baffled by the modes and mores of this bizarre territory — and probably wonder what the hell to wear to dinner here. But it's not easy to put this land of fruits and nuts into a nutshell, even though that's where it belongs. I have a library of books and articles on the subject of Los Angeles and I've spent thirty years on radio and television reporting its peculiarities, yet it still eludes my grasp. It is so diverse and perverse, so contradictory and conglomerate, so fluid and ridiculous and funky and dumb, it's delightful. But indescribable. So the best I can do is just pass along a few hints to help you get along here and then let you do your own scheming.

TRANSPORTATION. There isn't any. So buy, rent, or borrow a car. Or call up anybody you ever heard of who lives here and sponge. Bus tours of movie stars homes, Universal Studios, Disneyland, Knott's Berry Farm, etc. are fine and they'll probably use up all your money so you can go away happy.

RELIGION. Most Californians prefer to worship in the faith of their fathers: Astrology. Reading the Yellow Pages under "Churches" is certainly inspiring. Most of the migrating misfits wanted to try a new approach to God so starting your own cult was stylish. Meditation is popular but a Redemption Center is a Green Stamp Store.

POLITICS. This area is run by a couple dozen men who belong to the California Club. They do nothing to their disadvantage but it's a respectable operation. Don't try to categorize politicos as Democrats or Republicans. Most of them are Whigs. And they don't fix tickets. It's easier to get a zoning variance.

SPORTS. Los Angeles is the Sports Capital of the world, but only if you mean do-it-yourself participation sports. Every able-bodied man, woman, and child in the area is doing something non-productive but physically gratifying. Swimming is probably number one but sitting around and discussing what to do is a close second.

ARCHITECTURE. A delicious ethnic mix plus the efforts of unscrupulous developers have produced many variations in style, but the underlying motif is Corinthian Cardboard. Cheap and easy to dismantle, it was borrowed from motion picture studios whose sets look much more real than Los

Angeles itself. Doughnuts, hot dogs, derbies and upended matchboxes are favorite shapes for buildings.

CLIMATE. Fires in the fall, floods in the winter, winds in the spring, heat in the summer and earthquakes on call year-round. Generally, it will be hotter in the daytime and colder at night than you expect it to be. Smog is all-year now, but the Indians used to call this the "Bay of Smokes," so not much has changed.

CLOTHING. Clothes here are not worn to keep warm or show how much money you have. Looking inconspicuous is the whole point. Anything can be worn anywhere and the most ordinary gathering here would look like a costume party anywhere else. No hats, no ties, no gloves, no bras. And no mink stoles and no cameras.

MANNERS. Californians are open and friendly to the point of not giving a damn. Due to fast food chains, most young-sters don't use knives and forks until they're in their teens. Most people mumble because nobody's listening. The best way to start a conversation is to ask, "What's your sign?"

CULTURE. Art, music, fads and sex all flourish in this salubrious environment. Nobel prize-winners abound and the cutting edges of fashion in many fields surround you. However, Woody Allen says our only contribution to culture is the right turn on the red light. Woody, of course, is New York's only contribution to culture.

DOWNTOWN. This very midwestern term for the center of the city has special importance. Half a million people commute to work there each day but the other nine and a half million who live within two hours' drive of Downtown consider it very stylish never to go there. You will probably spend your time in the other 460-odd square miles of the County but some very fascinating experiences await the brave tourist who actually explores downtown Los Angeles.

FOOD. The Caesar Salad, the Margarita, the French-Fried Onion Ring and the Alfalfaburger were all invented here. However, the one word which best describes all Southern California cuisine is: sloppy. Most dishes dribble and the many deep-fat-fried foods are dipped into sauces so they dribble, too. The amalgam of Midwest and Mexican food is fattening fun but the finer points of all the wonderful places to gorge yourself comprise the rest of this book.

Perhaps I should add that both Mr. Wallach and I, being somewhat rootless, were also shaken loose and tumbled to the west coast some time ago. But we are now natives. Anyone who has been here sixty days and still has sixty dollars is a native. But this requires us to squeeze our own orange juice, rave about the weather, joke about the smog, ignore San Francisco, cheer for the Dodgers, read Jack Smith's column, barbecue all our food, pretend we have a swimming pool, lease a car, and stay away from downtown Los Angeles. Still, we must also boost Los Angeles, so I trust that my analysis of our locale will not be taken as criticism. Perhaps you should take this introduction just as you will take everything else you find in this book . . . with a dash of salt.

# INTRODUCTION
By Paul Wallach

My love affair with restaurants began when I was six years old and my father became the house physician for the Ambassador Hotel in Los Angeles. It was a lonely existence for a boy—the then-luxurious hotel tolerated no other children—and I found my only friends and happiness in the clattering, chattering, behind-the-scenes world of the busy kitchens, where I was immediately adopted by cooks and dishwashers, pantrymen and meat-cutters. After a while, I was allowed to set the tables in the banquet rooms, stir the stockpots and taste the Béarnaise and bordelaise sauces. The huge baker, his florid face dusted with flour, baked special cookies for me. The majestic chef would carry me on his shoulders during his inspection tour of the cooking area, rumbling things to me like, "What you think, little pigeon, is that souffle (or ice carving or salad dressing or duckling) *ready* for our people?"

My best friend was a Filipino apprentice, scarcely bigger than I and a superb mimic. We used to sneak into the private rooms favored by wine and food societies, and as the distinguished-looking guests would raise their glasses, my friend would ape each expression—the quivering nostrils, the closed, rapt eyes, the pursing of lips, the sage nods of approval—so perfectly that I was reduced to uncontrollable giggling and had to be dragged away to escape detection.

On those occasions when I joined my family for dinner in the main salon, my friends would pretend—except in little undetectable ways—not to know me. The maitre d' pinched me—hard—on the rear when I came in, and both of us maintained a straight face. Nor did I crack up when the filling in my baked potato turned out to be neither butter nor sour cream but *bavarois au marasquin* (my favorite cream dessert) nor when my souffle Grand Marnier had a grotesque cross-eyed face embroidered with *dragees* (sugar-coated bits of fruit). These eccentric, wonderful people were my friends, and I loved them.

I still do, and as a restaurant critic, I am unashamedly prejudiced in favor of the profession. As Oscar Wilde said: "A critic cannot be fair in the ordinary sense of the word. It is only about things that do not interest one that one can give a really unbiased opinion, which is, no doubt, the reason why an unbiased opinion is absolutely valueless."

My bias does not extend to the indifferent restaurateur. Like you, I deplore dirty menus, warm salads, poor service, watery cocktails and overcharging, to mention merely a few of the potential hazards of restaurant roulette that can exasperate the mind as well as the digestive process.

The profession of restaurant writer or critic is a relatively new one. By "critics," incidentally, I do *not* mean the free-loading "restaurant writers" of most newspapers and magazines who are, first and foremost, advertising salesmen. Their columns directly reflect, in space and enthusiasm, the amount of advertising dollars spent by the individual restaurants, or worse, the bribes (both under and on the table) they receive for the phony accolades—the "tasties" and "yummies" and "fantastics"—they hand out to their sponsors.

For the most part, restaurants have successfully dodged objective evaluation and criticisms. When you buy a set of tires or a pair of skis or a hearing aid, you can consult any one of several impartial rating guides from popular magazines to consumer digests. When you want to go to a movie or a play, you can read reviews beforehand in the daily press—before you invest in a $5 ticket. But if you're looking for a neighborhood pizzeria—or $100-a-couple *haute cuisine*—you have virtually no reliable guide to differentiate excellence from mediocrity. This, in spite of the fact that a recent study shows that $2 out of every $5 spent for food in California is spent in restaurants.

The restaurant ratings in this guide are based upon a complex system that takes into account every detail of the dining experience related to the premise of the particular restaurant—specifically, what it is trying to achieve. It would be unfair to measure seven different kinds of restaurants against one set of inflexible criteria, just as it is unfair to criticize the size of the wine list at a small restaurant when that restaurant quite properly offers the limited selection it can afford. My ratings, initially in the form of staff reports, were submitted to the distinguished advisory committee who serve as a blue ribbon jury, before I made the final decisions. It is the fairest method we can use.

Unlike most rating systems, mine accords considerable recognition to the smaller, less pretentious (but no less admirable) restaurateur along with the more familiar superstars. This book includes a wide range of restaurants. Like most restaurant writers, I've traveled the *haute cuisine* route and earned my ribbons. One of the early Paris critics commented, "Maxim's is perfection. Perfection can become a bore." Well, I don't totally agree. We have not been exposed to all that much perfection. The grand restaurants can still create the grand experience. However, it's the unexpected, undiscovered cafe—often concealed by a shabby storefront—that can provide that rare, rich adventure of which memories and cocktail conversations are made.

In the years since I became the restaurant critic for *Westways*, and on my KIEV talk radio program, I've learned a great deal about what you want—and need—to know. Tangible evidence of the need for this kind of guide is the tremendous amount of mail I get, letters that share comments and criticisms, suggestions, agreements and disagreements. I value that confidence above everything. I hope this *1982 Guide to the Restaurants of Southern California* will serve you well. Use it in good appetite.

# TIPS ON DINING OUT

**When you plan to visit a restaurant for the first time**, and it is an important occasion, you should arrange an advance call on the establishment to study the turf. The evening will be less of an obstacle course if you are familiar with the menu, the prices, the policies and the wine list. Besides, you are probably making a substantial investment, and it's not prudent to buy blindly.

**If yours is a party of four or more** you might consider pre-ordering the entire dinner. Your guests will be pleased by your thoughtfulness and you will avoid the awkward time when everyone is studying the menu and trying to hear what everyone else is ordering. You may arrange to have substitutions in the event Uncle Charlie is allergic— one man's meat may be another man's *poisson*. This foresight will enable a restaurant staff to better prepare each dish and choreograph the service.

Should you make **a reservation** and, for some reason find yourself unable to keep it, for heaven's sake call and cancel. Many still cling to the fear that the restaurant will roar in anger or, at the very least, acidly acquiesce. Nothing (well, hardly anything) could be farther from the truth. They will be pleased that you were considerate enough to call. There may be patrons waiting restlessly, staring dramatically at your empty table.

**If you are just running late**, a call to the maître d' will allow him to juggle the tables to accommodate. If you simply show up a half hour late your table may be gone, you'll be furious, and the restaurant will be upset.

You should be aware, and thus more tolerant, of the **problems the restaurant has in accepting reservations**. Often people will over-stay, tying up a table for hours and making your eight o'clock reservation impossible to arrange. (The maître d' can't very well push the dawdlers out the door, although he'd probably like to.) Another common

21

complaint by visitors without a reservation is that they were turned away "even though," as letters to me often rage, "there were several empty tables staring me in the face." Actually those tables were probably reserved by other parties and the fact that the restaurant holds them is a mark of integrity.

If you are served **a dish that is obviously wrong**—spoiled or curdled sauce, stringy or fat meat, cold soup, etc.—do not hesitate to send it back. It is neither rude nor inconsiderate. You should, however, be prepared to *precisely* explain your objection. Any restaurant of integrity will whisk away the offending dish and suggest either an alternative or a replacement.

Restaurateurs, when hearing a complaint related through a third party, often groan with exasperation. They'd much prefer to keep you as a customer by correcting the real (or imagined) error. The prospect of customers walking out muttering malevolently ("I ain't never coming back to this joint") is an operator's nightmare.

If you've had unusually **good—or bad—service, you should write a letter**. Most restaurants are starved for recognition and a complimentary letter may place you permanently in their hall of fame. (Waiter to kitchen: "It's that Mr. Heppledockler who wrote to us.")

A letter of complaint, if it's intelligent and precise (not just splitting enraged hairs), will often be appreciated more than the compliment. The professional restaurateurs I know tell me such letters are more valuable than accolades—praise is nice, but they can't improve with it.

**Don't get smashed before dinner**. I hate to shatter a comfortable myth, but most restaurants *don't* try to detour you over to the lounge to hike up the booze bill. Most would prefer that you not anesthetize your palate with more than two cocktails.

**Don't over-order**. Everything looks good when you're hungry, and there's always a tendency to order an eleven course marathon when a salad and an entrée would have sufficed.

**Don't order your dinner in increments**. "We'll order the soup now and decide on the entrée later," throws the kitchen into turmoil because they cannot coordinate the timing of each course. Dessert may be ordered after dinner, with one exception. If you want a soufflé it is a good idea to let your waiter know immediately. Some take up to an hour to prepare properly.

And do have some **feeling for the restaurant people**. Most try very hard to please you. Most restaurateurs are unflappable: the parking lot attendant may be ricocheting the Rolls, the kitchen ceiling may be leaking, the chef may be rendered *hors de combat* by lean broilerman who has finally erupted, and the freshly laundered napkins may have been lost, but he (or she) will not flutter an eyelash. It is an impossible, absurd, insane business hounded by bureaucracy and a million variables that can be the difference between success and failure. Most who work in restaurants are not primarily motivated by money and many have spent their youth apprenticed to the kitchen. The pride and the sense of satisfaction after a busy night is a great reward to the staff and it's helpful if you are on the same wavelength.

## ON DINING ALONE

Some of my richest experiences have occurred on the infrequent occasions when I have dined alone. I do not, of course, refer to efficient, hurried meals, the sole purpose of which is to fulfill our obligation to the stomach. What I have in mind is a leisurely appointment with one's self to savor special foods—perhaps an extravagant delicacy—with simple dignity.

It has been written with Lucullus, the Roman consul famous for his lavish feasts, decided one night to dine alone. He noticed the sauces were a touch indifferent and the fowl less succulent than usual. When summoned, his major-domo explained he thought there was no need to prepare a banquet "for just my lord alone."

"It is precisely when I am alone," the great epicurean

replied, "that you will take special care. At such times you must remember that Lucullus dines with Lucullus."

You are dining alone. If it is your intention to have a fine leisurely dinner, it is important that you let the restaurant know your plans in advance.

When placing the reservation, indicate, "I will be dining alone this evening, but I'm looking forward to a fine dinner. Please seat me at a comfortable table." Failure to do this may allow the maître d' to reach the understandable—if mistaken—conclusion that you are traveling alone and simply want to be refueled.

If you are shown to a table that is unsatisfactory (too close to the kitchen or to a service center), you should politely decline the table. Inform the host that you are willing to wait a bit longer, if necessary, to obtain a better table.

When you are seated, indicate to your captain that you are indeed looking forward to dinner at the restaurant and ask him for his recommendation. This also tells him that you expect good service and appeals to his sense of pride. Always find a way to ask his name. "I may be returning here again, and I want to be sure I know whom to ask for," is a polite way of getting the information. It also, gently, puts him on notice that you consider him the responsible party.

Take your time over both the menu and the wine list. Consult with your waiter and/or captain. Ask questions. Your concern with your dinner will be communicated to the staff and will generally bring you the best service the establishment has to offer.

It is quite common for a single diner to feel conspicuous and self-conscious. Thus some diners' process of placing the order is perfunctory, as though it were a ritual to be hastily concluded. The restaurant personnel feel that if you don't care, why should they?

When dining in unfamiliar cities at a new restaurant, I enjoy settling back and observing the patrons and the service. We all of us have the habit of fantasy. Dining alone can be marvelously entertaining.

**When a woman dines alone**, it brings up a few unique but conquerable problems. She should definitely reach an understanding with the maitre d' at the time she places the reservations. "I will be dining alone this evening, and I know that some restaurants do not like to serve a woman who dines alone. Your restaurant has been recommended to me." This introduction to the establishment will almost guarantee the pampering you deserve and the extra special attention it requires. After all, you might be a restaurant writer or the public relations director of a large company. Again, you should involve the restaurant in your total experience. When arriving at the desk, you should tell the maitre d' that you would like a lovely table to observe his restaurant. Consult with the captain about each individual dish you are considering, and take particular pains to talk with the wine steward. When the wine arrives, make sure that you follow the ritual and take a few seconds to inhale the aroma, take a little sip, and then—if acceptable—nod to the server, indicating permission to fill your glass. It is often more comfortable to request wine at the outset so you aren't sitting like a statue awaiting your first course.

I would like to emphasize the importance of working with the restaurant and letting them know your plans. Failure to do so makes you fair game.


## TIPPING MADE EASY

As a restaurant authority I've often been asked to appear before groups. Invariably during the question and answer period the subject most frequently mentioned is tipping.

I have begun to suspect that tipping might rate just below adultery or moral rearmament as a national concern. Reasonable men and women seem to dissemble in a restaurant.

Audiences tell me that a good portion of their deals are made in restaurants and yet they have trouble concentrating. They're constantly wondering who to tip, when to tip, how much to tip, how to tip, who's waiting on them, who the captain is, and more. When I suggest that 99% of all their tipping problems can be solved by uttering a single sentence their eyebrows raise like a field of brown butterflies taking off.

Tipping in America has always been shrouded in mystery. Even the act of giving the tip has become somewhat like a Masonic handshake. You "slip" the tip to the head waiter. You hide the tip under the plate. And for some silly reason you think it rude to ask how much to tip. But sillier yet are the restaurant people who rely on gratuities for their livelihood and still shy away from that question, mumbling something about, "Whatever you feel is fair, sir." Balderdash! We need to know the cost of things if we're going to pay for them. But I digress.

The single sentence I alluded to that will not only solve your tipping problems but save you money as well is:

**"KINDLY ADD 15% TO THE NET AMOUNT OF MY BILL AND SEE THAT IT IS DISTRIBUTED TO THE PEOPLE WHO WAITED ON ME."**

The reason for specifying the "net" amount is to avoid paying gratuity on top of taxes, something we all do.

In a splendid restaurant, you may want to tip 20%. If the experience warrants.

# HOW TO USE THIS GUIDE

The restaurants selected for this guide are listed alphabetically (with the exception of the Las Vegas headings which are in back of the book).

Just as many of the rules of etiquette are obsolete, so are the ways in which guide books are alphabetized. Technically, "Le Restaurant" should be filed under "R," but *you* don't think of it that way, so we start out with the first letter of the restaurant's full title. The only exception to this rule would be restaurants that start with the English word "The."

All the categories appear in the back of the book. Obviously no guide will list all the restaurants that deserve to be listed. I make the selections based upon a geographical, economic and "worth" basis.

Each listing contains the restaurant name, street address and map number plus all the data as to days and hours, credit cards, price, etc. Restaurants are rated from zero to three stars.

## RATING SYSTEM

Stars are awarded and restaurants are judged primarily on what the restaurant purports to be. If a restaurant says it is a veritable temple of *haute cuisine* it will be judged on that basis and its success or failure indicated.

I'm convinced that a hamburger restaurant that is among the best in the nation deserves as much recognition as a more complicated operation. Cassell's, a hamburger place in Los Angeles, makes its own mayonnaise, buys its beef in special lots in Colorado and even bakes its buns to specification. Surely Smitty works as hard as, say Peter Jepson at the Cove, a more sophisticated restaurant.

The ratings:

Zero stars: This may mean it is not recommended, although it could be part of a dining adventure in which food is less important than the overall experience.

One star ★: Good, above average, approaching excellence.

Two stars ★★: Excellent.

Three stars ★★★: Among the best in the nation.

DA: Dining Adventure is determined by all the component parts that add up to an experience that extends beyond just the food itself. DA may or may not be used in combination with stars, since it's a separate rating.

Stars are awarded with the help of an advisory committee. Every restaurant in this book has been contacted and all the information has been verified. Mistakes do occur, but we call each restaurant just before press time to make sure we are as accurate as possible.

## MAPS

See pages 30 to 39. Each is numbered and the map number appears in the restaurant listing. The maps in this book give you general area guidance and will often obviate the need to consult a road map. A missing map number means the restaurant is located beyond the boundaries of the maps in the book and you may want to consult a road map of Santa Barbara, Ventura, San Diego County, Palm Springs or Las Vegas.

There's a rumor that no matter where you are in the Los Angeles area, no place is more than twenty minutes from your home, hotel or the service station from which you've received directions. While that rumor is sometimes true,

28

there are times when the restaurant you have chosen is far enough away to make it prudent to pack your toothbrush. It is not our intention to discourage such trips; but, neither do we want you to feel you've been taken for a ride by our recommendations.

## PRICES

It is virtually impossible to come up with a simple price formula. A $5 breakfast may be inexpensive at a hotel dining room and expensive in Jack in the Box. Prices have been translated into one of three categories as an opener for the data.

**Inexpensive:** $7 or less for dinner.

**Moderate:** from $7 to $14.

**Expensive:** Don't expect to get away for less than $25 per person.

### Dress Description

Resort—Leisure activity clothes appropriate to area and activity.

Casual—Men in sportshirts; women in slacks and jeans, but no bare feet or bathing suits.

Semi-dressy—Men in sportscoats (not necessarily ties); women in after-five dresses or pantsuits.

Dressy—Men in coat and tie; women in semiformal or formal.

### Credit Cards Accepted:

AX-American Express     MC—Master Card
CB—Carte Blance     Visa
DC—Diners Club

## Southern California Area Map

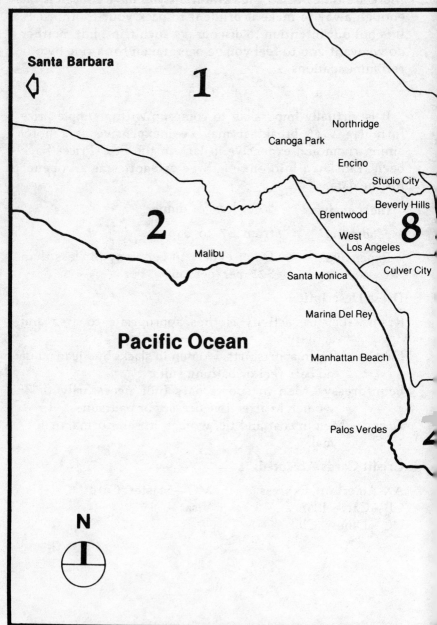

Santa Barbara

**1**

Northridge

Canoga Park

Encino

Studio City

Beverly Hills

Brentwood

**2**

West
Los Angeles

Malibu

**8**

Santa Monica

Culver City

Marina Del Rey

**Pacific Ocean**

Manhattan Beach

Palos Verdes

N

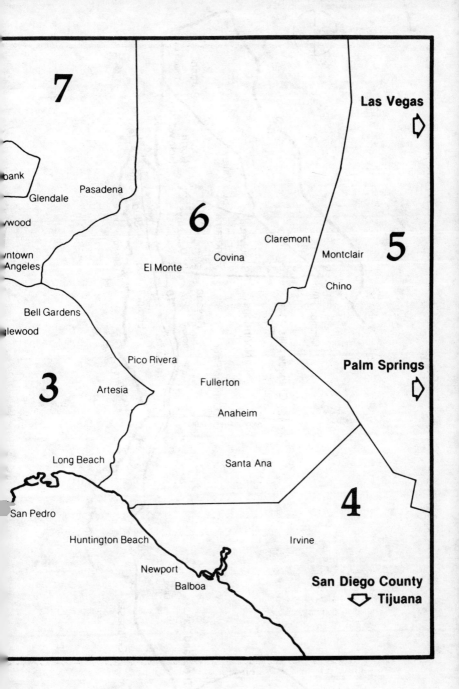

7

bank
Glendale   Pasadena
wood
ntown
Angeles

6

Claremont
El Monte   Covina   Montclair   5
Chino

Bell Gardens
lewood

Pico Rivera
3   Artesia   Fullerton
Anaheim

Long Beach   Santa Ana

San Pedro   4

Huntington Beach   Irvine

Newport
Balboa   San Diego County
Tijuana

Las Vegas

Palm Springs

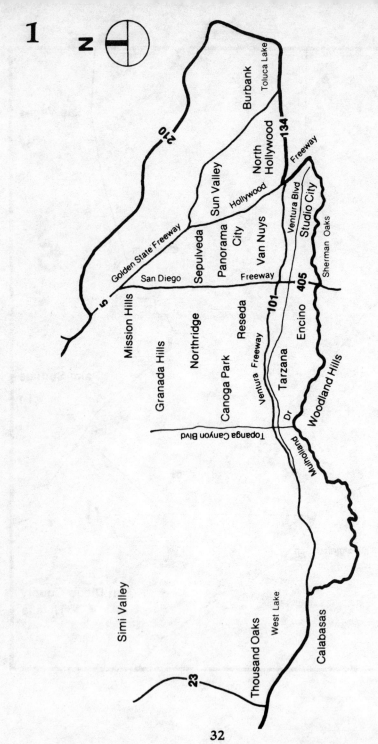

**1**

N

Burbank
Toluca Lake
210
North Hollywood
134
Freeway
Sun Valley
Hollywood
Ventura Blvd
Studio City
Sepulveda
Panorama City
Van Nuys
Golden State Freeway
Sherman Oaks
San Diego
Freeway
405
5
101
Mission Hills
Reseda
Encino
Granada Hills
Northridge
Tarzana
Canoga Park
Ventura Freeway
Woodland Hills
Dr
Topanga Canyon Blvd
Mulholland
Simi Valley
West Lake
23
Thousand Oaks
Calabasas

32

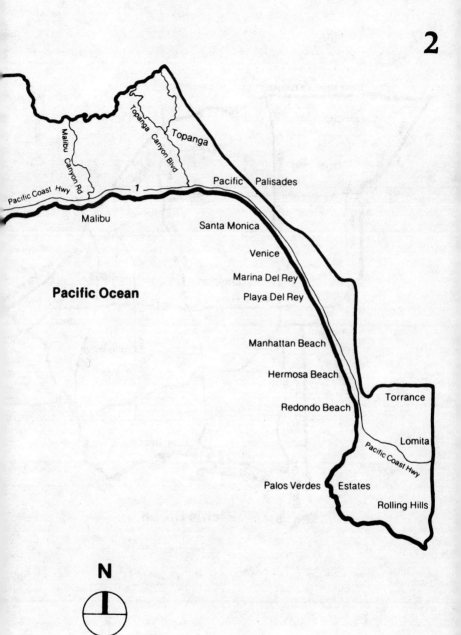

Malibu Canyon Rd

Topanga Canyon Blvd

Topanga

Pacific Coast Hwy

1

Pacific Palisades

Malibu

Santa Monica

Venice

Marina Del Rey

Playa Del Rey

**Pacific Ocean**

Manhattan Beach

Hermosa Beach

Torrance

Redondo Beach

Lomita

Pacific Coast Hwy

Palos Verdes Estates

Rolling Hills

N

N

Santa Monica Freeway

Culver City

San Diego Freeway

10

Maywood

Bell

Ingelwood

Bell Gardens

Harbor Freeway

Manchester Ave

405

Long Beach Freeway

Downey

Hawthorne Blvd

5

Santa Ana Freew

11

Compton

605

7

Artesia Freeway

91

Artesia

Lakewood Blvd

Lakewood

Pacific Coast Hwy

1

San Pedro

Long Beach

**Pacific Ocean**

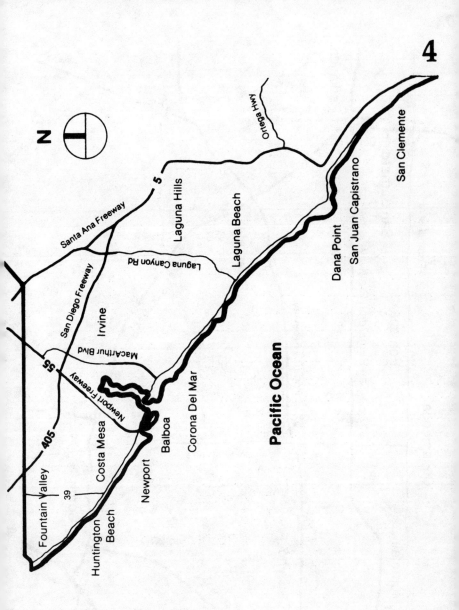

**4**

N

Ortega Hwy

Santa Ana Freeway

5

Laguna Hills

Laguna Beach

Laguna Canyon Rd

San Diego Freeway

Irvine

MacArthur Blvd

55

Newport Freeway

405

Fountain Valley

39

Costa Mesa

Huntington Beach

Newport

Balboa

Corona Del Mar

Dana Point

San Juan Capistrano

San Clemente

**Pacific Ocean**

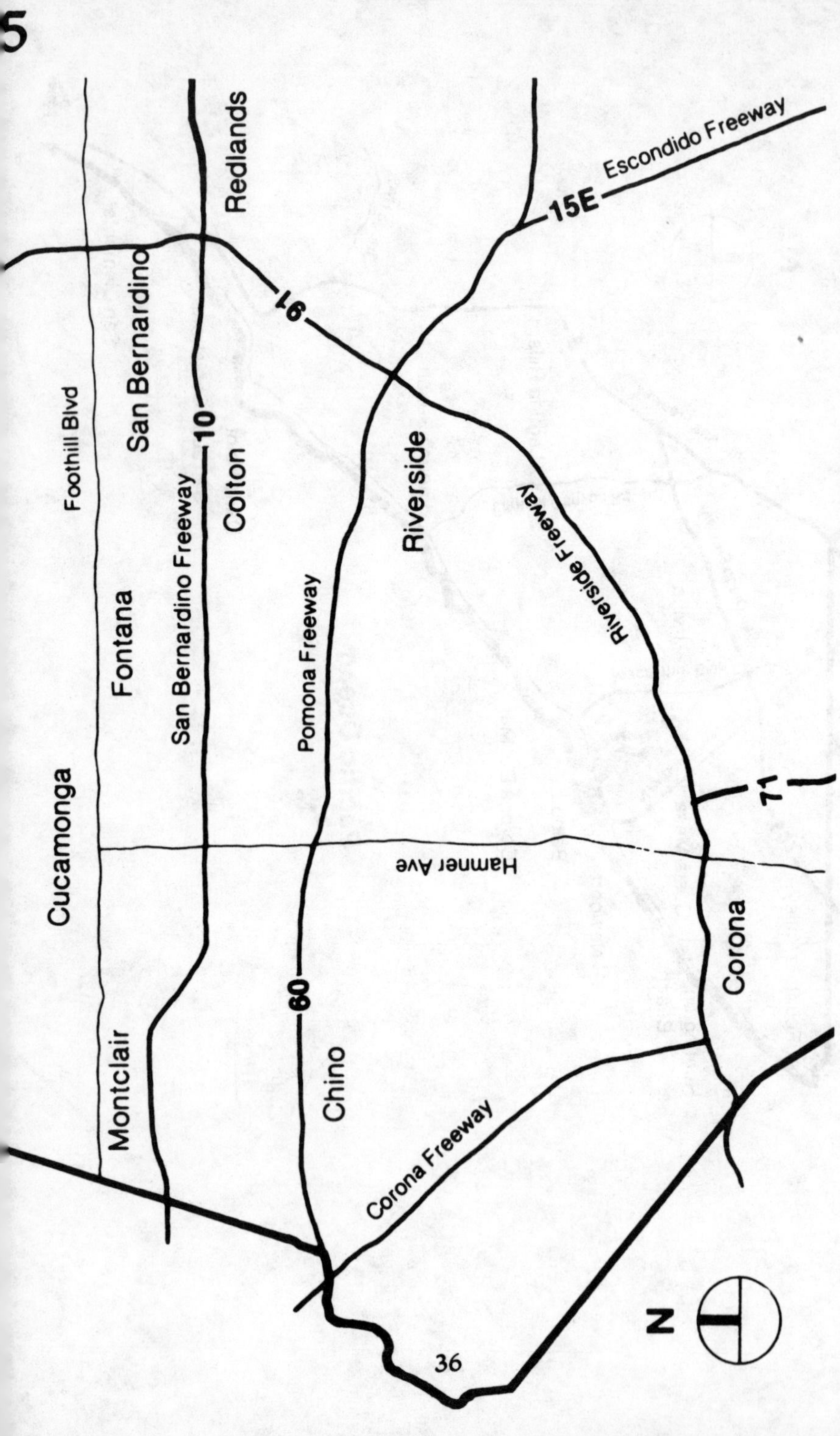
5
Redlands
Escondido Freeway
15E
San Bernardino
91
Foothill Blvd
10
Colton
Riverside
Riverside Freeway
San Bernardino Freeway
Fontana
Pomona Freeway
Cucamonga
71
Hamner Ave
Corona
60
Montclair
Chino
Corona Freeway
N

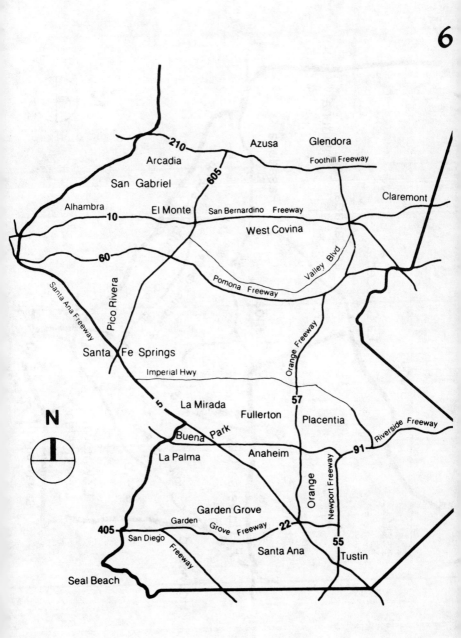

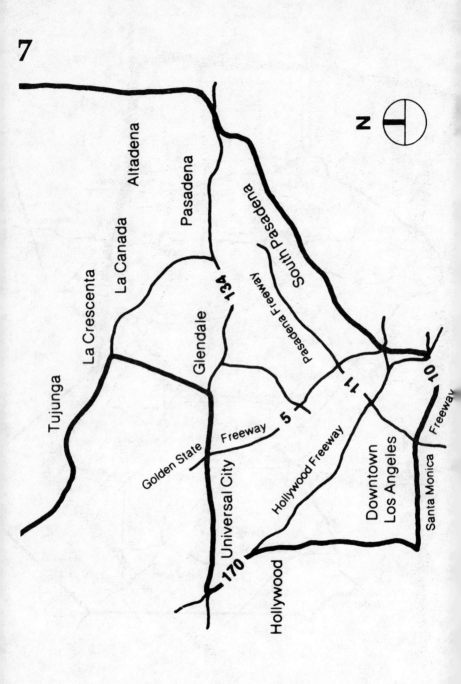

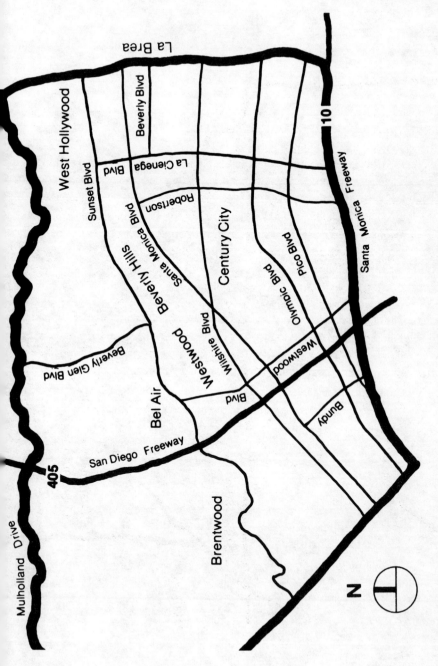

## ACAPULCO Y LOS ARCOS RESTAURANTS
**Mexican**

(Locations in Anaheim, Arcadia, Beverly Hills, Burbank, Encino, Escondido, Garden Grove, Glendale, Long Beach, Pasadena, Santa Ana, Santa Clara, Sun Valley and Westwood. See phone book for listings.)

Raymond Marshall proved that a young man from a small farming town in the east can find happiness as owner/chef of a thriving chain of Mexican restaurants in the west. Don't expect only authentic Mexican dishes. Ray is constantly concocting dishes for culinary contests. He wins a lot. So do his more adventuresome patrons. His crabmeat enchilada with his own tortilla is a winner, but I urge you to try other items from the expanded menu—now 18 pages instead of 14. I sneak previewed his cold avocado soup.

Look for it on the menu or ask about it. All restaurants serve from the same menu. Two have patio service— Encino and Escondido. Banquet facilities are available at Garden Grove.

**Inexpensive.** Open seven days. Closed Thanksgiving, Christmas. Hours and prices may vary at each location. No reservations. Full bar. Casual.

---

## ADAGIO
**Continental**
**★★**
5259 Melrose Avenue
Los Angeles  **Map 7**  (213) 465-8250

Most of us tend to hoard the special "little" discoveries. We astonish our friends—"You mean there is a restaurant *there*?"—and confound visiting New Yorkers who prattle on about their quaint little places. As a restaurant critic, I tend to shy away from such little delights on the theory that too much publicity will shatter their delicate structure and ruin the dining adventure for the very people who tout it to me. About Adagio, however, I have no such concern because this fine hideaway is insulated from the restaurant wobblies by layers of professionalism and good taste.

Adagio meets my criteria for a special favorite. It is (a) improbably located in the unchic part of Melrose, near Hollywood: (b) the kind of restaurant that can become a trusted friend, greeting and caring for you in a manner to impress your guests: and (c) full of surprises.

Ron Berenstein runs his place as near perfection as he can without breaking down. The look is his own statement, and he has transformed two rundown storefronts into a 70-seat charmer.

Berenstein admits to having been mesmerized by a dusty rose-hued color chip in a paint store, and his restaurant is unrelentingly dusty rose with the exception of the raw brick wall he discovered under layers of plaster. Tables and booths are set comfortably amid plush greenery, fresh flowers and high-ceilinged spaciousness.

Most à la carte entrées are under $10, and the hand-written menu may (or may not) include sliced duck with pepper game sauce, fresh veal scallops in a light champagne sauce, breast of chicken with fresh ginger and cream, or poached stuffed trout with a special lobster sauce.

Desserts are baked on the premises and the zabaglione, frothed tableside, is poured over fresh strawberries.

The wine list is selected with the menu in mind and explores some of the lesser-known California boutiques, along with the expected labels. Service is attentive and professional. Everyone there grew up to be a captain, even the lady. First-timers would do well to listen to the suggestions of the staff.

**Moderate.** Open seven days. Luncheon from 11:30 a.m. to 2:30 p.m. weekdays. Dinner from 5:30 to 10 p.m.; Friday and Saturday to midnight. Beer and wine only. Live entertainment. Reservations required. All major credit cards. Valet parking. Semi-dressy.

---

## ADAM'S                                          American
17500 Ventura Boulevard                              ★★
Encino          **Map 1**                     (213) 990-7427

This razzle dazzle of a restaurant could be the most excitement per square foot of any other restaurant in Southern California if not the universe. It has the *biggest* salad bar—55 feet of amazements. It has the *biggest* back bar in their saloon, over 450 brands, over 50 beers. It has the *most extensive* collection of historical photographs of the San Fernando Valley, 400 at last count, in the area. It has the *only* authentic soda fountain with a real soda jerk. It has the *only*

*In order to obtain the best results from this Guide, please consult "Tips on Dining Out" on page 21.*

bakery inside a restaurant to bake 12 inch layer (try the peanut) cakes. The girls are the prettiest, and more...much more. Almost too much more. If all this sounds like a Robert Morris production (the man who brought you Gladstones, Jetty's and R.J.'s for Ribs), it should. He sold Adam's to Mike Radel who has added a few touches of his own...such as an all-you-can-eat-special. His slow smoked ribs, beef and pork are cooked over oak wood and mesquite charcoal. And the chili is all beef with no beans about it. The seafood is fresh "this day." Fresh vegetables include, in season, corn on the cob, steamed artichokes and hugemongeous (pronounced hewg-mongus) bake potatoes.

To the right of the entrance is the long copper-topped bar and lounge. There's a piano above the back-bar and each of the three piano players is attired in an old-fashioned tuxedo as they grind out pretty good ragtime from 11 a.m. until 2 a.m. The piano serves as a room divider with the long bar and chaise lounges on one side and the dining area, surrounded by the salad bar that serpentines around the room, on t'other. Mike calls this area the "green grocer" and it's colorful with stacks of open crates or oranges, limes, lemons and grapefruit. Useful, too, because Radel insists on using freshly squeezed fruit in all their exotic concoctions and you owe it to yourself to have a fresh fruit—peach, banana or strawberry—daquiri.

This is a happy place to me because it is a celebration of Americana...Yankee food and ingenuity. It's taken us 200 years but we're beginning to respect the American cuisine, unique for its abundance of produce and seafood and fat livestock. Places like Adam's simply didn't exist until a few years ago when the only restaurants that served ribs or chili were the shabby storefronts or diners. Somewhere within the 350 (count them) potted plants there are people having a splendid time without red velvet chairs, tapestries, farcial French headwaiters, condescending sommeliers and menus written in a foreign language.

**Moderate.** Open seven days. Luncheon served weekdays and

Saturday 11:30 a.m. to 4 p.m. Dinner 4 to 10:30 p.m.; Friday and Saturday to 11:30 p.m.; Sunday to 10 p.m. Entertainment. Full bar. Reservations necessary. Visa, MC. No wheelchair access. Parking lot; valet in evenings. Casual.

---

## ADRIANO'S                Italian

2930 Beverly Glen Circle            ★★
Los Angeles     **Map 8**        (213) 475-9807

In that kind of no-man's land, Beverly Glen near Mulholland, we happened on to a restaurant that will probably become one of the darlings of the west side. Adriano Rebora has all the credentials from an apprenticeship at the famed Hotel Excelsior on Lake Como to top culinary management of such cruise ships as the *Leonardo da Vinci* and the *Michelangelo*. That he has brought this fantasy fare ashore is noteworthy. However, it is the stunning decor of the restaurant, improbably situated in a small, smart shopping center, that will excite the gourmets and gourmettes even more. The focal point of the vaulted, two story central area is the brass-trimmed pavilion where foods and wines are displayed. The walls are washed in a kind of pastel peach color and diners in the salon can view the tables on the mezzanine. The Italian cane-back chairs, the rich table settings and the spacious patio enclosed in trimmed hedges create the feeling of the *grand ristorante.* The fare is no less opulent and imaginative. Appetizers include *carpaccio*, paper-thin slices of beef sauced with mustard and pastas are homemade openshelled clams. Rainbow trout is presented with pine nuts and grapes and Adriano's medallions of lamb (*medaglioni d'agnello*) is marvelous. The menu is extensive, the wine list very comprehensive, including—unusual for an authentic Italian restaurant here—a splendid assortment of California wines including

45

some little-known boutique beauties. All desserts are home-made; the *sorbet* is especially piquant when compared to the bland snow-cones we have sampled at other Northern Italian restaurants. The service is that kind of Italian elegance that brings the captain respectfully to the table with gentle explanations and suggestions, instead of the too common imperious and patronizing attitude.

**Expensive.** Open Tuesday through Sunday. Luncheon served Tuesday through Saturday 11:30 a.m. to 2:30 p.m. Dinner Tuesday through Thursday 6 to 10:30 p.m.; Friday and Saturday to 11; Sunday to 10:30 p.m. Sunday brunch 11 a.m. to 3 p.m. Full bar. Reservations required. Patio. Visa, MC, AX. Parking lot. Dressy.

---

## AGOSTINO'S RISTORANTE
23683 Calabasas Road
Calabasas    **Map 1**

Italian
★
(213) 716-7001

Agostino and Alicia Costa have put their hearts and bankroll into Calabasas, an area not exactly rich in restaurants. The cuisine is difficult to pin down and is best sampled at luncheon when a bountiful array of dishes is aligned for a buffet at a modest charge. Specialties are homemade pasta, eastern milk fed veal and fresh fish. Evening service is a little formal for the location, the smartly dressed captains in sharp contrast with the Hawaiian sportshirts of some of the patrons. Agostino agonizes over each dish and you'll likely be quizzed in detail about your dinner, but that's a nice touch in an impersonal era. Entertainment nightly on the gentle side.

**Moderate.** Open for luncheon seven days 11:30 a.m. to 3 p.m. Dinner from 5:30 to 11 p.m. Sunday brunch. Closed Thanksgiving and Christmas. Live music nightly. Full bar. Reservations required. Patio. Visa, MC AX. Wheelchair access. Parking in adjacent shopping center. Dressy.

## AH FONG'S                                        Chinese
8005 Sunset Boulevard
West Hollywood          **Map 7**              (213) 656-2226

16240 Ventura Boulevard
Encino          **Map 1**                      (213) 783-8533

424 North Beverly Drive
Beverly Hills          **Map 8**               (213) 276-1034

1100 Glendon
Westwood          **Map 8**                    (213) 208-3976

Not to be taken seriously this Cantonese cuisine; even with
all the obligatory paper umbrellas in the exotic drinks it's
still just a step above the neighborhood chopsuery in food.
Service can be cranky. If you must—the lemon chicken is
the best on the menu. Owned by Benson Fong, Charlie
Chan's number one son, who can occasionally be seen
greeting special guests.

**Inexpensive to moderate.** Open from noon to 11 p.m.
weekdays; to midnight Saturday; 4 to 11 p.m. Sunday.
Closed Thanksgiving, Christmas. Full bar. Reservations
recommended. Visa, MC. No wheelchair access. Parking
lot; valet parking. Semi-dressy.

## AHIHEI                                          Japanese
3622 West Third Street                                 ★
Los Angeles          **Map 7**                 (213) 385-2536

Ahihei may be the only Japanese restaurant of any sort in
the whole world that doesn't serve tea. I don't know why it

*For best results, consult "How to Use This Guide" on page 27.*

doesn't, but it doesn't. So, since I couldn't have tea, I substituted the next most Japanese drink on the menu, which turned out to be 7-up, which went very well with Ahihei's many very tasty noodle dishes. Ahihei consists of a noodle bar and several booths against a wall. Behind the counter the noodle cooks dash about the kitchen wearing t-shirts that say "Ramen Fever." The selection of noodles is very much like that at Sapporo-Ya: there are *ramen* noodle soup dishes that can be eaten plain or flavored with soy sauce or bean curd, and topped with pork or bamboo shoots or butter or seaweed. As at Sapporo-Ya, the bowls of *ramen* are so large you could drown if you fell into one. The *yaki soba* (chow mein Japanese-style) is also filled with slices of pork and vegetables and a sauce that can be considered an honor to digest. And, there are *gyoza* and *tanmen* (a Chinese noodle dish in a pork broth with Chinese cabbage, mushrooms, bamboo shoots, carrots, pork and some spinach), and pleasant little rice balls called *onigiri*. And even though there's no tea, the 7-Up works very well indeed to subdue the inherent saltiness of Japanese cuisine. *M.S.*

**Inexpensive.** Open seven days from 11:30 a.m. to 3 a.m. Closed New Year's Day. No alcoholic beverages. No reservations. No credit cards. Street parking. Casual.

---

## AJETI'S ALBANIAN NATURAL FOOD     Albanian
425 Pier Avenue                            **DA★**
Hermosa Beach     **Map 2**           (213) 379-9012

We've had scores of enthusiastic letters and phone calls about this charmer, and even though many of them were obviously "plants," the restaurant withstands the closest scrutiny. None of my reference books clearly defines "Albanian" fare so we will accept the definition we see on our plates: fresh foods individually prepared *al dente*, marvelous lamb, imaginative salads.

**Moderate.** Open Monday through Saturday 5 to 10 p.m. Reservations accepted. Visa, MC. Street parking; parking lot after 6 p.m. Casual to semi-dressy.

---

## AKBAR INDIAN RESTAURANT
590 Washington Street
Marina del Rey          **Map 2**

**East Indian**
★
(213) 822-4116

Prior to the present new management, Akbar began with promise, then faltered. Now we'll have to see if culinary exorcism has been achieved. Like so many other restaurants in the Marina area, Akbar seemed to become lazy under the old management, responding to the general indifference to food—as opposed to schtick—that abounds in that watery haven for harried singles. However, recent visits indicate that this is a serious Indian restaurant. It is one of only a handful that has a tandoori oven.

**Moderate.** Open seven days. Luncheon from 11:30 a.m. to 2:30 p.m. Dinner from 6 to 10:30 p.m. Full bar. Reservations recommended. All major credit cards. Parking lot. Semi-dressy.

---

## THE ALBATROSS
1309 Camino Del Mar Street
Del Mar

**American/Continental**
★
(714) 755-6744

True to its name, the Albatross has stayed aloft. As though inspired by a cosmic Jacob's ladder, each booth setting was designed at a different level in this forsaken redwood benderboard church. There's nothing forsaken about the place now, especially since they've added a patio. You can still count on such well prepared entrées as seafood pizza,

---

*To obtain the best results from this Guide, be sure to consult maps on the various Southern California areas in the front of the book.*

teriyaki chicken and pepper steak. They have selected well for their short wine list. Happy Hour runs from 5 to 7 Monday-Friday.

**Moderate.** Open seven days from 5:30 to 10 p.m. Entertainment nightly. Full bar. No reservations. All major credit cards. Wheelchair access. Parking lot. Casual.

---

## ALBERTO'S RESTAURANT                    Italian
8826 Melrose Avenue                                    ★
Los Angeles          **Map 7**              (213) 278-2770

Sadly, this entire restaurant went flambé a while ago, and patrons held a premature wake for one of the fine, creative Northern Italian restaurants in the West Hollywood area. They did not reckon with the determination of Alberto (Pagliari) who managed to outwit the bureaucracy and open a smashing restaurant, lovelier than before with the same fine kitchen. Dishes like Alberto's artichoke bottoms, green peppers and cheese, and his linguine, *al dente* of course, round out a Northern Italian, imaginative menu served amidst wrought iron, gleaming wood panels and excellent paintings (see The Roman Senate). There are bookcases with real books and a piano bar with a real pianist.

**Moderate.** Open seven days. Dinner from 5 p.m. to 1 a.m. Closed Christmas. Full bar. Reservations advised. All major credit cards accepted. Valet parking. Semi-dressy.

---

## ALBION'S                                French
13422 Ventura Boulevard                                 ★
Sherman Oaks          **Map 1**              (213) 981-6650

A charmer that may have earned a spot in the *Guinness Book Of Records* by lowering the prices and not the quality of the exalted fare. Some time ago, for reasons unknown to me, Albion's was expensive, too expensive for most, and we received a number of complaints. Suddenly there was a turn-around; the prices dropped and we thought "Uh oh, back to Swanson's TV dinners." Not so. Nothing's frozen; everything is beautifully prepared and the selection of dishes fits the description of the *nouvelle cuisine*. In fact, it's as close to the basic flavors and textures as the food can be. Desserts are exciting, atmosphere is special-occasion and prices are now more than reasonable.

**Moderate to expensive.** Open Monday through Saturday. Luncheon served 11:30 to 2:30 p.m. weekdays. Dinner Monday through Saturday from 6 to 11 p.m. Full bar. Reservations advised. All major credit cards. Parking across Ventura in lot at lunch; behind restaurant at dinner. Semi-dressy to dressy.

---

## ALEXANDER'S                                        Continental
10444 Magnolia Boulevard                                    ★
North Hollywood          **Map 1**          (213) 763-4446

Chef Harold Alexander got ticked with me when I wrote a less-than-laudatory review of his first effort. Now I can happily eat my words. Whatever changes were made are clearly for the better: 10-course dinner priced at $45 is one of the best in the valley. Dinners start at 7:30 "promptly." Since yours will be the only party served that night—they prefer a maximum of 12 guests-you'll have to come up with a deposit, but you can cancel with two weeks' notice. The price is $5 less for nine or more and includes the hot and cold hors d'oeuvres, a champagne aperitif, dinner wines, tax and gratuity. Chef Alexander personally presents the major courses and, if invited, will join the guests for coffee after the dessert is served. A typical menu might include quiche Lorraine, soup made from fresh tomatoes, salad maison, boned rainbow trout with bay shrimp stuffing and dill butter

*Please be sure to consult "Tipping Made Easy" on page 25 of this Guide.*

sauce, broccoli with sour cream and then, after an intermission, melon with fresh pineapple, roast crown of lamb with mint sauce, fresh vegetables, French Brie, a sorbet, fruit, chocolate mousse and coffee. The appropriate California wine is selected for each course. I would recommend the veal courses, but you should consult with Chef Harold. On Thursday evening, you may make a reservation for a table for two for $60 per couple for an eight-course dinner.

**Expensive.** Open Wednesday through Sunday for dinner at 7:30 p.m. only. Wine only. Visa, MC. Street parking. Dressy.

---

## ALFREDO'S
666 Anton Boulevard
South Coast Plaza Hotel
Costa Mesa     **Map 4**

**Northern Italian**
★★

(714) 540-1550

Ivy cascades down from the towering skylight at Alfredo's in Costa Mesa, one of the loveliest rooms in Southern California. Multi-level seating, colorful banners, soft lighting, and a harpist help set the mood for a fine experience in the fundamental cuisine of Northern Italy. Nothing wild or outrageous here. The somewhat limited menu places no impossible demands on the kitchen, and the restaurant serves those dishes it can handle. Chef Larry Bowen is best with pasta and veal although the Porterhouse steak, marinated and broiled, had exquisite flavor.

*Antipasti* included a fine *mozzarella marinara* served in golden brown sections with garnish instead of the plain two-inch square of most restaurants. The *scampi provinciale* was sautéed in garlic with white wine and fresh tomato. The cream of spinach soup was too bland and sweet for my taste, but the chilled cucumber soup is a local favorite. Among the *insalate* is a salad of the week that enables the chef to express his whims in style. Entrées on the dinner list include broiled Dover sole with creamed butter, mint and parsely; breast of chicken baked with tarragon and white wine; and rack of lamb. Best are the veal dishes, particularly the *piccata al marsala* which is sauteed with shallots and mushrooms and finished with marsala at the table.

Pastas include the ubiquitous *fettuccine* Alfredo, *linguini* with clams, garlic and parsley, and a marvelous *cannelloni* that is filled with seasoned chicken and spinach.

The luncheon menu is lighter and less expensive, involving a different style of service. The special salad Alfredo is a colorful presentation of shrimp, lobster, tuna, crab and anchovies with artichoke hearts and romaine. Desserts are not particularly impressive, but this kind of cuisine is best topped off with fresh fruit, cheese and a rich coffee drink.

The wine list is—for me—one of the most intelligent collections for an Italian restaurant. There is no attempt to overwhelm with exotic sounding labels or a large variety of Italian wines that are difficult for Americans to understand. Instead, there is a real effort to present some of the fine California boutique "finds" along with some suitable Italian classics on a balanced list.

Host Angelo Capello is in charge of the choreography, and the service is deft, professional and pleasing.

**Moderate to expensive.** Open seven days. Luncheon from 11:30 a.m. to 2 p.m. weekdays. Dinner 6 to 10 p.m. Monday through Thursday; to 11 Friday, Saturday. Sunday brunch 10 a.m .to 3 p.m. Private party facilities. Harpist in lounge. Full bar. Reservations required. All major credit cards. Valet parking. Semi-dressy to dressy.

---

## ALICE'S RESTAURANT                                    American
1043 Westwood Boulevard                                        ★
Westwood          **Map 8**                        (213) 208-3171

A survivor of the funk period, Alice's was too good to be merely trendy. The building is still architectural graffiti but the eclectic—love that word—menu includes everything from sandwiches to Rock Cornish game hen and some sensational desserts. A good place for omelettes or a selection from their list of "munchies." Good, imaginative drinks as well. This is especially nice for lunch and the salads are real.

**Moderate.** Open seven days. Luncheon served from 11 a.m. to 2 p.m. weekdays. Saturday and Sunday from 10 a.m. to 2 p.m. Dinner from 4 p.m. to midnight; Friday, Saturday 4 p.m. to 1 a.m. Full bar. Reservations recommended. All major credit cards. Wheelchair access. Street parking. Casual to semi-dressy.

---

## ALOUETTE                                          French
7929 Santa Monica Boulevard                              ★
West Hollywood          **Map 8**          (213) 650-9119

An ambience of comfortable domesticity indicates immediately that Alouette is a family-operated restaurant. The genuine hospitality of Jean and Raymonde Bardeau enhances the image. Entrées at our last foray were *coq au vin* with delicately glazed skin and breaded veal cutlet Alouette, topped with mild cheese and slightly crisp at the edges, preceded by a marvelous potato leek soup and salad. For dessert there's a mellow *baba au rhum* and *mousse au chocolat* and Jean Bardeau's special chocolate-covered pear. House specialties range from the duck *à l'orange* to sweetbreads Chasseur. Bouillabaisse is now a specialty on Thursday and Friday.

**Moderate.** Open Wednesday through Sunday. Dinner from 5:30; 5 on Sunday. Closing times vary. Open all holidays. Wine and beer only. No credit cards. Reservations recommended. Parking next door at Chevron lot. Casual.

*In order to obtain the best results from this Guide, be sure to read the French, German, Italian and Oriental menu translators on page 705 to 710 of this Guide.*

## ALPINE VILLAGE INN

833 Torrance Boulevard
Torrance **Map 2**

**German**
★
(213) 323-6520

*Gemutlichkeit* galore at the Alpine Village, where genuine Germans, looking ever so much like the cast from "Ship of Fools," stroll among twenty-two shops on the village street, eat rich pastry with coffee, and dine heavily at the restaurant. You *vil* enjoy *kassler rippchen* (smoked pork loin with sauerkraut), mashed potatoes, salad, and apple strudel. Poodles and *lederhosen* are big here, and the imported grocery store makes for fascinating browsing. There is a soccer field, petting farm, kiddy rides, and a German cinema, or *kino*.

**Inexpensive to moderate.** Open seven days. 11 a.m. to 11 p.m. Closed Christmas. Entertainment. Full bar. Reservations suggested. Visa, MC, AX. Parking lot. Casual to semi-dressy.

## AMAGI RESTAURANT

6114 Sunset Boulevard
Hollywood **Map 7**

**Japanese**
★
(213) 464-7497

6890 Beach Boulevard
Buena Park **Map 6**

★
(714) 994-2730

There seems to be a fascination with the Old West at work here. One of the restaurants is on the site of the old Gower Gulch of early Hollywood and the other is within shootin' distance of Knott's Berry Farm. But that is where the similarity ends. Both restaurants are tastefully simple, with all the effort going into the food preparation. This is authentic Japanese cuisine; it would have to be with *Una-Ju* or teriyaki eel on the menu. I was less adventurous and had the ginger crab and seafood-suki—a delicate soup with seafood and vegetables. If someone with you refuses to get in the spirit, there's always steak teriyaki. There's a sushi bar at each restaurant and the sushi chefs are patient with questions, perhaps partly because they're not weighed down by ten gallon hats.

**Moderate.** Open seven days.
**Buena Park:** Luncheon from 11:30 a.m. to 2 p.m. weekdays. Dinner from 4:30 to 10 p.m. Parking in building.
**Hollywood:** Luncheon from 11:30 a.m. to 4:30 p.m. Dinner from 4:30 to 10:30; from 4 to midnight Friday, Saturday. Shopping center parking.
**Both:** Cocktails. All major credit cards.

---

## AMBER'S
16900 Burbank Boulevard
Encino          **Map 1**

10367 Balboa Boulevard
Granada Hills      **Map 1**

**American**
★
(213) 995-3200

★
(213) 366-1888

This reviewer has been whining about the lack of good chicken in this area and complaining about the pitiful pieces of greasy gunk the chain operations seem to insist upon making. Well, I've found an answer. It's Amber's in Sherman Oaks on the corner of Ventura and Woodman where they cook everything to order using extra large chickens that are cut into eight pieces instead of 9 or more like the chains. The chicken (and ribs) are marinated in special sauce and cooked under pressure to preserve the juices. They have a great potato, large, white and crusty but not greasy. They've been doing their thing for 15 years, and it's a good thing.

**Inexpensive.** Open seven days. Monday through Friday 11:30 a.m. to 9:30 p.m. Saturday, Sunday and holidays from 10 a.m. to 9:30 p.m. No alcoholic beverages. No reservations. No credit cards; checks accepted. Parking lot. Casual.

---

*Please be sure to consult "Tipping Made Easy" on page 25 of this Guide.*

---

# AMBROSIA

French/Continental

501 30th Street
Newport Beach  **Map 4**

★★★
(714) 673-0200

Newport Beach has everything—climate, breath-taking vistas, a teeming pleasure-craft harbor, paradise islands in a storied bay, million-dollar mansions alternating with cuddlesome cottages, enough beautiful people to overrun Beverly Hills. All this and Ambrosia too. Ambrosia is far more than a restaurant. It's an experience. People go to some restaurants to eat and drink. People go to Ambrosia to live like millinaires for an evening. The room reflects understated elegance with theme colors of subdued gold (chardonnay) and burgundy red (cabernet sauvignon), crushed velvet wall panels and high-back wing chairs surrounding dramatically arranged tables. There are long-stemmed roses almost a yard high reinforced by a ring of carnations atop the snow white linen. The exquisite silverware and B&G plateware are offset by graceful wine crystal. On every table a candle blinks at the 18th Century crystal chandeliers overhead. Your lady is provided with a velvet cushion on which to prop her feet. A menu composed with confidence offers a dozen hors d'oeuvres from oysters, pâté, prosciutto or galantine of veal with cognac-impregnated prunes to your chosen quantity of Osetra caviar. Our choice was scallops with pimiento and bell peppers sautéed in garlic butter. Chicken consommé with quenelles was the only order to fall short on taste. Six salads from spinach to endive to romaine to sliced lobster tail and crab leg challenged our powers of decision. With a fear that endives were not in season we settled for romaine/watercress/mushrooms vinaigrette. Twenty entrées graced this menu, marshalled in the German manner from least expensive at the top to dearest at the foot of the sequence. Multiple seafoods plus chicken, duck, pheasant, veal, lamb, and beef made decision a painful dilemma. My wife's petrale sole bore the taste and texture of the ultimate in crêpes. My abalone sautéed in sweet butter with chives and mustard sauce reinforced my memory of a previous visit: here is a kitchen where these little ear shells are pounded, cooked, and flavored. Broccoli and carrots al dente rounded things out. So how could we pass up veal chops with wild mushrooms, cognac and wine in crèe-fraiche, not to mention oven-roasted double prime sirloin with shallot wine sauce? Rome was not built nor is Ambrosia sampled in a day. Desserts to stagger the mind (speak not of the diet!) were headed by Geril Muller's immortal and now almost universal creation—strawberries washed in orange juice, dipped in coverture Swiss chocolate, refrigerated, then vaccinated with grand marnier. I should also mention crêpes Ambrosia enwrapping ice cream injected with anisette. Brothers/partners/owners Geril and Gosta Muller have outdone even themselves with a 600-label, 10,000-bottle array that may well be the noblest wine cellar of them all. Recently a quartet came in to blow $3,228.12 plus $400 tip. Their tab read $2,000 for an 1893 Chateau Latour, $575 for a 1955 Chateau Lafite plus a mere $56 and $100 for two lesser vessels of vintage. There was $259 for food and $182.72 for Gov. Jerry Brown. "Is it worth it?" If you have to ask, probably not. But for those who can afford the league it plays in, Ambrosia can represent one of the best true values-per-dollar-spent on the restaurant circuit. If you don't believe it ask one of the regulars who dine there weekly or more, or explain how Ambrosia can turn people away night after night, or why one-sixth of the trade comes down from Los Angeles regularly, or why 80% of the patronage is consistently repeat business. Or ask the couple who called for reservations one afternoon from Fairbanks, Alaska then flew their new Cessna Citation jet

*In order to obtain the best results from this Guide, please consult "Tips on Dining Out" on page 21.*

to Orange County airport, where limo'd to Ambrosia, spent $2,000 for a three-hour celebration and flew back home that same night. *Herb Baus.*

**Expensive.** Open seven nights. Dinner from 6 to 10 p.m. Closed Christmas and Thanksgiving. Violinist Sunday through Tuesday. Full bar. Reservations required; preferably three weeks' notice. All major credit cards. Valet parking.

---

## AMECI ITALIAN CUISINE
New York Italian
★
18912 Ventura Boulevard
Tarzana　　**Map 1**　　　　(213) 705-8232

When Sid Barlowe, financial advisor to the celebrity set, gets excited, I get excited. "Boy have I got an Italian restaurant for you." he enthused. "The real thing, New York Italian!" What is New York Italian you ask? It's a hard-to-define cuisine that eliminates the pretense-haughty captains, hand-kissing and 20th Century Fox accents—in favor of flavor. New York Italian is a touch spicier and richer than most and the menu must ring with Godfather dishes like fried *calamari, scungili,* mussels, jumbo shrimp with hot sauce "Mulberry Street style," and fresh seafood and veal in a variety of presentations. Nick Andrisano is the type of guy who would be cast to play the role of an Italian restaurant owner. If he's got the time, he'll kibbitz for awhile, and if you're from New York you're suddenly his cousin. He can't resist buying a glass of wine for his people—his accountant must have a fit—and he'll consult with you about your dinner selections as seriously as if it were the last supper. The decor is New York nostalgia with framed subway maps, newspapers and waiters with New York accents.

**Inexpensive to moderate.** Open seven days from 5 to 11 p.m. Beer and wine only. Reservations suggested. Visa, MC. Parking lot. Casual.

## AMELIA'S ON BALBOA ISLAND     Italian/Seafood
311 Marine Avenue                                    ★
Balboa Island      **Map 4**                (714) 673-6580

Amelia's on Balboa Island is an exquisite little Italian seafood restaurant that has become the most dearly beloved establishment in the Balboa area, and for good reason. Amelia Seaton's daughter Hetty is an artist who makes even the simplest dishes sing. She comes from a long line of restaurateurs in Capri—and her husband John acts as the host in the tiny homelike dining room furnished with antiques and personal memorabilia. The menu is limited and everything is extraordinary; but I would recommend the abalone Irma, the lady sole, and the *cannelloni* with white wine sauce. Bouillabaisse is prepared in the style of the Southern Mediterranean. The *tortellini* (pasta filled with meat, chicken, prosciutto, cheese and butter sauce) with soup or green salad is a great dinner on a cold night. The small listing of wines (no cocktails) has been very carefully prepared. Reservations are essential on weekends. Amelia's is a small restaurant with small tables, almost like a restaurant in miniature. Parking can be a big problem; it's all on the street.

**Moderate.** Open Tuesday through Sunday from 6 to 10 p.m. Beer and wine only. Reservations suggested. Wheelchair access. Bank cards only. Street parking. Casual to semi-dressy.

---

## ANCIENT MARINER                   American
2607 West Pacific Coast Highway                    ★
Newport Beach      **Map 4**            (714) 646-0201

Take note, a chain of restaurants without a weak link. Less than 15 years ago Pete Siricusa put together this chain gang with names like the Rusty Pelican, the Rusty Duck, and the Ancient Moose and then put them on the job in places like Walnut Creek, Alameda, Mill Valley, and Sacramento. At the Ancient Mariner you can come by land or by sea, and you are welcome as a family, a civic group, an after-prom partier, or a lone diner looking for friendly folks and foolproof food.

**Moderate.** Open seven days. Luncheon from 11:30 a.m. to 3 p.m. Dinner from 4:30 to 11 p.m.; to midnight Friday and Saturday. Early bird dinner 4:30 to 6 p.m. Sunday brunch 10 a.m. to 3 p.m. Closed Thanksgiving, Christmas. Entertainment. Full bar. Reservations recommended. Visa, MC, AX. Parking lot. Casual.

---

## ANDRE'S OF BEVERLY HILLS          Italian/Continental
8635 Wilshire Boulevard                              ★★
Beverly Hills          **Map 8**                 (213) 657-2446

West 3rd Street at Fairfax Avenue                      ★
Los Angeles          **Map 8**                   (213) 935-1246

The name of this popular, plush Beverly Hills location might lead you to believe that it is French and expensive. Wrong. The menu is continental in the truest sense of the word, with emphasis upon Southern Italy. The luncheons and dinners are gargantuan—and exceptional values. That, plus the fact that the food is well prepared and presented, is the reason for their great success. All meals begin with an appetizer platter of pâté, salads, garbanzo bean and peppers, followed by soup or salad. Then, if you have wisely eschewed potatoes, you will be served a bowl of *fettuccine verde* (green pasta) with piquantly seasoned meat sauce. Entrées include frog legs *provençales, coq au vin*, veal parmigiana, grenadine of veef, and more much more. Desserts come with dinner, although there are fancier and more dramatic á la carte desserts—cherries jubilee and crêpes suzette—as well. The wine list is educational and gives you an opportunity to delve into some Italian labels that may be unfamiliar but worthy.

**Moderate.** Open seven days. Luncheon served 11:30 a.m. to 2:45 p.m. weekdays. Dinner from 4 to 11. Hours and prices may vary at each location. Beer and wine only. Reservations Beverly Hills only. Patio. No credit cards, personal checks accepted. Parking lot. Casual.

---

## ANNA MARIA RISTORANTE Italian
1356 South La Brea Avenue ★
Los Angeles      **Map 7**      (213) 935-2089

## ANNA MARIA'S LA TRATTORIA
418 Wilshire Boulevard
Santa Monica      **Map 2**      (213) 395-9285

These are busy, inexpensive, colorful, little peasant Italian restaurants with a patio (La Brea) that's heated for off-season dining. When Anna Maria Dinardo and her husband Daniel opened in 1969 after operating similar restaurants in various parts of the United States, it seemed one of the restaurant ventures least likely to succeed; Los Angeles needed another Italian restaurant like it needed more smog. But the charm and the cooking of the *ristorantes* have momentarily repealed the law of probability. The *cannelloni alla* Genovese, the *polo imbottito*, and the *linguine del mare* are very special, and there is a full line of pizza-sandwiches-spaghetti, all about three notches above the norm. *Calamari* and mussels are specialties. I was glad to see the Santa Monica location almost double its size by adding a new dining room — standing out on the street waiting to get in put a chill on the evening.

**Inexpensive.** Open Tuesday through Sunday. Luncheon served 11 a.m. to 2:30 p.m. weekdays. Dinner Tuesday through Sunday 3 to 10:30 p.m. Beer and wine only. Reservations accepted. Patio. Visa, MC, AX. Parking in rear. Casual.

## ANNA'S RESTAURANT

Italian/American

★

10929 West Pico Boulevard

Los Angeles   **Map 8**   (213) 474-0102

Known for its *cannelloni*, this modest Italian-American restaurant is good but not a place you'll rave about. It's family-oriented and popular with students, probably because you can get a hearty luncheon or dinner for a moderate price. You can make this a dinner spot before a game at the Pauley Pavilion, where the once-undefeated UCLA Bruins play.

**Inexpensive to moderate.** Open seven days. Luncheon from 11:30 a.m. to 4 p.m. Dinner from 4 p.m. to midnight. Closed Thanksgiving, Christmas. Full bar. Reservations recommended. All major credit cards. Parking lot. Casual.

---

## ANTHONY'S HARBORSIDE

Seafood/American

★

1355 North Harbor Drive

San Diego   (714) 232-6358

Anthony's Harborside—used to be part of the Royal Inn—invites you to keep vigil over history-laden San Diego harbor as you dine behind the second-story picture windows. They've bent tradition only enough to blend with innovation in decor. Cauldrons of lusty chowder send up tantalizing steam signals that say it was worth coming and that there's more to come whether you concoct your own salad at the seafood salad bar or order from the seafood side or the landlubber side of the menu.

**Moderate.** Open seven days. Luncheons from 11:30 a.m. to 4 p.m. weekdays. Dinner from 4:30 to 10:30 p.m. Sunday

*In order to obtain the best results from this Guide, please consult "Tips on Dining Out" on page 21.*

brunch 10 to 3 p.m. Entertainment and dancing from 9 to 1:30 a.m. nightly. Full bar. Reservations accepted. Visa, MC, AX. Street parking; unvalidated parking at Holiday Inn. Semi-dressy.

---

## ANTHONY'S PIER 2     Seafood
103 North Bayside Drive     ★
Newport Beach    **Map 4**     (714) 640-5123

Charles Rivezzo has established his credentials in piscatorial matters with the successful Maxwell's—now under new ownership—and from his experience at the Fulton Fish Market in New York. The menu is vast, prices are low, and there's a good wine list in this former non-entity of a restaurant. Duffy's, I think it was called in its previous incarnation. Fresh Maine lobsters and the usual finny things abound with some unique Italian touches, a little humor and a lot of flair. A giant salad bar has recently been added.

**Moderate.** Open seven days from 5 to 10 p.m. Full bar. Reservations recommended. Patio. Visa, MC, DC, CB. Parking lot. Casual.

---

## ANTHONY'S STAR OF THE SEA ROOM    Seafood
1360 Harbor Drive     ★★★
San Diego     (714) 232-7408

The Star of the Sea Room is no ordinary seafood restaurant. It veers as close to haute cuisine as any in its genre. Under the guiding hand of Catherine Ghio, there are innovations as well as classics on the moderate-to-expensive menu. Abalone gourmet, a whole abalone served an inch thick, has the kind of sweetness and texture that is often sought but rarely found. (The Ghios own their own fish market.) *Cioppino* à la Catherine, the artist's version of the once humble peasant stew, has been elevated to new heights.

Fresh crab, lobster, gigantic shrimp, scallops and the like are served in a spicy, saffron-touched red stock. The dining room is beautifully appointed, with formal full-backed arm chairs at the tables and scalloped booths. Large picture windows surround the room with lovely views (the building is built out over the ocean) particularly effective at night. Table china and linens are elegant. The wine list is well put together; and, while it is not extensive, it reflects care in selection. The desserts are exquisite. Strawberries à la Martinique consists of six fist-sized, stemmed strawberries presented on a mound of crushed ice (for two). A sauce of equal parts sour cream and whipped cream is blended with Grand Marnier, orange curacao, Myer's rum, and brown sugar, mixed tableside, and served in a silver compote. The berries are dipped into the sauce: an ecstatic happening. When the berries are gone, the sauce remains, to be eaten with the long spoon that is thoughtfully provided. It is a triumph. Note: Please don't confuse the Star of the Sea with Anthony's Seafood Grotto, which shares the same building and is also owned by the Ghios.

**Moderate to expensive.** Open seven days. Dinner from 5:30 to 10:30 p.m. Closed major holidays. Full bar. Reservations required. Visa, MC, AX. Street parking. Dressy; ties required.

---

## ANTOINE'S SHEIK

Middle Eastern/Lebanese

2664 Fifth Avenue ★
San Diego (714) 234-5888

The walls are hung with ornate rugs, and the dining area is gently lightened by brass lanterns to suggest a sheik's tent. The dishes are mainly Lebanese from recipes handed down through countless generations to the owner, Letitia Estes.

The "sheik's specialty" is an education in the cuisine of Lebanon, rolled grape leaves (stuffed with meat and rice), stuffed eggplant, stuffed cabbage, *bulgur pilaf*, *kafta kabob* (skewer of onion, tomatoes, and bell pepper) *shishkabob*, and rice pilaf. The dinners include *hummus* (a garlicky garbanzo bean paste), homemade Lebanese bread and cheese, a vegetable, and green salad.

**Moderate.** Open Monday through Saturday. Luncheon from 11 a.m. to 3 p.m. weekdays. Dinner from 3 to 9:30 p.m.; 5 to 10:30 Friday; 4 to 10:30 Saturday. Full bar. Reservations recommended for dinner. Visa, MC, AX. Street parking. Casual.

---

## ANTONELLO
South Coast Village
Santa Ana      **Map 6**

**Nouvelle Northern Italian**
★
(714) 751-7153

Antonio Cagnolo wants his patrons to feel like they're in a real Italian restaurant so there are no plastic grapes, travel posters or red checkered tablecloths with breadsticks sprouting out of them. The use of lavish rugs and a kind of atrium patio could make this the setting for an elegant cuisine. The dishes are authentic, even to the fresh herbs grown in their garden. The Genovese style *cioppino*, the scampi in mustard sauce (*scampi alla sassi*) and the turkey breast in white cream of truffle sauce (*petti di tacchino al castel vetrano*) are different tastes to Southern Californians who are more accusomed to either the pastas—also served here—or the "cruise ship elegant," with little in between. Serious eaters won't mind the high prices.

**Moderate to expensive.** Open Monday through Saturday. Luncheon from 11:30 a.m. to 2 p.m. weekdays. Dinner from 6 to 10 p.m.; to 11 Friday, Saturday. Closed major holidays. Full bar. Reservations recommended. Visa, MC, AX. Parking lot. Semi-dressy.

## ANTONIO'S                                           **Mexican**

7472 Melrose Avenue                                        ★★

West Hollywood          **Map 8**            (213) 655-0480

I cannot imagine a more dramatic figure than Antonio Gutierrez, dressed in his finery (a suit of lights, as the matadors would have it) with his pencil-thin mustache and his proud stance. Antonio's is a Mexican restaurant in Hollywood that has grown immensely successful by presenting the fine cuisine of Mexico along with the more familiar varieties. The jicama salad with fresh tropical fruit, the chicken with *salsa verde* (hot green sauce), or better yet, with the incredible *mole* sauce of chocolate and chilis and scores of spices are the best I've had in the United States. Don't get me wrong—there are tacos, albondigas soup, and other standards, and they're good. But Antonio's allows you to experiment with stuffed fresh vegetables and desserts of fried bananas and flan in different flavors. The only jarring touch is the musical combo that insists on serenading each table, one of my pet restaurant peeves. They were a bit discomfited when Ralph Story, our dinner companion, and I began a loud discussion of funeral arrangements for a mythical aunt. But they all just smiled and played harder—and louder. However, foreknowledge is golden, and a word to Antonio will spare you the serenade.

**Moderate.** Open Tuesday through Sunday. Luncheon from noon to 3 p.m. weekdays. Dinner from 5 to 11 p.m.; 4 to midnight Saturday, Sunday. Full bar. Reservations recommended. Visa, MC, AX. Valet parking evenings. Casual.

---

*In order to obtain the best results from this Guide, be sure to read the French, German, Italian and Oriental menu translators on page 705 to 710 of this Guide.*

# AOBA

**Japanese**

201 West Harvard Street

★★

Glendale    **Map 7**

(213) 242-7676

I've rarely met a Japanese restaurant I didn't like. The big showly ones with tatami tables have become a significant part of the dining-out scene. Some are not exactly authentic. Rocky Aoki, affable young president of Benihana of Tokyo, once told me that he would be too embarrassed to represent his restaurants as "Japanese" in Japan; there they are called Benihana of New York. But of all Japanese restaurants, the favorites of our readers seem to be the small mamma and poppa establishments, and I have found a jewel. Aoba just may have the best sukiyaki (the Japanese pronounce it skee-yaki) I have tasted with a spicy, gingery stock. The sashimi was a delight. The fish teriyaki is fresh fish, gently broiled and seasoned with teriyaki sauce. If the prices seem to come from the twilight zone, the atmosphere does too; it's something else—a not unattractive odd bag of patio furniture, comfortably upholstered in lounge mats, and booths made of Z-brick. Even the music, while Japanese, is less discordant to Western ears. The waitresses are very special, helpful without being patronizing, and there is no language problem at all. Sake is served in *o'choshi* (tiny porcelain flasks in a Wedgewood blue). It is definitely casual; a pleasant departure from the bland, and ranks among the top dining experiences.

**Moderate.** Open seven days. Luncheon from 11:30 a.m. to 2 p.m. weekdays. Dinner from 5:30 to 9:30 p.m.; to 10:30 Friday, Saturday; 5 to 9:30 Sunday. Wine and beer only. Reservations recommended. Visa, MC. Parking lot across the street. Casual.

## THE APPLE PAN
American/Pie
10801 West Pico Boulevard ★
West Los Angeles          **Map 8**          (213) 475-3585

Now in their fourth decade of serving what some believe to
be the best hamburger in the area, and great apple pie, this
is an old-fashioned counter operation with all good sandwiches, homemade desserts, and sometimes cranky but
always fast service. (Our counterman suffered from fallen
archness, having once worked in a first-class restaurant,
and was grumpy about the whole thing.) This is one of the
best places in West Los Angeles for a late snack on your
way home from watching basketball, Lakers or Bruin style.

**Inexpensive.** Open Tuesday through Sunday from 11 a.m.
to midnight; to 1 a.m. Friday, Saturday. Phone orders
taken. Closed month of July. No alcoholic beverages. No
reservations. No credit cards. Parking lot; street parking.
Casual.

## THE ARCHES RESTAURANT
Continental
3334 West Coat Highway ★
Newport Beach          **Map 4**          (714) 645-7077

The Arches, the oldest restaruant in Newport Beach, is a
favorite of more Newport area residents and transplanted
celebrities than any of the plusher, more glittery spots that
proliferate along the Gold Coast. When I last visited here I
saw Chick Hearn and Tom Hayden. We were told Joey
Bishop had been in during that same week. The steak
Wellington *bouquetière* is a double center cut of filet, with
pâté, cooked in puff pastry; it is served, as are all entrées,
with choice of French onion soup (or du jour) or salad (try
the Roquefort). The dish takes 45 minutes to prepare, but
that gives you time to relax over a drink or two along with
the rest of the yachting crowd. There is a different daily
special, the most popular of which are roast duckling à

*l'orange flambé* (Sunday). Another favorite is the real saltim-bocca (real scallops with prosciutto ham and *fettuccini* noodles). Perhaps the specialty of the specialties is the rainbow trout stuffed with crabmeat, melted cheese, and rice pilaf.

**Moderate to expensive.** Open seven days. Luncheon from 11:30 a.m. to 2:45 p.m. weekdays. Dinner 5 to 1 a.m nightly. Full bar. Reservations recommended. All major credit cards. Parking lot. Casual.

---

## ARNOLD'S FARMHOUSE
6601 Manchester
Buena Park          **Map 6**

**American**
★
(714) 521-9450

Near Knott's Berry Farm, both geographically and philo-sophically, Arnold's is famous for the farmhouse buffet meal that includes three salads plus the entrée with two vegetables, rolls and butter, and beverage. James Arnold tries very hard to be good, wholesome, and inexpensive; and it shows. Homebaked desserts, children's menu—a family restaurant in the best sense of the word.

**Inexpensive.** Open Tuesday through Sunday. Luncheon from 11:30 a.m. to 3:15 p.m. Dinner from 4 to 8:30 p.m. Children's menu. Closed Christmas. No alcoholic beverages. No reservations. No credit cards accepted. Parking lot. Casual.

*To obtain the best results from this Guide, consult "How to Use this Guide" on page 27.*

## ART'S

**Delicatessen**

12224 Ventura Boulevard

★★★

Studio City **Map 1** (213) 769-9808

Every morning (except Monday, when it's closed), beginning at 7:30, cars start jockeying for parking spots alongside Art's on Ventura Boulevard. Nothing else is open on Ventura Boulevard in Studio City at that hour, yet in front of Art's (where "Every Sandwich Is a Work of Art"), there's a traffic jam. The reason people want to park so close to Art's is that after a meal like that, no one has the energy to stumble more than a few steps to his car. All the body's spare energy has gone to the digestive tract where a big job is underway.

Art's is one of the great delicatessens of the modern world. Indeed, though purists may scream, I do not believe there is a deli in all of New York City to compare with Art's. Art's is like a toy store for *fressers*; you can stand by the entrance and watch people with big appetites being literally poleaxed by the sight of the smoked sable and whitefish inside the deli case. Critics of Art's argue that it's too expensive (not more than Canter's or Nate 'n Al's), too crowded (so sue them; it's popular) and not kosher (few delis are; the euphemism is "kosher-style" or "New York-style"). Art's greatness comes from a variety of elements: the wit and panache of the waitresses; the sight of Art (a man of significant girth) behind the counter tasting the more-than occasional tidbit of corned beef, pastrami, brisket and tongue as it slides out of the slicer; the photographs of sandwiches that adorn the walls; and the food itself, the eating of which is virtually a religious experience. That corned beef—so moist with small rainbows of color flecking, the succulent chunks of meat. The Greek salad with herring—sweet, filled with crunchy cabbage, elegant squares of herring, and olives with a taste as ancient as the flavor of water. And the triple decker combinations (impossible on soft onion roll, fine on rye or pumpernickel): "Harold's Special," turkey, corned beef and chopped liver; "Kathy's Special," pastrami, chopped liver and

71

tomato; and the classic "Roberta's Special," corned beef, pastrami and tongue. The only clinker I've ever encountered at Art's was the matzoh ball in the chicken soup. It was a bowling ball which left hardly any room in the bowl for my soup. To make up for the disappointing matzoh ball, I bought myself a bag of chocolate covered raspberry jellies as I left. They made me feel much better.   *M.S.*

**Moderate.** Open Tuesday through Sunday 7:30 a.m. to 7:45 p.m. Closed most Jewish holidays. Beer only. No reservations. No credit cards. Street parking. Casual.

*In order to obtain the best results from this Guide, be sure to read the French, German, Italian and Oriental menu translators on page 705 to 710 of this Guide.*

# ART'S CHILI DOGS

1410 Florence Avenue
Los Angeles **Map 7**

**Hot Dogs**
★★
(213) 752-5796

Art's is a Los Angeles original. He's been making chili dogs at his small stand since 1939. Art ("Just say I don't have a last name") is a one time chemical engineer, now in his seventies, who started peddling hot dogs during the Depression when his wife was pregnant and he couldn't find a job in engineering. Art figures he's sold somewhere over six million hot dogs since then, and he's still every bit the perfectionist, the artist, the temperamental prima donna. Ask him for a hamburger and he'll snarl, "Go to a restaurant." Dare to compare his hot dog with any other—as I did once on a television show—and he'll sneer malevolently. Art expanded his operation a few years ago, increasing the seating capacity by nearly fifty percent, from ten stools to fourteen, but you won't mind being cramped at Art's, just as you get accustomed to his glares and growls. Art, in case you didn't know, just happens to make the best chili dog in town—and the sloppiest. If you're a favored customer, he'll sprinkle salt on top of your chili dog, lightly and precisely with a carefully calculated flick of the wrist. "I used to do it on all the chili dogs, but some jerks started asking me why. Now I only do it for the old timers." Art claims his customers come from all over the country and that "a few weeks ago I had a young lady say that even in Paris, France, she came across devotees of Art's chili dogs."

**Inexpensive.** Open Monday, Tuesday, Thursday through Saturday. Open 11 a.m. to 6:45 p.m. Closed major holidays. No alcohol. No reservations. No credit cards. Casual.

*To obtain the best results from this Guide, consult "How to Use this Guide" on page 27.*

## ASUKA
Japanese
★
1266 Westwood Boulevard
Westwood    **Map 8**        (213) 474-7412

Having expanded its sushi bar, this authentic Japanese restaurant now claims to have the largest one in Los Angeles. Samurai swords may be drawn with at least one other restaurant over this boast, but Asuka does serve 26 varieties of fresh seafood delicacies. Sano, the resident sushi expert, creates new combinations daily depending on the fish available. A complete selection of traditional Japanese cuisine is also on the menu. Japanese food, low in calories, appeals to diners on two levels, good taste and good figure — there are few overweight Japanese.

**Moderate.** Open Monday through Saturday. Luncheon served 11:30 a.m. to 2 p.m. weekdays. Dinner Monday through Thursday 5:30 to 10 p.m.; Friday and Saturday 5 to 11 p.m. Beer and wine only. Reservations suggested. Visa, MC, AX. Parking in rear. Casual.

---

## ATLANTIS
Seafood/American
★
2595 Ingraham
San Diego        (714) 224-2434

For a tourist attraction restaurant, Atlantis acquits itself well. Hangtown fries are a specialty and they have a really good champagne brunch on Sunday. They offer a sophisticated menu which includes cioppino, beef steak Neptune, choice filet mignon, butter fried and served with asparagus tips and crab legs, dressed in Bearnaise, and veal dishes. The place is expansive, but not expensive, considering the ideal location and the view of Mission Bay.

**Moderate.** Open seven days. Luncheon served 11:30 a.m. to 4 p.m. Monday through Saturday. Dinner from 4:30 to 10

p.m.; 11 p.m. Friday and Saturday. Entertainment. Full bar.
Reservation suggested. Ocean view. Most major credit cards
Parking lot. Casual.

---

## AT MARTY'S
8657 West Pico Boulevard
Los Angeles  **Map 8**

European
★
(213) 272-1048

The decor of the 20's has a certain innocent sophistication, if
those terms are not contradictory, that works well in a
restaurant. Marty (Tunick) had been with the Aware Inn and
La Masia and knew what people wanted on their plate—the
Art Deco with which he has literally surrounded himself,
and his patrons, is another matter. The menu is capricious-
Hollywood ("Fey Ray," "Roto-Rita") but the food is serious in
spite of itself with really good London broil, beef paprikash
(sic) and "zum zum sausages" seasoned with herbs and spices
in three varieties. Soup is made fresh daily and the vegetables
are brilliantly handled. Wines are very reasonable and
obviously intended to be a part of the attraction.

**Moderate.** Open Tuesday through Sunday. Dinner Tuesday
through Thursday from 6 to 11 p.m.; Friday 6 p.m. to 1 a.m.;
Saturday 6 p.m. to 1 a.m.; Sunday 5 to 11 p.m. Classical
guitar. Beer and wine only. Reservations suggested. All
major credit cards. Wheelchair access. Street parking. Casual.

---

## A TOUT VA BIEN
5730 East Second Street
Long Beach (Naples)  **Map 3**

French
★
(213) 439-9888

An American chef inspired by a French wife has created an
unpretentious French country inn that sings. Located in

that twilight zone known as Naples, adjacent to Long Beach, it has everything Long Beach needs in an important "little" restaurant; copper pots, antique sideboards and flowers; good sauces, butter lettuce salads, good imported wines. All these plus an aura of romance ensure that all *will* go well.

**Moderate.** Open Wednesday through Sunday. Closed major holidays. Dinner from 6 to 10:30 p.m. Wednesday through Saturday; 6 to 9:30 p.m. Sunday. Wine and beer only. Reservations required. Visa, MC. Wheelchair access. Street parking. Semi-dressy.

---

## AU CHAMBERTIN                                    French
708 Pico Boulevard
Santa Monica          **Map 2**          (213) 392-8738

International events of recent years have created an infusion of talented Orientals. It is not unusual to find a Texas barbeque stand or a pancake house well-operated by hard working and efficient people of the Pacific. Unfortunately with so many hits, it stands to reason that there will be an occasional miss, and Au Chambertin fits that latter category. The Vietnamese family is obviously dedicated, but their French restaurant is bleak and colorless. The kitchen needs some experienced hands at some departments. Dishes like oysters in curry and *croute* for sea bass in the shape of the fish and langoustines with a lime sauce are ambitious— perhaps too much so. However, the restaurant opened in '81 and may well settle in.

**Moderate.** Open Tuesday through Sunday 6 to 11 p.m. Closed major holidays. Full bar. Reservations recommended. Visa, MC, AX. Valet parking. Semi-dressy.

## AU PETIT CAFÉ

**French**

★

1230 North Vine Street

Hollywood    **Map 7**    (213) 469-7176

Now over 17 years old, Au Petit Café stood with Gallic disdain of the crazies that inhabited the Hollywood Ranch Market next door on Vine Street. Quite a bit better than most French restaurants in Southern California. Au Petit has character: Blackboard menus, a narrow basement level where the ceiling pipes are all painted black, and beautiful food served well. Luncheon includes sole amandine, sand dabs·Véronique, steak tartare, and roast leg of lamb. But it is at dinner that the little restaurant glows, with contented diners savoring chicken tarragon or fresh pompano or crisp roast duck with peaches. There is a small cocktail bar, the intime Sous Sol with red cut-velour walls and over fifty gold-framed mirrors, an interior by Serge Sassouni of Paris. The restaurant was opened and is still owned by Kit Marshal, who runs a well-disciplined house with an extensive (if preponderantly imported) wine cellar.

**Expensive.** Open Monday through Saturday. Luncheon 11:30 a.m. to 2:30 p.m. weekdays. Dinner Monday through Saturday 6 to 11 p.m. Full bar. Reservations suggested. Visa, MC, AX. Parking lot. Casual.

## AUX DELICES FRENCH RESTAURANT

**French**

★

15466 Ventura Boulevard

Sherman Oaks    **Map 1**    (213) 783-3007

This is one of those near-perfect little French restaurants that seem to thrive in the Southland, except that Aux Delices (pro-

*In order to obtain the best results from this Guide, please consult "Tips on Dining Out" on page 21.*

nounced "oh delees" for my nonlinguistic friends) is nearer to perfect than most. Perhaps the main difference between this somewhat severe and classic restaurant and its counterpart along St. Germaine in Paris is the price — and the quality of some of the vegetables. (Try to find a good tomato in America I dare you.) Dinners at Aux Delices begin at $12.50, less than half the cost of either Paris or New York. Owners Roger Martini and Marcel Frantz present a style of cooking that can best be described as French-authentic. The first such restaurant to open in the Valley, it does a thriving business; and reservations are important, particularly on weekends. If cream of watercress or cream of cauliflower is the soup du jour, you are in gustatory heaven. Seafood is particularly well prepared in this kitchen, and I can speak with enthusiasm about the filet of brook trout, poached au Chambertin, or their filet of sole sauté Murat. The scampi Marcel is flamed in cognac, an altogether delicious dish. There is a different chef's special every day made from whatever looks freshest in the marketplace. All dinners include soup and salad with the special house dressing and, of course, fresh vegetables. If you have to wait a bit, you might enjoy a Delices cocktail (no hard liquor is served) made with sherry, dry vermouth, orange bitters, and a lemon twist. Even though this is a small (48-seat) restaurant, you will feel more comfortable if you are dressed up a bit.

**Moderate.** Open Tuesday through Sunday for dinner 5:30 to 10 p.m. Beer and wine only. Reservations suggested. All major credit cards. Street parking; lot in rear. Semi-dressy.

---

## AZTEC DINING ROOM
2811 San Diego Avenue
San Diego

Mexican
★
(714) 295-2965

The food is good, but the fun is better. From 7 to 11 on Fridays, mariachi music and singing set a tempo that encourages sing-a-longs and toe tapping. There is no dance floor, a small matter when the tempo is right. The dishes are made in the tradition of the owner's hometown, Tepic. Order à la carte and get a sample of everything. Put out the spicy fire inside you with honey on your *sopapilla* for dessert.

**Inexpensive.** Open seven days from 11 a.m. to 8:30 p.m. Sunday brunch from 9 a.m. Closed two weeks at Christmas. Full bar. No reservations. No credit cards. Parking lot. Casual.

*To obtain the best results from this Guide, be sure to consult maps on the various Southern California areas in the front of the book.*

# b

## BAGATELLE
8690 Wilshire Boulevard
Beverly Hills     **Map 8**

French
★★
(213) 659-0782

Frustratingly, this is one of the best French restaurants in Los Angeles, but few people know it. It began as a French delicatessen some years ago and was one of the first such in the West with a selection of homemade *terrines, pâtés* and *charcuterie.* Now it is a serious dining room, although there are still take-out facilities and the cusine is essentially Burgundy provincial. *Lapin à la pron,* rabbit in a sauce of wine, cream and grapes, is my favorite dish here although the veal *villeroise* is extraordinary. They do their own pastries and a Napoleon here is a real one, not the cardboard and slush of most restaurants. It is not grand, not opulent, nor is it a momma and poppa cafe, but Bagatelle has its own distinction, largely from the kitchen.

**Moderate to expensive.** Open Monday through Saturday. Luncheon served 11:30 a.m. to 2:30 p.m. weekdays. Dinner Monday through Saturday 6 to 10 p.m. Beer and wine only.

Reservations required. Visa, MC, CB. Wheelchair access. Parking in rear and street. Semi-dressy.

## BAGEL NOSH

**Deli**

★

1629 Wilshire Boulevard
Santa Monica      **Map 2**      (213) 451-8771

Well, it's not the kind of deli your grandma might remember—corned beef served in an atmosphere of Tiffany lamps, hanging plants and antiques is different. But the food is pretty good and they bake their own bagels, nine varieties, including onion, pumpernickel and cinnamon-raisin. A big salad bar, lots of beer and wine and dozens of homemade salads to eat in or take out make this a happy place.

**Inexpensive.** Open seven days. Breakfast from 7 to 11 a.m. Lunch served from 11 a.m. to 4 p.m. Wine and beer only. No reservations. No credit cards. Street parking. Casual.

## BAJA CANTINA

**Mexican**

311 Washington Street
Marina del Rey      **Map 2**      (213) 821-2250

23410 Civic Center Way
Malibu      **Map 2**      (213) 456-2021

The Baja Cantinas—in the Marina and in Malibu—are the most fun and fanciful of any of the Mexican experiences in Southern California and maybe in the universe. Both were charmingly, if capriciously, created with workmen bouncing in Herb Alpert albums. Both offer that extra light-year into the style and joy of Mexicana rarely found in gringoland. Serious foods with serendipity nomenclature like "T.J. Taxi" and "Forty Miles of Bad Road" are carefully prepared dishes that result from research into Mexican kitchens. Fresh fish, gargantuan salads and colorful combinations highlight the whacky menu.

On Monday evenings you may have all the barbecued tacos (*tacos al carbon*) you can possibly push past your esophagus for $6.95. The Mexican barbecued lobster featured on Tuesday nights is served with Spanish rice, cheese enchilada, fresh corn on the cob and a generous salad. They use whole Maine lobster and lose money on the deal (have you priced lobster lately?), but the dynamics of hungry hordes encountering an array of exotic drinks that would startle even Trader Vic adds up in the black.

Sunday brunch is a selection of eight egg dishes like "The Baja Hotfoot" (with *jalapenos*, tomato, onion, cheese and *tomatillo salsa*) or the "Baja Banana," an omelette made with fresh bananas baked in butter, cinnamon and spices, then folded into a fluffy omelette with jack cheese and *chiliquilles*. Brunches are $5.50 and that includes a choice of champagne, bloody Maria, orange juice, and all brunches include fruit and hot corn tortillas, butter and, generally, a few surprises.

Decor is tasteful funk with antiques, the kind of effortless and casual look that has to be carefully plotted. There's a 1900's bar in the Marina location from one of the famous J.P. Wilson auctions and colorful tile, great Mexican fireplaces, carved furniture, good and terrible paintings, banana trees and palms. The Malibu location is festooned with hundreds of personal photographs and artifacts picked up in Mexico by Pat Phinney, the improbably young and impossibly happy proprietor. There is a terrific view from the long, lazy patio in Malibu that includes the Sierra Retreat, once the Ringe family home and the birthplace of Malibu.

People are scenic too, and I would rather person-watch on the patio than go to Cannes during the cellulewd festival. The girls here are the prettiest, both customers and employees, and the guys have the surfer-so-good glow.

**Moderate.** Open seven days from 11:30 a.m. to 11:30 p.m.

Sunday brunch from 10:30 a.m. to 2 p.m. Full bar open to 1:30 a.m. Reservations accepted for parties of five or more. Patio and view (Malibu); patio (Marina). Visa, MC, AX. Casual.

---

## BALI HAI
Cantonese/American

2230 Shelter Island Drive
★
San Diego
(714) 222-1181

"A sight to see" is the way I first heard it described—and sight it is—sometimes even good with authentic Polynesian decor and floor shows at the Bali Hai, which looks over the boats tied at its doorstep and the city lights across the water. Luau luncheon buffets, Cup-of-Gold Sunday brunch, and Cantonese cuisine are their main attractions; however, seafood and charcoal-broiled steaks are available if you're not in an adventuresome mood. No entertainment on Monday and Tuesday but there is a Senior Citizens' Buffet on Monday and Tuesday.

**Moderate.** Open seven days. Luncheon from 11:30 a.m. to 3:30 p.m. Dinner from 5:30 to 10:30 p.m.; 5 to 11:30 Friday, Saturday. Sunday brunch 10 a.m. to 2 p.m. Senior Citizens' Buffet, $3.50. Monday, Tuesday. Full bar. Reservations recommended. Patio. All major credit cards. Parking lot. Casual.

---

## BAYANIHAN RESTAURANT
Filipino

2300 Beverly Boulevard
Los Angeles          **Map 7**          (213) 383-8357

As testimony to a growing interest in Filipino cuisine a new and larger Bayanihan Restaurant opened recently and is housed in an elegant new building (looking a bit out of place in a slightly tacky neighborhood). The main dining room looked much like any other new restaurant, and is identified as Filipino only by the rattan chairs and some travel posters and other minor decorations from the Phillippines. The food, however, is authentically Filipino. Several varieties of *pancit* (noodles); *lumpia* (egg rolls); and other typically Filipino dishes are served. It's just like home-cooking if you come from the Philippines.

**Moderate.** Open seven days. Luncheon from 11:30 a.m. to 2 p.m. Dinner 2 to 10:30 p.m. Sunday brunch 11 a.m. to 2 p.m. Cultural presentations Friday, Saturday. Wine and beer only. Reservations recommended. Patio. Visa, MC, AX. Parking lot. Casual.

---

## BEACHBUM BURT'S
**Polynesian**
605 North Harbor Drive ★
Redondo Beach  **Map 2**  (213) 376-0466

A super-sized, super-formula restaurant by Burt Hixson, the man who brought you the Warehouse in Marina del Rey and Newport. The setting is a plantation house in the South Seas, with a thatched roof, palm trees, and view windows overlooking the ocean, furnished with the same peacock chairs that are so much a part of the character of the Warehouse. There is a cocktail lounge done in the style you might expect, with tall rum drinks adorned with veritable bushes of garnish, where you can expect to wait up to 45 minutes until your name is called. Malaysian shrimp — startling in their size and succulence — are the house specialty here, too; and the iceberg salad is served in a unique bowl with a compartment for the dressing. The menu is imaginative, but the dishes are not great — in that large an operation it is tolerable if they are served hot and good. The ambience is sheer fantasy and simply boggles the minds of out-of-towners. (The rest of us are more accustomed to the gigantic Technicolor theme restaurants.)

84

**Moderate.** Open seven days. Luncheon served 11:30 a.m. to 2:30 p.m. weekdays. Dinner seven days 5 to 11 p.m. Sunday brunch from 10 a.m. to 2:30 p.m. Closed Thanksgiving, December 24, Christmas. Entertainment. Full bar. Reservations for lunch only; dinner for parties of eight or more. Patio. Ocean view. Most major credit cards. Wheelchair access. Parking lot. Casual.

---

## BEADLE'S CAFETERIA                    American
850 East Colorado Boulevard                              ★
Pasadena          **Map 7**                (213) 796-3618

This is a better-than-average cafeteria that manages to avoid the bleak look and ordinary food so characteristic of the genre. Everything is fresh and homemade, from soups to desserts, and the main courses are, well, plain courses. The prime rib and leg of lamb are particular favorites with the people in the area, who form long long lines between noon and 1:30 p.m., and in the evening between 5:30 and 7:00.

**Inexpensive.** Open seven days from 11 a.m. to 7:45 p.m. No alcoholic beverages. No reservations. No credit cards. Parking in rear. Casual.

---

## BEAUDRY'S                    Continental Pretentious
Bonaventure Hotel
404 South Figueroa Street
Los Angeles          **Map 7**                (213) 624-2664

The first obstacle to overcome when dining at Beaudry's is to find the place. One wanders around the lobby floor maze of the Bonaventure in confusion. It's somewhere over there," a security guard ventured, waving in the general direction of

New Jersey. "I don't know," was the truthful, if surprising, admission by a disinterested bellman. Quite frankly, my dears, they don't give a damn.

On my visit, I entered the foyer accompanied by two traveled and sophisticated attorneys. The maitre d', after a moment, looked up from his stand and waited for us to speak. "We have reservations in the name of Schroeder," I offered. He glanced down at the chart. "Yeah," he said and walked toward the dining room. As we obediently followed, we marveled at a hostess in a sort of Frederick's of Hollywood mini-top that was held up by a strap so tight as to provide horizontal cleavage across her back.

Beaudry's is an attractive room with circular booths entirely surrounded by gold mesh drapes. There are plush banquettes along the wall and a medley of brown and bronze tones, and there are fresh flowers. The table was set with two open books of matches displayed à la Holiday Inn and four giant goblets of water. A basket of thin cheese toast was placed on the table in the manner of Scandia. Unlike Scandia's, the cheese toast was cold and had been made some time before.

Service is casual. Our waiter, or Captain, announced himself—"My name is Tommy"—and asked about drinks. At that moment my guests and I were perplexed by a strong fragrance that was identified, upon return of Tommy, as a cologne. He was drenched with it, and it made it difficult to taste the dishes he served until we had breathing time. By a strange coincidence, on an earlier visit, one of our distinguished advisors thought that perfume had been spilled in his drink. He called the waitress over and gallantly asked to see her lovely hands. They were awash with scent.

Without going into details of previous visits, my dinner began with soup "Ninon" into which the waiter poured a good two ounces of champagne, enough to chill. Next were scallops "Alex Humbert" served on spinach leaves with Pernod sauce. The dish arrived tucked into four crips points which had to be separated. The scallops were cold and utterly tasteless. After tasting one, I called Tommy, and he whisked them away—"Sorry about that"—to bring it hot—and utterly tasteless. The sauce had the consistency of LePage's library paste and the overcooked scallops were slippery. The spinach was a dark substance at the bottom of the dish. Again I ate one scallop. When the fish was removed, no comment was made nor was there any effort to discover why. After paying $6.25 for two scallops, I did not bother further with the dish.

The main course, at the chef's suggestion according to the menu, was *la chateaubriand avec sa bouquetiere des legumes fraiche*, a rather pretentious description. The beef was marvelous, cooked to perfection and obviously of highest quality. The vegetables were eminently forgettable.

*Les laitues de limstone et le fromage de Brie* is their description of limestone lettuce with Brie. This was an astonishing course; the Brie, obviously not long removed from the refrigerator, was chilled to a putty-like consistency which destroyed any possiblity of flavor.

The dessert, described as *les fraises "jeanne d'arc"* (sic) was a dish of fine strawberries drowned in bottled maraschino syrup that had been slathered with cream and walnuts.

As I look over my notes, I feel a sense of frustration attempting to describe the inept manner in which this restaurant is—and has been—operated. If the reader thinks me unduly harsh, remember that I once cancelled a negative review of Beaudry's when a change in management was announced. I hoped for better things. Now, the same old tackiness remains.

What sounded like a piano bar in the next room, the vocalist singing "How can you do me like you *do do do*," which

---

*Please be sure to consult "Tipping Made Easy" on page 25 of this Guide.*

was loudly amplified in the main room, the cold rolls and the myriad other details lead me to the conclusion that there is poor management here. Ironically the banquets at the Bonaventure are among the best in Southern California.

The "chef's preference" dinner was $29 per person, not exorbitant by any means, if it had been tolerable. With wine, dinners should expect to pay about $30 per person. The wine list, while impressive, fails to deliver. On two previous visits, the California wine ordered was "not available."

One can temporize as to the reasons for mediocrity here. They do have a captive audience, seemingly indifferent to the fare. Other diners will happen on the place by accident in hopes of a good dinner—such a party at the next table was furious.

**Expensive.** Open seven days. Luncheon served 11:30 a.m. to 2 p.m. weekdays. Dinner served seven days 6 to 11 p.m. Entertainment in lounge. Full bar. Reservations necessary. View. Major credit cards. Hotel parking. Semi-dressy to dressy.

---

## BECKHAM PLACE
77 West Walnut
Pasadena　　**Map 7**

**English**
★
(213) 796-3399

In this era of long overdue recognition for the fairer sex (that's ladies, folks), it's nice to see a charmer like Barbara Prager as managing director of Beckham Place, an outstanding restaurant in the English manor. Barbara was an important part of Lawry's and Gulliver's and her training techniques have never shown to better advantage than at this comfortable, colorful, multi-level establishment. Of course, there are cute names for salads ("Crown City Sallet") and three cuts of prime rib with spinach soufflé and creamed corn at a reasonable price. But the difference here is that everyone seems so genuinely glad to see you that you'll look back over your shoulder to see if they've made a mistake. There is a good stuffed salmon, veal and chicken with

choice of salad, also moderately priced. The wine selection
is limited but they try to pick out the best wines of the
month to accompany your dinner and they're reasonable,
too, either by the bottle or, praise be, by the glass. On
weekdays it's a popular place for luncheon with a menu
revised for the businessfolk of the area. Elaborate sandwiches, good salads and some entrées like roast beef hash
or toad in the hole (filet chunks simmered in burgundy
with Yorkshire pudding) plus the most gracious service
around make Beckham a special Place.

**Moderate.** Open seven days. Luncheon from 11:30 a.m. to 3
p.m. weekdays. Ale and sandwich bar from 11:30 a.m. to 3:30
p.m. Dinner Monday through Thursday 5:30 to 10 p.m.;
Friday, Saturday to 11 p.m.; Sunday 4 to 9:30 p.m. Closed
Christmas, July 4. Private party facilities. Full bar. Reservations advised. Visa, MC. Valet parking. Casual to dressy.

---

## BEL-AIR HOTEL
701 Stone Canyon Road
Bel Air          **Map 8**

**Continental**
**DA★**
(213) 472-1211

This elegant hideaway, green-screened from the rest of the
world, has been the object of some controversy in the last
year or two. I've had a superb dinner there—the sand dabs
*meunière*—and then I had a terrible dinner—fatty rack of
lamb indifferently served—on the very next evening. I
believe they had a problem with a touch of arrogance at the
host's stand, but this is still one of the great fantasylands to
which out-of-town guests should be treated. The hotel,
favored by royalty from abroad and eastern aristocracy, has
bougainvillea-draped walkways along picturesque bridges
over mossy streams where swans glide and preen. The

restaurant is intimate, luxurious, and cozy, and the sometimes impeccable service can make one of those magic
evenings when you know everything's going to be all right.
Soups are fine, and the medallions of veal Veronese are as
good as you'll be likely to find anywhere. The wine list is
good, but with not as many of the fine California wines as
you would expect. There is a magnificent patio—supposedly
for hotel guests only—but you won't have any trouble if
there is a table available. In the mid-afternoon it's a great
place to order an iced bucket of wine and watch the swans.
The Sunday bruncheon is little known and little frequented
by the tourist set. It's not inexpensive; but beauty rarely is.
Cocktails (the lounge is great), valet parking, and you'll
want to dress.

**Moderate to expensive.** Open seven days. Breakfast served
Monday through Saturday from 7:30 to 10 a.m.; Sunday
from 7:30 to 10:30 a.m. Dinner served from 6 to 10:30 p.m.
Sunday Brunch from 11 a.m. to 2:30 p.m. Entertainment in
bar. Full bar. Reservations advised. Patio. All major credit
cards. Street parking. Casual for breakfast, semi-dressy for
dinner.

---

## BELISLE'S RESTAURANT American

12001 Harbor Boulevard ★
Garden Grove     **Map 6** (714) 750-6560

Harvey Belisle claims to serve a "cross-section of American
food," and he's apt to get little argument from anyone who
studies the voluminous menu. Harvey is a promotionally minded
soul — his bright pink restaurant on the corner of Harbor and
Chapman in Garden Grove used to have a midget chef, ringing
a bell (belisle, get it?) on the sidewalk out front, an attention-
getter if there ever was one. Once inside the converted house
that grew and grew, you can have your choice of almost anything from fresh channel catfish with hushpuppies, fried rabbit
with corn fritters, carrot cake and (a-one, a-two) shoo fly pie,
to apple pandowdy. Other down-home touches: everyone gets

a fresh fruit salad with everything; corn bread and biscuits are homemade; everyone in the area waits for the strawberry pie season; the toothpicks are carved out of quills. Belisle's is open 24 hours a day every day and has "graveyard specials" for the truck drivers who gave the place its start. There's beer and wine (no cocktails) — and dress can be overalls for all Harvey cares. You'll find a lot of family groups inside (it's near Disneyland).

**Moderate.** Open seven days, 24 hours. Breakfast any time. Luncheon from 11:30 a.m. to 4 p.m. Dinner 5 p.m. to 4 a.m. Children's menu. Open all holidays. Entertainment Friday, Saturday. Wine and beer only. Reservations recommended for parties of 10 or more. Visa, MC. Parking lot. Casual.

---

## BELLE-VUE FRENCH RESTAURANT
French
101 Santa Monica Boulevard ★
Santa Monica  **Map 2**  (213) 393-2843

When this French restaurant was established over forty years ago Santa Monica was considered a resort area, and one driving guide of the time indicated it was "remote" from Los Angeles. Belle-Vue then was the big toad in the little pond (I couldn't say big "frog" because I'd be accused of insensitive ethnic slurs), and it thrived. Now that the freeways have made Santa Monica merely another, albeit sandier, part of the great city, the Belle-Vue still holds its place, and with just cause. There is little excitement here, just the kind of classically simple escargot, pâté, frog's legs, and duckling you would hope for; the sweetbreads are exemplary and the seafood dishes are done well, except for the bouillabaisse—a big disappointment. This is a pleasant, competent, knowledgeable establishment that should please you.

**Moderate.** Open seven days. Luncheon served Monday through Saturday from 11:30 a.m. to 3 p.m. Dinner Monday through Thursday 4:30 to 9:30 p.m.; Friday, Saturday 5 to 10 p.m.; Sunday 12:30 to 9:30 p.m. Closed Christmas. Limited banquet facilities. Full bar. Reservations advised. All major credit cards. Parking lot. Casual.

---

## BELMONT PIER
Mediterranean Seafood

11954 Wilshire Boulevard        ★

Los Angeles     **Map 8**        (213) 477-1281

A seafood restaurant in the Mediterranean style — they bring you a platter of the fresh raw fish, you make your selection, and it's cooked to order. They have an unusually succulent scallop brochette with fresh rosemary and mushrooms, and the sturgeon is served with a delicate mustard sauce. Desserts are prepared by the chef, the wine list is adequate and it's lately become a California classic.

**Moderate to expensive.** Open Monday through Saturday from 5:30 to 11 p.m. Beer and wine only. Reservations advised. Visa, MC. Street parking. Casual.

---

## BEN BROWN'S
American-Continental

31106 Pacific Coast Highway        ★

South Laguna     **Map 4**        (714) 499-2663

One weekend when I wanted the world to stop so I could get off, I happened on Ben Brown's in South Laguna. It's a rustic charmer on the wrong side of the highway, away from the ocean and entered through a narrow canyon where its high-gabled cottages surround nature's landscaping and a golf course. There are still deer and rabbit and the feeling of how it must have been before neon and freeways and the sustained screech of progress.

The restaurant, with a snug fireplace and glass walls, makes you wish it was raining. Everything is fairly priced and good and served by friendly waitresses—"Come look!" ours said as she pointed out a doe trailed by two little ones frisking on stiff forelegs. Mrs. Brown, who runs things here, says the deer are a nuisance, then sighs and admits she loves them. Dinner includes an admirable bouillabaisse, trout, scallops and prime rib preceded by spinach salad with chopped egg, bacon bits and a secret dressing. The crab cocktail I ordered was a pleasant surprise—giant crab legs in a zesty sauce.

The hotel rooms are really small houses with chalet roofs, kitchens and patios, and prices begin at $50 depending on the season. You can breakfast the next morning on eggs Benedict with fresh sliced tomatoes, coffee and rolls in the restaurant's patio with its profusion of hanging plants. I'll go back to Ben Brown's on those weekends when there is not enough time to drive a long distance and when I want to read (or write) or just walk along the canyon and look for squirrels.

**Moderate.** Open seven days. Breakfast served from 8 to 11 a.m. Luncheon from 11 a.m. to 3 p.m. Dinner Sunday and Monday 5 to 10 p.m.; Tuesday through Saturday to 11. Sunday brunch 10 a.m. to 3 p.m. Full bar. Reservations accepted. Patio. View. Visa, MC. Parking lot. Casual to semi-dressy.

---

## BENIHANA OF TOKYO         Japanese
(Locations in Anaheim, Beverly Hills, Encino, Marina del Rey, Newport Beach, Torrance. See phone book for listings.)

Are these gimmick-Japanese? Well, Rocky Aoki, the affable proprietor, in a moment of candor told me that his location in Tokyo was called "Benihana of New York." "They'd laugh me out of Japan" he reflected, "if I called these typical

For best results, consult "How to Use This Guide" on page 27.

Japanese." But they're good, damn good, at what they do and what they do is train a Teppan chef like a samurai who makes your dinner—you're probably seated at a horseshoe shaped table—with lightning flashes of his knife. It's dazzling, fascinating, and fun but it ain't Japanese. Cocktails with some mixed tropical drinks, sake, some wine and fine Japanee beer is available at all the locations.

**Moderate.** Open seven days. Check specific location for hours and prices. Some locations have entertainment. Full bar. Reservations advised. No reservations Friday after 7 p.m. some locations. All major credit cards. Valet parking. Casual to semi-dressy.

---

**BENJIE'S**                                    **Jewish Delicatessen**
1828 North Tustin Avenue                                           ★
Santa Ana          **Map 6**                        (714) 541-6263

If someone were to tell you that some of the best Jewish delis in the area are in Orange County — WASP country — you might understandably be surprised. This one is several notches above Fairfax Avenue in every respect, and the mile-long menu is a guide to good eating. Breakfast is a favorite with the stock-broker-lawyer crowd, who get involved with things like a bagel brunch, deli omelettes, and lox. Entrées include sweet and sour stuffed cabbage, baby beef liver, and roast brisket of beef with horseradish. Sandwiches are mountainous. There's a take-out bakery that's worth visiting too.

**Inexpensive to moderate.** Open seven days from 11 a.m. to 11 p.m. Closed Yom Kippur, Thanksgiving, Christmas. Full bar. No reservations. Visa, MC. Parking lot. Casual.

*To obtain the best results from this Guide, consult "How to Use this Guide" on page 27.*

## BEN'S PLACE                          Danish/American
1823 Pico Boulevard                                    ★
Santa Monica        **Map 2**              (213) 450-1878

More people have "discovered" this comfortable dinner
house that offers Danish specialties available nowhere else in
Southern California, dishes as unpronounceable (*medisterpolse,
hakkebof, fricadeller, rod grod*), as they are good. Fresh fish is a
specialty of the house and Ben manages to serve full dinners
with soup and salad at winsomely modest prices.

**Inexpensive.** Open Wednesday through Sunday from 5 to
10:30 p.m. Beer and wine only. Reservations required. Visa,
MC. Parking lot. Casual.

---

## BERGIN'S WEST                                American
11600 San Vicente Boulevard                            ★
Los Angeles         **Map 8**              (213) 820-3641

## TOM BERGIN'S TAVERN
840 South Fairfax Avenue                               ★
Los Angeles         **Map 7**              (213) 936-7151

Since the old House of Murphy faded away, this has
become the headquarters for Irish goings-on. There's a
horseshoe bar, a dining room with a fireplace, and a New
York pub atmosphere; but most of all, there's built-in
conviviality. Corned beef and cabbage are a tip of the green
derby to the theme; but then the menu gets serious, with
roast Long Island duck, broiled halibut, prime rib, steaks,
and chop, and what some feel is the best hamburger in
town. It's also a favorite hangout for the postgraduates
who gather for Irish coffee to weep or whoop it up after a
big game.

**Bergin's West: Inexpensive to moderate.** Open seven days;
from 11:30 a.m. to 11 p.m. Sunday through Tuesday; to

midnight Wednesday, Thursday; to 1 a.m. Friday, Saturday. Entertainment Sunday, Tuesday, Wednesday. Full bar. Reservations recommended for more than six. Visa, MC, AX. Valet parking. Casual.

**Tom Bergin's Tavern: Inexpensive to moderate.** Open Monday through Saturday. Luncheon from 11 a.m. to 2 p.m. weekdays. Dinner from 4 to 11 p.m. Closed major holidays. Full bar. Reservations recommended. Visa, MC, AX. Valet parking. Casual.

---

## BERNARD'S
French Nouvelle Cuisine
★★★

Biltmore Hotel
515 South Olive Street
Los Angeles  **Map 7**  (213) 624-0183

Bernard Jacoupy and his chefs have impeccable credentials that include Rothschild's restaurants abroad and the legendary Maxim's. The dishes are a revelation to our less sophisticated American palates: poached sea bass in lime sauce (*le loup demur au citron vert*) and the fillet of shark served in a light mint sauce are a mere glimmer of what comes from this talented kitchen. The poached clams served in a light cream sauce, perfumed with *pastis* or the delicate soup of mussels, are unequalled in the area. Desserts are awe-inspiring, particularly the white chocolate cake. Decor is dramatic: African sumac trees, black table service, gleaming silver (some from the old Biltmore opulence) on rush colored napery. Style, too, is important here. Plates are elegantly dressed and there are hand-shaped rosettes of butter, baskets of freshly baked banana bread, and fan-shaped pita. There is always light, unobtrusive musical background. Like many such restaurants,

*In order to obtain the best results from this Guide, be sure to read the French, German, Italian and Oriental menu translators on page 705 to 710 of this Guide.*

Bernard's is not as good at lunch as it is at dinner—the demands are different—but at its worst, it is still better than most French restaurants at their best. It is a splendid restaurant.

**Expensive.** Open Monday through Saturday. Luncheon 11:30 a.m. to 2 p.m. weekdays. Dinner Monday through Thursday 6 to 9 p.m.; Friday and Saturday to 10 p.m. Live entertainment. Full bar. Reservations necessary. Visa, MC, AX, CB. Wheelchair access. Validated parking on Olive Street. Dressy.

---

## BESSIE WALL'S FINE FOOD & SPIRITS  American

1074 North Tustin ★
Anaheim     **Map 6**     (714) 630-2812

Back in 1927 John Wall, one of Anaheim's leading citrus growers, built a house as a present for his bride Bessie. It embodied every architectural and luxury feature of the age, a beautiful and graceful home with a dramatic stairwell that descended from the bedroom suite into the foyer. How astonished Bessie would be to know that her home, lovingly restored, has become a restaurant called Bessie Wall's, preserving the feel of that innocent era. Of course, some changes were necessary to satisfy the gods of commerce and the health department, but the only thing that would have shocked our Bess is that her upstairs bedroom is now the swinging cocktail lounge and entertainment center of the establishment. Otherwise, diners have a sense of dining with Bessie and her friends: authentic photographs from the family album decorate the walls along with other memorabilia and artifacts. One of her recipes has even become a dinner favorite: homemade chicken and dumplings is still rich and warming on a winter's night. The restaurant offers an unusually creative early California selection. Enchiladas del mar (two flour tortillas stuffed with fresh crabmeat and topped with sour cream) is another favorite and the steak enchilada is much better than it sounds. Bessie Wall's is a fine dining adventure, a chance to relive the richest and most colorful era of California. It's fun and it's good, and that's what they used to say about Bessie.

**Moderate.** Open seven days. Luncheon from 11 a.m. to 3 p.m. Dinner 5 to 10 p.m.; to 11 Friday, Saturday. Sunday brunch 10 a.m to 3 p.m. Closed Labor Day, Christmas. Entertainment. Full bar. Reservations recommended. Visa, MC. AX. Parking lot. Casual.

---

## THE BICYCLE SHOP CAFE                    French/Brasserie
12217 Wilshire Boulevard                                    ★
Brentwood          **Map 8**                  (213) 826-7831

The Bicycle Shop Cafe in Brentwood is an appealing brasserie where Andre Driollet (in the kitchen) and Andre Phillipe (in the front) achieved a lifelong fantasy. Their previous restaurant, Papillon in Woodland Hills, received more than its share of accolades and awards, but it was too small and too haute. Often, they talked about reproducing that uniquely French institution, the cafe where a greater number could be served. They visualized a contemporary atmosphere of raw woods and greenery and, of course, bicycles—suspended from the ceiling as partitions. Their success exceeds even their wildest expectations. There are waiting lines from 11 in the morning until 2 a.m., but the staff of young energetic waiters and waitresses manages to keep everything good-natured. The multi-page menu of hors d'oeuvres, soups (the best onion in town), salads (fresh artichokes!), cold plates, omelettes, sandwiches, crepes, seafoods, and desserts is a multicourse lesson in cuisine brasserie: it is not grand fare, but it conforms to the exceptionally hig standards that the Paris *boulevardier* takes for granted as he relaxes in his neighborhood cafe, unhurried, content. My favorite dishes are from the omelette list (omelette Basque with pepper, onions, and garlic)—a lovely way to top off a late evening. The wine list is a bit abbreviated, but I expect it will grow with time. If I were to select the perfect place in which to lull a companion into an agreeable state of mind, it would be the Bicycle Shop, one of the nicest foreign imports since Jacqueline Bisset.

**Inexpensive to moderate.** Open seven days from 11 a.m .to midnight; to 1 a.m. Friday, Saturday. Closed Thanksgiving, Christmas, New Year's. Full bar. No reservations. Visa, MC. Street parking. Casual.

---

## THE BIG YELLOW HOUSE American
(Locations in Santa Barbara, Montclair, Cerritos, Garden Grove, National City, Brea, Costa Mesa, Monrovia, Mission Viejo and Summerland. See phone book for listings.)

Yellow for caution? Along Highway 101 about five miles south of Santa Barbara you swing into the Yellow House (you can't miss it), dig in and enjoy home cooking served home style by waitresses in granny gowns. Remember your mother's bean and bacon soup? Here it comes (or the soup of the day) in a tureen plunked down in the center of your table. Of course you gotta have your greens, so here comes the salad with a cream dressing. Then they bring country fried chicken, or you have a choice of pork, pot roast, ham, or fish (on Friday). Call ahead to find out what the day's choices are. If you call before they open, a recorded message gives full details on the day's menu. With the entrée you get two vegetables, mashed potatoes, and hot corn bread with honey butter. Still hungry? Seconds are free, so are thirds. Children are charged by the pound—theirs—determined on an antique scale.

**Inexpensive.** Open seven days. Dinner served Monday through Thursday from 5 to 9 p.m.; Friday from 5 to 10

p.m.; Saturday from 4 to 10 p.m.; Sunday from 3 to 9 p.m.
Sunday brunch from 10 a.m. to 2 p.m. Full bar. Reservations
advised. Visa, MC, AX. Parking lot. Casual.

---

## THE BIRCHTREE                              Continental
445 South Figueroa
Los Angeles        **Map 7**              (213) 620-0567

The only consistency about this place is that it has been
consistently disappointing during the past decade and a
half. A pretty restaurant in a highrise, it's now beginning
to live up to its potential. The dinner menu has opted for
fewer but better prepared dishes and the location would
make it a natural for the Music Center. There are good
soups and a fine Caesar salad (for two), but my favorite
dish is the *zita carbonara*, egg pasta served with a cream
sauce, prosciutto and grated parmesan cheese. The broiled
chicken breasts are spiced with oregano and green peppercorns in a cognac sauce and their succulent rack of lamb is
served in Dijon mustard sauce with herbs. Prices are
moderate for dishes this serious at dinner and, as you
might expect, the luncheon menu is less expensive and
caters to the crowds that come spilling out of the highrises
at lunch. RMA-West has taken over the management here
and has made a noticeable difference.

**Moderate.** Open Monday through Friday. Breakfast from 7
to 10 a.m., in cafeteria only. Luncheon from 11:30 to 3 p.m.
Banquet facilities. Closed all holidays. Full bar 11:30 a.m. to
8 p.m. Reservations advised. All major credit cards. Parking
lot. Casual to semi-dressy.

---

*Please be sure to consult "Tipping Made Easy" on page 25 of
this Guide.*

---

## THE BISTRO
246 North Canon Drive
Beverly Hills    **Map 1**

**Continental**
★
(213) 273-5633

My pet peeve is that tables placed too close to each other force you to eat with your elbows whilst enjoying the unarguably good but extravagant fare here. There is far too much catering to the *hoi polloi*, Hollywood variety, but if you go on a weeknight it can be memorable.

**Expensive.** Open Monday through Saturday. Luncheon served weekdays noon to 3 p.m. Dinner served Monday through Saturday from 6 to 11 p.m. Closed major holidays and in the summer for lunch. Full bar. Reservations advised. All major credit cards. Parking lot; valet parking. Semi-dressy.

## BISTRO GARDEN
176 North Canon Drive
Beverly Hills    **Map 8**

**Continental**
★
(213) 550-3900

Tables jumbled one onto another display those who want to be scene and those who want to see in an outrageously expensive, arrogant, star worshipping silken trap. The people here could be served kibble and they wouldn't notice it. Desserts and soufflés are quite good.

**Moderate to expensive.** Open Monday through Saturday. Luncheon served Monday through Friday 11:30 a.m. to 3 p.m. Dinner Monday through Saturday 6 to 11 p.m. Closed Christmas, New Year's. Full bar. Reservations advised. All major credit cards. Valet parking at dinner. Casual.

*In order to obtain the best results from this Guide, please consult "Tips on Dining Out" on page 21.*

# BIT O'SCOTLAND

**Seafood/American**
★

1938 Westwood Boulevard
West Los Angeles  **Map 8**  (213) 474-0328

Not much on looks; but, oh, those cooks. Their long suit is shortbread of the homemade Scottish variety. The cheesecake is homemade too. Eat in or take out. A good place to drop by for shrimps or scallops with chips, ham or chicken.

**Inexpensive to moderate.** Open seven days. Luncheon 11:30 a.m. to 3 p.m. Friday only. Dinner 4 to 9 p.m. Sunday through Thursday; from 6 Friday, Saturday. Take out available. Wine and beer only. Reservations recommended for five or more. Visa, MC. Parking lot. Casual.

---

# BLACKBEARD'S GALLEY & GROG

**American**
★

4250 Martingale Way
Newport Beach  **Map 4**  (714) 833-0080

This is a feisty theme restaurant with decor to match the name. Yet the food is surprisingly serious and good. Menu includes Oscar Port Royale and fresh fish of the day. Among the meat choices of prime ribs and steaks, my favorite is the generous-sized marinated pork chop. A shrimp salad bar completes the meals. Hearty eating here as the name implies.

**Inexpensive to moderate.** Open seven days. Luncheon from 11 a.m. to 2:45 p.m. Monday through Saturday. Dinner from 5 to 10:30 p.m. Monday through Thursday; to 11:30 Friday, Saturday; 4 to 9:30 Sunday. Sunday champagne brunch 10 a.m. to 2:45 p.m. Closed Christmas. Full bar. Reservations recommended. Visa, MC, AX, DC. Parking lot. Casual.

## BOB BURNS RESTAURANT    American/Continental

37 Fashion Island                              ★★
Newport Beach        **Map 4**        (714) 644-2030

6343 Laurel Canyon Boulevard                   ★
North Hollywood      **Map 1**        (213) 984-2261

500 North Euclid                               ★
Anaheim       **Map 6**               (714) 722-2130

202 Wilshire Boulevard                         ★
Santa Monica      **Map 2**           (213) 393-6777

Promenade Shopping Center                      ★
Woodland Hills       **Map 1**        (213) 883-2145

There is nothing quite so bleak as a shopping center when all the shops are closed; it is a long and lonely walk down the mall with nothing but stylish, smiling mannequins for company. But this restaurant is worth the walk. The interior is warm and inviting, with vivid colors and plaids and textures of rough stone, contrasting with polished woods and sleek booths. Food is American/Continental, and in order of popularity, the more notable dishes include roast duckling, Scottich plaice, veal cutlet Oscar, and prime rib. Scottish lasses, looking not quite so self-conscious as their counterparts in other theme restaurants, provide lively and cheerful service during the hectic luncheon and less busy dinner hours. You can dress or go beach-casual, but you should make reservations for weekends and for luncheon when the surrounding office complexes take their quota of space.

**Inexpensive.** Open seven days. Dinner served from Monday through Thursday from 5 p.m. to 11 p.m.; Friday, Saturday to midnight. Sunday brunch 11 a.m. to 3 p.m. Entertainment. Children welcome. Full bar. Reservations advised. Parking lot. Semi-dressy. Hours may vary in some locations.

## BOBBY McGEE'S American/Seafood

★

(Locations in Brea, Long Beach,
Mission Viejo, Newport Beach,
San Bernardino. See phone book for
exact listings.)

The in inn of the Newport area is Bobby McGee's, a discotheque with recorded music (should one say "dead" as opposed to "live"?), a disc jockey, dancing, and middle-of-the-road food and prices. On the site of the old Hungry Tiger that deserved to move away, this is go-for-baroque brouhaha with staff dressed like story-book characters, (Red Riding Hood, Little Bo Peep) serving above-average prime rib and seafood. Their salad bar—in a bath tub with golden legs—is better than most and now they're all over Southern California and still people pleasin'!

**Moderate.** Open seven days. Dinner from 5:30 to 10:30 Monday through Thursday; 5 to midnight Friday, Saturday; 5 to 10:30 Sunday. Children's menu. Closed Christmas. Disco dancing. Full bar. Reservations recommended, especially weekends which may be made up to two weeks in advance. All major credit cards. Parking in shopping mall. Casual to semi-dressy.

## BOCCACCIO'S Continental

★

32123 West Lindero Canyon Road
Westlake Village      **Map 1**      (213) 889-8300

When you've got the only restaurant in the area, as Mr. Colucci had back in 1968, you can understand a little laxity existing for awhile. But then things began to tighten up, and now this popular lakeside restaurant attracts people from much farther away than just the surrounding housing developments. The tableside preparation of the Continental menu includes an excellent *fettuccine*, steak *au poivre* and many desserts. A partially enclosed patio offers a lovely view year round, especially for Sunday brunch.

**Moderate to expensive.** Open Monday through Saturday. Luncheon served 11:30 a.m. to 2:30 p.m. weekdays. Dinner from 5:30 to 10 p.m. Full bar. Reservations suggested. Patio. Visa, MC, AX. Wheelchair access. Parking lot. Semi-dressy.

---

## BOGART'S  Continental
6288 East Pacific Coast Highway  ★
Long Beach  **Map 3**  (213) 594-8976

The beautiful waterside Marina Pacific Shopping Center in Long Beach is the setting for this theme restaurant carried to its illogical end. One sits amidst lush greenery hung at varying levels from the lofty ceiling. In some rooms the Casablanca opulence of lazy ceiling fans and stylized furniture makes it easy—with the help of a few bloody Marys—to imagine Sidney Greenstreet at the next table and Peter Lorre peering anxiously around a corner. I had baked grapefruit and a seafood omelette larger than Rhode Island. Dishes include "Bogart's specials" from eggs Benedict to *friarde* Parisienne (sausages in pastry) and a good Holstein *schnitzel*. For dessert you owe yourself the fresh strawberries dipped in chocolate, injected with Grand Marnier and served with whipped cream.

Dinner is divided into the "African Queen" list of seafoods including fresh broiled salmon and good scampi, and the "Maltese Falcon" group that gets down to the serious business of steaks and veal. There is an oyster bar, beautiful ocean view and good service in this relatively new addition to an area that quite desperately needs good restaurants.

**Moderate.** Open Tuesday through Saturday. Dinner served

6 to 9:30 p.m. Tuesday through Thursday; Friday, Saturday to 10:30 p.m. Sunday brunch from 10 a.m. to 2 p.m. Banquet facilities. Live entertainment. Oyster bar. Full bar. Reservations advised. View. All major credit cards accepted. shopping mall parking. Casual.

---

## BORDEAUX RESTAURANT                              French
758 St. Clair Street                                     ★
Costa Mesa          **Map 4**                  (714) 540-3641

This tiny restaurant has had more owners than chairs. But for four years Chuck Dudley, a former waiter from Beverly Hills where he learned well the ways of the movie stars in their spas, has had a good grip on this place. Even though menus are in French and English, Chuck comes to each table as an interpreter and counselor to insure your complete pleasure. While it is not necessarily the specialty on the extensive menu, the roast duckling has become the most popular dish with a choice of orange, cherry, or green peppercorn sauces. Desserts are homemade with a marvelous carrot cake appearing now and then on the menu. He promised to come up with his date-nut torte soon, so if you don't see it on the menu, nag him.

**Moderate.** Open Monday through Saturday. Luncheon from 11:30 a.m. to 2 p.m. weekdays. Dinner 6 to 10 p.m. Closed major holidays. Wine and beer only. Reservations advised during week, required on weekends. Visa, MC, AX. Semi-dressy.

---

*To obtain the best results from this Guide, consult
"How to Use this Guide" on page 27.*

## BORRELLI'S                                    Italian
672 Silver Spur Road                                ★
Rolling Hills Estates      **Map 2**        (213) 541-2632

Mediterranean atmosphere does not necessarily mean Mediterranean food as we have learned the hard way. Borrelli's is an exception, a marvelous, always-busy exuberant restaurant in an area that appreciates it. A classic Northern Italian menu, fine veals and pastas are served with the kind of friendly concern that seems almost twilight-zone. Jammed on weekends but worth visiting anytime, even for lunch.

**Moderate.** Open Tuesday through Saturday. Luncheon served 11:30 a.m. to 3 p.m. weekdays. Dinner from 5 to 10 p.m. Sunday brunch 10 a.m. to 3 p.m. Full bar. Reservations suggested. Visa, MC, CB. Parking lots. Casual.

## BOUCHON                                       French
11620 San Vicente Boulevard                         ★
Brentwood         **Map 8**                 (213) 820-6619

"A machine to dispense wine? Are you mad?" sputtered my friend the sommelier when I told him about the latest technological achievement in the restaurant industry, a device that enables you to turn even great wines on and off like a tap.

From France comes La Wine Machine, which is intended to change the way you purchase wine at a restaurant. Making its debut at the new Bouchon restaurant in Brentwood, La Wine Machine is a stainless steel contraption that's seven feet by two feet with a glass showcase that displays 30 open bottles of wine. It is claimed by both the inventor and Kit Marshall, proprietor of Bouchon, that the marvelous machine will keep bottles at wine temperatures, perfectly decanted by way of a complex system involving nitrogen pressure. Great vintages keep their original character, fragrance and flavor, and there is no spoilage. The objective is to allow ordinary people to enjoy glamorous and rare wines by the glass. The offerings at Bouchon (which, appropriately, means "cork") range from a Dinehard Silvaner Dry 1976 at $2 a glass to the legendary Mouton Rothschild for $100. French wines predominate, but there is also a selection of Californian, German and Italian. Perhaps the most interesting opportunity is the chance to taste the rare Chateau d'Yqem, the wheat-colored, rich dessert sauterne that is one of a kind. You may enjoy a half glass (enough when you take into account the sweetness and richness of the wine) for $20.

Kit Marshall, who gave us Au Petit Cafe in Hollywood, has a comfortable, intimate restaurant here that for now will be overshadowed by all the attention given La Machine. Bouchon's two chefs are from France and their specialties include *pissaladiere* (a French pizza-style appetizer), mussels in cream, *cunard* Martinquaise and trout *en croute* on an à la carte menu. There is a dessert spectacular that combines the puree of fresh fruit with ice cream and *crème fraiche*, *kirschwasser* and sliced fresh fruit.

**Moderate.** Open for lunch Monday through Friday noon to 3 p.m. Dinner Monday through Saturday 6 p.m. to midnight. Closed major holidays. Wine bar serving 30 different wines by the glass. Reservations advised. Patio. Visa, MC, AX. Wheelchair access. Validated parking. Casual.

---

## BOUILLABAISSE                    Seafood
17000 Ventura Boulevard                    ★★
Encino        **Map 1**                    (213) 990-4850

Here is a dream come true — for the owners — and possibly for discriminating diners. Bouillabaisse is a small, specialty restaurant on the top floor of a business building, yet one has the feeling you've been invited into Rosemary and Eddie Spivak's home. They serve to one sitting at 7:30 on Wednesday, Thursday, Friday, and Saturday evenings only. Bouillabaisse is the main and only course of dinner which starts with a salad of romaine, red or green leaf lettuce, and blanched vegetables of the season, accompanied by their own French dressing. Warm sourdough bread (for dunking) comes with the bouillabaisse. Customers are encouraged to "dig in" with their fingers for complete enjoyment. The broth and soup art of the bouillabaisse are prepared the night before and only genuine Spanish saffron is used. After a finger-bowl ritual, the table is reset and dessert comes beginning with an Italian pure fruit ice with a fresh lemon slice hand-dipped in chocolate. Then comes the cheese board bearing three or four imported cheeses. Fresh fruit is offered from an ornamental basket. Coffee is their special blend of three kinds of beans ground each day, and is presented in a twist. The wine list is small, but well chosen. The house wine is Italian Soave or Valpolicella bottled in a sealed liter. There are also imported beers, apéritifs, and dessert wines. Reservations, of course, are essential, but do make a note of the phone number as information operators can't spell bouillabaisse. For parties of 25 or more, the Spivaks will arrange dinner on the off nights with the same menu. They give special attention to birthdays, anniversaries.

**Expensive.** Open Wednesday through Saturday. Dinner served only at 7:30 p.m. Entertainment. Beer and wine only. Reservations necessary. Visa, MC. Street parking. Semi-dressy.

---

*To obtain the best results from this Guide, be sure to consult maps on the various Southern California areas in the front of the book.*

## BRATSKELLAR
American
★

1154 Westwood Boulevard
Los Angeles    **Map 8**    (213) 208-6030

As the menu says, "Bratskellar tells it like it isn't." A decorator's orgy of Gothic arches, suits of armor, antique chests, shields, and stained-glass windows creates a knight-club with great atmosphere, almost enough to make you forget the mediocrity on your plate—fancy sandwiches, bratwurst, chicken, and great shrimp boiled in beer. A youthful management team makes up in enthusiasm and originality for what they lack in experience; they've gone for baroque here.

**Inexpensive to moderate.** Open seven days. Luncheon from 11:30 a.m. to 4 p.m. weekdays. Dinner from 4 to midnight. Closed Thanksgiving. Full bar. Reservations recommended on weekdays; no reservations on weekends. Visa, MC, AX, CB. Parking lot; street parking. Casual.

## BREAKERS SEAFOOD CO.
Seafood
★

11970 Venice Boulevard
Los Angeles    **Map 7**    (213) 390-8719

In recent years, I've noticed a commendable trend toward seafood restaurants like Breakers. They're marked as a rule, by simple decor, menus written on blackboards, a genuine interest in fresh fish, and an eminently simple cooking style which consists almost entirely on grilling the fish over mesquite charcoal.

You can purchase clams and oysters at Breakers for 49 cents apiece. And you can order thresher shark, Idaho trout, Boston bluefish and Atlantic cod plates, at prices beginning just under $5. But I went to Breakers to check out the lobster... and I was, for the most part, satisfied with the result.

There's a large tank near the entrance filled with lobsters

and crabs, and you can choose the lobster or your preference from that milling mass. The one-pounders go for $9.95, while larger lobster cost in the $15 area, which is still a reasonable fee. The lobster ritual is basically the same as at the Hungry Tiger, with bib, nut cracker, chowder and assorted vegetables. The difference at the Breakers is that the lobster can be had either boiled or broiled. As a rule, I prefer the broiled lobster (though purists would sneer at anything but boiling, and boiling in seawater at that), simply because I like the taste that broiling gives to the lobster meat. Butter, as always, is the dip supplied on the side—just in case your cholesterol level should be running a little low. A fish market is on the premises also. *M.S.*

**Moderate.** Open seven days. Luncheon served Monday through Friday 11:30 a.m. to 4 p.m. Dinner served Monday through Thursday 4 to 10 p.m., Friday and Saturday to 11 p.m.; Sunday to 9:30. Closed Thanksgiving, Christmas and legal holidays which fall on Monday. Full bar. Reservations accepted. Visa, MC. Parking lot. Casual.

---

## BROTHERTON'S FARMHOUSE American

2239 East Colorado ★
Pasadena **Map 7** (213) 796-5058

For 50 years this homey, converted bungalow has been serving good chicken—pan fried, baked or in a pie—to patrons indifferent to their surroundings. The lights are too glary and there's plastic on the tables but the good food on the plate, rabbit and fresh fish and hot biscuits and more, is served at down home prices. No foolishness like credit cards or booze but you can get all the biscuits you want.

**Inexpensive.** Open Tuesday through Sunday. Luncheon and dinner served from 11:30 a.m. to 8:30 p.m. daily. Closed Christmas, New Year's. No alcoholic beverages. Reservations accepted but not necessary. No credit cards accepted. Casual.

# BROWN DERBY
**American/Continental**

1628 North Vine Street ★
Hollywood **Map 7** (213) 469-5151

9537 Wilshire Boulevard ★
Beverly Hills **Map 8** (213) 276-2311

Their celebrity lounge is replacing the famous forecourt as the stars hall of fame with caricatures that are certain to evoke nostagia in even the pre-Bette Davis set. The Hollywood Derby is decorated with crystal chandeliers, red banquettes and rich carpeting, fending off the shabbiness of some of its neighbors. One of its better companions is the Huntington Hartford Theatre, making the Derby a convenient, pleasant place for before-and after-theatre dining. The menu with a few exceptions is the same as the Beverly Hills Derby. Cobb salad is still big—chicory, chives, romaine, watercress, iceberg lettuce, celery, tomato and avacado chopped finely with chicken breast, crisp bacon and crumbled Roquefort cheese. The innovation, or concession, to the New Hollywood is a coffee shop annex that serves breakfast, soup and salad or sandwich combinations. Informality is the rule here; the prices are reasonable and the food good. Hollywood's Derby displays its famous caricatures of the stars and is still frequented by some of the personalities in the flesh, a few of whom have become caricatures of the caricatures.

**Inexpensive to moderate.** Open seven days both locations. Luncheon from 11 a.m. to 2 p.m. Monday through Saturday. Dinner from 5 to 11 p.m. Tuesday through Sunday (Hollywood); 4 to 11 (Beverly Hills). Sunday champagne brunch noon to 3 p.m. Closed major holidays. Entertainment, Hollywood only. Full bar. Reservations recommended. All major credit cards. Valet parking. Casual to semi-dressy.

## BRUNO'S CHARTREUSE

**Continental**
★

10275 West Pico Boulevard
Century City    **Map 8**    (213) 552-2521

Relatively new, this charmer created in the image of a firehouse scores both as a saloon and a restaurant. Next to 20th Century Fox it accommodates the more mundane thirsts of the studio executives and a host of recognizables. The menu is imaginative with such happy tastes as toasted Camembert in a good tossed salad, duck that tastes hauntingly like it has been dressed with a sauce of Chartreuse, and lamb chops that are sautéed, topped with *duxelle* and baked in pâté. Bruno Moeckli has proven once again that it doesn't take a million dollars to build a splendid restaurant. Just good taste, flair and some caring.

**Moderate.** Open Monday through Saturday. Luncheon served 11:30 a.m. to 2:30 p.m. weekdays. Dinner from 6 to 9:30 p.m. Full bar. Reservations advised. Patio. Visa, MC, AX, DC. Street parking. Semi-dressy.

## BUDAPEST HUNGARIAN RESTAURANT   **Hungarian**

★

432 North Fairfax Avenue
Los Angeles    **Map 7**    (213) 655-0111

This twenty-four year-old Budapest Hungarian Restaurant in Los Angeles' Fairfax district is one of those dining adventures in which the total experience transcends the component parts. In other words, the food isn't wonderful, but it's hearty, cheap, and fun. When you're ushered to your booth, it seems for all the world as though you're seated among a giant cast party for *Fiddler on the Roof*. The expressive faces, quick laughter, and spicy aromas that waft from the tables are a far cry from the harsh clatter of the neighboring delis; but many of the dishes are the same: the herring, chopped liver, matzo-ball soup, borscht (exceptional), and chicken in the pot. The Hungarian influence is reflected in goulashes, a good but surprisingly bland chicken paprikash served with nockerels and peas, savory stuffed cabbage, and a roast goose in season that tasted as though it had been cooking since last Rosh Hashanah. Dinners include relishes, appetizer, soup, dessert, and beverage. Seltzer is served instead of water, in the European tradition, and there are some rare California values like a Concannon burgundy, along with Hungarian reds and whites. With your dinner you might enjoy a *spritzer*, a tall glass of white wine and soda. Service is by pleasant, brisk, no-nonsense waitresses (none of this "Hi there, my name is Alice and I'm thrilled to serve you" jazz). Recommended dessert — a ritual there — is the strudel, which I found only passingly good. You would do better to go to one of the little bakeries in the area and buy fresh pastry. Open for dinner only.

**Moderate.** Open Tuesday through Friday 4 to 9:30 p.m.; Sunday 1 to 9 p.m. Beer and wine only. Reservations suggested. Visa, MC, AX. DC. Wheelchair access. Street parking. Semi-dressy.

---

**BULL 'N BUSH**                                          **Steakhouse**
3450 West 6th Street                                              ★
Los Angeles          **Map 7**                      (213) 385-4271

The fact that this popular place happens to be near the thicket of high-rise buildings on Wilshire Boulevard makes it no less the neighborhood restaurant, but it's better than most. Specialties include lamb chops, prime rib, pork chops, and steaks. Service is cordial and efficient, the bar is hospitable, and the overall effect is un-plastic.

---

*To obtain the best results from this Guide, be sure to consult maps on the various Southern California areas in the front of the book.*

---

**Inexpensive to moderate.** Open seven days from 11:30 to midnight; Sunday to 10 p.m. Closed Thanksgiving. Full bar. Reservations advised. Visa, MC, DC. Valet parking. Casual.

---

## BULLOCK'S WILSHIRE TEA ROOM American
3050 Wilshire Boulevard ★
Los Angeles **Map 7** (213) 382-6161

The only official landmark I know that serves a fine luncheon is Bullock's Wilshire. Once you get over the feeling you are dining in Marie Antoinette's boudoir, you can select from an array of exotica that would overwhelm Auntie Mame. How about (one of scores) the Wilshire Tower Five sandwich? It includes breast of turkey, bacon, Swiss cheese, avocado, and sliced egg layered between wafer-thin bread and topped with Russian caviar dressing, served with frozen fruit salad. According to the management one of the most frequently served specialties is the Bombay cold shrimp and crab platter. Prices are reasonable, and the atmosphere is old-rich, and the maitre d' calls everyone "honey." The building is a landmark itself and worth a visit.

**Moderate.** Open Monday through Saturday. Luncheon from 11:30 a.m. to 4:30 p.m. High tea from 2:30 to 4:30 p.m. Children's menu. Closed major holidays. Full bar. Fashion shows daily. Reservations recommended. Bullock's credit cards only. Parking lot. Semi-dressy.

---

## THE BUTCHER'S ARMS English
281 East Palm ★
Burbank (213) 843-1424

This little touch of Blighty in the midst of downtown Burbank is a royal charmer. More pub than posh, the steaks and prime beef are served with a hearty greeting. There is pub food available for take out along with good old fashioned deli items.

**Inexpensive.** Deli open Monday through Saturday from 10 a.m. to 6 p.m. Restaurant open for lunch only  Monday through Friday 11 a.m. to 3 p.m. Pub Monday through Saturday 11 a.m. to 1 a.m. Butcher shop Tuesday through Saturday 10 a.m. to 6 p.m. Closed Memorial Day, Labor Day, Christmas, New Year's. Entertainment Thursday, Saturday; dart tournaments Monday, Friday. Full bar. Reservations not necessary. Visa, MC, AX, DC. Wheelchair access. Parking lot. Casual.

---

## THE BUTTERY
6581 Manchester
Buena Park      **Map 6**

American
★
(714) 521-8309

If you think that dining in Buena Park is fraught with peril, perish the fraught, or let the Arnold's people do it for you. Buena Park is several quantam leaps—backwards—in restaurant excitement but the Buttery and its nearby sister, Arnold's Farmhouse have become an oasis of reliability and good food. Everything is done well here, and the menu—if a little limited—ranges from *scampi en casserole* to abalone steak to English beefsteak and mushroom pie with confidence. This is a little more sophisticated atmosphere than the Farmhouse. There are cocktails and entertainment, and there are palate savers at luncheon with a really uptown Monte Cristo.

**Inexpensive to moderate.** Open Wednesday through Monday. Luncheon Monday through Friday from 11:30 a.m. to 3 p.m. Dinner from 4 to 9 p.m. Closed July 4, Christmas, Labor Day. Organ music Wednesday through Saturday. Full bar. Reservations accepted. All major credit cards. Parking lot. Casual to semi-dressy.

*For best results, consult "How to Use This Guide" on page 27.*

# C

## CAFE CALIFORNIA American
2917 Main Street ★
Santa Monica **Map 2** (213) 396-4122

In restaurant-rich Santa Monica the Cafe is unique for its laid back attitude. Brick walls glow from the skylighted room, and there is a back garden to stroll in and admire. Fresh fish is prepared precisely as you want it. Soups and vegetables are not complex but are served well. Desserts include a big bowl of fresh whipped cream. Music is classical guitar.

**Moderate.** Open seven days. Luncheon Monday through Saturday 11:30 a.m. to 2:30 p.m.; light menu 2:30 to 6 p.m. daily. Dinner Monday through Thursday 6 to 10:30; Friday, Saturday to 11 p.m. Saturday, Sunday brunch from 10:30 a.m. to 2:30 p.m. Cabaret with light menu open from 9:30 p.m. to midnight daily. Closed Thanksgiving and Christmas. Classical guitar Friday, Saturday. Wine and beer only. Reservations accepted. Visa, MC. Street parking. Casual.

## CAFE CASINO                                    French Buffet

9595 Wilshire Boulevard                                    ★
Beverly Hills        **Map 8**              (213) 274-0201

1299 Ocean Avenue                                          ★
Santa Monica         **Map 2**              (213) 394-3717

Casino is the leading restaurant chain in France and provides a low cost answer to the curiosity of Western palates who would like to try French dishes. More buffet than cafeteria, the idea is still self-service but the food and ambience are the difference.

The festive cafe with a lively sidewalk atmosphere uses hand-painted tiles, etched glass, copper mirrors, decorator woodwork and awnings as a setting for fine croissants and pastries. Selections include homemade soup, a dozen salads, exotic hors d'oeuvres and specialties like quiche Lorraine, roast pork, chicken curry, eggs Benedict and much, much more. Prices are very low, by far the lowest for this kind of cooking and I predict the concept will be a great success in America.

**Inexpensive.** Open seven days. Monday through Thursday 7 a.m. to 10 p.m.; to midnight Friday, Saturday; 9 a.m. to 10 p.m. Sundya. Santa Monica location open Sunday through Thursday 7 a.m. to 11 p.m. Wine and beer only. No reservations. Patio. Visa, MC. Parking in building garage. Casual.

---

*In order to obtain the best results from this Guide, be sure to read the French, German, Italian and Oriental menu translators on page 705 to 710 of this Guide.*

# CAFE COURTNEY

French/American
★★

2701 Pacific Coast Highway
Hermosa Beach          **Map 2**          (213) 544-0370

Cafe Courtney presents one of the easiest introductions to French cuisine I've experienced—not French enough to be arrogant and intimidating, and American enough to be comfortable. Chuck Lehman, Michael Franks and Robert Bell have hit upon an expandable formula. They already operate Courtney's and Courtney's Bistro in Manhattan Beach and a Courtney's in Palos Verdes. The formula: an inexpensive, colorful, cozy, unpretentious cafe that is youth oriented. If there are nicer people anywhere than the waitresses or management at this establishment, it would be difficult to find them. Our mail and phone calls are effusive about the friendliness and hospitality, and Cafe Courtney is constantly being "discovered" by readers, and brought to my attention. While not *haute cuisine*—certainly they do not compete in preparation (or price range) with the Tower and its ilk—their duck *à l'orange* and the quiche Lorraine are very nicely done. The *bouchée de mer,* a flaky pastry shell filled with Alaskan bay shrimp, langoustine and king crab, would do credit to any restaurant here or abroad and is reasonably priced. Desserts include a fudge vanilla Lisa—vanilla custard, waffles and French vanilla ice cream topped with hot fudge, and a splendid carrot cake. There's a patio with a view for Sunday brunch, which has become a tradition in the area; and *al fresco* dining is encouraged on summer evening or for luncheon.

**Inexpensive.** Open seven days. Luncheon from 11 a.m. to 5 p.m. Dinner 5 to 10 p.m.; to 10:45 Friday, Saturday. Saturday and Sunday brunch from 11 a.m. to 2:30 p.m. Closed major holidays. Wine and beer only. Reservations accepted. Garden room. Visa, MC. Parking lot. Casual.

## CAFE DEL SOL                    Spanish/Continental
516 San Ysidro Road                              ★
Montecito                          (805) 969-0448

The Spanish-style complex of elegant shops houses this beauty and is part of the romance of this area. The cafe serves many wines from neighboring vineyards and is a photo-buff's paradise for the Hispanic decor. Luncheon salads are well constructed—as are the waitresses—and dinner includes some Spanish dishes. There's a patio that's become popular with residents and the Sunday brunch features *huevos rancheros*.

**Inexpensive to moderate.** Open seven days. Luncheon served noon to 3:30 p.m. Dinner from 6 to 10 p.m. Sunday brunch 10 a.m. to 2:30 p.m. Full bar. Reservations advised. Patio. Visa, MC, AX. Street parking. Casual to semi-dressy.

## CAFE EUROPA                             Continental
1733 South Hill Street                           ★
Oceanside                          (714) 433-5811

Good restaurants frequently provide a training ground for future restaurant proprietors. Thee Bungalow, a fine restaurant in San Diego, once boasted of Siegfried Heil (sounds like a name in a Wagnerian opera) who chefed there for a respectable period of time before opening his own restaurant. Oceanside is a city more noted for marines than marinas but there are people here, and this midpoint along the gold coast from Newport to San Diego has universities and industry and thus a large bedroom community; whether they are sophisticated enough for Cafe Europa remains to be seen. The atmosphere is not grand by any stretch of the imagination (it used to be a Mexican restaurant and it still shows the remnants), but the food is light years above anything in the surrounding territory. The menu varies according to what's fresh and good but you'll frequently find dishes like goose, stuffed lobster in whiskey sauce, duck pâté made with hazel nuts, quenelles in Americaine sauce and a great salad dressing that Siegfried made for Thee Bungalow: light oil, French mustard and tarragon. He has a nice touch with veal in a variety of dishes but he should skip the veal Oscar, an unholy combination made popular by American palates. The wine list is carefully thought out to blend imported with good Californians, and if you believe that "life is a cabernet, my friends"—try their 1975 Sterling.

**Inexpensive to moderate.** Open Tuesday through Sunday. Luncheon from 11:30 a.m. to 2 p.m. weekdays. Dinner from 6 to 9:30 p.m.; to 10 p.m. weekends. Full bar. Reservations required. Visa, MC. Parking lot. Casual.

---

## CAFE FOUR OAKS

2181 North Beverly Glen
Bel Air     **Map 8**

Continental
★
(213) 474-9317

This charming old Victorian house in the lush loveliness of Bel Air has been a continuing favorite of the Hollywood set. Created by actors, it manages the chemistry, the mix of things — color, fireplace, open windows, view and attitude — that imparts a feeling of expectancy from the moment of entry. The menu is changed seasonally so the clientele won't tire of it, although there are certain creative and fascinating dishes that have become identified with the place, such as beef'n bourbon — thin strips of lean beef marinated in bourbon. Veal scallops, fresh seafood, and roast duckling are favorites as well. There is a lovely patio, more a large garden with veranda, and the aroma of freshly baked croissants on the soft summer evening will be a haunting memory. Dinner only, except for Sunday brunch that has become a tradition in the area.

**Moderate to expensive.** Open Tuesday through Sunday for dinner 6 to 9:30 p.m. Sunday brunch 10:30 a.m. to 2:30 p.m. Live entertainment Sunday. Beer and wine only. Reservations required. Patio. No credit cards. Parking lot. Casual.

---

## CAFE LE MONDE
915 North Glendale Avenue
Glendale    **Map 7**

**Continental**
★★
(213) 243-0359

An improbable restaurant with a strangely eclectic menu—French with a Philippine influence—situated in an unlikely corner of Glendale. The building used to house a bleak coffee shop which was succeeded, if that's the word, by an indifferent Mexican attempt. André Guerrero is the manager of this little beauty. Cafe Le Monde is a son-and-mom-and-pop-and-sister effort that has attracted a great deal of attention. I met André, a lithe, shy, and handsome youth, not long after he removed the sheets from the windows. ("I didn't want anyone to know what we were doing.") With his degree in graphic arts from UCLA and a host of willing friends, he transformed a greasy spoon into a graceful, comfortable, spacious cafe. That he was able to do it at all is surprising. There are pin lights along the interior columns, careful use of color and a baby grand piano (sister Yvette plays classical music during dinner) in the entrance. Service is by smartly attired youngsters, very willing but still working out the intricate choreography of their profession. Never mind that it takes a little longer between appetizer and entrée; it's worth it. I began my dinner with a small portion of Chinese chicken salad—crisp, spicy and good. Others in my party tried the oysters *remoulade* and the marinated mushrooms. The homemade vegetable broth with glazed carrots was excellent, far better than I've had at most

Beverly Hills restaurants. The entrées include chicken *adobo* (from the Philippines: one half chicken braised and simmered in a sauce of fresh garlic, freshly cracked black peppers and soy.) My favorite is the *lengua de Malaga*: beef tongue simmered in red wine, fresh tomato sauce, mushrooms, capers and cognac. There's a splendid *coquille au saffron*; scallops simmered in a sauce of shallots, mushrooms, wine, cream, saffron, and sour sauce with pimientos and tomatoes. Desserts are prepared by Guerrero Sr., a talented baker. His lemon crunch cake filled with a kind of lemon mousse has nearly replaced Bernard's white chocolate cake in my dessert hall of fame. The wine list is as extensive as storage will allow, with some exciting Californias. The house wine is Robert Mondavi burgundy, chablis or rosé.

**Moderate.** Open Tuesday through Sunday. Luncheon served from 11 a.m. to 2:30 p.m. weekdays. Dinner 5 to 10 p.m.; Sunday 5 to 9 p.m. Entertainment. Full bar. Reservations advised. Visa, MC. Parking lot. Semi-dressy.

---

## CAFE MONET

French
★

9045 Burton Way
Beverly Hills          **Map 8**          (213) 858-7779

Cafe Monet is the creation of Roger Bourban, Los Angeles' famous running waiter ("Le Garcon Rapide"). Bourban, who used to be a waiter at Ma Maison has run in races carrying open bottles of Perrier, of wine and of beer, usually on a tray with a couple of glasses, either filled or unfilled as the case may be.

Roger Bourban's life as Le Garcon Rapide is a nice sidelight to his lovely little bistro on Burton Way, but it's certainly not the place's defining quality. That's left up to the food, which is very simple, relatively inexpensive, and exccedingly pleasant. In terms of its informality, and its intimacy, Cafe Monet may be as close as any restaurant in town comes to being a genuine bistro. The tables are small and nicely spaced. Candlelight casts long shadows against the walls.

Waiters in black ties and vests come and go, speaking of Michelangelo, Caesar salad and cold poached salmon with mayonnaise sauce on the side.

The food at Cafe Monet is basic, beloved textbook French-quiche Lorraine, crepes Florentine, trout almondine, duck with orange sauce, minute steak, salade Nicoise. For those too familiar with the most basic of French cookery, there are also some slightly advanced dishes, like a beguiling mackerel in white wine, almost too fishy, but not quite; and a duck in cranberry sauce, prepared like the duck in orange sauce, but much more tart, with a contrast that both shocks and allures.

The fruit tarts are wonderful, and fresh. The coupe colonel (a vodka lemon sherbert) is a dessert to linger over. So is the cappuccino. And linger you can with ease at Cafe Monet. The candles twinkle until two in the morning, long after the streets have been rolled up along Burton Way, and some hours before Roger Bourban begins his morning run. *M.S.*

**Expensive.** Open Monday through Saturday. Luncheon served noon to 3 p.m. Dinner served Monday through Thursday 6 p.m. to midnight: Friday and Saturday to 2 a.m. Closed Labor Day. Full bar. Reservations advised. All major credit cards. Wheelchair access. Parking lot. Semi-dressy.

---

## CAFE PARISIEN                                    French
3100 Washington Boulevard                               ★
Marina del Rey        **Map 2**              (213) 822-2020

It is difficult to understand the paucity of respectable restaurants n the Marina del Rey area. After all, isn't this the Leisure World for folks in their early 30's, the swinging, Marlboro-smoking, single Nirvana where men wear the required number of gold chains and macho leather wrist-watch bands, and girls wave picturesquely from little boats, hanging on with white-knuckled determination? Affluence and influence abound. But good food, it's practically non-existent. A rare and delightful exception to this deplorable condition is Cafe Parisien, a quietly competent, authentic, and honorable establishment. Odette and Raymond de Robert supervise everything with the same demanding attitude of proprietors in France. The table must be set just so; the napkins folded thus; the bouillabaisse stock (a Friday specialty) cannot vary. And this gently lighted cozy cafe is appreciated, not only by the Marina corps but by the celebrity set as well. (We saw two A's and a B on our last visit.) We began with a salmon mousse, followed by a fresh mushroom salad before graduating to the entrée list: *coq au vin* (real *coq au vin*, not a naked chicken with goosebumps that's sauced to order, but one that has simmered until all the flavors permeate); duck *à l'orange; coquille* St. Jacques, and my lovely fresh bouillabaisse. Other variations on the dinner, which includes soup or salad, are the medallions of veal d'Anjou, the jumbo shrimps à la Parisienne and their specialty, rack of lamb. Desserts are good and homemade. The addition of a garden patio next to the restaurant adds the option of dining under the sun or stars.

**Moderate.** Open Tuesday through Sunday. Luncheon from 11 a.m .to 5 p.m. Dinner from 5 to 11 p.m.; to 10 Sunday. Wine and beer only. Patio. Reservations recommended. All major credit cards. Parking lot; valet parking. Casual.

---

*To obtain the best results from this Guide, be sure to consult maps on the various Southern California areas in the front of the book.*

# CAFE PIERRE

**French**
★

317 Manhattan Beach Boulevard
Manhattan Beach · **Map 2** · (213) 545-5252

The style is that of southern France with lots of garlic and vegetables. There are hors d'oeuvres, soups, salads, crêpes, omelettes, and sandwiches, all better than average at less than average prices. It grew from a crêperie into a bistro. A nice little café. The crêpe Neptune, filled with (you guessed it) crab meat and shrimp, is enormous. Their quiche at night (just a quiche in the dark) is interesting, particularly the seafood variety. Their Sunday brunch and a stroll through the neighborhood shops has become a very popular pastime among the locals—probably because their brunch menu with soup, coffee and a glass of champagne costs little more than coffee shop prices.

**Inexpensive to moderate.** Open seven days. Luncheon from 11:30 a.m. to 2:30 p.m. weekdays. Dinner from 5:30 to 10:30 p.m. Sunday brunch from 10 a.m. to 2:30 p.m. Beer and wine only. Reservations suggested. Patio. Visa, MC. Wheelchair access. Parking lot. Casual.

# CAFE RODEO

**American/Continental**
★

360 North Rodeo Drive
Beverly Hills · **Map 8** · (213) 273-0300

Max Baril opened up the front of his Cafe Rodeo to provide the most colorful living mural in the world, Rodeo Drive. Flair is the motif from the room designs to the bar to the European-elegance of no particular region. The continental menu may be taken seriously with a filet of sole *bonne femme* as the winner of a worthy list of contenders. The intimacy and charm would make kibble taste good though, and this is one of the great places for people viewing.

**Expensive.** Open seven days. Breakfast from 7 to 10 a.m. Luncheon from 11:30 a.m. to 5 p.m. Dinner from 5 to 10 p.m. Full bar. Reservations recommended. Patio. Most major credit cards. Valet parking. Casual.

---

## CAFE SWISS
450 North Rodeo Drive
Beverly Hills    **Map 8**

**Swiss**
★
(213) 274-2820

Authentic, regional dishes from all parts of Switzerland—German, Italian, and French—are served in a flowery patio and in the early-Edelweiss dining room. For an appetizer, I like *the wurst* salad (no puns, please) or anchovies on toast. Among the entrées are veal cutlet Amphytrion with *foie gras*, asparagus tips, and mushrooms, as it is served in the Cafe Amphytrion in Geneva. The *wienerschnitzel* is uninspired, but the *holsteinschnitzel* (breaded veal cutlet with fried egg, anchovies, and capers) is good.

**Moderate to expensive.** Open Monday through Saturday. Luncheon served 11 a.m. to 4 p.m. Dinner from 4 to 11 p.m. Full bar. Reservations recommended. Patio. All major credit cards. Parking lot. Casual.

---

## CALABASAS INN
23500 Park Sorrento Drive
Calabasas Park    **Map 1**

**American**
★
(213) 888-8870

Take a very knowledgeable restaurateur, place him in charge of a beautiful restaurant in a scenic area just far enough from Los Angeles to be interesting — it used to be a historic stagecoach stop — and you have instant success. Right? Not quite. Or, at least, not immediately. Wally Hollenstein (he was the president of the Hungry Tiger chain) took a while to get things straightened out in his graceful restaurant, but the effort was worth it. The cuisine covers a wide variety of dishes; his New England lobster clambake is one of the best such presentations you'll find. The wine list is discriminating, with emphasis on the best of California as personally selected by the proprietor; and the service staff is well trained to make intelligent suggestions of wines that will go well with your order. A great place for weddings *al fresco*.

**Moderate.** Open Tuesday through Friday. Luncheon from 11:30 a.m. to 3 p.m. weekdays. Dinner from 5 to 11 p.m. Sunday brunch from 10 a.m. to 3 p.m. Full bar. Reservations recommended. View. Visa, MC, AX. Valet parking; lot. Semi-dressy.

---

**CALDRON**                                      International/American
119 North Main                                                   ★
Fallbrook                                              (714) 728-1505

Now stay with us. First there was a restaurant in Fallbrook called the Caldron (Restaurant A). A few years ago they expanded to a larger location (Restaurant B), but kept the original (A) open. Restaurant B had a lot of problems, so the original Caldron people gave up and went back to restaurant A. So this review is about restaurant A or the original, smaller Caldron, not the fancier, newer Caldron. O.K.? All this trouble is worthwhile because this is one of the great luncheon destinations, worth the slight detour to Fallbrook off Coast Highway 101. The cheese enchiladas are sensational, and there is a different crêpe special every day. The sandwiches are served on home-baked bread, and there's a lot of them from which to choose. I like the fresh chicken or the hot crab and cheese. The salads are pretty and plentiful, from avocado stuffed with lobster to tomato stuffed with turkey. There's even a weight-watchers' list tht includes such un-diety sounding foods as stuffed clams, *chiles rellenos*, and turkey dragon over bean sprouts.

Desserts are homemade, too, cheesecake and chocolate mousse and the lemon melting moments is as dramatic as its name.

**Moderate.** Open Monday through Saturday. Luncheon from 11:30 a.m. to 2:30 p.m. Dinner from 5:30 to 9 p.m. Sunday brunch from 10 a.m. to 2:30 p.m. Closed major holidays. Wine and beer only. Reservations recommended. Visa, MC. Parking lot; street parking. Casual.

---

## CAMILLE'S
13573 Ventura Boulevard
Sherman Oaks          **Map 1**

French
★★
(213) 995-1660

Camille's is, well... different. This restaurant set out to carve its own personality in decor: emerald green, deep pastel rose and a random but tasteful selection of old photos and mirrors in gilt frames. The filet of sole is wrapped around smoked salmon and dressed with cream, mussels, white wine, mushrooms and shrimp (like Bernstein and Woodward, they don't reveal their sauces). Chicken breasts are simmered and poached with a kitchen of fresh vegetables. The beef with port wine is marvelous. You'll want to dress with some style to look good against the ornate candelabra and china vases.

**Moderate to expensive.** Open Tuesday through Saturday. Dinner served from 6 to 11 p.m. Closed major holidays. Taped classical music, classical guitar. Wine and beer only. Reservations advised; required for weekends. Visa, MC, AX. Parking lot. Semi-dressy.

*In order to obtain the best results from this Guide, please consult "Tips on Dining Out" on page 21.*

# CANARD DE BOMBAY

**Indian**

476 San Vicente

★★

Los Angeles    **Map 8**    (213) 852-0095

Canard de Bombay, at the site of the old Potluck on San Vicente Boulevard near Beverly Hills is a welcome addition to the few good Indian restaurants of Southern California. Chef-owner  Saad Ghazi operated an Indian restaurant in London, which has the best Indian restaurants in the world, and he uses the recipes of his family in this cozy split-level restaurant. At first impression, Canard de Bombay looks like a British regimental mess with starched reds and whites, white brick walls, a touch of brass, and portraits of the royal family. There is a delicate hand-blown globe at each table with an intricate and tasteful bouquet of dried flowers. Ghazi has wisely refused to adjust his menu to the "yankee palate" and you can enjoy the full rich flavor of the curries and the home-made chutneys. There is a star system depicting the degree of spicy-hot and we worked our way up through the three stars without more than a mild patina of perspiration. However Ghazi's star system must be based on the same logarithmic principle as the Richter scale. When I ordered the four star "chicken Phal" I was catapulted into a new gastronomic hemisphere. My fingernails curled and smoked, my hair perspired and I came very close to drinking the contents of an ice bucket, cubes and all, situated temptingly nearby. English-Indian curries differ from East Indian restaurants in that each area of India has its own spices and the chefs work with their familiar ingredients, hence Madras curry, Delhi curry and others. Curry, however, is merely a spice and 50 different restaurants serving lamb curry, for example, will turn out 50 different dishes. In addition to the curries Ghazi serves *tandoori* (named after the clay oven) and you should try the mixed grill that includes a sensational lamb sausage. There are 147 items on Canard de Bombay's dinner menu including Canard de Bombay which is not duck, as you might think. It is a kind of crunchy dried fish that someone must like — just as some people like parsnips — but not me. The young chef put together an intelligent winelist carefully suited to the dishes he serves. There is an interesting tea list as well including orange spice, jasmine, licorice spice, and chamomile. You can even have oolong, the tea made famous for me by the obscure Burt Kolmar and Harry Ruby song "So Long Oolong, So Long and Goodbye."

**Inexpensive to moderate.** Open Tuesday through Sunday. Luncheon 11:30 a.m. to 2:30 p.m. weekdays. Dinner from 5:30 to 10 p.m. Beer and wine only. Reservations advised. All major credit cards. Street parking. Casual to semi-dressy.

---

## CANNERY RESTAURANT American

3010 Lafayette Avenue ★
Newport Beach **Map 4** (714) 675-5777

We've dealt harshly with this beautiful theme restaurant in the past but new owners and a new, refreshing attitude have called for a new look. The building is interesting, an old building that was a forgotten cannery, and the ancient machinery is now part of the decor. The seafood is getting good reports from all over and Bill Hamilton and his manager, Ms. Beech, seem to be really trying. It's certainly worth a visit to explore.

**Moderate.** Open seven days. Luncheon served 11:30 a.m. to 3 p.m. Dinner from 5 to 10 p.m. Sunday brunch from 9 a.m. to 2:30 p.m. Closed Thanksgiving, Christmas. Entertainment. Full bar. Reservations suggested. Patio. Harbor view. All major credit cards. Valet parking. Casual.

*Please be sure to consult "Tipping Made Easy" on page 25 of this Guide.*

## CANTER'S DELICATESSEN                    Jewish
419 North Fairfax
Los Angeles          **Map 8**                    (213) 651-2030

Many years ago I remember feeling both intimidated and
loved by an irate Canter's waitress, a regular Jewish *tante*,
who demanded, "Whatsa matter, you didn't finish you
stuffed kishka? You know plenty of people in Europe would
love to have that. You better eat it, kid, or I ain't bringing
you no dessert." But that was many years ago, before
Canter's faded in its unrelenting fluorescent lights to a
ghost of the deli I once knew. Tides of people now rumble in
and out with a conspicious lack of enthusiasm, and the
waitress acts as if her feet hurt, and you better order, ready
or not, because this isn't really her table and she's doing
you a favor. The rich golden chicken soup that used to cure
terminal hangnails is now a watery reflection of its former
glory and can be counted on to heal no worse than minor
lesions. And try—just try—to order a C.B. (corned beef)
lean. I think there is a special demented cook who dispenses
equal parts blubber and meat for people of such temerity.
But it's still open 24 hours a day, and the bakery is still
good, and whatever action there is in the Fairfax area is
here. So—whoever promised you a rose garden?

**Moderate.** Open seven days, 24 hours. Closed Jewish holidays. Full bar. No reservations. No credit cards. Parking lot.
Casual.

---

## CAPTAIN'S ANCHORAGE                Steak/Seafood
24521 Del Prado                              ★
Dana Point          **Map 4**                    (714) 496-6116

A steak and seafood restaurant, long on atmosphere, with
good clam chowder and a do-it-yourself salad bar. The
theme is old Spanish-galleon, with ancient beams, columns,
lanterns, and aquariums with piranhas that separate the

bar from the dining area. The Alaskan king crab legs are a specialty (16-ounce serving), and the beef kabob is a favorite among the boating crowd.

**Moderate.** Open seven days. Dinner from 5 to 10:30 p.m.; to 11:30 Friday, Saturday. Full bar. No reservations. Visa, MC, AX. Parking lot. Semi-dressy.

---

## CAPTAIN'S TABLE                                         Seafood
301 South La Cienega Boulevard
Los Angeles          **Map 8**                    (213) 655-7555

There's scarcely a glimmer left of the glory days when this was a premier restaurant that catered to the who's who of the local celebrity set. The service is tired and indifferent. The food is bland and not everything's fresh. The only thing that's up are the prices. Sorry to see an old friend in such shabby condition.

**Moderate to expensive.** Open seven days. Dinner served Sunday through Thursday from 5 to 11 p.m.; Friday and Saturday to midnight. Full bar. Reservations advised. Parking lot. Semi-dressy.

---

## THE CARIBBEAN TERRACE                         Continental
Bel Air Sands Hotel                                          ★
11461 Sunset Boulevard
Brentwood            **Map 8**                    (213) 476-6571

Poolside dining during the warmer months is the attraction at this restaurant. The hotel underwent a $3 million renovation a while back which, happily, included the restaurant. The decor is now wicker with lush plants inside and wrought iron poolside. The menu is imaginative with veals, curried chicken, and Port Royale pork chops—cooked in port wine and surrounded by pineapple. Their Sunday brunch includes champagne, fruit juices, and lots of fresh fruit.

**Moderate.** Open seven days. Breakfast from 7 to 11:30 a.m. Luncheon from 11:30 a.m. to 3 p.m. Dinner 5:30 to 10:30. Sunday champagne brunch 10:30 to 2:30. Entertainment. Full bar. Patio view. All major credit cards. Parking lot. Casual to semi-dressy.

---

## CARL ANDERSEN'S CHATHAM      Continental
10930 Weyburn Avenue                ★
Westwood Village      **Map 8**      (213) 208-4321

A favorite with the UCLA campus crowd, it's not expensive, although it looks it. There are paneled walls, waiters with Transylvanian accents, and all the accoutrements of a poshery, with the five-course dinners. The *fricadeller* (Danish oval pork meat balls), Danish goulash, made to order, and stuffed trout are accompanied by fresh vegetables. The Danish sandwiches like duck leg (the rest of the fowl is on the dinner menu) are favorites at luncheon, and lines are long.

**Inexpensive to moderate.** Open Monday through Saturday. Luncheon from 11 a.m. to 9:30 p.m.; 11 a.m. to 10 p.m. Friday, Saturday. Closed major holidays. Full bar. Reservations essential on weekends. Visa, MC. Unvalidated parking lot. Casual.

*To obtain the best results from this Guide, consult "How to Use this Guide" on page 27.*

# CARLOS 'N CHARLIE'S

**Mexican Funk**

★

8240 Sunset Boulevard

West Hollywood          **Map 8**          (213) 656-8830

When they first opened in West Hollywood on the site of the former Marquis, the critics gave it little chance for success. They were wrong, but barely. It took a Jewish grandmother from the Bronx to finally get this place to pay off. Bernice Altschul is "Grandmother disco" according to the customers and her T-shirt, and she kind of stumbled on the place when the Altschuls moved west to be near their kids. Their qualifications consisted entirely of a lifetime spent in the hardware business but something happened to Bernice the minute she saw the place. "There were so many people who wanted to have a good time we decided to roll up our sleeves and help." That Bernice has "helped" is best illustrated by the packed houses every night for the private club disco and the public restaurant. Bernice and her gang made the menu more "serious," and they have an assortment of fresh fish, particularly the swordfish steak, that would rival any of their Mexican locations. The avocado soup, shrimp "scampini" and tequila shrimp are favorites and I liked the New York cheesecake that Bernice put on the menu. "Listen, if it's good it don't matter that it came from the Bronx." Bernices house rules are printed on the menu and include: "Sometimes we serve small portions, so yell for more;" "Please yell, it's our custom and it should work." The atmosphere is a strange mixture of Marquis elegance that still shows in some of the decor and the colorful funk.

**Moderate.** Open seven days 11:30 to 1 a.m. Full bar. Reservations advised. All major credit cards. Valet parking. Casual.

## CARL'S
**Barbeque**
★★

4988 West Pico Boulevard

Los Angeles    **Map 7**    (213)934-0637

A little more than a year ago, Lou's Bar-B-Que on West Washington burnt down. Lou's kept their fiery hot sauce in small red plastic squeeze bottles, and the word on the street was that after reaching the point of spontaneous combustion, the sauce went up by itself. Considering the heat that must have been generated by that sauce, I wouldn't have been surprised to have heard that the whole block had gone up in flames. With Lou's gone, I've turned to Carl's for regular hits of that good ole vitamin 'que. Like many of the best barbeque joints, Carl's offers no amenities whatsoever. There's not much room to eat there or even to sit down and wait; just a rectangular window through which can be seen the workings of the kitchen and the mighty barbeque oven beyond. And like most of the very best barbeque places, Carl's offers many combinations which allow you to satisfy any letch you may be harboring. You can mix and match the beef ribs, pork ribs, rib tips, beef and hot links as you wish. A simple combination of the meats quenches my desire.

I love the beef, soft and succulent, so good you barely need teeth to eat it. I love the ribs which are always meaty and leave lots of good gristle for gnawing on (ribs are not eaten politely; you gnaw on them, thereby getting in touch with your primal self). And I truly love the hot links, which taste dangerous and grainy and of which I never will get enough. Carl's has one other dish, the specialty of the house, which I also cannot get enough of. It's the "dirty" rice, a New Orleans dish made of long-cooked rice, touched with the much the same way that beans and rice together make for a complete portein, Carl's "dirty rice and an order of hot links together make for a complete barbecue experience.  *M.S.*

**Inexpensive.** Open seven days. Monday through Thursday from 11:30 a.m. to 11:45 p.m.; Friday and Saturday to 1:45 a.m.; Sunday from 2 to 9 p.m. Closed Christmas, New Year's, Easter. No alcoholic beverages. No reservations. No credit cards. Parking lot. Casual.

---

# CARL'S JR. HAMBURGERS American
Locations: See white pages ★

There's a special hamburger here that's prodigious. The Starburger consists of two patties, lettuce, tomato, special gooey sauce, and, if you ask them, onions, on a huge, fresh sesame bun. I order it rare with Ortega peppers (10¢ extra), and it looks like something from an old horror movie ("The Hamburger that Ate Chicago"), but it is a meal unto itself. If this loses me some points as a gourmet, so be it; there are times when this monstrous concoction is more satisfying than caviar blinis or watercress soup. The regular hamburger is not particularly exciting, although you can add the Ortega pepper to this one too. These sit-down hamburger stands are among the more attractive of the breed, with leather booths and practical pseudo-tile floors. Salad bars available for non-purists.

**Inexpensive.** Child's sandwich. No alcoholic beverages. No reservations. No credit cards. Casual.

---

# CARMINE'S Italian
10463 Santa Monica Boulevard ★
West Los Angeles **Map 8** (213) 474-3577

Carmine's in West Los Angeles is that recurring phenomenon, the "in" Italian restaurant that emerges every year or so, attracts an enthusiastic celebrity following, then fades away in favor of yet another, newer one. (I once had a theory that there is only one great Italian chef in Southern California, and as he is lured away by competitors, so restaurants' fortunes rise and fall.) Carmine's seem to justify this recognition, with a menu of familiar and sophisticated dishes and intense personal service. I saw more *embrazos* here than I saw in the entire movie *The Godfather*. Clams oregano proved a good appetizer, but the Carmine special salad was tepid and not particularly distinguished. The *cioppino* was... well, adequate, and surprisingly, vegetables are sometimes canned. Italian sausage with peppers was superb, and all the pastas we sampled—vermicelli, shells, linguine—were commendable. Desserts are an afterthought and not a very good one at that, although the zabaglione was good. It's a small place, and reservations are recommended. Booths are surrounded by wines you can select and hand to your waiter—a nice idea. Definitely not inexpensive, but a worthwhile experience anyway.

**Moderate to expensive.** Open seven days. Dinner from 5 to 11:30 p.m. Full bar. Reservations required. All major credit cards. Valet parking. Casual.

---

## CASABLANCA                                 Continental
409 South Main Street                                      ★
Orange          **Map 6**                   (714) 771-6200

The Casablanca in Orange is a stately, luxurious, tasteful and promising restaurant to rival the Chez Cary and Ambrosia in stature. Rich mahogany woods, mirrors, crystal and silver are complemented by warm wine-colored carpeting and white tapestry French provincial chairs. The chef, Roger Foy, served exacting Raymond Andrieux at The Tower and was at the Villa Fontana for a decade. Luncheon at the

Casablanca is the hautiest in the area, with escargot *en casserole* and the *petit medallion de filet de boeuf*, a rather long-winded way to describe good sautéed beef. At dinner the menu provides a tour from Escoffier to Naples to *nouvelle* at approximately $30 per person.

**Expensive.** Open Monday through Saturday. Luncheon from 11:30 a.m. to 2 p.m. weekdays. Dinner from 6 to 10 p.m. Entertainment (harp at luncheon; piano at dinner). Full bar. Reservations required. Visa, MC, AX, CB. Wheelchair access. Valet parking. Dressy, coat and tie required.

---

# CASA CARNITAS
4067 West Beverly Boulevard
Los Angeles  **Map 7**

Mexican
★
(213)667-9953

Those of a linguistic bent will observe that it is rather odd for a restaurant specializing in Yucatenecan seafood dishes to call itself Casa Carnitas, which translates as the "House of Meat." But then, logic and restaurant names have not always run hand-in-hand.

Mexico's Yucatan Peninsula is surrounded by bodies of water that thrive with huge prawns, myriad shrimp, clams and crabs and oysters and abalone, and fish of every possible hue and cry. I once sat in a beachfront cafe on the island of Isla Mujeres, just off the northeast tip of the Yucatan, ordered fish, and watched as my waiter walked up to a man fishing from the beach and bought my fish directly from him. The fish had been caught maybe five minutes earlier. It was, not surprisingly, very delicious.

That sort of freshness is, of course, impossible here in Los Angeles. But Casa Carnitas does do a great job of capturing the spirit of the Yucatan. As in virtually all Mexican seafood places, there are opening courses of *ceviche* (raw seafood "cooked" in lime juice), and cocktails of abalone, shrimp, octopus, oysters, clams, and a mixture of everything. The cocktails at Casa Carnitas are very good, filled to the brim with a taste made tingly by tabasco and vinegar, and lots of coriander and scallions. As is also often the case, the cocktails are served in good, old-fashioned ice cream sundae glasses: talk about cultures in collision.

Prior to the main course, there's also a selection of chowders to choose from, most notably the ubiquitous *caldo siete mares*, a spicy hodgepodge of this fish and that, which tastes like it's been cooking for a long time, and is filled with many fishy surprises, including the occassional batch of bones.

Though there are many tantalizing items among the entrees, the ones that grabbed my attention the tightest were the two lobster dishes. Not because of their names, but because of their prices, which lingered around $10. For lobster! Holy smokestack! The dishes were worth every penny, and more, too. There was half a lobster on my plate of *langosta a la Verucruzana*, flavored with a peppery tomato sauce and decorated with random olives. But that other lobster dish... it's called *langosta mantequilla*, which translates simply as "buttered lobster," though the menu better translates the dish as "lobster Mexico delight." And a delight it is: a half lobster sharing its shell with a mound of peppery guacamole and enough butter to stiffen your arteries on the spot. There was nothing left but a very clean shell at the end of that dish.

There are also a good selection of shrimp dishes (*camarones empanizada, camarones a la Mexicana en salsa ranchero*), octopus dishes (*pulpo en escabeche, pulpo a la Verucruzana*), and some excellent soft *tacos* filled with crabmeat. But aside from the lobster, the most memorable entree at Casa Carnitas is the *abulon en escabeche*. Where abalone is usually pounded flat, this abalone is served as thick discs, which makes it more chewy than usual. It was not a taste that I was crazy about, but I did enjoy the opportunity to taste the prohibitively expensive abalone in something akin to its native state of rubber-iness.  *M.S.*

**Moderate to expensive.** Open Monday through Thursday from 11 a.m. to midnight; Friday and Saturday to 1 a.m.; Sunday from 10 a.m. to midnight. Beer and wine only. Reservations helpful. Visa, MC. Casual.

---

## CASA CUGAT

Mexican
★

848 North La Cienega
Los Angeles     **Map 8**     (213) 655-7722

This casa is a beauty—very Spanish with its tiled courtyards, wooden beams, fountain, and brick oven. Aimed at pleasing those who enjoy traditional Mexican fare, the restaurant starts with appetizers of *empanadas* (small turnovers stuffed with chicken, olives, and spices) that go well with the generous margaritas. Fifty-five Sonora style dinners, including *quesadilla Cugat especiale* (a large tortilla filled with ground beef, tomatoes, onions, and melted cheese, topped with guacamole), chicken *en mole Pablano* (chunks of chicken simmered in mole sauce or *paella* (a combination of ham, chicken, and shellfish) are available. Strolling mariachis entertain every night for dinner.

**Inexpensive to moderate.** Open seven days. Luncheon from 11:30 a.m. to 3 p.m. weekdays. Dinner from 3 to 11 p.m.; 4 to midnight Friday, Saturday. Entertainment. Full bar. Reservations recommended after 7:30. Patio. All major credit cards. Valet parking. Casual.

---

## CASA DE CARLOS

Mexican
★

22901 Ventura Boulevard
Woodland Hills     **Map 1**     (213) 340-8182

On the Valley side of Malibu Canyon in Woodland Hills is a Mexican dinner house that looks like a dinner house instead of a taco-ria. The menu is deluxe with appetizers like the Mexican pizza made with salsa, strips of green peppers, ripe olives, and smothered with Monterey Jack cheese, then put on a tostada and topped with guacamole and sour cream. The enchiladas rancheros are stuffed with cheese, sauced, and garnished with green pepper, onions, and olives, then topped like a pizza. Margaritas are good and take-out is popular here.

**Inexpensive.** Open seven days from 11:30 a.m. to midnight Tuesday through Saturday; Sunday and Monday to 10 p.m. Full bar. Reservations suggested. All major credit cards. Street and lot parking. Casual.

---

## CASA DE PICO
Old Town State Historic Park
San Diego

**Mexican**
★
(714) 296-3267

More than just a bit of Old Mexico in decor and in food, this place is as authentic as you'll get it north of the border. Macho margaritas!

**Inexpensive.** Open seven days 10 a.m. to 10 p.m. Full bar. No reservations. Visa, MC, AX, DC. Parking lot; street parking. Casual.

---

## CASA DE SEVILLA
428 Chapala Street
Santa Barbara

**Continental**
★
(805) 966-4370

A charmer in a converted old home that has been serving good, fresh seafood and Spanish dishes for 52 years. Try the *chili conqueso*. The fireplace is cozy, the menu is continental and the service is friendly.

**Moderate.** Open Tuesday through Saturday. Luncheon from noon to 2 p.m. Dinner from 6 to 10. Full bar. Reservations recommended. Visa, MC, AX, CB. Parking lot. Dressy.

---

## CASEY'S BAR                                          American/Irish
613 South Grand Avenue
Los Angeles          **Map 7**                    (213) 629-2353

More a bawdy exchange than a restaurant. Orders for food around 5:30 are sometimes handled as a nuisance. It's got a sort of turn of the century office feel with mahogany paneling, colorful walls and sheet metal ceilings with red-curtained booths and a carefully hodgepodged arrangement of tables and chairs. Pretty waitresses have to shout to be heard over the noise level.

**Moderate.** Open Monday through Saturday. Closed Saturday night. Luncheon 11 a.m. to 5 p.m.; Saturday to 3. Dinner from 5 to 10 p.m. Closed major holidays. Entertainment Tuesday through Friday. Full bar open to 11:30. Reservations for lunch only. Visa, MC, AX. Street parking. Casual.

---

## CASINA VALADIER                                          Italian
4445 Lamont Street                                              ★
Pacific Beach (San Diego)                        (714) 270-8650

Guiseppe Ferrari is Italian and his menu reflects the heritage—with a bit of his French wife's cuisine included. You are literally in the Ferrari's home and treated as an honored guest. Game, lightly breaded veal Milanese style and veal *parma* wrapped in bread, baked locally, is astoundingly good. All in all, a real find.

**Moderate.** Open Tuesday through Saturday from 5:30 to 10 p.m. Closed major holidays. Full bar. Reservations required. Patio. All major credit cards. Parking lot. Dressy.

143

# CASSELL'S HAMBURGERS

**American**

★★★

3300 West 6th Street

Los Angeles　　**Map 7**　　　　　　　　　　(213) 480-8668

Open only five hours a day, Cassell's is the superstar of hamburgerdom. Once in *Westways*, I asked readers to send in their nomination for the best-in-the-West hamburger, and out of the nearly thousand replies (people in Southern California are fervent about their burgers), this midtown Los Angeles spot that has been in existence since 1950, drew more votes than any other. Smitty uses only graded prime steer beef from Colorado, makes his own mayonnaise, serves it on specially made buns, and with a buffet of homemade potato salad, sliced tomatoes, cottage cheese, peach halves and pineapple, condiments and dressing, homemade red relish, pickles, onions, and an illustrious Roquefort dressing. His other sandwiches are equally superior (he bakes his own ham, makes his own egg and tuna salad), and the price is right. This no-nonsense little restaurant (cafeteria style) with its small outdoor patio has been catering to the people that work in the high-rises around Wilshire, with plain premises, quick service and hearty sandwiches. Burgers are cooked in a special oven to taste: rare, well-done, medium, or — and this is for connoisseurs — "blue" (extra rare?). Fresh lemonade (and when was the last time you tasted that?) is a refreshing touch. Baked ham, potato salad, and great sandwiches "to go" as well.

**Inexpensive.** Open Monday through Saturday for luncheon from 10 a.m. to 3 p.m. No alcoholic beverages. No reservations. Patio. No credit cards. Casual.

*For best results, consult "How to Use This Guide" on page 27.*

## CASTAGNOLA'S LOBSTER HOUSE     Seafood

(Locations in Canoga Park, Encino, Long Beach, Marina   ★
del Rey, Oxnard, Pasadena, Redondo Beach, Santa Barbara.
See phone book for listings.)

It's okay to feel shellfish once in a while and this remodeled
emporium of piscatory delights will cater to the most
discriminating lobster lovers. The family started with the
arrival of Gio Castagnola from Italy in 1905. His fishing
business provided employment for his son Mario and the
other four boys and they graduated from purveying seafood
in Santa Barbara to operating restaurants. The oyster bar is
soothing on a hot afternoon and the blackboard menu has a
wide variety of seafood.

**Moderate.** Check for days and times at each location.

---

## CATCH OF THE SEA     Seafood

20521 Devonshire     ★★
Chatsworth    **Map 1**     (213) 998-5400

The fact that this fine restaurant survived a series of near
legendary battles with bureaucracy is a positive. That Bill
and Kathy Holt have the only seafood restaurant with a
homemade flavor in Southern California is important.
Everything at Catch of the Sea, improbably located in
Chatsworth, is fresher than you'll find at most of the
seashore restaurants. I particularly like the bouillabaisse
but for dessert you should have "mudpie," one of the
specialties of their house. No cocktails, but a good wine list
and it's much like being a guest in someone's home with
elegant service in a casual atmosphere. The fine food has
helped make this a favorite spot with many sports and
entertainment celebrities. There is a "light diner's special"
that has smaller portions at reduced prices. Be sure to
consider ordering this way unless you have a huge appetite,
because regular portions are hugemongous.

**Moderate to expensive.** Open seven days. Luncheon from 11 a.m. to 3 p.m. Monday through Saturday. Dinner from 5 to 10 p.m.; to 11 Friday, Saturday; 3 to 9 Sunday. Sunday champagne brunch 11 a.m. to 3 p.m. Children's menu. Light diner's special Sunday through Thursday. Wine and beer only. Reservations essential. All major credit cards. Self parking. Casual.

---

## CATHAY DE GRANDE          Mandarin/Szechuan
1600 North Argyle Avenue
Hollywood          **Map 7**          (213) 461-4076

I was tempted to drop them altogether from the book, but they were once so good and drew so much attention I thought we'd mourn together for a while. All the great dishes of Northern China, starting with the complimentary appetizers, sweet and sour cucumber, pressed soy bean curd with celery, sour Chinese pickle, and chopped mustard and the Cathay special chicken minced with green pepper, mushrooms, onions, and peanuts, or the steamed beef with rice flour, or the smoked duck prepared in the style of Peking duck but smoked with camphor and tea leaves, thinly sliced and rolled in a crepe with plum sauce and green onion are merely soggy shadows of their former substance and there is a disco that I suspect gets more attention, and action, than the dining room. Farewell, old friend.

**Inexpensive to moderate.** Open Monday through Saturday. Luncheon from 11:30 a.m. to 2:30 p.m. Dinner from 4 to 10 p.m.; to 11 Saturday. Full bar. Disco. Happy Hour 4 to 6 Monday through Friday. Reservations recommended. Visa, MC, AX, DC. Parking lot. Casual.

## CATTAILS
**French-Continental**
★
69369 Highway 111
Palm Springs
(714) 324-8263

A rare desert experience in subdued and elegant surroundings. The menu is presented on a blackboard, since it changes often to insure the freshest. Each offering is painstakingly described by your waiter. There is variety of continental dishes with seafood selections. Specialties of the house: the house pâté, a classic appetizer, beef Wellington, and tenderloin of pork stuffed with water chestnuts. Among the wonderful desserts are included a chocolate mousse crêpe and Elizabethan syllabub.

**Expensive.** Open Tuesday through Saturday. Dinner from 6 p.m. Open seven nights through Christmas holidays. Wine and beer only. Reservations required. All major credit cards. Wheelchair access. Self-parking. Semi-dressy.

---

## CATTLEMAN'S WHARF
**American/Continental**
★
1339 South Hacienda Boulevard
Hacienda Heights **Map 6**
(213) 968-1526

A really good operation that doesn't look it—it's too atmospheric to be true—you can slide down a real slide into the disco room after a splendid dinner of prime rib or fresh seafood and steaks. The Sunday brunch is a particular favorite with the area and for good reason. It's hard for me to understand that these same people who brought us Cattleman's Wharf could also bring us the El Adobe in Glendale and Riverside, as uninteresting and pedestrian as the Wharf is good.

**Moderate.** Open Monday through Sunday. Luncheon served 11 a.m. to 3 p.m. weekdays. Dinner from 5 to 10 p.m.; Friday and Saturday to 11. Sunday brunch 10 a.m. to 2:30 p.m. Entertainment, dancing. Full bar. Reservations suggested. Visa, MC, AX. Valet parking dinner only. Semi-dressy.

# THE CELLAR
**Continental**

Villa del Sol

★★★

305 North Harbor Boulevard

Fullerton    **Map 6**    (714) 525-5682

Louis Schnelli is the Cellar and vice versa. I had the privilege of introducing Louis to the owners of this building some time ago and they saw the same things I did: knowledge, perfectionism, drive, pride and ceaseless energy. They worked out an arrangement whereby Louis actually took over what used to be the drafty, dusty cellar, and from that inauspicious beginning has flowered one of Orange County's finest. The lovely room is impeccably European; it's nice to know that some restaurants still cling to the formality and rituals of early tradition. Yet the Cellar by no means should be classified as a structured clone of the glamour restaurants of hundreds of cities throughout the world. Louis is always restless, always exploring. He learned his trade the hard but classic way in a hotel school in Switzerland. When *nouvelle cuisine* glimmered, Schnelli recognized it for more than a passing fancy and went to the source, to France, where he learned the complexities of this first important new cuisine in centuries. The Cellar has become a comfortable blend of the two: traditional Escoffier and the new cooking from Europe. It's a sophisticated restaurant that would draw praise in any location, and the fact that it is literally buried in Fullerton has not dimmed its light—some of our friends, readers and listeners have traveled great distances to dine there, and I've never had a bad report. We're greatly impressed with Mr. Schnelli, his elegant but not stuffy restaurant, and the standards he works so hard to achieve.

**Moderate to expensive.** Open Tuesday through Saturday 6:30 to midnight. Full bar. Reservations necessary. All major credit cards. Parking lot. Dressy.

# CHADNEY'S
**American**
★

3000 West Olive Avenue
Burbank  **Map 1**  (213) 843-5333

From the moment I walked into Chadney's, across the street from the Johnny Carson Show in Burbank, I knew I was going to like it. It's just the kind of warm, hospitable, cozy, honest place that I covet on nights when I'm interested in just talking a bit and dining well. Bob Hoeller has built an expanded steak and lobster house that delivers a few culinary surprises. I had chicken "a la Chadney," boneless pieces of charcoal-broiled chicken that had been marinated in herbs, wine, and olive oil. It was served with fresh cold vegetables in the manner of a Malaysian dish. The contrast between the hot chicken and cold vegetables and the uncommon flavor was marvelous. My lady had the middle cut of prime rib, an enormous portion, served with a foot-long baked potato and preceded by a good salad. Sandie took excellent care of us and told us little things about each dish she served: "That beaujolais will be perfect with your order." "Be careful splitting the potato because the steam's hot." There's a before-7 p.m. menu too combining many of the house favorites at lower prices that include everything from soup to dessert, but you must order before 7. I'm not sure what it is that makes one place so relaxed and friendly, but whatever it is, Chadney's has it in abundance. Sounds of happy conversation, people enjoying their steaks and being alive, and help that makes sure you "Come back, you hear?" Luncheon is the same, although the menu and the portions are smaller.

There is a fine entertainment lounge and a banquet room that made me think of Christmas parties.

**Moderate.** Open seven days. Luncheon served 11:30 a.m. to 4 p.m. weekdays. Dinner 4 p.m. to 10 p.m. Sunday, Monday; to 11 p.m. Tuesday through Friday; 5 to 11 p.m. Saturday. Entertainment Monday through Saturday. Full bar. Reservations necessary. Visa, MC, AX. Valet parking. Casual to semi-dressy.

# CHALET DE FRANCE

**French**

23254 Robert Road
★
Torrance        **Map 2**        (213) 378-7576

This country inn, now celebrating its twentieth year, is just inland across Pacific Coast Highway and conveniently near the Palos Verdes area. Its culinary roots are in Monaco where the proprietor had a successful restaurant, and the cuisine is fairly standard, although the service is occasionally slow. The escargot is indistinguishable from a hundred others, but the scampi *à la diable* is a superior appetizer. The onion soup is good and hearty, and the entrées, about twenty of them in all, have been carefully and competently prepared. Of particular note is the lobster thermidor and quail in raspberry sauce. Desserts, excepting the crêpe suzette, are nothing special. The wine list is well done with a fine imported variety, and fairly priced. Proprietor Jacques Haon was formerly with La Rue, The Beverly Hills Hotel, and The Stork Club.

**Moderate.** Open seven days. Luncheon served noon to 2 p.m. weekdays. Dinner Sunday through Thursday from 5 to 10 p.m.; Friday and Saturday to 11 p.m. Children's menu. Closed Thanksgiving. Full bar. Reservations advised on weekends. All major credit cards. Parking lot. Casual to dressy.

*In order to obtain the best results from this Guide, be sure to read the French, German, Italian and Oriental menu translators on page 705 to 710 of this Guide.*

# CHAMBORD

**French**

★

8689 Wilshire Boulevard

Beverly Hills      **Map 8**                    (213) 652-6590

There's a place on Wilshire Boulevard near Robertson in Beverly Hills that's confusing. First it was the Adriatic, then it wasn't. Then it was the Adriatic again. Then it wasn't. What it is now—and we think this time for keeps— is Chambord, a very French, very charming restaurant that seems designed for assignations. Its gilt mirrors, fresh flower arrangements on pink linen tablecloths, lush ferns, and deep rose walls are a fitting setting for an imaginative approach to the art of French cuisine. In Paris, it would be called creative. At Chambord, it is exciting; soups made from the very essence of bouillabaisse, saffron-rich and hearty, topped with homemade croutons of big slices of French bread (not the little cubes that crunch like dried kibble); *le grenadin de veau valée d' auge* (veal loin with cream sauce), *les filets de truite sautés Cléopatre* (filet of trout with sautéed bay shrimps and capers), along with all of the dishes we have come to expect and sometimes take for granted. Here they are performed a bit better than in most French restaurants, and the à la carte menu reflects it. It is not inexpensive, but they're worth it. A nice touch; you are brought full bottles of the featured wine but are only charged for the amount you consume. The plates are beautifully dressed, with the foods carefully composed. But the triumph of the evening was *la coupe* Chambord. It was— ahh!—fresh strawberries, vanilla ice cream, candied orange peel, rosettes of whipped cream with sugar crystals topped with melba sauce, and a soupçon of Grand Marnier. It was triumph. Luncheon is a more modest affair, as befits the palates and purses of the people in the neighborhood. There is a daily special, of course, with a choice of two meats or two fish dishes. Now several years old, Chambord is here to stay and vies for the ribbons.

**Expensive.** Open Monday through Saturday. Luncheon from 11 a.m. to 2:30 p.m. weekdays. Dinner 6 to 10:30 p.m. Mondya through Saturday. Full bar. Reservations recommended, especially for lunch. Visa, MC. AX, CB. Valet parking. Semi-dressy to dressy.

---

## CHANG'S                                          Chinese
21800 Victory Boulevard
Woodland Hills          **Map 1**                (213) 704-6891

The handsome pagoda-style blue roof of Chang's of Hong Kong gives the impression that it might be a branch office of a powerful Oriental bank. The riches here, however, are culinary. Inside, two garden atriums with carp pools and other touches of the Orient lend atmosphere. The staff seems to have been chosen as much for their friendliness as for their efficiency. Our waiter carefully explained that many of the dishes we had ordered were quite spicy and asked if we were prepared to pay the price. When I, for one, said I was not, he asked how much "heat" would be acceptable. When he was told "on the warmish side," he suggested an alternate dish with the same ingredients that would not singe the palate. With his aid, we were able to order unfamiliar dishes that, for the most part, filled the bill admirably. While my concessions have been made to Western tastes, the heart and spirit of Hong Kong-style cuisine remains. If the spirit of adventure has not gripped a member of your party, the dinner menu boasts a section featuring New York sirloin, lamb chops and barbecued chicken. The Champagne Sunday Buffet has traditional Chinese dishes existing alongside such things as lox and scrambled eggs.

**Moderate.** Open seven days. Luncheon served 11:30 a.m. to 2:30 p.m. weekdays. Dinner Monday through Thursday 5 to 10 p.m.; Friday, Saturday to 11 p.m.; Sunday 3 to 10 p.m. Banquet facilities. Children's menu. Reservations recommended. Piano Friday, Saturday nights. All major credit cards. Casual.

---

## CHAOS                                   Chinese-Cuban
834 South Vermont Avenue
Los Angeles          **Map 7**                    (213)384-7307

The sign in front of Chaos (a great name for a restaurant) says : "CHOP SUEY... FOOD TO GO." A traditional Chinese restaurant sign, which gives absolutely no inkling that Chaos is Los Angeles' only (far as I know) Cuban-Chinese restaurant. For fans of minimalist design, Chaos is also virtually a cathedral. The place has almost no design elements whatsoever. At best, it's bare. It is not a good place for those with agoraphobia to catch a quick bite.

Chaos does not coddle its customers. The lady at the cash register doesn't budge when you walk in. After you've found yourself a formica table to sit down at (the tables are festooned with bottles of *chiles preparados,* Trappey's Mexi-Pep Hot Sauce, soy sauce and catsup), a menu is dropped in front of you. A beer follows soon after. The waitress takes your order without the slightest interest. Some noise comes from the kitchen, along with chopping and sizzling sounds. Moments later, your dish is plopped down in front of you.

Whatever it is, the food is pretty good, and very inexpensive. The *wonton* soup is called *sopa China* (cup $1; bowl $4). Fried *wontons* are *maripositas fritas* ($1.50). *Chop suey* and *chow mein* are served with *pollo* (chicken), *camarones* (shrimp), *puerco* (pork) or *bif* (beef). The fried rice is called *arroz frito en stilo de Chaos.* As you can probably tell, the food here is pretty much traditional Chinese, served with a Cuban twist. I enjoyed my meal at Chaos, and was gladdened to find that one of my

153

favorite culinary combinations had made it out to the West Coast. *M.S.*

**Moderate.** Open Tuesday through Sunday noon to 9 p.m. Closed Christmas, New Year's. Beer and wine only. No reservations. No credit cards. Lot and street parking. Casual.

---

## CHARLEY BROWN'S American
(Locations in Anaheim, Huntington Beach, Long Beach, ★ Marina del Rey, Rosemead, Thousand Oaks, West Covina, Woodland Hills, Ventura. See phone book for listings.)

This is big business and getting bigger but, somewhat surprisingly, it's well done. The steakhouses have very limited menus but are marvelously furnished—at once striking and comfortable. The food is pretty good, the service excellent, the drinks great. Dinners are served with cool crisp salad (try their minted French dressing), and real San Francisco sourdough bread with crunchy crust served hot. Steaks are comparatively inexpensive, and there are a few "sides" worth considering. Mushrooms are sautéed in wine and butter, baked potato is served with your choice of condiments, and the onion rings are crisp and deep-fried in a beer batter. Luncheons present a limited and overpriced sandwich assortment, the kind that sounds simply marvelous when you read the menu but turns out to be cold beef on white bread when it's delivered. There are three salads, and all are better than average, particularly the lobster and avocado and the "salad supreme." The fruit salad isn't much. Wine is cheaper at lunch for reasons that only their C.P.A. could have doped out. Bruncheon is good if for no other reason than that they serve a sensational tequila sunrise or "bull shot" (bouillon and vodka on the rocks), plus crêpes and hash and steak and eggs and French toast. With apologies to my feminist friends, I must say the Long

Beach location has the most beautiful waitresses I've ever seen in a restaurant.

**Moderate.** Open seven days. Luncheon from 11 a.m. to 3 p.m. weekdays. Dinner 5 to 10 p.m.; 5 to 11 Friday, Saturday; 4:30 to 10 Sunday. Sunday brunch 10 a.m. to 3 p.m. Full bar. Reservations recommended. All major credit cards. Parking lot. Casual to semi-dressy.

---

## CHARMER'S MARKET                    American/Peculiar
175 Marine Street
Santa Monica          **Map 2**                    (213) 399-9160

Charmer's Market is unquestionably one of the strangest places I've ever eaten in. If I were rating it in terms of design, I'd give the place very close to four stars, but as they used to say in the ads for Horn & Hardart: "You can't eat atmosphere"... and unfortunately at Charmer's, you can't eat the food either.

Charmer's Market used to be a branch of the Bank of America, which it still resembles somewhat (the vault is off in one corner filled now with victuals). Strange and wondrous things have been done to the interior of Charmer's—stars have been installed in the floor, for instance, bearing mysterious words like "Passion"... "Tongue"... "Lust"... and "Magic" (in the men's room, of all places). There's a cheese department in one corner, a bakery in another, aisles are lines with a veritable cornucopeia of beers, oils, vinegars, and waters. In the center of this whole thing is a court-like dining rectangle, right next to an espresso bar. And the clientele is very *haute moderne*, very now, ultra hip. That's the good news.

The bad news is that you could die waiting for your food to come, and when it does come you may find death preferable. I'm speaking about 45 minutes wait for a cold plate to lollygag its way a distance of about 20 yards, and that's *real* slow. And, it seems to me that the dishes I finally got had neither departed nor travelled well.

155

There was a tiny, dessicated, unfortunate slice of quiche that was on the verge of losing its third dimension and turning into a matzoh. There was a slice of stuffed veal which could have been better described as stuffed leather, except that I think leather might have been more flavorful. There was an order of leeks vinaigrette which was stringy and tough in a sauce so vinegary it stung. Glancing into the delicatessen case, I could see the other dishes—the *poulet froid*; the patés of duck, seafood, rabbit; the eggs in aspic; the ratatouille. Like the Charmer's Market, everything seemed to work in concept... and nothing worked in practice.   *M.S.*

**Expensive.** Open seven days. Sunday through Wednesday from 11 a.m. to 10 p.m.; Thursday to 11 p.m.; Friday and Saturday to 12:30 a.m. Full bar. No reservations. Covered patio. Visa, MC. Parking lot. Casual.

---

# CHARTHOUSE                                    Steakhouse
(Locations in Coronado, Dana Point, Idylwild, La Jolla,   ★
Long Beach, Malibu, Marina del Rey, Newport Beach,
Oceanside, Rancho Mirage, Redondo Beach, Santa Barbara,
Westwood. See phone book for listings.)

I have great admiration for these people. One of the best of the beef and seafood houses, the Chart House was started in Aspen by a group of skiers with a respect for spectacular views, whose aim was to build restaurants with a set of architectural and decor values that fit with the location. The food is pretty ordinary, although you should ask for the "baseball steak" (not on the menu) a fist-shaped cut of prime beef that is unusually hearty. Service, by young people, is impeccable—swift, friendly, and personal. Wines are carefully selected.

**Moderate.** Open seven days from 5 to 10 p.m.; Friday, Saturday to 11. Sunday brunch some locations. All major credit cards. Parking lot. Casual.

---

## CHASEN'S                                     Continental
9039 Beverly Boulevard                                ★
Los Angeles          **Map 8**                  (213) 271-2168

I'm sorry that Maude Chasen, the lovely proprietor of this legend, is distressed with me. I still believe the restaurant to be expensive—she does not—and I've been hustled there a few times. "A little seafood appetizer?" my waiter asked when I brought a party of four there. "Certainly," I replied, thinking it a nice touch to begin a dinner. It was little, but not in price: $66 for the party. I also got the fisheye when I asked for an inexpensive California wine, one of my favorites here. The waiter, patronizingly said: "Why don't you let *me* select the wine." I told him it was fine with me if he'd pay for it, which seemed to end the discussion. Nearly fifty very odd years ago David Chasen opened this small but friendly cafe that early on became the favorite of what then would have been called "the pack." John Barrymore, Errol Flynn, W.C. Fields, F. Scott Fitzgerald, Gene Fowler, and a shy aircraft executive known these days as H.R. Hughes, exulted in the camaraderie, the ribald practical jokes—and the chili—in this nonentity of an eatery that quickly became a legendary haunt for actors, producers, writers, and a bevy of starlets. Sadly, most of the grand names have departed. Predictably, Chasen's has not. Instead, its kitchens were enlarged to accommodate the demands of palates grown sophisticated by travel and affluence. The decor gradually took on that soft, well-worn, luxurious patina that now makes it one of the more comfortable restaurants in the area. There are still some who claim that Elizabeth Taylor wooed Burton with Dave's chili, flown to the *Cleopatra* set daily; and chili remains on the menu, along with such homespun favorites as chicken pot pie, and hobo steak for two. Yet it is the extraordinary dishes that tend more to *haute cuisine* that make this establishment difficult to categorize. It was Chasen's that invented the spinach salad. It is prepared tableside with the usual ingredients and flourish (depending upon your captain), but sufficiently seasoned with cayenne pepper and English mustard to provide the zest that imitations lack. The hors d'oeuvres include Beluga caviar, but traverse a zigzag route that includes, among many selections, French white asparagus vinaigrette. Entrées, as such, are not listed. They appear under the heading of "Specialties"—all forty of them—combining the great dishes of many nations with such fancies as "deviled beef bones." Everything is à la carte, and no credit cards are accepted.

**Expensive.** Open Tuesday through Sunday. Dinner from 6 to 1 a.m. (service to 11). Closed Thanksgiving, Christmas. Reservations recommended. No credit cards. Valet parking. Dressy.

---

## CHEF GREGOIRE
15464 Ventura Boulevard
Sherman Oaks      **Map 1**

French
★★
(213) 789-2711

"Not for me,—the richest man in the cemetery, *mon ami.* Not for me," protests Chef Gregoire, proprietor of the small but respected French restaurant, Chef Gregoire, in Sherman Oaks. He is a genial, gentle, talented man who has learned to enjoy life. He has served as the chef of the grand L'Escoffier and other gustatory legends, but it is obvious that here he is most content—browsing, incandescent, animated, embracing old customers and introducing his son, the captain, with pride. "Chef," as he is called by everyone, does not attempt more than he can do easily and well. The menu is limited, strictly French, with blackboard supplements that depend upon what's fresh and good, who's coming for dinner, and the whims of the chef. In the afternoons he conducts a cooking school, where he shows charmed ladies in expensive jeans how to make *cordon bleu* and a variety of dishes. They return again and again as customers, and their reverence for the chef approaches awe. Chef is best with duckling and serves it with pepper sauce, not the ubiquitous sweet gook that most French restaurants feel the American palate requires. His poached salmon is perfectly executed and removed from the fire at the precise moment. His soufflés (order before dinner, please) are so light and tall, they virtually float away. This is a restaurant for conversation, for questions, and Chef will not be at all reticent about showing you his kitchen. It is a slightly unorthodox restaurant, but Chef Gregoire, like many geniuses, is a slightly unorthodox man.

**Moderate.** Open Tuesday through Sunday. Dinner 5:30 to 10 p.m. Sunday brunch 11 a.m. to 2:30 p.m. Wine and beer only. Reservations recommended. Most major credit cards. Parking lot. Casual to semi-dressy.

---

## CHEZ CARY RESTAURANT

571 South Main Street
Orange        **Map 6**

Continental
★★★
(714) 542-3595

Champions almost never come back — or so they say — and it was with mixed feelings, not the least of which was nostalgia and misgiving, that I revisited Chez Cary, once Orange County's greatest restaurant. I had been present on opening night in 1962. The Chez, all red velvet and crystal with highbacked chairs and a muted grandeur, was what we had hoped for. The food was rich and deftly presented in a graceful choreography of captains and waiters. The wine list was an inventory of rare treasures. But sadly, a series of management and policy changes resulted in a steady decline. Until now. My misgivings began to evaporate the moment I was seated. This was the Chez!

Gleaming tableware, expensive linen, a single tall rose in a simple vase and a Dresden doll centerpiece. The dinner began. I quaffed a glass of Scandinavian *aquavit*, served from a bottle frozen in a small block of ice, to clear the freeway dust from my palate. It left a splendid glow and so, naturally, I had another. Would I like scallops Provencale for an appetizer? I would, and the hot scallops were served in a zesty tomato and garlic sauce. I selected Chateau St. Jean Chardonnay, one of my all-time California favorites, as accompaniment. From there we moved to hearts of palm salad served in a Roquefort dressing and onward (ever onward!) to the *entrecote double marchand du vin*, a thick New York cut for two with a perfect Bordelaise and a *bouquetiere* of vegetables. This was accompanied by another California friend of mine, a silky cabernet from Beaulieu. At dessert my companions made rapturous sounds as they poked into their Grand Marnier soufflé while I, greedy and more Spartan, made do with raspberries. After-dinner liqueurs included a *pousse café*, served in a tall, thin cordial glass with layer upon layer of vividly colored liqueurs that must be poured ever so carefully to maintain the separation of layers. Ray Barrientos, one of the few who had been with Chez Cary since its opening, did the pouring in a production of such spectacular proportions that other tables kept him busy doing *pousse café*s through the evening. Chef Klaus Dornen has the kitchen back to its former glory but the moving force behind this renaissance would seem to be manager Sean Lewis who once served as a captain here. Even the special touches are to be found: a gold personalized box of matches; your car waiting with the door open as you leave. On the dashboard I found a gold medal with a bright ribbon as a souvenir.

**Expensive.** Open seven days for dinner from 6:30 to 10 p.m. Cocktails. Entertainment. Reservations required. All major credit cards. Valet parking. Dressy.

*For best results, consult "How to Use This Guide" on page 27.*

# CHEZ CLAUDE

700 North Gardner Street

Los Angeles        **Map 7**

**French**

★

(213) 651-5578

They like to serve things in a pastry shell at Chez Claude. I think this is fine because they make a very good pastry shell at Chez Claude. The *escargot en chablis* are served *en croute*, and the pastry coverlet over the snails keeps them juicy and tender, without becoming soggy from the rising garlic steam. The asparagus Claude are served inside a pastry wrapper, which keeps the tender white stemlets warm and comfy. The snapper *en croute* rests beneath a flaky crust in a sauce flecked with herbs and flavors which turn the oft-abused snapper into a dream of a dish.

The choice of rooms at Chez Claude is small, or large, as you prefer. The atmosphere is ever so slightly surreal. All looks well, but something feels pleasantly off-center. I don't know what makes Chez Claude seem so affably peculiar to me. Perhaps it's because I almost always dine there toward closing time, when the chairs are being put up, and the chamber music trio is beginning to wander from table to table playing everything from Mozart to Virginia reels. But whatever the reason, I like the effect. It always makes me a bit rakish, and has me feeling as if I'm strolling into the night in Montmartre, and not into the ambulatory shadows that scud along Melrose Avenue.   *M.S.*

**Moderate.** Open Tuesday through Sunday. Luncheon served Tuesday through Friday from 11:30 a.m. to 2:30 p.m. Dinner from 5:30 to 10:30 p.m. Sunday brunch from 11 a.m. to 3 p.m. Live chamber music during Sunday brunch. Closed July 4, Christmas, New Year's. Wine and beer only. Reservations advised. Visa, MC, AX. Street parking. Casual.

## CHEZ HELENE                                         French
                                                          ★
1029 West Washington Boulevard
Venice          **Map 2**                    (213) 392-6833

This is a highly personal restaurant, created in a charmingly
restored area of Venice, around the life and times of Earl
Kennedy, who once possessed a key to the executive restroom
of a top advertising agency. He now creates such disparate
and delicious delicacies as *poulet* Chez Helene, ratatouille,
*scallopini piccata*, or *carré d'agneau*. Homemade desserts include
strawberries Romanoff, cream *chomeur*, and a delicate
meringue and whipped cream sandwich. The tiny restaurant
seats only 20 customers amid photographs and memorabilia
and imparts more of a feeling of being a guest — of some
very charming people — than any restaurant in this book.

**Moderate.** Open Tuesday through Sunday. Luncheon served
noon to 3 p.m. Tuesday through Saturday. Dinner from 6:30
to 10 p.m. Beer and wine only. Reservations necessary.
Patio. Most major credit cards. Street parking. Casual.

---

## CHEZ JAY                                Continental/American
                                                          ★
1657 Ocean Avenue
Santa Monica        **Map 2**                 (213) 395-1741

Chez Jay is Daffyland at the ocean, a Santa Monica
eccentric that caters to the muscle-beach look-alikes and
the Marina set in their expensive poor-look clothes. If it
looks run down from the outside, that's the best part.
Operated by hot air balloonist and actor Jay Fiondella, it's
part put-on and fun, but serious about the food and wine.
It may be the only authentic "personality" cafe in the area.
The seafood is fresh, the martinis are the best in town,
there are peanuts on the floor and best of all, there's Jay. If
he doesn't enthrall you with stories of his latest hair-
raising escapade (if you can hear him over the jukebox)
then you are unenthrallable. The salad is served with big

chunks of Roquefort, the potatoes are prepared with bananas, and the cheesecake is, in the words of Allen Sues, "A little slice of Paradise." The menu ranges from Jay's seafood salad to such unlikely haute food as shrimp curry à l'Indienne with rice pilaf, and broiled swordfish served with béarnaise. The specialty of the house is a pepper steak, but my favorite single dish there is the scampi sautéed with fresh garlic and shallots and offered as appetizer. Dilapidated though it may appear, this is a good restaurant at very modest prices and the always-packed bar is the friendliest extant. We once heard a winsome blonde beauty yell, "Whoever pinched, I'm sorry, but I've already got a date." It's a trifle noisy.

**Moderate.** Open seven days. Luncheon from noon to 2 p.m. weekdays. Dinner 6 to 10:30 p.m.; to 11:30 Friday, Saturday. Full bar. Reservations recommended. All major credit cards. Valet parking. Casual.

---

## CHEZ LOMA
1132 Loma Avenue
Coronado

**Continental**
★
(714) 435-0661

Chez Loma is on Coronado Island, just around the corner from the grand and magnificent Hotel del Coronado where *Some Like It Hot* and *The Stuntman* were both shot and where the Duke of Windsor met the woman who would cause him to abdicate his throne. The very best place to eat is at the nearby Chez Loma, which would be a good restaurant no matter where it was located. The food at Chez Loma tends toward sort of a born-again French motif—not quite as light as *nouvelle cuisine*—not nearly as heavy classic French. The

*To obtain the best results from this Guide, consult "How to Use this Guide" on page 27.*

*escargot Nicoise* is a terrific variation of the classic snails in garlic butter. In this case the snails are served Provencal-style, simmered in white wine seasoned with garlic, tomatoes and herbs. There's also an appetizer of *brochette du Saint Jacques* $4.95—scallops and cucumbers skewered and grilled, and then served with a dipping sauce of garlic and saffron. The salad with goat cheese dressing is so revered that when I asked the desk clerk at the Coronado for directions to Chez Loma, he made sure to tell me it must be tried. It was very tart, though it could have been goatier, a personal preference and an acquired taste. The entrées at Chez Loma are adventurous, in a low key way. There is a fine *poulet braisees au Madeira,* a half chicken in a sauce of Madeira wine and mushrooms. And there are *escalopes* of veal in either marsala wine or lemon butter and vermouth. But best of all, there are the duck dishes, which are superb—crispy on the outside, moist on the inside, very succulent. The duck is served *poivre vert* (with Madagascar green peppercorns) or Montmorency (with sweet cherry port wine sauce and lingonberries). Both were topnotch. The wine list, as befits this sort of restaurant, was small but select, with special attention given to California wineries.  *M.S.*

**Moderate.** Open Tuesday through Sunday.  Lunch served 11 a.m. to 2 p.m. weekdays. Dinner from 5:30 to 10 p.m. Tuesday through Sunday. Closed Christmas, New Year's. Beer and wine only. Reservations essential. Patio. Most major credit cards. Wheelchair access. Street parking. Casual (bring a jacket as it can be cool on the patio in the evening).

*To obtain the best results from this Guide, be sure to consult maps on the various Southern California areas in the front of the book.*

## CHEZ NATUREL
**Health Food/Organic**
★

11836 Ventura Boulevard
Studio City  **Map 1**  (213) 763-1044

The cornbread may be the best west of the south and the steamed vegetables are meticulously prepared to preserve their freshness, color and most of all their flavor. These are healthy people and they don't let you forget it for a minute. No booze, cigarettes, preservatives or artificial anything. Emile's "natural wines" might fall under a boozy classification but they're terrible to my palate and I suggest you stick with the stuff they do best. The atmosphere is far better than the bleak storefront feeling of most organic places and I was surprised that I liked it.

**Moderate.** Open seven days. Luncheon from 11 a.m. to 5 p.m. Dinner from 5 to 10 p.m. Sunday through Thursday; to 11:30 p.m. Friday, Saturday. Sunday brunch 11 a.m. to 3 p.m. Wine and beer only. No reservations. Patio. All major credit cards. Parking lot; street parking. Semi-dressy.

---

## CHEZ ORLEANS
**French Creole**
★

302 Midway Drive
Escondido  (714) 743-1772

An opulent, Art Deco atmosphere with great brass chandeliers and black and white photographs of New Orleans, this is a winner from detail to detail. The menu lists Louisiana crab claws, shrimp Creole and more than its fair share of flown-ins (scallops, salmon, oysters). Desserts are exquisite with the chef's mudpie, a fantasy of chocolate tastes and textures. There's gentle background music.

**Expensive.** Open seven days. Dinner Sunday through Thursday 5 to 10 p.m.; to 11 p.m. Friday, Saturday. Sunday brunch 10 a.m. to 2 p.m. Dixieland jazz at Sunday brunch. Full bar. Reservations required. Disco. Visa, MC, AX. Parking lot. Semi-dressy.

# CHEZ SATEAU

**French/Continental**

850 South Baldwin Avenue ★

Arcadia **Map 6** (213) 446-8806

If Chef Ryo Sato were to wear all the gold medals he's won at international culinary competitions, the dimunitive Japanese chef would not be able to move. Named "chef of the year" and a winner of the culinary Olympics in Frankfurt, Chef Sato attracted respect and admiration for his work at Francois, a superior French restaurant. Now, as it must happen to all talents, Chef Sato is on his own. He took over a lovely property, formerly the Park Ritz in Arcadia, and has transformed it into a chef's dream. Salmon is smoked on the premises. Dishes like grapefruit consomme, and oyster and veal musse will draw the epicures in their Rolls Royces up the freeway like salmon in spawning season. Prices are amazing for this kind of *haute cuisine*, much like buying a Picasso at bargain rates. Two could dine, with wine, for under $50. There's even a Sunday brunch, rarely served at fine restaurants like this. Luncheon menu is lighter and less expensive. The wine list is extensive, and the desserts are wondrous to behold.

**Expensive.** Open seven days. Luncheon from 11 a.m. to 2:30 p.m. weekdays. Dinner from 5 to 10 p.m. Sunday brunch 10 a.m. to 2:30 p.m. Reservations required. Visa, MC, AX. Valet parking. Casual.

*In order to obtain the best results from this Guide, please consult "Tips on Dining Out" on page 21.*

## CHIANTI RISTORANTE · Northern Italian

7383 Melrose Avenue ★★★
Los Angeles **Map 8** (213) 653-8333

This ingratiating turn-of-the-century Art Nouveau restaurant serves *alta cucina* with a flair and style that would appeal to the aristocrats of royalty and industry who adopt such places in Northern Italy. While it is definitely an "In" show-and-tell spot of the celebrity scene here, it is also highly respected by serious aficionados of the more luxurious school of Italian cuisine. The handsome murals, etched-glass screens, polished woods, and elegant table settings provide the perfect setting for such dishes as calf's sweetbreads *alla marsala* (sweetbreads rolled in bread crumbs and egg and served with a wine sauce) or *lombatina di vitello* (a veal T-bone more than two inches thick), the most dramatic presentation of veal I've encountered. The antipasto is an assortment of less familiar— because they are very expensive—delicacies like clams on the half shell, cheeses, vegetables, meats, and greens. This gem is as small as it is beautiful, which makes it a little cramped for parties larger than four. Its immense popularity suggests you avoid weekends and reserve well ahead.

**Expensive.** Open seven days for dinner 5:30 to 11:30 p.m.; Sunday to 11. Closed July 4, Thanksgiving, Christmas. Full bar. Reservations required. Visa, MC, AX. Valet parking. Dressy.

## CHICAGO PIZZA WORKS · Italian

11641 Pico Boulevard ★
West Los Angeles **Map 8** (213)477-7740

In Chicago, muscular, thick-crusted pizza, (as a rule is heavy on the cheese and the goodies, but a trifle thin on the tomato sauce. The defining factor of Chicago-style pizza is the crust, which has bite, substance, great dignity, and is very filling, too. In New York, you can get a heart-shaped pizza or one with lox on it. In Los Angeles, we go to the Chicago Pizza Works, where an exceptionally fine pizza is created in an atmosphere of what appears to be wild abandon and madcap revelry.

There's a sawdust on the floor at the Chicago Pizza Works, and there are kitchen scales on the tables, which are there for no purpose other than to support the pizza upon its arrival (although if you peek at the scale, you can get a disconcerting idea of how much more you're going to weigh after you finish your pie).

According to the menu at the Pizza Works, "Our Chicago Style Pizzas are all custom prepared and may require up to 30 minutes. Please be patient." This is truth in advertising-in-action, since my pizza arrived 28 minutes after I ordered it. I didn't mind the wait at all. I spent it working on an order of the North Shore Antipasto of pickled cauliflower and *pepperoncini,* crumbled Canadian bacon, slices of salami and mozzarella and cheddar cheeses, olives and various other pleasant things, concealed in and around a bed of relatively lively lettuce. Had I more time, I would have tried the Foreman Starting Whistle—an appetizer of stuffed mushroom caps—or the rolls, which the menu noted as being, "Baked fresh from scratch in our own oven," but by that time my Assembly Line had arrived, and my comely waitress was already dishing the pepperoni and sausage and onions and mushrooms and bell peppers that topped the cheese and the thick crust onto my plate.

I wondered about the signs that said, "Hola! Jalapeno Pizza!" and "Aloha! Pizzazz your pizza with pineapple!" I thought about how living in Los Angeles and eating a Chicago-style pizza is the best of all possible worlds.   *M.S.*

---

*In order to obtain the best results from this Guide, be sure to read the French, German, Italian and Oriental menu translators on page 705 to 710 of this Guide.*

**Moderate.** Open seven days. Monday through Thursday 11:30 a.m. to 11 p.m.; Friday to midnight; Saturday from 4 p.m. to midnight; Sunday from 4 to 10 p.m. Beer and wine only. Visa, MC. Wheelchair access at rear. Parking lot. Casual.

---

## CHICKEN NATURAL American

(Locations in Canoga Park, North
Hollywood, West Los Angeles)

★

Just when it seemed the muck would inherit the dearth of lousy chicken take-outs, this beauty comes along with great chicken. They may be the only fast food restaurant to be approved by the American Heart Association because the chicken is prepared without oil and batter, and it's naturally low in calories, fat and cholesterol. All stores feature a natural wood fire where the chicken is roasted on a rotisserie after it is marinated with a special blend of lemon and spices. The menu lists *empanadas* (a flaky pastry stuffed with either beef, chicken or vegetables); chicken salad; cole slaw, bean salad; chicken sandwiches and special desserts like caramel custard and chocolate mousse pie.

**Inexpensive.** Open seven days 10:30 a.m. to 10 p.m. No alcoholic beverages. No reservations. No credit cards; personal checks accepted. Street parking. Casual.

---

## CHINA PALACE Chinese

3905 Sepulveda Boulevard ★
Culver City **Map 3** (213) 391-8389

416-C South Atlantic Boulevard ★
Monterey Park **Map 6** (213) 289-0489

In a plain concrete building next to a freeway ramp is some of the best Mandarin cooking, Szechwan style, in the area. The impressive interior includes a hardwood mural of the

Chinese coastline, there are Ming-red columns with Chinese lettering, hand-carved wooden screens, and festive lanterns. What makes me think that all this is a reasonably authentic reproduction of a fine mainland restaurant is the fact that it is patronized mainly by Chinese. The prices are a bargain, with a dinner that begins with "sour hot soup" and continues with egg rolls filled with fresh lettuce, cabbage, and meat (fried golden brown and ungreasy), then fried rice, then Mongolian beef and "dry sautéed string beans" (sautéed with chicken liver, onions, and mushrooms), then sweet and sour—and spicy—pork. The large menu also includes some good desserts. The "fried candied apple," fried at your table and immediately immersed in ice water to emerge crunchy on the outside and sweet and soft on the inside, is served at the Culver City location only. The wines are very inexpensive.

**Inexpensive to moderate.** Open seven days. Luncheon from 11:30 a.m. to 2:30 p.m. weekdays. Dinner from 5 to 9:30 p.m. Full bar. Reservations recommended. Visa, MC. Parking lot. Casual to semi-dressy.

---

## CHINA TRADER
Chinese/American
★
4200 Riverside Drive
Toluca Lake          **Map 1**                    (213) 842-8109

It's not hard to tell that this venerable valley institution was the brainchild of a Hollywood fantasy artist. It has that unmistakable Warner Brothers look, as though it would be perfectly natural for Bogart and Sydney Greenstreet to be nonchalantly matching wits at a table before the widescreen waterfall window. As a matter of fact, it is a favorite with nearby residents like Bob Hope and Jack Webb, who seem to enjoy the Cantonese and American cuisine and sometimes the shows, featuring acts that haven't quite made it yet. There is a choice of thirty-six tropical drinks, and a professor from Cal Tech set a record by working his way through sixteen before succumbing to a rum torpor, a record that doubtless will stand (which is more than he was able to do). This outpost of Polynesia now seats more people than populate some of the islands, but they've managed to maintain a cordial, even personal relationship.

**Moderate.** Open seven days. Luncheon served 11 a.m. to 2:30 p.m. weekdays. Dinner from 2 p.m. to 2 a.m. Sunday brunch 11 a.m. to 2:30 p.m. Full bar. Reservations advised. All major credit cards. Parking lot. Casual.

---

## CHINESE FRIENDS RESTAURANT                 Chinese
984 North Broadway                                               ★
Los Angeles          **Map 7**                    (213) 626-1837

If you're not prepared for the unusual, you're liable to become dis-Oriented here. I mean sea slugs are scarcely the egg foo yung of the ordinary places. This out-of-the-ordinary restaurant presents the cuisine of Hunan in plain surroundings that belie the complex sweet and sours, the good sauces, and the interesting combinations. These very pleasant people will help you understand their cuisine.

**Inexpensive.** Open seven days. Luncheon from 11:30 a.m. to 3 p.m. Dinner from 4 to 9:30 p.m. No alcoholic beverages. No reservations. Visa, MC. Plaza parking. Casual.

---

## CHRISTIAN'S DANISH INN                 Scandinavian
8235 University Avenue
La Mesa                                          (714) 462-4800

Your hostess greets you at the door with your glass of sherry in hand; if you prefer, she comes up with champagne instead—instant hospitality that grows at your table for the evening. Everyone orders from the same hand-scripted menu passed from table to table. For faithful fans of Christian's a monthly newsletter is sent forth heralding upcoming entrees to be sure they don't miss their favorites. If you're a first timer, put yourself in their care for selections. If you don't, by the time you are tempted with the desserts you'll have gone mad; and no one in his right mind would pass up dessert here. Mr. Hansen may even show you his working wine cellar, but please don't touch the dust.

**Expensive.** Open Tuesday through Saturday. Dinner from 6:30 to 9 p.m. fixed price of $24.50. Beer and wine only. Reservations required. Visa, MC, DC. Parking lot. Semi-dressy.

---

## THE CHRONICLE

**Continental**

★★

897 Granite Drive
Pasadena        **Map 7**                    (213) 792-1179

2640 Main Street
Santa Monica    **Map 2**                    (213) 392-4956

One into two does not always equal two in food-biz math. One good restaurant like the Chronicle in Pasadena adding another in Santa Monica did not come up with two winners at the beginning. The Santa Monica location suffered from early staggers but Lud Renick moved decisively. He acquired a Scandia alumnus: chef Rolf Nonnast—and together they have moved this beautiful restaurant, in a beautifully restored Victorian mansion, to the top ranks. Emphasis is on seafood although there is a full menu from chicken Kiev to veal chop *forrestière*. Like every artist, Rolf has his special talent—the night I was there the fresh fish of the day was smelt, a rarity. Consistency prevails from the hot or cold appetizers to the salads—try the Caesar—to savory clam chowder. Listen to the waiter; he'll recite a litany of specialties. The wine list is one of the best in this or any other area if you, like me, enjoy California wines. There's a banquet room that seats 60 but not for the usual service club type fare. Frankly, I wouldn't go near the place on weekend evenings but a Monday or Tuesday can be serendipity.

**Moderate to expensive.** Open seven days. Luncheon served 11:30 a.m. to 2:30 p.m. Monday through Saturday. Dinner from 5 to 10:30. Full bar. Reservations advised. MC, AX, CB. Valet parking. Semi-dressy.

---

## CHUCK'S STEAK HOUSE                    American
(Locations in Los Angeles, Westwood, Sherman                  ★
Oaks, Marina del Rey, Santa Barbara, Escondido, La Jolla.
See phone book for listing.)

Recently some colleagues of mine were discussing the derivation of that ubiquitous phenomenon, the steak-and-lobster house. There were nearly as many theories as there were restaurants. Yet all of us felt that somewhere, somehow, some inspired soul had to be the first to place entrées on a single plate, and I was inspired to make an effort to find the man. I'm pretty sure it was Chuck Rolles. Who's he? Well, Chuck is the Chuck of Chuck's Steak House of Hawaii that originated in the old Edgewater Beach Hotel in Honolulu and has proliferated to include restaurants from Hawaii to Connecticut, which is as literally "coast to coast" as the term can ever be. It came about because the patrons of Chuck's first restaurant were agonizing between succulent Australian lobster and the Black Angus beef, items that form the basis of the present menus. From the rough wood exteriors to the wood and textured interiors to the crackling fireplace to the warm and friendly people, these are restaurants of character and quality—where a bevy of attractive young people serve remarkably good food. The menu is lettered on a wine bottle, a much imitated device, but Chuck's is where that started, too. You begin at the fresh salad bar among a wide variety of selections and a choice of excellent salad dressings, including a Roquefort that would hold its own in any company. The à la carte artichokes weren't overcooked. (Try them with Italian dressing instead of melted butter.) There's a marvelous teriyaki steak with just the right combination of all the ingredients. The baked potato was not served in a foil wrapper nor was it watery and thin-skinned. It was an honest-to-Idaho delight and, inasmuch as I come from a long line of potato-skin eaters, that is quite important to me. Each Chuck's Steak House of Hawaii is apparently entitled to its own personality, and there is a flexible manual of operation. We particularly like the enthusiasm of the staff and the long dresses of the waitresses, and the fact that each operator prepares his own wine list. The restaurant is open for dinner only every day except Christmas and Thanksgiving, and also serves such fare as beef-kabob, lobster, and top sirloin steak. Its very limited menu (after all, how much can you write on a wine bottle?) presents the highest quality attainable. (They cut their own meat to ample twelve-and thirteen-ounce portions.) Salad is included with entrées, but baked potato is à la carte, which is proper. Children's portions are available on some items. All in all, it's good to see people who really care about what they are doing.

**Moderate.** Open seven days. Dinner from 5 to 11 p.m.; To midnight Friday, Saturday. Closed Christmas Thanksgiving. Full bar. No reservations. Visa, MC, AX, DC. Parking lot. Casual.

---

**CHU DYNASTY**                    **Mandarin/Szechewan**
1033 B Avenue                               ★
Coronado                              (714) 435-5300

1400 Camino del Arena ★
Mission Valley (714) 298-4680

7612 Fay Avenue ★
La Jolla (714) 454-3336

All tolled, I think you'll be glad you drove across the bridge to be pampered by the Chester Chu family and to view their etchings, sketchings, and portraits of their ancestors. Unless you know Mandarin/Szechewan cuisine well, why not let them order for you, as each dish is specially prepared to order. If you do your own ordering, don't overlook the *chow san shein* (beef, chicken, shrimp, and vegetables) or the Peking duck and pancakes. Yes, they have seafood.

**Inexpensive to moderate.** Open seven days. Luncheon from 11:30 a.m. to 2:30 p.m. weekdays. Dinner from 5:30 to 10:30 p.m.; to 11:30 Friday, Saturday. Full bar. Reservations recommended. Visa, MC, AX, DC. Parking lot. Casual.

---

## CHUNG KING RESTAURANT      Chinese/Mandarin
11538 West Pico Boulevard ★
West Los Angeles    **Map 8**      (213) 477-4917

A favorite of the art colony, this is one of the oldest restaurants serving good Szechwanese cuisine in the area. As you've been warned, these spicy, warming foods from the cold districts of China can cauterize the palate unless approached with respect. You might begin with sizzling rice soup and work your way up to Chungking salad (mixed vegetables with peanuts and chicken that have been soaked in a searing marinade.) Items that are particularly singeing are thoughtfully marked with an asterisk on the menu, but I urge you, my friends, urge you not to miss the symphony of flavors. One nibbles and takes little sips of water and eats soothing rice and noodles until there is at least a psychological callous that lets you experience new tastes not only from Szechwan, but in the great cuisines of India, Korea, and Indonesia, when you get to them.

**Inexpensive.** Open seven days. Luncheon from noon to 2 p.m. weekdays. Dinner from 5 to 10 p.m.; to 10:30 Friday, Saturday. Closed Christmas. Beer only. No reservations. No credit cards. Parking lot. Casual.

---

## CHURCHILL'S RESTAURANT
209 North Glendale Avenue
Glendale          **Map 7**

Continental
★
(213) 247-3131

A simply gorgeous setting for the shoppers by day and the diners by night who frequent Robinson's and the adjoining stores in Glendale. There is a gigantic portrait of Churchill (who else?) in the main dining room, much flowers, comfortable booths, good sounds and smells, and lots of artifacts along the ceiling display shelf. A patio for leisurely dining is shaded from the harsh sun—and, yes, smog—yet comfortable on chilly days. Serviceware, drinks, and most everything is first class—you'll see a lot of the old money here, established Glendale citizens—but how come the prices are so reasonable? Their enchilada is made with crab and avocado and topped with sour cream and comes with special salad and desert. I had roast leg of lamb, a lovely salad with Roquefort, baked potato, fresh vegetables, and hot bread plus a complimentary dessert. Their prime rib is choice, toad in the hole, good; and the stuffed flounder is exceptional. There's even that endangered species, lobster à la Newburg, and more. One of my favorite spots in Glendale.

**Inexpensive to moderate.** Open seven days. Luncheon from 11 a.m. to 3:30 p.m. Monday through Saturday. Dinner from 5 to 10 p.m. Monday; to 11 Tuesday through Thursday; to 11:30 Friday, Saturday; 4 to 10 Sunday. Closed Christmas. Piano bar Tuesday through Saturday. Full bar. No reservations. Visa, MC, AX. Shopping center parking. Casual.

---

## CIGO'S
915 South Pacific Avenue
San Pedro        **Map 3**

**Yugoslavian/Adriatic**
★
(213) 833-0949

How about a 10-course fisherman's dinner? San Pedro is beginning to emerge with a restaurant identity and some good Yugoslavian restaurants like Paragon. This one, Cigo's, has been around for a long time serving sautéed abalone chips, octopus salad, and squid along with the more familiar finny stuff. The cioppino is more authentic and not quite as bland as most.

**Inexpensive to moderate.** Open seven days from 11:30 a.m. to 10 p.m. Full bar. Reservations advised. Visa, MC. Casual.

---

## CITY CAFE
7407½ Melrose
Los Angeles      **Map 7**

**Continental cafe**
★★
(213) 658-7495

A dream of the owners Gai Gherardi and Barbara McReynolds and Margo Willits, this cafe was to bring the wonderful world of Italian cafe life to L.A. To accomplish their laudable objectives they introduced a relatively novel concept of restaurant operation, the take *in*. Most of the food is prepared somewhere else and brought to the premises. And why not? Why not get the best croissants (Croissant Show) and the best pasta (Pasta Pasta Pasta) and the best of everything from specialty places? After all, we don't care where the food is prepared, only that it tastes great and looks good. The cafe is a statement in contemporary graphics with a zolatone look from the 50's, high tech lights, pop art, black tables with chrome chairs and a gleaming black counter. Fresh fruit is heaped on a gondola shaped dish. Cappuccino, espresso and mocha blend American coffee and desserts are served all day. There were many who expected these ladies to stumble over their own feat but the trio has trimphed. There is an air of lazy Italian convivialty that is both charming and novel to this area.

**Inexpensive.** Open Monday through Saturday 8:30 a.m. to midnight. No reservations. Closed major holidays. No alcoholic beverages. No credit cards. Wheelchair access. Street parking. Casual.

---

## CLEARMAN'S STEAK 'N STEIN American
9545 East Whittier Blvd. ★
Pico Rivera **Map 6** (213) 699-4716

John Clearman has become a legend with his restaurants of solid and honest character. Real wood crackles and spits in the fireplace, the menu offers a few good steaks, fried chicken, and lobster, and dinners include a tossed green salad with a huge baked potato. No reservations are taken but none are really needed. The turnover is fast so you won't have to wait long. My favorite dish here is the ground steak, and I like the onion rings and cheese bread. Clearman's is much imitated but rarely topped.

**Moderate.** Open Tuesday through Sunday. Dinner served Tuesday through Saturday from 5 to 10 p.m.; Sunday from 3 to 9 p.m. Closed Thanksgiving and Christmas. Full bar. No reservations. Visa, MC. Parking lot. Casual.

---

*Please be sure to consult "Tipping Made Easy" on page 25 of this Guide.*

## THE CLIFF HOUSE RESTAURANT    American
6805 Vista Del Mar Lane                   ★
Playa del Rey    **Map 2**      (213) 823-1530

This old favorite is as cozy inside as it looks outside and the patio is the prettiest around. Pine woods, real Tiffany lamps and hanging plants form the setting for omelettes, salads, specialty sandwiches, steaks and fresh seafood. They're open all the time it seems, and the Sunday brunch, is often the start of something big.

**Inexpensive.** Open seven days. Breakfast served from 8 a.m. to 5 p.m. Luncheon from 11 a.m. to 5 p.m. Dinner from 5 to 10 p.m. Sunday brunch from 10 a.m. to 4 p.m. Beer and wine only. Patio. No reservations. No credit cards. Casual.

---

## CLIFTON'S CAFETERIA    Cafeteria
648 South Broadway at 7th Street      ★
Los Angeles    **Map 7**      (213) 627-1673

515 West 7th Street
Los Angeles    **Map 7**      (213) 485-1726

10250 Santa Monica Boulevard
Century City    **Map 8**      (213) 277-1760

Lakewood Center
Lakewood    **Map 3**      (213) 634-6555

West Covina Plaza
West Covina    **Map 6**      (213) 960-4741

Once upon a time, about fifty years ago, when people liked and trusted each other, there was a cafeteria that let you pay whatever you wanted to pay for your meal, and no one was turned away hungry. It was a fantasy of ferns, waterfalls, free limeade, and troubadors. Times and temperaments have changed—drastically—and the old Clifton's is dead; but the new ones, a chain of five, live on. The Broadway one, most resembling the original, still has the redwood forest atmosphere with waterfall and brook. Prices are reasonable, the food is good, and the strawberry pie is exceptional. The big old 700-seater is a fine place to bring the children on the rare occasions you find yourself downtown. The 7th Street one was originally a jewelry store built in 1922 and is closed on Saturday and Sunday. The Lakewood one has a Sunday brunch. Only the Broadway and 7th Street places are open for breakfast. The others open at 11 a.m.

**Inexpensive.** Broadway location open 6 a.m. to 9 p.m. West 7th open 7 a.m. to 3:30 p.m. Century City from 11 a.m. to 8 p.m. Lakewood from 11 a.m. to 8 p.m. West Covina from 11 a.m. to 11:30 p.m. All open seven days, except West 7th which is open Monday through Friday. Children's menu. No alcoholic beverages. No reservations. No credit cards. Wheelchair access. Parking lot. Casual.

---

## COCK'N BULL RESTAURANT    English
9170 Sunset Boulevard                           ★★
West Hollywood        **Map 8**        (213) 276-7814

The oldest and one of the coziest restaurants on the Sunset Strip, the Cock 'N Bull, is where agents and celebrities meet to discuss their deals and enjoy the British pub atmosphere and food. The steak and kidney pie, and beef dishes are better than most anything you'll find in the British Isles—which, admittedly, may not really be saying much. The long, cool building paneled in dark woods is an ideal place for Sunday hunt breakfast, which can be eggs,

180

sausage, grilled mushrooms, finnan haddie, chicken, and fresh fruit. This is a busy spot for cocktails; Pimm's cups and Moscow mules (a Cock 'n Bull invention) are particular favorites.

**Moderate.** Open seven days. Luncheon from 11:30 a.m. to 2:30 p.m. weekdays for fixed price of $5.50. Dinner from 6 to 11 p.m.; 5 to 11 Saturday, Sunday for fixed price of $12.50. Sunday brunch 10 a.m. to 2:30 p.m. for fixed price of $7.50. Open all holidays. Full bar. Reservations recommended. Visa, MC, AX, DC. Valet parking. Casual.

---

## COLONEL LEE'S MONGOLIAN BAR-B-Q   Chinese
(Locations throughout Southern California.   Bar-B-Q
See phone book for listings.)

Mongolian cuisine is unique among all foods because the dishes were prepared by scouring the countryside and tossing together the vegetables and meat on a warrior's shield with a little oil and spice. Few of us carry shields today, but the particularly spicy and satisfying flavors are still prepared as Genghis Khan enjoyed them in A.D. 1211.

At Colonel Lee's Mongolian Bar-B-Q you will select from a buffet of raw vegetables and sliced meats—turkey, pork, lamb or beef—and greens (cilantro, onions, peapods and beansprouts), then hand it to a chef who takes the raw food from you, throws it into an iron stove top about the size of a manhole cover, tosses it for a few seconds with a little oil and returns your plate with food that's crisp, crunchy and spicy (you add the sauce).

These are unpretentious little places ranging from semi-tacky to Sizzler modern but the "all-you-can-eat" is extremely popular, especially among college students. Takeout is handled well here at luncheon with a more varied menu. Hours differ with the locations—there are 60 in California—and some have beer and wine; many do not. Service is buffet-style.

**Moderate.** Hours differ at each location. Check with individual restaurant.

## COOK'S STEAK AND CHOP HOUSE American
645 South Olive ★★
Los Angeles **Map 7** (213) 627-1711

Cook's is cousin to the Pacific Dining Car, and the resemblance
is clearly reflected in the quality of the steaks and hearty beef
dishes in the masculine-elegant establishment — and in the
high prices. It's not that the operators are overcharging; it's
simply that the cost of superb beef is nearly out of sight. You
can pay plenty for a steak; but if you (or your expense account)
can handle the tariff, you won't find better prepared or better
served prime rib and beef anywhere. Fresh garden vegetables
are used, and the wine list has been carefully, intelligently,
almost whimsically thought out. They've been here since 1935.

**Moderate to expensive.** Open Monday through Saturday.
Luncheon served 11 a.m. to 5 p.m. weekdays. Dinner from 5
to 10 p.m. Saturday 4 to 11 p.m. Full bar. Reservations
advised. Visa, MC. Validated parking next door. Casual to
semi-dressy.

## CORDON BLEU French
859 Laguna Canyon Road ★
Laguna Beach **Map 4** (714) 494-1911

On a trip to Brussels, I eschewed the grand and majestic
restaurants in favor of momma and poppa operations, where
food is still seasoned with pride. Maxim's was classic but
colorlessly perfect. But, ah, the world of the tiny bistro,
where one man acts as maestro of his kitchen, turning out
fragrant and savory dishes under the watchful eye of
madame. No electronic ovens. No stainless steel. No frills.
Perhaps you can imagine our satisfaction at discovering just

such an adventure in Laguna. Here, at the end of a bleak and dismal shopping center, exists Cordon Bleu—a diamond in the rough, tough world of restaurant competition. Cordon Bleu used to be called Chez Gerard, a delightful oasis of French cuisine with somewhat rickety chairs and questionable oil paintings. Then it was purchased by the Bouchés. Now all the chairs match, the oils have been replaced by tasteful memorabilia, and the food is still exceptional. "Poppa" is Jean-Jacques, whose flashing Gallic eyes contradict a modest and gentle demeanor. Everything is prepared from scratch in his tiny kitchen. "Momma," Denise Bouché, is a gracious woman who provides more than her presence to the eighty-seat establishment. She was once chef for the British Embassy in Brussels. While she is adamant that Poppa is a vastly better chef, I cannot help but feel that there must be some animated discussions about the vichysoisse, succulent frog's legs garnished with fresh broccoli and baby carrots, and tripe à la Monegasque, a classic test of the chef's talent. Other entrées include a superior Dover sole Véronique, veal Oscar, *canard à l'orange*, and some steaks, although I can never understand why someone will go to a continental restaurant and order American steak. Three house specials depend on what's fresh and on the mood of the chef. Desserts, like everything else, disdain premixed, preportioned fare; we enjoyed the *mousse aux fraises*, although the more complex crêpes, omelettes, and cherries jubilee are available. They are located across from the Pageant of the Masters.

**Moderate.** Open Tuesday through Saturday (seven days in summer). Dinner from 5:30 p.m.; 5 on Sunday. Closed major holidays. Full bar. Reservations advised. Visa, MC. Parking lot. Semi-dressy.

---

*To obtain the best results from this Guide, consult*
*"How to Use this Guide" on page 27.*

# CORIANDER

**Continental**
★

12254 Ventura Boulevard
Studio City    **Map 1**      (213) 762-5544

According to a sign in front of Coriander, the multiple cuisine represented here is "French-Italian-Thai-American-Seafood," not to be confused with that hodgepodge called "Continental." This is food that takes a bit from each culture and results in a new cuisine that's a bit greater than the sum of its parts. The chicken *gai young*, for instance, is mostly an Oriental dish—marinated in five-spice powder, served with hot & sour dipping sauces—but then, what could be more American than half a baked chicken which you tear apart with your fingers. The same is true of the spareribs which taste like they've been broasted in an Oriental smoke cooker, but reek of the sort of barbecue sauce that could make a soul food restaurant puff out its chest with pride.

Not all the dishes at Coriander (one of my favorite herbs, also known as cilantro and Chinese parsley) walk that thin line between cuisines. The French onion soup is French only, and very traditional, too. The London broil with mushroom gravy is a perfectly American concoction. The *moo sate* Thai-style—marinated beef on a stick served with a dipping sauce—has few antecedents outside of Thailand. And the *linguine* with fresh seafood sauce is not only very Italian, but also very delicious. The roast Long Island duckling, on the other hand, is sort of a utility outfielder, served as it is with a different sauce everyday.

Aside from the pleasures of its food, Coriander is also symbolic of the many ways in which lower Ventura Boulevard is becoming one of the most interesting dining areas in Los Angeles. Ventura already boasts the city's best deli (Art's), best sushi bar (Terusushi), and a slew of terrific French restaurants (Wine Bistro, Le Cafe, Camille's, Albion, La Serre). Coriander adds a new texture to the street.   *M.S.*

184

**Moderate.** Open Monday through Saturday. Luncheon served 11 a.m. to 3 p.m. weekdays. Dinner from 5 to 10:30 p.m. Beer and wine only. Reservations advised. Visa, MC, AX. Parking lot. Casual.

---

## THE COTERIE                             Continental
9641 Sunset Boulevard
Beverly Hills          **Map 8**                    (213) 276-2252

The major restaurant at the Beverly Hills Hotel has major problems to surmount, and they haven't succeeded as of now. The problem of identification blurs most every function—is it a laid-back, casually-elegant establishment, or is it a proper dining room for proper people (not necessarily the hotel guests)? Dinner is served well; there is talent in the kitchen and Nino Osti is an experienced maitre d' but the dishes are pedestrian and the room simply doesn't have much life to it.

**Expensive.** Open every night for dinner from 6:30 to 9:30 p.m. Cocktails. Reservations recommended. Major credit cards. Wheelchair access. Valet parking ($2). Dressy; jacket required.

---

## COURTNEY'S                              Continental
900 Manhattan Avenue                            ★★★
Manhattan Beach         **Map 2**                  (213) 544-1020

Possibly the coziest, the loveliest and simply the best restaurant to come to Southern California in a while. There are presently a Cafe Courtney (Hermosa Beach), a Courtney's Bistro (in Manhattan Beach), Cafe Courtney in Manhattan Beach, Courtney's Palos Verdes and this one, simply called Courtney's, all named after Chuck Lehman's five-year-old daughter. Courtney's was created from the lumber of an old church in Oregon augmented by wood from farmhouses. The carpet is wheat colored and textured, as if forming itself to the peg floor, and the restaurant makes the first great use of color photography as decor that I've seen. Each photograph is gallery lighted and provides a highlight of color. Room dividers are ancient church pews topped with marble, and the feeling and view from the lacy second-story windows—the first floor is a massive sunken bar—is pure magic. Lehman and his management team have injected the flair that made their previous adventures so profitable. The dinner menu is kept confined to those dishes that the kitchen can prepare very well. The menu changes frequently and on the occasion of my last visit, included eight entrees including *aubergine* Suzanne—fried eggplant with mozzarella, ricotta and parmesan cheeses baked in fresh tomato sauce (including a salad of marinated mushrooms), plus three daily specials or more. Starters include soft shelled crabs in tempura butter, Scotch eggs and my favorite, Chinese chicken salad. Other entrées listed were *poulet à la crème*, boneless breast of chicken over fettuccine with Parmesan cheese cream and bay shrimp; *filet oignons nois*, a Scandinavian dish of filet mignon with sauteed onions and creamed horseradish; and *veau Francais* medallion of milk-fed veal dipped in egg, sautéed with creamed lemon sauce. The essential difference between this and other restaurants is that they refuse to accept any detail as ordinary. Every aspect of the food and service is constantly, almost ruthlessly under review. For example, Courtney's is one of the few restaurants where fine cheese is served at room temperature. Many of the so-called superstar establishments either have little or no selection or worse: they refrigerate their cheese to the consistency of putty. If I sound uncharacteristically enthused, it's because I am. Courtney's is living proof that good taste, hard work and courage still pay off. The atmosphere is casual—"laid back" might be a more appropriate term—with a young serving staff that really cares. The luncheon menu is more for the business folk in the area. The serendipity of Courtney's has probably contributed to afternoon absenteeism at nearby business. Entertainment from Thursday through Saturday is gentle.

**Moderate.** Open Monday through Saturday. Luncheon from 11:30 a.m. to 2 p.m. weekdays. Dinner from 6 to 10 p.m. Monday through Thursday; to 11 Friday; 5 to 9 Sunday. Closed Memorial Day, Labor Day. Reservations recommended. Entertainment. Ocean view. Visa, MC, AX. CB. Street parking; city lot. Casual.

---

## COURTNEY'S BISTRO

American/Continental
★

124 Manhattan Beach Boulevard
Manhattan Beach     **Map 2**     (213) 544-0810

After going through a forgettable period of operation as the Incredible Pub 'n' Grub Company, Courtney's Bistro has emerged as the most commercially successful of the present "Courtney" restaurants. Although the smallest of the group, it possesses its own special *joie de vivre* that keeps it vibrant yet cozy. The menu (same for lunch and dinner) exemplifies the well-established "Courtney" style. Selections range from sandwiches, omelettes and salads (including a traditional Cobb salad) to more serious entrées such as a cassoulet, chicken Bombay, the daily veal special, two or three fresh fish and other daily specials like duck, quail or lamb. The wine list is extensive and several of the wines from the list are offered by the glass each week, giving diners a chance to sample something new without investing in a whole bottle. Follow dinner with a stroll on the pier (about a hundred yards down the street) and your evening should rate very well on the 1 to 10 scale.

**Inexpensive.** Open seven days. Luncheon from 11 a.m. to 2 p.m. Monday through Thursday; to 2:30 Friday. Dinner from 5 to 10 p.m. Sunday through Wednesday; 5 to 11 Thursday through Saturday. Closed major holidays. Wine and beer only. Reservations recommended. Visa, MC. Street parking. Casual.

---

## THE COVE                                         Continental
3191 West 7th Street                                        ★★
Los Angeles          **Map 7**                    (213) 388-0361

The Cove is one of those restaurants in which you could order a steak, then leave on impulse to spend ten years in a monastery; when you return the same waiter would greet you with, "And how would you like it done?" At The Cove, nothing seems to change—not the personnel, not the ambience, not the quality, not even, it seems, the prices. One of the reasons The Cove is relatively inexpensive is because it was established before it cost a million dollars to build a restaurant, back in 1951, in the basement of the Chancellor, then a quiet, semi-elegant hotel in Los Angeles' Wilshire district. The Chancellor has changed, and her once chic lobby now processes budget tour groups from abroad. But The Cove is still as soothingly luxurious as it was twenty-seven years ago when Jersey Joe Walcott ad Harry Truman were champions and Bobby Thomson's home run destroyed the Dodgers. The continental dinner menu tilts slightly toward the Rhineland, with dishes like *wienerschnitzel*, an epochal sauerbraten with potato pancakes and red cabbage, and *rahmschnitzel* with noodles. The long menu lists the classic French dishes, a large selection of seafood, and from-the-broiler selections. There are some who feel that The Cove's roast rack of lamb *bouquetière* (only fresh vegetables are served) is the best in Southern California. All the dishes are prepared and served well, by people who have been doing it long enough to get it right. To me, the most noteworthy aspect of this restaurant is the comparatively low prices for cuisine that is among the finest in the area. The entrées come with choice of soup or salad (Caesar or mixed green). The dressing for the Caesar salad is pre-prepared in a blender. While this is not as theatrical as having it made tableside, it makes for a better, smoother blend. They serve carefully selected wines by the glass, an all-too-uncommon convenience if you want different wines with different courses or different dinners.

The Cove does a brisk luncheon business because of the food, the location, and the low prices. Continental luncheon is soup or salad and entrees like sauerbraten, roast pork, veal scallopini, or the chef's daily suggestion. Desserts are made on the premises, and I particularly recommend the *Schwarzwalder Kirschtorte*, a rich chocolate cake with cherries and whipped cream.

Entertainment is by strolling violinist Tony Doria.

**Moderate.** Open seven days. Luncheon served 11:30 a.m. to 3 p.m. weekdays. Dinner from 4:30 to midnight. Entertainment. Full bar. Reservations suggested. All major credit cards. Valet parking. Semi-dressy to dressy.

---

## COZZA'S
500 North Brookhurst
Anaheim      **Map 6**

Italian
★
(714) 776-0500

Almost an extension of the Big A in Anaheim, this is where Ray Malavasi parks his elephantine bod while contemplating the vagaries of Ramsball and staring into a short cold one. The Angels come here as well, not because it's convenient but because the food is good and portioned for hungry athletes. Veal Frank Sinatra is sautéed in sherry with mushrooms, green peppers and onions (Sinatra does not like green peppers), linguini with clam sauce and trout picatta are especially good. There's a banquet facility that can handle from 20 to the population of New Jersey.

**Moderate.** Open seven days. Luncheon from 11 a.m. to 4 p.m. weekdays. Dinner Sunday through Thursday 4 to 11:20 p.m.; Friday and Saturday to 12:30 a.m. Live entertainment. Full bar. Reservations preferred. Visa, MC, AX. CB. Wheelchair access. Parking lot. Casual.

---

## THE CRAB COOKER                                    Seafood
2200 Newport Boulevard                                    ★
Newport Beach          **Map 4**                (714) 673-0100

This is a wait-in-line combination fish market and restaurant with plastic forks and paper plates in plain surroundings, but the seafood dishes are good and fresh, and the house white wine (Cribari) is just right with the variety of charcoal-broiled seafood, clam chowder, and cole slaw.

**Inexpensive.** Open seven days. Sunday through Thursday 11 a.m. to 9 p.m.; Friday, Saturday 11 a.m. to 10 p.m. Closed Easter. Wine and beer only. No reservations. No credit cards accepted. Street parking. Casual.

---

## CRAB SHELL                                          Seafood
10 Washington Street                                      ★
Maina del Rey          **Map 2**                (213) 399-5717

5374 East 2nd Street                                      ★
Belmont Shores, Long Beach      **Map 3**       (213) 434-1856

George Batsakes started something good. When a fish market decides to become a restaurant, it usually purveys the best of both worlds. Although there are 75 seats and a kind of underwater flotsam decor in which fancy cocktails are served, the humble beauty of the mongery remains in the freshest fish served above sea level. There is a salt water tank in which clams and Pacific lobsters are kept. All cooking is kept simple, as it should be, thus making the most of the full fresh flavors of the fish. Entrées are served with French fries or baked potato and good cole slaw. Clam chowder is best than most. My favorite is the fresh cracked crab. The newer Crab Shell in Long Beach is similar in philosophy and menu but serves smaller portions for less money. An upstairs balcony overlooks the ocean and is a pleasant place to have cocktails.

**Marina: Moderate.** Open Tuesday through Sunday. Luncheon from 11:30 a.m. to 4 p.m. Full bar. Dinner from 4 to 10:45 p.m. Reservations suggested. Ocean view. Visa, MC, DC, CB. Parking lot. Casual.

**Belmont Shores: Moderate.** Open seven days. Luncheon from 11:30 a.m. to 4 p.m. Dinner 4 to 10 Sunday through Thursday; 4 to 11 Friday, Saturday. Beer and wine only. Reservations recommended, especially for five or more. Visa, MC. Parking lot. Casual.

---

# CROSSROADS
18050 Brookhurst Street
Fountain Valley          **Map 4**

**American**
★
(714) 963-6711

Most suburban areas like Orange County are blanded to death with steak-and-lobsteries and few imaginative restaurants. This one started out with high hopes and an eclectic menu and was forced to scale down to the tastes of the area. What has emerged here is a better than average limited menu operation with good seafoods and very good abalone. The rest of the menu is predictable and pedestrian with the welcome exception of a splendid vegetarian plate. While I think their slogan "sooner or later all people meet at the

Crossroads" is a fantasy, I'd still meet you there for the live Maine lobster and the good karma.

**Moderate.** Open seven days. Luncheon Monday through Friday from 11 a.m. to 4 p.m. Dinner Sunday to Thursday 4 to 10 p.m.; Friday, Saturday to 11 p.m. Sunday brunch 10 a.m. to 2 p.m. Children's menu. Closed major holidays for lunch. Full bar. Reservations advised. Visa, MC, AX. Parking lot. Casual.

---

# CYRANO
8711 Sunset Boulevard
Los Angeles     **Map 8**

**Continental**
★
(213) 655-9836

Cyrano's has come a long way from its humble origin as one of the first coffee houses in Hollywood, and traces of that casual insouciance remain. The omelettes are extra fine and there are interesting specials, though it's not the kind of place where the chef gets up at 4 a.m. to start the stock pots and buy the produce. You can wear what you want and, for that matter, be whoever you want. It's open and serving until 2 a.m. and you'll enjoy the tapestry of characters that weaves in and out and around the place.

**Moderate.** Open seven days. Dinner Sunday through Thursday from 6 p.m. to 1 a.m.; Friday, Saturday to 2 a.m. Private party facilities. Closed July 4, Christmas. Full bar. Reservations advised. Patio. All major credit cards. Casual.

*In order to obtain the best results from this Guide, be sure to read the French, German, Italian and Oriental menu translators on page 705 to 710 of this Guide.*

## DAISY'S MARKET

American
★

1700 South Harbor Boulevard
Anaheim Hyatt House
Anaheim     **Map 6**          (714) 772-5900

Finally there's a place near Disneyland (across the street)
with a reputation good enough to improve on. So they did.
Daisy's Market came up with new uniforms to add to an
operation that I had already found hopelessly cheerful. Yes,
they still have all that lush greenery, but they don't worry
about being overdone—they've even done over the lounge.
You'll find a good salad bar (most salad bars leave me cold)
with fresh spinach, mushrooms, bay shrimp, marinated
baby corn, herring in sour cream, and Greek olives. After
the main course, it's back to the bar—the do-it-yourself ice
cream bar—where you get to run the soft-ice-cream machine
and choose and ooze your favorite toppings. Sunday brunch
is one of the best in the area.

**Moderate.** Open seven days. Breakfast from 6:30 to 11:30
a.m. Luncheon from 11:30 a.m. to 2:30 p.m. Snack menu

2:30 to 5 p.m. Dinner 5:30 to 10 p.m. Sunday brunch 9:30 a.m. to 2 p.m. for fixed price of $8.50. Open all holidays. Full bar. Reservations recommended. All major credit cards. Parking lot. Casual.

## DAL RAE

Continental
★

2151 North Harbor Boulevard
Fullerton        **Map 6**        (714) 870-1711

This is one of those big, showy places with an entertainment lounge, huge dining rooms, and banquet facilities, that is a special favorite with the industrialists of Orange County. Mostly, the clientele seems so swoozled they would have difficulty telling the soups from the salad; often there's not much to tell. I have had some good dinners here, but they've been after 8 p.m. which is probably when the chef comes on—or wakes up. There are more than 100 items on the menu, with complete luncheons and à la carte dinners. Drinks are superb.

**Moderate.** Open seven days. Luncheon from 11 a.m. to 4 p.m. weekdays. Dinner 4 p.m. to midnight Sunday through Thursday; to 1 a.m. Friday, Saturday. Children's menu. Closed Labor Day, Christmas. Entertainment. Full bar. Reservations recommended. All major credit cards. Parking lot. Semi-dressy.

## DAL RAE

Continental
★

9023 East Washington Boulevard
Pico Rivera        **Map 6**        (213) 723-4427

This is a fine older restaurant. It's a favorite with the horse and track crowd, who know—and can afford—good food. If you ever find yourself in the unlikely eastern part of Los

Angeles known as Pico Rivera, you can't go wrong by stopping here for either luncheon or dinner.

**Moderate to expensive.** Open seven days. Luncheon from 11 a.m. to 4 p.m. Dinner from 4 p.m. to 1 a.m. Piano bar. Full bar. Reservations recommended. All major credit cards. Valet parking. Casual.

---

## D'AMICO'S
2710 East Chapman Avenue
Orange     **Map 6**

Southern Italian
★
(714) 639-4610

Papa D'Amico runs the most determinedly cheerful Italian restaurant in Orange County, and he has built a large and loyal following with Southern Italian specialties like *speidini Siciliana* (tender slices of rolled beef stuffed with cheese and herb dressing) and milk-fed veal. His *cioppino* is made with clams, shrimp, *calamari*, and scallops in a tangy red sauce. Papa sings, as do the waiters and waitresses—everything from folk to opera. The cappuccino is Old World, and there's an array of Italian liqueurs that tastes like home to the paisanos. Robust in the kitchen and the front of the house as well.

**Inexpensive to moderate.** Open seven days. Luncheon from 11 a.m. to 4 p.m. Dinner 4 to 10 p.m. Sunday brunch 10 a.m. to 3 p.m. Entertainment. Full bar. Reservations advised. Visa, MC, AX. Wheelchair access. Shopping center parking. Casual.

---

## DANISH INN
1547 Mission Drive (Hwy #246)
Solvang

Scandinavian
★
(805) 688-4813

This is not as touristy as the others in Solvang, and it's the place most likely to be selected when local residents go out. The windmill makes it an easy landmark to spot, and it's an unusually pleasant place with a bar that serves Danish beer. Dishes tend to be more authentic: pig's knuckles, *medisterpolse* (Danish sausage), and *okesteg* (pot roast). In addition to the menu there is a smorgasbord daily.

**Moderate.** Open seven days. Luncheon from 11:30 a.m. to 3 p.m.; smorgasbord from 3 to 5 p.m. Dinner from 5 to 10 p.m. Full bar. Reservations advised. Visa, MC, AX. Parking lot. Casual.

---

## DAN TANA'S RESTAURANT     Italian/Continental
9071 Santa Monica Boulevard     ★
Los Angeles   **Map 8**     (213) 275-9444

A celebrity hangout but good. (Most aren't.) The proprietor's credentials are in order. Dan Tana was formerly maître d' at La Scala, but he always had the urge to open a small restaurant with the foods of his native Trieste, more familiarly to be found on the Northern Italian menus. The exquisite food here approaches *alta cucina*, the highest standard of a cuisine that even the legendary Brillat-Savarin admitted was influential in the *haute cuisine* of France. Chicken Florentine is plump chicken breasts with spinach and cheese, baked in cream dressing and flavored with lemon. *Cioppino* is robust. *Cannelloni* is meltingly smooth. Giovanni's parfait is a dessert made with pear liqueur, pure cream, *kirschwasser*, and *marrons glacés*. The celebrity and sports personalities gather in the room just to the right as you enter. It's two doors from the Troubador night club, and I once saw the ultra-reclusive Bob Dylan slip into Dan Tana's after watching John Prine from a dark corner table. It's also Jerry Buss's hangout, Buss being a credentialed expert on the Lakers, Kings, women and food, not necessarily in that order.

---

*For best results, consult "How to Use This Guide" on page 27.*

**Moderate to expensive.** Open seven days. Dinner Monday through Saturday 5 p.m. to 1 a.m.; Sunday to 12:30 a.m. Closed Thanksgiving, Christmas. Full bar. Reservations advised. All major credit cards. Valet parking. Casual.

---

## DANTE                                   Northern Italian/Continental
1032 Swarthmore                                                    ★
Pacific Palisades           **Map 2**                    (213) 459-7561

This restaurant deserves far more attention than it has received to date. They strive for perfection with Northern Italian dishes served in a correct, authentic, noble little place. Starched white tablecloths, good wineglasses and low-keyed surroundings provide the setting for superior pastas, excellent veal and sauced seafood. The *gnocchi*, cannelloni Angele, eggplant *parmigiana* and sautéed zucchini are not perfect perhaps, but headed in the right direction under good management. Zaboglione is served in an original style, partly frozen. Dante's is particularly recommended for lunch when you need a quiet place to talk.

**Moderate.** Open Tuesday through Sunday. Luncheon 11:30 a.m. to 2:30 p.m. weekdays. Dinner from 5:30 to 10:30. Beer and wine only. Reservations required. Visa, MC, AX. Parking lot. Semi-dressy to dressy.

---

## DARIO'S IMPORTED FOODS          Italian Delicatessen
410 Ord Street                                                     ★
Los Angeles             **Map 7**                        (213) 628-4736

The Godfather is a 14-inch-long sandwich—big enough for two or more—with provolone cheese, mortadella, salami cotto, San Francisco salami, ham, roast beef, turkey, lettuce, tomato, bell peppers, and pickle chips with Italian dressing. A member of my advisory committee swears this is the best "submarine" in the area. There's a super Primo Carnera that's six feet long and serves 25 people. There are 35 other sandwiches, plus lasagne and macaroni, both with meatballs.

It's been in business since 1925 and is now operated by Dario Cortopassi with the same care his dad gave to this take-out or sit-on-a-barrel restaurant. Near everything downtown.

**Moderate.** Open Monday through Friday 9 a.m. to 6 p.m.; Saturday 9 a.m. to 5 p.m. Open to 7 on Dodgers game nights. No reservations. No credit cards. Small parking lot. Casual.

---

## DAR MAGHREB
7651 Sunset Boulevard
Hollywood    **Map 7**

Moroccan
★
(213) 876-7651

42300 Bob Hope Drive
Rancho Mirage    (714) 568-9486

"Almost from the minute I entered the joint I knew we'd never hit it off. The restaurant was built around an open air patio — and I have always nursed a prejudice against restaurants that encourage my dinner to fly in through a hole in the roof," Burt Prelutsky once commented to me about the once-impressive Dar Maghreb in Hollywood. M. Dupart's restaurant was a major contribution, a dining adventure that combined exotic surroundings, good taste, and competence. He designed the building to be everything he hoped for at his Marrakesh in San Francisco but didn't quite have the room for. (It was in a basement.) The understated exterior has as its only decor the words "Dar Maghreb" ("House of Morocco") in Arabic against the flat white walls. I entered a small interior courtyard, dramatic pillars, and a peaceful fountain and experienced a sense of culture shock when I found myself in the gentle far-away Morocco of my

Warner Brothers-inspired fantasies. Diners sit on low benches stacked high with cushions, and the low round tables are ornately inlaid with ivory and wood. Bright Moroccan rugs, vividly hand-painted tiles, costumed waiters, and a convivial, not unpleasant din of people add to the illusion. I feel, however, the Dar Maghreb has lost most of its original magic. Perhaps it's more Arabian plights than nights. The food has not maintained the original promise. There are four dinners, similar except for the entrée, which may be chicken, pigeon, lamb, or rabbit. The price is fixed (except for the pigeon), and dinner begins with the ceremonial washing of hands in rose-scented water. There is hot pita bread, helpful as an eating utensil (there's no silverware), to scoop the authentic salad from a large bowl brought to the table for all to share. *B'stilla* is the second course — chicken and nuts served in a pastry shell, then a small squab with lemon sauce, next *couscous* with lamb, followed by a bowl of fruit and nuts, then hot mint tea and *baklava*. Warm wash cloths and a concluding handwashing ritual complete the dinner. M. Dupart has selected wines to complement the experience, and there are cocktails, although they seem more an intrusion than an accommodation. They're busy but pride themselves on keeping reservations on time, so you may be asked to call back and confirm on the day of your reservation.

**Expensive.** Open seven days. Dinner from 6 to 11 p.m., Monday through Saturday; 5:30 to 10:30 Sunday. Fixed price of $14 for seven courses. Closed Christmas, New Year's. Full bar. Reservations essential. Visa, MC. Wheelchair access. Valet parking. Casual.

---

## DELANEY'S SEA SHANTY                            Seafood
(Locations Anaheim, Anaheim Hills, Laguna Hills, Newport Beach. See phone book for listings.)

Fresh fish from the boats of Delaney's fishing fleet are served in undisguised glory. The fish are poached, broiled, or sautéed; little is added to alter their flavor. An oyster bar serves a savory *cioppino* for those too hungry to wait for tables (no reservations here—you can hang around for two hours waiting to be called) and oysters and clams on the half shell. This was "the" destination for bruncheon if you could stand the long line. Lobster Benedict, poached finnan haddie, and shrimp ranchero are some of the reasons. Of late, the rudeness and impatience of the Newport location during Sunday brunch has been nearly tragic. Delaney's has apparently gotten too big for its boats. It's incredible that restaurants don't realize their patrons travel for miles and look forward to a special occasion. When they're treated like cattle, it hurts and becomes memorable for all the wrong reasons.

**Moderate.** Open seven days 11 a.m .to 11 p.m. Sunday brunch 10 a.m. to 2 p.m. Closed Thanksgiving, Christmas. Full bar. No reservations. Harbor view. Visa, MC. Parking lot. Casual to dressy.

---

## DELIUS
3550 Long Beach Boulevard
Long Beach    **Map 3**

American
★★
(213) 426-0694

In Long Beach, an unlikely setting for a dining adventure, there is a charmer called Delius (after the composer), operated by Kay and Elsa Klopfenstein, sisters who learned to cook in some of the best kitchens. The price is about $23. That includes on one given day as an example: good champagne (Korbel), a quiche fromage, cream of leek soup, chicken breasts, filet mignon, tomatoes, brussel sprouts and endive, fresh fruit, a lime soufflé, apple tart, mocha cake and too much more. The rest of the wines included Eye of the Swan, Mirassou Beaujolais, and a fine cognac. This may well be the bargain of all the *prix fixe* dinners. Certainly the sisters do everything in their vast talent to provide a delightful evening.

**Moderate to expensive.** Open Tuesday through Saturday 7 p.m. seating only. Fixed price of about $23. Closed August, major holidays. Wine only. Reservations essential. No credit cards. Wheelchair access. Semi-dressy.

---

## DEM BONES                                    Barbeque
11619 Santa Monica Boulvard
West Los Angeles          **Map 8**          (213) 475-0288

In the world of low rent barbeque joints, Dem Bones is something of a rare find. It's clean and neat and decorated with prints from *Harper's Weekly* (which is not to say that other 'que joints should be shut down by the Board of Health; just that ambience is usually an afterthought, if it's thought about at all). There are pleasant stained-wood picnic tables to eat at, and there's music in the background, rather than the standard basketball game. The sauce is not fiery at Dem Bones, but the bones are meaty and very smokey. There are pork ribs, beef ribs, beef, ham, pork, hot links, chicken and rib tips—the usual assortment of meats—all served with a choice of barbequed beans, cole slaw, potato salad, black-eyed peas, corn on the cob and collard greens. There's also an anemic salad bar, which is not recommended, particularly with the option of collard greens so much more appetizing. Dem Bones corn bread is vital to the enjoyment of any meal there. And Big Daddy's Texas chili is served without beans—just as God surely intended one of His favorite foods to be served.   *M.S.*

**Moderate.** Open Monday through Saturday 11 a.m. to 11 p.m.; Sunday from 2 to 10 p.m. Closed Thanksgiving, Christmas. Beer and wine only. No reservations. No credit cards. Parking lot. Casual.

## THE DERBY
233 East Huntington Drive
Arcadia    **Map 6**

American
★
(213) 447-2430

Built by the late, great jockey George Woolf to accommodate his racetrack friends from nearby Santa Anita, this restaurant has a decor, as you might imagine, built around the colorful memorabilia of that sport. The food is intended as an honest answer to hunger—steaks, chicken, pot roast and duckling. There's a "daily double" cocktail from 11 a.m. to 7 p.m., middle-of-the-road entertainment, and a nice woodsy-leather-folksy feel.

**Inexpensive to moderate.** Open seven days 11 a.m. to midnight; Sunday brunch 11 a.m. to 3 p.m. Entertainment. Dancing. Full bar. Reservations recommended. All major credit cards. Parking around building. Casual.

## DI AMICO'S STEAK HOUSE
1180 South Palm Canyon Drive
Palm Springs

American
★
(714) 325-9191

An above-average steakhouse in both style and food, with an unlikely specialty called liver steak Vaquero. Son-of-a-gun stew is savory and flavored with red wine. There's a salad bar. Popular for luncheon.

**Moderate.** Open seven days. Luncheon from 11 a.m. to 3 p.m. Monday through Saturday. Dinner from 5 to 11 p.m. Entertainment in lounge. Full bar. Reservations required. Visa, MC. Parking lot. Casual.

# DIAMOND SEA FOOD RESTAURANT

**Chinese/Seafood**

724 North Hill Street
Chinatown  **Map 7**  ★  (213) 617-0666

The Diamond is a more formal restaurant than either Mon Kee or Young Sing, and not nearly as crowded. But the cooking is competent and the food is good. And the choice of dishes, as at the other two restaurants, is ridiculously vast (11 shark's fin dishes, five abalone).

There are also some dishes at Diamond that I don't recall seeing at either Mon Kee or Young Sing. There's a shrimp with satay sauce, for instance, which combines the Chinese-style of cooking shrimp with Filipino satay sauce, very pungent with a strong taste of dark chilies and much garlic. There is pan-fried milk with crab meat, a dish I first encountered at a Cantonese restaurant in New York in which the milk is fried and coagulated along with the crab. Crab and milk seem an impossible combination, but some of the best cooking often skims along on the edge of the impossible, and this dish makes crab and milk appear born for each other.

Diamond is actually rather masterful with its crab dishes. There's a crab meat sauce here that makes the old standby of lobster sauce taste like dishwater by comparison. It's served with straw mushrooms, a combination so elegant I found myself brushing tears from my eyes before ordering a second portion.  *M.S.*

**Expensive.** Open seven days from 10 a.m. to 1 a.m. Beer and wine only. Reservations for parties of 10 or more. Visa, MC, AX. Limited wheelchair access. Valet parking. Casual.

---

*In order to obtain the best results from this Guide, please consult "Tips on Dining Out" on page 21.*

# DINO'S

**Italian**
★

2055 East Colorado
Pasadena    **Map 7**    (213) 449-8823

"What does a 26-year-old punk know about running a restaurant," was the intriguing lead-off sentence from their publicist. Plenty, as it turns out. Russell's uncle, Michael Scrantino, opened the restaurant in 1949 when most people never heard of pizza, let alone *fettuccine, scalloppine* or *Stromboli*. The locals took to the authentic cuisine like "meat balls to spaghetti" and by the time John was born, Dino's was a hangout for students from Pasadena High and City College. At 13, much like his European counterparts, John Russell apprenticed himself to a restaurant and at 20 he finally accepted an offer to learn Italian cooking at Dino's for a buck and a half an hour. He has taken over completely and the food remains as good as ever. What's new is the youth orientation. John has added live jazz. Two groups with opposite styles appear Wednesday through Saturday starting at 9:30. (There's no drink minimum but there is a small cover charge if you're not having dinner.) Dino has a spoon in about 60% of the dishes that leave the kitchen to make sure they're up to his standards, and the dinners include both soup and salad. Baked *mostaccioli* Sorrento, scampi à la Dino, *manicotti* and *cannelloni* are big favorites. It's a good place.

**Inexpensive to moderate.** Open Tuesday through Sunday. Luncheon served Tuesday through Friday from 11:30 a.m. to 2 p.m. Dinner Sunday through Tuesday from 4:30 to 10 p.m.; Wednesday through Saturday to 1 a.m. Banquet facilities. Closed Christmas. Entertainment. Children's menu. Full bar. No reservations. All major credit cards accepted. Parking lot. Casual.

*For best results, consult "How to Use This Guide" on page 27.*

# DISNEYLAND HOTEL

**Continental**

★★

1150 West Cerritos Avenue

Anaheim      **Map 6**      (714) 778-6600

The Disneyland Hotel at night rivals the Disneyland park in the daytime yet I find the hotel more fun. There are brilliant laser sculptures, torch-lighting ceremonies in their water world, dancing waters complete with a full-on show, an international collection of shops and bazaars featuring everything from Australian pottery to colorful tropical fish to raisins covered in yogurt... and much, much more. Now that they've finally got their act together and created a virtual restaurant row within the hotel grounds we can include them for the first time in our guide. Whether it was Jack Wrather (the Wrather Corporation owns the hotel) or God Almighty, serious changes for the better have been wrought here. **The Shipyard Inn** has expanded its kitchen. "So what?" you ask. So plenty. Now they can serve fresh fish and dishes like the best *cioppino* I've had in quite a while, the stock zesty and rich with Spanish saffron. You can see all the activities from your table and enjoy seafood that would be graded well even if it were in a free standing restaurant. (The Wrather people didn't *have* to have good food. Let's face it, with a hotel that has no occupancy rate in the high 90's, it's almost always full. They could serve cat food and their captive audience would tolerate it.) The fact that somebody really cares is a tribute to their management. They're open seven days a week and lunch is served from 11:30 to 2:30, dinner from 5 to 11. If you want to watch the summertime fireworks after dinner, ask to have your cognac or whatever on the floating barge adjacent to the Shipyard. On a soft summer night it's serendipity. **The Oak Room** has been a favorite of mine since the days it used to be a private club. It's paneled in oak (you expected knotty pine?) and their specialties are beef and veal. Lunch is served from noon to 2:30, Tuesday through Friday, and dinner is served nightly from 6 to 11.

**El Vaquero** is an Old West hacienda-like beauty with *huevos Mexicanos* or eggs Benedict for breakfast, a salad bar and sandwiches for lunch, and a meateaters haven at night. They're open from 7 to 11:30 for breakfast, lunch is served from noon to 2:30 and dinner from 5:30 to 11 nightly. In addition there's **Mazie's Pantry,** a bright cheerful country farmhouse atmosphere with hugemongous sandwiches, quiche, salads, ice cream concoctions, and chocolate chip cookies. **Señor Campos** has Mexican cuisine like tacos, burritos, tostadas, tamales, enchiladas and quesadillas. It's a great place to view Water Wonderland and the Seaports of the Pacific. They're open 7 days from 11 a.m. to 11 p.m. The **Chef's Kitchen** is a lavish buffet with a great Sunday brunch offering bourbon-glazed ham and leg of lamb along with roast beef and the usuals. Open 7 days for breakfast, lunch and dinner. For earlybirds there's a **Coffee House** with good food open 7 days from 7 a.m. to 11 p.m. One of the surprising facts about their food operation is that the prices are comparable or even lower than at many of the surrounding restaurants in Anaheim. A stupendous fact is that you can see the frenzy of entertainment from dancing waters to fireworks to water shows to dancers and much more... for free. Congratulations to the folks there. They've finally scored big.

---

## D'JIT POCHANA                                            Thai
15627 Ventura Boulevard                                      ★
Encino          **Map 1**                        (213) 981-9095

There's nothing like old family Thais. Charlermpol Charn-vises—he likes to be called "Charlie"—is managing director here and at D'Jit Pochana One and Two in Bangkok, huge palaces dedicated to the artform of Thai cookery. It is a family operation that dates back beyond remembrance. As you enter you'll hear the traditional greeting, "Ma Gin Kow"—come eat rice—and the interior appointments let you know immediately that this isn't just another Thai restaurant. The dishes are prepared by chefs trained in Bangkok and cover a broad range of rice culinary treasures with a third dimension in flavor—hot and spicy, sweet and sour, crisp and soups that are a revelation to the Yankee palate.

**Inexpensive to moderate.** Open Tuesday through Sunday. Luncheon from 11 a.m. to 2 p.m. weekdays. Dinner from 5:30 to 10:30 p.m. Tuesday through Friday; 5 to 10:30 Saturday, Sunday. Special buffet luncheon Tuesday, Friday. Closed Christmas, New Year's. Full bar. Reservations recommended for 4 or more. All major credit cards. Valet parking. Casual.

---

## DOMO                                        Japanese

11680 Ventura Boulevard                              ★
Studio City          **Map 1**          (213) 761-6151

Located in a small shopping center, Domo has a simple, under-stated exterior of natural wood panels, accented by a row of bright red lanterns. Inside, however, Domo is a large, two-story room of stunning and innovative design. There are dramatic, high-beamed ceilings of darkened wood, and colorful Japanese kites hang from the rafters. Two separate stairways lead to a sushi bar and a tatami room — both are constructed like balconies and are visible from the dining area below. The sushi bar has a handsome, bamboo railing and seating for ten; the tatami room partially projects over the first floor and seats six. Wood partitions throughout the spacious dining room lend a feeling of privacy to the booths, and the mood is relaxed and unhurried. Dinners come with soup, salad and rice, and combination dinners include *sunomono*. As an alternative to the somewhat limited dinner menu, you might assemble your meal from Domo's selection of appetizers. We recommend the spareribs teriyaki and *tofu* steak — warmed *tofu* and ground beef in a thick, ginger-and-soy-based sauce. *Kushi-age* (skewered chicken) and chicken *kara-age* (deep-fried chicken) are both attractively served but disappointingly bland. We also had a shrimp *sunomone* with carrot and seaweed, halibut, clam, and tuna sushimi and scallops *iso-age* (scallops wrapped in seaweed and cooked tempura style). The scallop appetizer was accompanied by an appealing arrangement of deep-fried buckwheat and rice noodles, but was also not seasoned enough for our tastes.

*— Shinobe Ishizuka*

**Inexpensive to moderate.** Open Tuesday through Sunday. Luncheon 11:30 a.m. to 2 p.m. weekdays. Dinner 5 to 11 p.m. Tuesday through Saturday; 5 to 10 Sunday. Open all holidays. Wine and beer only. Reservations accepted weekdays, but not on weekends. Visa, MC, DC. Parking lot. Casual.

---

## DON HERNANDO'S HIDEAWAY

Mexican/
Continental

Beverly Wilshire Hotel ★★
Beverly Hills **Map 8** (213) 275-4282

Named after that majestic gentleman Hernando Courtright, this little hideaway in the Beverly Wilshire Hotel is a favorite of the celeb set and the folks who live permanently in the hotel. The cuisine is continental but, more exciting to me, rich Mexican. You can have chicken sauced with a splendid *mole poblano* or choose from other complex and rare (in Los Angeles) dishes. Open for breakfast, luncheon and dinner. They have dancing to live music most nights.

**Expensive.** Open Tuesday through Saturday. Dinner from 6 p.m. to midnight. Entertainment. Dancing. Full bar. Reservations required. All major credit cards. Valet parking. Casual.

# DON JOSE RESTAURANT                    Mexican

(Locations in Anaheim, Artesia, Fullerton, Huntington Beach, Laguna Hills, Orange, Tustin. See phone book for listings.)

There is in Orange County a small chain of Mexican restaurants almost too good to be believed. Don Jose has superb Mexican food served in attractive surroundings by efficient and pretty girls, and the most expensive dinner, including albondigas soup or salad, with a choice of three main dishes served with rice or refried beans, is under $5. Their special taquito, not to be confused with any other aquito you've seen, consists of plump morsels of chicken ·olled in a corn tortilla, covered with guacamole sauce and nelted cheese, served with rice or beans. The margaritas ire great, if you like the kind that resemble a lime Orange Julius, and an item modestly called "fritos with cheese" is a good-sized basket of hot, crisp chips covered with layers of melted white cheese that may leave you too full for dinner if you aren't careful. This is not an undiscovered miracle, as the long lines (no reservations on weekends) and the hour-long wait on weekends indicate.

**Inexpensive.** Open seven days. Monday through Thursday 11 a.m. to 10 p.m. Friday, Saturday to 11 p.m. Sunday 10 ı.m. to 10 p.m. Sunday brunch 10 a.m. to 2 p.m. Closed Thanksgiving, Christmas Day. Entertainment. Reservations accepted during week, not on weekends. Visa, MC. Parking lot. Casual.

---

*In order to obtain the best results from this Guide, be sure to read the French, German, Italian and Oriental menu translators on page 705 to 710 of this Guide.*

## DONKIN'S INN
American
★
2454 Wilshire Boulevard
Santa Monica          **Map 2**                     (213) 828-6053

I went to a bad party here once — it was a fête worse than death; so I was skeptical about the good reports from the staff and advisory committee. When I revisited, however, I found everything shipshape at this waterfront restaurant, where mariners may tie up and drop in for a drink or four, or fill up on nourishing if unexciting food. There are dockside tables on the patio.

**Moderate.** Open seven days. Luncheon from 11:30 a.m. to 3 p.m. Dinner from 5:30 to 11 p.m. Monday through Saturday; 5 to 10 Sunday. Sunday brunch 10:30 a.m. to 3 p.m. at fixed price of $6.95. Closed major holidays. Entertainment. Full bar. Reservations recommended. Patio open during luncheon. Visa, MC, AX. Valet parking. Casual.

## DON RICARDO'S
Mexican
★
400 South Baldwin Avenue
Santa Anita Fashion Park
Arcadia          **Map 6**                     (213) 445-6750

Northridge Fashion Center                           ★
Northridge          **Map 1**                     (213) 886-7735

Sun Valley Civic Center                             ★
8022 Vineland Avenue
Sun Valley          **Map 1**                     (213) 767-9553

Fine Mexican family restaurants that do their best with innovative touches to overcome the size (most locations seat hundreds). Colorful restaurants with authentic decor and artwork from Mexico, they're proud of their shrimp enchilada sautéed in wine sauce and the chili Colorado, cubes of choice beef simmered in red chile sauce. The mahi mahi is grilled and served with house sauce. Their "magic margarita machine" spurts a rainbow of strawberry, pineapple, peach, banana, or coconut along with the traditional margaritas. A good place for birthdays and special events.

**Inexpensive.** Open seven days. Breakfast 9 to 11 a.m. Luncheon 11 a.m. to 5 p.m. Dinner 5 to 11 p.m. Full bar. Reservations suggested. Patio (Sun Valley location). Visa, MC, AX. Parking lot. Casual.

---

## DON THE BEACHCOMBER         Polynesian

1727 North McCadden Place         ★
Hollywood      **Map 7**          (213) 469-3968

13530 Bali Way
Marina Del Rey      **Map 2**          (213) 823-5435

120 Via Lola
Palm Springs          (714) 325-2061

22878 Pacific Coast Hwy
Malibu      **Map 2**          (213) 456-1818

Depending on your point of view, Don Beach should be given the credit or the blame for starting the first Polynesian restaurant anywhere. (He also invented rumaki.) These tastefully designed locations have been quietly turning out high-quality food and good rum drinks for so long that there is a tendency to take them for granted. The usual "Polynesian" dishes are prepared unusually well here, and the rum drinks are a sensation. There is more to the menu than South Seas fare—good seafood dishes and some less exotic staples. The Hollywood location is a great late place to know about — a little away from the lunacy of Hollywood Boulevard on a quiet street — and there are a number of supper items from which to choose after the theatre or whatever.

**Moderate to expensive.** Open seven days. Buffet luncheon from 11:30 a.m. to 2:30 p.m. weekdays. Dinner 5 to 10 p.m. Sunday through Thursday; 5 to 11 Friday, Saturday. Sunday brunch 10 a.m. to 3 p.m. for fixed price of $7.95. Hours vary slightly at different locations. Open all holidays. (Palm Springs location closed from July 7 to October 1.) Entertainment at Marina only. Full bar. All major credit cards. Valet parking. Casual.

---

## THE DRAGON PEARL
6000 Monterey Road
Los Angeles    **Map 7**

**Chinese**
★
(213)254-3415

The style of this Cantonese restaurant has remained pretty much the same for a quarter century in spite of the management turnover to the second generation. There's a new cocktail bar with TV and piano entertainment, but the good values and the large portions keep loyal customers. There's a special dinner including soup, almond chicken, pork chow mein, fried shrimp, pork fried rice, barbecued spareribs, fried noodles, tea, and almond cookies. With three or four, you get more. Hungry two hours later? Not likely. The good news is for the odd couples (vegetarians vs. carnivores)—there's a vegetarian menu.

**Inexpensive.** Open Tuesday through Sunday. Luncheon from 11:30 a.m. to 3 p.m. Tuesday through Saturday; 12:30 to 3 Sunday. Dinner 3 to 9:45 p.m. Closed Thanksgiving, Christmas. Take out. Full bar. Entertainment Thursday through Saturday. Reservations recommended. Visa, MC. Parking lot. Casual.

# THE DRESDEN ROOM
## American/Continental
### ★
1760 North Vermont Avenue
Los Angeles          **Map 7**          (213) 665-4294

This one-step-above-a-neighborhood-restaurant has been an undercover sports celebrity hangout for twenty-five years. It has a steak menu but with a decided Italian tilt. Veal dishes are good. They serve late—until midnight—and that's notable if you're on your way back from the ball game at Dodger Stadium or from the Music Center. Really good cocktails; entertainment in the lounge.

**Moderate.** Open seven days. Luncheon from 11:30 a.m. to 3:30 p.m. weekdays. Dinner Sunday through Thursday 4 to 10; Friday, Saturday to 11:30. Full bar. Reservations accepted. V, MC, AX. Valet parking. Semi-dressy.

---

# DUNBAR'S AT THE BEACH
## American
### ★
16360 Pacific Coast Highway
Huntington Beach          **Map 4**          (714) 840-1391

72291 Highway 111
Palm Desert          (714) 568-9388

This multi-level beauty originally opened as Reuben's and although it's under the same ownership—Far West Services, Inc.—they've changed the name "to avoid confusion." Why confusion? Dunbar's is the prototype for their top-of-the-line restaurant with a broader menu and a different philosophy. Highland trout topped with shrimp and mush-rooms, roast duckling and fresh fish are well prepared and the potted pies with a different selection for every day of the week have become an early favorite. There's an oyster bar (did you know oysters drink?), and *joie de vivre* that augers well for this concept. The name Dunbar's comes from a line in a Robert Burns poem if that excites you. They've made it in my book because they have hangtown fries on the brunch selection.

**Moderate.** Open seven days. Luncheon from 11:30 a.m. to 3 p.m. weekdays. Dinner from 5 to 10 p.m. Sunday through Thursday; 5 to 11 Friday, Saturday. Brunch Saturday, Sunday 10:30 a.m. to 2:30 p.m. Sandwiches in oyster bar 4 to 7 p.m. Closed Thanksgiving, Christmas Eve, Christmas. Full bar. Private party facilities. Reservations recommended. Patio. View. Visa, MC, AX. Semi-dressy.

---

## DU PAR'S American

★

(Locations in Encino, Glendale, Los Angeles, Studio City, Van Nuys. See phone book for listings.)

An excellent chain of convenience restaurants with lots of homemade dishes like pea soup, Swiss steak, beef and kidney pie, and sandwiches, at tolerable prices. Each location has a bakery showcase, and you can buy the same freshly baked pie and cakes and rolls that you enjoyed as part of your meal. Counter and booth service is alert and the restaurants are immaculate.

**Inexpensive.** Open seven days. Sunday through Thursday from 6 a.m. to midnight; Friday, Saturday 6:30 a.m. to 3 a.m. (at most locations). Closed Christmas. Full bar at some locations. No reservations. Visa, MC. Wheelchair access. parking lot. Casual.

> *To obtain the best results from this Guide, be sure to consult maps on the various Southern California areas in the front of the book.*

## EDWARD'S MANSION
2064 Orangetree Lane
Redlands     **Map 5**

**American**
★
(714) 793-2031

At first glance you may think the colorful refurbishing of this ancient home is a pigment of your imagination. But, it's all for real; it's a classic exhibit of Victorian architecture restored. This relic was literally cut in two, moved a mile, and is now one of the fun places in the Southland. To add to the charm, a museum, a wedding chapel, and a citrus grove enhance the solarium, or go for Sunday brunch and enjoy their specialty, orange muffins. If you are a chicken and dumpling buff, you've come home the minute you set your feet under the table at Edward's Mansion.

**Moderate to expensive.** Open seven days. Luncheon 11:30 a.m. to 2 p.m. Dinner 5 to 9, except Monday. Sunday brunch 10 a.m. to 2:30 p.m. Full bar. Reservations suggested. All major credit cards. Parking lot. Casual to semi-dressy

# THE EGG AND THE EYE
5814 Wilshire Boulevard
Los Angeles    **Map 8**

American
★
(213) 933-5596

This gracious luncheon spot is a favorite of the visitors to the L.A. County Museum. The icy gazpacho is made fresh and zesty. There are 55 (count 'em) omelettes, entrées that range from chicken *marechal* to *cannelloni salsa* to salads, and there are great homemade desserts (try the cheesecake). The house wine is Summit, an especially good Californian. Balconies overlook galleries of crafts and folk art from civilizations around the world. Some say the egg is the most perfect object in the world—I don't know where that leaves Bo Derek—but omelettes are definitely the thing here and luncheon's the time (although they're open until 8:30).

**Inexpensive to moderate.** Open Tuesday through Sunday. Open from 11 a.m. to 5 p.m. Tuesday through Thursday; 11 a.m. to 10 p.m. Friday, Saturday; 10 to 5 Sunday. Closed all major holidays. Craft and folk art exhibits. Full bar. Reservations recommended. All major credit cards. Parking lot. Casual.

# THE EGGCEPTION
1208 State Street
Santa Barbara

American
★
(805) 965-7942

970 Linden
Carpenteria

(805) 684-6041

Now there is a brace of Eggceptions. The rather dowdy mother hen in Santa Barbara has a chic chick in Carpenteria.

Omelettes in both locations are eggzactly what they're cracked up to be—all 100 varieties of them—all without benefit of milk or water. You can scramble for any six ingredients of your choice, but tell them you want #113, My Own Thing. You will find hot cakes, salads, and sandwiches on the menu.

**Inexpensive.** Open seven days from 6:30 a.m. to 3 p.m. Closed Thanksgiving, Christmas, New Year's Day. Wine and beer only. No reservations. Visa, MC. Street parking. Casual.

---

## EL ABAJENO DE GUADALAJARA                    Mexican/ International

101 Agua Caliente Boulevard
Tijuana, Baja                                      (70-668) 385-6980

If you loiter here long enough you are bound to see friends or creditors from back home, no matter where back home is. This is a popular stop for tour agencies to book their dazed clients chiefly because the food is typically Mexican. There's mariachi entertainment, and they can accommodate 300 people. Friday night there's cockfighting at their Fiesta Mexicana. You might hear the boasting and toasting of the bullfight aficionados at the next table who are either going to or coming from the arena. While soaking up all this atmosphere, you can soak up a triple surprise, the *casuelas voldadoras*. For food, I like the *carnitas* (chunks of beef and pork prepared Jalisco style) or you won't go wrong ordering the *carne asada* (charcoal steak). The menu is a la carte. If you have a choice, try to sit near the interior garden with a flower fountain.

**Inexpensive.** Open seven days from 7 a.m. to 1 a.m. Entertainment Friday through Sunday only. Full bar. Reservations accepted for large parties only. All credit cards. Parking lot. Casual.

## EL ADOBE DE CAPISTRANO     Mexican/Continental

31891 Camino Capistrano                         ★
San Juan Capistrano      **Map 4**       (714) 493-1163

In San Juan Capistrano, where tourists love—and residents hate—the swallows, there is an establishment with a peculiar and not unattractive mixture of Old California and gadget-modern. Dating from 1778, El Adobe has gracious gardens and lovely old woods. There is also a push-button sliding roof on the patio for dancing under the stars (or the swallows). Food is good, with a sort of Leo Carrillo-Hollywood-Mexican menu, and the dining room is one of the most attractive and gracious anywhere. Run by Ellie Allen, it is a good family restaurant when you're in the South Coast area.

**Inexpensive to moderate.** Open seven days. Luncheon from 11:30 a.m. to 4 p.m. Monday through Saturday. Dinner 4 to 10; Friday, Saturday 4 to 11 p.m.; Sunday 3 to 10 p.m. Sunday brunch 11 a.m. to 3 p.m. Entertainment. Full bar. Reservations suggested. Parking lot. V, MC, AX. Casual to semi-dressy.

## EL CHALAN                             Peruvian

5621 La Jolla Boulevard                         ★
La Jolla                                     (714) 459-7707

Peru is exotic fare for San Diego and it's good to find it served so well here. The menu tends to be simple and chatty: *lomo a la huancaina* is "my grandmother's secret recipe," topping a filet mignon served with Peruvian style potatoes. Among the appetizers you should try the *antichuchos*, beef

---

*Please be sure to consult "Tipping Made Easy" on page 25 of this Guide.*

---

218

hearts marinated in wine and spices, charbroiled and skewered. Victor Villar attends to everything here and loves to talk about his food. Did you know the potato was first discovered in Peru? Did you care?

**Inexpensive to moderate.** Open seven days. Luncheon 11 a.m. to 2 p.m. weekdays. Dinner 5:30 to 11 p.m. Cocktails. Reservations suggested. All major credit cards. Parking lot. Semi-dressy.

---

## EL CHOLO                                    Mexican
840 East Whittier Boulevard                       ★
La Habra          **Map 6**              (213) 691-4618

1121 South Western Avenue                         ★
Los Angeles       **Map 7**              (213) 734-2773

777 South Main Street                             ★
Orange         **Map 6**                 (714) 972-9900

It was a very good year... Lindbergh flew the Atlantic, Los Angeles neared a million population (the city extended all the way to Western Avenue) and it was the year, 1927, that George and Aurelia Salisbury opened a little Mexican restaurant in a tiny store front on Western, across the street from a farm. Food was cooked on a hot plate which heated tortillas on top, melted cheese underneath. All they had were six booths, a counter, one genial cook, one philosophical waiter and one of the best values in town. In 1931 they moved across the street to their present site, but the giant servings of real Mexican food, careful service and colorful surroundings haven't changed much except that luncheons are no longer 45 cents, and dinners cost more than 60 cents.

In 1962, a second El Cholo was opened in La Habra, a mission-style building that managed to survive the expansion without any loss of character. They're still growing, adding patios and using their expertise. The formula works and you can get one of the best Mexican dinners in gringo-land for very little money. They love families and won't be mad if you bring infants.

**Inexpensive to moderate.** Open seven days. Luncheon from 11 a.m. to 3 p.m. Dinner from 4:30 to 10 p.m. Sunday brunch from 11 a.m. to 3 p.m. Full bar. Reservations advised. Patio. V, MC, CB. Wheelchair access. Parking lot. Casual.

---

# EL CID                                    Mexican
4212 Sunset Boulevard                              ★
Los Angeles      **Map 7**            (213) 668-0338

Frank Romero, the man that brought you Gardens of Taxco in West Hollywood, loves a good time, good friends and flamenco, so it was only natural that he would buy El Cid. The cabaret restaurant is a charmer. Located in what used to be a seedy area—on Sunset near Alvarado in mid-Los Angeles—it's now becoming that kind of funky bou-tiqueland familiar to San Franciscans. The cabaret used to be the home of the Blackguard and has been remarkably restored. Downstairs, off the boulevard, the entrance is festooned with bright murals painted by former owner Clark Allen. Mrs. Allen, statuesque in a fantastic costume of silks and lace, still greets her guests at the door. The main room facing the stage has tables with brightly printed cloths and napkins, hand-painted ladder back chairs, flick-ering candles and good Latin art. There is a small balcony that offers the choicest seats, eye-level to the performers with a feeling of intimacy. Clark Allen, mural painter, historian and former owner, is an impossible combination of Irish and Welsh, and as the master of ceremonies he pulls his hat low to hide his gringo-blue eyes and ruddy complexion. On stage he guides the show effortlessly, segueing from the traditional songs and dances of Spain to the thrilling flamenco of Juan Talavera—heel-clickin' good—before an audience comprised mostly of Latinos. Clark is a compelling man, full of the lore of Mexico and Madrid and eager to share his knowledge. He's full of "didjanos." Did you know that flamenco is a gypsy dance originated by two despised minorities of Spain, the Jews and the Moslems? Or that "ole" is a shortening of "Allah"? Or that famous Spanish dancers like Escudero (Jose Greco is from Brooklyn) felt that they were dances of defiance? I haven't checked all the facts but Clark has had a lifelong love affair with the Latin culture and I prefer to believe everything he says. For dinner you may select your choice of eight entrées including shrimp in a cilantro cream sauce, chicken in a spicy chocolate-chili sauce or a thin Tampico-style steak. All are moderately priced and include a soup and salad, tortillas and a good flan. There's a full bar with margaritas a specialty of the casa.

**Moderate.** Open Tuesday through Sunday from 6 p.m. to 1:30 a.m. Flamenco guitar. Full bar. Reservations advised. Patio. V, MC, AX. Street parking. Casual.

---

## EL COYOTE SPANISH CAFE                    Mexican
7312 Beverly Boulevard
Los Angeles        **Map 7**                    (213) 939-7766

They call themselves "Spanish," but they mean Mexican. The euphemism dates back to the time when we would discriminate against our neighbors to the South and anything Mexican was not acceptable. Unfortunately, this may be the worst Mexican family restaurant in town and is in this book primarily because it is in a good location. It's cheap, but that's about it.

**Inexpensive.** Open seven days 11 a.m. to 10 p.m. Full bar. No reservations. Patio. Visa, MC. Parking lot. Casual.

## EL DORADO RESTAURANT            Colombian
4273 Beverly Boulevard                       ★
Los Angeles        **Map 7**         (213) 660-7746

What is Colombian food? It's the *especial*, ground beef with
rice, beans, one fried egg, fried pork skin, and fried
plantains. It's *sobrebarriga*, flank steak on sauce. It's breaded
pork cutlet with rice or beef liver or tongue in red wine
sauce. It's *morcilla*, blood sausage. It's also soup like a creole
of beans with fried pork skin or *mondongo*, a beef tripe soup.
Desserts include figs in heavy syrup with cheese, guava
paste, or corn dessert with milk called *mazamorra*. As in
Colombian restaurants, Coca Cola is listed as an important
beverage in this tiny, 36-seat Colombian adventure.

**Inexpensive to moderate.** Open Tuesday through Sunday.
Luncheon from 11 a.m. to 3 p.m. Dinner from 5 to 10 p.m.
Beer and wine only. Reservations suggested. Visa, MC, CB
DC. Parking lot. Casual.

---

## EL ENCANTO            American/Continental
9360 North San Gabriel Canyon Road               ★
Azusa        **Map 6**         (213) 334-2311

There's a joyous warmth that accompanies your dinner at the
El Encanto Inn in Azusa Canyon. Less than five miles from the
hustle and bustle of civilization, the El Encanto is nestled against
the mountainside just a few hundred yards off Highway 39.
The atmosphere inside and outside is rustic and comfortable.
Owners Bill and Donna Hinkley have quietly expanded their
facility over 17 years to two main dining rooms and a banquet

*To obtain the best results from this Guide, consult
"How to Use this Guide" on page 27.*

room that seats about 100. Both the banquet and dining room have a fireplace enhancing the mountain cabin atmosphere. In spite of what its name suggests, the El Encanto's menu is strictly American, featuring fresh seafood, steaks, chicken and the specialty of the house, prime rib. Dinners include a delicious corn fritter dipped in syrup, and a green salad that is a half-head of lettuce, with your choice of dressing. Youngsters under 10 may select from the child's menu. Altogether a quality dining experience.

**Moderate.** Open seven days 5 to 10 p.m. Sunday from 4 to 10 p.m. Closed Christmas, New Year's. Entertainment. Full bar. View. Reservations advised. Visa, MC, AX. Parking lot. Casual to semi-dressy.

---

## EL GATO GARDENSIDE RESTAURANT    Mexican
7324 Sepulveda Boulevard    ★
Van Nuys    **Map 1**    (213) 781-1580

Very popular, this massive place is a favorite in the valley with pretty good, if unimaginative, dishes, entertainment, and an interesting street scene mural or stage drop. Dancing, mariachis, and performers liven up attractive rooms that make good use of greenery and pools. An unhurried, unworried restaurant, it carries on the old style of early California hospitality and partying. Along with the familiar Americanized Mexican dishes, there are some that are authentic, like *menudo* (tripe Mexican-style), *chorizo* (a highly seasoned sausage), and *arroz con pollo* (chicken with rice) served during the Sunday fiesta.

**Inexpensive.** Open seven days. Luncheon from 11 a.m. to 4:30 p.m. weekdays. Dinner from 6 to 11:30 p.m.; to 1:30 a.m. Saturday, Sunday. Sunday brunch 11 a.m. to 4 p.m. for fixed price of $5.95. Children's menu. Entertainment Wednesday through Sunday. Full bar. Reservations recommended. All major credit cards. Parking lot; street parking. Casual.

## ELMER'S PLACE
323 North State College
Fullerton

**American**

★

(714) 870-7400

One of the best family restaurants in Orange County is operated by one of the best restaurant families. Big brother Chick owns Mr. Stox; his wife Phyllis develops recipes for both places and kid brother Ron with his wife, Debbie, operates this sparkling family oasis named after their father, Elmer Marshall, who was also a restaurateur. Everything is better than it need be from burgers to fresh pasta to the *croustade*, a giant hollowed out crouton brushed with butter and filled with your choice of savories. There's an innovative snack list. Wine is fairly priced. Cocktails are good, and Elmer's "fruit extravaganza" is a fine dessert. Good for the tot-lot.

**Moderate.** Open seven days. Luncheon served weekdays 11 a.m. to 3 p.m. Dinner Monday through Saturday 5 to 10 p.m. Sunday brunch from 10 to 2 p.m. Entertainment Wednesday through Saturday. Full bar. No reservations. Visa, MC. Wheelchair access. Parking lot. Casual.

## EL PADRINO
Beverly Wilshire Hotel
9500 Wilshire Boulevard
Beverly Hills        **Map 8**

**Continental**

★

(213) 275-4282

Two of the best luncheon destinations in Beverly Hills are located at Hernando Courtright's elegant Beverly Wilshire Hotel — one of them La Bella Fontana — with a separate listing in this guide, and the other the less formal El Padrino. The decor is dramatic: early California ranchero with saddles

*For best results, consult "How to Use This Guide" on page 27.*

and sterling silver horseshoes in a leather and dark wood interior. In addition to a luncheon menu with dishes like California sand dabs Véronique (sand dabs sautéed in butter with small seedless grapes) and calf's liver (sautéed with bacon), there are the usual beef, chops, salads, and sandwiches. The "market salad" bows to the health food fans, consisting of avocado, mixed greens and bean sprouts, mushrooms, carrots, radishes, alfalfa sprouts, tomato, grated cheese, and dressing. Appetizers or soups, pâté, ham and melon, and gazpacho Andaluz can turn luncheon into an elaborate meal. The extensive dinner menu (including soup or salad) ranges from piccata of veal to large shrimp *en brochette provençale* to a New York steak in a superior Bordelaise sauce. There's a supper menu from 10:30 p.m. to 12:30 a.m. including from-the-broiler dishes, omelettes and some super sandwiches. Champagne brunch in this always-busy room provides a broad selections of entrées.

**Moderate to expensive.** Open seven days. Luncheon from 11:30 a.m. to 3 p.m. Dinner from 5:30 p.m. to 1:30 a.m. Sunday brunch 11:30 a.m. to 3 p.m. Entertainment. Full bar. Reservations suggested. All major credit cards. Valet parking. Semi-dressy.

---

## EL PASEO INN RESTAURANT

Olvera Street
Los Angeles　　**Map 7**

Mexican
**DA**
(213) 626-1361

There is a predisposition to be wary of restaurants in tourist areas, but I'm pleased to report that Mexican food and entertainment are alive and surviving together—if a bit uneasily—on Olvera Street. The food is Sonora-style peasant fare authentically prepared. There is a colorful fiesta show three times each night, and the flamenco dancers and exuberant singers (we were engulfed by a cloud of talcum powder from an over-enthusiastic senorita) are well received.

**Moderate.** Open Tuesday through Sunday from 10 a.m. to midnight. Entertainment Saturday, Sunday at 7:30, 9:30, 11 p.m. Full bar. Reservations recommended. All major credit cards. Street parking. Casual.

---

## EL PESCADOR                                      Seafood
1342 Camino Del Mar                                        ★
Del Mar                                      (714) 755-1919

This charming Del Mar favorite started out as a fish market nearly a decade ago serving clam chowder and seafood cocktails on the side. It may be the only good place for good *cioppino* in the San Diego area served up spicy and hearty as opposed to the tomato sauce gunk of other concoctions masquerading by that name. Their house salad is an interesting admix of smoked fish, shrimp and scallops, and they serve fresh lemonade along with wine and iced beer.

**Inexpensive.** Open seven days 11 a.m. to 8 p.m. Closed Easter, Thanksgiving, Christmas, New Year's. Wine and beer only. No reservations. Patio. Visa, MC. Small parking lot; street parking. Casual.

---

## EL TORITO                                        Mexican
Consult phone book for listings.

Not my favorite Mexican restaurants, although these are massive investments in upgrading the atmosphere and variety of dishes. They've a little too commercial and some of the dishes like *camarones flores*, shrimp wrapped in bacon, seem out of place. The margaritas at the ones I've visited were squirted through a hose and while that probably works well for quantity, the drink is uninteresting. Noise level is high particularly during the mariachis.

**Inexpensive.** Open Monday through Thursday 11 a.m. to 11 p.m.; to midnight Friday, Saturday; 1 to 11 p.m. Sunday. Sunday brunch 9 a.m. to 1 p.m. Extended summer hours. Full bar. Reservations recommended. All major credit cards. Parking lot; street parking. Casual.

---

## EMILIO'S RISTORANTE                     Italian/Continental
6602 Melrose Avenue                                          ★★
Los Angeles          **Map 7**                    (213) 935-4922

Some restaurants are popular with me as soon as I hear their names. Emilio's Ristorante rolls so trippingly and continentally off the tongue that it makes you feel sophisticated for having selected it. One literally squeezes into the place. The bar is a shade too intimate, but the back room is spacious and the pace there is gentler. There is a central fountain in a piazza, and marble, tile, statuary, carved paneling, plush greenery, a stained-glass dome — even a grand staircase leading up to a balcony. When a friend of mine asked: "Is the food good?" I answered: "Is the Pope Italian?" "Not always," replied my friend. "Not always" either at Emilio's. When the stars are right — which is most of the time — the food can be very, very good. The Northern Italian cuisine offers some creative side trips like *carciofini alla Guidea*, a deep-fried artichoke recipe that goes back to the times of the Jewish ghetto in ancient Rome (yes, even then — even there). There are such delicacies as *zuppa pavese*, a soup of chicken broth topped with a slice fried bread that is topped with a poached egg and covered with romano cheese. Fish is fresh, and the entire menu offers a wide variety of dishes.

**Moderate.** Open seven days. Dinner from 5 p.m. to midnight; Friday, Saturday to 12:30, a.m. Limited banquet facilities. Closed Thanksgiving, Christmas. Full bar. Reservations advised. All major credit cards. Valet parking. Casual to dressy.

# EN BROCHETTE
**American**
★

9018 Burton Way
Beverly Hills     **Map 8**     (213) 276-9990

The last time I dined at En Brochette, a dog kept barking on one side of the restaurant's awfully pleasant "gazebo garden," as they like to call it. The dog would bark in a deep "rowff" sort of a sound, then stop long enough so that you thought he might have gone off to bite a mailman, then the "rowffs" would start again. The barking dog was a real nuisance, since he (or she) laid an air of irritable expectation over what otherwise is a truly fine outdoor dining experience.

En Brochette has a pair of outdoor dining areas. One is in the front, facing on sedate Burton Way. The other is the "gazebo garden," a long, thin area stretching along the side of the restaurant. In between is a brick courtyard and a hairstylist. Wandering between the two outdoor dining areas are a pair of young minstrels, classically playing much Mozart and various Vivaldi on violin and flute. Very civilized, very pleasant. A truly fine outdoor experience except for that confounded dog, that is.

The meals at En Brochette are pleasant and simple, as outdoor meals really should be. There are appetizers of guacamole, broiled mushrooms caps and quiche (imported from the incomparable Ms. Tish). They are "light suppers" of cold shrimp served with mustard and cocktail sauce, guacamole omelettes and chicken crepes. And there are, of course, the house specialty of skewered dishes.

At En Brochette, you can have your skewer packed with fresh yellowtail ($12.25), or filet mignon or lamb, or rainbow trout, or just vegetables. The skewers are served with a functional selection of dipping sauces (a very garlicky butter for the yellowtail). Desserts lean heavily toward the obscene, especially in the area of the various mousse pies. And up above, this being Beverly Hills and all that, you can see stars. *M.S.*

**Expensive.** Open seven days. Luncheon from 11:30 a.m. to 2:30 p.m. Dinner Tuesday through Sunday 6 to 10 p.m. Sunday brunch. Closed Thanksgiving, Christmas. Entertainment. Beer and wine only. Reservations required. Patio. Most major credit cards. Wheelchair access. Valet parking $2. Casual to semi-dressy.

---

## ENCINA
**Continental**
★
2220 Bath Street
Santa Barbara
(805)682-7700

Sometimes it's hard to tell the good guise from the bad ones when looking for good food in a hotel or motel restaurant. This is one of the good ones, and will probably stay good as long as Chef Ron Ousey from England stays around. His specialty is seafood, though you'll find about 25 reliable entrées to choose from. His crab mornay and shrimp dishes are talked about most. Desserts are homemade and vegetables are not given the tourist treatment. The wine list is modest in length and in prices and offers both domestic and imports. While the decor is not a gateway to heaven, you will hear harp music on Friday and Saturday nights. There's a view of the pool every day.

**Moderate.** Open seven days. Breakfast from 7:30 to 11:30 a.m. Luncheon 11:30 a.m. to 2:30 p.m. Monday through Saturday. Sunday brunch 11:30 a.m. to 2 p.m. Dinner 5 to 9 p.m. Wine and beer only. Reservations recommended for dinner. Enclosed patio. Visa, MC. Parking lot. Casual.

*In order to obtain the best results from this Guide, be sure to read the French, German, Italian and Oriental menu translators on page 705 to 710 of this Guide.*

## ENTOURAGE

French
★

8450 West 3rd Street
Los Angeles  **Map 8**

(213) 653-1079

Smart, trendy with skylighted solarium and an air of expensive relaxation, but it's not quite right. A study of the menu is like a dissertation in sauces, everything seems sauced but the waiters (and I was suspicious of one of them). *Artichauts a la Grecque* is served in a marinade sauce, of course, and the *carpaccio*, the transparently thin slices of beef, are covered with mustard sauce. The classic dishes here show little straying from the fold, but desserts are a disappointment. Astonishingly, on the two occasions I visited them they had no cheese, a serious omission for a restaurant with pretensions of high cuisine. I recognize that it is expensive to keep cheese at room temperature and that many restaurants prefer not to serve it all rather than purvey the chilled, putty-like consistency of refrigerated Brie or whatever, but there must be a way. Maybe they could charge it off to advertising.

**Moderate to expensive.** Open Monday through Saturday. Luncheon from 11:30 a.m. to 3 p.m. weekdays. Dinner 6 to 11 p.m. Full bar. Reservations essential. Visa, MC, AX. Valet parking. Semi-dressy.

## EPICURE INN

Continental
★★

7625 Topanga Canyon Boulevard
Canoga Park  **Map 1**

(213) 888-3300

If this fine restaurant were located two miles further south, it would be filled nightly. As it is, the Epicure Inn is still waiting to be discovered, almost hidden between a gas station and a motel. The decor had been skillfully transformed to a comfortable European country inn (it was formerly very British when the restaurant was the Generous Briton). Booths have high wooden backs; candles and fresh flowers accent the warmth of the restaurant. The specialty of the house is owner/chef Manfred Fuehr's beef Wellington. Like everything else on the menu, it is cooked to order, and more than worth the approximately 20 minute wait. Chef Manfred has been working in and around some of the finest European kitchens since he was 14 and his years of experience are well evidenced in the outstanding quality of everything he prepares. In addition to the complete menu, dinner specials each week include authentically prepared *weiner schnitzel, sauerbraten* and *rouladen* of beef.

**Moderate.** Open seven days. Luncheon from 11:30 a.m. to 2 p.m. weekdays. Dinner from 5:30 to 10 p.m. Full bar. Reservations advised. All major credit cards. Adjacent parking. Casual to semi-dressy.

---

## ERAWAN                                                    Thai
5145 Colfax Avenue                                            ★
North Hollywood          **Map 1**              (213) 760-1283

If first rate star-gazing (Hollywood style), fair prices, friendly service, cleanliness, and superb food appeal to you, join the "in" crowd here. For this unassuming Thai cottage may be low on atmosphere, but it soars with exquisite flavors. And there's always a possibility you might catch a glimpse of Dick Van Dyke, Angie Dickinson, Robert Mandan (*Soap*), Richard Paul, Roger Perry and Joanne Worley, Susan Seaforth and Bill Hayes (*Days of Our Lives*), Jon Walmsley (*The Waltons*), Pat Hingle, Karen Morrow, Nancy Dussault or Earl Holliman dining under the straw shrimp mobiles. Many of us have developed strange cravings for sour shrimp soup, *yum yai* (shrimp, chicken, Romaine, onion, and lemon-spiced salad), *sateh* (skewered beef with peanut sauce and cucumbers), *mee grop* (sweet, crispy noodles with pork and shrimp... *do* drown it in lime juice), *paht Thai* (rice noodles, sprouts, ground peanuts, shrimp, pork, dried chili), *paht pick khing* (fried pork, crunchy green beans, red chili), chicken and mint, plus sixty other selections. The hot dishes are starred, and can be ordered mild, medium or spicy hot. The creamy Thai tea or coffee helps sooth a sizzling tongue. The Erawan is family owned and operated, and within four years Sam and Cora Thomloi have won a firm place in the hearts of the underground Thai food eaters. The takeout is packed and ready for entertaining. There is no loss of flavor when the food is heated in a microwave.  *Jackie Joseph, actress and gadfly.*

**Inexpensive to moderate.** Open Tuesday through Saturday. Dinner from 5 to 10 p.m. Take-out. Closed Chrismas. Wine and beer only. No reservations. No credit cards. Street parking. Casual.

*In order to obtain the best results from this Guide, please consult "Tips on Dining Out" on page 21.*

## FAMOUS ENTERPRISE FISH COMPANY    Seafood
174 Kinney    ★
Santa Monica    (213) 392-8366

This renovated brick warehouse has become one of the area's most popular restaurants. If you're in a shellfish mood this is the place. Virtually all fresh seafood, in season, is broiled over mesquite charcoal in an exhibition kitchen. The wharfside atmosphere, genial service and reasonable prices add up to a winner.

**Moderate.** Open seven days. Sunday through Thursday 11 a.m. to 4 p.m.; Friday, Saturday to 11 p.m. Full bar. No reservations. Visa, MC, AX. Parking across from restaurant. Casual.

## FAR EAST TERRACE

**Chinese**
★

4123 Lankershim Boulevard
North Hollywood          **Map 1**          (213) 985-1139

Far East Terrace in North Hollywood is probably the favorite Chinese restaurant of motion picture personalities for two reasons—it's been around as long as they have, and it's good. The won ton soup is as good as I've had in Southern California—notice I didn't say Northern California—and the essentially Cantonese cuisine is served well prepared and without surprises. The restaurant is handsome, the service friendly, and there is good piano bar entertainment. Arthur Wong former honorary mayor of North Hollywood, a position that matters insignificantly in the SALT talks, perhaps, but he does know nearly everybody—and it shows. As an indication of the esteem in which he is held by his fellow restaurateurs of all persuasions and cuisines, Mr. Wong was recently the president of the Southern California Restaurant Association. This is definitely not a neighborhood chop suey-ry, and you'll want to dress a bit for dinner.

**Moderate.** Open seven days. Luncheon 11:30 a.m. to 3 p.m. weekdays. Dinner 3 to 11 p.m. Piano bar. Full bar. Reservations recommended. All major credit cards. Valet parking evenings. Semi-dressy.

## FARMER'S MARKET

**American/Continental**
**DA**

West 3rd Street
Los Angeles          **Map 8**          (213) 933-9211

For decades the Farmer's Market has been a favorite luncheon place to entertain out-of-town guests, or simply to spend a leisurely noon, wandering down the long rows of small booths picking out their specialties: an enchilada here, hamburgers there, or fresh papaya, hot fudge sundaes, or blintzes, or spaghetti, or pie, or tarts, a slice of melon, fragrant coffee, corn on the cob, candy, or just one perfect orange. You pick everything up on trays, find a table, and leave the tableware to be somehow sorted out by the busboys in the open-air market. It's ideal for people-watching, from celebrities to Viola Hopness, a piano teacher from Klamath Falls. Afterward you can load up on the fresh fruit and produce and groceries to take home if you can afford to.

**Moderate.** Open Monday through Saturday. Winter months from 9 a.m. to 6:30 p.m. Summer months from 9 a.m. to 8 p.m. No alcoholic beverages. No reservations. Patio. No credit cards. Ten acres of parking. Casual.

---

## FEASTBOARD American
777 South Main Street ★
Orange **Map 6** (714) 547-0879

The incredible edible of Orange County is under $10, the highest price you can pay at the Feastboard. It is a two pound (two pound!) cut of prime rib, a mammoth mountain of beef served on a 15 inch platter with fresh steamed vegetables, corn on the cob, fresh fruit and choice of salad. The Feastboard is an improbably located—in the exclusive Town and Country Shopping Center in Orange)—as it is improbably priced. Within an attractive castle interior, stone fireplaces, gargoyles, stone walls and rich wood chairs and tables, you can order a "Viking feast" of baked chicken and barbecued ribs on a bed of brown rice also with fresh fruit and vegetables for under $8. Or you can order up a "poultry feast" (if you have the stomach for it) of chicken *and* turkey *and* duck. "Beef and bird" is a petite cut of top sirloin served with baked chicken. There's no catch to this food bargain except that the low prices are intended to produce high volume and the restaurant, in defiance of accepted accounting procedures, is willing to take less profit per person. Luncheon is served on weekdays with similarly low prices for sandwiches and omelettes and lighter fare. Dinner is served every night. There are great desserts all day including a "super" banana split, "Mad dog's Sundae" of hot fudge, banana nut and ice cream flambéed, and a chocolate orgy called "flaming devil" with chocolate ice cream and hot fudge on chocolate cake. There are a variety of old-fashioned malts and phosphates, and a combination phosphate that my kids used to call a "suicide." There are teas, hot chocolate combination and a dozen exotic coffees. I expected a no reservation policy at a restaurant that lives by volume but I was wrong; reservations are honored. Children are welcome here although the decor is full-on major league and the service is cheerful.

**Inexpensive.** Open seven days. Luncheon served Monday through Friday from 11 a.m. to 4 p.m. Dinner Sunday through Thursday from 4 to 10 p.m.; Friday and Saturday to 11 p.m. Banquet facilities. Closed Christmas. Children welcome. Full bar. All major credit cards accepted. Parking lot. Casual.

---

**FELFELA**                                    **Egyptian**
270 North Beverly Drive                              ★
Beverly Hills        **Map 8**              (213) 274-6366

This is the first of the chain of restaurants to open outside of Egypt, and they may have some adjusting to do. Four complete dinners provide an opportunity to sample the exotic fare, cuisine quite distinct from any other. *Koshari* is a delectable dish created with rice, pasta, beans, onion, garlic, sausage, vinegar and cumin. Lamb shoulder with brown rice and nuts in another of the entrées.

The atmosphere is serenely Egyptian—the restaurant used to be Marty's deli in a previous incarnation—and the service is attentive and helpful.

**Moderate to expensive.** Open for lunch Monday through Saturday 11:30 a.m. to 3 p.m. Dinner from 6 to 11 p.m. Closed Christmas and New Year's. Cocktails. Reservations recommended. Visa, MC, AX. Wheelchair access. Valet parking. Semi-dressy.

---

## FELLINI'S                                    Italian
6810 Melrose Avenue                              ★
Los Angeles          **Map 8**          (213) 936-3100

A favorite with the theatre folk since it's open until 2 a.m., this is the hub of legitimate theatre in Los Angeles. Spinach soup, crêpes and omelettes, fresh trout and the usual pasta fare is served with flair. Eggplant Fellini and the excellent desserts like creamy cheesecake, carrot cake and pecan pie are my personal favorites at this plant-bedecked intimate.

**Moderate.** Open seven days. Lunch from 11:30 a.m. to 4:30 p.m. Dinner from 4:30 p.m. to 2 a.m. Sunday brunch served from 10:30 a.m. to 2:30 p.m. Full bar. Reservations advised for five or more. Patio. Visa, MC. Valet parking. Casual.

---

## FERRARESE FAMILY DELI          Italian/Deli
14456 7th Street                                 ★
Victorville                        (714) 245-5632

Victorville is not a destination point except for the hardy few who live there. It is, however, a way station on the journey to the attractions of the high desert including an obligatory visit to Roy Rogers' stuffed horse Trigger in Apple Valley, and for those with a Vegas notion.

Hugo and Bruna Farrarese moved to the area in 1955 and established a modest gourmet liquor store and delicatessen.

Then retired major leaguer Don Farrarese (Orioles, Cubs, Phillies) joined the team and remodeled an old A&W Root Beer stand into a jewel of a dine 'n' take-out restaurant, called The Ferrarese Family Deli. The soup is homemade and good, particularly the minestrone. My favorites among the blimp-sized sandwiches are the meatball with mozzarella cheese and the fresh mushroom with cheese melted on rye. They have chicken from the rotisseries, homemade spaghetti, ravioli and pastas. There are 22 (I counted) salads and a daily special.

**Inexpensive.** Open seven days from 8 a.m. to 9:30 p.m. Beer and wine only. Bank cards only. Parking lot. Casual.

---

## FIASCO                                American/Continental
4451 Admiralty Way                                        ★
Marina del Rey        **Map 2**                (213)823-6395

The glassed-in patio overlooking the main channel in Marina del Rey is not the only reason this is one of the better spots in the area. There are open fires, imaginative decor, and some good dishes — along with some ordinary ones. Among the best are the scampi, lamb chops, Alaskan king crab for brunch, and homemade soups. The bouillabaise is another matter, and one of no importance. There are good omelettes at luncheon. Peter Soracco obviously wanted to offer more than location and view when he opened this popular spot in 1969.

**Moderate.** Open seven days. Luncheon from 11:30 a.m. to 5 p.m. weekdays. Dinner 5:30 to 10 p.m. Sunday brunch 10 a.m. to 3 p.m. Full bar. Reservations recommended. Patio. View of Marina. Visa, MC, AX. Parking lot. Casual to semi-dressy.

*Please be sure to consult "Tipping Made Easy" on page 25 of this Guide.*

## THE FINE AFFAIR

**French Continental**

666 North Sepulveda Boulevard
Bel Air    **Map 8**    (213) 476-2848

Mr. Zivic's dream did not come about easily. This restaurant had piques and valleys and traces of arrogance in its past, but now it is serenely sailing back to the top of the West Side restaurants. In the foothills of Bel Air you'll see lots of latticework and plush plants. Elegant touches include hand painted French china and crystal. Their Sunday brunch is one of the best around.

**Expensive.** Open Tuesday through Sunday. Luncheon 11 a.m. to 2:30 p.m. weekdays. Dinner 6 to 11 p.m. Sunday brunch 11 a.m. to 2:30 p.m. Full bar. Reservations recommended. Patio. Visa, MC, AX. Valet, street parking. Semi-dressy.

---

## FIORE D'ITALIA

**Northern Italian**
★

14928 Ventura Boulevard
Sherman Oaks    **Map 1**    (213) 995-9074

There was a time when almost all Italian restaurants in America looked like this, when food was generous and the waiters were patient; but that was before even my time. Here are the "grapes" hanging from a trellis, the statues that always remind me of Forest Lawn, and the shrimp and pastas of yesteryear. The only things that changed are the prices, and they changed plenty.

**Moderate.** Open Wednesday through Monday. Dinner from 5 to 11 p.m. Monday, Wednesday through Thursday; 5 to midnight Friday, Saturday. Closed July 4, Thanksgiving, Christmas. Full bar. Reservations recommended. Patio room. Visa, MC, CB. Parking lot. Semi-dressy.

## FIRENZE KITCHENS                      Italian
612 North La Brea                          ★
Los Angeles          **Map 7**          (213) 932-8859

If you like antipasto — and I'm an addict — you'll find it at its best in this tiny, seven-table cafe. Most Americans have never tasted the real thing — all kinds of sausages, cold cuts, olives, deviled eggs, fresh and marinated vegetables, anchovies, and salads drenched in a strong garlicky dressing that's guaranteed to keep the mosquitos (and everything and everyone else) away from you for hours. Some menus offer this as an appetizer, but if you are having dinner, I would suggest that two or three people share a single antipasto serving. Veal parmesan is also good here. Nine pasta dishes are served to order.

**Inexpensive to moderate.** Open Monday through Saturday. Dinner from 6 to 10 p.m. Monday through Thursday; to 10:30 Friday, Saturday. Closed major holidays. Wine and beer only. Reservations recommended. Visa, MC. Street parking. Casual.

## FIVE CROWNS                          English
3801 East Coast Highway                    ★★
Corona del Mar        **Map 4**          (714) 760-0331

For more than a decade I've been a pleased patron of the Five Crowns in Corona del Mar, and I've always been intrigued with the story behind that graceful building. It is a faithful reproduction of England's oldest inn, Ye Old Bell, dating back to 1135 A.D. Ye Old Bell is still functioning as a highly respected restaurant and inn at Hurley-on-Thames,

---

*To obtain the best results from this Guide, be sure to consult maps on the various Southern California areas in the front of the book.*

about an hour out of London. By contrast Five Crowns in Corona del Mar is as successful and American as Ye Old Bell is continental. It certainly is newer. It was a farmsite as recently as the 1920's, about the time the highway was paved from Los Angeles to San Diego, just wide enough for two cars to pass. The Hurley Bell, as it was called in its earliest days, was the inspiration of a Balboa resident, a Mrs. Atkinson who was so impressed with Ye Old Bell that she literally brought it back from England with her. Five Crowns is much larger and brighter than its clone although the exterior will startle those that have been to the source—it's that close a replica. Once inside the cozy bar area with a great hearth, you can order a Pimm's Cup Number One (gin and ginger, sweet and sour that has soda) and watch the colorfully-dressed English maids and barmen at work. If you've got the time, ask them to serve you a half yard of Watney's. The glass resembles a thermometer with a bulb on the bottom and it is 18 inches of fun to drink. The dining rooms are bright and attractive and my favorite is the Greenery, a room with hanging plants and lovely decor. The food is consistently good and priced at less than half that of Ye Old Bell. I like the pride salad made with Bibb lettuce, walnuts, bacon bits, gruyère cheese and homemade dressing. Among the main courses you'll find the kind of beef dishes we have come to expect of a Lawry's operation but their special selections include less familiar dishes like sesame chicken, fresh snapper, fresh scallops, whole baby salmon (in season) and a super Bristol Cream chicken. The wine list is notable because of its confidence in presenting some of the lesser-known but fascinating California "boutiques." Philip Crowley is the manager here, and much like his counterpart in Hurley, he's everywhere at once. To his credit he solved a chronic problem that plagued the Five Crowns in an earlier time when it was often an hour before reservations were called. As an added attraction the Showcase Singers perform opera and light classics on Sunday and Monday from 8 p.m.

to midnight. Brunch is a favorite with the locals and provides a selection of about a dozen dishes.

**Moderate to expensive.** Open seven days. Dinner from 5 to 10 p.m. Sunday through Thursday; to 11 Friday, Saturday. Sunday brunch 10:30 a.m. to 2:30 p.m. Closed Thanksgiving, Christmas. Patio entertainment nightly. Full bar. Reservations essential. Visa, MC, AX. Valet parking. Semi-dressy.

---

## FONTAINEBLEAU ROOM
Little America-Westgate Hotel
San Diego

French
★★
(714) 238-1818

Westgate Plaza in San Diego was originally conceived by C. Arnholt Smith to be super posh. Mrs. Smith shopped the world for high-profile opulence — rich tapestries, antiques, gold plumbing fixtures, crystal chandeliers, and statuary. There were some mistakes — there's no swimming pool in this resort-area hotel, and the banquet rooms are small — but Esquire magazine has described the hotel as the "fifth most beautiful in America," high praise for this high-rise located alongside the edifice wrecks in downtown San Diego. Mr. Smith encountered a spate of financial and legal difficulties necessitating the sale of the hotel and a change of management. The fact that Westgate Plaza was sold to Little America, a highly successful accommodations corporation, is certainly understandable — it was the highest bidder — but what is incomprehensible was the buyers' insistence (based, I presume, on chauvinistic pride) to change the name to Little America. Of all the names that could convey the regal splendor and dignity of this hotel, "Little America" would seem among the least appropriate. Imagine a wealthy

*To obtain the best results from this Guide, consult "How to Use this Guide" on page 27.*

couple visiting their travel agent, insisting on deluxe standards, only to be referred to Little America in San Diego — images of Route 66 motels, right? The food is a different and happier story. The Fountainebleau Room serves *haute cuisine* at unusually reasonable prices. The classic Escoffier dishes are well represented, along with "creations of Chef Roger" whose crêpes Maxim (with crabmeat and brandy sauce) and *scampi petite jolie*, winner of the Grand Prix Gastronomique in London in 1954, are the highlights.

**Moderate to expensive.** Open Monday through Saturday. Luncheon 11:45 a.m. to 2 p.m. weekdays. Dinner Sunday through Friday 6:30 to 10 p.m.; Saturday 6 to 10 p.m. Banquet facilities. Piano and harp entertainment. Full bar. Reservations advised. All major credit cards. Garage (pay) parking. Semi-dressy to dressy, jackets required.

---

## FORTUNE FOUNTAIN                                    Chinese
8408 West 3rd Street                                          ★
Los Angeles          **Map 8**                    (213)655-3917

A little, yet dignified restaurant with a distinguished kitchen and a strong Szechwan flavor, although the selections include some Shanghai and some "safe" dishes. The circular tables have revolving, lazy-Susan type centers. Soup is not necessarily part of every dinner although the "sweet and hot" was delectable: spicy with vegetables and tart with vinegar. Chinese like to enjoy their soup during the entire meal and if you want to dine *de rigueur*, put your soup bowls aside and ask the waiter to leave the tureen. We exulted over diced chicken in brown sauce, beef and scallion, shrimp with Chinese peas and pork Szechwan style, all simple names for rich and complex dishes, and a fascinating combination of flavors, textures and colors. It was one of the more delightful dinners I'd had in a long while. Some tips on eating in a fine Chinese restaurant like this are: don't order a set dinner; they're dull and the kitchen doesn't feel challenged. I ask the proprietor to make the selections, having indicated my preference in meats. Order one main dish per person plus soup, unless the party is for more than six people. Try to achieve a balance between spicy dishes and the milder ones (ask). Don't order two dishes with the same flavor like oyster sauce with pork and oyster sauce with beef. There is a limited wine list, but Wan Fu goes well with Chinese food. Desserts are sparse but I like the lichee, served on crushed ice, similar in appearance and texture to Crenshaw melon balls. The atmosphere is distinctly Chinese and there is some good art and wood paneling on the walls. Prices are reasonable for food of this character.

**Moderate.** Open Wednesday through Monday. Luncheon from 11:30 a.m. to 3 p.m. Dinner 5 to 9:30 p.m. Wine and beer only. Reservations recommended. Visa, MC. Street parking. Casual.

---

## THE FORUM RISTORANTE                      Northern Italian
1529 East Valley Parkway                                    ★
Escondido                                      (714) 741-4111

What flair! What imagination! What courage it must have taken to open this charmer of a *ristorante* in Escondido. The wine cocktails and apéritifs are well chosen for a change. The menu in this dramatic and semi-formal room advises that your menu selection will take from 20 to 25 minutes to serve—it's prepared to order. Someone got the quaint idea of fashioning the menu after a showbill—I usually find such touches distracting—and this one consists of preludes, Act I, Act II, etc. The antipasto is terrific and the cheese *à la Forno* is a good "prelude." The *ricotta ravioli* is homemade and tastes like it and the semolina spaghetti is as good as I've had recently. It's sauced with Sicilian tomato paste and sautéed meat sauce, and served with meatballs or Italian sausage if you like. The *fettuccine, linguini* and clams, and *cannelloni* are uptown in quality and the *gnocchi* is served here as it should be served. There are veal dishes galore, seafood, and poultry, and the Forum wisely does not feel that offering varieties of pizzas will compromise their dignity. I took one home for breakfast. Itsa good place.

**Inexpensive.** Open Tuesday through Sunday. Dinner Tuesday through Thursday; Friday, Saturday to 11 p.m.; Sunday 5 to 9 p.m. Private party facilities. Closed Thanksgiving. Wine and beer only. Reservations advised. Parking lot in shopping center. Semi-dressy.

---

## FOURNO'S OVEN WEST                               Greek
550 Via del la Valle
Del Mar                                        (714) 481-5150

Fourno's moved to this Del Mar location from Cardiff, and the Greek *taverna* is still renowned for their lamb Wellington, done in filo dough. I can recommend the seafood Mephistopheles, having once consumed a portion and a half there—perhaps a Guinness record. There's Greek joy and spirits abound.

**Expensive.** Open Friday, Saturday only from 7:30 to 10 p.m. Closed month of October. Belly dancer Friday. Full bar. Reservations advised. Covered patio. No credit cards; personal checks accepted. Parking lot. Semi-dressy.

---

## FRANÇOIS                                     Continental
18151 Beach Boulevard                                    ★
Huntington Beach          **Map 4**            (714) 842-1919

This has been a favorite French restaurant for a decade in an area (Huntington Beach) where restaurant age is measured in months. Frank Richmond, proprietor of this understated establishment, presents flaming duck as his speciality of the house,

245

but I find virtually all the familiar dishes on the classic menu to be well prepared and professionally presented. The art of flambé — flaming puddings, duck, desserts, and so on — is more complex than it appears. In most places it is ignition for purely theatrical reasons; here, the flame serves a cooking purpose — imparting the finishing flavor to the dish. The sauces are better than average, though a little bland.

**Moderate to expensive.** Open Monday through Saturday. Luncheon from 11:30 a.m. to 3 p.m. weekdays. Dinner from 6 to 11 p.m. Piano bar. Full bar. Reservations advised. All major credit cards. Adjacent parking lot. Casual to semi-dressy.

---

## FRANÇOIS                                          French
555 South Flower Street                              ★★★
Los Angeles          **Map 7**              (213) 680-2727


Gold medal-winning entrees from the Culinary Olympics Competition in Frankfurt are served at Francois' on a rotating basis as the special of the day. The entrées include turkey breast Oklahoma (minced, rolled and stuffed with fresh vegetables, ham and mushrooms) served with mushroom-shaped potatoes and pearl onions in a vegetable nest: Black Sea bass St. Augustine with lemon sauce, stuffed with crab meat and served with sautéed peapods, tomatoes and new potatoes baked with cheese: chicken breast stuffed with crab meat and served with stir-fried vegetables and lemon noodles. Sato has gone on to open his own restaurant, Chez Sateau, in Arcadia, but the kitchen at Francois carries on in style.

Francois' is a very luxurious, very French restaurant situated in the seven acres of underground shopping area of ARCO Plaza. There's a splendid value in pre-theatre dinners including a choice of hors d'oeuvres (try the baked oyster on a bed of creamed spinach), entrées (try the duck with calvados or the pepper steak in creamy cognac sauce) and your selection of desserts baked and prepared in their kitchens. The price is $15, and the dinner is served from 6 p.m. to 7:30. There is a large à la carte selection and an excellent wine list at fair prices.

**Expensive.** Open Monday through Saturday. Luncheon from 11:30 a.m. to 2 p.m. weekdays. Dinner 6 to 10 p.m.; Friday from 5:30. Entertainment. Full bar. Reservations required. All major credit cards. Validated parking days at 400 South Flower, evenings in ARCO Plaza and Flower. Semi-dressy to dressy.

---

## FREDERICK'S
512 West Main
Santa Maria

**Italian/Continental**
★
(805) 925-1166

Frederick's is the originator of sourdough pizza, but not until it had been in business for nearly 30 years as a neighborhood Italian grocery and deli did it become a Pizza Parlour. In 1961 the founder sent back to the old country for a mail-order bride and part of the dowry was her pizza recipe. They have their own smokehouse, and all meat and sausage here is processed and cooked in their own kitchens and in the plant where the equipment dates from 1911. Slicers, grinder, and walk-in boxes have been restored. Everything is made from scratch, even the pizza sauce. Only fresh vegetables are used. Each day there is a different luncheon special such as knockwurst and sauerkraut with German potato salad in addition to soups, salads and sandwiches. If you can't find what you like on the menu, they will gladly prepare any dish not listed (I can't imagine what it could be). Dessert decisions are calmer because with cheese cake as good as theirs, there's no contest.

**Moderate.** Open seven days. Luncheon from 11 a.m. to 2 p.m. Dinner from 5 to 10 p.m. Sunday through Thursday; to 11 Friday, Saturday. Sunday brunch 10 a.m. to 2 p.m. for fixed price of $6.95. Children's menu. Closed Thanksgiving, Christmas. Full bar. Reservations recommended. Visa, MC. Parking lot. Casual.

## FRENCHY MARSEILLES                             French
8th and C Streets                                      ★
San Diego                               (714) 233-3413

Besides having what might be the most terrible name for a
French restaurant I've come across, this one has really good
food. Convenient to the theatres and the nightlife that does
exist in San Diego (there is some), the menu won't
confound or astound with beef Wellington, quiche, omelettes, and fresh fish, but they do have freshly baked bread.

**Moderate.** Open Monday through Saturday. Luncheon 11
a.m. to 2:30 p.m. Monday through Saturday. Dinner 5 to
11:30 p.m. Tuesday through Saturday. Closed most major
holidays. Oyster bar. Full bar. Reservations recommended.
Visa, MC. Parking at 9th and "C" days; street parking
evenings. Casual.

## FUJI GARDENS                                  Japanese
424 Wilshire Boulevard                                 ★
Santa Monica          **Map 2**          (213) 393-2118

A tranquil place with the traditional personal service that
the bigger Japanese restaurants can no longer provide. Mrs.
Song will guide you through the menu if there is a
language problem with the waiter. The menu lists 10
combinations and a dozen full dinners but really exotic
cuisine may be prepared on 24 hours notice. While the
familiar dishes are here, you really should try the sushi
dinners. This is also a favorite luncheon place.

**Moderate.** Open Tuesday through Sunday. Luncheon 11:30
to 2:30, Tuesday through Friday. Dinner from 5 to 10 p.m.
Sunday, Tuesday through Thursday, and 5 to 11 p.m.
Friday, Saturday. Reservations recommended. Street parking
(public lot nearby). Visa, MC. Wine and beer only. Casual.
Closed Thanksgiving, Christmas.

## FUJIYA                                    Japanese
8339 Reseda Boulevard                               ★
Northridge          **Map 1**              (213) 885-0562

A new sushi bar has been added as if this splendid Japanese restaurant needed any embellishment. The suburbs are usually the last to get good ethnic food, but the proliferation of Japanese restaurants in Southern California is such that you might find one in your backyard some day. And why not? The food is healty, delicious, pleasing to the eye and—usually—graciously served. Here are the familiars: tempura, sukiyaki and sashimi but there are also specialties of the house. The *yosenabe,* described sometimes as an Oriental bouillabaisse, and the *shabu shabu* are better than most. There is full cocktail service with some unusual liquers—try the melon—and you can sit in the tatami rooms if you like.

**Moderate.** Open Monday through Saturday. Luncheon Monday through Friday from 11:30 a.m. to 2 p.m. Dinner Moday through Friday from 5 to 10 p.m.; Saturday to 10:30 p.m. Full bar. Reservations advised. Visa, MC. Parking lot. Casual.

## FUNG LUM                                    Chinese
Universal Studios                               ★★
Universal City          **Map 7**              (213) 760-4603

The Pang family objective in this magnificent restaurant overlooking Universal Studios is to bring the Chinese experience to the United States. Toward that end they have created a unique restaurant—the sixth of the family's—that is a celebration of Chinese art and cuisine. All the chefs are from Hong Kong and Taiwan as are many of the staff of 200 who can serve up to one thousand diners in the two-level restaurant. Custom design of the multi-million dollar establishment was under the supervision of Sing Bing Pang, whose creation could serve as an art museum if the tables were removed. There are over a thousand pieces of rosewood and teak furniture, 2,000 handcarved, painted and embroidered decorative panels and 16,000 square feet of gorgeous handwoven carpeting. The wall bronzes are breathtaking. There are small VIP rooms for intimate feasts, and the main rooms, big and busy, are somehow subdued in sound, a touch I appreciated. The food explores the art of Cantonese cooking, and Chef So is as respected here as he would be in China—he has his own private courtyard to which even the owners canot come without an invitation. The food is extremely reasonable—less than the price of admission to tourist attractions that are less colorful than the restaurant. Dinner can run under $10, but with wine and a cocktail, about $40 a couple would be reasonable. There are a few spicy dishes here, but the waiters will guide you through the long menu made simple by color illustrations and descriptions.

**Moderate.** Open seven days. Luncheon 11:30 a.m. to 2:30 p.m. Monday through Saturday. Dinner 5:30 to 10:30 p.m. Monday through Thursday; to 11:30 Friday, Saturday. Sunday from 11:30 a.m. to 10:30 p.m. Banquet facilities. Full bar. No reservations. View. Visa, MC, AX. Free valet parking. Casual to semi-dressy.

---

**FUTAMI**                                          **Japanese**
10650 Zelzah Street
Granada Hills          **Map 1**          (213) 368-1717

I hate the name of the street—Zelzah—and I swear it didn't prejudice me against this rather ordinary establishment. I suppose it's a luxury of sorts to have so many good

Japanese restaurants that we are able now to distinguish between the level they attain or, in this case, fail to attain. The hostess is lovely, but even Rae Jean Kashiwaya can do little to bring this to excitement except for the fresh broiled fish of the day.

**Inexpensive to moderate.** Open Tuesday through Sunday. Luncheon from 11:30 a.m. to 3:30 p.m. Dinner 4 to 10 p.m. Wine and beer only. Reservations recommended. Parking lot. No credit cards. Casual.

*To obtain the best results from this Guide, be sure to consult maps on the various Southern California areas in the front of the book.*

# g

## THE GALLEY STEAK HOUSE
2442 Main Street
Santa Monica     **Map 2**

**Steakhouse**
★
(213) 399-9727

Billed as "Santa Monica's oldest restaurant" (but how can that be? There must have been some restaurants there before 1934), this is an eccentric steakhouse with a no-nonsense approach to food (no baked potato, one salad dressing, no desserts, no soup) in an atmosphere they describe as "nautical." In addition to the one-to-two-pound steaks, there are steamed clams, lobster, and abalone; everything — despite the appearance — is well above average.

**Moderate.** Open seven days. Dinner from 5 to 11 p.m. Full bar. No reservations. No credit cards. Street parking. Casual.

## GARDEN ROOM
Century Plaza Hotel
Los Angeles **Map 8**

American/Continental
★
(213) 277-2000

One of the best places to have luncheon is this appropriately-named room. The crab and shrimp salad is especially good, and there is a flavorful Swiss fondue omelette and a thick cut of cold prime rib that are more than satisfying. Bruncheon includes champagne, choice of fruits (well-known and exotic), assorted pastries, and beverages. I'm partial to lox with scrambled eggs that have been lightly seasoned with herbs and onions. Breakfast and dinner are competently prepared and served.

**Moderate.** Open seven days. Breakfast from 7 to 10:45 a.m. Luncheon 11:30 a.m. to 2:30 p.m. Dinner 5:30 to 10:30 p.m. Entertainment. Dancing. Full bar. Reservations recommended. Garden view. All major credit cards; Western International card. Valet parking; validated self parking. Semi-dressy.

## THE GARDENS OF TAXCO
1113 North Harper Avenue
Los Angeles **Map 8**

Mexican
★
(213) 654-1746

"Our food here is quite different. If this is your first visit, we have a special dinner so you can taste a little of everything, just as if you were in Mexico City and a guest in my home." That's how we were greeted by the gracious waiter at The Gardens of Taxco on North Harper around the corner from the weirdsville porn part of Santa Monica Boulevard near the massage parlors of West Hollywood. Taxco is Frank Romero's dream fulfilled. He was formerly maître d' at the Biltmore in Santa Barbara and at the San Clemente Inn. "Somehow, some day, I wanted a place where people could taste the real foods of Mexico," Frank reminisces. And it works. Everything is made painstakingly from scratch and served on colorful tablecloths with floral napkins folded like fat pigeons at every place. The drinks (wine and beer only) are different, too; there's a glistening pitcher of pastel-pink "margarite" that is utterly refreshing and unlike anything of a similar name I've had yet, made with guava and other fresh fruits and a blend of wines. There is the house sangria, worlds apart from most, and the fine beers of Mexico. Depending on your dinner selection and mood, you may choose from seven appetizers ("margarita pie" is like a Mexican pizza with three different sauces, topped with melted cheese and guacamole) and eleven desserts (*empanadas de cajeta*, bananas in cream, flan and more).

**Inexpensive.** Open Tuesday through Sunday. Dinner served Sunday, Tuesday through Thursday from 4:30 to 11 p.m.; Friday and Saturday to midnight. Children's menu. Closed Thanksgiving, July 4, Christmas. Classical guitarist nightly. Wine and beer only. Reservations advised. Visa, MC, AX. Casual.

*In order to obtain the best results from this Guide, please consult "Tips on Dining Out" on page 21.*

## GATSBY'S

**Continental**

★

11500 San Vicente Boulevard
Brentwood **Map 8**

(213) 820-1476

God's favorite restaurant, or George Burns' as he is known on this planet, is a splendid one. Bill Rosen, his beautiful wife Helen (stage name, Helen Grayco), and brother Tony all work together as a team to come up with a beautiful, relaxing favorite of the stars. They've weathered some storms together and we did not give them a favorable review in the past, but they have emerged triumphant with a continental menu, great steaks, and the best karma (don't try to order it) in town. If you're lucky, Helen and some of her show business buddies might gather around the piano bar and give you a million dollars worth of entertainment. Even without that inducement, just the place and the prices—stars watch their budgets, too—make this a fine evening out.

**Moderate to expensive.** Open Monday through Saturday. Luncheon 11:30 a.m. to 3 p.m. weekdays. Banquet facilities. Dinner 5 to 11:30 p.m. Piano bar. Reservations recommended. All major credit cards. Valet parking. Semi-dressy.

---

## GENERAL LEE'S RESTAURANT

**Chinese**

★

475 Gin Ling Way (in New Chinatown)
Los Angeles **Map 7**

(213) 624-1825

This big, touristy restaurant serves basically Cantonese food and has been doing an agreeable job for nearly fifty years. There's little to get enthusiastic about, and one has the feeling that the enthusiasm that once won it recognition as an outstanding restaurant has given way to the pragmatism of the accounting department. A lot of the serving staff from Trader Vic's eat here, but they must know something I don't know (and be getting food that I didn't get).

**Moderate.** Open Tuesday through Sunday. Luncheon from 11:30 a.m. to 2 p.m. weekdays. Dinner 5 to 10 p.m. Tuesday through Thursday; to 11:30 Friday, Saturday; 4 to 10 Sunday. Banquet facilities. Closed Thanksgiving. Piano bar. Full bar. Reservations recommended on weekends for Mandarin Room (exclusive dining room with different menu). All major credit cards. Street parking; Broadway lots next to Chinatown. Semi-dressy.

---

## GENIO'S
1420 West Olive
Burbank     **Map 1**

Italian/American
★
(213) 848-0069

Eugene (Genio) Cecchini opened this exuberantly Italian restaurant in 1952, and at the age of 80 he still runs things with the help of son Marvin (manager), son Gene (chef), daughter Paula (hostess), grandsons Dave, Gregg, James, and John (busboys) — and his brother-in-law is not only the maintenance man but he painted the oil paintings in the dining room. There's something for everyone on the big menu, but if you've never tried *gnocchi* (potato dumplings, here served with meat balls and spaghetti sauce), this is the place. It's informal ("but we don't allow tank shirts or bare feet"), fun, a good value, and a particularly appropriate place to bring the kids. Prices for huge dinners are reasonable. Try the French fried potato skins with cocktails.

**Inexpensive.** Open Monday through Saturday from 11 a.m. to 10 p.m. Full bar. Visa, MC, AX, CB. Casual.

---

## GERARD'S FRENCH RESTAURANT
9814 Magnolia
Riverside     **Map 5**

French
★
(714) 687-4882

An old friend, Gerard Thiry, has developed a fine French restaurant in Riverside, that gustatory wasteland. We knew Gerard when his little restaurant, now in different hands, was the rage of Laguna, and the fact that he has chosen

Riverside bodes well for the epicurean future of this blighted territory. Nothing too innovative here but good duckling *à l' orange*, splendid onion soup, rabbit in red wine sauce and scallops are worthy dishes. No cocktails but an adequate wine list.

**Moderate.** Open seven days. Breakfast and lunch from 8 a.m. to 2:30 p.m.; dinner from 5 to 11 p.m. Closed summers. Reservations advised. All major credit cards. Parking lot. Casual.

---

## GINGERMAN
369 Bedford Drive
Beverly Hills　　　　**Map 8**

American/Continental
★
(213) 273-7585

When I asked Carroll O'Connor where he went wrong—meaning, how did a nice guy like you get in the restaurant business, he gave out with an Archie Bunker look and said, "For an investment and—it's a good one." It appears he's right, surprisingly, for celebrities find their most difficult roles as restaurateurs. Stars like O'Connor or the legion of others who have tried their hand at inn keeping will give $10,000 worth of their time for free, if it helps the gross, that's what this crazy business does to you. O'Connor noted the success of his partner Patrick O'Neil with the Gingerman in New York and was glad to get aboard this gleaming, relaxed, old New York decor restaurant-pub. Specialties are the specialty here with items like beef Wellington on Thursday, bouillabaisse on Friday, and lots of fresh fish. It's jammed at lunch and stays open with a supper menu—good to know—until 1 a.m. You'll see O'Connor around; he's not an absentee owner, and he had the sensitivity to have some of the French items translated from the original menu to more understandable — to most of us — English. Thank you, Carroll.

**Moderate.** Open seven days. Lunch from 11:30 a.m. to 4 p.m. Dinner from 5:30 to 10:30 p.m. Supper served from 10:30 p.m. to 1 a.m. Sunday brunch 11 a.m. to 3 p.m. Piano 9 p.m. to 1 a.m. Monday to Thursday, Saturday; jazz Sunday 4 to 7 p.m. Full bar. Reservations advised. Visa, MC, AX. Valet parking from 6 p.m. Casual to semi-dressy.

---

## GIN LING
### Chinese
3644 South Bristol Street      ★★
Santa Ana    **Map 6**    (714) 751-4666

The Gin Ling restaurant in Santa Ana has attracted a great deal of interest and may well be the long overdue important Chinese restaurant in Orange County. The entire kitchen staff travels every day by company van from Chinatown to assure the kind of competent help a fine Chinese restaurant requires. Every time I've passed or visited this shopping center location there has been a line waiting for their tables. The menu is Chinese-electic, a refreshing departure from those authoritarian restaurants that proclaim themselves Szechwan or Cantonese. Gin Ling combines the best of both. Luncheon is priced from $2.75 but the dinner explores the stratosphere of Chinese cooking and the prices range to $140 banquet for eight to ten people (bird's nest soup with crab meat. Peking duck, chicken with Chinese greens in white sauce, steak Chinese style, sauteed shrimp and scallops, squab, black mushrooms in oyster sauce, sweet and sour whole fish, yang Chow fried rice and dessert). The Chinese perfected the art of communal dining, and the banquet facilities here are impressive.

**Moderate.** Open seven days. Luncheon served weekdays from 11:30 a.m. to 3 p.m. Dinner Monday through Saturday 4 to 10:30 p.m.; Sunday to 9:30. Closed Labor Day, Thanksgiving, Christmas. Full bar. Reservations advised. All major credit cards. Wheelchair access. Valet parking. Semi-dressy.

---

*Please be sure to consult "Tipping Made Easy" on page 25 of this Guide.*

---

# GIO'S

**Continental**

★

7574 Sunset Boulevard

Los Angeles　　**Map 8**　　(213) 876-1120

I like Gio's (pronounced Jee-oh's), the continental restaurant with Brazilian dishes. Located on the site of L'Auberge in West Hollywood, it is more comfortable, with less anxiety, than its predecessor. I had a spectacular new dish, escargots in pasta. The escargots were plump, the spaghetti *al dente*, and the grated fresh cheese added zest to a dish that was invented as a compromise between proprietor Gio Casara— he wanted snails—and his wife who hungered for pasta. Perhaps the highlight of a memorable rainy evening was the entrée from Brazil called *peixada a Brasileira* (I just eat it, I don't pronounce it). It consisted of lobster, shrimp, scallops, red snapper, tomatoes, bell peppers, and coconut milk on spicy, firm rice. The *xin-xin de Galinha*, chicken in a sauce made with coconut milk, cashews and dry shrimp, may be the best moderately priced adventure in town. Italian touches include a fine chicken *cacciatori*, chicken *Romanesca* (with tomato, cream sauce and artichokes), *tortellini*, and an unusual dish, *pasta al pesto Genovese*, (nuts, fresh basi, olive oil and your choice of pasta). There's lobster thermidor; scampi prepared with apples, champagne and shallots; and grilled salmon with a bouquet of fresh vegetables. All entrées are accompanied by salad, vegetables and hot rolls. Everthing we had rated excellent, even the desserts, with an unlikely avocado mousse and a terrific Grand Marnier soufflé that has to be ordered well in advance. The wine list is ample. Decor is sort of European country inn, with dark wood beams, whitewashed walls, old prints, copper and brass. The main room, divided by washed brick and iron grille, has comfortable brown leather booths.

**Moderate.** Open seven days. Luncheon from 11:30 a.m. to 3:30 p.m. weekdays. Dinner 5:30 p.m. to 1 a.m. Entertainment. Full bar. Reservations recommended. Patio. All major credit cards. Parking in rear. Casual.

# GIOVANNI'S
**Italian**
★

922 Williamson Avenue
Fullerton     **Map 6**                    (714)526-5561

The role of the restaurant in our society is changing. As
supermarket costs go up, with both husbands and wives at
work all day, the restaurant has become not just a place for
special occasions or quick snacks, it has become a necessity.
Small take-out/sit-down operations have taken over the
function of food retailers. They can buy for less and can
prepare entire meals, many of them excellent, more cheaply
than one can prepare them himself. A fine example of this
concept is Giovanni's in Fullerton; they've been turning out
homemade Italian food for nearly two decades, and now many
of the people in the area depend on them. Beginning as a
pizzeria, they took over adjoining storefronts and broadened
their menu to include a large selection of grinders (sandwiches
of sliced cold meats, cheeses, onion, tomatoes, and pepperoncini with warm vinegar and olive oil dressing on a hot
Italian roll), roast chicken and ribs. You can phone ahead to
have everything ready to go, but the fun is coming here in
parties of four, trying different things and sitting at tables in
the middle of what appears to be a grocery store — shelves
of imported canned goods, pastas, a long deli counter and a
refrigerator with beer, wine, and soft drinks. There's a unique
honor system here. After placing and receiving your order,
you take it to your table and pick out anything you want to
drink. Then on the way out you tell them what you had and
they charge you for it — a nice throwback to less cynical
times when people trusted each other. The pizza combinations are on medium-thick bread-style crust, but my favorite
item is *cannoli*, a wonderful dessert of ricotta cheese with
bits of candied fruit, served in a crisp pastry tube. I find the
place warm, friendly, and happy, and the prices inexpensive.

**Inexpensive to moderate.** Open Monday through Saturday

from 11 a.m .to 9 p.m. Children may order half order dinners. Closed major holidays. Wine and beer only. No reservations. No credit cards. Parking lot. Casual.

---

## GITANJALI                                          Indian
414 North La Cienega Boulevard                    ★
West Hollywood        **Map 8**        (213) 657-2117

The family is the attraction for me here—always attentive and eager to please. The food is better than it used to be and tends toward the more sophisticated *tandoori* and *tikka* specialties like marinated chicken, lamb or shrimp. *Masala* and *vindaloo* dishes and the Kathmandu chicken sautéed in butter and spices are all enjoyable. There's a much better than average wine list and beer—that perfect accompaniment to spicy food—is available in many varieties.

**Moderate.** Open seven days. Dinner from 6 to 11 p.m. Catering and take-out. Private party facilities. Wine and beer only. Reservations required on weekends. All major credit cards. Casual.

---

## GIULIO'S RESTAURANT              Northern Italian
809 Thomas Avenue                                   ★
Pacific Beach                          (714) 488-9126

If you haven't noticed Giulio's in San Diego, it's set back from the street on Thomas Avenue and it's worth searching for. An old style fill-em-up Italian *ristorante*, this one has some touches of flair along with the garlic. Veal is offered in twelve variations and the saltimbocca is as good here as at restaurants that would charge three times the price. The antique furniture is a pleasant variation from the checkered tablecloths and candles of most such places and the Northern Italian cooking may be as good as San Diego can produce.

**Moderate.** Open seven days. Dinner from 5 to 10 p.m. Sunday through Thursday; to 11 Friday, Saturday. Private party facilities. Closed Thanksgiving, Christmas, Easter. Full bar. Reservations recommended, especially weekends. All major credit cards. Valet parking. Semi-dressy.

---

## GIUSEPPEI!                                                    Italian
8256 Beverly Boulevard                                              ★★
Los Angeles        **Map 8**                        (213) 653-8025

To dream the impossible dream—for a maitre d'—is to have your own restaurant. Guiseppi Ballisario was the maitre d' at Scandia and managed to inspire a number of his patrons to back him in the ultimate. The ultimate table ware, silverplate and crystal. Designed by Juan Forteza, the skylights sets off an artful continental/California decor that is both gracious and efficient. From Scandia they borrowed an appetizer: *boccanini di aragosta* (lobster tail cooked with a cold sour cream and caviar sauce). The pastas are homemade and the linguini with *scungilli* is spicy and good. The wine list is gargantuan—too big—but they are reasonably priced for this kind of a poshery. The service is incredible. The Captains and waiters and Guiseppi would self-immolate if that contributed to your evenings enjoyment.

**Expensive.** Open Monday through Saturday. Luncheon served 11:30 a.m. to 3 p.m. weekdays. Dinner Monday through Saturday 6 to 11 p.m. Full bar. Reservations necessary. Visa, MC, AX, CB. Valet parking. Dressy.

---

*To obtain the best results from this Guide, consult "How to Use this Guide" on page 27.*

## GIUSEPPI'S
Agua Caliente #700
Tijuana

**Mexican/Italian/Continental**
★★
(70-668) 385-1910

## GIUSEPPI'S AT 5TH STREET
Calle 5 A
#1738 y Niños Héroes
Tijuana

(70-668) 385-0577

## GIUSEPPI'S DE LA MESA
Baja California #100 A
y Boulevard Diaz Ordaz
Tijuana

(70-668) 386-8751

## GIUSEPPI'S PLAZA
Calle 3 A
Estacionamiento America #19
Tijuana

(70-668) 385-4777

## GIUSEPPI'S DE ROSARITO
Avenida Juarez #300
Rosarito, Baja California

(70-668) 382-1261

## GIUSEPPI'S
Revolucion 914
(between 5th and 6th street)
Tijuana

(70-668) 388-2993

Giuseppi's, a Mexican/ Italian/continental beauty, is on the road to Agua Caliente. Giuseppi's is clean, attractive, innovative and inexpensive. Their own creations deserve attention, dishes like *calabresa brochet*: small rolls of prime beef wrapped with bacon and stuffed with sharp cheese. Chicken *a la Saverios* is prepared with Marsala wine, home-cured olives and onions and includes soup, good salad, pasta and hot garlic rolls. The back room of this particular location — there are eight in all — has what is easily the most spectacular mural I've seen in the West. It is a canal scene of Venice around the 15th century and is authentic to every detail including colors, clothing worn by the pedestrians and the apartments (you can look in the windows). It surrounds the large room and took three years to research and paint. The fact that fluorescent paints were used to transform the daytime panorama into gradual evening with flickering lights probably sounds tacky, but it really works here and it is wonderful to watch. There's a complete list of pasta, all made of the premium Durum semolina, high in protein and low in calories. A pizza kitchen occupies one room with some exotic combinations on the menu. The wine list is limited but good.

**Inexpensive.** Open seven days. Monday through Saturday from noon to 11 p.m., Sunday 1 p.m. to 10 p.m. Closed Christmas, New Year's. Full bar. Reservations required for large parties. Visa, MC, AX. Public parking. Casual.

---

## GLACIER GOURMET
**Mediterranean Fruit Ices**
★

2915 West Magnolia Boulevard
Burbank    **Map 1**    (213) 849-4616

The news is that Glacier Gourmet now offers more than "the best fruit ice in the universe." Mediterranean sandwiches turn this taste temple of dessert-dom into a cheerful luncheon stop. The storefront eatery is sprinkled with ice cream tables (appropriate, since they make their own ice cream too). There you can relax and enjoy the *empanadas* (Argentinian meat pies), pita sandwiches or submarine *pizziolas*... before the star attraction... the desserts. The walls are adorned with photos of famous glacé eaters and newspaper clippings that vainly attempt to describe how divine the desserts really are. You simply have to taste their pure and savory specialties made from natural produce. This is a true "old country" art form, carried on by proprietors Vic and Mae Tortolano (whose names sound like one of their desserts). Take your pick from totally fat-free ices to tortoni with 40% (!) cream. The tortoni comes in six flavors, including anisette, strawberry, rum and cappuccino. The pina colada sorbet transports me to the Caribbean. Scooplets are available to eat in, bulk take-home packs are available, and for show off entertaining there are fruit ices frozen in their natural shells. Some of their fantasies are rum spumoni loaf, *torta semifredda alla strega* and chablis glacé. And there are boozy ices galore. Think of a fruit in season, and they ice it. Glacier Gourmet supplies some of our finest restaurants and gourmet markets, but why not go to the creators? They love to tell you how they do it, while you sample the latest fresh fruit ice. Naturally, their theme is "Have an Ice Day."   *Jackie Joseph*

**Moderate to expensive.** Open Monday through Friday 9:30 a.m. to 6:30 p.m.; Saturday 10 a.m. to 5 p.m.

---

## GLADSTONE'S 4 FISH
17300 Pacific Coast Highway
Pacific Palisades          **Map 2**

**Fish**
★★
GL-4-FISH

When Bob Morris gets excited I get excited, because excitement is the essence his restaurants from Gladstone's 4 Fish to R.J.'s For Ribs in Beverly Hills. Morris seems to break all the rules of the restaurant business, but whatever he's cooking with works because his places are jammed even in these uncertain times. His latest and most ambitious project is to move Gladstone's 4 Fish to the site of the burned-out Jetty's restaurant in Pacific Palisades where Sunset meets the ocean and his parking lot. Gladstone's was named in that innocent era when the first two digits of a telephone number were the first two letters of colorful words. There were, among many, DRexel for mid-Wilshire, CRestview or BRadshaw for Beverly Hills and Gladstone for Hollywood—where Bob happened to be living at the time. When he was pressed for an instant decision to come up with a name for the sign painters who were waiting at the restaurant he glanced at the phone. *Voilà!*

I met Morris on a cold, cloudy day. He took me on the cook's tour fairly bubbling with enthusiasm. "Look," he said, "We found this neat old fishing dory but it was too big so I cut it in half. One part is upside down over the entrance for the canopy and the other half is our host's stand." The place is nautical (but nice). Ships' wheels are covered with glass and made into cocktail tables in the lounge. Floors are made of pegged deck planking covered with sawdust.

There are four tanks for live lobster and rock crab and a glassed-in room where customers can watch their dinner weighed and dropped into the boiling pots. There are even steps up to a small platform so that children may watch as well. The luxuriously appointed President's Room will seat 14 for private dinners in a dining salon much like that of an extravagant yacht. It is separated from the public areas by a jeweled and beveled 1850 stained glass window.

Gladstone's breakfasts, served from 7 a.m., will include a wide range of omelettes, and a "fisherman breakfast" of eggs, a half pound of ham or swordfish and potatoes sautéed with their skins. Luncheon and dinner will feature the Morris familiars: ribs and chili and steaks along with the seafood.

**Moderate.** Open seven days. Breakfast and lunch from 7 a.m. to 3:30 p.m. every day. Dinner to 11 p.m.; Friday, Saturday to midnight. Full bar open to 1 a.m. Closed Chrismas. Reservations accepted after 5 p.m. only. Patio. View. Visa, MC. Valet parking. Casual.

*In order to obtain the best results from this Guide, be sure to read the French, German, Italian and Oriental menu translators on page 705 to 710 of this Guide.*

# GOLDEN BOWL                              Chinese
16733 Ventura Boulevard
Encino      **Map 1**                   (213) 995-3500

Somehow Chinese restaurants rarely seem romantic, and many share certain weaknesses like tiny highball glasses, tacky tableware and lime green vinyl everything. Not so at the Golden Bowl in Encino, a restaurant with a name like a take-out but an atmosphere of elegance.

Once the smashing, widely-heralded Concorde Restaurant that featured Brazilian food and South American pizzazz (Brazilian fare has never made it for long in the States). The Golden Bowl has retained the plush interior of the former establishment, soothing lighting and gentle colors, but the personality of the place is subdued. Smart. Chic. Romantic.

Perhaps, most important, the food is splendid. The menu provides set dinners ($9.95) that are not tokens reminiscent of the chop suey days. These dinners are carefully selected and prepared by chef Ching Yee Cheung, who has received the "Best Chef" award from the *Washington Post*. The $10.95 "Bowl Dinner" includes General Tso's chicken, *kung pao* shrimp, crispy roast duck, shredded pork with Peking sauce and a special beef dish along with a platter of appetizers, soup, tea and the obligatory fortune and almond cookies. For the more adventurous, the long à la carte menu lists and explains a variety of dishes that range from my favorite, Hunan Chow San Shin ($6.95) (tender beef, shrimp and chicken sautéed in wine and garlic sauce) to *moo shu*, scallops with spicy sauce, and sesame chicken.

At luncheon he has brought a Szechwan chicken salad to its highest art form, and, at ($4.25), it is ample. Bar drinks are generous and well served. Waiters are gracious and helpful, and even the fortune in my cookie sounded a little less inane than most. Ther is a good wine list, but you would be well advised to order Wan Fu, a wine especially prepared to accompany Oriental food.

**Moderate.** Open Monday through Friday 11 a.m. to 10 p.m.; Saturday and Sunday 4 to 10:30 p.m. Closed Thanksgiving. Full bar. Reservations accepted. Visa, MC, AX. Parking lot. Casual.

---

## GOLDEN GOOSE PUB

**Seafood/Mediterranean**
★

3809 Pacific Coast Highway
Torrance    **Map 2**                    (213) 375-9122

Owner Paul Marinkovich is a creative chef, and that's what makes this establishment worth visiting. He's at his best with seafood (he visits the San Pedro fisherman's wharf twice a day to get fresh fish and is on call at any hour of the 24 to bid on an especially desirable catch). Grilled mahi mahi and charcoal-broiled and marinated Catalina blue perch are among his specialties. The *cioppino* is not the bland tomato soup stock and crazy mixed-up squid of other restaurants; here it is the hearty, spicy peasant stock, a stew of shell and fin fish, perfectly served in a base of herbs and tomato and wine. The blackboard in front lists the fresh fish of the day, although the good cooking doesn't stop with the take from the ocean. Charcoal broiled steak is also featured. A number of Yugoslavian wines — a reflection of the proprietor's origin — are priced reasonably. There is a cocktail lounge with entertainment that seems — to us — to be entirely unnecessary, but obviously fills someone's need.

**Moderate.** Open Monday through Sunday. Dinner 5 to 10:30 p.m. Monday through Friday; to 11:30 p.m. weekends. Full bar. Reservations advised. All major credit cards. Parking in rear. Casual.

---

*To obtain the best results from this Guide, be sure to consult maps on the various Southern California areas in the front of the book.*

## GOLDEN PAGODA

**Chinese**

950 Mei Ling Way

New Chinatown    **Map 7**    (213) 628-4244

This is Chinatown at its best and its most mediocre, the two standards being not far apart. Nothing in this familiar Cantonese menu is bad — but nothing is really good or great, either. It's tourist-oriented; and if I had to pick, it might be the foil-wrap chicken, golden fried shrimps, or spareribs.

**Inexpensive to moderate.** Open seven days from 11:45 a.m. to 10 p.m. Children's menu. Entertainment in bar. Full bar. Reservations recommended for parties of 8 or more. Visa, MC. Street parking. Casual.

---

## GOLDEN TEMPLE OF CONSCIOUS COOKERY

**Vegetarian**

7910 West 3rd Street    ★

Los Angeles    **Map 8**    (213) 655-1891

A sincere attempt to merge the spiritual with the culinary in this stunning vegetarian restaurant kitty cornered (okay, Jack Smith?) across from the Farmer's Market. This food is not without its blandishments. French appetizers, stir-fried vegetables, and pastas with herb sauce are well prepared and served but most of the dishes seem to come from India, the Middle East, and Mexico. Fruit and vegetable juices are, of course, fresh, and there is a delectable array of non-alcoholic beverages from shakes to banana "aura," a blend of orange juice and banana. Even the desserts are something special: "papayan sunset" is fresh strawberries, served with rich papaya ice cream, whipped cream, and nuts. There are other Conscious Cookeries in other states and countries from Alaska to Georgia to the Netherlands and all operate with the same gentle philosophy that makes this one a success.

**Moderate.** Open Monday through Saturday. Luncheon served

from 11:30 a.m. to 4:30 p.m. Dinner 5:30 to 10 p.m.
Entertainment Friday night. Non-alcoholic cocktails. No reservations. Patio. Visa, MC. Parking lot. Casual to semi-dressy.

---

## THE GOOD EARTH                           Health Food
12712 Ventura Boulevard                               ★
Encino          **Map 1**                   (213) 986-9990

1002 Westwood Boulevard                               ★
Westwood        **Map 8**                   (213) 208-8215

23397 Mulholland
Woodland Hills       **Map 1**              (213) 888-6300

21 West Canon Perdido
Santa Barbara                               (805) 962-4463

More than likely the mention of nutritious food conjures
up the thought of a parsnip parfait consumed at a bleak
counter in a health food store. Well, not anymore.

The Woodland Hills location has hanging plants, lots of
wood and a general feeling of warmth and spaciousness.
While care has been taken to avoid refined sugar and over-
processed foods, one bite of their homebaked whole grain
rolls asks the question: Can anything that tastes so good
really be good for you?

Breakfasts include omelettes, sour-dough cakes and hot
or cold granola cereal. At lunch the sandwiches are made
with freshly-baked ten-grain bread or there are interesting
salads and the Good Earth's burrito or tostada.

Dinner is reasonably priced. My favorite was the country
French lasagne—spinach pasta, three cheeses and a white-
and-red sauce with almond slivers—not your usual lasagne,
healthy or no. Other choices include Zhivago's beef stroganoff, curried chicken or shrimp. Malaysian cashew beef and
more. Fresh juices and shakes are provided along with beer

and a not-so-good homemade wine sold by the carafe. They're also a bit weak on the desserts.

**Moderate.** Open seven days. Breakfast from 8 to 11 a.m. Full lunch and dinner menu 11 a.m. to 11 p.m. Sunday through Thursday; to midnight Friday, Saturday. Sunday brunch 9 a.m. to 3 p.m. Wine and beer. No reservations. Visa, MC. Parking. Casual. Hours differ at each location.

---

## GRAND AVE. BAR

Continental
★★

510 Grand Avenue
Los Angeles　　**Map 7**　　　　　　　(213) 624-1011

Show me the interior of some restaurants and I can tell you who the operators are. Contemporary artwork here by Jim Dine, Helmut Jahn and Michael Graves; a sensuous long marble topped bar, Mies van der Roh velvet chairs could only be those folks at the Biltmore and their competent v.p. in charge of food and beverage, Bernard Jacoupy. GAB, as it is called, will be where the elite meet to eat (with apologies to Duffy's Tavern). A luscious cold buffet is served at luncheon with a great hors d'oeuvres list. There's a disc jockey who provides varied mood music for dancing on a marble dance floor and high tech lighting that sets this place apart. It's got style.

**Moderate.** Open Monday through Friday 11:30 a.m. to 1:30 a.m.; Saturday 6:30 p.m. to 1:30 a.m. Luncheon served 1:30 to 3 p.m. Entertainment. Full bar. Reservations required. All major credit cards. Valet parking $2 from 7 p.m. Semi-dressy to dressy.

---

*In order to obtain the best results from this Guide, please consult "Tips on Dining Out" on page 21.*

## GRAND STAR RESTAURANT        Chinese
943 Sun Mun Way        ★★
New Chinatown
Los Angeles     **Map 7**       (213) 626-2285

This graceful restaurant started life as a penny arcade operated by Him Gin Quon, back in 1939. Sons Frank and Wally helped create a family corporation with their 80-year-old mother and the building was improved to become a modern and tasteful addition to the restaurants of New Chinatown. There are reasonably-priced multi-course dinners but it is the à la carte selection that offers the enchantment. For winter melon soup a whole melon is hollowed out and steamed with chicken broth; the contrasting textures and flavors are especially satisfying. The Mongolian beef is marinated in wine; the crystal shrimp is succulent and the sweet and sour whole fish is an artistic achievement. Flaming clams with black bean sauce is a specialty and the piano bar is the best in the area. This restaurant has too much dignity to pander to the tourists' tastes; it would be a fine restaurant whatever the location.

**Moderate.** Open seven days. Monday through Thursday 11:30 a.m. to 11:30 p.m.; to midnight Friday; Saturday noon to midnight; Sunday noon to 11 p.m. Piano bar. Full bar. Reservations recommended. All major credit cards. Validated parking. Semi-dressy.

---

*For best results, consult "How to Use This Guide" on page 27.*

## THE GREAT AMERICAN FOOD
## AND BEVERAGE COMPANY American

9th and Wilshire
Santa Monica     **Map 2**     (213) 451-1411

8500 Santa Monica Boulevard
West Hollywood     **Map 8**     (213) 652-9594

The Great American Disaster might be a more appropriate name for this post-funk, youth-oriented, semi-organic restaurant that started with some good ideas, one of them being a "feast" that a party of two or more could order with whole chickens, ribs, pineapples, bananas, and other good things heaped on a gigantic platter. The problem was that this mass was virtually inedible and bore an unfortunate resemblance to an accumulation of garbage. Since then we've tried the other items and have found nothing that was (a) worth the money or (b) particularly appetizing. Entertainment is good, however, and some of the help are nice people.

**Moderate to expensive.** Open seven days. Hours vary according to location. Closed Christmas and New Year's. Reservations Santa Monica only. Wine and beer only. Full bar in West Hollywood. Parking lot. Visa, MC. Entertainment. Casual.

## THE GREAT SCOT English/Prime Rib
2980 Los Feliz Boulevard ★★
Los Angeles     **Map 7**     (213) 664-0228

No one operates theme restaurants on the scale of Lawry's, and their experience in providing a great atmosphere, good food, and crowd control pays off in this rambling inn, where the waitresses wear Scottish plaid, and there are upholstered chairs in front of the fireplace. Pennants hang from the high-beamed ceiling, and many of the chairs suggest thrones (a subtle ploy to the subconscious). The food is uniformly good. Dishes like roast sirloin of beef with Yorkshire pudding and skewered beef are an old story at Lawry's; the service is intelligent and attentive.

**Inexpensive to moderate.** Open seven days. Luncheon from 11 a.m. to 3 p.m. weekdays. Ale and sandwich bar Saturday 11 a.m. to 4 p.m. Dinner 5 to 10 p.m. Monday through Thursday; to 11 Friday, Saturday; 4 to 10 Sunday. Sunday brunch 10:30 a.m. to 2:30. Closed Thanksgiving, Christmas. Full bar. Reservations accepted. Visa, MC, AX. Parking lot. Casual.

---

## GREENBLATT'S
8017 Sunset Boulevard
Hollywood          **Map 8**

Deli
★★
(213) 656-0606

Boy, do I remember Greenblatt's. As a young and hungry writer I used to stand at their counter and gobble down lean corned beef sandwiches and good dill pickles for breakfast. The starlets (Marilyn Monroe and Kim Novak among them) would come tottering in around early afternoon for a nutrition break on their way to Victor's, a cocktail bar that used to be located a half block east on Sunset where Walter Gross played his "Tenderly" at the piano bar to the mingling singles. Roy Kavin was my friend then—he's been operating Greenblatt's since 1952—and his fascination for wine made him the maven of the celebrity set. *Everyone* sent out to Greenblatt's for homemade deli and wine and their truck, parked in front of your house/apartment/pad was a status symbol. Roy was a trusting soul who papered his display case (in those early days) with the bounced checks of the famous, near famous and infamous.

Years later, driving down Sunset, I noticed that Greenblatt's had moved to the center of the block. "Aha," I thought, "another guy's cashed in on the big bucks." I was wrong.

The deli is as delectable as ever, although now it is a full on restaurant, different only from most in that you place and receive your orders at the counter (for take out or sit-down). The food is good—ribs and ham are prepared in special smokers on the premises—and Diane Kavin keeps an eye on things and protects her sources of supply with the ferocity of a mother hen. The wine cellar, still quietly catering and advising the real celebrities from Palm Springs to Santa Barbara now offers one of the largest selections of wine for sale in the United States. It's still a favorite with the show biz crowd and still very special.

**Moderate.** Open seven days 9 a.m. to 2 a.m. No alcoholic beverages served. No reservations. Visa, MC. Parking lot. Casual.

---

## THE GREENHOUSE
**Continental/French**
5900 Wilshire Boulevard
★
Los Angeles     **Map 8**     (213) 933-8333

This first opened as a monument to the taste and wealth of former owners Jerry Magnin and Larry Mindell (they operate the superb Chianti). Unfortunately, a series of problems not the least of which was the acoustics (it really did sound as though you were seated in the timpani section of the Boston Pops) caused this beauty spot to change faces. Now operated by R.M.A. West which seems to specialize in improving things, the emphasis is still on luncheon—they're part of a high rise complex—with the Cobb salad, a sandwich board and about a dozen entrées, but dinner's the real challenge. The food is really good if you can avoid the embarrassment of the stage happenings with fresh vegetables, fresh fish, and good daily specials. All juices for the bar drinks are freshly squeezed, a thoughtful touch that we'd like to see imitated by other restaurants with bars. There are fresh loaves of pumper-nickel and rye, free hors d'ouevres during cocktail hour and imaginative hors d'oeuvres like potato skins and marinated chicken dumsticks for a small fee.

**Moderate.** Open Monday through Friday. Breakfast from 7:30 to 11 a.m. Lunch from 11:30 a.m. to 4 p.m. Dinner served from 4 to 9 p.m. Full bar. Reservations advised. All major credit cards. Underground parking. Casual.

---

## GREEN JADE
### 747 North Broadway
**Los Angeles**    **Map 7**

Hunan
★★
(213) 680-1528

Some years ago, a small storefront restaurant called the Hunan opened in San Francisco. Within a few weeks, this restaurant had lines of famished souls stretching around the block. The reason, aside from the extraordinarily low prices, was that the Hunan's cooking was so fiery as to make even the peppers of Szechwan seem like pablum by comparison. This was a cuisine marked by its use of smoked ham and smoked duck and peppers so potent they would make you sweat on the clammiest of San Francisco nights.

Our local Hunan is no relation to the one in San Francisco, and neither is the Green Jade, which grew out of some Hunan staff members striking out on their own. But the Green Jade is a wonderful restaurant nonetheless, even if its dishes aren't "10"s, hotnesswise. There are plenty of "9"s at the Green Jade, and I've tried quite a few of them. There are, for instance, both the spicy bean curd and the Szechwan bean curd, which make the best use I can possibly imagine for bean curd, outside of using the normally bland stuff as a grout. There are a pair of pungently hot fish dishes— steamed fish with bean sauce and steamed fish with broad bean sauce—both of which raise the normally prosaic sea bass to the level of manna from Hunan. There are mythically hot dishes using gammon (an old-fashioned word for bacon) and using whelk (an old-fashioned word for sea snails), and there's a very fine abalone with cinnamon sauce that, strangely, doesn't taste all that much of cinnamon. There are also a few non-hot dishes. I wouldn't know much about them. I always go for the hottest of the hot. *M.S.*

**Moderate to expensive.** Open seven days for luncheon from 11:30 a.m. to 3 p.m. Dinner from 4:30 to 9 p.m. Beer and wine only. Reservations essential. Visa, MC. Parking lot. Casual.

---

# GREEN LEAVES
727 North Broadway
Los Angeles **Map 7**

Chinese/Thai
★
(213) 626-4929

One of the great frustrations of the Chinese restaurant maven are those items that appear on menus, and sometimes on walls, in Chinese. The maven *knows* that those are the most incredible dishes in the history of the civilized world... but can't translate a single syllable. And Chinese restaurant waiters are never willing to tell you what those funny little ideographs will taste like on your plate. How unwilling? Let me tell you.

A full 26 of the items on the menu at Green Leaves are in Chinese (which means more than half the menu). I asked my waiter if he could translate some of them for me. He told me, "You won't like those dishes... they contain medicine that are for Chinese people only... you order from the English side." So much for the mysteries of the menu. Luckily, there are enough wonderful dishes on the English side of the menu to make for several terrific Taiwanese meals. Taiwanese food appears to be very different from the food of the Chinese Mainland. The eggrolls, for instance, have soft, thin shells that taste almost steamed, and are filled with a most peculiar sweetish rice packed around pork chunks. Nothing at all like those crispy eggrolls we were weaned on.

There's a strong reliance on seafood at Green Leaves, though nothing as overwhelming as the seafood at the nearby Mon Kee. But the salty, spicy shrimp with garlic is a dish I would crawl on my knees across the downtown interchange for: poetry in about a dozen medium-sized, crispy shrimp, very salty and covered with a thick layer of finely-chopped garlic, that's been cooked ever so slightly. This dish could make Taiwan more popular than Mexico hereabouts.

Add to the salty, spicy shrimp a plate of plump, succulent sauteed oysters in a hotcha-hotcha black bean sauce, perhaps some squid fish balls and an order of red cooked bean curd, and you not only have quite a feast, but also a great sampling of the foodstuffs of Taiwan.  *M.S.*

**Moderate.** Open Thursday through Tuesday from 11 a.m. to 9 p.m. No alcoholic beverages. Reservations accepted. Patio. No credit cards. Validated parking under Food Center. Casual.

---

## GRISWOLD'S INDIAN HILL     Continental/American
555 West Foothill Boulevard                                    ★
Claremont        **Map 6**                       (714) 626-2411

Griswold's Indian Hill restaurant, part of the complex that includes Griswold's Smorgasbord and Casa Ramon, was opened to accommodate the need for a more luxurious operation. Early-California decor, less plastic than most such interiors, provides an attractive setting for the imaginative cuisine. Dinners include such entrées as brochette of seafood Wellington, stuffed Spanish shrimp, veal Oscar with béarnaise, along with the expected steak. Rack of lamb "epicure" is a particularly good value. Luncheon features the "beef bar" and such sandwiches as pastrami with Camembert served with apple slices, or La Granada — ham, turkey breast, Ortega chili, cheese, avocado, and bacon, served on sheepherder's bread. Indian Hill serves a lavish buffet as well. Sunday brunch includes champagne, iced juices, exotic fruit, crab Newburg, lox, eggs Benedict, steak and eggs, shrimp and bacon rarebit, plus dessert. Sunday buffet-dinner — one of the best in Southern California — is served with some unusual touches — steamed octopus, pickled shrimp, gazpacho — along with the usual entrée items. Everything is included in the reasonable price, even the wines and dessert.

**Moderate.** Open seven days. Breakfast Monday through Saturday from 7 to 11:30 a.m. Luncheon from 11:30 a.m. to 2:30 p.m. Dinner MOnday through Saturday from 5:30 to 10 p.m. Gourmet banquet Sunday from 5 to 9 p.m. Sunday brunch from 10 a.m. to 2 p.m. Early evening dining special between 5:30 and 7 p.m. Banquet facilities. Full bar. Patio. Visa, MC, AX. Parking lot. Casual.

---

## GRISWOLD'S SMORGASBORD                    Scandinavian
Interstate No. 10 at Ford Street offramp
Redlands          **Map 5**                    (714) 793-2158

At Griswold's Smorgasbord the American preoccupation with numbers is apparent all around. There are signs above the line comparing the number of meals served that day with a year ago and revealing "served to date." The restaurant attracts such throngs because it is both inexpensive and good. There were sixteen fresh salads set out with six hot dishes. On the theory that one man's meat may be another man's *poisson*, the entrées are changed frequently. Smorgasbord is not properly appreciated by most Americans. Somehow there is a feeling that going back to the buffet several times is a disgrace. As a result, plates are piled high with such incompatibles as marnated herring, fruit tart, sliced beef with gravy, and creamed corn. The intermingling of the juices can be exotic, if not exactly palatable. To avoid this, three or more trips are usually in order—salad, entrée, dessert—and you are encouraged to return as often as you like. The huge adjoining bakery offers the largest array of cakes, pies, cookies, and breads (over thirty kinds) you are apt to find anywhere. To cope with the sometimes frantic demands—as many as 853 pies in one day—Griswold's will purchase a farmer's entire crop for a season's baking. Griswold's in Claremont really started about 1909. It was then that Professor George Griswold opened a roadside stand to sell fruit and jams. The property grew to include a marmalade factory, bakery, smorgasbord restaurant, art exhibits, shopping center, and Griswold's Indian Hill, a major restaurant.

**Inexpensive.** Open Monday through Saturday. Breakfast from 7 to 11 a.m. Luncheon from 11:30 a.m. to 4 p.m. Monday through Saturday. Dinner Monday through Thursday 5 to 8:30 p.m.; Friday, Saturday to 9 p.m.; Sunday noon to 8:30 p.m. Banquet facilities. No alcoholic beverages. Reservations accepted. Patio. Visa, MC, AX. Parking lot. Casual.

---

## GUADALAJARA INN                                  Mexican
4466 East Gage                                          ★
Bell        **Map 3**                          (213) 773-9882

Specialty dishes prepared on weekends bring in homesick Latinos by the hundreds—try the *costillas en salsa negra* (spare ribs in black chili sauce) or the *carne adobada* (pork steak marinated for 36 hours in chili sauce). There are the usual dishes but the friendliness and hospitality and the immaculate appearance is that of a good Mexico City family restaurant. Augustin Delgadillo knows good food, he was a captain with La Famiglia in Beverly Hills, Scandia and Chianti. Now he's sharing it with the folks who couldn't afford it.

**Inexpensive.** Open seven days Monday through Saturday from 11 a.m. to 10 p.m.; Sunday 10 a.m. to 8 p.m. Closed Thanksgiving, Christmas. Wine and beer only. No reservations. Visa, MC. Parking in rear. Casual.

---

*In order to obtain the best results from this Guide, please consult "Tips on Dining Out" on page 21.*

## GULLIVER'S American/English
18482 MacArthur Place ★★
Irvine (714) 833-8411

13181 Mindanao Way ★★
Marina del Rey **Map 2** (213) 821-8866

One of the most successful of the Old Britain restaurants is
Gulliver's in Irvine. From the moment you enter Gulliver's,
everything is meticulously planned. The atmosphere, roughly
from the time of Jonathan Swift, is a kaleidoscope of
color—walls festooned with artifacts and old prints, bright
costumes, sounds of conviviality, and the aroma of roasting
beef from an open kitchen where the chefs are slicing-to-
order. At Gulliver's, the limited dinner menu has been
refined to its ultimate—a single entrée. While the stylized
bill of fare offers a selection of "fore dishes"—either a
"Tureen of Today's Pottage" or "Glubb-dubdrib Sallet"
(chopped romaine with baby shrimp, crumbled egg and
radishes served in an icy bowl and topped with special
dressing)—the only decision on the main course is how well
you would like your prime rib roasted and how thickly you
would like it sliced. The succulent beef is served with its
own juices and accompanied by Yorkshire pudding, a
superb spinach soufflé, and yet another fresh vegetable of
the season. By preparing so few items and doing it well the
pub proprietor, Mr. Levie, is able to keep his costs quite
low, a saving that is passed on to his patrons. Five
homemade desserts are modestly priced, and the fresh
strawberry torte is a near-masterpiece. If the menu seems
limited, the wine list is, well, slender—emaciated, in fact.
One good wine is selected each month. That's it. No choice.
This policy, originally a gamble, has proven as popular with
the guests as it is profitable to the management. It is at the
art of showmanship, however, that Gulliver's excels. Serving
wenches are carefully selected and trained, and they are as
pampered as any star performers. Their floor time is

described as being "on stage." They memorize their "scripts of greetings." Rehearsals are held periodically. The employee's locker room is a theatrical dressing room, even to the traditional make-up mirrors. Wenches work a four-day week so they will be alert and rested. They are given few enough tables to allow more time for flippant dialogue with the guests. Together with their "squires" (busboys), they can make a birthday a traumatic experience. Luncheon (steak and prime rib sandwiches, eggs Benedict, fish and chips, etc.) is more subdued.

**Moderate.** Open seven days. Lunch served Monday through Friday frm 11:30 a.m. to 3 p.m. Dinner from 5:30 to 11 p.m. Full bar. Reservations advised. Visa, MC. Parking lot. Casual.

---

**GYPSY'S**                                    **East Indian**
1215 4th Street                                        ★
Santa Monica        **Map 2**         (213) 451-2841

This little place is a good beginning for palates ready to explore curry flavor. Tina is Eurasian with an elegant British accent and an ability to make you feel you are dining in her home. She handles her own herbs, makes her own chutney and offers a limited menu of only what she can do well. Each of her curry bases is prepared to fit the specific dish and its "hotness" can be changed to fit the tastes of the diner (you'll have to ask, however). Don't be surprised to see many of the local Indian residents from UCLA. It's their favorite. Try a good pinot chardonnay with this spicy fare.

**Inexpensive to moderate.** Open Tuesday through Sunday. Dinner from 6 to 10 p.m. Private party facilities. Closed Christmas. Wine and beer only. Reservations recommended. Visa, MC. Public parking lot across street. Casual.

# h

## HAMAYOSHI
3350 West 1st Street
Los Angeles    **Map 7**

Japanese
★
(213) 384-2914

The fact that sushi is great here is not Occidental. It's Japanese talent, unduplicated in any other cuisine, that makes these little jewels taste as good as they look. There are other items on the menu, but you should be prepared to pig out on the wide variety that is carefully illustrated with English subtitles. My favorite is the *irigiku*, or red roe atop gingered rice wrapped in seaweed.

**Inexpensive to moderate.** Open Monday through Saturday. Luncheon Monday through Friday from 11:30 a.m. to 2 p.m. Dinner from 5 to 11 p.m. Sushi served till 3 a.m. Full bar. No reservations. Visa, MC, AX. Parking lot. Casual.

## HAMBURGER HAMLET American

(Locations in Beverly Hills, Brentwood, Century City, ★
Costa Mesa, Encino, Hollywood, Los Angeles, Palm Springs,
Pasadena, Sherman Oaks, West Los Angeles, Westwood,
Woodland Hills. See phone book for listings.)

The hamburger has gone big-time, in plush locations far
removed both geographically and atmospherically from
their starting place, a small counter-patio operation on the
Sunset Strip. The secret is not just in the fancy hamburgers—at fancy prices now—but in the same insistence
upon quality that was noticeable from the beginning.
Cocktails, lighthearted menus, and good service at most
locations.

**Moderate.** Casual dress.

## HAMBURGUESA American

4016 Wallace Street ★★
(Old Town) San Diego (714) 295-0584

The ubiquitous hamburger strikes again! This time in a
couple dozen disguises—all of them good and just as you
ordered. I remain partial to the *ensalada* Cobb served with
a green salad, three cheeses, avocado, and bacon. Steaks are
available for the less adventuresome. Desserts are worth
saving room for. You have a choice of indoor or outdoor
sipping and dining at this refurbished saloon/museum
embellished with antiques. "Show up Saturday or Sunday
morning for the best omelettes in the west," says a friend.

**Inexpensive.** Open seven days from 11 a.m. to 10 p.m.; to
midnight Friday, Saturday. Brunch Saturday, Sunday 9
a.m. to 3 p.m. Full bar. Reservations recommended. All
major credit cards. Parking lot. Casual.

## HAMBURGER HENRY'S

**Hamburgers**

3001 Wilshire Boulevard

Santa Monica     **Map 2**

★

(213) 828-3000

4700 East 2nd Street

Long Beach (Belmont Shores)     **Map 3**

★

(213) 433-7070

In my not necessarily humble opinion, the restaurants that prepare the perfect hamburger deserve every bit as much recognition as European ones. Now it's time to make way for a new contender. Hamburger Henry's in Long Beach and Santa Monica not only bake their own buns, but they do it so well that they've won the gold medal at the California State Fair an amazing eight times. And it's the extras—tomatoes that taste like tomatoes, crisp lettuce, pickles with that out-of-the-barrel taste, big Bermuda onions and fresh fruit that make a big difference. Although there are dozens of hamburger variations—even a Romanoff with imported caviar—there's much more. Their egg salad is made from an old recipe and other sandwich combinations are served well. The à la carte dinner menu, with entrées ranging from ground steak to chicken to seafood are all served with a mixed green salad. Soups are a meal in themselves and there are fanciful salads. The breakfasts are served with three eggs, even the dozen omelettes. Belgian waffles come with a variety of toppings.

**Moderate.** Both locations open 24 hours, seven days. Closed Thanksgiving, Christmas. Beer, wine and sake in Long Beach. Full bar in Santa Monica. No reservations. Patio. Visa, MC. Parking lot. Casual.

---

*Please be sure to consult "Tipping Made Easy" on page 25 of this Guide.*

## HAMPTON'S
4301 Riverside Drive
Burbank        **Map 1**

**Hamburgers**
★★
(213) 845-3009

1342 North Highland Avenue
Los Angeles        **Map 7**

★★
(213) 469-1090

These are marvelous gourmet hamburger establishments rumored to be owned in part by Paul Newman. The beef is ground fresh daily and perfectly prepared to order. There is a wine list with some surprisingly uptown selections, and the salad bar is fresh and dewy. Light classical entertainment at Sunday brunch. (Let Big Mac top that!) And reasonable prices top off the ultimate hamburger haven.

**Burbank: Inexpensive.** Open Monday through Friday during the day; seven nights. Monday through Thursday 11:30 a.m. to 10 p.m.; to 11 p.m. Friday, Saturday; 5 to 10 Sunday. Closed major holidays. Full bar. Reservations requested for six or more. Patio. Visa, MC. Valet parking. Casual to semi-dressy.

**Hollywood: Inexpensive.** Sunday through Thursday 11 a.m. to 10 p.m.; to 11 Friday, Saturday. Sunday brunch 11 a.m. to 1:30 p.m. Closed all major holidays. Classical music on Sunday. Wine and beer only. Reservations requested for six or more. Patio. Visa, MC. Valet parking. Casual to semi—dressy.

## HANABISHI
334 East 1st Street
Los Angeles        **Map 7**

**Japanese**
★
(213) 680-1989

This is another "if you knew sushi like I know sushi" place but there's seafood here prepared in the complex Japanese style. It's close enough to the downtown pressures to offer a tranquil afternoon before going home to face the crab grass, and you can eat as much as you like without perishing from sudden debt. Charred bonito will be an experience for you if you haven't tried it before, and you probably haven't. I particularly like to start with a Japanese boilermaker: hot sake with cold Kirin beer. Convivial atmosphere.

**Inexpensive.** Open Friday through Wednesday. Luncheon served from 11:30 a.m. to 2:30 p.m. Dinner Monday through Wednesday; Friday through Saturday 5 to 10:30 p.m.; Sunday 11:30 a.m. to 9:30 p.m. Closed Christmas, Halloween. Wine and beer only. Reservations advised. Visa, MC. Parking lot. Casual.

---

## HANIL
2851 West Olympic
Los Angeles          **Map 7**

**Korean**
★
(213) 480-8141

One must develop a taste for Korean food, and this is among the best authentic restaurants in the area. Mostly Korean people go there—they can't be all from Central Casting—and the dishes that are difficult to pronounce (*seng song chige*) are easy to eat. The hostess speaks English well and will guide you into this exotic fare.

**Inexpensive to moderate.** Open seven days 11 a.m. to 4 a.m. Wine and beer only. Reservations recommended. Visa, MC. Street parking. Casual.

---

## HARLEQUIN DINNER PLAYHOUSE   Dinner Theatre
3503 South Harbor Boulevard          ★
Santa Ana          **Map 6**          (714) 979-7550

While not new, dinner theatre seems to be steadily gaining in popularity. So much so that the Harlequin's owner-producer-management team, Al and Barbara Hampton, have built the first theatre in the area designed exclusively for that purpose. The most modern staging is possible; a flying stage appears over the platform when dinner is over, and the play begins. The staging of the buffet is equally impressive. The service consists of a choice of hot entrées, salads, vegetables, and fresh fruits. Desserts and drinks served by the young waiters and waitresses, are extra, but it's fun to eat and drink during intermission like continental theatre-goers. Dressing for the theatre, a lost art, seems to have been revived at the Harlequin. You'll be comfortable in a jacket and tie, or cocktail or long dress.

**Moderate to expensive.** Open Tuesday through Sunday. Dinner served Friday at 7 p.m. Tuesday, Wednesday, Thursday and Saturday at 6 p.m.; Sunday at 5:30 p.m. Sunday brunch 11 a.m. Broadway shows performed, dancing. Full bar. Reservations required. All major credit cards. Parking lot. Dressy.

---

## HARRY'S BAR AND AMERICAN GRILL          Italian
2020 Avenue of the Stars                                                  ★
Los Angeles          **Map 8**                    (213) 277-2333

I suspect that my good friends and fine restaurateurs Jerry Magnin and Larry Mindel are ticked with my reviews of this restaurant but it still misses for me. The idea was great: take the legendary Harry's Bar in Florence—the one made immortal by Hemingway—spare no expense to reproduce it in Century City and voilà! But as previous reviews have mentioned, flounder is not a seafood here, it's sort of a policy—or the absence of one. When they're good they are very, very good with *carpaccio* (paper thin raw beef with mustard sauce) and *vitello tonnato* (slices of cold veal in an inspired tuna mayonnaise).

The feeling is stylish. Archways are rounded, tables and chairs are elegant, tablecloths are pink and starched and the wood panels are decorated with small brass nameplates bearing the etched signatures of regular customers.

The service, however, can be dreadful. The waiters act as if money grows on trays, and they make little effort to work for it. When it is bad it is because, (I think), it is

288

difficult to staff a restaurant adjacent to a major legitimate theatre like the Shubert. Will the play or musical be a hit (and thus require a full floor staff and kitchen) or a miss (resulting in bored waiters exchanging yawns across a disenchanted room), or will the Shubert be dark, a situation wherein the restaurant—not inexpensive—must attract its own clientele. If I'm wrong, I'll get a mildly reproving letter from Larry or Jerry but fellas, this is not even in the same league with your lovely Chianti or MacArthur Park in San Francisco in terms of professionalism. After saying all this, however, the restaurant is a good luncheon destination and is usually packed with the noontime residue of the surrounding highrises.

**Moderate.** Open seven days. Luncheon from 11:30 a.m. to 3 p.m. Monday through Saturday. Dinner 5:30 to 11:30 p.m. week nights; 4:45 to 11:30 Saturday; to 10:30 Sunday. Closed Christmas, New Year's. Full bar. Reservations recommended. Visa, MC, AX. Valet parking in front of Shubert Theatre. Semi-dressy.

---

**HARRY'S DELI**                                         **Jewish Deli**
416 West 7th Street                                             ★
Los Angeles          **Map 7**                    (213) 622-6703

The lines begin forming by 11:30 a.m., but don't think you can beat the lunch rush by waiting until 2:00 p.m., the lines may still be long. Lines at Harry's, however, are not like lines anywhere else. Even at the height of the noon-time crush, I have never had to wait more than ten minutes for a table. I still don't understand how the hostess can escort you to the table so quickly, nor how the waitress can bring you the menu, take your order, and deliver your lunch all within three minutes' time — and all, somehow, without making you feel the least bit rushed or uncomfortable. This experience of speed without hustle or hassle is only part of the lure of Harry's. Harry's, quite simply, serves the best deli sandwich in Los Angeles — the Boston Special: pastrami, cole slaw, and Russian dressing on a long onion roll. Wash it down with a bottle of Dr. Brown's cream soda, and you'll think you're on New York's Lower East side. The matzo ball soup is also excellent, the corned beef lean, and the pastries taste as good as they look and smell — a rarity at even the best of Jewish delicatessens.

**Inexpensive to moderate.** Open Monday through Saturday. Monday through Friday 7 a.m. to 4 p.m. From 7:30 a.m. Saturday. Closed all major holidays, some Jewish holidays. Beer and wine only. Reservations accepted. Visa, MC. Street parking. Casual.

---

## HARRY'S OPEN PIT BAR-B-QUE Barbecue
1470 Sepulveda Boulevard ★
Westwood **Map 8** (213) 478-9097

1434 North Crescent Heights Boulevard
Hollywood **Map 7** (213) 654-4773

12924 Ventura Boulevard
Studio City **Map 1** (213) 789-3880

For 16 years Harry's has been purveying ribs to the populace. It's a big democratic portion that will fill the hungry who don't necessarily think neatness counts. Other specialties are beef and ham. Fun for the hearty eaters.

**Inexpensive.** Open Monday through Saturday 11 a.m. to 11 p.m. (to 2 a.m. at Hollywood location). Closed Thanksgiving, Christmas. Wine and beer only. No reservations no credit cards. Parking lot. Casual.

---

> *To obtain the best results from this Guide, consult "How to Use this Guide" on page 27.*

## HEART OF EUROPE RESTAURANT          European
476 North Western Avenue          ★
Hollywood          **Map 7**          (213) 467-8910

An honest and hearty European restaurant, all tables and chairs, where you can have a delicious dinner, with wine, reasonably. Generous portions of entrées — roast pork, chicken paprika, *wienerschnitzel*, and veal parmesan—are accompanied by spaghetti. The homemade apple strudel is better than most.

**Inexpensive to moderate.** Open Wednesday through Sunday. Dinner from 5 to 11 p.m. Open all holidays. Entertainment. Wine and beer only. Reservations recommended. Visa, MC. Parking lot; street parking. Casual.

## HEMINGWAY'S          Continental
2441 Pacific Coast Highway          ★★
Corona del Mar          **Map 4**          (714) 673-0120

Since owners Randy and Allyson Johnson opened this offspring of the Balboa Hemingway's they have settled into a routine that gives well-paced, personalized service. The new place looks and acts much like an English country inn. For openers, I suggest the "Flaming Cheese"... Greek cheese lightly broiled, flavored with lemon juice, and flamed with brandy at your table. They are particularly proud of their fresh fish and veal entrées. For closers, the homemade French chocolate cake layered with raspberry purée and whipped cream is a winner. On your next Sunday drive along the Gold Coast you might look in on them for Sunday brunch.

**Expensive.** Open Tuesday through Sunday from 5:30 to 11 p.m. Sunday brunch from 10 a.m. to 3 p.m. Closed Thanksgiving, Christmas Eve, Christmas Day. Full bar. Reservations necessary. Patio. Visa, MC, AX. Valet parking. Semi-dressy, jackets preferred.

## HIRO SUSHI
**Sushi bar**

1621 Wilshire Boulevard
Santa Monica    **Map 2**    (213) 395-3570

While the sushi bars around Little Tokyo tend to be filled mostly with Japanese customers, the *sushi* bars in the more outlying areas are often filled with no Japanese at all (outside of the chefs and other serving persons). Teru is one such place; Hiro Sushi is another. Hiro is rarely as mobbed as Teru, probably because there are about half dozen other *sushi* bars nearby. But in reputation, it is no less popular. There are several Asteroid machines (the table models) in the waiting room at Hiro, which eat up your quarters faster than a slot machine in Vegas. (It's amazing how, after a few sake, Asteroids becomes a particularly cosmic game.) And, there's a selection of *sushi* that looks to be as broad as the one at Teru. In fact, Hiro even offers a *sushi* checklist almost identical to the one at Teru, on which you can simply mark the *sushi* you desire—everything from Yellowtail and Spanish mackerel to jellyfish and our home-grown California roll (a seaweed roll filled with rice, cucumber and avocado). My singular problem at Hiro is that one part of the *sushi* bar is not really a *sushi* bar, but rather a bar in front of the area in which *tempura* is made and plates are assembled. So, even though you are sitting at the *sushi* bar, the creation of the *sushi* is really happening some distance away. And, at that section of the bar, the temperature is a bit on the sticky side. In fact, it's darn hot, which makes eating *sushi* less fun than it should be.   *M.S.*

**Moderate.** Open Wednesday through Monday. Luncheon from 11:30 a.m. to 2 p.m. weekdays. Dinner 5 to 10 p.m.; 5:30 to 11 p.m. Friday, Saturday. Closed all major holidays. Beer and wine only. No reservations. Visa, MC. Street parking. Casual.

## H.M.S. BOUNTY

**Continental**

★

3357 Wilshire Boulevard
Los Angeles        **Map 7**                    (213) 385-7275

Brought to you by Gordon Fields, the man who brings you Bull
'n Bush; if you love one you'll be at home in the other. After a
few drinks you may forget which of the two you're in; the
limited choice menu and the enthusiasm of the patrons virtually
produce a clone. They go by bus to every place that's busable,
Dodgers, (Anaheim?) Rams, Lakers, etc. A favorite with the
Dow Jones and Janes set.

**Inexpensive to moderate.** Open Monday through Friday 11
a.m. to 11 p.m. Closed holidays. Juke box. Full bar. Reservations recommended. Visa, MC, AX, DC. Parking lot. Casual
to semi-dressy.

## H.M.S. SANDCASTLE

**Seafood**

★

16821 Pacific Coast Highway
Sunset Beach        **Map 6**                    (213) 592-2103

Here's a little seaside restaurant that really reflects the personality of the owner. Eric Bakker is a marine antique buff
and his seafood and steak restaurant, the Sandcastle, looks
more like a museum than a fine dinner house. But it's the
food that brings the customers back. The sign on the highway
boasts "The Most Crab On The Coast" and king crab lovers
cue up for the juicy 2-pound-plus servings. When available,
the Sandcastle collects raves for its abalone — quickly sautéed
in butter with a splash of lemon. A seafood platter, lobster
tail, and superbly aged steaks highlight the menu. The
homemade New England clam chowder is thick and sinful,
and the honey-mustard salad dressing is a great complement
to the seafood. Ten years of culinary success have not
changed Eric and his charming wife, Elaine. They personally
oversee the intimate floor which bristles with polished brass
gauges, plaques, lamps and marine hardware. So many cus-

tomers wanted to buy the decorations that Eric recently opened Antiques Of The Sea across the street — worth the drive alone. You'll find The Sandcastle a mile past the old wooden water tower after Seal Beach.   *Jackie Olden.*

**Moderate.** Open Tuesday through Sunday from 5 to 10 p.m. Closed Christmas, New Year's. Full bar. No reservations. Visa, MC. Parking lot. Casaual.

---

**THE HOBBIT**                                  **Continental**
2932 East Chapman                                    **DA** ★
Orange        **Map 6**                       (714) 997-1972

When some good wine folk saw this gracious old hacienda that formerly housed a respected Ukrainian restaurant (The Ukramada), they realized it was the culmination of their search and fantasy: a place in which to prepare "customized" set menus for a discriminating clientele with room enough for the kind of wine cellar they visualized. Dinner begins promptly at 7:30, when guests are admitted to the wine cellar to nibble on appetizers, drink complimentary champagne, and discuss their wine selections for the evening. The dinner itself is a multi-course affair; an example of one week's menu includes stuffed mushrooms, gazpacho, breast of chicken Raphael, fresh spinach salad, coquille St. Jacques, sherbet, then a roasted New York Steak with Madeira sauce, vegetables, and a *crêpe de maison*. The dinner is interrupted somewhere between courses for a much-needed intermission; the guests are encouraged to stroll through the art galleries or perhaps walk around the block. Reservations are booked months in advance, but there are cancellations from time to time that may allow you to sneak in. The cuisine as served here is not without fault (which of us is?), but it's good and improving. Service is cordial and informal.

**Expensive.** Open Wednesday through Sunday. Dinner (one seating only at fixed price $35) 7:30 Wednesday through Saturday; 7 on Sunday. Private party facilities. Closed major holidays. Wine only. Reservations required four to five months ahead. Visa, MC. Parking lot. Semi-dressy.

## HOB NOB HILL

**American**

**★★**

2271 First Avenue
San Diego

(714) 239-8176

In San Diego, the place to go for breakfast is Hob Nob Hill. Hob Nob Hill has not always been known as Hob Nob Hill. When it opened as a 14-seat diner back in 1944, it was called the Juniper Cafe. Later it became the Melody Grill, Dorothy's Oven, and finally (with a seating capacity of 120) Hob Nob Hill. It's one of those wonderful places you come across now and again which seems t be completely out of time and place. Like the Tick Tock in L.A., it's a working tribute to the joys of culinary Americana. The breakfast menu, for instance, is rich with such delights as "Three Musketeers"—a trio of buttermilk pancakes, light and scrumptious, rolled in turn around a slice of ham, a sausage and a dollop of sour cream. Then, there's the pancake sandwich, in which you can choose between having ham, bacon, or a sausage squeezed between two pancakes, with an egg tossed in for company. There are golden pecan waffles and eggs Florentine and tall or short stacks of wonderful Canadian blueberry hot cakes. And then, there are the pastries. The pastries are the first thing you smell when you walk into Hob Nob Hill, which does all its own baking. There's coffee cake, sweet rolls of every description, muffins and many sorts of biscuits. They're all served warm, fresh and reassuringly good. As an odd touch, the jams are served in orange halves, which is more cute than it is practical.   *M.S.*

**Inexpensive.** Open Sunday through Friday 7 a.m. to 9 p.m. Visa, MC. Reservations suggested. Casual.

---

*To obtain the best results from this Guide, be sure to consult maps on the various Southern California areas in the front of the book.*

## HOLIDAY HOUSE                    Continental
27400 Pacific Coast Highway                      ★
Malibu     **Map 2**               (213) 457-3641

Malibu, where the favorite sport is body searching, where Jerry
Brown walks the beach with Linda Ronstadt, where Mel Brooks
and Anne Bancroft skip along the ocean in the rain, where
Jason Robards, wearing one of his funny hats, tap-danced "April
Showers" on Sam Peckinpah's roof. Malibu. It's come a long
way since Leon Victor Prudhomme bought the mile-long
beachfront and adjacent property for $400 ($200 of which was
to be paid in "groceries and wines") back in 1884. Now summer
rentals average $5,000 a month for a one-bedroom home where
the plumbing is as eccentric as the madcap community. It's not
without significance that the organizers of tennis tournaments
— the colony's favorite legal pastime — have to remember
which couples are still together, and who will steadfastly refuse
to volley with an ex-husband (or ex-wife). Tennis brings out
the blood lust in otherwise civilized millionaires whose marital
ties are strained as frequently as their hamstring muscles. It
was in 1937 that a talented architect, Richard Neutra, suc-
cumbed to the inexplicable charisma of this improbable, uncomfortable, beautiful beach and created Holiday House, a resort
and restaurant complex that figured frequently in the history
of the era and area. Dudley Murphy, no stranger to legends,
was the proprietor of the restaurant and property, and it flour-
ished until shortly after Murphy's death, when it disintegrated
alarmingly. Since then, it has gone through a couple of ownership changes and some brutal treatment by nature. Its beautiful
patio was literally washed out to sea during one of the area's
not infrequent storms. Current owners Daniel and Marylou
Perlmutter have made a sustained effort to right the ship. The
multi-level patio has been rebuilt. The food is expertly prepared,
though not inexpensive by any standards. It's a popular gathering place for many of the area's entertainment stars. Its
biggest drawback is that it's a very long drive from most of
southern California, although it's reasonably close to much of

the San Fernando Valley through Topanga Canyon. If you're willing to travel the distance and spend some bucks, it can be a lovely experience.

**Moderate to expensive.** Open Tuesday through Sunday from 11 a.m. to 10 p.m. Sunday brunch 11 a.m. to 3 p.m. Full bar. Reservations recommended. Patio. Ocean view. Visa, MC. Valet parking. Semi-dressy.

---

## HOMER AND EDY'S BISTRO                          Creole
2839 South Robertson                                 ★
Los Angeles        **Map 8**                (213) 559-5102

The seafood is flown in fresh from New Orleans; red fish, shrimp, flounder, crab, trout, frog's legs, catfish, crawfish, oyster, and pompano. The chicory coffee and spices such as filé also come from down home. The pecan pies, hot praline sauce, and bananas Foster are made in their own Creole kitchen, and served in candlelight on napery. Best of all is the oyster loaf and the French dishes with a Creole flavor like *poisson en papillote* although I do like the baked ribs with red beans and rice. It's all here and it may be the best Creole in town.

**Moderate.** Open Tuesday through Sunday. Luncheon from 11:30 a.m. to 2:30 p.m. Tuesday through Saturday. Dinner from 6 to 11 p.m. Tuesday through Thursday; 5 to 10 Sunday. Piano nightly. Mardi Gras Jazz Festival in February. Wine and beer only. Reservations recommended during the week; essential on weekends. Patio. All major credit cards. Wheelchair access. Parking lot; valet parking weekends. Casual to semi-dressy.

---

*In order to obtain the best results from this Guide, be sure to read the French, German, Italian and Oriental menu translators on page 705 to 710 of this Guide.*

## HOPPE'S OLD HEIDELBERG

German

13726 Oxnard Street

★

Van Nuys    **Map 1**    (213)997-9396

Everything is from Germany: the food, decor and most of the help. Wood carvings, mugs and ceramics give this a Milwaukee-German flavor but the food is heavy — if hearty —and it's not easy to polka after downing one of these feasts. It's beer-hall big and great for banquets.

**Moderate.** Open Tuesday through Sunday. Luncheon from 11 a.m. to 3:30 p.m. Tuesday through Saturday. Dinner from 4 to 10 p.m.; Sunday, Tuesday through Thursday; 4 to 11 Friday, Saturday. Children's menu. Banquet facilities. Closed Christmas, month of July. Entertainment on weekends. Full bar. Reservations recommended. Visa, MC, AX. Valet parking. Casual.

## HORIKAWA RESTAURANT

Japanese

111 South San Pedro Street

★★

Los Angeles    **Map 7**    (213) 680-9355

South Coast Village

Santa Ana    **Map 6**    (714) 557-2531

If this Japanese restaurant seems a little more authentic than most, it should be; Horikawa is part of a major chain of good restaurants in Japan. The management brought some of the Tokyo-trained chefs to this location, where they perform (and that's the word for the lightning-fast preparation) at the teppan, a grill set into tables with seven diners on three sides and the chef on the fourth. Also at one location is the longest sushi bar outside of Japan, with fresh seafoods served to order. Now there is a second Horikawa located in Santa Ana (without a sushi bar), and both are fair representatives of their country and cuisine.

**Moderate to expensive.** Open seven days. Luncheon from 11:30 a.m. to 2 p.m. weekdays. Dinner 5:30 to 10:30 p.m. Monday through Thursday; to 11 Friday; 5 to 11 Saturday; 5 to 10 Sunday. Closed Thanksgiving, Christmas, New Year's. Full bar. Reservations recommended on weekends. All major credit cards. Parking. Casual to semi-dressy.

---

## HOT LICKS
French-fast food
12740 Culver Boulevard
★
Los Angeles
(213) 823-0075

One block East of the Marina freeway this *routier* is better than most French truck stops and it is open 20 hours a day. Onion soup gratinée, escargot, quiche, omelettes, salads and crepes are all under $4. There are daily specials as well.

**Inexpensive.** Open seven days. Sunday through Thursday 7 a.m. to 3 a.m.; Friday and Saturday to 4 a.m. Beer and wine only. No reservations. No credit cards. Wheelchair access. Parking lot. Casual.

---

## HO TOY'S
Chinese/Cantonese
4630 Van Nuys Boulevard
★
Sherman Oaks    **Map 1**
(213) 783-0460

Simple, honest Cantonese dishes, with appetizers of egg roll, fried shrimp, and good egg flower soup, have been bringing them in from Van Nuys since Ho Toy's opened as a take-out spot over twenty years ago. Now it's a 125-seat restaurant with a cocktail bar, and the success of Ho Toy's enabled brothers Robert and William Lee to open the fabulously opulent Jade West in Century City, which bears little resemblance to this humble ancestor.

**Moderate.** Open seven days. Luncheon from 11:30 a.m. to 6 p.m. Monday through Saturday. Dinner Sunday through

Friday 3 to 10 p.m.; to 11 Saturday; Sunday 1 to 10 p.m. Closed Thanksgiving Day. Full bar. Reservations recommended. All major credit cards. Street, lot parking. Casual.

---

## HOULIHAN'S OLD PLACE     American
(Locations in Encino, Long Beach, Newport Beach,    ★
San Diego and Torrance. See phone book for listing.)

I'm not going to pull the chain comparisons this time, all of these seem to have their own personality and to operate independently. They are right on target for the people they hope to attract—the young and affulent (although the prices are surpisingly moderate). There is attention to detail here I've not seen in most multiple operations and the attitude of the staff couldn't be friendlier or more sincere. Each location has lush greenery and a cozy interior. All have appetizers from the increasingly popular fried zucchini to pita bread pizzas and escargot. Entrées include roast duck with an onion or live or less sweet accompaniment?), daily fresh seafood specials, omelettes and more, with a respectable salad bar. They've also got good hamburgers here. The full bar is professional and the glasses are man-sized.

**Moderate.** Open seven days from 11 a.m. to 10:30 p.m. Sunday brunch from 11 a.m. to 3 p.m. Closed Christmas. Disco. Full bar. Reservations advised. Visa, MC, AX, DC. Parking in front. Casual to semi-dressy.

---

## HUGO'S     Continental
8401 Santa Monica Boulevard    ★
West Hollywood    (213) 654-3993

A classic, informal European restaurant that includes a display of cold entrées and homemade pasta for take-out, Hugo's cuisine may best be described as Northern Italian and Southern France. The butcher shop claims, and may be, the only veal specialty shop in the country. Additional take-out items include selections from the shelf-lined walls containing fine "gourmet" items. Terry Kaplan, fourth generation butcher, purchased Hugo's in 1980 with a dream of creating a setting worthy of his product. Terry is also an artist of some note; his charcoals are in increasing demand. A complete renovation transformed the former warehouse appearance into a light, airy multi-windowed structure and furnishes the vibes in which Kaplan and his chefs work.

At any given time the creations on display might include fresh Santa Barbara prawns in Pommery mustard dressing with fresh tarragon; whole chicken roasted in herbs and lemons; hearts of palm with pesto and pine nuts; chicken with walnuts, lemon and truffles, or one of the extraordinary veal salads. There are frozen entrées such as veal or vegetable lasagna, filet of salmon in lobster sauce, veal cannelloni and chicken *cacciatore*. Forty-five contented diners are served breakfast through dinner. Wine list is fine and there is fresh orange juice.

**Moderate.** Open seven days. Breakfast from 9 a.m. Luncheon from 11 a.m. Dinner from 4 to 9 p.m. Sunday 11 a.m. to 7 p.m. Beer and wine only. No reservations. Visa, MC, AX. Wheelchair access. Parking lot. Casual.

---

## HUNAN                                    Chinese
980 North Broadway                              ★
Chinatown      **Map 7**            (213) 626-5050

Hunan is the first restaurant in the area to present the food of Hunan Province, considered by many to be the best of the spicier (as compared to Cantonese) Northern Chinese cuisine. Still brand-new — but so busy they haven't had time to have a grand opening — Hunan is an immaculate but unpretentious establishment with a long counter adjoining the dining room. Dishes like minced chicken in a bamboo cup and steamed fish, with broad bean paste are revelations. The abalone with cinnamon and peanut sauce will wake up your palate, and the sea slugs in a stew-like concoction are, according to hostess Antonia Chen "*very* good for your complexion." (Her mother made her eat some "nearly every day," and it worked . . . at least for her.) There are 154 dishes on the menu, but the attentive serving staff will help you select a dinner with just the right ratio of spicy dishes to the less spicy but no less robust creations, like butterfly shrimp in Chef Leu's special sauce. Oh, yes, don't expect individual place settings of dinner plates. The steaming platters are placed in the center of the table to be shared by all — an old Hunan tradition — and a very pleasant one.

**Moderate.** Open seven days. Luncheon from 11:30 a.m. to 2:30 p.m. weekdays; to 3 p.m. Saturday, Sunday. Dinner from 5 to 9 p.m. weeknights; from 4:30 Saturday, Sunday. Special Prime Minister's dinner (9 courses) starts at $15. Banquet facilities. No alcoholic beverages served; diners welcome to bring their own. Reservations recommended for parties of six or more. Visa, MC. Validated parking. Casual.

---

## HUNGRY TIGER                                Seafood/Steaks

(Locations in Hollywood, Sherman Oaks, Westwood, Westchester, Palos Verdes, Buena Park, Santa Ana, Thousand Oaks, Marina del Rey, Palm Springs. See phone book.)

I approach my review of this restaurant as warily as if I were literally approaching a hungry tiger; whatever the Latin word for "inconsistency" is, it should be emblazoned across the Hungry Tiger's coat of arms. This chain—for the most part in the purgatory of mediocrity—can, on occasion, rise to great heights. Fresh oysters, cherrystone clams, Maine lobster and a seafood bar with cioppino sound great, right? But somehow, some of the locations muck it up (particularly Palm Springs, which must be totally out of the range of quality control). One day the food may be good enough to shout about, another day it may be barely good enough to eat. Frustratingly, the two extremes can be—and often are—experienced at the same location. So with the

302

forwarding above, I suggest you explore a location or two and look into their great cocktail hour bargains—oysters and fresh clams at giveaway prices—and maybe even try a bowl of *cioppino*. You might be one of the lucky ones.

**Moderate.** Open seven days. Breakfast at some locations. Luncheon from 11:30 a.m. to 4 p.m. at most locations. Dinner from 4to 11:30 p.m. Sunday brunch from 10 a.m. to 3 p.m. Closed Christmas. Entertainment at some locations. Full bar. Reservations advised. Visa, MC, AX, CB. Valet parking for dinner only. Semi-dressy.

---

# HYANG MI                               Korean
966 South Western Avenue                    ★
Los Angeles     **Map 7**        (213) 734-7794

Hyang Mi is slightly less opulent than Korea Gardens and, unlike most Korean restaurants, does not offer *hwaros* for cooking. What it does offer is an incredible Korean sampler referred to simply as "Special Korean Dinner." Holy M.A.S.H.! What a spread! Within minutes after we orderd, dishes started arriving at a frantic pace. So fast and furiously did the dishes arrive at our table, in fact, that we had to just sit back and watch, unsure of where or when to begin.

Ultimately, there were 26 dishes of every size and configuration arranged before a group of four persons. Since we had no *hwaro* to cook on, the *bulkogi* (a spicy, marinated beef dish) was brought out sizzling on a platter and, unlike my table-cooked version, was not burned to a sizzle. Sorting through the dishes, I found some tender fish filets which had been fried in egg to the consistency of an omelette. There was a salty soup with beef ribs in it, and another soup with what seemed like meatballs. And there were many dishes of vegetables in every possible configuration of pickledness.

Some of the pickles, like a cabbage and a raddish *kimchee*, were exceedingly, almost bonecrushingly, hot. Others, like the pickled bean sprouts and the radish in brine, tickled the palate more than they scorched it. And, there were other vegetables, less easily identified—like a ream of fried, flattened seaweed, a dish that crunches and tastes like something your mother would tell you to eat because it's good for you. Or the salads or pickled cucumber, or the potato salad with green beans, or radish-and-carrot salad, or the crunch black beans, or... obviously there were just too many dishes on the table to keep track of.

And, perhaps, too many to taste as well. Which may be the point of Korean food: It is possible that one is not meant to eat everything, but rather is given far more choice than in other types of cuisine. In dining in a Korean restaurant, you can let your spirit roam free over more dishes than the mind and body could possibly assimilate. How you deal with all that largesse becomes in a way, a mirror of who you are.   *M.S.*

**Moderate.** Open seven days from 11 a.m. to 10 p.m. Beer and wine only. Visa, MC. Reservations accepted. Parking lot. Casual.

*For best results, consult "How to Use This Guide" on page 27.*

# i

## ICHABOD CRANE'S
### American
### ★
2808 West Sepulveda Boulevard
Torrance    **Map 2**                  (213) 539-3131

Quantity supersedes quality in this theme restaurant with cute
menu nomenclature ("Roast'd beefe"), pretty girls galore and
interesting, woodsy-rich decor. Harry Prod was with the
blandest of them all, the Red Onion (pretty, but I don't like to
eat there), and here he's playing it safe with a menu that can't
be messed up and the kind of drinks that would make you not
care if it was (messed up). There are all kinds of interesting
drink combinations, entertainment of a casual but good sort;
and success. The place is jammed — there's a disco — with
what looks like stewardi on a night off the planes and on the
town. Harry will get rich, his customers are happy, and if this
kind of hype appeals to you, you'll find no better.

**Moderate.** Open seven days. Luncheon from 11 a.m. to 3
p.m. Monday through Saturday. Dinner 5 to 11 p.m.
Monday through Saturday; 4 to 10 Sunday. Sunday brunch

10 a.m. to 3 p.m. Closed Christmas. Entertainment 9 p.m. to 1:30 a.m. Monday through Thursday; disco Sunday through Tuesday. Full bar. No reservations. Visa, MC, AX. Valet parking. Casual to semi-dressy.

---

## IGNAZIO'S ITALIAN RESTAURANT      Italian
3532 West Eighth Street                      ★
Los Angeles     **Map 7**             (213) 387-8308

An attractive pizza restaurant with inexplicable designs to become another "gourmet" establishment—they should stick to the pastas and pizzas. *Cannelloni* is good, and if you're not careful people, will poke fun at your expanse if you gorge on this kind of fare. The portions are large and dinner for two would feed four comfortably. Wine is given importance, and there are some unfamiliar labels that are worth looking into. Luncheon is more of a merchant's affair, but dinner has real possibilities.

**Inexpensive to moderate.** Open seven days. Luncheon 11:30 a.m. to 2:30 p.m. Dinner Monday through Thursday 5 to 11 p.m.; Friday 11 a.m. to midnight; Saturday, Sunday 5 p.m. to midnight. Closed Christmas and Thanksgiving. Full bar. Reservations advised for eight or more. Visa, MC, AX. Parking lot. Casual.

---

## IMPERIAL DYNASTY          Continental
2 China Alley                       **DA** ★★★
Hanford                        (209) 582-0087

The pleasantly bucolic community of Hanford, about thirty-five miles southeast of Fresno, is an improbable location for an epicurean restaurant. Yet it was in Hanford, where there are more livestock than people, that I had one of my most memorable dining adventures. The Imperial Dynasty stands on China Alley, an ancient backstreet of shaded buildings where herbs, opium, and all-night gambling were once dispensed to Chinese laborers who worked on the railroads and in the mines around the turn of the century. The restaurant has been part of the Wing family since Henry Gong Wing, an acclaimed chef, established it in 1881. The Imperial Dynasty is merely one of the jammed-together buildings with Chinese markings that give no clue to the pleasures inside. Behind the massive, somewhat forbidding door there is a surprising jumble of vivid Oriental color, wall hangings, huge lanterns with red tassels, exquisitely carved jade, and the murmur of people happily dining. Richard Wing presides here. A creative artist, he blends the classic French cuisine with touches of Mandarin. His *escargots à la Bourguignonne*, stuffed into shells with chopsticks and prepared with the unorthodox ingredient of cashew butter, has won two major awards as "Best Dish of the Year" from national wine and food societies. Most dinners include a soup du jour (my night: consommé of oxtail with whole mushrooms), half a head of lettuce with special house dressing, crab *fu yung*, an entrée (there are forty), dessert, and coffee — or tea. I tasted petite lobster tails in sauce diablo under crisp leaves of fried spinach, a coquille St. Jacques (scallops in a delicate white wine sauce) topped with shrimps and Mandarin orange, tournedos of beef Bordelaise covered with a gigantic mushroom cap, followed by a dessert of honey pastry (similar to the Greek baklava) laid across a circle of crenshaw melon, then drenched with Grand Marnier. Order 24 hours in advance for special dinner as described. Service is informal, mostly by members of the family. Richard himself makes frequent trips from the kitchen to see how his guests are faring and to chuckle appreciatively over the compliments. He may disappear for a moment into the vast wine cellar, which once served as an escape tunnel for the opium smugglers, to emerge with a bottle he feels would be particularly suitable. The collection of wine was assembled by his brother, the late Ernie Wing, and includes private reserves, special selections, and many rare labels virtually unavailable anywhere else. The private party facility — more museum than banquet hall — contains 400 pieces of art, some priceless, in recessed wall cabinets. The most magnificent room of all, the highlight of the interior, is . . . the ladies' room. It is about the size of a hotel lobby, with a foyer surrounded by richly upholstered chairs. Two ornate, hand-carved, wooden pagodas contain the essentials, and they are surrounded by wall tapestries, paintings, screens, and Oriental carpets. Mr. Wing's ladies' room was used for a cocktail party by the San Francisco press corps on one occasion, an honor which has not before been bestowed on any lavatory of my acquaintance. Hanford is located just west of State 99 about 200 miles north of Los Angeles (look for China Alley). It's about four hours, all freeway, and worth the drive.

**Moderate to expensive.** Open Tuesday through Sunday. Dinner from 4:30 to 10 p.m. Full bar. Reservations advised. AX only. Parking in rear. Semi-dressy.

---

## IMPERIAL GARDENS                                  Japanese
8225 Sunset Boulevard                                      ★
Hollywood          **Map 7**                    (213) 656-1750

A historic building — once a gambling casino, then a bordello, then the Players Club for actors, and, finally, a fine and unde-servedly underrated Japanese restaurant. The third-floor dining room is as far from the Strip, spiritually, as you can get, with a peaceful tatami room. The next floor down houses the enter-tainment lounge and sushi bar where, if you're hungry and impatient enough, you can have a satisfying dinner of the fish morsels, rice and pickled ginger. Other dishes, more common to the dining room than to a seafood bar, are available here as well, including a golden, flaky tempura.

**Moderate to expensive.** Open seven days. Dinner served Monday through Saturday from 6 to 10:45 p.m.; Sunday to 9:30 p.m. Closed major holidays. Sushi bar closed Sunday. Entertainment Friday, Saturday. Full bar. Reservations advised. Visa, MC, AX, DC. Valet parking. Semi-dressy.

## IMPERIAL HOUSE RESTAURANT     Continental
505 Kalmia Street (Across from Balboa Park)     ★
San Diego     (714) 234-3525

There'll always be an England at the fringe of Balboa Park. For more than 16 years, this gem has carried on admirably, turning out flaming entrées and desserts fit for the Queen. The specialty is seafood, but don't snub the chateaubriand bouquetière or the individual rack of lamb (still a rarity). Indeed, give the entire menu a good run through to discover some delicious surprises at this old "English" restaurant. Banquet facilities and outside catering are available. On Thursday and Friday nights jam sessions happen from 4 to 7. Do take time to enjoy nature exposing herself across the street in Balboa Park.

**Moderate.** Open Monday through Saturday. Luncheon 11 a.m. to 2 p.m. weekdays. Dinner from 5 to 10 p.m. Banquet facilities. Entertainment. Full bar. Reservations recommended. All major credit cards. Valet parking. Semi-dressy.

## THE INAGIKU ORIENTAL PLAZA     Japanese
5th and Flower     ★★
Los Angeles     **Map 7**     (213) 614-0820

Finally. Finally I can report a good restaurant in the new Bonaventure Hotel in downtown Los Angeles, those five circular towers that look like a set from H. G. Wells' "Shape of Things to Come." It's also, I'm happy to report, the first major Japanese village: they have 15,000 square feet divided into six dining concepts: *kaiseki* dinners (fabulous), *sushi* bar (try the red roe), *teppan* (frying on a large griddle, steaks, etc.) *tempura* (deep-fried batter dipped), a Chinese room and another offering Western cuisine (why?). The dinner lists 60 items, not inexpensive, with the best prepared in the tradition of the Shojin, the elders of Japanese cuisine. Owners, the Asano family, have been operating restaurants in the Orient and New York (at the Waldorf-Astoria) since the mid-1870's.

**Moderate to expensive.** Open seven days. Luncheon from 11:30 a.m. to 2 p.m. weekdays. Dinner from 5:30 to 10:30 p.m. nightly. Banquet facilities. Closed major holidays. Polynesian bar open to 10:30 p.m. Reservations recommended. All major credit cards. Validated parking at World Trade Center. Casual.

---

## INN OF THE SEVENTH RAY   Continental/Vegetarian
128 Old Topanga Road                   ★
Topanga    **Map 2**           (213) 455-1311

This place has gone through more perils than Ma Perkins since it's located in an area where there seems to be annual floods, rockslides and breaking up. Mt. St. Helens seems bucolic by comparison. However, survive they have in all their rustic glory. Here you can dine *al fresco* besides a brook or in the unpretentious interior. Organic and fresh are the key words here. Fish is served within hours of the catch and the vegetables are privately grown to be free from pesticides and cellophane. Chicken and eggs and dairy products are all natural but when they serve unpasteurized wine, that's going a bit far for my tastes. Bread is baked fresh daily. The Inn was once a church and the vibes still remain.

**Moderate.** Open seven days. Lunch from 11:30 a.m. to 3:30 p.m. Dinner from 6 to 10 p.m. Sunday brunch from 10 a.m. to 3:30 p.m. Wine and beer only. Reservations required for dinner only. Patio. Outdoor seating by creek. Visa, MC. Parking on premises. Casual to semi-dressy.

---

*Please be sure to consult "Tipping Made Easy" on page 25 of this Guide.*

## INTERNATIONAL HOUSE OF  American/Coffee Shop
## PANCAKES
(Locations throughout Southern California)          ★

Bigness doesn't always mean badness. This massive chain operation serves up fine breakfasts — three eggs with ham or bacon or sausage plus a stack of really good pancakes — all day long. When you veer away from breakfast dishes on the massive menu, though, you are in the as-yet-unconquered world of convenience foods. Children have a particularly good time with colorful special menus and balloons, and very friendly people.

**Inexpensive.** Hours and prices vary at various locations. Children welcome. No alcoholic beverages. No reservations. No credit cards. Parking lot. Casual.

---

## THE IRON GATE RESTAURANT          American
45-406 Highway 74                                    ★
Palm Desert                            (714) 346-4453

At the foot of the palms to pines highway, the long mountainous road that serpentines its way from the desert to Idyllwild is a quietly competent restaurant almost hidden on the grounds of the Adobe Garden Hotel. The three intimate dining rooms are charmers. Nothing has been spared in decor or imagination to create the aura of an oasis of tranquility. The patio overlooks a lovely, tender garden. The menu is somewhat limited to the expectables, but everything's good and there is live entertainment and dancing.

**Moderate.** Open Tuesday through Saturday. Luncheon served Tuesday through Saturday from 11:30 a.m. to 2:30 p.m.; dinner from 6 to 10 p.m. Private party facilities. Closed Thanksgiving and Christmas. Live entertainment and dancing 9 p.m. to 1:30 a.m. Full bar. Reservations advised. Visa, MC. Parking lot. Casual.

# ITCHEY FOOT
**Italian American**
★

801 West Temple Street
Los Angeles     **Map 7**     (213) 680-0007

A restaurant with a name like Itchey Foot and a slogan that reads "food like mama used to send out for" would seem to have two strikes against it. However, this charmer, located within walking distance of the Music Center, is colorful, inexpensive, fun and open until midnight on weekends. With the downtown area enjoying a renaissance with the emergence of central condominiums, many of the customers of the Itchey Foot are well-to-do neighborhood regulars. Many more, however, are people smart enough to figure out that this is the best before and after theater restaurant around.

The food is that of a high-class *ristorante* with the standard American list of steaks and chops, but then it flies off into beautiful pastas, pizzas, sandwiches and the best chicken *cacciatore* I've had in a long time (it's served boned here).

The atmosphere is Italian funky, there's a full bar and the price is right. At luncheon their combination sandwiches draw a bigger crowd than the unemployment office and the beer is served in gigantic schooners, the way God intended beer to be served.

**Inexpensive to moderate.** Open Monday through Saturday. Luncheon from 11 a.m. to 5 p.m. Dinner Monday through Thursday 5 to 10 p.m.; Friday, Saturday to midnight. Banquet facilities. Children welcome. Closed major holidays. Entertainment Sunday provided by the Mark Taper Forum. Full bar. Reservations advised. Visa, MC, AX. Parking lot next door. Casual.

---

*For best results, consult "How to Use This Guide" on page 27.*

# j

## JACK'S AT THE BEACH    Seafood
2700 Wilshire Boulevard
Santa Monica    **Map 2**    (213) 396-1831

Where to begin? There is no Jack, and it's not at the beach, and they don't produce as they claim, "the best seafood procured worldwide," but it is a comfortable, luxurious restaurant. They have a special occasion room—the Mirror Room—that's one of the most beautiful in town. Celebrities still come here though not as many and not as often. Once Jack's was a top restaurant, but then a dollar was once a dollar.

**Moderate.** Open seven days. Luncheon served Monday through Friday from 11:30 a.m. to 2:30 p.m. Dinner from 5:30 to 11 p.m. Limited banquet facilities. Closed major holidays. Full bar. Reservations advised. All major credit cards accepted. Valet parking. Semi-dressy.

## JACQUES RESTAURANT          Continental/American
2256 East Alosta                                    ★
Glendora          **Map 6**                (213) 963-2511

Edna Cooke, who owns Jacques Restaurant, prepares everything herself, from the minestrone soup to the chocolate
soufflé and cheesecake. Having learned to cook in Europe at
her mother's apron hem, she now presides over a comfortable Swiss chalet located in a desolate Glendora shopping
center. The steak Diane, steak au Madeira, chicken *cordon
bleu*, or steak *marchand de vin*, all at moderate prices, may
make it worth the trip. Every entrée comes with plenty of
vegetables. For American tastes there's fried chicken, ham
steaks, and ground round steak dinners.

**Moderate.** Open Wednesday through Sunday. Dinner from
5 to 10 p.m. Wine and beer only. Reservations advised.
Visa, MC, DC. Ample parking. Casual.

## JADE WEST                                      Chinese
2040 Avenue of the Stars                          ★★
Century City          **Map 8**            (213) 556-3388

Jade West may well be, square foot for square foot, the most
expensively constructed restaurant in the area. More importantly, the money was invested with good taste. From the
instant you step into the spacious foyer with its deep carpet,
carved antique screens, and recessed lighting that glows through
vibrantly colored silk, it is obvious that this is an extraordinary
place. Nearly all of the decorative pieces were done by hand in
China. A mural was commissioned by the restaurant to depict
myriad scenes of Chinese life through the ages. Seemingly
hundreds of feet long, it continues through each room of the
massive restaurant, blending unobtrusively with the decor.
Captains prepare many dishes at the table, where service is on
fragile, hand-painted china. An elaborate menu offers a wide
selection of à la carte items including a good, thick bird's nest

soup, sesame chicken, lobster with salty Virginia ham, and Jade West beef, served with fresh, crisp asparagus. The entrée I enjoyed the most was the abalone, served in thick chunks (rather than the more commonplace thin slices); the flavors and textures of an oyster sauce with mushrooms complemented the delicate freshness of the abalone. Complete dinners include the exotic Yang Chow melon soup, and a long wine list offers some unusual selections. (My recommendation: the *gerwurztraminer* from Alsace, a spicy, chilled white wine that goes prticularly well with Cantonese food.) Desserts are the weakest, but perhaps the least important, part of the menu. If you feel that your evening must have some sort of dramatic climax, you may select colorful drinks with fanciful names, some of which are flambéed at the table. Luncheons are far less expensive to appeal to the business and professional community in the area. Jade West is located in the same complex that houses the Shubert Theatre and if you dine before or after the show, your parking ticket remains good for the entire evening. In fact, given the unpardonable crush of humanity that invariably occurs when the shows break, this is an excellent place to visit for a drink while the other theatregoers grumble and jostle each other on the one set of escalators that leads down to the parking basement.

**Moderate to expensive.** Open seven days. Luncheon served from 11:30 a.m. to 3 p.m. weekdays. Dinner Monday 3 to 9 p.m.; Tuesday through Friday to 11; Saturday 4:30 to 11:30; Sunday 4:30 to 10:30. Closed Thanksgiving. Entertainment Tuesday through Saturday. Dancing. Full bar. Reservations recommended. Visa, MC, DC. Valet parking. Semi-dressy to dressy.

---

*To obtain the best results from this Guide, consult*
*"How to Use this Guide" on page 27.*

## JAILHOUSE CHILI COMPANY American/Mexican
4050 Laurel Canyon Boulevard ★
Studio City **Map 1** (213) 766-4794

There have been more culinary wars over the preparation of chili than any other dish in recent years. Here it is prepared with tomatoes, onion, masa, suet, cumin, and—a sacrilege to some—beans. There is more meat than beans, though, and it is very good. But then so are the combinations of steak and chili and the spareribs and the tostada. There's even a special price for the little critters if you want to expose their innards to the hot truth.

**Inexpensive.** Open Monday through Saturday. Luncheon from 11 a.m. to 6 p.m. daily. Dinner from 6 to 10 p.m. Children's menu. Wine and beer only. Reservations advised. Visa, MC, DC. Street parking. Casual.

## JAKE'S DEL MAR American
1660 Coast Boulevard ★
Del Mar (714) 755-2002

Would you believe that this used to be the garage of the great old Hotel Del Mar? Now it's one of the charming spots on the ocean with good food (live lobster, rack of lamb, fresh dungeness crab) great drinks and a spectacular view. Great spot for Sunday brunch.

**Moderate.** Open Tuesday through Saturday. Luncheon Tuesday through Saturday 11:30 a.m. to 2:30 p.m. Dinner 5 to 10 p.m.; to 11 Friday, Saturday. Sunday brunch 10 a.m. to 2:30 p.m. Check for summer hours. Full bar. Reservations recommended. Ocean view. Patio. Visa, MC, AX. Parking lot. Casual.

## JANTHINA'S                                        Seafood

24880 San Jacinto Street                                ★
San Jacinto (near Hemet)        **Map 5**        (714) 652-7551

There is a seashell by that name, and this restaurant, given
the utter poverty of acceptable establishments in the general
area, is noteworthy because it is of average quality. Looking
much like a franchise operation—they intend to have other
restaurants—the menu lists 50 dishes which is far too many
for the talent in the kitchen. However they are new to the
area and doubtless will adjust. The salad bar is o.k., the cocktail bar is great, and the service is inept, albeit friendly in a
simple-minded way.

**Moderate.** Open for lunch Monday through Saturday 11
a.m. to 4 p.m. Dinner from 4 to 10; Friday and Saturday to
11 p.m.; Sunday from 11 a.m. to 10 p.m. Sunday brunch.
Full bar. Entertainment. Reservations recommended. View.
Visa, MC, AX. Wheelchair access. Parking lot. Semi-dressy.

## JB'S LITTLE BALI                              Indonesian

217 East Nutwood Street                                 ★
Inglewood        **Map 3**               (213) 674-9835

Only one complete dinner, the multicourse, palate-expand-
ing Indonesian *rijsttafel*, is prepared in this small, attractive
place. Decor includes Indonesian artifacts, batik wall cover-
ings and tablecloths, and more than 4,000 Christmas cards
received over the years by Diane and Hans Qui from their
devoted customers. "Spicy" is the best single word to
describe this kind of feast, but boring it's not. Dinner
begins with gado-gado, a salad of stewed vegetables topped
with peanut-based sauce. You'll receive eight entrée items,
including marinated, skewered filet mignon; *pangsit goreng*
(chicken meatballs in ginger sauce), and *kare ayam* (chicken
cooked in coconut milk and curried). Condiments, five in
all, are the soul of the dinner and include ground spiced

317

shrimps, fried coconut and peanuts, and homemade pickled vegetables. Dessert and beverage (java coffee or Chinese jasmine tea) are included, but I would strongly recommend the beer on draft as the perfect accompaniment. Not for children (too spicy).

**Moderate.** Open Thursday through Sunday. Dinner 6 to 10 p.m. Thursday through Saturday; 5 to 9 Sunday. Wine and beer only. Reservations recommended. Visa, MC. Street parking. Semi-dressy.

---

## JERRY'S FAMOUS DELI        Deli
12655 Ventura Boulevard      ★
Studio City     **Map 1**      (213) 980-4245

The San Fernando Valley seems to attract more good delis than any other area and this one is certainly better than the tired delis on Fairfax. Jerry Seidman imports his pastrami, salami, Kosher franks, knockwurst and cheese cake from New York and keeps a sharp watch on quality control. When they opened in 1978 they knew it was going to be competitive, but they're hanging in there with the best.

**Inexpensive.** Open seven days 7 a.m. to 11:15 p.m. Sunday brunch. Piano bar. Cocktails. Reservations accepted for 10 or more. Terrace. Visa, MC. Wheelchair access. Parking lot. Casual.

---

## JIMMY'S        French
201 South Moreno Drive      ★
Beverly Hills     **Map 8**      (213) 879-2394

Poshest of the posh, it's difficult to argue with Jimmy Murphy's description of his widely publicized new manse as a place to dine "in elegant splendour with unending charm and ambience." The question is, dine how well? Jimmy is unquestionably one of the most gracious hosts extant; his years as maître d' at the Bistro have polished his charms to a silky finish. Jimmy's aspirations were certainly laudable. But the service is not faultless and sometimes, too often, a little simple-minded. Some of the service faults, fundamental errors that would be difficult to overlook in lesser establishments become glaring errors in a self-proclaimed temple of haute cuisine. Pâtés were good—if not spectacular—the blinis were excellent but the vegetables were overcooked, the sauces hesitant, the captain unfamiliar with the wine list, the busboys clumsy, and the desserts were like starlets, beautiful but vacuous. The tables seem unattended; except during the moments of service, no dining room supervision is in evidence and we had needs that went unattended. In a magnificent attempt like this it would be premature to sound the knell. Paris doesn't like to rate their restaurants for a year or two. Americans are less patient and, at this time, Jimmy's is hype, hip, but not haute.

**Expensive.** Open Monday through Saturday. Luncheon from 11 a.m. to 3 p.m. weekdays. Dinner 6 to 11 p.m. Closed major holidays. Full bar. Reservations essential. All major credit cards. Valet parking. Dressy.

---

## THE JOLLY ROGER                          American
(Everywhere—see white pages)

This large chain of restaurants located all over Southern California is the answer to family dining at reasonable prices. The expected hamburgers, steaks, and seafood are on the menu, but more intricate dishes such as boneless breast of chicken—marinated in teriyaki sauce, broiled, and served on rice pilaf—and vegetable crock, a combination of vegetables baked with cheese, can also be enjoyed. Ice cream specialties and frozen yogurt complete the all-American dining here. Cocktails and entertainment at some locations.

**Inexpensive to moderate.** Open seven days. Times and prices vary. Breakfast, lunch and dinner menus available at any time. Closed Christmas. Full bar at some locations. No reservations. All major credit cards. Wheelchair access at some locations. Casual.

---

## JOSEPHINA'S                                    Italian
4102 California                                   ★★
Bakersfield                              (805) 324-0981

10369 Santa Monica Boulevard
Century City      **Map 8**              (213) 553-6955

8930 Corbin
Northridge        **Map 1**              (213) 349-3030

110 East Holly Street
Pasadena          **Map 7**              (213) 796-8333

13562 Ventura Boulevard
Sherman Oaks      **Map 1**              (213) 990-0411

In the middle of a particularly wet sunset, an old and mellow friend called me, barely able to control the excitement in her voice, to tell me about "the best pizza in Southern California." It was perhaps the nine-hundredth time I'd heard that phrase, and I muttered malevolently as I slipped into my ancient Aquascutum and, collar turned up against the drizzle, prepared one more time to put the pizza where my mouth was (and still is). I nosed the old car out, the steel-belted radials churning up a shallow river of sparkling confetti in the early neon of Santa Monica Boulevard. Past Sears, past the Oriental Massage and Meditation Parlor, past Beverly Hills, I found Josephina's, a turn-of-the-century, fantasy-Italian restaurant. The bar was packed, damp shoulder against shoulder—a good sign— as the hostess slunk cordially out to greet me. I was seated amidst a decorator's frenzy of stained glass, whiskey mirrors, dress-making dummies and antique bicycles, just a few feet from an antique gas pump with its top converted into an aquarium filled with suspicious-looking fish. I browsed through the menu—the veal, the "Showcase" sampler—the cioppino and—my favorite—the shellfish marinara. Then I turned to the waitress and muttered, "Gimme a Ziegfeld's Folly—the works." Shortly thereafter the waitress (she was tall, peppy, and half-Hungarian) reappeared with an incredible dish with more resemblance to a casserole than a pizza. It had the usual—sausage, olives, pepperoni, cheese—but the sauce was made with fresh tomatoes (I checked), and it was topped with artichokes and avocado. I dipped in. It was great. It was fantastic. It was the best pizza I'd had in California. I beckoned to the hostess and asked to meet the boss. David Sidell seems all wrong for a restaurant tycoon. He's very young and very American, and he entered the business with no experience. I soon wormed out of him that he's opened a series of successful places called the Bratskellars (I made a note to try them), and he copped this secret pizza formula from a pal in Chicago from whence he came (or so he claims). After some top-secret experimenting he opened Josephina's. I asked, "How come Josephina's?" He shrugged and shot his cuffs. It was an instant success in Denver, in Sherman Oaks, and now here in Culver City. The prices are right, there's take-out service, a great bar, entertainment; it's kind of an adult Shakey's, only the real thing if you know what I mean. And the desserts, my God, the desserts are good. Try the chocolate chip cheesecake.

**Moderate.** Open seven days. Luncheon from 11:30 a.m. to 2:30 p.m. Dinner 5 to 10 p.m. Sunday through Tuesday; to 10:30 Wednesday, Thursday; to midnight Friday, Saturday. Closed major holidays. Full bar. Reservations accepted. Visa, MC, AX. Valet parking. Casual.

# JUNGRY JOSE

Seaport Village
Long Beach Marina          Map 3

**Mexican**
★
(213) 594-8666

You may resist mariachis, a colorful ethnic interior, or Mexican food, but the view from Jungry Jose's is haunting. Overlooking a waterfall next to the bay with sailboats coming and going, this restaurant offers mariachis, a complimentary champagne at Sunday brunch, and traditional Mexican fare. Fresh seafood includes red snapper, swordfish, and sea bass so you won't suffer unless it's from over-indulgence. Maybe not gourmet, but good for the eyes, and you won't be "jungry."

**Inexpensive to moderate.** Open seven days. Luncheon served from 11 a.m. to 4 p.m. weekdays. Dinner from 4 to 10 p.m. Sunday brunch from 10 a.m. to 3 p.m. Children's menu. Closed Thanksgiving, Christmas. Banquet facilities. Entertainment at Sunday brunch. Full bar. No reservations. Visa, MC, AX. Parking lot. Casual.

---

# JUNIOR'S

2379 Westwood Boulevard
West Los Angeles          Map 8

**Delicatessen**
★
(213) 475-5771

Recently, a publicist called to inform me that Junior's, rather than Art's, is the best deli in Los Angeles. He also said that the local Junior's is no relation of the one in New York, but that I shouldn't hold that against it. I don't. Junior's is a large deli, filled with smaller side rooms that you can lose yourself in. It's certainly the best deli in the neighborhood, what with Art's being in Studio City, and the other major deli in West Los Angeles—Shep's—having fallen on hard times, corned beef sandwich-wise.

As is the case in many large delis (like Katz's in New York, or Wolfie's in Miami), you can easily feel lost amongst all the noise and confusion. Waitresses come and go and quickly become lost in a sea of brisket, and that motherly touch isn't often there. What you do get is a menu large enough to serve as a pretty substantial coffee table book. You also get an ersatz pickle barrel filled with some half-sours which get devoured mighty fast, even though they're not all that great.

For whatever reason, the sandwiches at Junior's are named after cars. A Bugatti is a roast beef sandwich with onions and chicken fat. A Packard is corned beef with cole slaw and Russian dressing. You order a Cadillac; you get pastrami. You want turkey; you ask for a Pierce Arrow. None of the sandwiches bear any resemblance to the cars they're named after. And all of them include a side order of a tiny potato pancake, which is an incredibly civilized piece of serendipity.   *M.S.*

**Moderate.** Open seven days from 7 a.m. to 1 a.m. Beer and wine only. Reservations for six or more. Visa, MC. Parking lot. Casual.

---

**JW'S**                              **Nouvelle Cuisine**
700 West Convention Way                        ★★
Anaheim       **Map 6**                (714) 750-8000

The "J.W." here is for J.W. Marriott, and the boss would not allow the use of his name unless he thought his restaurant to be a super star. It isn't, but the effort is professional and commendable. *Nouvelle cuisine,* fresh game and seafood are served in a formal atmosphere that provides glimpses of the decor of many countries. Service is part formal and part Magic Castle—they whisk the domed cover off your entrée after everything is in place with a "voila!"—at least from my waiter. A harpist provides suitable background to this innovative restaurant that could become among Orange County's finest. Will Anaheim support this venture? They didn't in similar situations (The Three Greenhorns from Vancouver opened at the Quality Inn to a resounding silence) and tourists are not a dependable market for this fare.

**Expensive.** Open Tuesday through Saturday. Dinner from 6 to 10 p.m. Monday through Thursday, and 6 to 11 p.m. Friday, Saturday. Harpist nightly. Full bar. Reservations required. All major credit cards. Valet parking. Dressy.

*In order to obtain the best results from this Guide, be sure to read the French, German, Italian and Oriental menu translators on page 705 to 710 of this Guide.*

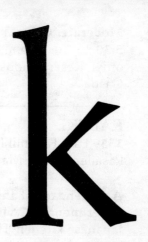

## KABAKIAN'S RESTAURANT    Armenian/Lebanese
3746 East Foothill Boulevard          ★
East Pasadena    **Map 7**    (213) 684-2551

This is a touchingly sincere place, serving over one hundred Middle Eastern dishes, with the emphasis on Lebanese. Nercess Kabakian tells us that all the dishes are prepared from recipes of the old country "taught to us by our dear departed mother." "We have a bakery adjoining the restaurant. You are free to bring your own wine, and we will furnish you glasses at no cost." All the dinners in this plain but charming restaurant include a choice of soup, *hemmos be tehineh* (a dip from Lebanon made of sesame seeds, garbanzo beans, and spices); three Armenian vegetables, and the dessert of the day with coffee. Entrées on these huge dinners range from an assortment of charcoal-broiled shishkabobs to such fantasies as *kufte* (meat, rose petals, and spices rolled in cracked wheat and nuts), with lots of familiar and unfamiliar dishes in between. The pastry is heavy, in the style of the Middle East, but it is all home-baked and good. There are special vegetarian dinners as well.

**Moderate.** Open Tuesday through Saturday. Dinner from 5:30 to 10:30 p.m. Closed major holidays. Wine and beer only. Reservations advised. No credit cards. Parking lot. Casual.

---

# KABUKI                                                          Japanese
3539 East Foothill Boulevard                                         ★
Pasadena          **Map 7**                              (213) 351-8963

A descendant of the respected Shogun restaurant, Kabuki is experimenting with *kaiseki ryori*, the *haute cuisine* of the Japanese kitchen The Shogun continues as *teppanyaki* restaurant with a sushi bar, and the Kabuki takes form as a general or family-style restaurant with emphasis on full dinners. Perhaps more imagination should have gone into the new enterprise. It had a very old, very familiar look, but it is nevertheless pleasant enough, and the service is particularly extraordinary.

Their specialties include beef *shabu-shabu* (thinly sliced with vegetables in broth, two sauces and a king crab version of that dish that is spectacular). My piece of crab looked as large as a baseball bat.

The sukiyaki and tempura (lobster tempura is a luscious dinner for ($16.50) are listed, but the *kaisaki* is served as well—an assortment of Japanese dishes on a complete dinner for about $25. The exotic names ripple as musically as splashing water in a pebbly brook—*tsukidashi, mizoreae, san shioyuki, tokkuri muschi, isobeoge* all unfamiliar, but then, we didn't know about sukiyaki or tempura until the early '50s. The manager, Mr. Sada, will guide you through the list.

Sushi chef Itaro Osawa prepared sushi for Henry Kissinger, and his presentation on a "boat" was as colorful and perfectly executed as any I've seen outside of Toyotaland. Chef Iwao Noritake was trained at Horikawa and his dishes are artfully arranged to appear as still lifes.

**Medium to expensive.** Open for luncheon Monday through Friday 11:30 a.m. to 2 p.m. Dinner Monday through Thursday 5 to 10 p.m.; Friday, Saturday to 10:30 p.m. Cocktails. Reservations suggested. Visa, MC, CB. Free parking. Casual to dressy.

---

## KALEMEGDAN
328 Redondo Avenue
Long Beach **Map 3**

Yugoslavian
★
(213) 434-4327

A real sleeper, this tiny taste of Yugoslavia has been satisfying the homesick fisherfolk in the area since it opened in '79. Not long on atmosphere or amenities, the emphasis is on solid food at reasonable prices and home cooking under the exacting supervision of Mike Miladinovich. There's a long list of strudels made with filo dough for luncheon, and they are stuffed with everything from sweet cabbage and onions to chicken and mushrooms resembling a European *dim sum*. There are 17 dinners with a whole range of unfamiliar dishes, but all are carefully explained on the menu. The Kalemedian salad as an appetizer consists of ham, feta cheese, eggs, agvar and tomato.

**Moderate.** Open for luncheon Wednesday through Friday 11 a.m. to 2 p.m. Dinner Wednesday through Saturday 5:30 to 9:30 p.m.; Sunday 5:30 to 9 p.m. Closed July 4, Thanksgiving, Christmas, New Year's Day. Beer and wine only. Reservations recommended. Visa, MC, CB, DC. Wheelchair access. Street parking. Casual (no shorts) to semi-dressy.

---

## KANDEL'S
20825 Sherman Way
Canoga Park **Map 1**

Jewish Deli
★★
(213) 704-1444

You can take the kid out of Brooklyn, but you can't take Mott Street out of a neighborhood guy like Jack Kandel who made mucho bucks as a developer. The results are a strange but workable combination of all that tastes good from his childhood and all that looks good in Bel Air. There are polite waiters, a self contained laundry to keep the massive restaurant—the Cadillac of Kosher—clean. Gone are the bleak florescent lights of Fairfax and the agonized and irritated countermen. Even the customers are different: well dressed, discerning and obviously not in a hurry. There's a chocolate eggcream, the Chateau Lafite of fountain drinks—two dozen entrées, great appetizers, homemade soups, bagel brunches and sandwiches by the ton.

**Inexpensive to moderate.** Open seven days. Sunday through Thursday 7 a.m. to 10 p.m.; to midnight Friday, Saturday. Banquet facilities. Closed Yom Kippur. Full bar. No reservations. Visa, MC, AX. Free valet parking. Casual to semi-dressy.

---

## KINGS                                    American
(Locations in Compton, Downey, El Segundo, La Palma, Long Beach and Los Angeles. See phone book for listings.)

This coffee-shop restaurant has been brought up to the highest state of the art of good food served fast and friendly. A family-owned, family-run operation, each location is plastic-plush with booths, counters, banquet halls, cocktail lounges, and entertainment. A big menu offers the usual fare with better-than-usual service and some pleasant touches, like casserole dinners and luncheons. Luncheon buffet is a good bet.

**Inexpensive.** Open seven days. Hours and prices vary according to location. Children's menu. Closed Thanksgiving, Christmas. Full bar. Reservations accepted in dining room; otherwise, no reservations. All major credit cards. Parking lot. Casual.

*Please be sure to consult "Tipping Made Easy" on page 25 of this Guide.*

## KIN JO

**Japanese**

980 North La Cienega Boulevard · ★

Los Angeles **Map 8** (213) 652-2443

This is not yet a great Japanese restaurant but it has a lot going for it. There is a sushi bar under the direction of chef Yuichi Mikan. He has implanted a more creative type of cuisine to appeal to the sophisticated Los Angeles diner (at least sophisticated insofar as Japanese food is concerned). There is a tempura bar that seats about 25 and it too is under the direction of some great chefs. The positive aspect is that Kin Jo is open until 2 a.m. and we have had hundreds of requests for after-theatre dining in Los Angeles. The late crowd will love it.

**Moderate.** Open Monday through Friday from noon to midnight; Saturday from 6 p.m. to 2 a.m. Full bar. Reservations advised. Visa, MC, AX. Valet parking. Casual.

## KIYO'S

**Japanese**

3365 5th Avenue ★★

San Diego (714) 298-4583

Kiyo Matsumoto once worked for the Benihana chain although he had yearnings to bring his Osaka-style cuisine to his own restaurant. He is adept at the art of sushi and often drives over a hundred miles of coastline to get fresh fish. The tempura, teriyaki *gyoza* are better prepared here than at most Japanese restaurants which is high praise because all Japanese restaurants maintain the highest standards of food preparation.

**Inexpensive.** Open Monday through Saturday. Luncheon served Monday through Friday from 11:30 a.m. to 2:30 p.m. Dinner 5 to 10 p.m. Closed lunch for Labor Day. Full bar. No reservations. Visa, MC. Street parking. Casual.

## KNOLL'S BLACK FOREST INN

**German**

124 Santa Monica Boulevard

Santa Monica     **Map 2**

★

(213) 395-2212

This place may be bad for your breadth. Definitely not to be confused with the Black Forest on Pacific Coast Highway—that one's a Bavarian bust—it is an authentic replica of typically small, hearty German restaurants of no great distinction. The roast goose, in season, can be good; but it can also be dry (I've had both), depending on the time of day and the mood of the kitchen and your horoscope. The proprietor's wife, Hildegard Knoll, is a charming hostess and makes sure you are as pleased as the food will allow. I did like the smoked pork loin with homemade sauerkraut washed down with draughts of good German beer.

**Moderate to expensive.** Open Tuesday through Saturday. Dinner Tuesday through Thursday 5:30 to 10 p.m.; Friday, Saturday 5:30 to 10:30. Full bar. Reservations required. All major credit cards. Parking on 2nd Street. Casual.

---

## KNOTT'S BERRY FARM

**American**

8039 Beach Boulevard

Buena Park     **Map 6**

★★★

(714) 827-1776

A three-star rating for a tourist attraction restaurant? You bet. Three stars means the recipient is among the tops in the nation and Knott's Berry Farm has undeniably the finest restaurant of any attraction in America. It's best understood when you realize that Knott's started as a restaurant. Walter and Cordelia Knott were farming back in the 20's and 30's but when the Depression came, that revered lady began cooking chicken dinners in her kitchen, and on her first day she served eight customers using her wedding china. From these modest beginnings a giant developed but it grew carefully, always—and now—under the supervision of the Knott family and in-laws. Walter

Knott indulged his interest in the West by buying and moving remnants of ghost towns to Buena Park in an effort to keep the hungry throngs, waiting in line for their chicken dinner, occupied. The ghost town kept expanding until now the complex includes the Fiesta Village, the Roaring 20's area, the heart-stopping rides and a theatre that presents "family" attractions. They serve millions of dinners a year in the Chicken Dinner Restaurant and the Steak House, and the quality is still there.

Even if the restaurants were standing alone they would represent a unique value. You're served a cherry rhubarb appetizer, green salad with French dressing, mashed potatoes with country gravy, cabbage seasoned with ham, hot buttermilk biscuits, berry preserves, choice of dessert: farm baked berry pie, ice cream or sherbert, and choice of beverage. If the folks that wait on you seem to enjoy what they're doing it's because they do. The Knott family makes every employee a partner in a unique profit sharing system, and they just gave them a voluntary raise to compensate for inflation.

Knott's Steak House serves up a pound of porterhouse or an extra large cut of prime rib for about $10, and that includes soup or tossed salad, baked potato, steak, and fries or rice pilaf. The breads, hot from the oven and served with preserves, are savory There's lots more on the menu—seafood, country-fried steaks, pork chops and beef stew. But the big news for the people who live around here is the fact that they have begun to serve wine—albeit quietly (to avoid jarring their image)—and the wine's a good one, C.K. Mondavi. Both restaurants have children's plates.

I've two secrets about the chicken dinner that I'll share with you. Secret #1: Ask for cucumber pickles. They're free, though not on the menu, and they taste kitchen fresh. #2: Order vanilla ice cream for dessert. When the waiter-person brings it, ask for lots of boysenberry jam and make yourself a sundae.

The fast food restaurants, and there are a lot of them, are better than average but our top rating really is shared by the two majors we have described. If you ge the time, browse through the shops and visit Virginia's gift emporium. You can buy homemade preserves, candy, chicken-to-go, magic tricks, pies, and so much more it's wearying to describe.

**Chicken Dinner: Inexpensive to moderate.** Open seven days. Breakfast seven days 7 to 11:30 a.m. Luncheon Sunday through Friday noon to 5 p.m. Dinner 5 to 9 p.m.; Friday, Saturday till 10 p.m. No alcoholic beverages. No reservations. All major credit cards accepted. Casual.

**Steak House: Inexpensive to moderate.** Open seven days. Luncheon and dinner Sunday through Thursday noon to 8:30 p.m.; Friday, Saturday to 9 p.m. Closed Christmas. Wine only. Reservations advised, especially on weekends. All major credit cards accepted. Casual.

---

## KONDITORI SCANDINAVIA  Scandinavian

362 North Camden Drive  ★
Beverly Hills  **Map 8**  (213) 550-9950

The smorgasbord here is among the best in the area; authentic dishes and a profusion of colorful salads and desserts. But that's not all—there's a full dinner menu with a variety of meat and fish selections as well as omelettes. Any repast should begin with a snort or two of *aquavit*, the colorless Scandinavian libation that is served icy cold and tastes of caraway. My Norse friends tell me that this national drink is used for everything—an aphrodisiac, stomach settler, even rubbed on the scalp to grow hair. I suspect (if they're not putting me on) that the only time *aquavit* is used externally is immediately after it has been used, in rather copious amounts, internally. Open-faced sandwiches join the smorgasbord at lunch, and it is a busy place at dinner, when reservations are a good idea. The decor, formerly rather stark, has been softened and lit with table lights that make the dining experience more flattering as well as appetizing.

**Moderate.** Open Monday through Saturday. Luncheon from 11:30 to 3 p.m.; light specials from 3 to 5 p.m. Dinner from 5 to 10 p.m. Closed major holidays. Full bar. Reservations required for dinner. Visa, MC, AX. Parking lot. Casual.

---

## KOREA GARDENS
950 South Vermont Avenue
Los Angeles    **Map 7**

Korean
★
(213) 388-3042

As in many Japanese restaurants, but few Korean restaurants, there are two different ways of dining at Korea Gardens—either sitting at a table in the standard Western manner, or sitting cross-legged at a low table. Though I find chopsticks an enjoyable excursion into Oriental etiquette, low tables have never worked for me. As a rule, part way through the meal, I begin to wonder if I'll ever walk again, which interferes with my dining enjoyment quite a bit.

The most popular dish at Korea Gardens, as it is at most Korean restaurants, would appear to be *bulkogi* (also spelled *bool koko, pulgogi,* and just about every other way you can imagine), which is a spicy, marinated beef dish, brought raw to the table for cooking on a *hwaro*. But as one of the most ornate and complex restaurants in Koreatown, Korea Gardens also offers a sizeable selection of dishes available at few other restaurants.

There's *shinsullo* (literally "wizard's barbeque"), for instance, a sort of Korean variation on the Mongolian *huo kuo* (or hot pot) in which a melange of fish, meat and vegetables are stewed at your table in a brass firepot filled with a beef broth. *Shinsullo* must be ordered in advance, and varies from serving to serving—I've found lamb, meatballs, chicken, mushrooms, noodles, fishballs and God-knows-what-else in *shinsullos* I've ordered. Another unusual dish at Korea Gardens is the *koo jul pan*, an hors d'oeuvres tray of sorts, served in an octagonal, black lacquered box with a center well-filled with tiny soft pancakes. In small cubby holes radiating from the pancakes are eight different types of snack—recently, some fried fish, shredded zucchini and carrots, sliced bamboo shoots, some marinated shrimp, mushrooms and so forth, all of which are intended to be wrapped—burrito-style—in the pancakes. The dish, curiously, is far more satisfying in the presentation than in the eating. The ingredients lean a bit toward the bland side, which is most appropriate—a meal, after all, cannot be *all* fire.   *M.S.*

**Moderate.** Open seven days from 11 a.m. to 10 p.m. Beer and wine only. Reservations suggested (essential for *shinsullo* and *koo jul pan*). Visa, MC, AX. Parking lot. Casual.

---

## KOUTOUBIA
2116 Westwood Boulevard
Westwood        **Map 8**

**Moroccan**
★
(213) 475-0729

Koutoubia provides a unique experience in Moroccan food, which has become the new rage in Southern California dining adventures. How much more romantic can a spot get than to offer an authentic wedding feast to its customers? Along with romance and adventure, variety also comes into play with courses that include everything from a good *b'stilla* (chicken, almonds, eggs, cinnamon in a filo pastry crust) to the soul food of the area, couscous. Here you can delight in the naturalness of eating with your fingers and sharing community platters. Hopefully, the romance and earthiness of this spot won't drive you to hold hands before the final handwashing, for the immediate results of all this lusty eating is terminal stickiness, but the experience is well worth it.

**Moderate to expensive.** Open Monday through Saturday. Dinner from 6 to 10 p.m. Monday through Thursday; 6 to 11 p.m. Friday, Saturday. Wine and beer only. Reservations required. All major credit cards. Street parking only. Casual to semi-dressy.

1

---

**LA BELLA FONTANA**                    **French/Continental**
Beverly Wilshire Hotel                              ★★
9500 Wilshire Boulevard
Beverly Hills          **Map 8**              (213) 275-4282

A strikingly formal dining room with soft rose walls, a
three-tiered fountain, and magnificent table settings with
fresh daisies to lighten the mood. Henry Becker (on some
occasions) wheels a gleaming silver cart festooned with row
upon row of his special hors d'oeuvres (he's been making
them there for nearly twenty years) and is delighted to
explain each dish ("Wait till you taste this one") with an air
of conspiratorial consultation. Hernando Courtright, operator of the great Beverly Wilshire Hotel in which this
restaurant is situated, is a man of consummate good taste,
a true gourmet, a perfectionist whose concern for every
detail is reflected by the attentive staff. The Bella Fontana's
menu includes some French specialties with a touch of the
exotic. Appetizers such as scampi with wine sauce, country
pâté, and *escargots forestière* on mushroom caps lead to such
entrées as salmon poached on a bed of sauerkraut with
mushrooms and white wine, whole lobster, split and lightly

seasoned with curry and cream, *noisette* of lamb on artichoke bottoms, tournedos St. Michel, and forced meat of veal and chicken. Salads are major productions, artichokes and sliced tomatoes with crab meat for instance, but I particularly liked the fresh mushrooms and watercress. The wine list—Mr. Courtright is a renowned connoisseur—is extensive, with some real bargains. Wines are sold at the original price and are not marked up until the supply runs out, and we had a fine dessert sauterne at about half the tariff many other, less notable restaurants charge. Luncheon at La Bella Fontana is a social and epicurean experience. I had a lamb stew that was the best I'd ever tasted, and in addition to daily specials and seafoods, there is a selection of salads for the more calorie-conscious people who frequent the Beverly Wilshire.

**Expensive.** Open Monday through Saturday. Luncheon from 12 to 3 p.m. Dinner from 6 to 11 p.m. Entertainment. Full bar. Reservations required. All major credit cards. Valet parking. Dressy.

---

## LA BRASSERIE                        French
202 South Main                              ★★
Orange          **Map 6**          (714) 978-6161

La Brasserie, a stunning yet informal French restaurant owned by a fine chef, Joseph Vieillemaringe, and restaurateur, Paul Rossi. It is a multi-level house of many moods and textures with a great bar-lounge and, my favorite, a warm and intimate library-dining room. The menu at dinner provides for a dozen hors d'oeuvres and a score of entrées that include homemade soup or salad and fresh vegetables. Joseph and Paul wanted a relaxed atmosphere; both are critical of the coldly arrogant restaurants that intimidate and bully their patrons. The chef begins his day at the produce mart in Los Angeles where he personally selects the fresh fruits and vegetables. He's liberal in his use of garlic (don't plan to kiss anyone for an hour or two after dinner). The partners met in France and both are from families rich in the tradition of fine restaurants. Both appear to be vibrating with enthusiasm and touched by their warm reception in Orange County, often thought of (but not by me) as a sort of gustatory blight area. Luncheon is busy. Cocktails and wines are reasonably priced and the wine list is appropriate for this type of restaurant.

**Moderate.** Open Monday through Saturday. Luncheon from 11:30 to 2 p.m. Dinner from 5 to 10 p.m. Full bar. Reservations advised. Patio service. All major credit cards. Parking lot. Semi-dressy.

---

## LA BROCHETTE                                    French
2424 Pico Boulevard                                    ★
Santa Monica          **Map 2**              (213) 450-5555

This family-owned bistro in Santa Monica, though new in years, reminds its patrons of old European intimate spots. Operated by Judy and Larry Buschnell, La Brochette offers beef bourguignon, breast of chicken braised in champagne, charbroiled brochette seasoned with herbs, and other specialties, some of which are prepared tableside. Wines are inexpensive but quite wide-ranging. Genuine hospitality seems to be the aim here with a touch of candor. For instance, a menu is posted to make sure the customer knows just what he may expect. Fair enough.

**Moderate.** Open Tuesday through Sunday. Luncheon from 11:30 a.m. to 2:30 p.m. Dinner from 6 to 11 p.m. or later. Private party facilities. Closed month of September. Full bar. Reservations recommended. Visa, MC. Parking lot. Casual.

## LA CABANA RESTAURANT      Mexican
738 Rose Avenue      ★
Venice     **Map 2**      (213) 392-6161

*Mole pablano*, an incredibly complex sauce of forty-six ingredients including chocolate and chili, provides a completely new dimension of taste—when it's done right. Watch someone's face closely at the first taste of *mole*, and you will see the expression continue to change moments after the encounter. This sauce, used most often with chicken dishes, continues its symphony of flavors with a *diminuendo* of aftertastes. Even though it's not done exactly right here, it's good enough to give you the idea. You can watch them make their own tortillas here, and the beef dishes are good, the sauces rich.

**Inexpensive.** Open seven days. Luncheon served 11 to 5 p.m. Dinner 5 to 3 a.m. Closed Thanksgiving and Christmas. Wine and beer ony. No credit cards. Casual.

---

## LA CAVE      American
1695½ Irvine      ★
Costa Mesa     **Map 4**      (714) 646-7944

Bill Boyer has quickened the pulse of all nonprofessionals who aspire to become restaurateurs (and who doesn't?). After release from the Marine Corps in 1962, he opened a small 55-seat steak-house that was a success from the beginning. It's a cozy charming, friendly room where intelligent and attentive waitresses seem to be happy with what they are doing. The salad with Caesar dressing and a hint of anchovy is served properly

---

*To obtain the best results from this Guide, be sure to consult maps on the various Southern California areas in the front of the book.*

chilled accompanied by hot, crunchy, aromatic cheese toast. We ordered steak and lobster (what else?), and we were served massive hunks of beef carefully charred to our order after being brushed and basted with what we were told is their secret sauce. Lobster was light and tender. Stuffed baked potatoes were served, not as an afterthought but as a well-prepared separate item. Drinks are hefty and the Bloody Marys were good enough to enter in a contest. An ample wine list supports the dinners, but most of all you know that you are in a place that really cares about you, and that's nice.

**Moderate.** Open Monday through Saturday. Luncheon from 11:30 a.m. to 2:30 p.m. Dinner 5:30 to 10:30 p.m. Monday through Thursday; to 11, Friday, Saturday. Closed major holidays. Children welcome. Full bar. Reservations recommended. All major credit cards. Parking lot. Casual.

---

## LA CHAUMIERE                           French
1305 State Street                                ★
Santa Barbara                          (805) 962-5607

One of Santa Barbara's finest small bistros — they seat 50 — a restaurant that would do credit to major metropolitan areas and would probably even do well in Barstow. Their escargot (did you know there's a shortage of imported escargot? Do you care? California's now breeding its own) is succulent and the lobster thermidor actually has lobster aboard. The menu is limited but each dish is an example of what the kitchen can do best although the dessert list, with our friend Monsieur Mousse au Chocolat, is uninspired.

**Expensive.** Open Tuesday through Saturday. Luncheon Tuesday through Friday 11:30 to 2:30 p.m. Dinner Tuesday through Saturday 6 to 10 p.m. Wine and beer only. Reservations advised. All major credit cards. Street and lot parking. Semi-dressy.

## LA CHAUMINE

French

★★

1466 Garnet Avenue
San Diego

(714) 272-8540

This restaurant looks more like its present name, the cottage, but acts more like its former name, La Fenière, which means silo or barn. Before you jump to confusions, give me a chance to say that an alert diner reading the menu might imagine a herd of inquisitive pigs out back sniffing out truffles to go with the tournedos of beef while a herd of contented cows could be whipping up a batch of fresh cream to top off the homemade apple tarts. It's true, the truffles are fresh and the cream is fresh. This is still the kind of correct cafe that is favored by professional people in Paris and has established a reliability that recommends calling for reservations three days in advance. Each night a different specialty, such as fresh salmon from Washington, is offered. The formerly scant wine list has been expanded to 160 choices. They've expanded their seating to 100 and added a new kitchen entrance, and now have banquet facilities. Roland Chassang has a winner here.

**Expensive.** Open Tuesday through Sunday. Dinner from 6 to 11 p.m. Full bar. Reservations required. All credit cards. Street parking. Casual.

## LA CHINOISE

Chinoise

★

23600 Rockfield Boulevard
Lake Forest

(714) 830-9984

My relentless investigation has disclosed that Chinoise cuisine may have been a gift to the world of Madame Chiang Kai-Shek. When this regal lady was in exile in Paris, after the revolution made China a Communist country, she hungered for foods from home but was fascinated with French cooking as well. She assigned her chefs the task of studying the art of classic French cooking to combine it with Cantonese. Richard

Wing, founder of the famed Imperial Dynasty, was one of those chefs, and his restaurant has become a beacon that has attracted epicures from the world around.

This restaurant in Orange County does not appear ready to be regarded as a legend, but it does have some imaginative touches of what could as well be called *nouvelle* Chinese. Appetizers of oysters with ginger, fresh mushrooms with oyster sauce and Chinese chicken salad were served adequately. The wine list is limited but appropriate. The atmosphere is attractive but, sadly, they seem eager to please the midwestern finicky palates of Leisure World, and the excitement is missing.

**Moderate.** Open seven days. Luncheon served 11 a.m. to 2 p.m. weekdays. Dinner Monday through Saturday 5 to 10 p.m. ; Sunday 5 to 9. Closed all major holidays. Full bar. Reservations suggested. All major credit cards. Parking lot. Casually-elegant.

---

**LA COSTA**                                    Mexican (seafood)
Calle 7a., No. 150                                         ★★
Tijuana                                      (70-668) 5-84-94

I asked the border guard on my way into Mexico, "Where should I eat in Tijuana?" Border guards are famous for their knowledge of the cuisine of the country whose border they're guarding, due to their spending most of their time sampling that cuisine while waiting for something to happen at the border. "Eat," he said, "at La Costa." The border guard was right. La Costa serves some of the best Mexican seafood I've ever sampled. And judging from the crowds that surge in and out of La Costa, its reputation is

*In order to obtain the best results from this Guide, please consult "Tips on Dining Out" on page 21.*

far from underground. La Costa is just around the corner from the Jai Alai Fronton, and it appears to be one of the few sitdown restaurants in Tijuana, even though Tijuana is relatively close to the Pacific Ocean. It obviously caters heavily to Americans (the menu is in Spanish and English), but La Costa never condescends. The seafood is full-flavored and even bold in its presentation. And it's also somewhat zany in its descriptions. You can have your lobster (*longosta*), for instance, prepared in eight styles—"Watergate," 'Hawaiian," "Seville," "New Burg" (sic) and so on. Oysters (*ostiones*) are prepared *diabla* ("the she devil") and *crilloa* ("Creole Indian") among other ways. In many ways, ordering a meal at La Costa can be a bit of a crap shoot—you choose a likely sounding dish and hope for the best. According to my experience, you can hardly ever miss. The meals begin with a complimentary piece of fried fish pieces, salty to inspire your beer drinking. Then comes a fish soup, sort of a pepper pot filled with all manner of unidentifiable fish pieces, and a fair collection of treacherous bones. At this point, an à la carte order of one of La Costa's mammoth seafood cocktails works as a decent break before plunging into the main course. There are cocktails of clams *(almejas)*, shrimp (*camaron*), abalone (*abulon*), oysters *(ostiones)*, scallops *(callos de hacha)*, lobster (*langosta*) and king crab (*congrejo Alaska*), though I usually opt for the mixed seviche, for the sake of all the lemon on it. For the main course at La Costa, the choices go ever on. There are 20 fried fish dishes (Aztec red snapper, sweetwater smelts and such), another 18 shrimp dishes (Blue Coast shrimp, Riviera shrimp, Bombay shrimp, etc.) Frog's legs are cooked "to taste" (*ancas rana al gusto*) and the octopus in garlic sauce is first rate. When I declined dessert at the end of the meal, my waiter brought me an order of Kahlua and cream anyway, on the house. La Costa is that kind of place.  *M.S.*

**Moderate.** Open seven days from 10 a.m. to midnight. Full bar. Reservations accepted. All major credit cards. Parking lot. Casual.

## LA CREPERIE BRETONNE

12130 Santa Monica Boulevard

West Los Angeles     **Map 8**

**French**

★

(213) 826-8177

A splendid crêperie that should do better than it's doing. A half-full Friday night is insufficient tribute to Charles Van Doan and his staff who work their buns off in an effort to please everyone who wanders in off the street. Crêpes are made one-at-a-time and the list is long and savory, including crêpes à la Bretonne (crab, asparagus and mushroom with sauce Normandie), *le palmier* with shrimp and hearts-of-palm zinged with Dijon sauce, veal Marengo, and many more. The *soupe de poisson* (fish soup) was much like bouillabaisse stock, and Charlie's Special includes shrimp and smoked salmon on a bed of freshly-cooked spinach, baked in lobster sauce and topped with Gruyère. The eight dessert crêpes are luscious combinations calculated to tempt you beyond reason. The atmosphere is quite charming, the wine list ample and the staff efficient and very pleasant. So why aren't there lines in front? There should be and may be.

**Moderate.** Open Tuesday through Sunday. Luncheon from 11 to 2:30 p.m. Dinner from 5:30 to 11 p.m. Saturday brunch. Wine and beer only. Reservations preferred. Visa, MC. Parking lot. Casual.

## LA CUISINE OF NEWPORT

1400 South Bristol

Costa Mesa     **Map 4**

**French**

★★

(714) 751-4252

## LA CUISINE OF DANA POINT

24312 Del Prado Street

Dana Point     **Map 4**

★★★

(714) 661-6801

Bill Discenzo, in this second of what may be the most exclusive chain of restaurants in the world, has accomplished a minor miracle here. Because of peculiar lease provisions, he literally had to transform a fast food restaurant in a motel into a temple of *haute cuisine*... in two weeks. From ground zero. The fact that he accomplished it in such luxurious style is noteworthy. The fact that the restaurant is performing so well is mind-boggling.

La Cuisine has the air of an elegant restaurant in the provinces of France with Queen Anne chairs, gleaming china, heavy crystal and lovely place settings. There are fresh flowers everywhere, even in special containers on the back of the doors. The long and elaborate menu includes many of the classics but it also shows a certain flair. The scallops in the Coquille St. Jacques were studded with caviar. *Feuillete d' enoki*, *dahi* and *shitaki* are three varieties of Japanese mushrooms diced and sauteed in white wine sauce, herbs and fresh tarragon, butter and dressed with puff pastry. There are many of the over-elaborate concoctions that seem to please the Orange County gastronome. Desserts are a specialty of the house. The wine list is huge with wine fairly priced at about twice wholesale.

**Expensive.** Newport location open seven days for brunch 9 a.m. to 2:30 p.m. Dinner both locations served seven nights 6 to 11 p.m. Sunday brunch Dana Point 10 a.m. to 2:30 p.m. Closed Christmas and New Year's. Full bar. Reservations requested. All major credit cards. Wheelchair access. Valet parking. Dressy.

---

## LA DOLCE VITA
Italian
★★

9785 Little Santa Monica Boulevard
Beverly Hills      **Map 8**      (213) 278-1845

In 1966 two ambitious young men who worked at Casa d'Oro, (now Carmine's,) in West Los Angeles, decided they were tired of accepting tips and tired of the heavy southern Italian cuisine they served. Beverly Hills deserved some.hing better. The unlikely marriage of George Smith and Jimmy Ullo would offer a subtler Northern Italian cuisine in a warm ambience; La Dolce Vita was the fruit of their union. Gentility is the keynote here. There is a small comfortable bar where you can actually hold a conversation, and you are unlikely to spend a half hour waiting for your table if you scowl at either Jimmy or George, one of whom is always in attendance. La Dolce Vita has the intimacy of a wine cellar and the feel of a study with its brick walls and beautifully finished woodwork. Nobody rushes you and the low key atmosphere may explain why many celebrities, including "Old Blue Eyes," make it a point to have dinner there. The faces are not always familiar since the real power brokers from studios and networks don't often get their pictures in the papers, but at the next table you may overhear someone planning a twenty million dollar film or deciding on how to program a key TV series. There is a good reason for their attendance . . . the food. Everything is done with care and the finest materials are used. Calamari salad in a light olive oil, vinegar, and garlic dressing is an irresistible appetizer. Steamed clams *posillippo*, or Jimmy's version of *moules mariniere* (in season) are continuing favorites. Except for the dried pastas which are imported, all pastas are made on the premises. Despite the fact that there are 19 pastas on the menu, the captain will apprise you of such specials as *Tagliarni Tree*, noodles finer than fettuccine, in a sauce of fresh peas, *prosciutto*, cream and parmesan cheese, served *al dente*. Lasagna *verdi bolognese* and *pasta pesto* (in a fresh basil sauce) are extraordinary. There are daily fish specials ranging from sand dabs to swordfish. Jimmy's *osso bucco* (knuckle of veal) is served only on Thursday and if you are an aficionado of this dish, I suggest you order it when you make your reservation or it may be sold out when you arrive for dinner. The veal dishes cover the range from veal *piccata* to the redoubtable *scaloppine pizzaiola* in a garlic tomato sauce. Veal steak is another specialty, broiled and served pink with a wedge of lemon. Desserts include the richest spumoni I've ever tasted to the best cheese cake this side of Ferraro's in New York. As befits a restaurant of the calibre of La Dolce Vita, the wine list is extensive without being imperious, although there are eighteen pages of it. You will find a remarkable variety of bordeaux and burgundies, from a California cabernet sauvignon to Chateau Lafite-Rothschild 1966. One delightful surprise on the wine list in Corvo di Salaparuta, a dry fragrant Sicilian white wine.

*Norman Bogner*

**Expensive.** Open Monday through Saturday. Dinner from 5 to 11 p.m. Closed Thanksgiving, Christmas. Full bar. Reservations essential. All major credit cards. Valet parking. Semi-dressy.

---

## LA ESPECIAL
Revolucion 718
Tijuana

Mexican

(70-668) 5-66-54

One needs a touch of cleverness to find La Especial, since it is very well hidden. It's one story below the main street in Tijuana, on the edge of a large marketplace, where the eye is drawn constantly left and right by hawkers selling *serapes* and bullwhips and onyx ashtrays. There's a small neon sign on Revolucion which says La Especial, and if you can find the sign and descend the stairs at that point, you can't miss the place. It's well worth not missing. La Especial is the Mexican restaurant I've been looking for here in Los Angeles for as long as I can remember. Though we have restaurants that come close, there's nothing that quite duplicates the simplicity and style of La Especial. There's almost always a line in front of people waiting hungrily to sit at plain wooden tables, and eat some of the world's most straight-forward Mexican cuisine. As at many Mexican restaurants, the working principle is the combination plate, mixing every imaginable permutation: *tacos* and *tamales*, *enchiladas* and *quesadillas*, *tostadas* and *chile rellenos*, common enough Mexican restaurant dishes, but rarely have I tasted them as equisitely prepared as at La Especial. The *chile relleno*, for instance which is so often a pathetic creation made out of an anemic chile filled with some miserable excuse for cheese, is in this case, long and elegant, stuffed with tangy *queso de Oaxaca*, breaded and fried to a turn. At La Especial, there are *huevos rancheros* cooked with care and served with a fiery salsa. There is baked pork (carne de puerco adobada), and fine *guacomole* served chunky rather than pureed. Even the *frijoles* taste as if they've been fried and refried with love. My last image of La Especial is of pulling several napkins from the wooden napkin holders with flowers painted on them, and wiping my lips. Then gobbling a last handful of marinated carrot slices from the complimentary *jalapeno* and carrot dish on my table. And then I realized with a painful swallow that I had gotten a *jalapeno* pepper in the bargain.   *M.S.*

**Inexpensive.** Open seven days from 9 a.m. to 10 p.m. Closed November 20. Beer only. Reservations accepted. Visa, MC. Street parking. Casual.

---

## LA FAMIGLIA
453 North Canon Drive
Beverly Hills    **Map 8**

**Italian/Continental**
★
(213) 276-6208

Across town in Beverly Hills, La Famiglia demonstrates the *alta cucina*, the high art of Italian cuisine from which the *haute cuisine* of Escoffier borrowed sauces and ideas. This intimate, sparkling creation is a tribute to the finesse developed by owner Joe Patti during his decade at La Scala. Everything on the à la carte menu is very special, from the list of a dozen antipastos to the pasta (*al dente*, of course), the fresh fish (three scampis), and a talented handling of veal in a variety of dishes that allows the delicate flavor to come through. It's a celebrity haven as well, and you'll usually be dining with the likes of Wilt Chamberlain or Liz when she's in town. The Amaretto mousse should make someone's dessert hall of fame, although I opt for the zabaglione. If you get the idea that this is not an inexpensive restaurant, you're right. The wine list is one of the best in town, and you'll want to linger over cappuccino or the caffé espresso. Casual but chic.

**Expensive.** Open Monday through Saturday. Luncheon from 11:30 to 2:30 p.m. Dinner from 5 to 10:30 p.m. Full bar. Reservations preferred. All major credit cards. Validated parking days; valet parking evenings. Casual.

---

## LA FAYETTE
12532 Garden Grove Boulevard
Garden Grove       **Map 6**

French
★★
(714) 537-5011

This is about as French as you can get in Orange County—or anywhere else, for that matter. The mussels *poulete* (mussels in a white cream sauce) and the rabbit sautéed in red wine are my favorites here, and the pâté—a blend of duck and pork liver with fresh peppercorn—is marvelous. The setting is one of growing grandeur (I watched it grow from a rustic, unfinished mademoiselle to this sophisticated lady-of-the-world). You're served amidst fine oil paintings and artifacts. The desserts (try the rum cake or the Napoleon mocha) are baked fresh every day except Monday.

**Moderate to expensive.** Open Tuesday through Saturday. Luncheon from 11:30 a.m. to 2 p.m. weekdays. Dinner from 6 to 10 Tuesday through Thursday; to 10:30 Friday, Saturday. Special dinners served to groups. Banquet facilities. Closed major holidays except New Year's. Full bar. Reservations recommended. Visa, MC, AX, CB. Parking lot. Wheelchair access. Semi-dressy.

---

*To obtain the best results from this Guide, consult "How to Use this Guide" on page 27.*

# LA FONDA

2501 Wilshire Boulevard
Los Angeles    **Map 7**

**Mexican**
DA ★
(213) 380-5055

I prefer to take my guests from out of town to La Fonda instead of to Olvera Street. At the risk of committing tourist heresy, Olvera has a certain boring sameness about the souvenirs, the refried beans and the entertainment. La Fonda, on the other hand, has surprisingly good food *and* the world-famous Los Camperos. Nati Cano has assembled a group of splendid musicians who are talented singers and comedians, and the fame of Mariachi Los Camperos is such that they have played to audiences throughout the nation. Las Vegas, Carnegie Hall, Hawaii and Hollywood Bowl audiences seem surprised to find that a Mexican orchestra is just that — an orchestra. The violins, French horns, brass section and harpist are a truer reflection of the culture of Mexico than the stereotypical strolling assortment of guitarists. The performances are thrilling, the musicians costumed brilliantly, and the architecture of the room, especially its massive balcony, seems to surround the stage. The menu included the best *mole poblano* chicken in a sauce of red chiles, peanuts and chocolate that I've had in gringo land. The *arroz con pollo* is cut breast of chicken in a zesty Spanish cheese. The menu is somewhat limited but confined to the dishes that the kitchen can do best. La Fonda may be one of the best places ever to celebrate anything from birthdays to divorces. They serve a drink that's a special favorite of mine called the sangrita (not sangria, that's wine punch), a combination of tequila and spicy tomato juice. There are four shows nightly.

**Inexpensive to moderate.** Open seven days. Luncheon from 11 a.m. to 2 p.m. weekdays. Dinner from 5:30 p.m. to 2 a.m. Closed for lunch major holidays. Four shows: seatings at 5:30, 8:15, 10:15, 12:15. Full bar. Reservations essential. All major credit cards. Street parking. Casual.

## LA FONDUE BOURGUIGNONNE                     French

1085 Gayley Avenue                                  ★
Westwood Village          **Map 8**         (213) 208-8542

13359 Ventura Boulevard
Sherman Oaks          **Map 1**             (213) 501-0181

Expensive, but fondue lovers will exult at the variety and
the attractive dunking gear. Everything is fresh and raw,
and you do the cooking in the bubbling concoction that
occasionally can make life interesting for your dry cleaner.

**Expensive.** Open Monday through Saturday. Dinner from
6 to 9:30 Monday through Thursday, from 6 to 10:30 p.m.
Children's menu. Wine and beer only. Reservations preferred. All major credit cards. Street parking. Casual.

---

## LA FRITE                                    French

15013 Ventura Boulevard                             ★
Sherman Oaks          **Map 1**             (213) 990-1791

22616 Ventura Boulevard                             ★
Woodland Hills          **Map 1**           (213) 347-6711

These joyous, sensible, informal restaurants of French
specialties and snacks encourage diners to split all kinds of
dishes for round-robin tastings. There are cocktails in a
capricious bar with the famed French cartoon character
"Asterix" as part of the decor. Seventeen different crêpes, a
good *ratatouille* (tomatoes, onions, eggplant cooked in olive
oil and served hot as a vegetable or sometimes cold as an
appetizer) are part of the carte.

**Inexpensive.** Open Monday through Saturday in Sherman
Oaks. Open Tuesday through Sunday, in Woodland Hills.
Lunch and dinner from 11:30 a.m. to midnight on weekdays,
and until 2 a.m. on Friday and Saturday. Reservations
advised. Visa, MC. Parking lot in Woodland Hills. Casual.

## LA GRANGE AUX CREPES                    Crêperie
1025 West Washington Boulevard                 ★★
Venice        **Map 2**              (213) 396-6005


15472 Ventura Boulevard                        ★★
Sherman Oaks        **Map 1**        (213) 986-9332

**Ten years** ago this restaurant would have been considered a
**posher-than-usual** Venice coffeehouse. Today it's full of hanging
**plants,** suspended candles, good smells, happy conversation,
**and** the real people of the Marina, enjoying an improbable
array of crêpe combinations at reasonable prices. Along with
this variety of crêpes they have good soups (try the fresh
garlic) and some of the best desserts in the hemisphere. I had
the Meryle, which consisted of (ready?) fresh thin slices of
orange, slathered with hot melted fudge and slivered almonds,
served on a crêpe and flambéed with orange liqueur. My God!
This is a great place to sip inexpensive wine (you can bring
your own with no corkage fee), people-watch, and unwind. La
Grange is a bit hard to find. It's on West Washington
Boulevard, not Street.

**Inexpensive to moderate.** Open seven days. Lunch from 11
a.m. to 3 p.m. weekdays. Dinner from 5:30 to 11:30 p.m. in
Venice; 4 to midnight in Sherman Oaks. Sunday brunch 11
a.m. to 3 p.m. Banquet facilities. Closed Thanksgiving. Wine
and beer only. Reservations recommended. Patio. Visa, MC.
Street parking. Casual.


## LA GRANGE RESTAURANT          French/Continental
2005 Westwood Boulevard                         ★
Los Angeles        **Map 8**         (213) 279-1060

La Grange means "the barn" in French, but there is nothing
rustic or unsophisticated about this restaurant in Westwood,
which has won passionate devotees from the time it opened

in 1968. Owners Rudolphe nd Monique Valle have provided interesting and colorful settings for the exceptional food, with antique farm implements and stuffed owls and ducks above the brown leather banquettes. Chef Rudolphe makes his creations sing. The great dish here is chicken *poulet jurassienne*, skillet-browned chicken cooked in a sauce of white wine with shallots, onions, and morels. The flavor is as nearly indescribable as a taste can be, and will offer new dimensions to your palate. The stuffed eggplant *hongroise* is a favorite, and the white fish is great. Desserts are baked on the premises. Cherries Jubilee here is what it should be, not the ridiculous concoction served under that name by many restaurants; but the tarte Normande is my favorite. The wine list is heavily into the wines of France; both the famous and modest are priced quite reasonably. The California wines are listed by variety, but instead of indicating the label (or brand name), there are the words "our selection," with the exception of Korbel Brut. Ostensibly, only the wines that most appeal to the exacting palate of M. Vallee are selected. The menu is basically à la carte, although all entrées are garnished with appropriate vegetables. There are often specialties, and the menu changes frequently. The fresh artichoke Bretonne is a fine appetizer. *Terrine maison* is good, as is the *scampi niçoise*. I was disappointed with the snails *bourguignonne*, all-too-ordinary in this otherwise extraordinary restaurant—rather like coming across a pedestrian chapter in a Hemingway novel.

**Moderate to expensive.** Open Monday through Saturday. Luncheon from 11:30 a.m. to 2 p.m. weekdays. Dinner 6 to 10 p.m. Monday through Thursday; to 10:30 Friday, Saturday. Closed major holidays. Full bar. Reservations recommended. All major credit cards. Parking lot. Casual.

For best results, consult "How to Use This Guide" on page 27.

## THE LAKESIDE

Continental
★★

4110 MacArthur Boulevard
Newport Beach   **Map 4**   (714) 752-7841

Irwin Milman started with an impossible dream, a man-made lake and waterfall, a massive menu, and the kind of atmosphere that boggles New Yorkers when they discover it in the so-called boondocks, near the Orange County airport. The entire structure is made of wood (an endangered species in this plastic age) and there are high ceilings, an atrium of glass with a massive fireplace — almost like entering a different dimension in restaurants. Their specialty is everthing; the 86 entrées are cooked to order and you can ask the captain to guide you through the nine page menu. I've watched this beautiful restaurant from its beginning, through growing pains and adolescence into the confident, mature place it has become. I recommend it.

**Expensive.** Open seven days. Luncheon served from 11 to 4 p.m. Dinner served from 4 p.m. to 12:30 a.m. Entertainment. Full bar. Reservations preferred. All major credit cards. Valet parking. Semi-dressy.

## LA MARINA

Continental
★

Santa Barbara Biltmore
1260 Channel Drive
Santa Barbara   (805) 969-2261

On summer days, the bougainvillea-covered patio is a lovely setting for luncheon, for omelettes or fresh halibut with *mousseline* (a light airy version of hollandaise mixed with whipped cream) and for sipping cold drinks. The elegant, dimly lit dining room is rather formal and grand. Boeuf bourguignon, lamb stew, and beef stroganoff are the best of the sophisticated menu. The dessert cart is filled with home-baked pastries, fresh and appealing. This beautiful spot has been here since 1928.

**Moderate to expensive.** Open seven days. Breakfast served Monday through Friday from 7 to 11 a.m.; Sunday 7 to 9 a.m. Luncheon from noon to 2:30 p.m. weekdays. From 2:30 to 7 light snacks served. Dinner from 6 to 10 p.m. Sunday brunch from 10 a.m. to 2 p.m. Full bar. Reservations advised. All major credit cards. Parking lot. Semi-dressy to dressy.

---

## LA MASIA
9077 Santa Monica Boulevard
Los Angeles          **Map 8**

**Spanish**
DA★
(213) 273-7066

A good place to learn what *paella* is all about, La Masia features some Castilian dishes of Barcelona, including stuffed little-neck clams, *canalones de Mariscos* (cannelloni stuffed with crabmeat, shrimp, and fish), *mariscada* (particularly thick bouillabaïsse), and beef *Andaluza*, a filet mignon stuffed with ham and mushrooms. Dinners include fresh mixed salad, entrée, vegetables, and rice. From 8 to 10:30 business is very brisk, and you'll want to call ahead to reserve.

**Moderate.** Open Tuesday through Saturday. Luncheon from 11:30 a.m. to 2 p.m. Dinner from 5 to 10:30 p.m. Sunday brunch from 10:30 a.m. to 2 p.m. Closed major holidays. Entertainment weekends only. Full bar. Reservations advised. Visa, MC, AX. Parking lot. Casual.

---

## LAMONICA'S
10925 Weyburn Avenue
Westwood          **Map 8**

**Italian**
★
(213) 208-8672

New York-style pizza is defined in two ways. The first way is that it's basically a thin-crusted pizza—usually created by throwing the dough high into the air with a twirling motion so that it centrifugally flattens itself—topped with a thick tomato sauce heavily spiced with oregano, and plenty of cheese. The pepperoni, sausage, et. al. are usually scattered carefully over the surface of the pizza to provide for an aesthetically pleasing visage. The other way that New York-style pizza is defined is that it's sold by the slice, and is eaten as you walk.

There are many purveyors of New York-style thin-crust pizza in Los Angeles but the walk-and-eat aspect of the stuff has suffered badly. But there is one part of Los Angeles where walking is a noble occupation, and that's Westwood. And, it's in Westwood that Lamonica's New York Pizza has found its rightful home.

Lamonica is the guy behind the counter tossing the pizza high in the air. As he sloshes the sauce and tosses the cheese across yet another pie, he explains in a nonstop New York accent how he's made pizza in Manhattan and Brooklyn. Lamonica and all his helpers wear t-shirts bearing the clever Lamonica logo—a California license plate with the words "LAMONICA'S NY PIZZA" on it. Their motto is, "It's tossed in the air—then sauced with a flair." A slice of pizza costs 70 for the regular model, and goes up to a dollar for either mushrooms, sausage or pepperoni. Lamonica's has something of the air of an emigré cafe about it, where displaced persons from New York gather to talk about the old days over a slice of pizza with a wonderfully tangy sauce, accompanied by a cup of Fanta orange, or maybe a Tab.    *M.S.*

**Moderate.** Open seven days. Monday through Thursday 11:30 a.m. to 10:30 p.m.; Friday, Saturday to midnight; Sunday 3 to 10 p.m. Closed Easter, July 4, Thanksgiving, Christmas. No alcoholic beverages. No credit cards. Limited wheelchair access. Street parking. Casual.

*To obtain the best results from this Guide, be sure to consult maps on the various Southern California areas in the front of the book.*

# LAND'S END
Seafood

323 Ocean Front Walk

★

Venice    **Map 2**    (213) 392-3997

The European version of the seafood restaurant I most admire is, again, the simpler, more sincere one. A restaurant that attempts only what it can do well—no more—and is not embarrassed to offer a limited menu where the selections are dishes prepared with skill and served with pride. Such a discovery, for me was Land's End in Venice. There were thirteen seafood entrées, and all were fresh and served beautifully in this informal cafe where a woodsy atmosphere coaxes you into loosening your tie or slipping out of your shoes. Red snapper with capers and imported lotte with shallots were served with a magnificent mussel chowder—rich, creamy and colorful. The wine list was a revelation, with intelligent selections from abroad and a representative listing of California varieties (try the Novitiate pinot blanc). Land's End is an interesting Sunday brunch spot, too, with a continental breakfast: croissants, orange juice, and muffins or the champagne special, which is the Continental plus omelettes or poached egg with hollandaise sauce, caviar, and quiche du jour, as well as a choice of other egg dishes, salads, and sandwiches à la carte. Nice touches: classical music in the background, helpful, friendly waiters, experienced wine service, sweet butter and good bread. And, of course, fresh flowers. Sidewalk dining when the weather permits, for the romantic and young at heart.

**Moderate.** Open seven days. Dinner from 5:30 to 10 p.m. Sunday brunch 10 a.m. to 2:30 p.m. Wine and beer only. Reservations accepted. Ocean view. Visa, MC. Public parking by beach. Casual.

## LANNATHAI                                    Thai
4457 Van Nuys Boulevard                            ★
Sherman Oaks      **Map 1**              (213) 995-0808

This is Thai elegance situated on the site of a former
swimming pool display company that left behind some
pools to reflect the soft lighting. A pagoda transforms one
pool into an event in which guests lounge around the pool
and grapple with the huge menu. Owner Surapol Mekpon-
satorn—try that with your mouth full—will consult with
you and you'd be wise to leave your taste of Thai to him.
There are cocktails served with flair, and the low prices
seem almost incongruous here.

**Inexpensive to moderate.** Open seven days. Luncheon served
Monday through Friday from 11:30 a.m. to 2:30 p.m.;
dinner Sunday through Thursday from 5:30 to 10:30 p.m.;
Friday and Saturday to 11 p.m. Closed Christmas and New
Year's. Full bar. No reservations. All major credit cards.
Valet parking. Casual.

## LA PARISIENNE                              French
1101 East Huntington Drive                       ★★
Monrovia       **Map 6**                 (213) 357-3359

I have had my share of disappointments on gastronomic
safari. I once traveled 70 miles to a highly touted resort
where the "great souffle" turned to library paste, the
"terrific little house wine" had the viscosity and flavor of
milk of magnesia and the "great view" overlooked a tennis
court where spavined players looked as though they'd been
drenched in cocoa butter as they scuttled around the net
like brown crabs—hardly the tanned graceful nymphs of

my freeway fantasy. Perhaps the most improbable—and rewarding—adventure was to La Parisienne, then located in the bleakest industrial section of El Monte. The food was worth the lack of ambience and I had a surprise place to talk about! Imagine my disappointment when my favorite "find" went flambé: poof and it was gone.

When I heard that La Parisienne was relocating in Monrovia I was skeptical. Old favorites that upgrade usually wind up in a vinyl resting place of no special virtue. But the proprietors had a dream and El Monte was merely the prelude.

The graceful restaurant is fashioned in the style of a luxurious countryside inn of France. Two brick fireplaces, dark wood and beams set against the white walls, crisp linen, fine china, crystal and fresh flowers create the new atmosphere. Highbacked chairs upholstered in print—the same material used in the draperies—are worlds apart from the family-style seating of earlier days, but, most importantly, the quality of the food has not changed.

The successful French restaurants are team-operated to implement the two highly complex and dissimilar halves: the kitchen and the front of the house. Julien Espériquette is a fine chef. Jean Jacques Sarfati and Robaire Belestra are thorough, professional restaurateurs.

Luncheon is no mere accommodation to the merchants of the area. Filet of *sole meunière*, *foie de veau* sauté Parisienne and an excellent trout served in the style of the South of France are a sampling of entrées. Dinner lists the dishes you would expect to find in a fine French restaurant with a modest effort to provide a suggestion of that indefinable *nouvelle cuisine*. On Friday their famous bouillabaisse is served; and desserts are made on the premises, rich with the flavors of fruit, chocolate and cream.

Dinner for two with wine is in the $50 range; luncheon is much less. The wine list is an education in some of lesser known—but enjoyable—wines along with the old familiars.

**Expensive.** Open Monday through Saturday. Luncheon from 11 a.m. to 2 p.m. weekdays. Dinner from 5:30 p.m. Closed July 4, Labor Day, Thanksgiving, Christmas. Full bar. Reservations required. All major credit cards. Valet parking evenings; parking lot days. Casual.

---

## LA PETITE MAISON French/Continental
8828 Sunset Boulevard ★
West Hollywood **Map 7** (213) 652-2555

Alas, times change and old friends disappear. This used to be The Aware Inn, a far above-average organic theme restaurant. The new owner, D.N. Nadumoff, had his eye on the location for several years and finally made his move. The new premises are tastefully designed to retain the terrific view. While the kitchen now features dishes like *papillotte*, scampi peri-peri and souffles, the concern for natural foods has remained. Everything's fresh. Perhaps this restaurant reflects the change in the record company personnel who used to lounge around in questionable jeans and white socks with fruit flies buzzing around their heads. Now there is more of a Mike Curb look and the new establishment would be comfortable for the New Republicans.

**Moderate to expensive.** Open seven days. Luncheon from 11:30 a.m. to 2:30 p.m. weekdays. Dinner from 6 to 11 p.m. Full bar. Reservations advised. View. Visa, MC, AX, DC. Valet parking. Casual to semi-dressy.

---

## LA PIZZA Italian
4454 Van Nuys Boulevard
Sherman Oaks **Map 1** (213) 986-0581

I happened upon L.A. Pizza completely and totally by accident. After a couple of hours of staring blankly at a film notable mostly for its intense lack of plot, I wandered over to the nearby Sherman Oaks Shopping Center in search of a margarita and some *nachos*. And there it was, an Italian restaurant I had never seen before. I meandered in, and was immediately poleaxed by a sight that screamed contradictons.

Seated in what looked like the world's most average Italian restaurant were table after table of men wearing *yarmulkes*, some of them in the traditional black garb and long side curls of the Hasidim. There, in one corner was a pizza oven, yet the clientele was definitely not Sicilian. I picked up a copy of the menu and found, just beneath the words "L.A. Pizza Ristorante," the phrase "A Kosher Italian Restaurant."

Any cuisine can be kosher, as long as it adheres to the basic dietary tenet. And though La Pizza does a few fancy steps to keep their dishes in line, everything is not only kosher, but quite good as well.

The pizza, for instance, is very fine—thin skinned in the New York style, with a thick layer of cheese, a piquant sauce, and a choice of such toppings as mushrooms, anchovies, black olives, green peppers, onions, jalapenos (which I tried, and which gave me the hiccoughs) and pepperoni. Or more specifically, "pepperoni"—like the "meatballs" and the "salami"—are vegetarian versions of meat products made out of soy protein and flavorings which approximate the original ever so slightly.

Aside from the lack of meat, the Italian cuisine at La Pizza is on the good, wholesome level to be found at most neighborhood Italian restaurants. There's spaghetti with a tomato sauce, mushrooms, garlic and oil, or eggplant. The *cannelloni* is heavy but hearty. And a *pita* bread sandwich (called a *panini*) is served, filled with tomatoes and cheese, or sauteed vegetables, or tuna.   *M.S.*

**Moderate.** Open Saturday through Thursday. From 4 to 11 p.m. weekdays; 9 p.m. to 1 a.m. Saturday; 11 a.m. to 9 p.m. Sunday. Closed Jewish holidays. Beer and wine only. Reservations accepted weekends. Visa, MC. Parking lot. Casual.

---

## LA PLACE
French/Continental

10323 Santa Monica Boulevard ★

West Los Angeles  **Map 8**  (213) 277-1333

An intimate, romantic French restaurant across from Century City—one of the rare ones that manage to combine good food with entertainment. Owner Verita Thompson hosts an unusual number of celebrities: politicians prefer the rack of lamb and T-bone steaks, and show businesses people are more involved with the continental entrées and each other. An open fire, fresh flowers, and a patio soften the setting. Usually there is also a classically oriented entertainer who is not obtrusive; I remember a couple who played great guitar on my last visit. The menu is limited, but you should try the shrimp La Place.

**Moderate to expensive.** Open Monday through Saturday. Luncheon from 11 a.m. to 3 p.m. Dinner from 5 to 11 p.m. Wine and beer only. Patio. Visa, MC, AX. Valet parking. Semi-dressy.

---

## LA POLONAISE
French

225 South Beverly Drive ★

Beverly Hills  **Map 8**  (213) 274-7246

There is a Basque influence here in specialties found in these parts. *Ttoro de Saint-Jean-de-Luz* is from the Pyrenees, a cross between *cioppino* and bouillabaisse. *Farcie d'agneau en croûte* is the Saturday night fever here, a boned and rolled leg of lamb stuffed with ham, veal, beef, and spinach and served with a splendid mint sauce. Seafood is well prepared and served, and soups change daily. Try the Basque's delight for dessert. It is richer than anything I've had but I finished it, damn it. Salads are exceptional.

**Moderate to expensive.** Open Tuesday through Sunday. Dinner served Tuesday through Saturday from 6 to 11 p.m.; Sunday from 5 to 10 p.m. Closed Christmas and New Year's. Full bar. Reservations essential. All major credit cards. Valet parking. Semi-dressy.

---

## LA SALSA
Mexican
11075 West Pico Boulevard ★
West Los Angeles      **Map 8**      (213) 478-2106

10959 Kinross Avenue ★
Westwood Village      **Map 8**      (213) 208-7666

2600 West 6th Street ★
Los Angeles      **Map 7**      (213) 384-9935

The La Salsa restaurants in Los Angeles are the most authentic reproductions of the *tacorillas* of Mexico City imaginable. Hard tacos of the kind with which we have become familiar are virtually unknown in the interior of Mexico. The soft taco is the delicacy served with *carne asada* (charcoal-broiled steak) or *pastor* (marinated pork). They are most frequently served with the *cebollita*, a scallion that's split down the middle and charbroiled—and is seriously thought to be a digestive aid. Soft tacos are accompanied, as is virtually every dish, with a tiny wedge of lime.

La Salsa excels in the preparation of fresh sauces. The

three basic include *salsa Mexicana* made with fresh tomatoes, chile Serrano, chopped onion and lime; *salsa cebolla* made with chopped onion, fresh cilantro, oregano and lime; and the *salsa fuego* (muy hot! muy hot!) made with *chili de arbol*.

Behind the long counters, the cooks, recruited from butcher shops and produce markets, are in constant motion. They chop as quickly as a *teppan* chef, they trim the slowly rotating skirt steak, they hand out the tacos to the starving mob and somehow, manage to remain impertubable. English is rarely spoken and gringo customers must point to what they want. Then the tacos are taken to the salsa bar where they help themselves from the fresh bowls.

The *quesadilla* is served on flour and corn tortillas. The *tortas*, a kind of Mexican Grinder, is served on a special *balillo* (five-point bun) that is split to hold *carne asada* or pork, with black beans and sour cream. The burrito, a purely American invention, was added to the menu as an accommodation but has proven one of the more popular dishes. *Huevos ranchero* are served all day and virtually all night as these restaurants struggle to keep up with the demand, and most will soon be open 24 hours.

Make no mistake, these are little more than taco stands. The La Salsa on Pico does not yet have a beer license but the Westwood and downtown locations serve Carta Blanca, Dos XX and Superior. There's a soft drink—*orchata*—made with rice flour, burled cinnamon and milk that's especially suited to the spicy fare. *Caffe del olla* is a Mexican coffee that's strong enough to make you forget your hangover.

**Inexpensive.** Open seven days. Hours vary, but most are open from early morning to late. Beer only. Little English is spoken. No reservations. No credit cards. Parking lot. Casual.

---

*In order to obtain the best results from this Guide, please consult "Tips on Dining Out" on page 21.*

## LA SCALA                                    Italian
9455 Little Santa Monica Boulevard                ★★★
Beverly Hills        **Map 8**              (213) 275-0579

Unlike most nations, restaurants are best run with a
dictator at the helm. There can be no indecision, no
faltering in matters of taste and judgment, and the grand
restaurant is an instrument the proprietor is always fine-
tuning. So it is at La Scala, a marvelously professional
operation, under the firm and total control of Jean Leon, a
man of supreme (and not misplaced) confidence. Here,
pouilly fuissé is the "cooking wine," the veal is perfect, the
cuts of meat treated and priced like the precious commodities
they have become. Fettuccine is cut by hand, and everything
that can be fresh. The further mark of an important
restaurant is the myriad little things that in themselves
would scarcely be detectable to the diner; taken together, as
a philosophy, they comprise the soul of a restaurant. The
wine cellar is one of the great ones; Mr. Leon has his own
vineyard in Spain. As you might imagine, a superb restaurant in Beverly Hills attracts a mighty celebrity following,
and, although autograph hunters would be disintegrated by
the laser glare of the maitre d', one can see here more of
the superstar pack and the authentic jet-setters than in any
other single location. The service can be a bit intimidating.
Unless you are somebody, or unless you obviously know
good food and how to order from the lavish menu, you may
get about as much personal attention as from a railroad
conductor taking tickets. On the other hand, if you are
obviously someone coveted by the waiter, captain, or
management, you will start in motion a choreography of
service that is as delightful to see as it is to receive. The
cuisine is from Northern Italy, although hardly the peasant
fare that is often identified with that region. The pastas are
triumphant and the *fettuccine* Leon was not named after
the boss without just cause. The chicken *cacciatore* here
reveals nearly all the other chicken cacciatores as imposters—

without richness and without the sauces permeating the chicken. You shouldn't go if you're on a budget. There are too many expensive and seductive diversions. The bar is one of the swingingest and brightest.

**Expensive.** Open Monday through Saturday. Luncheon from 11:30 a.m. to 2:30 p.m. Dinner from 5:30 to 11:00 p.m. Full bar. Reservations necessary. All major credit cards. Validated parking at lunch; valet parking at dinner. Dressy.

---

## LA SCALA MALIBU
3835 South Cross Creek Road
Malibu      **Map 2**

**Continental**
★
(213) 456-1979

There are few enough good restaurants in the Malibu area that survive the annual disasters of flooding, earthquake and more. This one is a charmer with a patio, large floral arrangements and a flower-bedecked patio with awnings to shelter diners against sudden sea gusts. The *ratatouille alla niçoise* served cold and the *mozzarella marinara*, deep-fried and sauced with just a kiss of anchovies, were promises of good things to come from their sophisticated kitchen. *Fettuccine* and *spaghetti carbonara* are the rcommendations here although the *cannelloni* and the fresh vegetable plate are favorites with the eccentrics who chose that area in which to live. As one might expect from Jean Leon, the wine list is an index to treasures, some obscure, but all selected for the palate rather than pretension.

**Moderate.** Open Tuesday through Sunday. Luncheon served Tuesday through Friday from 11:30 a.m. to 2:30 p.m. Dinner Tuesday through Thursday from 5:30 to 10:30 p.m.; Friday, Saturday from 5 to 11 p.m.; Sunday to 10 p.m. Closed Thanksgiving and Christmas. Full bar. Reservations advised. Patio. Visa, MC, AX. Parking lot. Casual.

## LAS CASUELAS NUEVAS                          Mexican
70050 Highway 111                                    ★★
Rancho Mirage                              (714) 328-8844

This Mexican restaurant of exalted cuisine is a delight
There are 14 different complete dinners and the Lobster
Ensenada is simply wonderful. It is delightful to find a
restaurant like this that doesn't take advantage of the
captive resort community. Even though they're a half mile
east of Frank Sinatra Drive, it hasn't gone to their head or
their prices, so if you don't like this spacious, colorful
hacienda you may be the first not to do so.

**Moderate.** Open seven days. Luncheon from 11 a.m. to 4
p.m. Dinner 4 to 11 p.m. Sunday brunch from 10 a.m. to 3
p.m. Entertainment. Cocktails. Patio. Mountain view. Visa,
MC, AX. Valet parking. Casual.

---

## LAS CASUELAS TERRAZA                          Mexican
222 South Palm Canyon Drive                          ★★
Palm Springs                               (714) 325-2794

In three years of operation, this restaurant in a downtown
Palm Springs landmark has won three national awards: one
for design and two consecutive from *Restaurant Hospitality
Magazine*, "one of the 500 leading commercial food service
operators in the United States." All that, plus the food's
good. Recipes reflect the special touch of third-generation
Delgado family care and know-how. The unique menu
allows 50,640 combination choices. (A Delgado in-law came
up with that one.) House specialities include a spectacular
*tostada supreme, burrito ranchero* and *chimichanga*. If cousin Louise
is uninitiated and no adventurer, try tuna salad and fruit or a
fruit salad she'll talk about back in Pawtucket.

**Inexpensive to moderate.** Open Monday through Saturday from 11 a.m. to 10 p.m.; Sunday from 9:30 a.m. Closed Thanksgiving and Christmas. Flamenco guitar entertainment. Full bar. Reservations suggested. Patio. View. Visa, MC, AX. Wheelchair access. Parking lot. Casual.

---

## LA SERRE                                   French
12969 Ventura Boulevard
Studio City        **Map 1**               (213) 990-0500

Beautiful. Gracious. Over-rated. Overpriced. In spite of the beautiful interior with a botanical garden, flowers, trellises and patio brick floors (La Serre means "greenhouse") the honeymoon is over and the beautiful bride has suddenly emerged as something less, far less than perfect. The *coquille* St. Jacques is still fine and firm and the Côte de Veau Forestiere is good, but neither are worth the inflated price or the necessity to endure condescending service.

**Expensive.** Open Monday through Saturday. Luncheon from noon to 2:30 p.m. weekdays. Dinner 6 to 10:30 p.m. Closed major holidays. Full bar. Reservations essential. Visa, MC, AX. Valet parking. Semi-dressy.

---

## LAS LOMAS                                 Mexican
5638 East La Palma Avenue                      ★★
Anaheim          **Map 6**                (714) 779-1200

Is this the best Mexican restaurant in Orange County? Many of our readers and listeners think so and I'm beginning to feel the vibes as well. Sometimes the "best Mexican" is a hole-in-the-wall like Blanco's in Rowland Heights where you can pig-out on a pound and a half of burritos. But most of the time the ideal Mexican experience is in a restaurant like this: graceful, hospitable and with dishes that reflect the Spanish influence. In addition, this charmer is not afraid to be innovative.

The range of appetizers, salads and soups is representative of the aristocracy of the sophisticated Mexican cuisine but the stars here are the entrées. There's a splendid *paella* with seafood, chicken, and *chorizo* served on a bed of saffron rice. The *huachinango*, or red snapper, is fried in butter and served with a slightly spicy sauce made with tomatillas (little green tomatoes). The beef dishes like *carne asada* are strong points of the kitchen and I'd recommend an inexpensive one, the "especial" that is made up of marinated beef slow-cooked, shredded and served with homemade salsa. The large menu lists an array of burritos, omelettes and my favorite egg dish, *machaca con huevos*. They take shredded beef, eggs, chopped onions, diced tomatoes, spices and herbs and scramble them together; then they serve it with beans and rice. On Sunday, brunch is served with complimentary fruit and champagne. They're now in their third year and going strong; along with El Cholo, they make Orange County the best Mexican restaurant area in Southern California.

**Moderate.** Open seven days from 11 a.m .to 10 p.m. Sunday brunch from 10 a.m. to 2 p.m. Full bar. Entertainment. Reservations preferred. Visa, MC. Parking lot. Casual.

---

## LA STRADA                    Northern Italian
3000 Los Feliz Boulevard                            ★
Los Angeles        **Map 7**            (213) 664-2955

Opera and musical comedy are the added elements at La Strada. You wouldn't go there for the best Italian food in town, and you wouldn't go there just to hear music, but the combination of the two is fun. It's an old five-and-ten store

---

*Please be sure to consult "Tipping Made Easy" on page 25 of this Guide.*

which was converted into a colorful Hollywood-Italian restaurant in 1961, with murals, awnings, and fountains, and it became a hang-out for actors and singers who performed in exchange for wine and dinner. Now there is a company of singers who perform portions of opera, Broadway shows, and random selections with the aid of scenery and costumes. On an early visit, the show began with the pianist pounding out "Red Sails in the Sunset" and then reached a level of musical pandemonium as the tenors, sopranos, and baritones entered, beating tambourines and triangles and each other. Our ringside seat proved a little disconcerting as the singers wandered about, occasionally colliding with waiters, to perform to individual tables. We had *Figaro* with our *fetuccine* (both a little heavy), and selections from *La Boheme, Rigoletto*, and *La Traviata* with our *scampi marinara* (good but bland) and *pollo alla cacciatore*. Dessert was a splendid zabaglione whipped tableside with five eggs, sugar, and marsala, and accompanied by "A Cup of Coffee" from Caratella, while the tenor banged a cup dramatically against a saucer in syncopated rhythm.

**Moderate.** Open seven days. Luncheon served 11:30 to 3 p.m. weekdays. Dinner Sunday through Thursday from 5:30 to 11 p.m., Friday and Saturday to 11:30 p.m. Closed Thanksgiving and Christmas. Entertainment at 8 and 10 p.m. on Sunday; 8, 10 and 12 Friday and Saturday. Full bar. Reservations essential. All major credit cards. Valet parking. Semi-dressy.

---

**LA STREGA**                                      Italian
400 South Western Avenue                              ★
Los Angeles        **Map 7**              (213) 385-1546

La Strega (which means "the witch") is a place awash with not only good food, but also good fun. The waiters and waitresses are snarky and wry, and burst into song at the drop of a *cappeletti*, accompanied by an unobtrusive pianist. The wine list is massive, (my waitress claimed it was the largest in the city) and actually as exhausting to look through as it's exhaustive—the Italian wine section seems to go on forever, and under the California wines there are a solid 58 chardonnays, many of which are real finds.

But don't let me give you the ideas that La Strega is just a wine list with a restaurant built on as an annex. The menu here is a virtual encyclopedia of Italian cooking. Among the 35 pasta entrees, for instance, there's a fabulous house *lasagna* made with four different cheeses, three different sauces and heaps of meat—balls and sausages. *Gnocchi*—those wondrous potato dumplings—are served *alfredo, verdi alfredo, bolognese* and *al burro*, while *pesto* runs amok throughout the menu, covering the *fettuccini* and the spaghetti with equal green garlickiness.

And then there's the pizza. The crust is thick here, though not thick like a Chicago-style pizza. The cheese is heavy, and the sauce is cluttered with oregano and basil. And the toppings! There are all the usual ingredients—the pepperoni and the sausage and the anchovies—but there is also shrimp, octopus, chicken, eggplant, tuna, even spinach with a white sauce. This is pizza that breaks down the old clichés about what a pizza is here in America. In Italy, pizza—more than being a pie—is really an open-faced sandwich. La Strega treats this old favorite just like that... and the results are nothing short of marvelous.   *M.S.*

**Expensive.** Open seven days. Luncheon served Monday through Saturday 11 a.m. to 2:30 p.m. Dinner from 4:30 p.m. to midnight. Full bar. Reservations accepted. All major credit cards. Parking lot. Casual.

---

*In order to obtain the best results from this Guide, be sure to read the French, German, Italian and Oriental menu translators on page 705 to 710 of this Guide.*

## LA TERRAZZA

11701 Wilshire Boulevard
Brentwood          **Map 8**

**Northern Italian**
★
(213) 820-2802

For the pause that refleshes, this new self-service antipasto buffet is fun and fancy. Serious dishes like spaghetti Estive and veal Lucchese are featured on the dinner menu. There's patio service with a view with interesting imported beer and wine.

**Inexpensive to moderate.** Open seven days. Luncheon from 11:30 a.m. to 3 p.m. Monday through Saturday. Dinner 6 to 11:30 p.m. Closed Christmas. Wine and beer only. Reservations accepted. Patio. Visa. Shopping center parking. Casual.

## LA TOQUE

8171 Sunset Boulevard
Los Angeles          **Map 7**

**Continental/Innovative**
(213) 656-7515

This restaurant is—for us—impossible to rate. There are flashes of genius, and chef-owner Ken Frank has been a chef in many major restaurants. However, the inconsistency, arrogance and, most recently, an illness, may affect the quality. Frank is young, American and one of the celebrated whiz kids of *nouvelle cuisine*. He is also petulant—he brought a great restaurateur to a labor relations hearing on a relatively minor matter—and seemingly immature. We tend to make our heroes too fast these days, and some of them can't stand the heat of the kitchen.

**Expensive.** Open Monday through Saturday 6:30 to 10:30 p.m. Five-course fixed price dinner $35. Closed most major holidays. Full bar. Reservations recommended. Patio. Valet parking. Semi-dressy.

## L'AUBERGE

**Belgian/French**
★

1237 Prospect
La Jolla

(714) 454-2524

The cuisine of Belgium has moved perilously close to the high standards of Paris, and there are many who feel that Brussels may soon become the epicurean capital of the world. Belgian-born owner Roger Purnelle prepares three or four entrées daily in his small but lovely restaurants; all illustrate the subtle differences of the cuisine of his home region. A typical day's offerings might include *lapin au vin blanc* (rabbit in white wine sauce) *filet à la flamade* or *brochette de fruit de mer* (fresh tender morsels of shellfish and fish on a skewer). The prawns and scallops stuffed with almonds—and the sweetbreads with Madeira sauce—are compliments to the chef-owner. Desserts include—surprisingly—a zabaglione and cherries with Cointreau, both substantially above the dessert offerings of many more pretentious establishments.

**Moderate.** Open seven days for dinner from 6 to 10 p.m. Wine and beer only. Reservations preferred. Visa, MC, AX, DC. Parking lot; street parking. Casual.

---

## LA VALENCIA HOTEL SKYROOM

**Continental**
★

1132 Prospect
La Jolla

(714) 454-0771

One of the smart swinging centers for the beautiful people (money gives one such a relaxed look), this lovely hotel has a good steakhouse restaurant downstairs (Cafe La Rue) and a good lounge (The Whaling Bar). The main dining room is the Skyroom from which the view is stunningly beautiful, one of the most spectacular along the coast. Here is where they serve their Sunday buffet. (The true European buffet is an art unto itself, and should not be confused with chuck-wagon lines.)

**Moderate to expensive.** Open Monday through Saturday. Luncheon from 11:45 a.m. to 2 p.m. Dinner from 6 to 9 p.m. Closed major holidays. Full bar. Reservations essential. View. Visa, MC, AX. Valet parking. Semi-dressy.

---

## LA VE LEE

12514 Ventura Boulevard
Studio City    **Map 1**

**Middle Eastern**
★
(213) 980-8158

For months I drove past La Ve Lee twice daily, hardly paying it any mind. The restaurant sits at something of a Dead Man's Curve in Studio City, and it's easy not to see it as you jockey for position heading for the Sportsman's Lodge. But La Ve Lee is very much worth looking for, and very much worth stopping at for lunch or for dinner. Like Tempo, La Ve Lee faces onto Ventura Boulevard, and like Tempo it has an outdoor dining area and a counter. But the food at La Ve Lee isn't quite a clone of the food at Tempo. There are similarities... and there are differences.

The menu at La Ve Lee proclaims: "For the much traveled gourmet, a chance to experience Middle Eastern Israeli cuisine... Nine nations, one cuisine." The menu doesn't go on to say which nine nations make up the one cuisine of Israel, but several of them don't seem to be the same nations that make up the cuisine at Tempo. La Ve Lee is not a home away from home for the eggplant, as at Tempo for instance, but it is a terrific place to sample *kibbeh bis-sayniyyi* and *kibbeh niyyeh*, the national dish of both Lebanon and Syria. *Kibbeh* is an addictive dish made of bulghur wheat, ground lamb, onions, spices and pine nuts, baked in the case of *kibbeh niyyeh*. I have been known to eat *kibbeh* hot and cold, day and night, to the exclusion of all other activities. It is on my list of dangerous dishes to keep away from me during periods of Santa Ana winds. Who knows what I might be driven to with a belly full of *kibbeh nivveh*?

Although, given my choice, I would probably eat *kibbeh* until I dropped, I have to admit that there are other dishes at La Ve Lee which could easily tempt me away from *kibbeh*. There are La Ve Lee's wonderful stuffed grape leaves, for instance, which are not served cold in the Greek tradition, but quite hot. The result is a surprising shift in taste, making them less like a snack and more like a substantial entree. There's *moussaka*, and lamb shanks, and short ribs, and the most marvelous *lahm hajeen*, a sort of Middle Eastern pizza, which is sometimes served flat like a pizza, but in this case is served rolled up like an egg roll. And though eggplant does not rule the menu here, there is eggplant *tahina* and fried eggplant, both of which do much honor to the noble aubergine.   *M.S.*

**Moderate.** Open Monday through Thursday 11:30 a.m. to 11 p.m.; Friday and Saturday until midnight. Closed Thanksgiving. Beer and wine only. Reservations accepted. Patio. Visa, MC. Parking lot. Casual.

---

**LA VILLA**                                  **Central/South American**
5724 Melrose Avenue                                              ★
Los Angeles        **Map 7**                        (213) 463-4001

While superstar restaurants deserve the attention they get, they have a sameness that can be boring. The rituals, the shtick, the captains and sommeliers, and valets all tend to run together in my mind after a time—like a mural dissolving in the rain.

The little restaurants are fun. Impudent, inexpensive and often improbable, they deserve the coverage they get and, in these oh-so-hard times, can use a little support.

La Villa is like that, and the Melrose-district Los Angeles restaurant is simply waiting to love you. The tiny former storefront was transformed some few years ago by Roger Castro who had a dream of bringing the *grande cuisine* of Central and South America to his friends. In that regard, the menu that ranges from Argentina (breaded sirloin steak with one egg over), Bolivia (half a roast chicken with black cherry sauce) with many other stops along the way is perhaps too ambitious, but it does manage to deliver. Besides that, the dinners are served with a delectable rice and black bean combination that I could eat forever.

Luncheons offer a choice of many combinations: filet of rex sole simmered in chablis, sour cream, sweet butter and tropical spices; or a seafood omelette with avocado, scallops and fresh tomatoes.

The brunch selection of seven combinations (#1 is breast of chicken with fresh spinach, lean bacon and sliced tomatoes in an egg batter) is $5.75, and that includes unlimited champagne.

This is the kind of gem that we must join forces to support if they are to survive the financial EKG. In this case, with the fresh-flower ambience and the grand piano accompanying Roger's murmured suggestions, it just could be one of your nicest dining adventures in some time.

**Inexpensive to moderate.** Open Tuesday through Sunday. Luncheon from 11 a.m. to 3 p.m. weekdays. Dinner from 3 to 10 p.m. Sunday through Thursday; to 11 Friday and Saturday. Sunday brunch 11 a.m. to 3 p.m. Closed Thanksgiving, Christmas, New Year's. Entertainment. Beer and wine only. Reservations suggested. Visa, MC. Parking lot. Casual.

---

## LAWRY'S CALIFORNIA CENTER          California
570 West Avenue 26                                    ★★
Los Angeles          **Map 7**                (213) 225-2491

Mention California dining to me and I immediately think of Lawry's California Center. Improbably situated in a drab industrial area just north of downtown Los Angeles is this oasis of beautifully landscaped gardens, outdoor dining areas, a gift shop and wine purveyor all set amidst fountains and lush greenery.

It's a great place to go for luncheon on any weekday but it is the annual Fiesta Dinner that excites the native Californian in me.

This year they've made it bigger, better and grander with the menu broadened to include hickory-smoked half chicken, fresh swordfish or salmon and the New York steak. All dinners include the distinctive cartwheel salad, fresh corn on the cob, sour cream tortilla casserole, fresh green vegetables and hot herb bread. There are mariachis plus special entertainment to accompany the general feeling of serendipity that is helped along by some of the richest daquiris and margueritas extant.

Thank the Lord, sez I, for the Frank family who brought us—finally—a suitable place to bring out-of-town guests in the California tradition. There's a grand wine selection and you can choose your bottle at the wine shop to enjoy with dinner.

**Moderate.** Open year round for luncheon seven days 11 a.m. to 3 p.m. Dinner from May to October 31: Tuesday through Saturday 5 to 10 p.m.; Sunday 4 to 9 p.m. Entertainment at dinner, Sunday afternoon. Full bar. Reservations for six or more only. All outside dining. All major credit cards at dinner only. Wheelchair access. Parking lot. Casual.

---

## LAWRY'S PRIME RIB

55 North La Cienega Boulevard
Beverly Hills          **Map 8**

American
★★
(213) 652-2827

There is little that can be said to add to the legend that Lawrence L. Frank created some two decades ago, when he established the premise that a restaurant with a single entrée — prime rib — served well would be received. And well received it has been, by millions of Californians and tourists who put their names on a list (no reservations taken) and wait a surprisingly short time for a booth. Service by the waitresses is competent and there is nothing whimsical about the beef, roasted in rock salt and carved from silver carts at your table, served with Yorkshire pudding, a crisp well-tossed salad (actually it's spun on a bed of ice) and fine creamed spinach. There is a child's plate. Cocktails and house wines are available. Now there's a gift shop.

**Moderate.** Open seven days. Dinner from 5 to 11 p.m. Monday through Thursday; to midnight Friday, Saturday; 3 to 11 Sunday. Children's menu. Closed Thanksgiving, Christmas. Full bar. No reservations. Visa, MC, AX. Valet parking. Semi-dressy.

---

## LAWRY'S WESTSIDE BROILER
116 North La Cienega
Beverly Hills          **Map 8**

American
★
(213) 655-8686

When the guys at Lawry's want to do something, they do it with style. Their latest venture (formerly Stears) on La Cienega is an absolutely smashing room, the first in which color, band-box red and ivory plus design, are specifically aimed at the newer era. The younger diner-outer will feel comfortable in a casual ensemble but the elegance is full on. Families that grew up with Lawry's restaurants will not be disappointed. The staple items are listed: culotte steak, filets and lamb chops. Now more imaginative dishes have been added, such as coconut chicken tempura and broiled Indonesian shrimp. Their broiler is fired with a blend of mesquite hardwood charcoal imported from Mexico. One of the best appetizers I've had anywhere is the mussels in escargot butter with pistachios. About half a dozen mussels

For best results, consult "How to Use This Guide" on page 27.

are placed in individual white porcelain cups shaped like white thimbles, and they are all served in a white bowl. Vegetables are fresh and the salads—as in all Lawry operations—are special; my favorite was the beef-steak tomatoes with Maui onions. The bar is a good place to come for an after-theatre cappuccino or espresso.

**Moderate.** Open seven days. Luncheon from 11:30 a.m. to 2:30 p.m. weekdays. Dinner from 5 to 11 p.m. Monday through Thursday; to midnight Friday, Saturday; to 10 Sunday. Closed Christmas. Piano bar. Full bar. Reservations essential. Visa, MC, AX. Parking lot. Casual to semi-dressy.

---

## LE CAFE                                              French

14633 Ventura Boulevard                                   ★
Sherman Oaks        **Map 1**              (213) 986-2662

Le Cafe is a pleasant cafe of the sort found in New York's Soho region. Very High Tech, if you catch my drift. Hard edges. Newspapers decorating the walls (*French* newspapers, that is to say). Exposed pipes. Lots of metal. And a small dining area in front facing the hubbub of Ventura Boulevard, and the many tales of human anguish that drag by nearly every night of the week. There is a broken heart for every skid mark on Ventura Boulevard...

In the evening, when the traffic thins down a bit, and the world's longest parking lot (the Ventura Freeway) picks up the slack from the boulevard, Le Cafe is a fine place to sit, and watch the people come and go. The food at Le Cafe is pleasantly light, nearly *nouvelle* in its understated use of sauces, and almost fanatical in its use of lemon, which is fine with me. Along with salt and garlic, I consider lemon to be one of the great pleasures of the world, a flavoring that gives satisfaction well beyond its meagre cost.

I've enjoyed most everything I've eaten at Le Cafe. The boneless breast of chicken citron has a bite like a glass of cool lemonade on a hot day, if lemonade could be made with buttery slices of chicken floating in it. The fresh fish dishes—filet of sole *meuniere*, eastern scallop *provencal* and Pacific red snapped *dijonaise*—were flakey and fine, playing off their sauces rather than drowning beneath them. This is more difficult to pull off than you might expect—often a dish served awash in a sauce is buried because of some abomination committed upon the main ingredient.

Le Cafe has a small but tidy menu—top sirloin steak *forestiére,* filet mignon cubes in peppercorn cream sauce, tournedos *au poivre,* many salads, many more omelettes, Haagen Dazs ice cream (which is made in the Bronx, contrary to the map of Denmark on the label—and what's wrong with ice cream made in the Bronx anyway?) and some terrific sidewalk desserts, including a banana split. The waiters and waitresses at Le Cafe wear quasi-punk looking t-shirts with the restaurant's name on them, which probably makes for far happier service than if they were made to wear formal dress or, heaven forfend, tennis gear. *M.S.*

**Moderate.** Open Monday through Saturday 11 a.m. to 11 p.m.; Sunday from 3 p.m. Closed major holidays. Entertainment upstairs Thursday, Friday and Saturday. Full bar. Reservations accepted. Patio, Visa, MC, AX. Parking lot in rear. Casual.

*In order to obtain the best results from this Guide, be sure to read the French, German, Italian and Oriental menu translators on page 705 to 710 of this Guide.*

## LE CELLIER
French
★

2628 Wilshire Boulevard

Santa Monica    **Map 2**    (213) 828-1585

This restaurant would be my choice for those who are just beginning to fall in love with cuisine Française. I can think of no more gracious guide than Jacques Don Salat who, in partnership with Jean Bellodre, operates one of the more reliable French restaurants in all of Southern California. The high standards of the food—I loved my bouillabaisse and the *coquilles St. Jackes*—are pleasantly disproportionate to the moderate prices. Diners, include a rich soup and fresh salad. I was taken with the mixed bag of patrons at Le Cellier. Young college students, post-graduate instructors, affluent middle-class celebrants, and just off-the-street hungry folk are a colorful lot, served by mustachioed waiters in a soothing, pleasant, softly lit atmosphere. (A Mr. and Mrs. Schneider, both young psychiatric social workers, spotted me and bet that as a restaurant writer I would be recognized and served first. I wasn't.) The menu is not unusual—you could probably write it yourself if you've been to enough restaurants—but the total experience is delightful and well worth the trip to Santa Monica when, I trust, it will be less foggy than on our foray. The imported wine list is excellent (try the white burgundy from Armand Roux).

**Moderate.** Open Tuesday through Sunday. Dinner from 5:30 to 10:30 p.m. Tuesday through Thursday; to 11 Friday and Saturday; 5 to 10 Sunday. Banquet facilities weekdays. Closed Christmas, New Year's. Full bar. Reservations essential on weekends. All major credit cards. Valet parking in rear. Casual.

# LE DOME
French
8720 Sunset Boulevard
★★
Los Angeles     **Map 7**
(213) 659-6919

There is elegant informality with bistro-style service of everything, even single dishes, at any time. The menu promises tastes that are new to us, courageous departures on the part of the restaurant and the patron. *Boudin noir* (blood sausage) is typical of daily specials that might include a cold veal tongue with sauce *remoulade*. The country flavor of the selections allow for interesting combination—*fromage de tete* (head cheese) and smoked meat. The pastry chef is from the kitchen of the late Jean Bertranou and the desserts are colorful and abundant. The view from the windows is tranquil and this is, perhaps, the most romantic and interesting of the big three.

**Moderate to expensive.** Open Monday through Saturday. Luncheon from noon to 6 p.m. Dinner from 6 p.m. to 1 a.m. Closed all major holidays. Full bar. Reservations essential. All major credit cards. Valet parking. Semi-dressy to dressy; jackets required.

---

# LE HOT CLUB
American
15910 Ventura Boulevard
★
Encino     **Map 1**
(213) 986-7034

Marilyn and Harry Lewis those wonderful folks who brought you Hamburger Hamlet, have come up with a razzle dazzle of a place that has virtually every diversion and game known to man (and woman). The place really jumps with excitement. A disco with style and good food at reasonable prices are a formula that works well in disco-land. You can play backgammon whilst deciding between Southern style ribs, Iowa grain-fed beef, catfish, and much more.

**Moderate.** Open seven days. Luncheon from 11:30 a.m. to 5:30 p.m. weekdays. Dinner from 5:30 to 1 a.m. Same menu for lunch and dinner. Monday buffet 4:30 to 7 p.m. Open all holidays. Full bar; Happy Hour 4 to 7 p.m. Dancing 9:30 p.m. to 2 a.m. No reservations. Visa, MC, AX. Valet parking. Casual.

---

## LE HUYEN                                    Vietnamese
21614 Ventura Boulevard
Woodland Hills        **Map 1**              (213) 340-3131

Perhaps the only distinction here is the immutable fact that this may be the only Vietnamese restaurant in the S.F. Valley. But old familiars like pork satay ($3.25), eggroll, chicken with cashews ($4.35), or stir-fried shrimp with baby corn ($5.55), are just that—old and maybe tired. No wine, so you may bring your own, a situation I find cheerful.

**Moderate.** Open Thursday through Tuesday 11:30 a.m. to 9:30 p.m. No alcoholic beverages. Reservations accepted. Visa, MC. Lot, street parking. Casual.

---

## LE MONACO                                      French
2325 Palos Verdes Drive West                          ★
Palos Verded Estates    **Map 2**          (213) 377-6775

Jean Paul Wulc is a masterful restaurateur who has built a steady following for his traditional French middle class restaurant with such entrées on the blackboard as *coq au vin*, frog legs Niçoise, lobster Cardinal, and about half a dozen more, all served with soup and salad, vegetables, and tomatoes. Among the rather ordinary list of hors d'oeuvres, I liked the mushroom salad, but I found little excitement among the desserts. The brunch has become a social ritual in the Palos Verdes area.

**Expensive.** Open seven days. Dinner from 5:30 to 10 p.m. Sunday brunch from 10:30 a.m. to 2:30 p.m. Full bar. Patio. Ocean view. Reservations preferred. All major credit cards. Parking lot. Casual.

---

## LEMON TREE BY THE SEA
444 Culver Boulevard
Playa del Rey                    **Map 2**

**American**
★
(213)827-1444

The owner has a real thing for lemons, and his obsession has turned out a refreshingly different theme restaurant. Set in an early California style restaurant, Lemon Tree serves lemon chicken, mushrooms stuffed with crab, lemon soup, and great lemon meringue pie. The California wine list they offer for accompaniment is a joy to the palate as well as the pocket. Although lemon wine is not included on the wine list, the theme *is* carried almost to excess with lemon trees on the porch, panels of lemon tree graphics, and of course, the lemony menu. Although spots of yellow might be dancing before your eyes by the time you leave, this place is basically quite apeeling.

**Moderate.** Open Tuesday through Sunday. Luncheon from 11:30 a.m. to 2 p.m. weekdays. Dinner from 5:30 to 10:30 Tuesday through Thursday; 5 to 11 Friday, Saturday. Closed Labor Day. Full bar. Reservations recommended. Visa, MC, AX. Valet parking. Casual.

---

*To obtain the best results from this Guide, be sure to consult maps on the various Southern California areas in the front of the book.*

---

## THE LEMON TURTLE

French/Mid-Eastern
★★

1054 South Seaward Avenue
Ventura

(805) 643-4160

Terribly out of place in restaurant-bleak Ventura, and isn't it nice? This small European style gallery and sidewalk cafe is rich with the character of its owner Don Ulrich, a distinguished artist. Fresh quiche, casseroles, homemade soups, fresh mushroom and cream clam chowder, omelettes, pita salad sandwiches, Cheyenne coffee cake (like a heavy apple strudel) and baklava will give you an idea of the dishes served in the tiny—20 seats inside, 20 seats outside—gem. Serious dinners are multi-course productions with exotic hors d'oeuvres, cold vegetable or egg and lemon soup; *dolmas, boureks, moussaka,* shish kebobs, and Turkish coffee. An interesting wine list complements the selections.

**Inexpensive to moderate.** Open Tuesday through Sunday. Luncheon from 11 a.m. to 5 p.m. Dinners to special groups by reservation only. Beer and wine only. Reservations accepted. Patio. Visa, MC. Street parking. Casual.

## LE PAPILLON

French
★

22723 Ventura Boulevard
Woodland Hills          **Map 1**

(213) 347-2900

Some of my favorite memories reside in this tiny jewel — it's about that size — that might well have been converted from a dry cleaners. A Christmas Eve when I had the choice of all the city to celebrate this precious moment, I happily chose Le Papillon and was treated to a power failure. When the lights went out the proprietors, acting as though it stormed and raged like this every night, nonchalantly lighted candles. How the kitchen functioned I do not remember, but the dinner was exquisite. It was purchased a few years ago by Jacques and Gigi Goessens, and for a brief time—as it must happen to all new owners—gremlins were unleashed. Now it is back to the serendipity of a French/Belgian restaurant with a fine blackboard menu, good service, and the best apple tarts I've tasted. The warm country inn feeling is romantic, and an evening here is something very special.

**Moderate.** Open Tuesday through Sunday. Luncheon from 11 a.m. to 2:30 p.m. weekdays. Dinner 6 to 10:30 Tuesday through Saturday; from 5 on Sunday. Closed mid-August through September. Wine and beer only. Reservations essential on weekends. Visa, MC, AX. Parking lot; street parking. Casual to semi-dressy.

---

## LE PAVILLON

**French Cafe**
★

12161 Ventura Boulevard
Studio City    **Map 1**                      (213) 980-0225

Le Pavillon used to be a little place, but recently it's expanded slightly to the west, and has become sort of sizable. The size hasn't hurt the old intimacy of Le Pavillon—it's still a mildly zany, good French cafe situated in the middle of Studio City.

The staff at Le Pavillon understands their customers. They respond to off-center questions with witty asides, and the occasional lapse in fluent English; which is okay, since this is as much a theatrical version of a French cafe as it is a French cafe. The menu is under glass at Le Pavillon, and it tells us that there are many crepes, many salads and many omelettes. The crepes come filled with ham, with spinach, with ratatouille, with cheese, with turkey slices and mushrooms, and with wine asparagus (canned, I'm afraid, and limply soggy). The top-of-the-line house crepe contains spinach, mushrooms, bacon and Swiss cheese, and like the

*To obtain the best results from this Guide, consult "How to Use this Guide" on page 27.*

other crepes at Le Pavillon would be a fine creation, except for the kitchen's decision to serve the crepes baked in small casseroles, covered over with large dollops of sauce. This decision makes for a tasty, but unfortunate concoction, with the crepe itself getting lost among the sauce and the heat.

Aside from that singular complaint, the food at Le Pavillon is more than adequate, for lunch. The hollandaise on the eggs Benedict is top notch. The crab bisque is fine and dandy. The mackerel in white wine is an interesting change of pace from the usual cold fish appetizers. And the salads—mushrooms, spinach, Russian, Greek and the house salad of turkey, ham, salami, Swiss cheese and shrimp—are all generous to a fault, and constructed with a reasonable balance between the greens and the more adventurous ingredients. The salads at Le Pavillon do not feature sprouts.

Neither do the omelettes of mushroom, ham, cheese, bacon or apples cooked in brown sugar. Le Pavillon is a very nourishing, very wholesome cafe, and a pleasure for lunch. There are moments when the most French thing in the place seems to be the accents, but then as Steve Martin has pointed out, all it really takes to be French is the ability to speak like Maurice Chevalier.   *M.S.*

**Moderate.** Open Monday through Thursday 11 a.m. to 10 p.m.; Friday and Saturday to 11 p.m. Closed major holidays. Beer and wine only. Reservations accepted. All major credit cards. Parking lot. Casual.

---

## LE PETIT CHATEAU

French
★★

4615 North Lankershim Boulevard
North Hollywood          **Map 1**          (213) 769-1812

This North Hollywood was a charmer when it opened nearly 20 years ago to serve the stars and such of the San Fernando Valley. It was then, as now, purveying an uncompromisingly high quality of French cuisine at affordable prices. It was Francois Sirgant's dream and the chef-owner created a castle like interior with high ceilings and walls festooned with antiques and artifacts such as copper cooking utensils that had been in the family for many years. Twelve years later, the Sirgants went into semi-retirement after appointing their niece, Christina Vives from Toulouse, as managing partner.

The warm ambience with booths and banquettes in pale green leather, a fine fireplace amid the memorabilia of a kitchen family seemed the proper setting for the kind of familiar dishes that attract a loyal following. From *la sélection des hors d'oeuvres* the generous serving of the *pâté maison* was the most impressive, served coarsely ground in the style of the provinces. The sautéed mushrooms and *coquille* were flawless.

Among the entrées I tasted were frogs' legs prepared in the manner of the chef, succulent and savory with garlic. The *coquille*, made with pearl scallops, was not overdone and was, therefore, unique and superior. The roast rack of lamb *bouquetière* is served with a garden of fresh vegetables, and the pan-fried sweetbreads with Béarnaise ($13.50) is the favorite of many long-time patrons.

Desserts are not an afterthought—the mighty mousse is homemade and triple-chocolated. *La coupe aux marrons* is a heavenly concoction of preserved chestnuts and French vanilla ice cream and—strangely—the trifle is better than at most British-style restaurants.

The long menu seemed to me a representation of *cuisine bourgeoise* (simpler, heartier, generous portions) with a dash of haute cuisine (ceremonial, elegant, traditional). There are no except for the prices which seem miniscule compared to the newer restaurants. Two can dine splendidly for under $40, and all entrées are served with either the salad bowl or the homemade *potage du jour*. The wine list is carefully selected and the Rothschild Mouton Cadet at $12 would be $18 at most restaurants.

**Moderate.** Open Tuesday through Sunday. Dinner from 5 to 10:30 p.m.; 4 to 10 Sunday. Full bar. Reservations recommende. All major credit cards. Parking lot; street parking. Casual to semi-dressy.

---

## LE RESTAURANT                                          French

8475 Melrose Place                                             ★
Los Angeles        **Map 8**                    (213) 651-5553

My first visit could have come from the pages of a Ross McDonald novel. "The thin rain slicing down transformed Melrose into a shallow river of sparkling confetti, churned into oblivion as Lew Archer swung his roadster into the driveway in front of the salmon-colored bungalow. His footsteps echoed self-consciously as he passed through the iron grillwork gates — more decoration than protection — into the courtyard, lush with hanging planters." The breeding here is the best: St. Germaine and La Chaumiere are represented by the ownership. Chandeliers, fresh flowers, attractive lithographs, sparkling crystal, and dramatic tablesettings provide the ambience. The dishes are well done throughout the long menu, but somehow do not live up to the excitement and promise of the exquisite setting. Belgian endive and walnut salad are a refreshing beginning. Smoked salmon was perfect in flavor and texture. Salmon poached in wine and sole *belle meuniere* (in a simple sauce of browned butter, chopped parsley, and lemon) were beautifully served, but a trifle bland. The wine list is as comprehensive as you might expect — and as expensive. Cheeses are served properly here, at room temperature.

**Expensive.** Open seven days. Dinner from 6 to 11:30 p.m. Monday through Saturday; 5:45 to 11 Sunday. Closed all major holidays. Full bar. Reservations recommended. All major credit cards. Valet parking. Dressy.

# L'ERMITAGE

730 North La Cienega Boulevard
Los Angeles          **Map 8**

**French**
★★
(213) 652-5840

Jean Bertranou established a restaurant that quickly became one of the superstars locally and is rated among the top 20 nationally. Following the tragic loss of this modest chef-owner we received notes and calls about service problems. I'd avoided visiting the restaurant during the days of readjustment but decided that—sentiment aside—we had to report facts. The serenely beautiful room is unchanged. White is an accent color that contrasts with soft suede walls, and brocaded high back chairs. White candles in silver candle sticks flicker over fresh flowers. There is style and a relaxed elegance. Michael Blanchet worked side by side with Bertranou and is as familiar with the philosophy of L'Ermitage as the maestro was. I had—and these are the English translations of the French dishes: Maine lobster pâté with lobster sauce, beautifully presented; a salad of Chinese peas and duck confit (the duck was warm and the plate was dressed as though it were a still-life); chilled oysters and spinach soup, and saddle of lamb with eggplant and mushrooms. The food was perfect to behold, to taste, and to enthuse over. However, the problems with the service were much in evidence. The waiter who accommodated the beautiful but intimidated people at the next table was cold and arrogant. When they toyed with their wine selections and asked about a local winery he replied, "California wines are much alike. We emphasize imported wines." My waiter was sullen and mildly argumentative, and the service, while technically okay, was perfunctory.

Several days later, when I was asked my opinion of the restaurant by the fine PR people, I gave it candidly. It is still a great restaurant but if something is not done about the service, I suggested it will lose stature, if not business. People will still go to L'Ermitage, but now only to see, be seen, and enjoy *haute cuisine*. Shortly after my conversation,

I was called by a member of the Bertranou family who expressed great concern with the problem, but unfortunately, after subsequent visits by our staff, the problem still remains. L'Ermitage will overcome eventually. The house that Bertranou built has become a legend and its founder brought the greatest chefs of Europe to cook in his restaurant as a contribution to our dining culture. However, my bill was nearly $200 for two—I did order lavishly to taste more than would be normal under other circumstances—and the experience was not worth the investment.

**Expensive.** Open Monday through Saturday. Dinner served 6:30 to 10:30 p.m. (two seatings). Enclosed patio for private parties Monday and Tuesday. Closed major holidays. Full bar. Reservations required. All major credit cards. Valet parking. Dressy.

---

## LE ST. GERMAIN French

5955 Melrose Avenue ★★
Los Angeles     **Map 7**     (213) 467-1108

There is some kind of extrasensory signal that emanates from new restaurants destined to be the darlings of the "in" crowd. It's like a signal pitched too subtly for the ears of people who drive less than a Rolls or a Mercedes, who don't wear caviar-spotted Levis and Gucci shirts and "I am allergic to penicillin" bracelets of solid gold. Just such a signal went out when this small stunningly beautiful French restaurant opened, and the call was instantly answered by the Beautiful People. The fact that these usually fickle souls have supported the restaurant unflaggingly since its opening is a tribute to the artistry of the kitchen and the relaxed competence of the dining rooms.

Perhaps because Le St. Germain does not take itself too seriously—there are touches of Gallic humor—it has become a serious restaurant. By the same sort of peculiar reasoning, the flowerbedecked multilevel, sunny rooms make no effort to be pretentious—which may be the reason that it has become the place in which to be seen. Like an athlete who performs incredible feats with an air of nonchalance, the French cuisine is served here as perfectly—and effortlessly—as in the popular (as opposed to "great") restaurants of Paris. While there is some sort of printed menu, it is rarely used. Instead, the youthful waiter will recite the half-dozen appetizers and entrées in a sometimes difficult-to-understand accent. (The bentwood wicker-bottom chairs here always remind me of George S. Kaufman's great, embarrassment-dispelling line when the wicker gave way and Edna Ferber, his dinner companion, suddenly fell through: "Edna, I've told you that's not funny.") The scampi, served with fragrant and crunchy-crusted French bread, are a delight. The *saumon a l'oseille* is that barely remembered beautiful pink in a cream sauce with sorrel. The roast chicken in champagne sauce was festooned with small squares of lemon, and flavored with curaçao. Desserts, particularly the fruit tarts, are in keeping with the high standards of the other dishes. Casually dressy, if you know what I mean. Men without neckties are the rule.

**Expensive.** Open Monday through Saturday. Luncheon from noon to 3 p.m. weekdays. Dinner from 6 to 11 p.m. Closed Christmas and Thanksgiving. Full bar. Reservations essential. Patio. All major credit cards. Valet parking. Semi-dressy.

---

## LE SAINT MICHEL                                              French
3218 Santa Monica Boulevard                                        ★
Santa Monica          **Map 2**                    (213) 829-3173

It seems to me that the French underrate the American palate. Duck served in almost all French restaurants here is turned out sweetly, with sauces of plum, orange, Grand Marnier, peaches — everything but saltwater taffy. Yet I recall some of the great duckling of Paris restaurants — smothered in onions and olives, turned golden with paprika, stuffed with turnips or artichoke hearts. At Le Saint Michel, where duck and seafood are the only concerns of the kitchen, I expected to find my unsweetened fowl — but it wasn't here either. What is here is splendid duck in familiar sweet sauces similar to those I've mentioned, along with some distinguished seafood dishes. *Langouste tour d' argent* (poached lobster in rich cream laced with cognac, and fresh tomatoes) is aristocratic, and the *moules à la marinière* (mussels poached in white wine) are exquisite.

**Expensive.** Open Monday through Saturday. Dinner from 6 to 10:30 p.m. Wine and beer only. Reservations necessary. All major credit cards. Street parking. Semi-dressy.

---

# LE SAINT TROPEZ
**French**
★

3012 Newport Boulevard

Newport Beach　　　**Map 4**　　　(714) 673-7883

This Newport restaurant has improved greatly since it opened. It was with some reluctance, akin to putting your finger back into a hot socket, that I returned with memories of an earlier disaster heavy on my mind and on my abdomen. But voilà! Dishes are classic: *cotes d'agneau* (lamb chop broiled) and *caneton a l'orange, flambé*, the first duck *à la orange* I've had where the flambé actually enhanced the flavor instead of burning it away—or worse, leaving a residue. The abalone and veal with zucchini were light and delicate. Desserts are unimaginative. However, the flowered wallpaper, fresh flowers, and Impressionist prints communicate warmth and care.

**Expensive.** Open Tuesday through Sunday. Dinner from 6 to 10:30 p.m. Full bar. Reservations necessary. All major credit cards. Parking lot. Semi-dressy.

---

## LES ANGES                                          French
14809 Pacific Coast Highway
Santa Monica          **Map 2**                       (213) 454-1331

I am not optimistic about the chances for this new restaurant. Formerly the Cape Cod Inn, this restaurant is in an area that has rarely supported a major establishment, and it is on the wrong side of the street with a fort-like appearance. They are terribly sincere, devastatingly dedicated and all that, but pretensions aside, the winters are long and wet here, good help is hard to find (how many dishwashers and busboys live around Malibu?) and the competition is overwhelming. The menu is printed in French, an arrogance that I find appalling. It makes as much sense as having an English menu in Paris, a condescension the French would not tolerate... for long.

**Expensive.** Open Tuesday through Sunday from 6:30 to 10 p.m. Dessert in the bar 8:30 to 11:30; to midnight Friday, Saturday. Closed Christmas Day, first two weeks in January. Piano. Full bar. Reservations recommended. Visa, MC, AX, CB. Valet parking. Semi-dressy; jackets preferred.

---

## LE SANGLIER                                        French
5522 Crebs Avenue                                     ★
Tarzana          **Map 1**                            (213) 345-0470

The sauces here are among the best in Southern California and the pâté is a specialty of the house. As the name implies, there is fresh wild game in season (wild boar in season is a specialty); and the classic dishes are well and faithfully prepared. The chef is the owner, which always bodes well for the consistency of such a restaurant.

**Expensive.** Open Tuesday through Sunday. Dinner from 5:30 to 10:30 p.m. Closed July 4, Christmas, New Year's. Full bar. Reservations advised, essential on weekends. All major credit cards. Parking lot. Casual.

---

## L'ESCOFFIER

Beverly Hilton Hotel
Beverly Hills     **Map 8**

**French**
★★★
(213) 274-7777

A restaurant that dares take the name of Escoffier, after that feisty little legend of French culinary art, is virtually asking for criticism. The fact that L'Escoffier, a Beverly Hills venerable, has withstood comparisons without loss of dignity or stature is a tribute to manager Leo Walters and his all pro team team. L'Escoffier is one of those favorite restaurants that has functioned so well for so long that restaurant writers tend to take them for granted in favor of the trendier, gaudier and generally more short-lived establishments. I was surprised to receive word that L'Escoffier, perched like a tiara atop the Beverly Hilton Hotel, had undergone "renovation." The beautiful room centered around a dramatic back-lighted mosaic mural with spacious windows that overlook Beverly Hills and Century City needed a change like Bo Derek needs a nose job. Any misgivings I had about the establishment becoming a vinyl resting place were dispelled on the occasion of my most recent visit. In truth, the differences are so subtle as to be scarcely noticeable. The heavy gold draperies have given way to a muted rose look, there are differences in the ornate candelabra, the dancing area has been changed most noticeably and there are gleaming blinds to soften the

---

*In order to obtain the best results from this Guide, please consult "Tips on Dining Out" on page 21.*

glare. It's still a very good restaurant. The dinner I ordered à la carte, from their lengthy classic French menu, was nearly faultless. (The Brie served with the salad was taken from the refrigerator and had the consistency of chilled putty but I've been assured that this is unlikely to occur again.) While you can go on a dining orgy here—I did— there is a simpler way to accommodate first-time visitors and others who might be intimidated by formal French menuspeak. Called *le diner classique* it is a preselected assortment of good eats like consommé Strasbourgeoise served with a *pâté* foie gras in tiny profiteroles. The salmon mousse that follows is garnished with shellfish. The entrée of roast tenderloin of beef is accompanied by fresh vegetables and an unusual presentation of puff potatoes. The dessert is marinated strawberries over rich vanilla bean ice cream baked in a crown of fluffy meringue. Another set dinner, *le diner* Escoffier, has an entrée that I like: loin of veal topped with pâté and delicate Madeira sauce. Nice touches include a slice of quiche served before the menu is presented and a platter of no little feats—French pastries, candies and *petit fours*—during the after dinner coffee. The wine list is extensive. Prices are reasonable for an important restaurant, about two-and-a-half times wholesale. The sommelier recommended a new (to me) California, Trefethin chardonnay (1977), that was rich and full. He supervised the chilling to make certain it was not served so icy as to destroy the subtle flavors—a mistake made by some restaurants where the sommelier is really just another gent with a silly key around his neck. There is dancing until midnight every evening except Sunday when the room is closed.

**Expensive.** Open Monday through Saturday. Dinner from 6:30 p.m. to midnight. Full bar. Reservations neccessary. City view. All major credit cards. Valet parking. Dressy.

## LES FRERES TAIX FRENCH RESTAURANT  French

1911 Sunset Boulevard ★

Los Angeles **Map 7** (213)484-1265

The direct descendant of the original Taix, a family-style restaurant where you sat at long tables and passed platters and bowls of hearty food boarding-house style, this newer, larger, and fancier restaurant, opened in 1962, still shows signs of its early honesty and skill. There's good sourdough bread, soup is still served in a tureen, but now there are leather banquettes and wine and gift shops — and seating for 600. While native Angelenos are wistful at the passing of the original Taix, this one still provides one of the best good food values in town, and nobody ever walked away mad or hungry.

**Moderate.** Open seven days. Lunch from 11 to 3 p.m. Dinner from 5 to 10 p.m. Monday through Saturday. Sunday 1 to 9 p.m. Child's plate. Full bar. Reservations preferred. Visa, MC. Valet parking. Casual.

---

## LES PYRENEES  French

2455 Santa Monica Boulevard ★

Santa Monica **Map 2** (213) 828-7503

A nearly perfect replica of a small Parisian restaurant, Les Pyrenees hung by a thread before they got their cocktail license and began to enjoy the success they deserve. Creative dishes abound; a "sole three-ways" and lamb "Wellington" are interesting. You'll enjoy this pleasant cafe.

**Moderate.** Open Tuesday through Sunday. Luncheon from noon to 2 p.m. daily. Dinner 6 to 10 p.m. Closed Tuesdays in summer; Christmas, New Year's. Full bar. Reservations recommended. Visa, MC, AX, DC. Street parking; Sav-On lot. Semi-dressy.

## L'ETOILE

**Continental**
★★

8941½ Santa Monica Boulevard
West Hollywood     **Map 8**          (213) 278-1011

Altogether charming — with liberal helpings of cozy, romantic and unique — and the food is simply marvelous. This tiny restaurant is further evidence that intelligence can transform a modest storefront into a dining adventure. Giancarlo Zaretti is there to greet you at the door, he is at your side to explain the chalked menu, he is in the kitchen and out — he is everywhere. The room is comfortable with chairs of antique burnished-copper velvet, fresh flowers on every table and elegant tableware. The walls are festooned with plates autographed by the stars who have dined there although, unexpectedly, there is a large upper plate bearing the scrawled signatures of the Sylmar High School Spanish class. One could be served kibble in such surroundings and still feel mellow, but the food was every bit as good as we dared to hope it would be. The escargot is served without the shell in a dish with thimble-sized compartments, and it's touched with curry to make it different. The appetizer of shrimp magenta, also served as a main course, was our old friend scampi — but with the added touch of saffron — and the shrimp were plump giants perfectly prepared. The calf's liver was simply the best I've had—delicate, gently crisped with bacon (topped with bananas, for God's sake) and a garniture of fresh vegetables. My companion had the tournedos, small filets blessedly not wrapped in lard or bacon but served in a rich and stately sauce. There is a selection of fresh fish, silken homemade *canneloni*, chicken L'Etoile, veal Maltese and much more. Nor have desserts been neglected. The list is long and sinful but I had — are you ready? — a presentation of simmering chocolate fondue with an artistic arrangement of fresh pineapple, berries, apples and grapes for dipping. Given a single dessert with my last dinner on my last day on earth it would be this concoction. The piquant flavors of the fruit enveloped in the rich Swiss chocolate (with just a touch of kirsch?) was almost more than I could bear. The wine list is individualistic, ranging from a good moderately-priced house wine to those that cost over $100. It is adequate because the wine was selected with the menu in mind and the fact that the list doesn't ramble on to include hundreds of exotic vintages really simplifies the evening. Service is informal and relaxed. The patrons are those folks fortunate enough to be described as beautiful people although they are obviously not there to see or be seen. They are there to eat. Mere mortals are treated with the deference usually reserved for rock stars.

**Expensive.** Open Tuesday through Sunday. Dinner from 5:30 to 11 p.m. Full bar. Reservations. All major credit cards. Street and lot parking. Dressy.

---

## THE LETTUCE PATCH — Vegetarian

(Locations in Brentwood, Encino, Manhattan Beach, Mission Viejo, Santa Monica, Torrance; Westlake will open early 1982. See phone book for listings.)

These are a fancy-schmancy semi-vegetarian and diet social centers with patios. They manage a massive salad bar operation with excellent quiches (there is bacon aboard), 20 varieties of fresh vegetables every day, and desserts made with pure ingredients that are a damn sight better than those served in most elegant restaurants. All dressings and soups are homemade and the fresh fruit salad is really made of fresh fruit. You might see Barbra Streisand or one of the jet set here, but if you don't you'll enjoy your salads and a glass of wine—right?

**Inexpensive.** Most locations open Monday through Saturday. Closed most major holidays. Wine and beer only. No credit cards, but personal checks accepted. Casual.

# L'EXPRESS
14910 Ventura Boulevard
Sherman Oaks      **Map 1**

**French Bistro**
★★
(213) 990-8683

In a recent issue of *Los Angeles Magazine*, Orson Welles—a gastronome against whom all other gastronomes should be judged—expanded on a comment he had made in 1959 about how, "Hollywood is the first show town in history without a pub or bistro in the traditional sense." Speaking of his favorite ersatz bistro, Ma Maison, the aging *enfant terrible* observed that, "Ma Maison is, of course, a fake bistro—fake in the sense that it's not *popular*, it's not for the bookkeeper next door."

In Los Angeles, of course, there are *no* bookkeepers next door, largely because there's really no next door at all. This is a city of destinations; you go from your home or office, to your restaurant or theatre. In between, there's nothing but miasma and clutter. The concept of strolling from your walk-up, cold water garret to the local cafe for a *cafe noir*, or a Pernod and water, works well in cities constructed along the old design paragons. Los Angeles is the city of the future... and there is no place to walk to.

There are, however, some very nice places to drive to, and if it is popularity that we're talking about, that is to say, mass appeal, then L'Express is certainly the finest and most popular bistro in town. Serious, good food is served in a casual setting without fuss or pretension. New Wave meets *pommes frites*. Jogging shorts linger over an order of trout stuffed with the silliest, most ephemeral sole mousse. In the background, the Eagles sing of the Hotel California while danty *cornichons* are scooped inelegantly from an oversized pickle jar. This is not a bistro like I remember from my poor days in Paris, but it is a bistro custom made for the fast and free life just a Frisbee throw away from the Pacific.

The first time I ate at L'Express, I ordered the *rillettes*. It was a shocking appetizer—a miniscule remekin sitting on a large plate, the ramekin stuffed with several dollops of what looked like pink lard. The *rillettes* came with part of a baguette, and a mason jar filled with *cornichons* and a pair of tongs. I ate twice my weight in cornichons (can one get enough of this enticing little pickle? can one eat too much caviar? or drink too much of Domaine Chandon's *blanc de noir*?), and devoured the *rillettes*, fascinated by its richness of flavor, and the fact that I was consuming about a week's worth of calories in ten minutes.

L'Express no longer carries the *rillettes*, I was told recently. My waitress, a comely young lady with Dick Tracy-style mascara around her eyes, and an involvingly direct manner, told me that nobody ever ordered it, so it was discontinued. More's the pity, since I expect I was on the verge of developing an addiction to the stuff. She told me of the specials of the day, which included something she called "baby chickens."

"Baby chickens?" asked I. "Fresh from the shell and still chirping?"

"I think they're squab," she said, and recommended the trout stuffed with sole mousse. She was right. The trout was boneless and succulent, bathed in a wondrous brown sauce. It had been cut into two pieces like a sandwich, and the sole mousse, heavy with herbs, was layered inbetween. On the side as a broiled tomato stuffed with some shards of broccoli and topped with a slightly-curdled hollandaise. A basic baked new potato lingered nearby, stoically observing the fresh steamed petit pois mixed with pearl onions and some happily lurking pieces of soft bacon.

Sitting on the sheltered patio, watching the traffic roar past on Ventura Boulevard, I could hear Jackson Browne singing a confessional ballad called "The Pretender." (In Paris, it would have been Piaf singing but the effect is the same.) On the walls, were ancient posters for things like "Rivoire & Carret Vermicelle Macaroni." Next to the bar, wine bottles sit brazenly in a lucite rack. I order a pizza *fruit de mer*, which arrives hot and bubbly, topped with shrimp and mussels, and a Campari and soda. My waitress asks me if I'd like to examine the dessert bar, which is awash with *flan nougatine* **and** *bavarois a l'orange.* Over the speakers come the strains of a song from *Urban Cowboy*, and I know I'm not in Paris. And I know that it doesn't matter a bit.   *M.S.*

**Moderate.** Open seven days from 11 a.m. to 1 a.m. Full bar. Reservations suggested. Patio. Visa, MC. Wheelchair access. Valet parking. Casual.

---

**LILLIAN'S**                                    **American**
962 North Cahuenga                                    ★
Hollywood        **Map 7**            (213) 462-0435

The soup's the thing at Lillian's, where everything is home-made except the silverware — and from the looks of mine I'm not sure about that. Your taste buds may have forgotten what long-simmered soup from a stock-pot tastes like, but what it doesn't resemble is Campbell's or Heinz. The bread (homemade, of course) could be a meal in itself, but when dinners also include soup, salad, entrée, two fresh vegetables, dessert, and beverage you must be careful to leave room. The front room and covered patios look — well, homemade as well, and it's the kind of inexpensive but good place that will make you feel comfortable, inside and out.

**Inexpensive.** Open Monday through Friday 10 a.m. to 10 p.m. Saturday from 6 to 10 p.m. Beer only. No credit cards. Street parking. Casual.

*To obtain the best results from this Guide, be sure to consult maps on the various Southern California areas in the front of the book.*

## LITTLE J'S
**American**
★

1119 South Olive
Los Angeles **Map 7** (213) 748-3646

Back before the building codes made anything but cubism impossible in the downtown area, Herr Hehneiser handbuilt a little cottage where he served chili from a South American recipe, and fantastic Grand Marnier pie, along with homey but good daily specials at homey prices. Now he's in a new building with a more extensive menu. The cocktails are only fair, but you can get some good wines here. Lousiana seafood gumbo served every Monday.

**Inexpensive.** Open Monday through Friday. Luncheon from 11 a.m. to 4 p.m. Dinner from 4 to 7 p.m. Cocktails. Visa, MC. Parking lot. Casual.

## LITTLE JOE'S RESTAURANT
**Italian/American**
★

900 North Broadway
Los Angeles **Map 7** (213) 489-4900

4248 Martingale Way
Newport Beach **Map 4** (714) 752-8000

Little Joe's Restaurant in downtown Los Angeles started in 1910 as the back room of a grocery store where spaghetti was served to the hired hands who were building the nearby Civic Center. From a varnished board nailed across two sawhorses, Little Joe's has sprouted room after room, added a food store, and now serves hearty Italian-American food to more than 2,000 people each day. In spite of its size—perhaps because the individual rooms are small—there remains a family feeling to the place. The ravioli are still made by hand, but of necessity, the spaghetti is pre-prepared, not served to order or *al dente* (literally translated "to the tooth") as in the uptown Italian restaurants that aspire to *alta cucina*. It's good, though, and served with freshly ground parmesan cheese, and the savory sauce with chunks of meat is the kind you sop up with the homemade bread after the pasta's all gone. A spaghetti dinner with a fresh antipasto salad, rich homemade soup, bread, special-blend coffee, and dessert (good spumoni or vanilla ice cream) is a bargain. Selecting from the six-course dinners, I had a succulent braised lamb shank, marvelously tender, served with fresh carrots and peas and potatoes au gratin. The menu is massive, but good. The luncheon menu is shorter, and there are three daily specials each day: Italian meat loaf, barbecued breast of lamb, or braised sirloin tips. You may select from modestly-priced California and imported wines, or order a litre of house wine. Little Joe's is great for banquets and special events and convenient before the Dodgers games or Music Center attractions.

**Inexpensive.** Open Monday through Saturday. Luncheon from 11:30 a.m. to 2:30 p.m. six days. Dinner 2:30 to 9 p.m. Closed major holidays. Full bar. No reservations. All major credit cards. Valet parking. Casual to semi-dressy.

---

# THE LITTLE KITCHEN American
2694 Arrowhead Avenue ★
San Bernardino **Map 5** (714) 883-7247

Most of their patrons have dined with them since they first opened in 1960. Serving midwestern-style home cooking, they bake their own goodies and use fresh, fresh, fresh products. Meals are served buffet-style.

There is a wide variety of dishes, and daily specials include pan-fried chicken (Monday and Wednesday), chicken and dumplings (Tuesday), lasagna and chicken fricassee (Thursday) and Swiss steak (Friday). Regular menu may include meat loaf, beef stew, spare ribs, corned beef and cabbage and salmon loaf. Desserts are scrumptious. The Little Kitchen prepares food to go from their regular menu for up to 50. Takeout orders include a variety of sandwiches, salads and whatever. It's an excellent place to stop en route to or from the mountain area as a trip-breaker at the foot of the mountain roads.

**Inexpensive.** Open weekdays only. Luncheon served 11:30 a.m. to 2:30 p.m. Dinner from 4 to 8 p.m. Closed weekends, major holidays, December 20 to January 5 and July and August. No alcoholic beverages. No reservations. No credit cards. Street parking. Casual.

---

## LITTLE SHANGHAI
13864½ Chase Street
Panorama City          **Map 1**

Mandarin/Szechwan
★★
(213) 894-0332

Like many of my favorite restaurants, this is one that you wouldn't dream of entering (Fortune Fountain in West Los Angeles is another) unless you knew it was great—and it is. In a shopping center in an undistinguished section of Panorama City is some extraordinary Szechwan cooking. Appetizers, suh as the *pupu (sic)* try—varieties of morsels arranged on a tray with a flame in the center to roast at the table. The snow white chicken with abalone soup is merely wonderful and the lemon chicken, barbecued pork with Chinese pea pods and fish in brown bean sauce (his own recipe) are marvelous. Hot and spicy dishes are clearly asterisked on the large menu, and these are the nicest people you'll find. They are eager to explain. Desserts include the famous toffee apples and bananas that are cooked, caramel coated, and plunged into ice before serving. I don't care much for their family dinners, preferring to explore the inexpensive à la carte less familiar territories, but they are better here than at most Chinese restaurants and may give you a good beginning point.

**Inexpensive.** Open Wednesday through Monday from 11:30 a.m. to 9:30 p.m. Monday, Wednesday and Thursday: to 10:30 p.m. Friday and Saturday; 4 to 9:30 p.m. Sunday. No alcoholic beverages. Reservations preferred. Visa, MC. Parking lot. Casual.

## LITTLE VIENNA

**Hungarian**
★

12461 Magnolia Boulevard
North Hollywood    **Map 1**    (213) 763-8149

I enjoy German food so much that friends are always having fun at my expanse. But there was so much going on at this fine little restaurant, I don't remember what I ate. The food, is however, top quality and well prepared. Concert violin music and other appropriate entertainment enhances the evening.

**Moderate.** Open Wednesday through Monday. Dinner from 5 p.m. to midnight. Full bar. Reservations advised weekdays, essential Friday and Saturday. Visa, MC. Parking lot. Semi-dressy.

---

## LLOYD'S RESTAURANT

**Continental**
★

32114 Hilltop Boulevard
Running Springs    (714) 867-2731

In 1953 a coffee shop opened in Running Springs, and in true Horatio Alger style, has expanded into a restaurant, bakery, and has become the fixture of the area. It opens early, closes late, and has a daily special menu. One of Lloyd's soups has even been featured in the good-enough-to-eat magazine *Bon Appétit*. There is still coffee shop service, as well as more complete dining.

**Moderate.** Open 7 a.m. to 2 a.m. Breakfast from 7 to 11 a.m. Luncheon from 11 a.m. to 3 p.m. Dinner 5 to midnight. Full bar. Reservations recommended. No credit cards except Lloyd's. Parking lot. Casual.

---

*Please be sure to consult "Tipping Made Easy" on page 25 of this Guide.*

## THE LOBSTER

1602 Ocean Avenue

Santa Monica      **Map 2**

**Seafood**

★

(213) 394-9751

The last time I was there they were out of lobster, which could be (a) because it's a popular dish or (b) it's become so expensive that it requires delivery by Brink's or (c) none of the above. This is a no-nonsense, plain little place that will tell you when your table is ready in no uncertain terms. But we are all willing to sacrifice ambience and mannerliness for fresh seafood, aren't we? And here the fish dishes are done well and are often reasonable. Occasionally they have barracuda on the menu, and it's something special.

**Moderate.** Open seven days. Luncheon from 11:30 a.m. to 4:30 p.m. Dinner from 4:30 to 10 p.m. Monday through Thursday; Friday, Saturday to 11:00 p.m. Sunday from 2 to 10 p.m. Wine and beer only. No credit cards. Parking lot. Casual.

---

## THE LOBSTER TRAP

3605 Peninsula Road

Oxnard

**Seafood/American**

(805) 985-6361

In the land of the tone-deaf, even the discordant sounds good. The Lobster Trap is no great shakes as a seafood restaurant—as a matter of fact, I liked the steak here better—but it is in an underprivileged (gastronomically speaking) area and the massive restaurant, while offering no surprises, tries to be sincere. They're not always successful. There's a piano bar that would probably render "Wabash Cannonball." If you requested it and some patrons do.

**Inexpensive to moderate.** Open seven days. Luncheon from 11:30 a.m. to 3 p.m. Dinner 5 to 10 p.m. Monday through Thursday; to 11 Friday, Saturday; 4 to 10 Sunday. Sunday brunch 11 a.m. to 3 p.m. Banquet facilities. Piano bar. Full bar. Reservations recommended. All major credit cards. Parking lot. Casual.

---

## LONGFELLOW'S American
2011 Pacific Highway ★
Lomita    **Map 2**    (213) 325-9616

5530 Van Nuys Boulevard
Van Nuys    **Map 1**    (213) 994-9418

The answer to family dining without bankruptcy. The motto of the original Big Green House, "Chicken, steak, and chocolate cake" now applies to five eat-alikes. There's reason as well as rhyme when soup, salad, vegetables, mashed potatoes, hot corn bread, and a whole chocolate cake for each party (half for a "party" of two) are added. The kids get on an old-fashioned scale for proportionately lower dinner prices. Three hundred thousand people were served in three years at the first "chicken, steak, etc." restaurant, proving nothing succeeds like excess.

**Inexpensive.** Open seven days. Dinner from 5 to 9 p.m. Monday through Thursday; 5 to 10 p.m. Friday, Saturday; and 3 to 9 p.m. Sunday. Full bar. Reservations preferred. Visa, MC, AX. Parking lot. Casual.

---

## L'ORANGERIE French
903 North La Cienega ★★★
Los Angeles    **Map 8**    (213) 652-9770

This has become one of the best French Restaurants in California after a shaky beginning. There was arrogance at the front desk, uncertainty in the service and some pricing that needed to be revised — and it was. Now the tall graceful windows and waterfalls from old stone, high ceilings, and bright pure colors blend to create character in a restaurant that inspires. The white fish *aux deux couleurs* is an example: the two sauces are the coral color of Americaine, made with lobster shells, tomatoes and herbs; the second color is the creamy ivory of a perfect Béarnaise. Among the appetizers is a seafood salad made with raspberry vinegar and the entrées include breast of duck in green pepper sauce, spicy calf's liver cooked in vinegar sauce, and a savory steamed leg of chicken with chervil sauce. Rack of lamb is a specialty and the desserts are exquisite: *tarte aux pomme chaudes* (paper-thin slices of undercooked apple fanned out across a shell of buttery pastry crust and accompanied by a silver pitcher of whipped cream). It is a beautiful restaurant, one that is at once comfortable and dignified and is ideal for special occasions. While this is certainly not inexpensive, the original L'Orangerie in Paris from which this has sprung is twice the price.

**Expensive.** Open seven days. Dinner from 6:30 to 11 p.m. Closed major holidays. Full bar. Reservations essential. All major credit cards. Valet parking. Dressy.

---

## LORD FLETCHER INN                                    English
70385 Highway 111                                          ★
Palm Springs                                      (714) 328-1161

One of the glamour spots, but the good Lord can be somewhat inconsistent. Prime rib and steak are the staples here, served by wenches who sometimes look a little annoyed with the whole thing. Food can be very good, drinks are above average, and atmosphere is plush and cool. You'll sometimes have to make reservations several days in advance.

**Expensive.** Open Monday through Saturday. Dinner from 5:30 to 10:30 p.m. Full bar. Reservations necessary. Visa, MC. Valet parking. Semi-dressy.

---

*To obtain the best results from this Guide, consult
"How to Use this Guide" on page 27.*

## LOS BURRITOS
300 South Alvarado
Los Angeles    **Map 7**

**Mexican**
★
(213) 483-0185

Have I discovered the best soft taco in town? I think so. It's at Los Burritos, a spotless, if bleak, restaurant with no alcoholic beverages. Everything is homemde and dishes like *chile relleno* (stem-in) and burritos are incredibly delicious, but the soft taco is sublime. They use *carnitas*, shredded pork, and a sauce that must be made in heaven. Everything is available for takeout. Parking is tough, street only. It might be easier to phone ahead and pick up your dinner.

**Inexpensive.** Open Monday through Saturday from 10 a.m. to 11 p.m. Take out. Closed major holidays. No alcoholic beverages. No reservations. No credit cards. Street parking. Casual.

---

## LOS FELIZ INN
2138 Hillhurst Avenue
Los Angeles    **Map 7**

**Continental**
★★
(213) 663-8001

A comfortable, clubby, semi-dressy establishment that has good vibes in the kitchen and the front of the house—they're partners. A fireplace, deep leather booths, and a feeling of special happenings are part of the charm of this traditional place. I had one of the best Christmas dinners ever here, including stuffed goose, coulibiac salmon baked in pastry, and more. Once, during an unusually hectic pre-Dodger game crush at this old and popular inn, a slightly swoozled cople attempted to share a table with a dignified gentleman who was savoring his soup. "Hi there, my name is Abernathy," the would-be interloper declared. "Mine's not," replied the old gentleman, without missing a spoonful. Fortunately, the food here is not also a put-down. There's fresh fish every day in this small, comfortable restaurant, and the veal and chicken dishes are well prepared. Vegetables are fresh as well. The location is ideal for the Music Center, Griffith Park, the zoo, and Dodger Stadium.

**Moderate.** Open for luncheon Monday through Friday 11:30 a.m. to 4 p.m. Dinner from 4 to 11 p.m.; Friday and Saturday to midnight. Full bar. Reservations recommended. Major credit cards. Valet parking. Semi-dressy to dressy.

---

## LOUISE'S PANTRY
124 South Palm Canyon Drive
Palm Springs

American
★
(714) 325-5124

There is always a line in front of this little — long counter, a few booths — coffee shop, a tribute to the homemade, home-on-the range, all-American cooking. The pies and cakes are three-star, and everything's reasonable. Groucho, in a bit of Marxmanship, opined that the joint must be a massage parlor; he couldn't figure out such stand-in-the-sun loyalty to mere food. However, several generations of Palm Springs regulars will attest to the fact that it's only the palate that gets tickled here; but it's a great tickle. Open for breakfast.

**Inexpensive.** Open seven days. Breakfast from 7 to 11 a.m. Luncheon from 11 a.m. to 3:30 p.m. Dinner from 3:30 to 10 p.m. Closed June 15 through September 15. No alcoholic beverages. No credit cards. Parking lot. Casual.

---

## LOVE'S WOOD PIT BARBEQUE
Everywhere (check phone book)

Barbecue

It's not chic to tout franchise operations, but Love's does its thing — and its thing is barbecue — about as well as anyone. It is a dynasty founded on a sauce of 48 herbs and spices that's good enough for you to feast on the beans alone. But there's more: dinners of ribs or chicken or ham or pork or combinations, and sandwiches piled high with meat. Some locations are better than others, but nearly all are satisfactory.

**Moderate.** Open seven days. Luncheon from 11 a.m. to 4 p.m. Dinner from 4 to 11 p.m. Children's menu. Full bar. No reservations. Visa, MC. Parking lot. Casual.

---

## LOWENBRAU KELLER
3211 Beverly Boulevard
Los Angeles     **Map 7**

German
★
(213) 382-5723

You will pass four gigantic wooden Clydesdale horses pulling a long beer wagon as you enter the colorful, vibrant interior, where pretty *frauleins* serve massive dinners. It's a where-have-you-been-all-my-life place, with the kind of haphazard decor—stuffed animals, glittering ornaments, wooden panels and carvings—that you can't fully absorb in a single visit. The *sauerbraten* is as good as I've found in the area, and the smoked pork chops and veal loaf, garnished with fresh fruit, are adequate. Sauerkraut is homemade, less spicy than most. Sandwiches and sausage plates at luncheon are a long way from Denny's and worth the trip from downtown. German beer is heavier, sweeter—but seemingly you can drink more of it.

**Inexpensive.** Open Monday through Saturday. Luncheon served Monday through Friday from 11:30 a.m. to 2:30 p.m. weedays. Dinner Monday through Friday from 6 to 10 p.m.; Saturday 5 to 10 p.m. Full bar. No reservations. No credit cards. Parking lot. Casual.

---

## LUBACH'S
2101 North Harbor Drive
San Diego

Continental
★
(714) 232-5129

The one-story red-and-white frame building with a washed-ashore fishing boat in the entrance belies the crystal and linen, leather and mahogany-paneling interior in one of the Southland's historic *haute cuisine* establishments. The breast of capon curry and the calf's sweetbread *financière* are near

411

perfection. The major weakness of this otherwise impeccable restaurant is the shockingly limited wine cellar. The 30 labels offered are mostly premium wines and would do a credit to a typically upper-middle-class restaurant. But Lubach's isn't typical. They aspire to, and sometimes achieve, grand cuisine. Their service is knowledgeable and confident. Even the desserts, usually more of a convenience than a thrill on most "continental" menus, are rich and freshly made. The steakhouse wine list is all the more out of place in such surroundings.

**Moderate to expensive.** Open Monday through Saturday. Luncheon from 11:30 a.m. to 4 p.m. weekdays. Dinner from 4 to 11:30 p.m. Closed major holidays. Full bar. Reservations required. Visa, MC. Parking lot. Semi-dressy; jackets required.

---

# LUCKY RESTAURANT
1643 North Cahuenga Boulevard
Los Angeles    **Map 7**

**Chinese**
★
(213) 463-0464

Restaurants with Mandarin and Shanghai cuisine, Szechwan-style, are becoming as familiar as the Cantonese egg roll variety, but they seem to be uniformly better. The fish dishes are best here, and this is one of the few Chinese restaurants where I would recommend the set dinners. They're a balanced selection of dishes. You should indicate whether you want mild-hot or shazam spiciness at the time your order is taken. If you add some of the innocent-appearing red sauce on the table to any food, be very careful — it's dynamite. Beer or a medium dry white wine is the best accompaniment to this kind of food.

**Inexpensive.** Open Wednesday through Monday. Luncheon from noon to 3 p.m. weekdays. Dinner from 5 to 9 p.m. Sunday, Monday, Wednesday through Friday; to 10:30 Saturday. Closed major holidays; Chinese holidays. Full bar. Reservations recommended. Visa, MC, AX, DC. Two-hour parking next to restaurant. Casual.

# LYON'S ENGLISH GRILLE

**English/Prime Rib**

233 East Palm Canyon Drive

★★

Palm Springs

(714) 327-1551

It is not surprising that one of Palm Springs' best—a laudable combination of ambience, cuisine, service and value—would be among the favored few wherever it might be located. The late Arthur Lyon was a canny Britisher whose three decades of restaurants in Palm Springs have given him special insight into the dining aspirations of his clientele. From the wood-and-rough-plaster exterior to the somewhat theatrical British setting—wall hangings of colorful heraldic banners, green booths, wooden tables and antique stained-glass windows, old pub signs and maps—he has achieved a luxuriously cozy atmosphere. The tastefully costumed serving wenches attentively serve the 13 dinners. All come with fresh green salad deftly tossed tableside (peppering it down from a five-foot pepper mill), hot sourdough bread, and a giant, honest-to-Idaho baked potato that is not roasted in foil. Among the entrées are whole trout stuffed with crab and shrimp and topped with capers and a lemon wedge; steak and kidney pie (the house favorite); Long Island duckling with wild rice; filet mignon and New York steaks; teriyaki on a flaming sword; and a calf's liver with bacon or onions. The prime rib was one of the most generous cuts I've encountered in recent memory, nearly two inches thick (they get 10 cuts form an 18-pound rib), and prepared precisely as ordered. The food is generally faultless—nothing frozen or canned—although desserts are not exceptional. The wine list is intelligent and moderately priced. Even the cocktail lounge has its special flair. It is a softly lighted, lovely place to sip an after-dinner drink and contemplate your golf score—or what it should have been.

**Expensive.** Open seven days. Dinner from 5 to 11 p.m. Full bar. Reservations preferred. Visa, MC, AX. Valet parking. Casual.

# m

---

## MADAME WU'S GARDEN
2201 Wilshire Boulevard
Santa Monica      **map 2**

**Chinese**
★
(213) 828-5656

The familiar Cantonese and the spicy Szechwan dishes are served in an atmosphere appropriate to an epicurean experience. Madame Sylvia Wu, whose background is more diplimatic than culinary, has created a gracefully beautiful restaurant where the standards of cuisine and service are among the area's highest. Ordering from the vast menu—there are 200 dishes—could be intimidating, and I suggest you have Madame or one of the captains do it for you if you like. There are complete dinners, but you would do well to consider the à la carte menu. The four most popular items are the sizzling *go ba*, mixed green vegetables with black mushrooms; Wu's beef, barbecued pork with vegetables, and (my favorite) the tossed shredded chicken salad, a blend of shredded chicken, crisp fried vermicelli, green onions, and toasted almonds. The Peking duck gourmet dinner required two days' notice and includes winter melon soup served in a whole melon, sweet and sour fish (whole fish, deep fried), along with an unending array of exotic dishes. The Peking duck is a whole duckling, marinated with honey and spices and barbecued to a crackling brown.

**Expensive.** Open seven days. Luncheon from 11:30 a.m. to 2:30 p.m. Dinner from 5 to 10 p.m. Full bar. Reservations preferred. All major credit cards. Valet parking. Semi-dressy.

---

# MADRID
1712 Sunset Boulevard
Los Angeles      **Map 7**

**Spanish**
★
(213) 483-9328

The restaurant profession is subject to periodic fads, as are other professions. We are approaching the end of a time in which so-called "theme" restaurants, more costume than cuisine, were in vogue. During this period, I have been served by restaurant personnel who have donned the garb of sheiks, gypsies, wenches, witches and corseted court-esans. I even had my car parked by a chicken in Chicago. The novelty is wearing away, and places like Madrid remain. Here in the Echo Park district of Mexican and Cuban restaurants, the main dining room is gracious and hospitable with heavy wrought-iron chairs and colorful wall hangings.

*Paella valenciana*, seafood à la Basque, ($9.95); shrimp in green sauce ($6.50); and red scampi with garlic ($9.50) have an authenticity that is inarguable. The long menu lists scores of Spanish regional dishes and the wine list is extensive. Desserts include guava shells with cream cheese, papaya and flan. Dishes are prepared to order so there may be a short wait, but it's worth it.

Luncheon is lighter, with slightly less to choose from.

**Moderate.** Open Monday through Thursday 11 a.m. to 11 p.m.; Friday, Saturday to midnight; Sunday noon to 11 p.m. Beer and wine only. Reservations advised, especially week-ends. All major credit cards. Parking lot. Casual.

## MA FACON

French

★★

1000 Wilshire Boulevard

Santa Monica          **Map 2**                    (213) 394-2718

This multi-level culinary jewel has gathered together a staff from such local legends as Michael's, Jimmy's, L'Ermitage, and L'Orangerie. These are young and dedicated artists who are free to be tastefully innovative. When you arrive, you are greeted by a serene lady seated at a desk, much like an intimate and exclusive club. Owners Phillip Stroud and Richard Mann allow the kitchen freedom from the strict disciplines of L'Escoffier, and the results are impressive. Pigeon with spinach and foie gras and raspberry sauce, scallops and artichoke hearts with watercress butter sauce, and petrale sole with mousseline and lobster sauce are favorites. Prices are more reasonable than espected, perhaps illustrating a trend downward and indicating resistance from the patrons of fancy restaurants who are weary of fanciful prices. Ma Facon is likely to be a winner.

**Expensive.** Open Monday through Saturday 6:30 to 10:30 p.m. Full bar. Reservations required. Visa, MC, AX. Valet parking. Dressy.

---

## MAGIC PAN

French

(Locations in Arcadia, Beverly Hills, Brea, Costa Mesa,     ★
Glendale, San Diego, Thousand Oaks, Torrance, Woodland Hills. See phone book for listings.)

I never expected to like any restaurant that's a wholly-owned subsidiary of the Quaker Oats Company—or any other large corporation, for that matter—having found that the corporate mentality does not deal at all well with temperamental chefs, waitresses in love, and the myriad other hazards of the restaurant profession. But the magic Pan crêperies are beautiful operations, and they do their thing—crêpes—very well. In addition to the fifteen locations in California, there are more than 60 Magic Pans throughout the nation in such uncrêpe-like locations as Skokie, Illinois; Paramus, New Jersey; and McLean, Virginia. The interiors are similar—a contemporary version of French country side—with provincial antiques, off-white and plaster walls, oak wood and earth-tone tile floors, polished wooden tables set with brass candle lamps and fresh-cut flowers, and abundance of fresh plants and greenery, Hansel and Gretel curtained windows, and waiters in red aprons and waitresses in colored dirndls. The heart of the restaurant is the crêpe-making machine invented by Lesli Fono, a Hungarian skiing champion and currently a San Francisco restaurateur. It is a circular rotating arrangement of eight upside-down frying pans, set over gas flames in a colorful tile well. Crêpes are made fresh in the dining room, and fillings for the dozen or so entrée types that include coquille St. Jacques, and spinach soufflé are added in the kitchen. The potage St. Germain, a thick pea soup with sherry, is excellent; the consommé less so. Desserts include crêpes made with fresh fruit, chocolte, or ice cream (the mocha is sensational), as well as crêpes Beigner—delicately crisped, twisted, powdered with sugar and served in a basket to be dipped into hot brandied apricot sauce. The house wine, an Inglenook burgundy, is especially pleasing—rich, fruity, and smooth. Service is friendly and very informal, and the waiters— often young working-their-way-through college students— will take all the time you need to describe every dish on the menu. Each location varies somewhat—cocktails at some, daily specials like steak kabobs and salads at others—but the quality is consistent, and you can have a satisfying experience at a modest price.

**Inexpensive.** Open seven days. Luncheon served Monday through Friday from 11 a.m. to 5 p.m.; Saturday and Sunday brunch from 11 a.m. to 3 p.m. Dinner served Sunday through Thursday from 5 to midnight; Friday, Saturday to 1 a.m. Closed Thanksgiving, Christmas, New Year's. Full bar. Reservations accepted. Visa, MC, AX. Parking lots except Beverly Hills. Casual.

## MAGNOLIA'S PEACH

**American**

560 North Mountain Avenue

★

Upland     **Map 5**

(714) 982-1366

Man-sized drinks are served in this charming, gas-lighted New Orleans atmosphere and their award-winning chili and hamburgers lived up to the expectations of our testing, tasting palates. "Whiskey chicken," good steaks and oven fresh peach cobbler makes this a serendipity stop on your way to somewhere—the mountains or the desserts. This would be a favorite of mine if I lived in Upland.

**Moderate.** Open seven days. Lunch and dinner served form 11 a.m. to 5 p.m. Full bar. Reservations preferred. All major credit cards. Parking lot. Casual.

---

## MAISON ALEXIS

**French**

2515 East Coast Highway

★

Corona del Mar     **Map 4**

(714) 673-0347

This San Francisco all star team: chef Spinace who was a cook at La Bourgogne, and Walter Pazos from Ernie's (where he tended bar) along with his father, Alexi Pazos, who practiced his profession at Ernie's, have noble intentions. That they have not achieved greatness yet is not surprising, even Frank Sinatra has to tune up a bit. The transplant of a fine restaurant staff from one of the dining capitals of the world to an area that doesn't have the same quality of raw materials necessary for the kitchen will cause some pause. The sauces are the strong point here, making this a kind of classic, somewhat heavy fare that is sauced. They took over the old Indonesia, a not-so favorite restaurant of mine, and the place is still a bit haunted by mediocrity and touches of Polynesia.

**Moderate to expensive.** Open Monday through Saturday. Luncheon from 11:30 a.m. to 2:30 p.m. Dinner from 6 to 10 p.m. Full bar. Reservations recommended. All major credit cards. Parking lot. Casual to semi-dressy.

## MAISON GERARD
**French Provincial**

224 South Beverly Drive
★

Beverly Hills  **Map 8**
(213) 273-5430

4100 Cahuenga Boulevard
North Hollywood  **Map 1**
(213) 766-3841

"Pleasant" is perhaps the most descriptive term to use for this French country-style restaurant that has been doing a good business in Beverly Hills for twelve years. They're best known for very good (not great) onion soup, *cassoulet*, sweetbreads, kidneys, and an acceptable coquille St. Jacques. Menu is semi à la carte; entrées are served with salad, two vegetables, potatoes, and rolls. A word about the *cassoulet*: this was originally a humble peasant dish and is made well here, a bean stew with sausages, pork, lamb, and other ingredients. It is usually served for dinner but it is sometimes available at noon if the chef has prepared it in advance. It's worth asking about.

**Moderate.** Open Monday through Saturday. Luncheon from 11:30 a.m. to 3:30 p.m. Dinner from 5 to 11 p.m. Closed major holidays except Mother's Day. Full bar. Reservations essential. All major credit cards. Validated parking for lunch only in garage next door; street parking at night. Casual to semi-dressy.

## MALDONADO'S
**Continental**

1202 East Green Street
★

Pasadena  **Map 7**
(213) 796-1126

One of the more successful opera-cabaret-restaurants, Maldonado's has won a following for their cuisine as well as their *Carmen*. Tuesday night they have a harpist, but on all other evenings there are singers galore performing light opera, musical comedy and often with Mr. Maldonado himself at the piano. Veal Oskar is good but the chicken Marengo may be the best dish on the menu.

**Moderate.** Open seven days. Luncheon from 11 a.m. to 2:30 p.m. Dinner seatings at 6 and 9 p.m.; Sunday 5:30 and 8:30. Closed July 4, Thanksgiving, Christmas. Entertainment, musical comedy and opera. Full bar. Reservations essential. All major credit cards. Parking lot. Semi-dressy; jackets requested.

---

## MALIK CARTER'S NEW ORLEANS                    Barbecue
## BAR-B-QUE & GUMBO HUT
8549 Santa Monica Boulevard
Hollywood          **Map 8**                    (213) 657-1817

For years, I've driven past Malik Carter's without noticing the place. This is easy to do, since it's in the back of a parking lot, on the side of the street where you're facing the other way when you go by. Actually it's kind of a miracle that I ever found Malik Carter's. Mostly, I'm glad I did. It is not a place to eat if you're in a hurry. I gave Malik my order, and he told me to come back in about 20 minutes. I took a walk, picked up some beer, walked back, lingered, looked at the many photographs on the wall of Malik's hut, lingered a while longer, window shopped and, on the verge of collapsing from anticipation, finally dove into shrimp creole (served without shells which, Malik says, is the only way to eat shrimp; otherwise they're "unclean"), beef hot links and beef ribs. The ribs were heavy with meat, though they were smallish ribs. The links tasted of garlic and were spicy. And though the shrimp seemed a bit overcooked, Malik's hot sauce made up for that.

The side orders of beans and salad, however, were not much fun at all. The beans had little taste, and the salad was dull, and served in a plastic-packaged dressing. But Malik himself more than compensated for failed beans and salad (one does not after all, go to a rib place for salad). Brooding and convivial at the same time, well-bearded Malik Carter will gladly declaim upon the joys and significance of barbecue and Creole cooking. He'll tell you all about his Creole monkey bread, fresh baked and soaked like a sponge in butter, and his New Orleans vegetable dish called "peacoo." For dessert, he served pecan pie and peach cobbler. But I would just as gladly opt for the pleasure of his company and his freely-dispensed conversation.   *M.S.*

**Inexpensive.** Open seven days. Monday through Thursday noon to 11 p.m.; Friday and Saturday to 2:30 a.m.; Sunday 3 to 10 p.m. No alcoholic beverages. No reservations. No credit cards. Parking lot. Casual.

---

## MA MAISON

8368 Melrose Avenue
Los Angeles        **Map 8**

**French**
★★★
(213) 655-1991

Ma Maison, casually observed, is a curiosity—the epitome of eccentricity that draws international attention to Southern California. First time visitors who are lured to the restaurant by tales of great food or the attraction of a truly stellar clientele, may have a sinking moment of doubt when they pull into the valet tended parking lot. In a city where flash and glamour are signs of success, a first class restaurant in a converted Melrose Avenue bungalow is a bit of a surprise. It has taken Patrick Terrail seven years of hard work to turn Ma Maison into a warm, ebullient establishment while diligently retaining the cottage's original homely, homey character. The roof no longer leaks, Ricard umbrellas that once provided shelter now merely add to the unique decor, the tilting fence that screened the patio from a busy street has been replaced by a solid wall, but the same astro-turf green indoor-outdoor carpet still covers the patio and plant-crowded entry. A subtle metamorphosis goes on steadily, with the goal of greater comfort and better service. There is a keen perception of Southern California manias for freshness, bodies beautiful, and health. With impish imagination Ma Maison creates dishes that use the best, the freshest, and the newest in our markets with some of the same from around the world. Salad for lunch?

Among the leafy green assemblages that Californians wolf down are showstoppers like hot grilled duck breast with warmed butter and a locally cultivated Japanese oyster mushrooms or hot Maine lobster with cool California avocado dressed with a silken sauce. Lunch, in fact, is worth a special plug because the skills of the kitchen are very much in evidence—unlike many establishments that resort to sandwiches and other dull simplicities for midday fare. In the evening, the choices grow in complexity. Two lasting favorites appear with frequent variations. Salmon (or other best catch of the day), filled with a contrasting fish mousse, baked in a whimsical fish-shaped puff pastry shell is served afloat one delicate version of buerre blanc or another. Duck arrives in two courses. Slivers of rare breast, in a light but sinful sauce, are embellished by fruit one day, peppercorns another, sometimes both as the discretion of the chef dictates. A bity salad of endives follows, topped with crisp morsels of duck skin, and a crisply roasted duck leg. But these are just starters. First courses, accompanying vegetables, other main dishes, desserts—all hold their own. The wine list grows and deserves study—while the house wine holds its own. Service has been honed to an interesting expertise by a group of black-suited veterans, while maitre d' Claude Gourdal backs up Patrick's eagle eye and bark with gentle attentiveness.  *Jerry Di Vecchio*

**Expensive.** Open Monday through Saturday. Luncheon served noon to 2:30. Dinner from 6:30 to 10:30 p.m. Closed all major holidays. Full bar. Patio. Most major credit cards. Valet parking. Semi-dressy; jackets preferred.

---

## MAMMA FESADA'S                Italian/Continental
21 Sierra Drive                                      ★
Kernville                              (714) 376-3444

Kernville is the resting point for thousands of vacation-minded folks who pause and then continue on to Northern California via the High Sierras. Chef Richard Adamic was forced West by the recession of 1974. He got as far as Las Vegas but he didn't have the Vegas notion, and after five years of "hard knocks," as he puts it, he came to this charming area. Nothing fancy, but you'll feast on big portions of honest food like a double breast of chicken stuffed with broccoli and cheese, baked and topped with fresh mushroom sauce (chicken breasts "Mama"), or fresh trout amandine, or any of the pastas. If it's a hot day you might order a bottle of Piesporter Goldtrophehen, an unlikely accompaniment to Italian fare, but good. Their claim that the chicken soup is better than penicillin and even has an effect on your lovelife is a bit farfetched, however.

**Moderate.** Open Tuesday through Sunday. Dinner from 5 to 9 p.m. Children's menu. Wine and beer only. Reservations preferred. Visa, MC. Off street parking. Resort wear.

---

**THE MANDARIN**  **Mandarin/Chinese**
430 North Camden Drive  ★★
Beverly Hills  **Map 8**  (213)272-0267

"There were no red eggs sent out on my first birthday," the diminutive Madame Cecilia Chiang recalls. "Since I was a girl with twelve brothers and sisters, rejoicing at my birth was naturally subdued." Madame Chiang was able to resolve her personal identity crisis, first with an interest in competitive sports, unusual for a young girl from a family of great wealth in Peking, and later as an expert in Mandarin food. She opened her first restaurant in Tokyo, and, subsequently, The Mandarin Restaurant in San Francisco's Ghirardelli Square, where it has become one of that city's most exciting visual and culinary treasures. Her new Mandarin in Beverly Hills serves its famous Beggar's Chicken encased in clay, prawns à la Szechwan, and Mongolian firepot with highly flavored chicken broth and thinly sliced meats, seafoods, and vegetables. A Mongolian firepit is central to the decor, and as many as a dozen guests may grill their own food at the firepit or have the chef prepare it for them. Peking duck is an ancient Chinese art form, and it is done to perfection here.

After the duck is killed, a bamboo tube is inserted just below the neck, and the skin gradually separated from the flesh as air is blown into the tube. The duck is dried and coated with honey, then hung in a hot oven to allow the    to drip down. It's roasted until the skin — considered the choicest part — is a deep translucent brown, crisp and luscious. The duck is then carved into bite-sized pieces at the table, placed in an *paoping* (a Chinese crêpelike pancake), spread with *hoisin* (duck sauce), topped with scallions and rolled up in the pancake. Unlike the Chinese palace decor of the Ghirardelli Square location, the Beverly Hills restaurant takes on a different, more contemporary character. Floors are laid with bright blue and jade green tile and burnt orange carpeting, and the spacious dining rooms are rich in antiques and lush greenery. There is a feeling of openness, and in the front dining room a view of the street much like that of an aristocratic French cafe. Madame Chiang has personally supervised each detail of the operation from the waiters' silk Mandarin uniforms to luxurious table settings in an admirably understated elegance.

**Moderate to expensive.** Open seven days. Luncheon from noon to 3:30 p.m. weekdays. Dinner 5 to 11 Monday through Saturday; to 10 Sunday. Full bar. Reservations essential. All major credit cards. Wheelchair access. Valet parking. Casual.

---

## MANDARIN CHINA RESTAURANT　　Chinese
4110 West Point Loma Boulevard　　★
San Diego　　(714) 222-6688

Chinese junk food was literally prepared on the small boats and barges for use in Hong Kong and was no better than that served here, a kind of San Francisco connection to San Diego. The specialty of the house is Hong Kong style *dim sum* served daily for lunch and—a rarity—for dinner as well. These dumplings are steamed, baked or deep fried stuffed with curry beef or steamed shrimp or melon with crispy fried meat balls and more. The subdued atmosphere is a pleasant change from Charlie Chan decor.

**Inexpensive to moderate.** Open seven days. Sunday through Thursday 11 a.m. to 10 p.m; to 11 p.m. Friday, Saturday. Closed Thanksgiving. Wine and beer only. Reservations suggested for larger parties. Visa, MC, DC. Shopping center parking. Casual.

---

## MANDARIN GOURMET                              Chinese
1500 Adams Avenue                                      ★
Costa Mesa          **Map 4**                (714) 540-1937

A rarity: the good Chinese restaurant in Orange County. Michael Chiang purchased a used Cantonese store and transformed it into a competent—if not exciting—Hunan, Szechwan, Peking, Mandarin operation. The menu is pedestrian and certainly doesn't appear to take chances with the Orange County palate, a mistake in my opinion. However, the expected and usual list is prepared well. Service is good when the restaurant is not full.

**Inexpensive.** Open seven days. Luncheon served 11:30 a.m. to 3 p.m. Monday through Thursday. Dinner served from 4:30 to 10 p.m.; Friday and Saturday from 11:30 a.m. to 11 p.m.; Sunday from 11:30 a.m. to 10 p.m. Closed Thanksgiving. Full bar. Reservations advised. Most major credit cards. Wheelchair access. Parking lot. Casual.

---

## MANEEYA THAI                                     Thai
3737 Cahuenga Boulevard West                          ★★
Studio City          **Map 1**                (213) 760-9691

The first thing I noticed about Maneeya Thai that impressed me was that the waitresses were wearing very tight-fitting jeans. Considering the relative modesty of most of the Thai restaurants around town, the slickness of Maneeya comes as quite a surprise. After perusing the brand name on my waitress's back pocket, my eye wandered about the room, pausing on many an item of Thai memorabilia, but mostly resting on a large mural on the restaurant's west wall which portrays a day-in-the-life of a rural Thai village. In a cartoon-like fashion, priests collect alms, fishermen row out into a river, a band entertains. It's a mural for all seasons and all times of the day, just like the restaurant it's decorating.

I do not think there's a bad dish to be eaten at Maneeya, though, of course, some dishes are better than others. Actually, after eating there many times (it's near the Universal Tour, which I take every time a new attraction is added), I've found that as at many of L.A.'s Thai restaurants, though the entrées are good and reliable, and even often excellent, the Thai touch is best felt in the appetizers and the salads. Beyond reason I adore the house eggrolls at Maneeya. Without shame, I love the *mee krob* (or *mee grob*) a dish reminiscent of *pud Thai*, only the fried rice noodles are caramelized in a bean and tomato sauce ($4.25). My adoration for Maneeya's deep-fried shrimp (or squid, $3.75 in either case) is without bounds, as is my ability to eat terrifyingly large portions of most Thai appetizers.

But I've always felt my sins of excess on the bbq'd beef on a stick ($3.75), for instance, are well made up for by the reverence with which I hold the Thai salads, especially the *yum yae* ($4.75), a concoction of shrimp, pork, cucumber, eggs and onions, upon a few leaves of romaine, covered with a tangy peanut sauce. There's something so healthy about a salad, and something so rare about one that's actually edible. And by the way, in no way am I putting down the main courses. I think if I had to make a choice between Maneeya's sauteed baby clams and Bo Derek... well, I'm thinking, I'm thinking.  *M.S.*

**Moderate.** Open Monday through Saturday. Luncheon served 11:30 to 3 weekdays. Dinner from 5:30 to 10. Closed most major holidays. Beer and wine only. Reservations accepted. All major credit cards. Parking lot. Semi-dressy.

## MAN FOOK LOW RESTAURANT      Chinese
962 South San Pedro Street      ★
Los Angeles     **Map 7**      (213) 623-3375

Fewer people know what *dim sum* is than can tell who was Harry Truman's vice president in 1948. Although everyone knows something about Chinese food, hardly anybody knows anything about this Chinese tea feast. (One of the reasons it's been so long undiscovered is that most menus use Chinese characters to describe it.) Man Fook Low is one of the best purveyors of the various hors d'oeuvres-like dishes: dumplings, steamed and baked, and filled buns and sweet cakes. Served from 10 a.m. until 2 in the afternoon, the steamed dumplings filled with a mixture of ground meat are vaguely similar to ravioli in appearance, but the tastes and textures are likely to be a new and exciting experience for you and your palate. There is a standard Cantonese menu as well, but it fades into obscurity when compared to the *dim sum*, as served here for over fifty years. (The office of the vice president was vacant in 1948.)

**Inexpensive to moderate.** Open seven days. Luncheon and dinner from 10 a.m. to 10:30 p.m. daily. Closed Thanksgiving. Full bar. Reservations advised for large groups. Visa, MC, AX. Parking lot on 10th Street entrance. Casual.

---

## MANGIA      Northern Italian
10543 West Pico Boulevard      ★
(Rancho Park area)
West Los Angeles     **Map 8**      (213) 470-1952

The restaurant scene in Southern California is blessed with the emergence of small, stylish European delis and restaurants. The extraordinary cooking would draw raves in a superstar restaurant and has attracted a great deal of professional attention. The Florentine cuisine is really the source of many of the Escoffier recipes and its richness and complexity virtually defies description. Lasagne with fresh sliced tomatoes and cheese is delicate and light. Minestrone is made in small batches, and the vegetables retain their individual flavor. Prawns are served with fresh fennel, cream and Pernod, speckled with tiny red peppers. The antipasto changes with the whims of the kitchen and the availability of the freshest ingredients. Pastries are as good as any in town; pasta is fresh. There is a wide selection of good California and familiar Italian wines, most available at retail. Decor is a mix of bentwood chairs, flowers, Italian newspapers racked and tile floor. Best of all, for the too-hot-to-cook set, everything here is available for take out. Congratulations to Kathleen Ellsworth and Meg McComb, the hard working owners who share their enthusiasms and talent with a delighted following.

**Moderate to expensive.** Open Monday through Saturday from 11 a.m. to 10 p.m.; desserts served until midnight. Closed major holidays. Wine and beer only. Reservations required for dinner. Patio. Visa, MC, AX. Valet parking. Casually elegant.

---

**MARCO POLO RISTORANTE**  Italian/Continental
12223 West Washington Boulevard  ★
Los Angeles  **Map 8**  (213) 398-6106

A comfortable and quaint restaurant, with a friendly and efficient staff—and a sure hand with veal. Dinners come with homemade minestrone and special house salad, and there are about a hundred wines on the wine card. It recalls several upper middle-class restaurants in any of the large cities of Italy. Background music is Italian opera or folk.

**Inexpensive to moderate.** Open Tuesday through Sunday. Dinner from 5 to 10:45 p.m. Tuesday through Saturday; 4:30 to 9:30 Sunday. Entertainment. Full bar. Reservations recommended. All major credit cards. Street parking. Casual.

# MARCUS STEAK HOUSE

**Steaks**

633 South Olive Street ★

Los Angeles **Map 7** (213) 622-0773

This restaurant opened in 1924 dedicated to quality, and Stan Marcus keeps it that way for the downtown aficignados and the visiting Japanese who exclaim over the size of the great steaks as if they were the crown jewels. Ribs from the slow burning hickory ovens, seafood, salads and breakfasts take care of the hunger pangs although the wine list would be more suitable to a fancier restaurant. This is a cozy, comfortable, reliable place run by an outstanding professional.

**Inexpensive to moderate.** Open Monday through Friday from 7 a.m. to 8:30 p.m. Closed major holidays. Full bar. Reservations suggested. All major credit cards. Validated parking after 5 p.m. Casual.

---

# MARENGO

**French/Continental**

24594 Hawthorne Boulevard ★

Torrance **Map 2** (213) 378-1174

You dine in Napoleon's field camp, under a canopy of blue and white surrounded by battle flags, and the waiters wear the uniform of Napoleon's army. Chicken Marengo, a classy dish, was created — or so the story goes — at a special celebration of the victory at Marengo; it combines chicken, tomatoes, eggs, crayfish, garlic and more. This succulent dish is at its best here, but surprisingly, all the food is good. The soufflé is so light you have to keep catching it to bring it back down to the plate.

**Moderate.** Open seven days. Luncheon from 11:30 a.m. to 2:30 p.m. weekdays. Dinner from 6 to 10 p.m. Monday through Saturday; 5 to 10 Sunday. Closed major holidays. Full bar. Reservations essential. Visa, MC, AX. Parking lot. Semi-dressy.

# MARIANNE

French
★★

45 South Mentor Avenue

Pasadena          **Map 7**          (213) 792-2535

Georges Bardot and Gene Ronay, the chef-partners, have another winner in Marianne to add to their Véronique, both in unlikely but deserving locations. The Véronique in bleak Pico Rivera has been an oasis in the gastronomic wasteland and now the more sumptuous Marianne has finally given Pasadena the jewel it richly deserves. Marianne is splendid with its skylight, potted greenery, fresh flowers, and excellent selection of dishes. Its most unique touch is the wall of private booths, each one partitioned on both sides with lights that can be raised — or lowered — and lace curtains if privacy is desired — or required. I recall how astounded I was when several local columnists came to the simultaneous conclusion that there are virtually no good French restaurants in America (much less in Southern California) and even took one to task for being so gauche as to print English translations of dishes described in French. What pomposity. What snobbery! There are fine French restaurants here and to say otherwise is an affront to a joyous establishment like Marianne where the *poulet amandine*, or the sweetbreads, or the sensational baby salmon *moutarde* (the chef is from Dijon) are as good as one would find in many fine French restaurants. The blackboard menu is a tradition here (the dishes listed were copied from several days' presentation) and represent what the kitchen feels is freshest and most appropriate. At luncheon the prices are surprisingly modest. There's a wide variety of selections and an adequate wine list. Desserts are not an after-thought — we opted for fresh raspberries — and they are prepared in house. When you call for a reservation be sure to let them know if you want a private booth. In all, the Marianne is a charming experience and the patrons, from conservative Pasadena pinstripes to outlandish Scottsdale checks and plaids, were thoroughly enjoying the romantic atmosphere, professional service and the excellent dishes prepared by a great chef. Viva la Véronique! Viva la Marianne!

**Moderate.** Open Tuesday through Sunday. Luncheon from 11:30 a.m. to 2 p.m. weekdays. Dinner from 5:30 to 9 p.m. Tuesday through Thursday; 5 to 9:30 Friday, Saturday; 5 to 9 Sunday. Closed major holidays. Full bar. Reservations required for dinner. All major credit cards. Parking lot. Semi-dressy.

## MARIE CALLENDAR                                    American
Everywhere (check phone book)

This chain started as a little pie-to-go shop with a counter and then grew to become a formidable chain with unfaltering quality control. The pies are still splendid — the fresh strawberry in season is a masterpiece — but now there are also hamburgers and ham sandwiches and, in some locations, full dinner menus. Everything is about as wholesome — if not as good — as it can be, and they have their own little touches (a cup of stewed apples with sandwiches) that are nice. Emphasis is on bland, however, and the chili would be banned in Dallas or Tucson as counterfeit. Whole pies are still a big part of the business.

**Moderate.** No credit cards. Casual.

## MARINE ROOM                              Continental/American
2000 Spindrift Drive                                         ★
La Jolla                                          (714) 454-7126

Photography buffs, you're in for a royal treat here if you keep your cameras in focus and aim to the west. Voilà! Prints of whales. When the sun goes down and the moon comes up, point your camera skyward to shoot the stars through the open roof. Of course, the stars are there for dancing under, and you can until midnight all week long. Meanwhile back inside, focus your attention, if not your camera, on the aquariums with live sea horses. Oh, yes, the food, which is probably why you came. It's all good: abalone, lobster, chicken *cordon bleu*, prime rib, and steaks.

You'll be glad you got all dressed up for this marine experience. The effect is complete if you're there at high tide and the surf rushes up to the windows.

**Moderate.** Open seven days. Luncheon from 11:30 a.m. to 2:30 p.m. Dinner from 6 to 10 p.m. Sunday brunch from 10:30 a.m. to 2:30 p.m. Dancing. Full bar. Reservations necessry. Ocean view. All major credit cards. Parking lot. Semi-dressy.

---

## MARIO'S                                            Italian
71-730 Highway 111
Rancho Mirage                              (714) 346-0584

An excruciatingly embarrassing restaurant—mediocre food and oft-times simply horrible singing. This would be a great evening for conventioneers already fortified against the onslaught of sopranos or for Aunt Tilly from Patchy Pants, Arkansas, but for anyone who has ever heard serious music or eaten Italian food, it is an unmitigated disaster in the desert. However, now that I've warned you, I should add that people have fun here with the high camp.

**Moderate.** Open Tuesday through Sunday. Dinner served 5 to 10 p.m.; Friday and Saturday to 11 p.m. Closed Christmas. Entertainment nightly. Full bar. Reservations advised. All major credit cards accepted. Parking lot. Casual.

---

## MARIO'S ITALIAN RESTAURANT   Italian/American
1001 Broxton Avenue                                    ★
Westwood Village        **Map 8**          (213) 208-7077

This is a good Italian restaurant that transcends its spaghetti-house location in Westwood near UCLA. An original creation is *linguine sorrento al cartoccio*, linguine in a clam sauce with chunks of lobster, shrimp, and clams, cooked in a plastic bag. The *cannelloni alla Napoletana* (stuffed with ground beef and cheese) is a specialty, and I would urge you to try the *gnocchi* (Italian potato dumplings), here served *alla pie-montese*, with a meat sauce. The pasta is not prepared al dente unless you so request. There are steaks and chicken and seafood (shrimp alla Anna Maria is my favorite) and other house specialties. The desserts are poor. Wine and beer only, but they're creative with their offerings of wine cocktails. There are some Italian wines that may be a bit harsh to the palate of those used to the "softer" American and French varieties. Mario Angelini has a good thing going here, and the people in the area know all about it. Best yet, it's open until 12:30 on weekends, when the restaurant is especially crowded with UCLA and show-going crowds. Expect to wait.

**Moderate.** Open seven days. Luncheon from 11:30 a.m. to 2:30 p.m. weekdays. Dinner from 2:30 p.m. to midnight. Closed Thanksgiving, Christmas. Wine and beer only. Reservations advised. Patio. All major credit cards. Street parking. Casual.

## MARIO'S RESTAURANT                    Mexican
18603 Main Street

| Huntington Beach | **Map 4** | (714) 842-5811 |
| 15964 Springdale | | |

| Huntington Beach | **Map 4** | (714) 897-6664 |

Mario's, with two locations in Huntington Beach, serves thousands of luncheons and dinners each week with home-made tortillas. You can feast on a real *chile relleno* served with rice and beans for lunch at a mere $2. You can get a combination enchilada and tamale for $2.65. The menu is extensive and the food pleasantly served. I doubt if you could do it for the price at home. Margaritas are excellent at a buck and you can have a full liter of wine for around $3.

**Inexpensive.** Open seven days. Luncheon from 11 a.m. to 3 p.m. Dinner 3 to 10 p.m. Springdale location; to 11 at Main Street location. Children's menus. Full bar. Reservations recommended. All major credit cards. Parking lot. Casual.

---

## MARQUIS WEST                                    Italian
3110 Santa Monica Boulevard                              ★
Santa Monica          **Map 2**              (213) 828-4567

Their reputation will not be at steak. There are not enough good little Italian restaurants—the plush kind that put you in the mood for *calamari*, the dry white wines and robust reds, and the great pastas of Northern Italy. New to West Los Angeles area but old in friendship are Chef Pietro Giordano and his partner Pasquale Lombardo of the historic Marquis on Sunset Boulevard. The booths are commodious and comfortable, the carpeting lush, and lighting is through the stained-glass panels. There is a tiny hospitality bar as you enter, a friendly note to start the evening. Pasquale is everywhere, explaining, discussing, chatting, supervising the *fettuccine* Alfredo or—my favorite—the *puttanesca*. There is *calamari* as a main course here, too, as served in the style of the chef's hometown San Remo, simmered long in a zesty Italian sauce. The menu is immense, but everything is so well executed that the Italian set are already filling the main rooms. As with other such establishments, you'll see more *embrazos* here than in *Godfather* I and II combined, as good will flourishes, nourished by the rich foods.

**Moderate.** Open seven days. Luncheon from 11:30 a.m. to 2:30 p.m weekdays. Dinner from 5:30 to 11 p.m.; Sunday 4:30 to 11 p.m. Banquet facilities. Entertainment. Full bar. Reservations advised. All major credit cards. Valet parking. Semi-dressy.

## MARRAKESH

1100 West Pacific Coast Highway
Newport Beach         **Map 4**

Moroccan
★★★
(714) 645-8384

13003 Ventura Boulevard
Studio City         **Map 1**

★★★
(213) 788-6354

3146 Sports Arena Boulevard
San Diego

★★
(714) 223-6609

I did not expect the epicurean road to Morocco would lead so improbably to a Newport Beach restaurant. How brazen to call it the Marrakesh, considering the fame of the long-past-its-glory Marrakesh in San Francisco. But young Ali Rabbani is brazen, and his big black eyes glisten with excitement as he describes the attempt to create authentic Moroccan cuisine. It is a palace for sultans with a Hollywood-Arab decor of Valentino-era opulence. A restaurant that will dazzle Americans with its sumptuous setting—a caravan of luxurious tents pitched beneath the evening sky. the *djellaba*-gowned Rabbani used his unlimited lacquer license—from the gleaming hand-carved doors to the inlaid talbes—and an unlimited budget for assorted fountains, handpainted tiles, and gold filigreed glasses. The waiters have the familiar fezzes of Mideastern restaurants, but their attentiveness and skill are exceptional. The complex menu is explained patiently, even graciously. Hands are laved with hot scented Turkish towels between each course (you eat with your fingers; silverware is available only upon request), and thick mint tea is poured from five-foot heights. The four entrées of fish, chicken, rabbit, or squab (on which the entire party must agree for serving rituals) is accompanied by *harira* (spicy soup); fresh vegetables as salad (to be eaten between the fingers); home-baked bread; *b'stila* (chicken, egg, and sweatmeat pie in a powdered sugar pastry); couscous, mint tea, and that richest of dessert pastries, baklava. The combination of ambience, perfect service, and exceptional food adds up to one of the best values in dining adventures in Southern California. A limited but intelligent wine selection is available, and cocktails are served. No belly dancers (thankfully); no entertainment is needed.

**Newport Beach: Moderate.** Open seven days. Dinner from 6 to 10 p.m. Monday through Thursday; 5:30 to 11 Friday through Sunday. Full bar. Reservations advised. All major credit cards. Valet parking. Wheelchair access. Semi-dressy. **Studio City, San Diego:** Open seven days. Dinner from 5 to 10 p.m. Sunday through Thursday; to 11 Friday, Saturday. Full bar. Reservations recommended. All major credit cards. Valet parking. Casual to semi-dressy.

---

# MARTONI'S                                      Italian
1523 North Cahuenga Boulevard                       ★
Hollywood        **Map 7**                  (213) 466-3441

Among the hearty peasant fare of Southern Italy, there is *pasticcio verde* (layers of homemade spinach noodles and meats, topped with béchamel sauce), which is rarely found in the United States. This fine old Italian restaurant caters to fine old Italians who care about such plates of nostalgia, and other rarities like *scungilli* (a conch shellfish). To assure authentic tastes and aromas, owner Salvatore Marino has his own herb garden with *rugola*, a leafy salad green. There are all the other dishes you would expect of a good Italian *ristorante*, and the bistro atmosphere is a favorite of tourists and theatregoers who flock to the Huntington Hartford and the nearby Cinerama Dome, as well as radio and recording celebrities.

**Moderate.** Open Monday through Saturday. Luncheon weekdays from 11:30 a.m. to 3 p.m. Dinner form 5:00 p.m. to 1:00 a.m. Full bar. Reservations required. All major credit cards. Valet parking. Semi-dressy.

## MARV'S DELI                              Deli
12512 Magnolia Boulevard                      ★
North Hollywood        **Map 1**        (213) 763-0616

The deli competition has been great for Southern California. Marv's, recently remodelled, is giving Art's a run for its money by doing everything nearly as well and for less money. It really looks more like a French bistro but when you're starving for a lean (remember lean?) c.b. on rye (their ryes have seen the glory). You don't care where you get it, right? They are number two but moving up on the outside.

**Inexpensive.** Open Tuesday through Sunday for lunch and take-out only from 8 a.m. to 6 p.m. Closed Jewish holidays. No alcoholic beverages. No reservations. Wheelchair access. Parking lot. Casual.

## MATTEO'S                              Italian
2321 Westwood Boulevard                       ★
West Los Angeles        **Map 8**        (213) 475-4521

Matteo's in Westwood is an important Italian restaurant that has a sense of style—and humor. A celebrity haven from the first, this colorful, tasteful room with touches like toy trains chugging around the ceiling serves alta cucina, but the peasant dishes of Southern Italy are done best here.

*Moderate to expensive.* Open Tuesday through Sunday 5 p.m. to 2 a.m. Closed Thanksgiving, Christmas. All major credit cards. Reservations required. Full bar. Parking lot. Semi-dressy.

---

*For best results, consult "How to Use This Guide" on page 27.*

## MATTEO'S                                      Italian
2325 East Coast Highway                            ★
Corona del Mar          **Map 4**            (714) 673-8267

Matteo's in Newport is a graceful, lovely restaurant, more
sedate than its Westwood parent. A polished brass railing
set against rich deep red decor sets the style as you enter
the mirrored dining room, or descend to the cozily romantic
lounge below for an apéritif. Veals are reverently handled,
and the *fettuccine* is creamy-rich.

**Expensive.** Open Tuesday through Sunday from 5 to 11
p.m. Full bar. Reservations advised. All major credit cards.
Valet parking. Semi-dressy.

## MAURICE'S SNACK 'N' CHAT                    Soul food
5553 West Pico Boulevard                           ★★
Los Angeles             **Map 7**            (213) 931-3877

Maurice's Snack 'n' Chat is a restaurant with a fierce and
devoted following. It has been praised beyond all reason.
On one of my visits, I began to sense the charm that's
beguiled so many diners at this very interestng soul food
restaurant on Pico Boulevard. Service was quick and very
friendly, even though Henry Winkler was throwing a
birthday party in the front room, and an awful lot of
energy was going into that. My waitress, Barbara, was
having more fun than a proverbial pig in a poke. She would
giggle to us about the things going on at the Winkler table,
compliment us on our choice of beets for one of the
vegetables ("Beets mean you'll have good blood") and spent
more time than most would have wondering why fish is a
word both singular and plural ("Why not fishes... why not
sheeps?")

As a good waiter or waitress always can, Barbara made
this meal at Maurice's a memorable experience. Contrary to
general consensus, I don't find Maurice's to be the ultimate
soul food restaurant. (That's a nod I'd give to either Chez

Helene down in New Orleans or Nate Thurmond's The Beginning up in San Francisco.) But I do think it's a very good soul food restaurant. The short ribs, the smothered pork chops, the pan fried fish, the liver and onions are among the best versions of those simple home-cooked dishes to be found anywhere in Los Angeles. Unlike many home-cooked restaurants, the food here really does taste like someone's homecooking; and that includes all the imperfections of homecooking. But there is a note of untruth in the sign in front of Maurice's. It says: "Eat Here Cheaper Than At Home and Better Too." Possibly you'll eat better at Maurice's than at home, but you won't eat cheaper. Maurice's is more expensive than the average soul food restaurant. And unquestionably the only soul food restaurant with an unlisted phone number.   M.S.

**Moderate.** Open seven days from noon to 10 p.m. weekdays; 6 to 11 p.m. Saturday; 4 to 9 p.m. Sunday. Closed most major holidays. No alcoholic beverages. Reservations essential. No credit cards. Street parking. Casual.

---

# MAURO'S                                      Italian
514 South Brand Boulevard                      ★★
Glendale        **Map 7**              (213) 243-6908

An instant hit when it opened about two years ago, but then a lot of folks worried when Mauro left to conquer other locations. I am delighted to report that this elegant Roman restaurant is better than ever, perhaps the best southern Italian kitchen in the southland. Mauro's right hand Giovanni, took over a while back and made prudent menu changes. Chef Orlando Pelligrino remains to prepare a rich selection of dishes including veal, chicken, game bird, beef, seafood, pasta, *zuppa*, and several varieties of antipasto. The antipasto  enjoyed most was made of fresh vegetables arranged in an eye-boggling presentation. Vegetables are *al dente*. Pasta is homemade. I can state with confidence that the homemade ice cream and ices are the best I've ever tasted here or abroad. Italian equipment is used, preservatives are avoided, there is very little sugar added and the flavors of the fresh fruit are the flavors you taste. Among our bouquet of ice creams—all fresh—was banana, served in a banana skin; lemon and oranges in their shells; pistachio, raspberry, white chocolate and the most chocolatey chocolate you can order without a prescription. Mauro's is not inexpensive, you should spend about $40. There's a cozy bar, happy sounds, cappuccino, and espresso and Italian mineral water is provided without charge. The wine list is so extensive you'll need a guide, and they're obliging. A charming luncheon buffet is now served in a new addition that serves as a deli as well.

**Moderate to expensive.** Open Monday through Saturday. Dinner from 5:30 to 11 p.m. Harpist Tuesday through Saturday. Full bar. Reservations essential. Visa, MC, AX. Dressy.

---

## MAXWELL'S
317 Pacific Coast Highway
Huntington Beach          **Map 4**

**Seafood**
★★
(714) 536-2555

Seafood, flown in from the East or fresh caught nearby, is the main attraction here, but there are others as well. There's the view of the ocean and pier, live entertainment and an award-winning wine list. The seafood menu consists of ten to twenty varieties daily, including fresh Eastern scallops, Maine lobster, *cioppino*, and the Maxwell supreme. My own favorite accompaniment to the dinner is the complimentary basket of popovers, air-filled, and aromatic.

**Moderate.** Open seven days. Breakfast daily except Sunday 8 to 11:30 a.m. Luncheon from 11:30 a.m. to 4 p.m. Dinner 4 to 10 p.m.; Friday, Saturday and Sunday until 11 p.m. Sunday brunch 11 a.m. to 4 p.m. Child's menu. Entertainment. Full bar. Reservations advised. Ocean view. All major credit cards. Valet parking. Casual.

## MEDALLION RESTAURANT   Continental
3701 Wilshire Boulevard   ★
Los Angeles   **Map 7**   (213) 385-8191

Huge brass chandeliers, marble pillars, fountains, pools, lush greenery, and red-draped windows create a feeling of surreal elegance. Wine is emphasized — there is a unique "wine wall." Service is continental, leaning toward Russian, with entrées finished at the table. Among the best is a steak à la Phipps, a prime rib steak pan-fried at the table with a sauce of Dijon mustard and served with fresh vegetables, salad, or soup. The chicken or seafood crêpes are great for luncheon.

**Moderate.** Open Monday through Saturday. Luncheon from 11:30 a.m. to 3 p.m. weekdays. Dinner 5:30 to 11 Tuesday through Saturday. Closed most holidays. Piano bar Wednesday through Friday; disco Saturday. Full bar. Reservations recommended. All major credit cards. Parking lot. Casual.

## MEDITERRANEAN ROOM   Continental
18700 MacArthur Boulevard   ★
Irvine   **Map 4**   (714) 833-2770

For years this has been an exceptionally well run hotel dining room, and we have no reason to believe things will change. Owner Richard Duffy is committed to continuing the high caliber of the dishes, and keeping things swinging in the bar lounge where there's big band entertainment and dancing nightly. The Cafe Continental with its patio is available for private parties. There is Sunday brunch with a fruit carousel and nine entrées from which to choose.

**Moderate.** Open seven days. Luncheon from 11:30 a.m. to 2 p.m. weekdays. Dinner from 5:30 to 10:30 p.m. Sunday through Thursday; to 11 Friday, Saturday. Sunday brunch 10 a.m. to 3 p.m. Open major holidays. Entertainment. Full bar. Reservations recommended. Patio. All major credit cards. Valet parking. Casual.

## MEDIUM RARE                                    American
70064 Highway 111
Rancho Mirage                                (714) 328-6563

Four different owners, five different dining areas but one
entrée—prime rib—is the noteworthy dish in this limited
beauty with the ubiquitous turf and surf and boring
desserts. Nothing special here but for those who like chain
steakeries in the desert this may be the place.

**Moderate.** Open Monday through Saturday. Luncheon 11:30
a.m. to 2:30 p.m. weekdays. Dinner 5 to 10 p.m. Banquet
facilities. Children's menu. Full bar. Reservations recommended. All major credit cards. Valet parking. Semi-dressy.

---

## MEL'S LANDING                                    Seafood
8418 Sepulveda Boulevard                               ★
Sepulveda        **Map 1**                   (213) 893-7000

A phoenix among restaurants, this valley favorite has survived fire and catastrophe and re-emerged as a born-again
winner. Formerly a fisherman, Mel eventually learned to
cook the fish he caught, and now he views his finned friends
from a different perspective: they must first pass his inspection before entering his restaurant or fishmarket. Remember
Mark Spitz? Well, he's about the only denizen of the deep to
escape making an appearance on Mel's menu, since variety is
a key feature here. This is one of the pioneers of the low cost
American style seafood restaurants that include soup or salad
with all dinners.

**Moderate.** Open Tuesday through Sunday. Luncheon from
11:30 a.m. to 2:30 p.m. weekdays. Dinner 5 to 10 p.m.
Tuesday through Saturday; 4 to 9 Sunday. Wine and beer
only. No reservations. Visa, MC. Parking lot. Casual.

## MELVYN'S .

**Continental**
★★

200 West Ramon Road
Palm Springs

(714) 325-2323

Whether the candles are shimmering romantically or the brilliant sun streams across the terrace, Melvyn's is a place to unwind. A beautiful garden area is a setting for lovely *coq au vin* served in wine with tarragon and a poached turbot— true reflections of the chef's talent. There is also a long list of the obligatory steaks. Melvyn Haber makes this the best kept secret in Palm Springs but worth finding.

**Expensive.** Open seven days. Luncheon noon to 3 p.m. weekdays. Dinner 6 to 10 p.m. Saturday and Sunday brunch 9 a.m. to 3 p.m. Banquet facilities. Entertainment. Full bar. Reservations recommended. Patio. Visa, MC, AX. Valet parking. Casual.

## MICHAEL'S

**Continental**
★★★

1147 Third Street
Santa Monica          **Map 2**

(213) 451-0843

When the young (28) American chef-owner says: "We have built the number one restaurant to serve *haute nouvelle cuisine* in the city of Los Angeles," he is sticking his toque out. If the statement does not ring with the same drama as "I shall return" or Churchill's "blood, sweat and tears," it is not because Michael McCarty takes himself or his restaurant any less seriously. Indeed, it would be easy sport to poke a little fun at such pretentiousness. But the truth is, he may be right. Michael's is located in a restored '30s-ish private residence with a kind of *nouvelle* Queen Mary interior. The intimate and utterly charming dining room overlooks a terraced garden of flowering plants and a patio for lazy luncheons. Inside, the table settings are smashing. Thirteen-inch Villeroy and Boch plates, and Christofle silver provide the "stage" on which the food is presented. Fresh flowers are in abundance and Michael's private collection of contemporary art includes some of the superstars like Jasper Johns and David Hockney. McCarty's American roots are in nearby Malibu, but his credentials range from the Cordon Bleu—where he received the Grand Diploma—to the Academie du Vin and Cornell's School of Hotel Administration. Along with Wolfgang Puck formerly Ma Maison, Michael feels the term *nouvelle cuisine* has been misused and abused. To Puck it means that younger, more imaginative chefs are allowed freedom to break away from rigid formulae. To McCarty it means that a kitchen becomes "a laboratory of creativity" and his is staffed with American chefs as talented as their French peers. Michael will be likely to greet you and check often and earnestly with the progress of your dinner. All the male staff is dressed in the Annie Hall look of bulky knotted ties over open collars and pleated trousers. They are trained to guide you glibly through such wonders as an appetizer of hot *mousseline* of fresh fish with red butter sauce; a salad of chicory, hot goat cheese and walnut *vinaigrette* and entrées that include saddle of lamb with red currant sauce or an even more exciting breast of chicken with duck liver and morel mushrooms. Typical of the professionalism is the selection of cheeses, here served room temperature as God and Europeans intended. (By comparison some of the "grand" restaurants serve a Brie that has been chilled to the consistency and flavor of putty, inexcusable to say the least. To say the most, restaurants lose money on such cheese service, for the leftover unrefrigerated cheeses most often are thrown away. If they're going to do it they should do it right, right?) Desserts are flawless, as good to look at as to taste. The wine list, under the supervision of Philip Reich, is a phenomenon of taste and intelligence. After dinner we wandered upstairs to the lounge with huge overstuffed furniture adjoining what may be the most perfect private room—it seats about 24— I've come across. If it's not booked every night I'll be surprised. You'll like young Michael and his restaurant.

**Expensive.** Open Tuesday through Sunday. Luncheon noon to 2 p.m. weekdays. Dinner 6:30 to 9:45 p.m. Full bar. Reservations required. Patio. All major credit cards. Parking lot. Dressy.

---

## MICHAEL'S CANOGA INN      Continental
21129 Sherman Way      ★
Canoga Park     **Map 1**      (213)340-6446

When Count Michael Gaszynski sold this gustatory landmark to his manager Christian Bernaert, there was trepidation in the Valley. The European-style, intimate inn had become an important part of the life and times of a great many people of good palate, and they were pleasantly surprised to find the transition handled smoothly, and even some excitement added to the fare. The Continental-Polish cuisine became Continental-Belgian, with specialties like *anguilles au vert*, fresh river eel with spinach and sorrel sauce. There's duck, rabbit, boeuf *à la flamande*, and mussels in season. A great favorite is the lusty beer beef stew. This is an impeccable operation from kitchen to entrance and, at their modest prices for gourmet dishes, a good family restaurant as well.

**Moderate.** Open seven days. Luncheon 11:30 a.m. to 2:30 p.m. weekdays. Dinner 5 to 10 p.m. Full bar. Reservations recommended. All major credit cards. Parking lot. Casual to semi-dressy.

---

## MICHAEL'S ITALIAN CUISINE      Italian
2254 East Colorado Boulevard      ★
Pasadena     **Map 7**      (213) 793-1340

Friendly, happy, talented, colorful, expansive, but not expensive, all good things seem to come together in this charmer. Michael Pellicciotti (Sr. or Jr.) makes you feel good instantly and the food, Mama mia! it's good enough for Sinatra. The pasta, pizza, parmigiana, spaghetti and veal are a mere indication of the talent; there's even a splendid *fettuccine* Alfredo. There are individual alcoves for parties up to six. Take-out service is available.

**Inexpensive.** Open Wednesday through Monday. Dinner from 4:30 to 10 p.m. Monday, Wednesday through Thursday; to 11 Friday, Saturday; from 4 Sunday. Closed major holidays. Wine and beer only. No reservations. Visa, MC, AX. Parking lot. Casual.

---

## MICHELANGELO'S                                    Italian
435 North Beverly Drive
Beverly Hills          **Map 8**                  (213)273-2292

An implosion of Roman kitsch, an almost psychedelic experience, awaits you here. Some weeks ago on one of the television news teasers — you know, when the anchorman interrupts "Lawrence Welk" or "Real People" with a headline item—I heard one of them say, "Michelangelo has come to Beverly Hills." Being no fool, I realized it wasn't the real Michelangelo, and so I watched to discover that it was the name of a restaurant created with murals based on those in the Sistine Chapel. It seems that proprietor Vido Sasso is sort of a Michelangelo groupie, and he commissioned artist Stefano Angelo Falk to recreate some of the historic masterpieces. One is virtually overwhelmed by the huge murals, statuary and art, some of it a little beyond Michelangelo's era, plus an extra touch of kitsch. At a flick of a switch, for instance, the ceiling glows with a Milky Way of "stars" against the night background. There is more art on the walls than on the plate, although the fare is fair to good, particularly the pasta and seafood. The daily special is a bargain; my night, it was spaghetti with shrimp, and soup or salad with good bread. This should have been a dining adventure; the art alone is worth the price, and the kindly service is a pleasant touch.

**Moderate.** Open Monday through Saturday. Luncheon from 11:30 a.m. to 4 p.m. Dinner 5 to 11 p.m. Monday through Thursday; to midnight Friday, Saturday. Entertainment. Full bar. Reservations essential. All major credit cards. Parking lot next door. Semi-dressy.

---

## MICHEL RICHARD
Crêpes

310 South Robertson
★
Los Angeles          **Map 8**          (213) 275-5707

12321 Ventura Boulevard
★
Studio City          **Map 1**          (213) 508-9977

A small pâtisserie with a few tables, this is deservedly the darling of decorator row. Michel is the Michelangelo of the pastry chefs. Careme, the 19th century gastronome and philosopher said it: "There are six fine arts—painting, sculpture, poetry, music, architecture and... pastry." (I might have added one more.) You can have a crêpe or an omelette, and hear some spicy gossip, with love and quiches.

**Inexpensive to moderate.** Open Monday through Saturday 9 a.m. to 7 p.m. Wine and beer only. Visa, MC. Street parking. Casual.

---

## MIFUNE
Japanese

Japanese Village Plaza
DA★
Little Tokyo (Los Angeles)          **Map 7**          (213) 628-0697

In the Restaurant Plaza in the Japanese Village Plaza in Little Tokyo, you can sit at some central tables and order from one or all six of the restaurants under one roof, or you can sit at any one of the six counters and watch the chefs at work on your meal-to-be. In the case of Mifune, the Restaurant Plaza's noodle shop, you can watch the noodles being made on a large machine in the back of the shop. You can watch them being boiled and formed and flavored and spiced and placed in front of you. No *ramen* dishes are served at Mifune, but there's a huge selection of *udon* and *soba*. You can have your noodles with sweet fried bean curd or a poached egg or with cooked chicken or beef or seaweed or grated Chinese yam or horseradish or even herring. Some of the noodles are served in broth; some are served hot, and some are served cold, which I like best since cold seems to bring out the flavors more distinctly. This is particularly so in a dish called *yakatabune*, a combination of two types of cold noodles, served with a small order of *tempura* in a tiny wooden boat. The difference in taste between the *udon* and the *soba* is more pronounced in this tiny ship of foods. And it's the type of ship that could carry you through any manner of culinary storm.  *M.S.*

**Moderate.** Open Tuesday through Sunday 11:30 a.m. to 10:30 p.m. Full bar. No reservations for counter service; reservations accepted for dining area. All major credit cards. Parking lot. Casual.

---

## MIKISAN
2424 5th Avenue
San Diego

Japanese
★
(714) 235-6144

Mikisan is a large Japanese restaurant near Balboa Park with many interesting dining features. There is a *sushi* bar, a large *tatami* room (with a sunken floor and a capacity of 48), two *teppanyaki* dining areas, a step-down cocktail lounge, and even a small gift counter near the entrance. The decor is simple, the waitresses and lady *teppan* chefs are kimono-clad. On many nights, owner Mr. Takaki, can be seen behind one of the *teppan* counters, amusing patrons with his lively humor. Unfortunately, these *teppan* areas are situated in the main dining room and strong *teppan* smells can be distracting. Service is efficient and friendly. On weekends, live *koto* music makes a soothing accompaniment to the dining experience. The menu has an interesting variety of appetizers, including *tako su (sunomono* with octopus), *Kani (sunomono* with crabmeat) and *ika masagoae* (squid with smelt egg). The à la carte dinner menu offers many popular Japanese dishes, including beef and chicken *sukiyaki*, beef, chicken or salmon *teriyaki, tempura* and *tonkatsu* (pork cutlet). All dinners come with soup and *tsukemono*. For a little more, combination dinners also come with an appetizer and are available with many of the à la carte items. For example, the beef *teriyaki* combination is served with a choice of *sashimi* or *tempura*; the Mikisan special combination (for two or more persons) includes *sashimi*, beef *teriyaki, tempura* and chicken *sukiyaki*. *Omakase Ryori*, is the chef's special, and varies according to the availability of ingredients. It is served in the *tatami* room only, and requires advance notice for preparation. Mikisan will be moving to the Gas Lamp Quarter in downtown San Diego soon.   *Shinobu Ishizuka*

**Inexpensive to moderate.** Open Tuesday through Sunday. Luncheon Tuesday through Friday from 11:30 a.m. to 2 p.m. Dinner Tuesday through Thursday from 5 to 9:45 p.m.; Friday and Saturday to 10:45 p.m. Sunday from 4 to 9:45 p.m. Banquet facilities. Closed most holidays. Live *koto* music on weekends. Cocktails. Reservations advised on weekends. All major credit cards. Parking lot. Casual.

---

## MILLIE RIERA'S SEAFOOD

**Italian/Seafood**
★

1700 Esplanade
Redondo Beach          **Map 2**          (213) 375-1483

The "Italian grotto" style of cooking can be a splendid experience; and it is here, for the most part. The Riera family came to this building a quarter of a century ago, with recipes that have been handed down through the generations. Soups and salads are somewhat indifferently prepared, but entrées like *cioppino* Riera and shrimp diablo are—like the fish—right off the boat. The waitresses are cheerful, the view is fine, and cocktails are generous.

**Moderate.** Open seven days. Luncheon from 11:30 a.m. to 4 p.m. Dinner 4 to 10 Sunday, Monday through Thursday; to 11 Friday, Saturday. Closed July 4, Thanksgiving weekend, Christmas Eve, Christmas, New Year's. Full bar. Reservations recommended. View. Visa, MC, AX. Valet parking. Casual.

---

**MIRIWA**                                                    Chinese
750 North Hill Street                                              ★★
Los Angeles          **Map 7**                          (213) 687-3088

Miriwa is on the second floor, up a graceful stairway and into a rich rosewood and fabric foyer that divides the massive dining room. It's arced by a semicircle of plush booths that overlook a busy, tiny shopping area. Chinese dishes do not comfortably survive translation. "Shark fin and chicken soup" is a shark fin, first simmered in chicken broth with leeks and ginger, then seasoned with wine and sesame oil, combined with a mixture of beaten egg white and chicken that has been minced. "Soyed squab" is a whole squab that is first sautéed in light oil, then simmered in oyster sauce, soy ginger, and wine—a delectable entrée. "Deep fried oysters" is asterisked as the Hong Kong chef's favorite and I'd like to add my little asterisk. This magnificent concoction consists of oysters marinated in ginger root and onion juices, lightly breaded and deep fried to be served with little side dishes of sauce. I could go on, through the broth and soup menu to the listing of abalone, seafood, appetizers, duck, squab, chicken, beef, pork, and more, much more, but I think I have conveyed the enormity of the menu and my enthusiasm. While I am usually reluctant to recommend complete dinners in a Chinese menu, preferring to travel the more adventurous à la carte path, I would suggest that the Cantonese special or the Miriwa— three appetizers, abalone with vegetable soup, shrimp with lobster sauce, lemon chicken, fried rice, tea, preserved fruit and cookies—are an intelligent introduction to this exciting restaurant. A more limited menu is served at luncheon, but *dim sum*, the delightful stuffed Chinese dumplings that have caught on here, are served every day instead of once a week as in most Chinese restaurants. There is full cocktail service, but the wine list at the time of my third visit was still limited. I would like to see The Fu Jin, a California and inexpensive wine, available here as an appropriate accompaniment to the Chinese food. This is a great place to bring the kids but the reservation policy is still unwieldy and I suggest you ask for Donald Cheng, the vice president, or Sam Wong, the manager. Both speak English well.

**Moderate to expensive.** Open seven days. Luncheon from 10 a.m. to 2:30 p.m. weekdays. Dinner from 5 to 9:30 p.m. Full bar. Reservations recommended for dinner. All major credit cards. Shopping center parking lot. Casual.

---

## MISCHA'S
7561 Sunset Boulevard
Los Angeles     **Map 8**

Russian/European
★★
(213) 874-3467

Ah, how Joseph Wambaugh transformed this once semi-tacky location when he used it as the location site for his *Black Marble*. It was a complete redecorating job that transformed this restaurant into a winner that will live far after the movie is relegated to the late-late-late show (or on cable, a fate worse than debt). The restaurant could have been any of the ones that Carole Lombard, Jean Arthur or Loretta Young visited, after being urged to go there by her lovable, gruff doorman (Lionel Stander or Mischa Auer) who later turned out to be a czarist on his uppers, tattered but proud. The restaurant was always small, always atmospheric, with moustachioed Russians good. And so it is with Mischa's the Russian cabaret restaurant in Hollywood. Mischa Markarian has a background almost as romantic as the fabled doorman's. Born in Shanghai, he's lived in Paris and Rio de Janeiro, the third generation of an international restaurant family. The rooms at Mischa's are sort of

Byzantine with arches and stained glass windows. There's a stage where the entertainment, both amateur and professional, is presented in its pure essence of gaiety. The food is uncommonly good. There's chicken Czar Alexander made with a cream sauce and cucumbers and mushrooms; *galbutzi*, delicious stuffed cabbage; and a dish called veal Mischa, made with avocado, tomato and tilsit cheese in brown sauce. All entrée prices include a fine borscht or salad and rolls and butter but, as the menu admonishes, everything is cooked to order so it may take time. There are vodkas galore and a wine list with over 100 labels, mostly Californian. Service is friendly and willing and it's a great place for a late stop after the Music Center. They will still take a food order at 1 a.m.

**Moderate.** Open seven days. Dinner from 5 to 11 p.m. Entertainment until 2 a.m. Catering. Take-out. After theatre dining. Cocktails. All major credit cards. Street parking. Semi-dressy.

---

## MISSION INN                     Spanish/Continental
3649 Seventh Street                                    ★
Riverside          **Map 5**              (714) 784-0300

That great sprawling San Simeon of the inland empire has had its death knell sounded so often folks just don't pay any attention any more. Now it's a landmark, the hotel where Taft, Coolidge and Roosevelt, and I cavorted, ate boar in the dining room and met the citrus nobility of the area. Part has been restored as an office structure, part as a museum. When I was a child, some of my pals locked me in a room with a mummy-case which frightened me no end. Anyway, the restaurant opened for the umpteenth time and has a beautiful patio with splashing fountains, belltowers and arches. In the background you hear the music of a classical guitar. Cuisine is Early California, Spanish and continental with an opulent Sunday brunch and a good wine list.

**Moderate.** Open seven days. Breakfast served Monday through Saturday from 7 to 10 a.m. Luncheon buffet Monday through Saturday from 11 a.m. to 2 p.m.; dinner Tuesday through Sunday from 5:30 to 10 p.m. Sunday champagne brunch from 10 a.m. to 2:30 p.m. Banquet facilities. Children welcome. Full bar. Reservations advised. Patio. Visa, MC. Parking in the library; municipal parking lot; street parking. Semi-dressy

---

## MISTER A'S RESTAURANT
Atop the 5th Avenue Financial Center
San Diego

**Continental**
DA
(714) 239-1377

This decorator's tour de force has achieved a timeless opulence with authentic antiques and fine art that provide a lavish setting for the panoramic view of the city. It is one of the more beautiful penthouse restaurants and deserving of better support from the kitchen and serving staff. There is a New York aloofness at the maître d' station, and a doesn't-quite-make-it look and taste to the continental dishes listed on the huge menu. The rack of lamb *à la persillade de provence* with *jardinière* of garden vegetables is not well trimmed, and the vegetables were overcooked. The Long Island duckling—quite different from the duck of Paris—was presented well, with a good sauce of Grand Marnier, but the wild rice was cold. All the Old World charm and thick carpets and swag draperies and painted cherubs could not help the grenadine of beef *chasseur*, which was tougher than any other in recent experience.

**Expensive.** Open seven days. Luncheon from 11 a.m. to 3 p.m. weekdays. Dinner 6 to 10:30 p.m. Closed for lunch major holidays. Entertainment. Full bar. Reservations requested. All major credit cards. Parking at 5th Avenue Financial Center garage. Dressy.

## MR. CHOW, L.A.                                      Chinese
344 North Camden Drive
Beverly Hills        **Map 8**                    (213) 278-9911

Mr. Chow is from London, where it was a smashing success as
the "in" Chinese restaurant of the monied set. Decor is black
and white (no cute lanterns here), modern, surreal, and more
like a stage setting for a ballet than a restaurant. Everything is
cooked to order, and you may have to wait interminably
between courses, although that provides the advantage of
nonchalant study of the other people in the room. (They'll be
nonchalantly studying you.) Service is formal, with serviceware
of silver and crystal and all manner of things you wouldn't
expect in a Chinese restaurant. Trouble is, after all this panoply,
the food isn't all that good. And it's expensive.

**Expensive.** Open seven days. Luncheon noon to 2 p.m.
weekdays. Dinner 6 to 11:30 p.m. Full bar. Reservations
required. All major credit cards. Street parking days; valet
parking evenings. Dressy

---

## MR. "H"                                American/Continental
The Hilton Hotel                                           ★
9876 Wilshire Boulevard
Beverly Hills        **Map 8**                    (213) 274-7777

The amount of dining pleasure derived from eating at Mr.
"H" depends almost equally on the quality and the quantity
of the buffet. The salad and dessert selections are among
the most beautiful and lavish in town. The adventure for
gourmands (overachievers) begins after the soup course
when the hors d'oeuvres buffet in all its glory is approached.
There's the usual tossed green salad with the choice of
additions and dressings and dozens of other appetizers
ranging from chopped liver, shrimp, egg and potato salads,
picture-pretty jello molds, cheeses, ham, lox, and on and on.
It's a wedding spread that would make a bride's mother

proud and a bride's father faint from checkbook anemia. But you've only begun to fight. Entrée time at the steaming board offers sautéed filet of sole, roast beef and chicken (duck on Saturday) with vegetables and rice. Theser are honorable but unexciting. Desserts include cakes, tarts, fruit and cream pies, custard and fresh fruit. An à la carte table service is also available. Luncheon is similar but with less filling entrées. Sunday brunch, served with champagne, is equally awe-inspiring. Service is pleasant and efficient; the dining room is elegant and subdued; a carafe of mediocre house wine is included in the *prix fixe* dinner, so meet your serious eating friends at Mr. "H." We whom are about to dine salute you.

**Expensive.** Open seven days. Breakfast from 7 to 11 a.m. Luncheon from 11:30 a.m. to 2:30 p.m. Dinner from 5:30 to 10:30 p.m. Sunday brunch from 10 a.m. to 2:30 p.m. Full bar. Reservations advised. All major credit cards. Validated parking. Casual to semi-dressy.

---

## MR. STOX                                                  Continental
1105 East Katella                                                  ★★
Anaheim        **Map 6**                          (714) 634-2994

Chick and Phyllis Ann Marshall were ideally selected by fate to take over this massive, plush, California-style restaurant and get it moving again. Originally opened about a decade ago, Mr. Stox was a splendid restaurant, then. For reasons that are unclear, it was allowed to deteriorate and the team that put it together gradually went their separate ways. The menu is kept simple, fresh fish, aged beef, and some interesting combinations. There is a lobster tank, great service, fine lounge entertainment, and Chick's Lawry's background is evident throughout (he was general manager of Lawry's restaurants). There's an exceptional wine cellar, one of the best in Orange County. As a personal note, I dropped in one Halloween to visit the Marshalls in their new acquisition only to find the help—

from owners down—costumed to participate n a city-wide promotion. Imagine the difficulty I experienced talking restaurant business with a witch—warts, blackened teeth and all. It wasn't easy, but an example of the sacrifices made in the name of producing a guidebook.

**Moderate.** Open seven days. Luncheon served 11 a.m. to 3 p.m. weekdays. Dinner 5 to 10 p.m. Sunday through Thursday; to 11 p.m. Friday, Saturday. Full bar. Reservations recommended. Entertainment. Dancing Tuesday through Saturday. All major credit cards. Valet parking. Semi-dressy.

---

## MIYAKO RESTAURANT                    Japanese
139 South Los Robles                    ★
Pasadena        **Map 7**               (213) 795-7005

24 Del Amo Fashion Square               ★
Torrance        **Map 2**               (213) 542-8677

33 Town & Country                       ★
Orange          **Map 6**               (714) 541-3303

Southern California is blessed with the finest Japanese restaurants in America—I don't know a single bad one—but Miyako is the most devoted to the authentic preparation and service of *sukiyaki* (pronounced skee-yah-key). The word *sukiyaki* comes from two idiographs— *suki*, which means "plow," and *yaki*, "roasted." In early times, meat for sukiyaki was cooked on plowshares by farmers in their fields. Beef is the prime ingredient—although you can use chicken or even seafood. The meat is combined with green onions and celery, bamboo shoots, bean sprouts, onion, mushrooms, yam noodles, bean curd cake, and a seasoned sauce. The restaurants are designed in the 13th-century style of architecture, and the waitresses are meticulously trained in the art of preparing the *sukiyaki* at the table. The other dishes are not overlooked; the *tempura* and *teriyakis* are artistic, and there are interesting appetizers like ginger beef and *sashimi*. But this is the place that pays reverence to *sukiyaki*.

**Moderate.** Open seven days. Luncheon 11:30 a.m. to 2:30 p.m. weekdays. Dinner 5:30 to 10 p.m. Children's menu. Full bar. Reservations advised. Visa, MC. Parking lot. Casual.

---

# MIZUHO
## Japanese
314 South Brookhurst Street ★
Anaheim        **Map 6**        (714) 956-8510

Mizuho in Anaheim served us the best sashimi, the best sukiyaki, and the best tempura I've tasted in a long while. Two pieces of the sashimi were rolled in home-grown herbs; the beef for the sukiyaki was vivid pink and lean and beautiful; and the tempura was light and delicate, particularly the asparagus. "Mixed fresh fruit," turned out to be a wedge of cold tangy pinapple beside an orange, peeled and halved in the manner of the ancient kitchen artists, and a cool slice of melon. Mizuho is on the site of a deserted Kentucky Beef building turned into a simple, tasteful, charming restaurant. There's an elevated tatami room where people of lesser girth than mine can sit on cushions and dine off teak tea tables. While I generally prefer to have my sukiyaki prepared in the kitchen by the chef, our waitress was so deft and skilful I could scarcely imagine it better made or served. Dinner includes *suimono*, made from chicken stock and garnished with a few small noodles and a leaf or two of watercress, and *sunomono*, a marinated salad of cucumber and shrimp. Luncheon (weekdays only) is even less expensive, and there are good Japanese beers and hot sake to keep things tranquil.

**Moderate.** Open seven days. Luncheon from 11:30 a.m. to 2 p.m. weekdays. Dinner Sunday through Thursday 5 to 10 p.m.; Friday, Saturday to 11 p.m. Children's menu. Entertainment. Wine and beer only. Reservations preferred. Visa, MC. Parking. Casual.

## MOBY'S DOCK

420 Santa Monica Pier
Santa Monica    **Map 2**

**Seafood**
★
(213) 395-5643

Now that they've re-piered, repaired and remodeled, the patrons have reappeared to appreciate the fresh seafood at low prices. New owners Eve and Clarence Harmon have transformed this into a serious restaurant with appetizers that are as good as any (and as large). Their "Fishmonger's platter" is unique. They, along with 211 other restaurants, claim the "best clam chowder anywhere," and it is good. In combination with an unimpaired view of Santa Monica clear out to Avalon on a clear night (and there are one or two of those a year), it can be a slice of paradise. Certainly the best use of this 40-year-old landmark.

**Moderate to expensive.** Open seven days 11 a.m. to 11 p.m.; Friday, Saturday to midnight. Entertainment. Full bar. Reservations advised. Ocean view. All major credit cards. Parking lot. Casual.

## MOGHUL

163 North La Cienega Boulevard
Beverly Hills    **Map 7**

**Indian**
★
(213) 652-7065

The newest kid on La Cienega's fabled Restaurant Row is Moghul, a very comfortable and nearly elegant Indian restaurant that promises (according to the menu) that, "Tonight you will dine as the Great Moghul Emperors of India did, for these recipes are recreated from the royal kitchens of the Moghul Empire." The Moghuls are descendents of Tamerlane and Genghis Khan. It was a Moghul who built the Taj Mahal. And, if we are to judge by the cooking at the Moghul restaurant, it was also the Moghuls who developed the highest level of Indian cooking, much as the Mandarins brought Chinese cooking to its peak.

The menu at Moghul is so filled with new and unusual

458

dishes that the temptation is to bring everyone you know and order one of everything. There's *chooza pakoora*, for instance, deep-fried, battered chicken hunks, which taste sharply of yogurt, ginger and garlic. *Kashk-E-Badamjan* is sort of a distant cousin of Italy's *caponata*, without tomatoes, but with yogurt. And *Piazzi Kulcha* takes the theme of stuffed breads and expands on it, filling a pastry with onions and mango.

Some of the best dishes at Moghul come from the tandoori ovens which sit in the middle of the restaurant behind a large glass window. The tandoori mixed grill is a great introduction to the wonders of tandoori cooking (in which marinated, skewered shrimp, chicken, fish, bread, what-have-you, are cooked very quickly in a round oven heated to blast furnace proportions). Otherwse, Moghul creates miracles with lamb, which is served marinated in yogurt (*gosht patiala*), stewed in gravy (*lamb do piazza*), spiced to the very edge of reason (*lamb vindaloo*), curried (*ragan josh*), creamed (*lamb bhuna*) and stewed with spinach (*saag gosht*).

And, to save shy diners the embarrassment of not knowing what to eat, Moghul also has three preassembled dinners—a Moghul Dinner, a Nehru Thali and a Vegetarian Bhajan—which give a fair sampling of the various tastes of the Moghuls. *M.S.*

**Expensive.** Open seven days. Luncheon buffet from 11:30 a.m. to 2:30 p.m. Dinner from 6 to 11 p.m. Full bar. Reservations suggested. Visa, MC, AX. Parking lot. Semi-dressy.

---

**MOLLERKROEN**                              Scandinavian
435 Alisal Road                                       ★
Solvang                                    (805) 688-4555

Jack and Marianne Larsen set out a first-rate groaning board in this quaint and mercenary village. There's *biff* Lindstrom and Danish sausage with red cabbage for dinner and a parade of open-faced American and Danish sandwiches, including a French dip (no nationalist prejudice here) for both lunch and dinner.

**Moderate.** Open seven days 11:30 a.m. to 9 p.m. Weekend entertainment. Full bar. Reservations advised. All major credit cards. Parking lot. Casual.

---

## MON GRENIER

18040 Ventura Boulevard
Encino    **Map 1**

French
★★
(213) 344-8060

Mon Grenier means "my attic," and that's the theme of this Gallic whimsy, with a sloped ceiling and the menu written in crayon on a dressmaker's dummy. Salmon *en croute* (in a crust) and *faisan aux girolles* (pheasant with a rare kind of mushroom) are extremely well prepared. Duck with wild cherry sauce and veal are specialties. All the sauces are exceptional, carefully constructed to blend with the entrée, one of the secrets of a good *saucier*. The *salade de champignons* (fresh mushrooms sliced with house dressing) is a fine way to clear the palate for the rich dishes to come.

**Expensive.** Open Monday through Saturday. Dinner 6 to 9 p.m. Closed major holidays; month of September. Full bar. Reservations essential. Visa, MC. Parking lot. Casual to semi-dressy.

---

## MONIQUE

618 Shoppers Lane
Covina    **Map 6**

Hungarian
★★
(213) 332-4902

I've found a real gem among the restaurant flotsam of Covina, an area not especially noted for gustatory pleasures. Monique is equal parts charm and marvelous cooking. It is a delightful (lace-covered windows, potted palm, taped gypsy music), improbable (nestled between rather grim and grungy little shops) and an altogether joyous adventure.

460

Guests are greeted at the front door by Monique, a gracious hostess with the exuberance and the accent of a younger Charo. Renée, the waitress, who is dressed like a French schoolgirl, and an energetic busboy are all that is required to handle the 48-seat café. The kitchen is presided over by chef-partner Sandor Fekete who cooks up exciting Hungariqan dishes—along with examples of French Provençal fare.

For an appetizer, I selected a full order of scallops and mussels that was served in a deep bowl with a savory and zesty stock of oregano, fresh tomatoes, parsley, scallions, chile peppers and white wine. This marvelous concoction accompanied by *langos*, a raised dough, deep-fried Hungarian round bread that you rub with a garlic bud.

Duckling Sandor ($8.50) was roasted in its own juices, served crisp and fine with braised red cabbage. Beef goulash is prepared in the Old World tradition and served with homemade *spätzle*. The Gypsy steak is pan-fried pork steak seasoned with pepper, paprikash and a kiss of garlic.

Prices on the à la carte menu are about $3 for appetizers, with most entrées under $10. The homemade desserts are gorgeous, the wine list adequate and the small establishment fairly bursts with pride and talent that's a pleasure to experience.

**Moderate.** Open Tuesday through Saturday. Luncheon from 11:30 a.m. to 2:30 p.m. Dinner from 5 to 10 p.m. Wine only. Reservations suggested. Bank cards only. Parking lot. Casual.

---

## MON KEE LIVE FISH SEA FOOD     Chinese/Seafood
679 North Spring Street     ★★
Los Angeles    **Map 7**     (213) 628-6717

Chinese get the yen for seafood, too. The Chinese seafood restaurants—there are few in America—exhibit the same meticulous care in preparation that we have come to expect of the best Chinese restaurants. Exotic sauces and a wide variety of presentations of the same dish are some of the more interesting features. It's not likely you'll taste either lobter or crab served as flavorfully as it is in this restaurant because the centuries-old recipes are at their best with delicate and subtle seafod. Mon Kee lists grouper, bass, gopher cod, long-nosed sucker and sculpin: all sound like performers in a punk rock band but all are delicious and distinct. The list is seemingly endless with a dozen variations of rock cod, eight lobster dishes, and a stir-fried lobster in garlic sauce that's a delight. The restaurant is unpretentious to the point of tackiness, the prices are low, and the eatin' is great.

**Inexpensive.** Open seven days from 11:30 a.m. to 10 p.m. Take-out. Beer only. Reservations recommended for large parties. Visa, MC. Small parking lot; public lot nearby. Casual.

---

## MONTELEONE'S                                    Italian
19337 Ventura Boulevard
Tarzana     **Map 1**                    (213) 996-0662

16911 Ventura Boulevard
Encino     **Map 1**                    (213) 986-2245

It looked like an off night. I had to do an interview with Roberta Linn (Lawrence Welk's original champagne lady), who, I had decided, would turn out to be a sort of a middle-aged Shirley Temple. All sorts of put-down lines went through my mind like "The fizz is gone" or "It wasn't so wunnerful." When I found out she was appearing at an unfamiliar Italian restaurant in Encino, I really got depressed. Visions of soggy, starchy, lumpy food added to my gloom. Well, I was wrong on both counts. Monteleone's looks like a supper club, perhaps a bit larger than most, but that's where the resemblance ends. The food was genuinely exciting, the first creative Italian cuisine I'd had in some time—dishes like *saltimbocca* with spinach, fresh and firm "shrimp soave" in good wine sauce; rich house dressing for the crisp salads; and a splendid *cannoli*, dessert that's a pastry shell filled with minced fruit and whipped cream and brandy and special cheese. The wine list, like the menu was modestly priced with some Italian reds that had obviously been carefully selected. And Roberta Linn was devastating. Instead of the oldies and moldies, her act consisted of up-tempo arrangements, impressions, and a take-off à la Ella, on a jazz flight. If Roberta is typical of the entertainment—and I think she is—then this may be one of the few restaurants that breaks the rule about combining entertainment with good food. I mean, it just isn't done.

**Moderate to expensive.** Open Tuesday through Sunday. Dinner from 5 to 11:45 p.m. Tuesday through Thursday; to 12:45 Friday, Saturday; to 10:45 Sunday. Closed Easter, Thanksgiving, Christmas. Live entertainment nightly. Full bar open to 1:30 a.m. Reservations required. All major credit cards. Parking lot. Casual.

---

# MONTEREY JACK'S                    Steak/Seafood
11940 Bernardo Plaza Drive
Rancho Bernardo                    (714) 485-1263

A chain restaurant with corporate thinking in the kitchen that extends to the costumes and decor in front. The beef and seafood menu lists some safe and good dinners and some ghastly combinations like the Alaskan king crab legs with teriyaki steak. There is a good California wine list. This would be ordinary in most locations, but it is notable in Rancho Bernardo.

**Moderate.** Open seven days. Luncheon from 11:30 a.m. to 2:30 p.m. weekdays. Dinner 5 to 10 p.m. Monday through Thursday; to 11 Friday, Saturday; Sunday 4 to 10. Sunday brunch 10 a.m. to 2 p.m. Closed Christmas. Entertainment Tuesday through Saturday. Full bar. Reservations accepted. Enclosed garden dining room. Visa, MC, AX. Parking lot. Casual to semi-dressy.

## MONTY'S STEAKHOUSE

**American**

★

1100 Glendon Avenue

Westwood Village     **Map 8**          (213) 272-2000

17016 Ventura Boulevard                          ★

Encino     **Map 1**          (213) 783-1660

592 South Fair Oaks Avenue                        ★

Pasadena     **Map 7**          (213) 681-0129

Monty's in Westwood passes the rare-but-charred test; their steak, shrimp scampi and Dungeness cracked crab with Swedish dill sauce are all tantalizing, as are the oysters and clams served on the half shell or steamed. Ribs are great, too, but it's the side dishes that show the class of the house with items like charred baked potato skins and the second best onion rings I've tasted. I've not begun to describe the huge dinner and luncheon menus. The menu is à la carte, but entrées include potato and salad. Everything's good, and the view from atop the Westwood building can be spectacular. Not as good as Pacific Dining Car, but what is?

**Moderate to expensive.** Open seven days. Luncheon from 11:30 a.m. to 3 p.m. Monday through Saturday. Dinner 5 to 11:30 p.m. Monday through Thursday; to midnight Friday, Saturday; 4 to 11 Sunday. Hours vary slightly at each location. Full bar. Reservations recommended. All major credit cards. Validated parking. Casual to semi-dressy.

## MOONRAKER

**American**

★

18542 McArthur Boulevard

Irvine     **Map 4**          (714) 833-9600

The city may be Irvine, but you'll consider it a part of Newport Beach in the new restaurant row (Gulliver's, Red Onion, Harry's Airporter Inn) that shows signs of becoming the restaurant capital of the area. The Moonraker is architecturally stunning, drinks are fine, service is friendly, but the food is the ordinary steak and lobster and scampi of less pretentious establishments. This place really swings around cocktail time, thronged with smartly dressed executive persons of the area.

**Moderate.** Open seven days. Luncheon from 11 a.m. to 4 p.m. weekdays. Dinner from 4 to 11 p.m. Closed Thanksgiving, Christmas Eve, Christmas. Full bar. Reservations recommended. Visa, MC. AX. Parking lot. Semi-dressy.

---

## MOONSHADOWS                                     American
20356 Pacific Coast Highway
Malibu          **Map 2**                    (213) 456-3010

Malibu is so restaurant poor that even mediocre food, as served here, is tolerable. The view is magnificent and the atmosphere is romantic. They've a heated outside patio and a sumptuous salad bar but the steak and lobster and fresh fish are only fair.

**Moderate.** Open seven days. Dinner from 5 to 11 p.m. Monday through Thursday; to midnight Friday, Saturday; 4 to 11 Sunday. Closed Thanksgiving, Christmas. Full bar. Reservations suggested. Patio. View. Visa, MC, AX, DC. Valet parking. Casual.

---

## MORT'S DELI                                     Hot Dogs
18452 Clark Street                                     ★
Tarzana         **Map 1**                    (213) 345-3700

233 Woodland Hills Promenade                           ★
Woodland Hills        **Map 1**              (213) 887-0400

The sign out front says, "We have the famous Coney Island hot dog." They don't but they're close. It's the same hot dog all right, with the goose fat that gives it its special flavor. But Nathan steams his; Mort boils, then grills his. Catering service.

465

**Inexpensive.** Open seven days from 6:30 a.m. to 9 p.m. Sunday 7 a.m. to 8 p.m. Closed Thanksgiving, Yom Kippur (Woodland Hills); major holidays (Promenade). Wine and beer only. No reservations. Visa, MC. Casual.

---

## MOULING
11620 Wilshire Boulevard
West Los Angeles    **Map 8**

**Chinese**
★
(213) 477-5041

This enterprising restaurant specializes in Szechwan and Hunan cuisine. From hot sour soup to a more subdued crab and cucumber kind, the chef demonstrates his versatility. A particularly intriguing event occurs on Saturday and Sunday. That's when the Northern style tea cakes are served — over fifteen varieties — and they are absolutely delectable. The tropical drinks are good here, with one of the better mai tais in town, and they even have a small patio.

**Inexpensive.** Open seven days. Luncheon 11:30 a.m. to 2:30 p.m. Dinner 5:30 to 10 p.m. Sunday through Thursday; to 11 Friday, Saturday. Sunday brunch 11:30 a.m. to 3:30 p.m. Full bar. Reservations advised. Patio. All major credit cards. Parking lot. Casual.

---

## MOUN OF TUNIS
7445½ Sunset Boulevard
West Hollywood    **Map 8**

**Tunisian/Moroccan**
★
(213) 874-3333

The fez is becoming familiar in Southern California. Decor is not in the same league with Dar Maghreb, or my favorite Moroccan restaurant, Marrakesh, but the food is good and they are really earnest about authenticity in the kitchen. Mamoun Asli has provided the low stools around brass tables where you will learn to enjoy eating with your fingers. Rose-scented water, as is the custom, is poured on the hands at appropriate intervals so you won't stay forever stuck to whomever you shake hands with.

**Moderate.** Open seven days. Dinner from 6 p.m. to midnight. Belly dancing on weekends. Wine and beer only. Reservations required. All major credit cards. Parking lot. Casual.

---

## MOUSTACHE CAFE                                    French
8155 Melrose Avenue                                          ★
West Hollywood          **Map 8**              (213) 651-2111

1071 Glendon Avenue                                          ★
Westwood          **Map 8**                    (213) 208-6633

464 North Bedford                                           ★
Beverly Hills          **Map 8**               (213) 276-2321

Cinzano unbrellas drape over the white lattice fence of the patio at this café in the herat of the little theatre district. A superstar team collaborated on this trendy, casual delight— it used to be a gas station. Soups are marvelous and duck is served without the sweet gook of many pseudo-French restaurants. The house omelette is made with Swiss cheese, ham, fresh mushrooms and tomatoes.

**Moderate.** Open seven days from 11:30 a.m. to 1 a.m. Closed Christmas. Full bar. Reservations recomended. Visa, MC. Wheelchair access. Valet parking West Hollywood, Beverly Hills; public parking Westwood. Casual.

---

## MULBERRY STREET                                Italian/Jazz
12067 Ventura Place                                         ★
Studio City          **Map 1**                 (213) 980-8405

In an area and an era not noted for its nightlife, Mulberry Street in Studio City is a phenomenon: the perfect jazz restaurant, with marvelous entertainment and (surprise) excellent food at (surprise) miniscule prices.

Allen Goodman, a studio musician, along with his wife

Bobby opened Mulberry Street as an outgrowth of a nearby pizza stand they operated. It was to be a spot for jazz groups, informal enough to accommodate the many celebrities who may want to perform unannounced. Hal Linden occasionally drops in to play clarinet and Byron Janis of "Mork and Mindy" and his group are a regular weekly feature. Each night is different, from performers like Tommy Newsom (on a recent Sunday), to John Pisano and Oscar Casto-Neves (Wednesday). Janis and Segal (Tuesday) and Bud Shank on Friday and Saturday.

Tuesday night is my favorite because it features an improbable aggregation comprised of actors, philosophers, producers, teachers and movie stars that are known as the Beverly Hills Unlisted Jazz Band. These guys have so much fun performing that it is impossible not to be caught up in their joy. None of the musicians, with the possible exception of Goodman, who sets the pace with his drums, are dependent upon music as a means to survival. Fortunately, perhaps. There may be better banjo players than actor George Segal (oh, yes) and better trombonists than comedian-actor Conrad Janis, who is the marvelously wry frontman; obviously, there are *better* jazz groups than the BHUJB, but none, I suspect, so entertaining. It speaks to the good breeding of the audience—only 40 can fit into the small room—that celebrities performing or simply enjoying are left alone, which is what they want here.

The food is wonderful. Everything is homemade including the pizza crust (try #9: pizza with baby clams, special herbs, olive oil and two cheeses, from $6.25); the calzone, a pocket sandwich with your choice of fillings (try the #3: meatball, onions and cheese, $3.50). Soups, specials and desserts are listed on the blackboard menu or will be recited by an attractive and genuinely friendly waitress (I was seated at Victoria's station). Inglenook wines and beer are the only alcoholic beverages served, but there is a wide selection of soft drinks, coffees, tea, mineral water and juices.

Most surprising to me was the low prices, which enabled a full evening's dining and entertainment for not much more than a hard-ticket event. Admission is $5 at the door (all musicians perform for scale) and a large cheese and tomato pizza is $5. That's it. No hidden charges, no minimum, nothing but pure enjoyment in an intimate atmosphere that is like a gift to the entertainment-starved San Fernando Valley.

**Inexpensive.** Open Tuesday through Sunday. Dinners show only from around 8:30, 7 on Sunday. Closed Christmas and some Jewish holidays. Jazz entertainment. Wine and beer only. Call for information regarding reservations and who is performing. Visa, MC. Wheelchair access. Street parking. Casual.

---

## MURRAY'S CAFE

5974 South Broadway
South Central Los Angeles

Southern/Soul Food
★
Map 7          (213) 750-1211

You don't argue with Deacon Jones, five time all-pro people-maimer of the NFL. At least I don't. When Deacon tells me that Murray's Cafe on South Broadway is about the best soul food around, I agree; and that's nice, because I really do. Deacon is one of the most knowledgeable experts on soul food I've ever had on my T.V. show. He used to bring gangs of pro athletes here for their introduction to "soul" and still shakes his head in wonderment at the tonnage put away in a single seating. Soul food is a tribute to the resourceful slaves. When the plantation owners gave them their leftovers they would take them home and, inspired by equal parts imagination and necessity, season and cook the dishes until it was a feast far more flavorful than the white gentry enjoyed in the big house. It was so good, as a matter of palate, that these recipes have lingered on to become treasured epicurean dishes. The gumbo (served on Friday nights only) is a combination of shell-fish, turkey wings, ham, and other improbable ingredients and people line up for it with empty stomachs and faraway looks in their eyes. Murray knows what to do with turkey; he stuffs it with oyster dressing on Sundays. Of course there are collard greens, black-eyed peas, yams, pigs' feet, neck bones, and chitlins. Beer only. It goes well with this kind of heavy, rich food. You don't really believe that Deacon scared me, do you?

**Inexpensive.** Open seven days from 11:30 a.m. to 9 p.m. Sunday through Thursday; to 10 p.m. Friday, Saturday. Closed July 4, Christmas. Beer only. Reservations accepted. Visa, MC. Parking lot. Casual

---

## MUSSO & FRANK GRILL

**Continental**

★

6667 Hollywood Boulevard
Hollywood    **Map 7**    (213) 467-7788

This grand old establishment opened in 1919, back when Hollywood Boulevard really meant Hollywood. Somehow, it has managed to retain its dignity and status as a fine restaurant despite the disintegration of the area into honkytonkville. As a matter of fact, the contrast between the quiet restaurant and the pandemonium outside is quite startling. The atmosphere is comfortable, old, traditional, competent and cordial, although the waiters can be a little grouchy. The food includes daily specials like sauerbraten and potato pancakes, homemade chicken pot pie, corned beef and cabbage, minced chicken, baked ham, veal sautée, and flannel cakes. Fear that Musso's might change for the worse due to the death in 1976 of Chef Rue, who presided over the kitchen from its beginning, has proved unfounded. John Helman, a newcomer (only 31 years at Musso's), continued the familiar varied menu without a dropped stitch—or egg. Now Michel Bourger continues the tradition. There is a sense of theatrical history here, far more meaningful than the goldplated stars they put into the sidewalks as a tourist attraction. Breakfasts are particularly satisfying here.

**Moderate to expensive.** Open Monday through Saturday from 11 a.m. to 11 p.m. Closed major holidays. Full bar. Reservations required. All major credit cards. Valet parking. Casual to semi-dressy.

---

## NANTUCKET LIGHT Seafood
22706 Pacific Coast Highway
Malibu    **Map 2**                          (213) 456-3105

The view is the thing... the food certainly isn't. My Maine
lobster might have been "live" but it was senile, and tough.
If you can stick to the salad bar and the booze you'll have a
good time. Cappuccino is prepared to order (it sounds like
the wreck of the Cannonball Express) and you can browse
among the display of salt water aquariums. In fairness,
Malibu is a ghastly place in which to try to run a
restaurant. Not only do they have the natural calamities
like the annual washing-out-to-sea and mudslides, but they
have a tough problem getting help. It's too expensive for
waiters and busboys and their female counterparts to live
in the area so they have to commute from long distances.
The restaurants are also at the mercy of the elements. In
all, it's a miracle that any of the Malibu places survive and
one wonders what sort of death wish the operators have in
selecting their site.

**Moderate.** Open seven days. Brunch from 11 a.m. to 2:30 p.m. for a fixed price of $6.95. Dinner from 5 to 11 p.m. Monday through Thursday; to midnight Friday, Saturday; 4 to 11 Sunday. Closed Christmas. Full bar. View. No reservations. Visa, MC, AX, DC. Valet parking. Casual to semi-dressy.

---

## NATE 'N AL'S                               Delicatessen
414 North Beverly Drive                            ★
Beverly Hills       **Map 8**            (213) 274-0101

This is the New Yorker's decompression chamber—where they go for great lox and sandwiches while they're trying to adjust to California freeways and mores and tacos and doughnuts. It is a bit plusher than most delis and a bit better, with all home-cooked dishes. Orange juice is freshly squeezed (which is un-deli-like), and the huge menu has chicken giblets with rice, chicken blintzes, knockwurst and beans, and on and on and on. The combination sandwiches are expensive, but you can't get much better anywhere. I wish I could wave a giant salami and have them open for after-theatre noshes instead of closing at the horribly unreasonable hour of 9 p.m.

**Moderate.** Open seven days from 7:30 a.m. to 8:45 p.m. Same menu all day. Closed Jewish holidays. Wine and beer only. No reservations. No credit cards. Wheelchair access. Street parking. Casual.

---

## NATE'S DELI                                    Kosher
283 North Palm Canyon Drive                        ★
Palm Springs                          (714) 325-3506

Reading the menu here will put you under the whether—to choose this sandwich or that sandwich from the list of 100. On top of that the sandwiches are about as high as the list is long. Nate's nickname is "Mister Corned Beef of Palm Springs," which may be a clue to help you select. If you can't find a suitable sandwich, come between 4 and 6 and order the 9-course dinner. Entrée choices on this are fried chicken, filet of sole, corned beef and cabbage, or brisket of beef.

**Inexpensive to moderate.** Open seven days 8 a.m. to 8:30 p.m. Take-out service. Wine and beer only. No reservations. Visa, MC. Parking lot across street. Casual.

---

# NEPENTHE

**American**
★★

Big Sur                                                    (408)667-2345

The term "romantic," when applied to a restaurant, is frustratingly ambiguous. To some, it conjures visions of strolling musicians and a single red rose placed across madame's plate. To others, it may be a favorite downstairs bistro, all bread sticks and checkered tablecloths (with that rare, discreet waiter who understands the precise moment when not to serve). But whether it's an intimate countryside pub or a cozy cafe with a jukebox, we've all got one — our personal place more valued for the memory than the menu. To me, the truly romantic restaurant must possess a special aura that affects the mood with everything that is seen, heard, smelled, and touched. It should be a private fantasyland —an emotional light-year away from the real world. These are few, of course, and one of the best is Nepenthe. Located amidst the rugged, wild beauty of Big Sur, the restaurant has been handcrafted from natural elements — adobe, rock, oak, and redwood — which make it seem part of the cliff it tops. Man strives to establish himself in proportion to this beauty. Some ninety miles south, William Randolph Hearst met the challenge by building a castle on a mountain at San Simeon, and filling it with priceless treasures. William Fassett, however, decided that Big Sur itself was the treasure, and designed Nepenthe as an unobstrusive entity from which the spectacle of nature can be fully absorbed. Hearst's achievement seems somehow less significant when compared to a single exquisite sunset at Big Sur. At Nepenthe, vast windows surround the room to provide a breathtaking, living gallery. Raging white surf crashes against the huge rocks some eight hundred feet below, and beyond is a Pacific sometimes so blue that it blends almost imperceptibly with the horizon. Landward, dense pine and redwood forests tower cloud-high above sheer cliffs and precipitous gorges. Nepenthe is a gathering place for the intellectuals — the writers and artists of Big Sur drawn from the world over — who sip liqueur and draft beer around the enormous fire pit on the terrace. Occasional *al fresco* entertainment is as unplanned as it is unpaid: chamber music ensembles creating a fragmentary Bach festival — or folk dancers — or those gentle musicians who play the music of the air — primitive rhythms in which the musician himself seems an instrument of the environment. Inside, oak logs crackle to life as the dusk chill draws the crowd around the circular fireplace, to the tables or, best of all, to the long stretches of wooden window seats that surround the dining area. A profusion of cushions in every size and color provides comfortable backrests for gazing at the outside view or sharing the inside warmth and rapprochement. Modern conveniences have been accepted reluctantly at Nepenthe. The room is lighted by candles only, and it was not until recently that Nepenthe acceded to the need for a telephone. The food is simple, though perfectly prepared. Luncheon consists mostly of good sandwiches, desserts, and the cheese board with port wine, which seem to be preferred by the chess players. For dinner, I enjoyed the cheddar steak, lean ground steak topped with melted cheddar cheese and chopped green onions, served with fresh green salad and herb dressing. The limited menu includes excellent steaks, broiled chicken, and a local favorite: roast squab — served on weekends only. Every entrée has a wine recommendation on the menu, and the list is surprisingly diverse. Cocktails are served, though there seems more concern about liqueurs (C&C — chartreuse and cognac — is a favorite), reflecting the sophisticated taste of the patrons. On a level beneath the restaurant is the Phoenix, a gift shop and arts and crafts gallery where much of the local talent is represented. Nepenthe is thirty-two miles south of Carmel on Highway 1. Look for a rustic gate, leave your car in the compound, and follow the footpath.

**Moderate.** Open seven days. Luncheon from 11:30 a.m. to 4:30 p.m. Dinner from 5 to 10 p.m. Closed Thanksgiving, Christmas, New Year's Eve. Full bar. Reservations recommended for parties of 5 or more. Patio. View. Visa, MC, AX. Parking lot. Casual.

---

## NEW MOON RESTAURANT      Chinese
912 South San Pedro      ★
Los Angeles     **Map 7**      (213) 622-1091

Situated in a bleak block in the produce section of downtown Los Angeles, this used to be an epicurean fantasyland of great and creative Cantonese food. It's come down considerably since then, but it's still worth a visit if you're in the area. Appetizers of foil-wrapped chicken, and main dishes like crystal shrimp, shrimp in black bean sauce, and beefsteak cubes are still an improvement over the usual Cantonese fare. I particularly like their "chicken salad," a dish that bears no resemblance to the Western dish of the same name. Decor is pleasant with large rooms and a cocktail bar. You are encouraged to let the waiter order for you — a great idea, except I thought my waiter was wearing a hearing aid until he bent over to serve my soup and I heard the unmistakable voice of Vin Scully seep out from the earplug: "It's two balls and no strikes on Garvey . . . "

**Moderate.** Open seven days. Luncheon from 11:30 a.m. to 2:45 p.m. Dinner from 3 to 9:30 p.m. Full bar. Reservations recommended. All major credit cards. Casual.

*Please be sure to consult "Tipping Made Easy" on page 25 of this Guide.*

# NIEUPORT 17

**Continental/American**
★

1615 East 17th Street
Santa Ana　　**Map 6**　　(714) 547-9511

This is a restaurant with in-depth good taste and character in every department — concept, decor, cuisine, and service. The Nieuport 17 was an early French bi-wing fighter plane; and owner W. F. Bettis, a former pilot, has blended airport history and memorabilia — murals, paintings, photos — into a stunning decor. The food, basically American-gourmet, is marvelous — from one end of the colorful menu to the other. I particularly liked the chicken marsala with saffron rice and mushrooms. All dinners include choice of homemade soup or wilted spinach salad — or fresh green, for that matter. Veal *piccata* is tender, sautéed with lemon and served with zucchini and eggplant. If you're just there for cocktails, be sure to try the shrimp *escaddrille* hors d'oeuvre made with their own *remoulade* sauce, spicy with horseradish, curry, and ginger. There are chef's daily luncheons like shrimp almond Cantonese or veal parmigiana. House wines reflect — as they should — the care and integrity of the establishment. Unlike most restaurants, where house wines are all from one vineyard, the management wisely selected Sebastiani for the burgundy and Almaden for the rosé and chablis. There are a number of other wines listed, all among the top of their variety. As you may gather, this is more than an ordinarily good restaurant — it is an experience and one I'd recommend. Reservations are a good idea, particularly on weekends. There is a cocktail-entertainment lounge, and you'll want to dress a bit for dinner.

**Moderate to expensive.** Open seven days. Luncheon from 11 a.m .to 4 p.m. weekdays. Dinner 5 to 1 p.m. Sunday through Thursday; to 11 Friday, Saturday. Closed major holidays. Entertainment. Full bar. Reservations recommended. All major credit cards. Valet parking. Semi-dressy to dressy.

## NIKOLA'S

**Continental/Yugoslavian**

★

1449 Sunset Boulevard

Los Angeles     **Map 7**

(213) 628-8005

Despite the fact that this is essentially a Yugoslav restaurant, the *pièce de résistance* is abalone. I believe the secret of the marvelous abalone here is simplicity. Only the freshest abalone is fried for the least possible time to emerge golden-crisp, succulent, sweet, and tender. The rest of the menu is hearty and heavy: brisket of beef, potato pancakes, beef stew, and homemade soups.

**Inexpensive.** Open Monday through Saturday. Luncheon from 11 a.m. to 4 p.m. Dinner from 4 to 11 p.m. Closed major holidays. Children's menu. Full bar. Reservations recommended, essential when Dodgers are in town. Visa, MC. Valet parking in back. Casual.

## NINO'S

**Italian**

★★

4501 Mission Bay Drive

San Diego

(714) 274-3141

Everyone in New York has a favorite Italian restaurant that's comfortable, colorful and competent; and Nino's is the West Coast equivalent. The *alta cucina* of Northern Italy is well handled here, but the veal dishes are sensational, and we've never been tempted to order anything else. Veal is milk-fed, Eastern, and somehow — in some way — superior to the veal at restaurants more expensive and pretentious than this one. They have cappuccino and the bartender says, "I smile at everyone for the entertainment."

**Moderate.** Open Tuesday through Saturday. Luncheon from noon to 2 p.m. weekdays. Dinner from 5 to 10:30. Closed July 4, Thanksgiving, Christmas. Full bar. Reservations recommended. All major credit cards. Parking lot. Casual to semi-dressy.

## NIPA HUT
**Filipino**
★

326 South Alvarado
Los Angeles    **Map 7**    (213) 483-8988

Although it's much upgraded from the coffee shop atmosphere, it's not likely to be confused with Perino's, but you can get some fine dining adventures here. The *pansit malabon* (imported noodles with port and shrimp) and *adobo baboy* (marinated spicy pork in gravy) are two dishes you'll like. The *tortilla hipon* (shrimp and vegetable wrapped in egg) is my personal favorite, and the *inihaw carne* (grilled strips of beef with tomatoes and onion) is unique to this cuisine. Best of all, according to my friend, the Philippine expert, is *adobo manok* (marinated chicken). Philippine beer goes well with all this.

**Inexpensive.** Open seven days. Luncheon and dinner Tuesday through Friday from 11 a.m. to midnight; Saturday from 2 p.m. to midnight, Sunday from 2 to 10 p.m., Monday from 11 a.m. to 10 p.m. Closed Thanksgiving. Wine and beer only. Reservations accepted. Visa, MC. Parking lot. Casual.

## NOEL'S
**Seafood**
★

16281 Pacific Coast Highway
Seal Beach    **Map 6**    (213) 592-2051

The most laid-back and best seafood restaurant around is in this jam-packed little place in Seal Beach. The days, hours, months, and policies are subject to change — frequently. You have to call just to make sure they're open (no reservations though). You'll stand in line a half hour, or much more, but you'll meet some nice people.

**Inexpensive to moderate.** Open seven days. Dinner from 5 to 10 p.m. Closed Easter, Thanksgiving, Christmas. Full bar. No reservations. Visa, MC. Casual.

## NO NO'S ITALIAN RESTAURANT                Italian
1866 Tustin Avenue                                    ★
Orange        **Map 6**                    (714) 998-7001

"No No" means "Grandpa" in Italian—of course you already knew that—and this is an eat-till-you-die low-priced Italian restaurant with more than pastas. They have fried mozzarella cheese, fish chowder, and casseroles of veal. At luncheon there are eight sandwiches shaped like dirigibles and eight children's plates, a nice touch for a place called No No. If the food takes some abrupt geographical zig zags you should know that it is owned by a Lebanese cook who learned Lebanese cooking from his family and then trained in Mexican, French and Armenian kitchens.

**Moderate.** Open Monday through Saturday. Lunch from noon to 3 p.m. weekdays. Dinner from 4 to 9:30 p.m. Child's menu. Full bar. Reservations advised. Visa, MC, AX. Parking lot. Semi-dressy.

---

## NUCLEUS NUANCE             Continental/Organic
7267 Melrose Avenue                                   ★
West Hollywood      **Map 7**             (213) 939-8666

The changes here have made this hard-and fun-to-find gem scarcely recognizable to its clientele. When the Nuance opened in 1967, Rudy Marshall served apocalypse chow—grimly vegetarian—to the celebrity-studded set who brought their own wine. Now, recently sold to Bruce and Katherine Veniero, it has been transformed into a cozy, chic corner of Hollywood. Thick lamb chops, steaks, scampi, veal California and a fine linguini are only a portion of the selections. Desserts seem to throwback to the health food orientation, homemade but not great. The wine list is intelligently prepared and wines are inexpensive; there is a wine tasting every Wednesday to add to the collection.

**Moderate.** Open Monday through Saturday. Luncheon Monday through Friday 11:30 a.m. to 2:30 p.m. Dinner Monday through Saturday 6 p.m. to midnight. Full bar. Reservations required. Patio. Wheelchair access. Visa, MC, AX, CB. Valet parking. Semi-dressy.

---

## THE NUTSHELL                                                French
21020 Ventura Boulevard                                          ★
Woodland Hills        **Map 1**                      (213) 883-4136

This small French restaurant has some attractive German accents and is one of the few places where you can enjoy the *Berliner weisse*, wheat beer with a dollop of raspberry juice. The French onion soup is thick and hearty, and there are at leat four shellfish dishes every night. Their Black Forest cake—not always available—is an extravagant dessert. Otherwise the luncheon and dinner menus offer few surprises, although the quiche Lorraine and the omelettes are pleasant.

**Moderate.** Open Monday through Saturday. Luncheon served 11:30 a.m. to 2:30 p.m. weekdays. Dinner Monday through Thursday from 5:30 to 10 p.m.; Friday, Saturday to 10:30. Closed most holidays. Wine and beer only. Reservations advised on weekends. Visa, MC. Parking lot. Casual.

---

*In order to obtain the best results from this Guide, be sure to read the French, German, Italian and Oriental menu translators on page 705 to 710 of this Guide.*

---

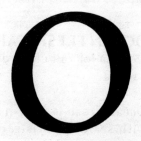

## OAK TREE
7811 Herschel Avenue
La Jolla

**American**
★
(714) 454-1315

Tie a blue ribbon 'round the old Oak Tree for the popovers here. They also know how to carve the New York strip — thin enough to please the Queen herself. However, thin doesn't mean skimpy. This, and other entrées, such as veal *cordon bleu*, filet of sole and jumbo shrimp, *cordon bleu* and breast of chicken are served up in hefty portions, as are the cocktails. All in all, a pleasant, leisurely dining-by-candlelight evening. Or, you may decide to come at midday to dawdle over luncheon on the patio thoughtfully stocked with heaters for year-round enjoyment. Luncheon can be a hearty homemade soup, a variety of salads, and a choice of nearly a dozen sandwiches. Their bacon, lettuce, and tomato sandwich is reputed to be addictive. Saturday luncheon is limited to the bountiful Caesar salad, cheeses and fresh fruit offered with sourdough bread. Homemade cheesecake is the only exciting thing on the dessert menu.

**Inexpensive to moderate.** Open Monday through Saturday. Luncheon from 11:30 a.m. to 2 p.m. Dinner from 5:30 to 9 p.m. Monday through Thursday; to 10 Friday, Saturday. Closed major holidays. Full bar. Reservations recommended. Patio. Visa, MC. Street parking. Casual.

---

## OCEAN FRESH CAFE
5509 La Jolla Boulevard
La Jolla

**Seafood**
★
(714) 459-4149

Ocean Fresh is their name. Ocean fresh is their game. And, with seafood purists, ocean fresh is their fame. What local fishermen cannot supply each day is flown in from the East and Pacific Northwest without benefit of the deep-freeze, allowing a choice that includes littleneck clams on the half shell and silver salmon. This family-type restaurant offers big choices and big servings. With dinner you get brown rice, vegetable, salad, and rolls. New England chowder and Italian-style cioppino come by the cup, bowl, or tureen. Chips and sandwiches are available at lunch, and there's an above average wine list. Sunday brunch on the patio is reminiscent of fish and eggs over an open fire. Maybe not the fanciest seafood place in California, but certainly one of the fussiest.

**Moderate.** Open seven days. Breakfast 8 to 11 a.m. Monday through Saturday. Luncheon from 11:30 a.m. to 2:30 p.m. Monday through Saturday. Dinner 5 to 10 daily. Sunday brunch 10 a.m. to 2 p.m. Closed Easter, Christmas. Full bar. No reservations. Patio. All major credit cards. Parking lot. Casual.

---

*In order to obtain the best results from this Guide, be sure to read the French, German, Italian and Oriental menu translators on page 705 to 710 of this Guide.*

# OLDE MANHATTAN SPAGHETTI FAIRE    Italian

124 North Sepulveda Boulevard                    ★
Manhattan Beach        **Map 2**        (213) 379-4849

A good pit stop to refuel the just plain folks in the beach area. Nine different spaghetti dinners are served with soup *and* salad *and* garlic bread for a pittance. There's a child's menu. Plenty of beer and wine with not much atmosphere at this bargain dine-in or take-out place.

**Inexpensive.** Open for dinner Wednesday through Sunday 5 to 10 p.m. Closed major holidays. Wine and beer only. View. Visa, MC. Wheelchair access, but call in advance. Parking lot. Casual.

# OLD SPAGHETTI FACTORY    Italian

275 5th Avenue                                    ★
San Diego                            (714) 233-4323

5939 West Sunset Boulevard
Hollywood        **Map 8**                    (213) 469-7149

2110 Newport Boulevard
Newport Beach        **Map 4**        (714) 675-8654

Pots and pans and piles of pasta. Spaghetti obviously is the thing here and simply delights the young crowd. Antiques, an indoor street car and an ancient bar from Yuba City are standouts in this Early Funk motif. This is an inexpensive family restaurant with something for everyone.

**Inexpensive.** Open seven days. Dinner from 5 to 10 p.m. Monday through Thursday; to 11:30 Friday, Saturday. Sunday from 4 to 10 p.m. Closed Thanksgiving, Christmas. Full bar. No reservations. No credit cards. Parking lot. Casual.

## OLD TOWN MEXICAN CAFE Y CANTINA  Mexican
2489 San Diego Avenue
San Diego Old Town                          (714) 297-4330

The Old Town Mexican Cafe may be a better place to drink and meet young singles than it is a place to eat; but it's really not a bad place to eat. Fresh *tortillas* are pounded out in a window in the front of the cafe; the *salsa* is very hot and very good, not watered down for the sake of the gringo clientele; and the food is much better than you'd expect. Especially good is the house specialty of pork *carnitas*—deep-fried, chopped pork meat, served with *tortillas*, cilantro onion, slices of avocado, tomato, peppers and beans. You can make your own *tacos*, or just eat everything at once, or do whatever you wish. It all works very well. So do the side orders of *nachos* and the *quesadillas*. The *chile rellenos* and the enchiladas do not work nearly as well; nor does the red snapper Veracruz or the shrimp in garlic sauce. The food that works best at the Old Town Mexican Cafe y Cantina is food that can be eaten as you drink a margarita or a fine Mexican beer.   *M.S.*

**Moderate.** Open Monday through Friday 11 a.m. to 11 p.m.; Saturday and Sunday from 9 a.m. Closed Christmas, Thanksgiving, New Year's. Full bar. Reservations for parties of 10 or more weekdays only; no reservations weekends. All major credit cards. Parking lot. Casual.

---

## OLD TRIESTE                          Northern Italian
2335 Morena                                        ★★
San Diego                                   (714) 276-1841

The cuisine of Trieste is essentially that of Northern Italy—simple, hearty, and heavy. Specialties include veal dishes, scampi, fresh fish, and smooth cannelloni served in a tiny paneled room with ten tables. There is a "Nino's Special" that includes filet mignon, veal, chicken livers, eggplant, and cheese. Tommy Tomicich is a wine buff, and he has put together one of the more serious selections of wine in the San Diego area, including some of the rare French superstars.

**Expensive.** Open Tuesday through Saturday. Luncheon from noon to 2 p.m. weekdays. Dinner from 5:30 to 10:30 p.m. Full bar. Reservations accepted. All major credit cards. Parking lot. Semi-dressy.

---

## OLD VENICE NOODLE COMPANY   Italian/American
2654 Main Street                                     ★
Santa Monica      **Map 2**             (213)399-9211

The exuberance of this imaginative restaurant is contagious. Good spaghetti, lasagna, chicken, and steaks are served in a striking ambience — stained glass, antiques, and artifacts — highlighted by a trolley car in the restaurant. This is precisely the kind of place that Santa Monica needs, and it is showing evidence of becoming a nerve center for the area.

**Inexpensive.** Open seven days. Lunch and dinner 11:30 a.m. to 10 p.m. Monday through Thursday; to midnight Friday; 2:30 to midnight Saturday; 2:30 to 10 Sunday. Children's menu. Banquet facilities. Closed Thanksgiving, Christmas, New Year's. Full bar. Reservations recommended for parties of eight or more. All major credit cards. Parking lot. Casual.

---

*In order to obtain the best results from this Guide, please consult "Tips on Dining Out" on page 21.*

## THE OLD WORLD

**California funky**
★

8782 Sunset Boulevard

Hollywood     **Map 7**     (213) 652-2520

1019 Westwood Boulevard     ★

Westwood     **Map 8**     (213) 208-4033

216 North Beverly Drive     ★

Beverly Hills     **Map 8**     (213) 274-7695

262 South Palm Canyon     ★

Palm Springs     (714) 325-5502

One can sit outdoors at the Old World in Hollywod and watch a veritable caravan of extraterrestrials parade hither and yon. The Old World just smacks of wholesomeness, a testament to the basic virtues of meat and vegetables, working hand in hand to make this a better world to eat in for all of us. They are not beyond declaring their wholesomeness in a menu blurb that declares that, "Our hamburger meat comes from beef that has not been lot fed. This means a healthier piece of meat as well as a better product." It is a fine product that is served here and also a puzzlement in terms of creative menu writing. The burgers at the Old World have colorful names which I've never had much luck at matching up with their titles. Why, for instance, does the Leonardo burger feature bacon and Swiss cheese? What metaphorical explanation is there for a burger topped with sautéed mushrooms, onions and cheddar cheese called a Picasso? Is mozzarella cheese with ham reason enough to peg a burger with the moniker Michelangelo? The bottom line at the Old World is that the hamburgers are just fine, and so are the home-fried potatoes which you can opt for as an adjunct. I'm particularly fond of the swinger burger, which is filled with onions, cheddar cheese, green peppers, olives and tomatoes, all hidden here and there within the burger, somewhat like a miniature meatloaf on a bun.    *M.S.*

**Moderate.** Open Monday through Thursday 8 a.m. to 11:30 p.m.; Friday and Saturday to 12:30 p.m. Hours vary at Palm Springs location. Full bar in Hollywood, Westwood; wine and beer only at Beverly Hills. No reservations. Visa; MC. AX. Wheelchair access. Street parking: lot parking in Westwood, no validation.

---

## OLIVE MILL BISTRO
1295 Coast Village Road
Montecito

French/Continental
★
(805) 969-4900

"Bistro" has the connotation of local cafe, but this draws patrons from as far away as Los Angeles with its carefully created illusions: white table linens, flickering candlelight, and warm woods. Dinner begins with a fresh, iced relish tray. Among the appetizers is a notable clams *mariniere* while entrées include supreme of chicken Suzanne, *entrecôte* Cafe de Paris, and best of all, shrimp curry Bombay served with chutney, raisins, toasted coconut chips, and almonds. Desserts are prepared for two or more and are just so-so.

**Moderate to expensive.** Open seven days. Dinner from 6 to 10:45 Monday through Saturday; 5 to 10 Sunday. Closed New Year's. Full bar. Piano bar; trio. Reservations recommended. Visa, MC, AX, DC. Valet parking. Semi-dressy to dressy.

---

## ONE THOUSAND EAST
Biltmore Hotel
1000 East Palm Canyon
Palm Springs

Continental
★
(714) 323-1811

For dinner I liked the Maine lobster, though they offer a good complete menu. Not to worry if you choose wrong, you can still enjoy the waterfall in the lush gardens or watch the swimmers from your table. There is nightly entertainment. A word of caution: When the heat's on in the desert, the natives relax any and every way they can think of. One of those ways is to keep irregular hours, so during the summer better verify their hours before steaming across town.

**Moderate.** Open seven days. Breakfast and lunch 8 a.m. to 12:30 p.m. Dinner 5 to 11 p.m. Closed summer months. Reservations recommended. All major credit cards. Parking lot. Resort wear.

---

## OPASO 2 Thai

Town and Country Shopping Center ★★
Orange          **Map 6**                    (714) 542-5654

It really should have started in Hollywood or Beverly Hills, where exotic fare is better welcomed, rather than in less-experimental Orange, where there is not even a good Chinese restaurant. The food is simply lovely; influenced by, but distinct from, the cuisines of the East. The feeling is a Thai village, with thatched bamboo ceilings and teak tables, certainly a great improvement over the usual ethnic restaurant that frequently opens in a bleak storefront with a Bangkok poster and a recorded score of *The King and I.* Here it is served in a Thai temple, a magnificent restaurant with a creaking foot bridge and soft, delicate lighting, creating a soothing effect over all. I had coconut soup, rich and spicy with vegetables and shrimp, an original creation of Opaso. The beef curry with peanuts and the stuffed chicken roll (*wing kai*) are exciting. Thai iced tea and iced coffee are a revelation, always served thick and sweet and strong. The staff are virtually all Thai and seem delighted with the opportunity to share and explain their culinary heritage. After serving dinner, they are likely to change from tuxedo and dresses to magnificent Thai costumes and perform folk dances. The only jarring note is the Western-style dance lounge, but you can ignore it, and it doesn't intrude into the dining rooms.

**Moderate.** Open seven days. Luncheon from 11:30 a.m. to 2:30 p.m. Dinner 5 to 10 p.m. Sunday, Monday through Thursday; to 11 Friday, Saturday. Closed most major holidays. Full bar 11 a.m. to midnight. Reservations recommended. All major credit cards. Parking lot. Casual.

---

## ORANGE HILL                                    Continental
19912 East Chapman Avenue
Orange        **Map 6**                       (714) 997-2910

For several years I've been lamenting that the beauty here is out of the window—not on the table. You can see all of Orange County, and on a clear day. Catalina. Inside decor has all good things too: dark wood beams, opulent chandeliers, a fireplace and waterfalls.

**Moderate.** Open seven days. Luncheon and buffet from 11 a.m. to 5 p.m. weekdays. Dinner from 5 to 11. Closed Christmas, New Year's. Full bar. Reservations recommended. Visa, MC, AX. Valet parking. Semi-dressy.

---

## THE ORIENT EXPRESS                              Chinese
5400 Wilshire Boulevard                              ★
Los Angeles      **Map 7**                    (213) 935-6000

What a swell name for a Chinese restaurant, and this one in the mid-Wilshire area is exciting. New, its design reflects the art of a master architect from San Francisco, Lin Chan. The bar is intimate with copper and brass appointments and it's furnished with contemporary rattan furniture much like an exclusive private club in Injah. Colors are subtle — faded shades of terra cotta, sand, and an occasional accent of Chinese blue. The stepped ceilings are impressive and there is a mezzanine designated for private parties. Specialties include *chaio-tzu*, cracked crab and fried *calamari* as an appetizer, sliced chicken soup and beggar's chicken, grilled shark, minced pigeon and barbecued pork chops as a main course. The menu is extensive for both luncheon and dinner with a wine list of nearly 40 wines, unusual for a Chinese restaurant. The best description of the cuisine would be Mandarin/Szechwan but I am impressed with the imaginative dishes and combinations listed.

**Moderate.** Open seven days. Luncheon served 11:30 a.m. to 3 p.m. weekdays. Dinner daily from 6 to 10:30 p.m. Limited banquet facilities. Entertainment. Full bar. Reservations recommended. Visa, MC, AX. Parking lot. Semi-dressy.

---

## THE ORIGINAL PANTRY American ★
877 South Figueroa Street
Los Angeles     **Map 7**     (213) 972-9279

For fifty-eight years they've been famous for wholesome homemade food with generous portions at prudent prices. As a matter of fact, there are generations of families to whom the Pantry is part of life. For reasons best known to the proprietor, the Pantry issued a Madison Avenue-type booklet containing remarkable statistics. They serve 2,500 people daily. An entire harvest of more than 20,000 coffee trees is required for a year's service. There are 68 on the staff, and the Pantry serves enough bread each year to supply an average family with three loaves a day for 143 years. All these facts and more are acceptable because no one took time away from the kitchen to figure them out. The ham hocks, beef stew, halibut fillets, soup, iced garnish, and home-baked breads are still good—and cheap. Breakfast is magnificent, dinner very good, lunch only mediocre—if that.

**Inexpensive.** Open seven days, 24 hours. No alcoholic beverages. Parking lot. No credit cards. Validated parking. Casual.

*To obtain the best results from this Guide, consult*
*"How to Use this Guide" on page 27.*

# ORLANDO-ORSINI RISTORANTE    Italian
9575 West Pico Boulevard
Los Angeles    **Map 8**    (213) 277-6050

The room is light, spacious and charming. The menu is a return-to-Italian, no-nonsense compendium of Roman delights. The fried *calamari* known here by the pseudonym of *tegamino calamari riccione* were a little pastry but everything else prepared by the two chefs was certainly above average. Veal roasted with garlic, rosemary, and brandy is a special favorite of mine and the *straccetti* of beef is new to this area, as is the pasta *pirato*, (with seafood). They opened in 1978, and they'll get better and their prices will be adjusted (they were a shade high at this writing). At luncheon (served weekdays only), they have a buffet.

**Expensive.** Open Monday through Saturday. Luncheon from noon to 3 p.m. weekdays. Buffet luncheon at fixed price of under $12. Dinner 6 to 1 p.m. Closed major holidays. Full bar. Reservations required. Patio for lunch. All major credit cards. Valet parking. Semi-dressy; jacket required.

---

# ORVILLE & WILBUR'S    Steak/Seafood
401 Rosecrans Avenue
Manhattan Beach    **Map 2**    (213) 545-2262

That's Wright; it's a theme steak house with a broader menu than most, including a chicken Oscar and a good scampi. There's fresh fish every day and a salad bar. The waitresses may be the prettiest in the area and are the best decor a place could have. Nothing else is very special.

**Moderate.** Open seven days. Luncheon from 11 a.m. to 2 p.m. Dinner from 5 to 11 p.m. Sunday through Thursday; to midnight Friday, Saturday. Closed Christmas. Entertainment nightly from 5 to 8; 9 to 1:30 a.m. Full bar. Reservations recommended weekends. Visa, MC, DC. Valet parking. Casual.

## O'SHAUGHNESSY'S DOWNTOWN

American/
★

515 South Flowr Street
ARCO Plaza
Los Angeles     **Map 7**        (213) 629-2565

This cozy castle in the highrise buildings of ARCO Plaza somehow manages to be all things to all people...and to do it well. Fine American cuisine includes fresh spinach salad, steaks, king crab legs, seafood and chips and more. Luncheon entrées include a daily special, seafood, crepes, quiche, salads and hot entrées. For the sports fan without time to get home before the big game there is a lounge with big screen t.v., camaraderie, special drinks and finger food. Going to the theatre? There's a pre-theatre special for around $10 that includes everything from appetizer to dessert. Best bet is the cold yoghurt soup. Happy hour includes—if you're ready for this—"crispie munchies for the drinkies," an array of Chinese egg rolls, homemade potato chips, quiche Lorraine, zucchini tempura, fried cauliflower and much more, at nominal prices.

**Moderate to expensive.** Open for lunch Monday through Friday 11 a.m. to 2:30 p.m. Dinner Monday through Saturday 5 to 10 p.m. Closed major holidays. Full bar. Reservations recommended. AX, CB. Wheelchair access. Validated parking. Casual.

## OTTO'S PINK PIG

Continental/American
★

4958 Van Nuys Boulevard
Van Nuys     **Map 1**        (213) 788-9971

The food is excellent, the decor lovely, and the American dishes, like brisket finished over hickory, are special. Bursting with flair and added touches, Otto's has a special senior citizen budget dinner served Tuesday through Thursday from 4 to 6 p.m., a complete dinner with smaller portions at reduced prices.

**Moderate.** Open Tuesday through Sunday. Luncheon from 11:30 a.m. to 4 p.m. weekdays. Dinner from 4 to 10 p.m. Monday through Thursday; to 11 Friday, Saturday; 3 to 9 p.m. Sunday. Full bar. No reservations. All major credit cards. Parking lot. Casual.

---

## OUR CONTRIBUTION
13230 Burbank Boulevard
Van Nuys     **Map 1**

**Vegetarian**
★
(213) 988-2332

If vegetarian's your thing—it's not mine—this just may be the place. There is no meat on the menu, nor chicken, nor fish, nor alcohol. The baked breads and the fresh juice combinations and blends are refreshing. Vegetable is king here whether raw or cooked (steamed or sautéed) and a canny use of cheeses and soybean curd provides a texture that you won't find in most vegetarian restaurants. (If they hate the thought of meat so much why do they have dishes like "burgers"?) The soups are homemade and really taste it. The salad dressings are good and the baked potato and guacamole are the real thing but it's all a bit bland.

**Inexpensive.** Open Monday through Saturday from 11 a.m. to 10 p.m. Child's menu. Wine and beer only. Reservations for parties of six or more. Patio. Visa, MC, DC. Parking lot. Casual.

---

## OVERLAND STAGE
1855 South Harbor Boulevard
Anaheim     **Map 6**

**American**
★
(714) 750-1811

Wild buffalo every night and boar, bear, rattlesnake, pheasant and rabbit on special nights make this an obviously unique restaurant. Authentic pieces from the California Gold Rush period add interest to the decorating, as does a bar from a Mississippi steamboat. If you know paintings, look for the famous Remington originals. An actual Overland Stage stands proudly atop the restaurant as a landmark.

**Moderate.** Open seven days. Luncheon served 11:30 a.m. to 2 p.m. weekdays. Dinner from 5:30 to 11 p.m. daily. Cocktails. Reservations accepted. All major credit cards. Lot parking. Casual.

---

*To obtain the best results from this Guide, be sure to consult maps on the various Southern California areas in the front of the book.*

# P

## PACIFIC DINING CAR American
1310 West 6th Street ★★★
Los Angeles      **Map 7** (213) 483-6000

It's rare that a love affair can be rekindled but it's happened. I am again enamored of the Pacific Dining Car, an institution near downtown Los Angeles for about a half century. Wes Idol is a direct descendant of the founders and while his stewardship has brought about some alterations, sophistication, and a splendid wine list, the emphasis on personal service is still there. Wes is definitely diffident when it comes to wine lore. Much like the "reluctant" poker player who suddenly begins to riffle the deck like Houdini, Idol is far more knowledgeable than he likes to appear. He frequently suggests moderately priced alternatives that are as good, or better than, the expensive super-star labels. He buys in quantity lots at seasonal lows and his avowed policy is to never mark up a bottle once the price has been set, regardless of market fluctuation. This has created some diplomatic problems with affluent patrons who order a Texas six-pack of say, an expensive cabernet to take home only to be told that the wine, priced as it is, is not available for takeout. Of course they are known for their steaks, but there are other endearments such as an appetizer of bay scallops and a beautiful tomato and onion salad (the onion tastes like the famed Maui variety). Pacific Dining Car is one of the few places left where one can order a boned saddle of lamb (for two); this cut is a revelation to anyone who has not tried it. They also have a fine abalone steak and soft-shelled crab, and all vegetables are fresh. The service is direct and correct in this atmosphere of early century plush. The cocktail lounge has become a bar away from the bar for lawyers who congregate to swap yarns and camaraderie helped along by free (free!) oysters, caviar toast points, and hors d'oeuvres of similar distinction. Desserts include hot green apple pie, excellent cheesecake, and best of all, ice cream that's made in Santa Barbara — vanilla with some of the beans left in; the taste is extraordinary.

**Expensive.** Open seven days, 24 hours. Breakfast from 1 to 11 a.m. Luncheon from 11 a.m. to 5 p.m. Dinner from 5 p.m. to 1 a.m. Sunday brunch from 10 a.m. to 4 p.m. Full bar. Reservations advised. Visa, MC. Valet parking. Casual to semi-dressy.

---

## PAL JOEY'S                              Steakhouse
233 East Saturnino Road
Palm Springs                              (714) 325-7444

Okay, so Frank Sinatra ate here. That draws the "in" crowd, for a while. Sooner or later, you've got to come up with good food if you want to keep that crowd. Manager Joe Hanna is making the effort. Recently he hired Chef Willie Moye, and brought out a new menu with 10 entrées such as ribs, roast Long Island duck, crab, lobster and an improved wine list. He's avoided accusations of chauvinism by laying in a supply of waiters to match the attractive waitresses. "Something for everybody," he explains.

**Expensive.** Open seven days. Dinner from 6 p.m. to midnight. Closed major holidays; summer until October 1st. Disco music 11 p.m. to 1:45 a.m. Cocktails. Reservations recommended. All major credit cards. Valet parking. Casual.

---

## THE PALM
9001 Santa Monica Boulevard
West Hollywood          **Map 8**

Steak/Lobster
★★
(213) 550-8811

New York steak houses are often noisy, brightly lighted, expensive operations that serve huge eastern lobster the way God and New Yorkers intended —broiled over charcoal and presented with deep dishes of melted butter. Thus, it is no surprise that The Palm in West Hollywood should reflect these characteristics — it is the offspring of the famous New York Palm, that has been assuaging appetites and depleting wallets for three generations, of the Ganzi family. Third-generation Walter makes sure the Nova Scotia lobsters are really flown in alive and kicking; they purchase tons of them by contract. The lobster may seem expensive, but the creatures are five-pounders and can be shared. They are without qualification, the best I've had. The steaks are also costly, but the "Steak Stone" sandwich is interesting: sliced mignonettes served with pimiento and sautéed onions. There's sawdust on the floor, caricatures on the wall, and celebrities. There are other items on the menu, from chops to shrimp, but they are there for those benighted souls who don't understand you only go to a New York steak house for steak or lobster. Potatoes are cottage fried, not exciting, and the cheesecake imported from the Bronx should be instantly deported. But the bread is lovely, and the wines — what there are of them — are fairly priced.

**Expensive.** Open seven days. Luncheon from noon to 4 p.m. weekdays. Dinner menu available from noon to 10:30 p.m. weekdays; 5 to 10:45 Saturday, Sunday. Closed major holidays. Full bar. Reservations recommended. All major credit cards. Valet parking. Casual.

# PANCHITO'S
### 261 South Mission Drive
### San Gabriel     **Map 6**

**Mexican**
★★
(213) 284-8830

Panchito's is worth the effort to find — a splendid restaurant somewhat remotely situated on the site of the first city hall in San Gabriel (across from the mission). For openers, I loved the margaritas, sensitively prepared, without ice (unlike the lime slush of most Mexican restaurants), served cold and fresh tasting in various sizes up to 17 ounces. But it is the atmosphere, hand-crafted by Frank Ramirez of tiles and adobe and·railroad ties and rough woods and wrought iron, that is the main feature here, the nearest to a Mexico City setting you'll find in gringo-land. I watched the broilerman deftly pare the fat from a filet strip and ignore the scales as he cut precise eight-ounce beauties. When I looked a bit skeptical, he put several — selected at random — on the scale, and they each registered exactly eight ounces. The broilerman, like so many of the help, has been there from the beginning, more than 20 years, and has that ease of hospitality that comes with long association. We dined on the patio in a serendipity mood beneath an ancient, gnarled grapevine. Señor Ramirez, reminding me much of Jack Smith's friend Mr. Gomez, said, "For you I have a special surprise." With that he turned out the lights on the patio. "I have the moon." Indeed he did—a large silvery beauty that added to the sense of timelessness in the type of feast enjoyed by the mission fathers. The Ramirez family is everywhere — cooking, slicing, greeting. Even the salsa is prepared fresh each day, and Mamacita complains if it's not thick enough. The huge menu contains everything you'd expect in a Mexican establishment, along with many dishes rarely found. The steak, *carnitas de filet*, is prepared in homemade marinade with 18 ingredients. The shrimp/steak combinations are a favorite, and the menu is very inexpensive for the quality of the food. For an authentic taste of early California history, I can think of no better restaurant than Panchito's. It should be easier to find.

**Moderate.** Open Tuesday through Sunday. Luncheon from 11:30 a.m. to 3 p.m. Dinner from 3 to 10 p.m. Children's menu. Full bar. No reservations. Patio. Visa, MC, AX, DC. Parking lot. Casual.

---

## PANDA INN                                         Chinese
3472 East Foothill Boulevard                             ★
Pasadena          **Map 7**                   (213) 681-2700

The spicy food of Northern China, and Mandarin and Szechwan specialties, should wake up the palates of Pasadena in this attractive restaurant. There are special arrangements for large parties (ten or more), feasts that include an array of exotic foods not ordinarily on the menu. If this cuisine is unfamiliar, tell Manager Andrew Cheng if you like mild, medium, or hot, and let him suggest the dinner.

**Moderate.** Open seven days. Luncheon from 11:30 a.m. to 3 p.m. Dinner from 3 to 10:30 p.m. Closed Thanksgiving. Full bar. Reservations recommended. Visa, MC. Parking lot. Casual.

---

## PAPA CHOUX                                   Continental
1925 West Olympic Boulevard                              ★
Los Angeles        **Map 7**                  (213) 380-2580

The service and food have improved—there was room for it—at Papa Choux, the showy midtown restaurant and banquet center. House specialty is veal and the seafood bar features half lobster au cognac and cracked crab with mustard mayonaise. There are several small booths tucked away in the corner with curtains to keep you from the curious and wandering musicians, one playing the 100-string salterio. Adding to the atmosphere are crystal chandeliers, aquariums with astonished fish, and plush galore.

**Moderate.** Open Monday through Saturday. Lunch from 11:30 a.m. to 2:30 p.m. weekdays. Dinner from 5 to 11 p.m. Full bar. Reservations advised. All major credit cards. Valet parking. Semi-dressy.

---

## PAPADAKIS TAVERNA
301 West 6th Street
San Pedro          **Map 3**

**Greek**
**DA★★**
(213)548-1186

A joyful Greek heart beats beneath this unexciting exterior in a shabby section of San Pedro. Waiters, cooks, and their wives dance and sing together almost every evening, and former USC linebacker John Papadakis is proud of his unpaid entertainment, which often involves the customers. The food's good here, too, particularly the moussaka, the *pastitsio*, and the cheese *tiropitas*. Greek wine at bargain prices are included on the wine list, and daily specials may include red snapper in tomato sauce, stuffed eggplant, squid, and octopus.

**Moderate.** Open Tuesday through Sunday. Dinner served Tuesday through Thursday from 5 to 9 p.m.; Friday and Saturday to 10 p.m. Sunday from 4 to 9 p.m. Private party facilities. Closed Christmas, New Year's and Greek Easter. Wine and beer only. Reservations required. Visa, MC. Parking lot across street. Semi-dressy.

---

## THE PARAGON INN
660 West Seventh Street
San Pedro          **Map 3**

**Yugoslavian**
★
(213) 831-2200

As good as you'll find outside of Yugoslavia, this former private home delights the Slavs of the area—the fishing families. Dinners include soup or salad and fresh rolls baked every day by Tanya Milojevicic in her immaculate kitchen. Stuffed cabbage, moussaka, shish kebab, and *satrash* (a rich stew), are a few of the main dishes but do try to save some room for dessert; the apple strudel is especially good. There is a "Paragon plate for two" that features a taste of this and that.

**Moderate.** Open Tuesday through Sunday. Luncheon from 11:30 a.m. to 2:30 p.m. Dinner from 5 to 10 p.m. Entertainment, dancing. Wine and beer only. Reservations advised. Patio. Visa, MC, CB. Street parking. Casual.

---

## PARU'S                                                    Indian
5140 Sunset Boulevard                                         ★
Hollywood        **Map 7**                          (213) 661-7600

Paru's is a terrific solution to the brown rice perplex. The food served here is the cuisine of Tamil Nadu, the southernmost (pointy) tip of India, where the people are exceedingly dark, the weather intolerably hot and sticky, and the cooking strongly vegetarian. And not the boiled zucchini school of vegetarian either. The food of Tamil, as served at Paru's, is spicy, alive with good flavors and bright colors. It's fun; and Awanijs Raj and Paru make it even more fun with their high spirits and quasi-silly menu.

There are six dinners listed on the menu. From one to six, they're called "Delite All India" ($7), "Mini Emperor" ($6), "Softy-Puffy" ($5), "Grandma's Goody" ($4.50), "Madras Special" ($4) and "Simple Glory" ($3.50). "Softy-Puffy" (my favorite name) consists of a wonderful lentil soup, *pongal* (rice and lentils flavored with ginger and cumin), *gotsu* (eggplant cooked with onions), and a couple of pieces of puffy *poori* bread stuffed with a potato curry. "Grandma's Goody" includes Paru's astounding homemade yogurt, which is served with cucumbers and tomatoes swimming around at the bottom of the bowl; a lentil gravy called *sambar* and a coconut chutney; and an amazing creation referred to coyly as a "superpancake." Superpancake is related to another Paru specialty called *masala dosa*. Both are a kind of a gigantic burrito, about the length and width of a clarinet, filled with lentils or potato curry or some such starcy concoction. Actually, many of the dishes at Paru's lean toward the starchy, rather than the green side of the vegetarian coin. But they're concocted with such verve that

501

the starchiness doesn't painfully whack you across the shins.

There is also a variety of desserts, strange and wondrous at Paru's, including a very nice dish with the very unfortunate name *barfi* which tastes strongly of cardamon. But my favorite taste is that of an extraordinary yogurt drink called *lassi*. This lightly-sweetened yogurt has far more bite than *kefir*, and a hint of rosewater. I think it might have been served in the Garden of Eden.   *M.S.*

**Moderate.** Open Thursday through Tuesday. Luncheon from 11 a.m. to 1:45 p.m., except Saturday; Sunday from 10 a.m. Dinner from 5:30 to 9:45. Closed Christmas. Beer and wine only. Reservations accepted. Patio. V, MC. Street parking. Casual.

---

## PAT AND LORRAINE'S COFFEE SHOP American
4720 Eagle Rock Boulevard                          ★
Eagle Rock     **Map 7**                (213) 256-9269

Remember the smell of bacon and eggs cooking on Saturday morning? P&L's offers the traditional American breakfast including fresh biscuits made daily. The cheery, elderly ladies who serve you the way Mom used to do, make sure everything is to your satisfaction. It is one of the few places where coffee refills are free. A nice way to start the day.   *C.W.*

**Inexpensive.** Open seven days 6:30 a.m. to 2 p.m. Closed major holidays. Take-out. No reservations. Visa, MC. Parking lot. Casual.

---

*For best results, consult "How to Use This Guide" on page 27.*

Announcing . . .
# The Paul Wallach Restaurant Newsletter

A monthly newsletter filled with items about restaurants: openings, closings, changes and gossip. You'll be up to the minute on wine values and newsletter subscribers will have the opportunity to participate in the monthly Epicurean dinners.

**HALF PRICE TO BOOK PURCHASERS . . .**Use of this coupon will entitle the subscriber to 50% off the $30 annual subscription rate and this permanent, introductory subscription will guarantee against increase in future subscription rates.

**Please send the PAUL WALLACH RESTAURANT NEWSLETTER at the special price of $15 a year to:**

Name _____

Address _____

City_____

Zip_____

TO REORDER THIS GUIDE BOOK:

In the event the book is not available in your local bookstore you may send $11.66 ($9.95 plus postage and tax) to GUIDE, P.O. BOX 1000, Glendale, Ca. 91209. Please include your correct address with zip code.

Your comments, questions, and suggestions are welcome.
Please write to:   American Guide Publications
                   P. O. Box 1000
                   Glendale, CA 91209

## PATIO RESTAURANT                          American
450 North Robertson Boulevard                     ★
Los Angeles        **Map 8**           (213) 659-8381

The rich man's Cassell's? It's The Patio in the West Hollywood design area near the Blue Whale. The Patio is just that, with outdoor dining and a special heating arrangement for the winter months. The third-pound hamburgers are freshly ground and served with your choice of homemade carrot/raisin salad, potato salad, tossed green with an assortment of dressings, or the homemade soup du jour. Best of all, their homemade potato chips accompany all orders. Patio burgers are broiled to your liking and served on a bun from Pioneer Bakery. There are chiliburgers and cheeseburgers, and for the nonpurist, such ridiculous (but good) combinations as bacon and avocado burgers. Obviously, this is a full-scale restaurant, albeit small, and the service and setting are delightful.

**Moderate.** Open seven days 10 a.m. to 11 p.m. Sunday brunch from 10 a.m. to 2 p.m. Wine and beer only. Reservations advised. Patio. Visa, MC. Street parking. Casual.

## PAUL BHALLA'S CUISINE OF INDIA          Indian
10853 Lindbrook Drive                            ★★
Westwood          **Map 3**            (213) 208-8535

Indian restaurants in America had a timid, hesitant beginning. Most often they were initiated by a handful of cheerfully unprofessional exchange students, homesick for the food and culture of their country. When their nest egg and optimism gave way to cold reality, it usually came in the form of a tiny converted store on the periphery of an academic community, with Air India Posters and Ravi Shankar records, and a harassed waitress in a perma-press sari serving compromised curry. Paul Bhalla's Cuisine of

India is near UCLA geographically, but light-years away from that kind of off-campus fiasco. It is as much a tribute to the proprietor's business administration—he has a master's degree—as to his cultural and ethnic origins. The small entrance opens into an unexpectedly spacious interior of quiet elegance. Murals and tapestries from Indian mythology, hand-carved teak chairs, dangling brass chandeliers, a tiger skin, and gold-colored napery have been artfully arranged. Service is informal, but quietly efficient. Your order is usually taken by Mr. Bhalla, or his statuesque wife from New Zealand, and served by young girls in Rajasthan costumes—bare midriffs with jingling bells and necklaces. All are patient and gracious in explaining the unfamiliar dishes. Dinners include a choice of soups—*mulligatawny* (vegetables cooked down to their essence and flavored with turneric, cumin, coriander, garlic and ginger) *dal shorba* (lentil soup), *raita* (vegetables in yogurt), *ordal* (a side dish of lentils), and a salad are also included with the dinner, as is a very delicious buttery bread identified as *naan*. Entrées include chicken *tandoori*, a beautifully prepared dish with saffron and paprika; *soor-kakorma*, pork curry of Punjabis; *masala* beef, tender morsels of beef cooked with blended spices, fruits and nuts; and—my favorite—*sang-wala-lela*, succulent pieces of lamb cooked in a sauce of spinach and greens. There is even a New York steak for the hopelessly incurious. Leaves of edible silver (unfortunately resembling aluminum foil) garnish the more elegant dishes, and a choice of chutneys—mango, mint, or hot pepper—is offered with the main course. The degree of "hot"—mild, medium, or fiery—is left up to the patron at the time the order is taken. Overly hot sauces will obscure the delicate flavors, although the staff remembers with glee the Japanese tourist who insisted that his food was never hot enough. Finally, in desperation, the kitchen gave it all they had—and watched with some anxiety as perspiration poured from the diner's deeply flushed face. As he paid the check he was asked, "Hot enough?" "Closer," he replied. As in all explorations into the relatively unknown, a few guidelines may prove helpful at Paul Bhalla's. Indians eat a lot of bread with their food as a sort of palate clearer between dishes. They never eat bread after rice or vice versa. In the pre-ordering consultation, you may be advised not to mix curries. The salad of fresh vegetables is served with the main course and placed in the center of the table to be divided by the diners. While a limited wine list is provided with, surprisingly, four champagnes ("We get very festive here"), I find that beer is the best accompaniment to the spicy fare. Otherwise, a light wine, perhaps the Gerwirtz-traminer, is suggested. I was not particularly excited about the desserts, although my guests were pleased with the rice pudding; and I did find the sweet cheese in cream sauce (*ras malai*) enjoyable, with a small bottle of Puilly Fuissé. The after-dinner dish of anise seeds is supposed to aid digestion, although I found the huge dinner rested lightly.

**Moderate.** Open Tuesday through Sunday. Dinner served Sunday through Thursday from 5:30 p.m. to 10 p.m.; Friday, Saturday from 5 to 11 p.m. Closed major holidays. Banquet facilities. Entertainment weekends. Full bar. Reservations required on weekends. Visa, MC. Street parking. Semi-dressy to dressy.

---

## PAUL'S FRENCH CUISINE French/Continental
3801 Riverside Drive ★
Burbank **Map 1** (213)848-1501

Heaping platters of hors d'oeuvres with baskets of hot French bread are included with the dinners at this respected Gallic restaurant, favored by the nearby studio workers and visitors. Paul S. Manod learned butchering from his father, as the prime and generous cuts of beef and veal indicate. Most popular dishes: pepper steak, scampi, veal with hearts of palm, rack of lamb, and duckling. Best desserts are the pear flambé and the crêpes suzette. Interesting decor items are originals of the Little Musicians of Montmartre by Etienne.

**Moderate.** Open Monday through Saturday. Luncheon from 11:30 a.m. to 3 p.m. weekends. Dinner from 5 p.m. to midnight. Closed major holidays. Full bar. Reservations recommended. All major credit cards. Street parking. Casual.

---

**PAVILION**                          **Continental**
135 North Grand Avenue               ★★
Los Angeles    **Map 7**           (213) 972-7333

For years the restaurants at the Music Center were barely tolerated, if that. We had become accustomed to the lifeless fare at the Curtain Call, little more than a coffee shop. We have become almost hostile to the arrogance at the Pavilion, ostensibly the crown jewel of the restaurants there. I recall an Academy Award evening when I courteously suggested that the service was virtually nonexistent. The maitre d' eyed my suit of lights—the Academy had just gone formal—and snapped: "Whaddya people care, you only come here once a year." As I rode down the elevator I thanked whatever fates were responsible for my becoming a restaurant critic. That night I wrote a deliciously detailed column that was good for my blood pressure, bad for theirs.

It is particularly gratifying therefore to describe the changes at the Music Center, all of them for the better.

After three incognito visits, I met with Marty Breverman, the improbably young, enthusiastic, apprehensive—this was his first meeting with a restaurant writer—vice president of Hungry Tiger, the new operators.

Imagine a fully-staffed restaurant, with a kitchen that would be the envy of the White House, that must do 99 percent of the dinner business in less than 90 minutes. Imagine further that the patrons of this restaurant arrive in a state of anxiety often bordering on hysteria, in a hurry to down the food and get to their seats on time. It would be impossible for any restaurant to meet that crunch with complete success. The Pavilion comes close.

Service is improved due to large measure to an intensive training program and the fact that the staff are top professionals. The appetizer buffet is an elaborate affair, cruise-ship festive, with the king crab legs, freshly shucked oysters and clams, jumbo shrimp and an array of colorful hors d'oeuvres. Entrées are selected from the menu. There are five, including poached salmon in sorrel sauce, roast duckling in tangerine sauce, rack of lamb with minted Bordelaise, New York steak "Madagascar" and medallion of veal "Pavilion." Dinners are $18.50 including appetizers. There is a limited wine list intelligently selected to accompany the menu, from which I would order the Parducci Chenin Blanc ($8) with the salmon. A respectable collection of cork-finished house wines include a stylish Zinfandel from Pedroncelli or, if you insist, a rosé made from Zinfandel grapes that is almost adorable. The Pavilion at dinner will never be a great restaurant; it would be impossible given the circumstances. However, it has become respectable, well worth the extra half hour you should allow to enjoy a cocktail, the soothing sounds of the harp, a pleasurable dinner and a liqueur. It could be half the fun of going to the Music Center.

For luncheon the Pavilion changes character to accommodate the court house and high-rise clientele. The entrées tend to the lighter variety with crepes, salads, sandwiches and a luncheon buffet.

**Moderate.** Open Monday through Saturday. Luncheon served 11:30 a.m. to 2:30 p.m. Dinner from 5:30 to 9 p.m. Sunday dinner only on performance days. Closed major holidays. Entertainment. Cocktails. Reservations required. View. Visa, MC, AX, CB. Wheelchair access. Parking is $2.50 in Music Center garage; $1.50 across the street. No validation. Dressy; jacket and tie.

---

*For best results, consult "How to Use This Guide" on page 27.*

# PEAR GARDEN
**Korean/Japanese**

666 North La Cienega Boulevard
Los Angeles **Map 8** (213) 659-3022

This place is particularly notable to me for the graffiti in the men's room. It read: "To do is to be—Schopenhauer." "To be is to do, Nietzche." "Do be do be do be do—Sinatra." The graffiti was the best part. This used to be a pretty good Korean restaurant, a fair Japanese teppan room, and now it's a confusing hodge-podge of Oriental mediocrity. There is also a sushi bar.

**Moderate to expensive.** Open Monday through Saturday. Luncheon from 11:30 a.m. to 2:30 p.m. weekdays. Dinner from 5:30 to 10:30 p.m. Sunday through Thursday; to 11 Friday, Saturday. Closed major holidays. Full bar. Reservations accepted. Visa, MC, AX. Parking lot. Casual.

---

# PELICAN RESTAURANTS
**Seafood**

The Pelican's Roost ★
8232 Sepulveda
Van Nuys **Map 1** (213) 988-6334

The Pelican's Catch
1715 Pacific Avenue
Venice **Map 2** (213) 392-5305

The Pelican
3801 Highland Avenue
Manhattan Beach **Map 2** (213) 545-6563

The Pelican's Nest
1717 Ocean Avenue
Santa Monica **Map 2** (213) 451-0818

Cafe Pelican
2720 Main Street
Santa Monica          **Map 2**                    (213) 392-5711

Not really a chain in the strictest sense, the Pelican
restaurants buy supplies as a group so they are able to offer
the widest variety of fresh fish each day. It isn't uncommon
for fifteen or twenty varieties to be offered on the
blackboard. If a fish can be sucessfully charbroiled, it will
be, simply and without a lot of elaboration. Those that
can't, such as clams, scallops or shrimp, are deep fried in
non-cholesterol oil. The basic difference among the five is
decor. Though basically nautical, each of the restaurants
shows the young, creative energy of the staff who are
encouraged to contribute. Each of the restaurants now has
some sort of patio (all are heated) and a Sunday brunch.
And although they are very good about it, if you like your
fish moist make sure to mention it.

**Pelican's Roost:** (Hours at other locations may vary)
**Moderate.** Open seven days. Luncheon Monday through
Friday from 11:30 a.m. to 4 p.m. Dinner from 4 to 10 p.m.
Sunday brunch 11 a.m. to 4 p.m. Closed July 4, Christmas.
Full bar. No reservations. Patio. Visa, MC, AX. Parking lot.
Casual.

---

## PENELOPE'S                          French/California
50 Los Patos Way                                    ★★
Santa Barbara                          (805) 969-0307

Penelope Williams operates a dazzling enterprise with imagination, ambience and flair. The young proprietress explained
that her food is not so much French as it is *nouvelle* and
California. Her chef is from London and Penelope is from
Santa Barbara.

Exciting dishes include: crab bisque with fresh corn,
whitefish with three caviars, semolina pasta and vegetables

so fresh they seem dewy. Scallops with fresh strawberries, warm rabbit salad and oysters baked with sorrel are all good dishes. There is a three citrus cake with chocolate truffles that is outrageous.

**Moderate to expensive.** Open Tuesday through Sunday for dinner 6 to 10 p.m. Closed Christmas and New Year's. Live entertainment. Greenhouse bar. Full bar. Visa, MC. Wheelchair access. Parking lot. Dressy; jackets required.

---

## PENGUIN PALACE                                    Chinese
3537 East Foothill Boulevard                              ★
Pasadena          **Map 7**                  (213) 351-8716

The specialty here is Mandarin, but to really enjoy it you should allow your waiter to select; just give him the amount you want to sepnd for dinner and he'll ask if you like beef or seafood and then he disappears—to reappear with a feast that you couldn't pronounce but will enjoy. They've never let me down, and I am sure that they'll perform well if you give them a chance. Stay away from the menu; it's for the unaware.

**Inexpensive.** Open seven days. Luncheon from 11:30 a.m. to 2:30 p.m. weekdays. Dinner 2:30 to 9:30 p.m. Sunday through Thursday; to 10:30 Friday, Saturday. Banquet menus. Wine and beer only. Reservations essential. Visa, MC, AX. Parking lot. Casual.

---

## PEPPONE                                    Northern Italian
11628 Barrington Court                                    ★★
Brentwood          **Map 8**                  (213) 476-7379

The menu suggests that Gianni "Peppone" Paoletti will prepare any special dish at your request. Indeed, this is the kind of Italian service that would have the waiters self-immolating if that was your desire. (In Venice the waiters will put a little plate of food in front of the customer's Pekingese as a custom.) But service is not all—the kitchen creates mighty concoctions with a battery of skillets sputtering in indignation, emanating a heady aroma of garlic and wine. I know a connoiseur basketball player who would kill for the liver Veneziana, and I've seen him down two portions. The pastas, especially the *paglia e fieno* ("straw and hay") and the green fettuccine with garlic butter and anchovy sauce is flawless. The wine list is awesome—and so are some of the prices.

**Expensive.** Open Tuesday through Friday for lunch from 11:30 a.m. to 2:30 p.m. Dinner Tuesday through Saturday 5:30 to 11:30; Sunday 4:30 to 10:30. Closed Thanksgiving. Full bar. Reservations required. Visa, MC, AX, DC. Wheelchair access. Validated parking behind restaurant. Casual to semi-dressy.

---

## PERINO'S
4101 Wilshire Boulevard
Los Angeles    **Map 7**

Continental/American
★
(213)383-1221

Forty-four years ago Alex Perino opened a restaurant of such consequence that it would become an epicurean landmark throughout the world. That it remains so is not only a tribute to the old maestro (he retired several years ago), but also to the staff, which carries on with a passion for perfection that is as much a part of Perino's as the damask-covered walls. Within the subtle magnificence of the circular dining room, beneath the massive crystal chandeliers, the ageless art of elegant dining resembles a living tapestry. The muted colors, tall silver wine buckets, fresh flowers, gleaming crystals, and impeccably correct headwaiters combine to create a general aura of well-being that exists in no more than a dozen grand establishments in the United States. The Perino patrons, like the restaurant, have an air of relaxed unostentatious wealth. They would have to, because they pay a high price for what they consider the ultimate in cuisine and personal service. For others it is a restaurant of special occasions where one can still dine, as I dine, as I did, on oysters Mornay, saddle

513

of lamb, and perfect Grand Marnier soufflé, or any of the 170 dishes on the menu, with the knowledge that all have been prepared from fresh raw materials in a kitchen where experience is measured by the decade. During a recent luncheon I found myself in that state of exultant well-being that accompanies the last of a bottle of Chateau d'Yquem and a dessert of fresh strawberries. I complimented the waiter and asked if he had noticed any significant changes since the founder departed. "No," he said, waving his arm to encompass the kitchen, the dining room, and lounge. "Here, now, we are all Perino."

**Expensive.** Open Monday through Saturday. Luncheon from 11:30 a.m. to 5 p.m. weekdays. Dinner from 5 to 11 p.m.; Saturday until midnight. Entertainment. Full bar. Reservations advised. All major credit cards. Valet parking. Dressy.

---

## PHILIPPE THE ORIGINAL
1001 North Alameda Street
Los Angeles        **Map 7**

Deli/French dip
DA★
(213)628-3781

A great old place in its sixty-ninth year near the Union Station (remember passenger trains?), where hordes of the hungry line up at the long counter and order the world-famous French-dip sandwiches made with your choice of beef, ham, pork, or lamb; homemade stew, soup, salads, chili and beans, pickled hardboiled eggs, and the like. Then they take their trays to long tables for some serious eating. Most of the trade isn't here because it's cheap, but because it's good. Coffee is still 10 cents! The atmosphere is fun, too.

**Inexpensive.** Open seven days. Breakfast from 6 to 10:30 a.m. Lunch and dinner from 10 a.m. to 10 p.m. Closed Thanksgiving, Christmas. Wine and beer only. No reservations. Parking available. Casual.

## PIERO'S SEAFOOD HOUSE    Seafood/Italian

2825 West Olive Street    ★
Burbank    **Map 1**    (213) 842-5159

Piero's kitchen is supervised by its namesake and his mother, who cooked for King Umberto, Italy's last king. Seafood is one of Italy's national glories, so the specialties of this restaurant come naturally. One such is the Neptune Sea Chest consisting of chunks of lobster, crab, shrimp and scallops sauteed with shallots and mushrooms in a light wine sauce with spices. Traditional Italian dishes *fettuccini* Alfredo and Provimi veal are to be had in the relaxing low-lit atmosphere. A special Sunday dinner from 5:30 to 10:30 p.m. at a fixed price of $25 includes all the wine and champagne you wish.

**Moderate.** Open seven days. Luncheon from 11 a.m. to 3 p.m. weekdays. Dinner Monday through Thursday 5 to 10:30 p.m.; to 11:30 Friday, Saturday; 5 to 10 Sunday. Closed Easter, Thanksgiving, Christmas. Full bar. Reservations recommended. Patios, covered and open. All major credit cards. Small parking lot; street parking. Semi-dressy.

## PIKE'S VERDUGO OAKS    American/Continental

1010 North Glendale Avenue    ★
Glendale    **Map 7**    (213) 246-5655

This type of operation is more prevalent in California than anywhere else. It's virtually a fine department store of dining with banquet rooms to accommodate the sales meetings, bar mitzvahs, and wedding receptions of the Glendale communities. In the public dining rooms there is nothing on the huge menu (there are nearly forty entrées) that is exquisite or by any stretch of the imagination (and palate) *haute cuisine*; but I get the feeling that it's not intended to be. Rather, there is an air of professionalism throughout — manifesting the good taste of the late owner Jack Pike — from the dance-entertainment lounge to the lovely public rooms and the banquet facilities. Buffet luncheons and dinners are popular here.

**Moderate.** Open seven days. Luncheon daily from 11:30 a.m. to 4 p.m. Dinner from 4 to 11 p.m. Sunday through Thursday; to midnight Friday, Saturday. Sunday brunch 11 a.m. to 2:30 p.m. Banquet facilities. Children's menu. Entertainment. Full bar. Reservations advised. Bank cards only. Valet or self-parking. Semi-dressy.

---

## PINK'S FAMOUS CHILI DOGS

711 North La Brea Avenue
Los Angeles     **Map 7**

Hot Dogs
★
(213) 931-4223

There are those who quite seriously believe these to be the greatest hot dogs in the world. Of course they're wrong. The greatest hot dog in the world is served at _____ (fill in your own favorite place). But this **could** be the third best hot dog (the second best being the legendary Coney Island red-hot steamers). Chili dogs are really their specialty. There are hamburgers and tamales as well, but I've never seen even Paul L. Pink eat one of those, and he owns the place.

**Inexpensive.** Open seven days from 8 a.m. to 3 a.m. Closed Thanksgiving, Christmas. Parking available. No reservations. No credit cards. Casual.

---

*In order to obtain the best results from this Guide, please consult "Tips on Dining Out" on page 21.*

## PINOCCHIO WEST                    Italian Deli
1333 Santa Monica Boulevard                    ★
Santa Monica          **Map 2**          (213) 394-2554

## MONTE CARLO'S PINOCCHIO
3103 West Magnolia Boulevard
Burbank          **Map 1**          (213) 849-5632

## PINOCCHIO WESTWOOD
1084 Glendon Avenue
Westwood          **Map 8**          (213) 208-4663

California seems to encourage the combination of Italian deli and restaurant, each a separate business operating within the same walls. These are for real with sausages that sound like the lyrics to an Italian opera: mortadella, zampone, salami, cotechino. Italian wines are in evidence everywhere, in every corner, and there're pizza pasta, with thin breadsticks (*grissini*) and cheeses: fontina, gongozola, parmigiano, asiago, fresh mozzarella, and ricotta. Fun to say and fun to eat.

**Inexpensive to moderate.** Open seven days (Westwood open Monday through Saturday only) from 11 a.m. to 9 p.m. Monday through Thursday; 5 to 10:30 p.m. Friday, Saturday; 4 to 9 p.m. Sunday. Closed major holidays. Wine and beer only. No reservations. No credit cards. Parking lot. Casual.

---

## PIONEER BOULANGERIE                    French
2012 South Main Street                    ★
Santa Monica          **Map 2**          (213) 399-1405

These are the folks who make a lot of big name French restaurants respectable: they bake the bread and other Gallic treasures. Now ensconced in their own restaurant, it almost seems as if they would not go into competition with any of the establishments that they provide. Certainly the prices are far lower as though the decimal point were moved one stop to the left. Yet everything is homemade—the half dozen soups, savory lamb, fresh fish and probably the richest stews extant. Boulangerie is typical of the large continental restaurants with window boxes and hanging baskets spilling with geraniums. There are even fresh flowers in the parking lot. Tuesday night is an adventure with a Basque menu. Their new upstairs room serves all Basque on a fixed menu. The wines are priced at retail plus $1, an intelligent approach that will ultimately sell much more wine and thus make more profit (if less on each bottle) than the "Mark it up, Charlie, here come the suckers" approach. Nice touch: you can watch the bakers at work and buy the savory breads. Buffet service.

**Inexpensive.** Open seven days from 11 a.m. to 9 p.m.; to 9:30 Friday, Saturday. Basque dinner served Tuesday at 7:30 p.m. for fixed priced of $9.75. Children's portions. Wine and beer only. Closed Easter, Thanksgiving, Christmas. Reservations essential in Basque room; no reservations necessary in other rooms. Patio open during lunch. No credit cards. Parking lot. Casual.

---

# PISCES
### 7640 El Camino Real
### Carlsbad

**Seafood**
★★★
(714) 436-9362

Marny De Vries is a graduate of the Hotel Industry School in Nice, and Pisces is the culmination of his acquired knowledge and objectivity. He has, in less than 10 years, created the second three star restaurant (Anthony's Star of the Sea) in the San Diego piscatoraial scene that is threatening to become second only to Boston for good seafood. The ambience—subdued colors, rich banquettes, gleaming crystal and fresh flowers—provides a setting for the *haute cuisine* of the kitchen. More fish than people arrive at the airports here—succulent mussels in a variety of presentations; rich chowders and a grand lobster bisque, nine (count 'em) variations of sole, Louisiana soft-shelled crab, scallops Florentine and much, much more. There are a half dozen souffles (try the lemon) and fresh fruit in and out of season.

**Expensive.** Open Thursday through Tuesday from 6 to 10 p.m. Closed Christmas. Full bar. Reservations recommended. Parking lot. Dressy; jackets required.

---

## PITRUZELLO'S                              Northern Italian
287 La Cadena Drive                                    ★
Riverside        **Map 5**              (714) 686-6787

Riverside is an improbable location for a memorable epicurean occasion; the last one on record was a feast (wild boar with turnips, roasted lamb, and five pies) to honor President William Howard Taft when he visited the Mission Inn during the heyday of both. But it was in South Riverside that we came upon Pitruzello's, a restaurant with a twilight zone ambience of old brick, stained glass, and statuary more gaudy than Getty. However, we've long pined for an oasis to break up the long drive twixt Los Angeles and resort destinations like Las Vegas, Palm Springs, and Arrowhead, and this is definitely it. Cuisine is Northern Italian imaginative. The "Three Musketeers" (for four) is a combination of chicken breast Albano, veal Francese, and New York pepper steak prepared with Academy Award drama at tableside. I haven't seen so much flambé since I was caught in an incendiary attack during one of our recent wars. On the gourmet list are *bagna cauda*, the traditional holiday feast of Northern Italy served fondue style, and all manner of pastas made from the recipes of Nana Pitruzzello, who still comes in frequently to check on things. Everything possible is homemade, and the wine list is among the most comprehensive I've seen. The night we were there, a single family occupied half of the spacious room. They had assembled from all over the world to celebrate the 50th anniversary of their grandparents. And celebrate they did, from five in the afternoon until nine at night, and they were, in a word, sloshed — but they were happy, God bless 'em. Luncheon is a favorite with civic organizations in the area — their flags are permanently hung in the banquet rooms. There is also dining on the patio during suitably sunny days. Prices are moderate, and the quality of the food is such that, if it were in Beverly Hills, it would draw raves from the discerning critics of the area. The wine shop sells at retail, and case prices are shown on the wine list if you should stumble across a vintage that you simply must take home. Gourmets and gourmands are advised that their own game — properly and legally obtained, of course — will be prepared upon adequate notice to the kitchen. Pitruzello's Continental Cuisine is located right off the Riverside Freeway. You can see it clearly, and the easiest way to get there is to take the Center Street offramp. The experience is worth the drive.

**Moderate to expensive.** Open seven days. Luncheon from 11:30 a.m. to 3 p.m. weekdays. Dinner from 5 to 10 p.m. Sunday brunch from 10:30 a.m. to 2:30 p.m. Closed Christmas, July 4. All major credit cards. Semi-dressy to dressy.

---

## PIZZA TIME THEATRE                                  Pizza
(Everywhere. See phone book for listings.)

A computer company has achieved what mere mortals couldn't: the perfect and badly needed children's restaurant. Pizza Time Theatre is the brainchild of Nolan K. Bushnell, a pioneer in video games. (He invented Pong). The fun and games parlors have three dimensional computer-controlled characters plus a dazzling array of electronic and arcade games, along with their pizza and sandwiches. The dining room shows run every eight minutes with characters like Dolli Dimples, a life-sized computer-animated hippopotamus that sings old standards and show tunes at the piano bar. Chuck E. Cheese—a costumed employee—appears at regular intervals to greet honored guests. Most of the characters go into hysterical frenzies at the idea of birthdays and other parties, while a number of four foot animated characters look on from their shelves above the diners.

This is handled as well and with as much class as a Disneyland attraction, and the food is at least average if not better. Having the figures computerized is probably the only way an operation like this could succeed, minimum wages being what they are. Another benefit of computerized help is that Jasper T. Jowls, the Mopsey Sisters, Mr. Munch and Dolli won't get temperamental or call in sick.

**Inexpensive to moderate.** Hours differ at various locations. Entertainment. Wine and beer only. Visa, MC. Casual.

---

**THE PLAYBOY CLUB**                      **American**
2020 Avenue of the Stars                        ★
Century City       **Map 8**            (213) 277-2777

That Hugh Hefner has managed to survive this enlightened age is a miracle of public relations and general obfuscation that rivals Barnum at his Phineast. Perhaps the Playboy clubs were relevant once—so was Captain Billy's Whiz Bang—but now they are simply tacky, idiotic, and, fortunately, fading. That Mr. Hefner still manages to survive as the Nadia Comaneci of chauvinism and guru of men's morals and machine-washables is a subject more suitable for a sociologist. But for me, the occasion marking the anniversary of the founding of the Los Angeles Playboy Club in Century City required some sort of comment. It is, after all, an institution. I arrived on this momentous evening to find the lobby looking ever so much like a penthouse from an old Doris Day movie, jammed with photographers, a B list of celebrities, "with-it" young stockbroker and lawyer keyholders and, of course, the ubiquitous Bunnies. They are presided over by grim, if not ferocious, "Bunny mothers," a euphemism for the combination teachers ("A Bunny shall not chew gum") and duennas ("A Bunny must not date a member"). The latter rule, I suspect, is as much to protect the image of the Bunnies as scintillating symbols of the feminine ideal—the Bunnies we saw seemed to carry their intellect in their silly cotton puff tails—as their morals. Besides, the club sells a plaque complete with Bunny tail and the inscription, "I caught it at the Playboy Club." The food in the opulently appointed dining room is actually rather good, although the selections are limited to beef-and-lobster fare. The entertainment, consisting largely of one time "names" who played the Playboy circuit of clubs and hotels, is inoffensive and bland. "These cats don't want no real stuff," an ancient jazz pianist complained. "They want us to sound like their tapes." Even though he had become a Muzak man, the money was steady, and he could wail after hours if he wasn't too tired. But members still sign up at $25 a key for the privilege of ogling the mammaries of girls without typing skills, and buying official Playboy memorabilia from the giftshop Bunny.

**Expensive.** Open Monday through Saturday. Luncheon from 11:30 a.m. to 2 p.m. weekdays. Dinner from 5:30 to 11:30 p.m. Closed major holidays. Entertainment. Full bar. Reservations recommended on weekends. All major credit cards. Non-validated parking. Casual.

---

**PLAZA FOUR**                                    Continental
2020 Avenue of the Stars                              ★
Century City          **Map 8**           (213) 556-2111

Plaza Four is that kind of New York Italian — smart, sophisticated, innovative — that ultimately had to find its way across country. Following the trend away from plush red velvet and crystal, Plaza Four (there are four partners, and it's on the Shubert plaza, *capisce?*) manages to be smart without being ostentatious; it's obvious that their trust in decorator Pepe Mathieu was not misplaced. The rooms are large and the aisles wide enough to facilitate Russian service with many dishes prepared at the table. An entire wall is banked with Roman shades, full-length draperies with a louvered effect. The room is a subtle blend of earth tones, from booths to table settings to fabrics. Chilled bay scallops with avocado was a welcome departure from the usual sea-food cocktail. Other appetizers included zesty seafood gazpacho and a silky-smooth cold cucumber soup with just a hint of fresh mint. *Linguini carbonara* has become an early favorite: but best of all, in my not-so-humble opinion, is the fish monger's stew, a piscatory paradise that includes clams, mussels, shrimp, scallops, and deep-water fish in a savory broth. The Caesar salad is deftly executed. Desserts are . . . my God, they are splendid. I mean, how about hot fresh pineapple served over ice cream, or real (and Easterners know what I mean) New York cheesecake? To top the list of improbables (remember the axiom about good food and entertainment?), there is dancing to live music — thankfully away from the dining area — every night but Monday; it has become kind of the date shake of the area. Plaza Four is moderate to expensive, but it's well worth the tab. The luncheon menu is less expensive, more given to omelettes and hash and salads, but all served with flair. Be sure to tell them if you're going to the Schubert so they can get you out in time. Call for the times when they book superstars like Bobby Short.

**Moderate to expensive.** Open Monday through Saturday. Luncheon from 11:30 a.m. to 3 p.m. weekdays. Dinner from 5:30 to 10 Monday through Thursday; 6 to 10 Friday, Saturday. Closed major holidays. Piano bar; disco after 10. Full bar. Reservations recommended. All major credit cards. Validated parking. Semi-dressy.

---

## PLUM TREE INN · Chinese

937 North Hill Street · ★
Los Angeles · **Map 7** · (213) 613-1819

A new Chinese restaurant in Chinatown is not necessarily news, but one of this stature is notable. The atmosphere is not luxurious by any standards but the rooms are colorful and well-lit, the service sure and swift, and the food is good. Dishes like squid in *sha cha* sauce, Hunan-style lamb, crab meat and asparagus soup, assorted seafood in sizzling rice, Szechwan shredded chicken and scallops in black bean sauce will give you an idea of their kitchen's range. We were the only Occidentals there during our visits and the Chinese we saw were far from stereotypical: young girls in jeans and Italian-designer glasses, Chinese businessmen in three-piece Brooks Brothers presiding at their family gatherings and smartly dressed ladies playing cards after dinner. Mark, the proprietor-chef, will be glad to order for you.

**Moderate.** Open seven days. Luncheon from 11:30 a.m. to 3 p.m. weekdays. Dinner from 5 to 10 p.m. Monday through Friday; 11:30 a.m. to 10:30 p.m. Saturday, Sunday. Full bar. Reservations recommended. Visa, MC. Parking lot. Casual.

---

## POLICE ACADEMY American

Los Angeles Police & Revolver Athletic Club ★
1880 North Academy Drive
Los Angeles          **Map 7**                    (213) 222-9137

The Police Academy is one of the real "finds" in this book. Conveniently located just a few minutes from downtown, they serve great breakfasts and luncheons. Those who into atmosphere will be glad this place is open to the public, for the Academy is a world within our world, almost like a retreat or a great old military officers club. Here is where the cops eat their good, hot, hearty chow, and the public receives the same wholesome fare. The inside man on this deal is Pete Guzzeti, who feels quite at home on his range. He was the chef at the Sportsman's Lodge in the San Fernando Valley when it was one of the top restaurants around. At one time, you could catch your own trout in the privately stocked streams right on the grounds of the Lodge, and the chef would prepare it any way you chose.

Breakfast prices are from the twilight zone which is fitting since they open at the twilight zone hour of 6:00 a.m. to serve the "joggers delight." The luncheon menu has a large selection of salads and a salad bar is available for those other-than-salad entrées. And entrées they have by the dozen, from Southern fried chicken to broiled halibut, although your best bet is usually Pete's Special. On my visit, this special consisted of braised short ribs of beef served with creamy mushroom soup and fresh vegetables.

Most exciting of all are the private party facilities. Unlike most public restaurants, they provide bar service for weddings, business meetings, pre-Dodger get-togethers, or whatever. The private room is paneled in rich wood, and one of the windows overlooks a miniature Sequoia. At luncheon banquets you can select from a wide variety of dishes. Banquet dinners include a tossed green salad, your choice of two dressings, potato, rolls, beverage and light dessert. The outdoor rock garden and waterfalls make a serene setting for weddings or barbecues. All baking is done on the premises and the decorated sheet cakes are a specialty. It's non-profit, so you'll get one of the best values in the whole Southern California basin. The necessarily masculine decor of the lunchroom includes historic photos of the police department that date back to the turn of the century.

**Inexpensive.** Open Tuesday through Friday. Banquet facilities. Breakfast and lunch from 7 a.m. to 3 p.m. Dinner from 4:30 to 9:30 p.m. Full bar. No reservations. No credit cards. Parking lot. Casual.

---

**POLO LOUNGE**          **Continental/American**
9641 Sunset Boulevard            **DA★**
Beverly Hills     **Map 8**        (213) 276-2251

Times and tithes may change, but the Polo Lounge has been the super-swinging celebrity social center since 1912, and it shows no signs of changing. It's a place to be seen in, if you are sufficiently high on the pecking order to merit a favorable location. There are gorgeous girls, gorgeous girl-watchers, and important show-biz types talking on the plug-in phones or closing some big package. F. Scott Fitzgerald fell off a bar stool twice here (once he was pushed), and John Barrymore claimed to have created the polo mural behind the bar. Luncheon is the only real meal served in these august rooms and on the charming patio — and, surprisingly, the food is really good. There are daily specials like chicken-filled crêpes and generous luncheon salads (the "Beverly Hills" is best) and a selection of exceptional sandwiches, including the Polo-ground sirloin.

**Expensive.** Open seven days. Luncheon from noon to 2:30 p.m. Supper 10:30 p.m. to 1 a.m. Sunday brunch from noon to 2:30 p.m. Banquet facilities. Evening piano entertainment. Full bar. Reservations required. Patio. All major credit cards. Valet parking. Dressy.

---

## THE PONDEROSA

**American**
★

10900 West Jefferson Boulevard
Culver City          **Map 3**          (213) 391-5206

Since 1967 they have been serving up one of the squarest deals in town — one price for a gargantuan buffet including roast turkey, baked ham, corned beef, and ribs, with seconds encouraged, and dessert. Decor is kind of plastic cowboy, but there's a feeling of warmth.

**Moderate.** Open seven days. Luncheon from 11:30 a.m. to 2:30 p.m. weekdays. Dinner from 5 to 10 p.m. Monday through Thursday; to 11 Friday; 4:30 to 11 Saturday; 1 to 10 Sunday for a fixed price of $6.95. Full bar. Reservations recommended for lunch only. Visa, MC, AX. Parking in front. Casual.

---

*Please be sure to consult "Tipping Made Easy" on page 25 of this Guide.*

## PONTEVECCHIO

**Northern Italian**

2518 Wilshire Boulevard
Santa Monica       **Map 2**                    (213) 829-1112

Mr. Zaretti, owner of the successful little L'Etoile in West
Hollywood, doesn't have it all together here. Atmosphere is
cold, the kitchen inconsistent, and the service slack. It is
obvious that there were lofty goals in mind and maybe
they'll be achieved, but not now.

**Moderate.** Open Tuesday through Sunday from 5:30 to 11
p.m. Beer and wine only. Reservations suggested. Visa, MC,
AX. Wheelchair access. Parking lot; valet on weekends.
Casual to semi-dressy.

---

## PORTS O' CALL

**Polynesian**

Berth 76
San Pedro       **Map 3**                       (213) 833-3553

One of the finest sea goings-on views, this tourist oriented
restaurant lets you watch freighters, tugs, yachts and
foam-waked pleasure craft with harbor helicopters hovering
overhead. At least, it's visually delicious. It is a gustatory
misadventure. It isn't that the brochettes and curries and
spare ribs are bad; they're not. They're just close to that
bland twilight zone that approximates the food in a
convalescent hospital. If the lights were out, you would
know you were eating something, but you probably couldn't
identify it.

**Moderate.** Open seven days. Luncheon served 11:30 a.m. to
3 p.m. Monday through Saturday. Dinner 3:30 to 11 p.m.
Sunday brunch 10:30 a.m. to 2 p.m. Closed Christmas.
Terrace. Reservations suggested. All major credit cards.
Parking lot. Casual.

## PRESIDENTE RESTAURANT

**Mexican**
★

11451 Sepulveda Boulevard
Mission Hills   **Map 1**                     (213) 365-7153

There's a lot to be learned from menus. Recently, I read that the tortilla was discovered by the Aztecs. It seems they used them as frisbees until a young Indian accidentally caught one in his mouth and found it delicious. At the impressive Presidente Restaurant in Mission Hills, the ten-page menu includes the traditional fare — albondigas soup, chicken tacos, tamales, and various mundane combinations — but then it veers upwards into relatively uncharted gustatory constellations in the Mexican galaxy: exotica like broiled salmon steak, crab relleno Vera Cruz (filled with crabmeat, topped with melted cheese, sour cream, black olives, and avocado slices), all served with beans or rice. There's even a salad list including an awesome "Ensalad Presidente" for $3 that's made with julienned ham, cheddar and jack cheese, chopped hard-boiled eggs, tomatoes, and avocados on lettuce on a tortilla shell. Best of all, there is a bouillabaisse, a potpourri of seafood and herbs in a delicate broth. Bob Jimenez, who would look at home on the French Riviera, helped design the massive multilevel premises with good taste and understated elegance rarely displayed in a Mexican restaurant. Raised banks of booths enclosed in wrought iron surround the central seating area and the stage where entertainers perform Tuesday through Saturday.

**Inexpensive.** Open seven days. Luncheon from 11 a.m. to 5 p.m. Dinner 5 to 10:30 p.m. Monday, Tuesday; to 11 Sunday, Wednesday through Thursday; to midnight Friday, Saturday. Children's menu. Closed Thanksgiving, Christmas, New Year's. Entertainment. Full bar. No reservations. Visa, MC, AX. Wheelchair access. Parking lot. Casual.

## PRINCE OF WALES GRILLE

**Continental/French**

Hotel Del Coronado

★

Coronado

(714) 435-6611

Hotel Del Coronado, last of the extravagantly conceived seaside hotels, stands like a monument to the opulence of the 1800s. Amid her turrets, cupolas, Victorian gingerbread roofs, and promenade gardens, there are several restaurants that strive to perpetuate the ritualistic service and lavish cuisine of those halcyon years — a time when people knew how to be rich, were not ashamed of it, and indulged themselves in proud magnificence. It was here that the dashing, impetuous Edward, Prince of Wales, met Wallis Warfield Simpson (at that time she was Mrs. Earl Spencer, and it would be many years before they met again) at a never-to-be-forgotten ball, a glittering affair that stunned Southland society. (It was reported that a half-dozen of the ladies fashionably swooned in the imperial presence, although another explanation might be the tightly corseted fashions of the time). Certainly it was a historic episode, and it became the premise for the restaurant. Red leather booths, heavy carved shields, stained-glass windows, and crystal chandeliers create an elegantly understated atmosphere at the Prince of Wales Grille, where graceful captains serve bountiful cuisine in high style. Dishes on the à la carte menu are splendid to behold. An appetizer of smoked salmon garni is as pink and artfully arranged as a float in the Rose Parade. Salads are tossed with the vigorously controlled gestures of Leonard Bernstein. Entrées, mostly familiar beef and lobster dishes, are presented with the sense of underplayed drama that seems to permeate the room. The crown roast rack of lamb was excellent and the fresh vegetables firm and flavorful. Our captain wisely recommended a baked potato in place of the garish mashed variety, which were dyed green and red in a garland of imitation roses. (Sometimes artistic license can go a bit too far.) The filet of veal à la Oscar was fine, attributable to a superior Béarnaise. Desserts include crêpes suzette and cherries jubilee. All in all, the Prince of Wales Grille offers no surprises, but presents itself with confidence and unusual care.

**Expensive.** Open seven days. Dinner from 6 to 9:30 p.m. Monday through Thursday; to 10:30 Friday, Saturday. Closed Thanksgiving, Christmas. Full bar. Reservations recommended. All major credit cards. Wheelchair access. Valet parking. Casual.

---

## PRINCESS LOUISE RESTAURANT     Continental
Berth 94                                            ★
San Pedro       **Map 3**                         (213) 831-2351

If there is a principal rule of eating out, it's "Don't dine at a tourist attraction." (This would be second only to warnings against restaurants that have dancing.) Thus, the *S.S. Princess Louise* was a ship I really didn't want to board. I had visions of rubbery steak and slippery lobster served by a crew wearing costumes left over from a high school production of *HMS Pinafore*. Happily, I was mistaken. From the moment I ascended the gangplank, I knew I was on a real ship, not a vessel converted into museums, hotels, and tap-dancing schools. From the slight list to the feeling of faded luxury—worn carpeting, wooden railings buffed by many hands, ancient draperies—there is somehow the excitement of imminent departure, as though all visitors might be ordered ashore at any moment. The restaurant is excellent by tourist-attraction standards, good by any other. I waited an additional twenty minutes to secure a table on the port side with a dramatic view of the busiest harbor on the West Coast. The starboard side has a less dramatic view of the busy parking lot. Dinners are moderately priced and include a fresh relish dish, choice of soup (gazpacho was good), tossed or spinach salad, entrée, beverage, and a selection from the pastry tray. Bouillabaisse, rack of lamb, mahi mahi macadamia, and crêpes of English sole were all above average. There is no admission charge for browsing, and that's a marvelous way to entertain the children while waiting for your call. There are the captain's and first mate's quarters, the wireless room, and staterooms, along with shops purveying quality merchandise. There is a display of the British crown jewels in replica that is educational, but could hardly be mistaken for the real thing. However, a real wedding can be performed in the ship's chapel. The restaurant is popular for luncheon among the locals, a usually reliable recommendation. There are numerous banquet rooms, a good bar, and a swinging dance lounge with gentle rock from 9 p.m. to 2 a.m.

**Moderate.** Open seven days. Luncheon from 11:30 a.m. to 3 p.m. weekdays; noon to 3 Saturday. Dinner 5:30 to 10 p.m. Monday through Thursday; to 11 Friday; to midnight Saturday; 4 to 10 Sunday. Sunday brunch 11 a.m. to 3 p.m. Children's menu. Closed Christmas. Piano bar. Full bar. Reservations recommended. All major credit cards. Valet parking; self-parking. Casual to dressy.

---

## PRONTO RISTORANTE                    Northern Italian
3333 Bristol Street                                          ★
(South Coast Plaza)
Costa Mesa          **Map 4**                    (714) 540-8038

Mr. John Lopes, the guiding force behind Pronto Ristorante, needed all of his acumen and experience absorbed from the Dorchester Hotel in London and the lovely Restaurant Folclore in Lisbon to survive the early wobblies that afflicted this stunning Northern Italian establishment. Orange County has long been the killer reef of restaurateurs who looked longingly at the demographics and thought all they had to do was open their doors.

With the *caveat* that all that melts in the mouth adds bulge to the stomach, you may revel in the homemade *fettuccine* ("Napoletana" with tomato sauce or *alla Bolognese*, with meat sauce); exclaim over the fresh idea salads and gorge on desserts like *zuppa Inglese*. As for me, I'll settle for the *fettuccine carbonara di pesce*, a masterful concoction of butter, heavy cream, smoked fish, Parmesan and red caviar. Of course, I would first have a half order of *scampi* "Pronto" sautéed in

531

garlic butter with fresh tomatoes and *calamari fritti*.

Happy hour at the Pronto is a jarring confrontation between the young execs and classic cuisine, but Pronto copes with a most elegant buffet of hot and cold hors d'oeuvres at fiveish—kind of a sampler of what to expect at dinner. Sunday brunch is a buffet as well, with 50 dishes from fresh roasted turkey and ham to eggs Florentine and flounder filet almondine, accompanied by freshly baked breads and pastries for $10, including champagne.
pagne.

**Moderate.** Open seven days. Luncheon from 11:30 a.m. to 2:30 p.m. Monday through Saturday. Dinner Sunday and Monday 5:30 to 8:30 p.m.; Tuesday through Thursday to 9:30; Friday and Saturday to 10:30. Sunday brunch buffet 10 a.m. to 3 p.m. Closed July 4, Christmas, New Year's. Full bar. Reservations suggested. Visa, MC, AX, DC. Wheelchair access. Valet parking. Casual; no shorts.

---

## THE PROPHET

**Vegetarian**
★

4461 University Avenue
San Diego
(714) 283-7448

At first glance this looks like a No-No. No meat. No fowl. No fish. No smoking. No booze. No credit cards. No matter, there are more fresh vegetables than you knew existed perfectly prepared in a Chinese wok and seasoned with taste. Add to that string of choices a soup, a kitchen sink salad, and hot-from-the-oven muffins. Don't be fooled into thinking that no alcohol means no appetizers. There is a fine selection to be accompanied by a no-hangover brew such as ginseng cocktail, for instance. This is truly a place to enjoy. Enjoy it even more by asking for one of the compartments with cushions on the floor, for private meditation.

**Inexpensive.** Open Tuesday through Sunday. Luncheon from 11:30 a.m. to 2:30 p.m. weekdays. Dinner from 5:30 to 10 p.m. Live music nightly. Non-alcoholic bar. Reservations for large parties only. Parking in lot after 6 p.m. Casual.

# PUERTA DEL SOL

**Mexican**
★

11669 Sherman Way
North Hollywood     **Map 1**     (213)982-1336

★
219 North Central Avenue
Glendale     **Map 7**     (213) 246-8296

California and many of the Western states are blessed with so many good Mexican restaurants it is difficult to list them all in any single guidebook. The restaurants appear in three categories: a variation of the taco stand; a modest establishment with emphasis on tamales, enchiladas and burritos; and the major ones with a wider bill of fare and a bit more atmosphere. Puerta del Sol in North Hollywood and Glendale are not grand restaurants, as, say, the Los Arcos, or El Toritos, but they are honorable purveyors of Mexican food prepared and served well. It is relatively easy to dine for around $7 here; I counted 26 entrées and combinations in that price range including rice and beans and tortillas. I had "number 9," a combination of chile Colorado, *chile verde, ropa vieja* (lean shredded beef with onions, peppers and tomatoes), sautéed chicken with vegetables, rice, beans, and sour cream. The homemade salsa and some corn tortillas rounded out a more than ample dinner (not counting a few good margaritas and some Carta Blanca). I like these restaurants for lunch instead of the usual champagne brunch. The *huevos con chorizo*, eggs scrambled with Mexican style sausage, were a delight, and there were four omelettes, including one made with ripe avocado and cheese in a special sauce that was very good. These are attractive restaurants and it is nice to know that you can have a large luncheon salad at the Glendale location or a complete luncheon of eight entrées for an exceedingly modest price. The bar is efficient, the atmosphere colorful and casual and the waiters friendly. Children would be welcomed here.

**Inexpensive.** Open seven days. Luncheon from 11 a.m. to 3 p.m. Sunday through Friday. Dinner 3 to 10 p.m. Sunday through Thursday; to 11:30 Friday, Saturday. Children's menu. Entertainment. Full bar. Reservations recommended. All major credit cards. Parking lot. Casual.

*To obtain the best results from this Guide, be sure to consult maps on the various Southern California areas in the front of the book.*

# q

## THE QUIET WOMAN
**Continental**

3224 East Coast Highway
Corona del Mar **Map 4** (714) 640-7440

The original public house of this name is located in Oxford-shire, England. About 1680, so legend relates, the tavern owner left his wife alone overnight whilst he gamboled with the boys. She, upon hearing a noise in the kitchen, quietly crept down the stairs, quietly picked up an iron skillet, and quietly killed the intruder, who turned out to be the infamous highwayman, Black Jack. Unfortunately, the legend is the most interesting part of this ordinary dinner house that has never really lived up to expectations.

**Moderate.** Open seven days. Luncheon from 11 a.m. to 3 p.m. weekdays. Dinner from 5 to 10 p.m. Sunday brunch from 10:30 a.m. to 2:30 p.m. Entertainment. Full bar. Reservations only for large parties. All major credit cards. Valet parking. Casual.

# r

---

**THE RANCH HOUSE**
102 Besant Road
Ojai

**Continental**
★★
(805) 646-2360

Situated in the middle of a vegetable garden beside a little
brook, this old inn is particularly appealing to health food
fanatics, although the cuisine is sophisticated French-Continental. The vegetables are extraordinarily fresh with that added
touch of flavor that can only come from just-picked. The waitress recites the menu and points out the dishes that are particularly good that day. Curried mushrooms are a rare and
zesty appetizer. Cream of fresh pea soup was full-bodied and
aromatic. The filet of sole Florentine is served with fresh spinach
in a rich but rather uninteresting cheese sauce. A dish that was
unavailable on the occasion of our visits is pork *cointreau*
(available only on weekends). I had read that it is a slice of
sirloin steak baked between two slices of pork roast and served
with an orange sauce. Desserts are homemade, and I like the
fudge pie.

**Expensive.** Open Wednesday through Sunday. Dinner seatings at 6 and 8:30 p.m. Sunday dinner also served at 1 and 3:30 p.m. Entertainment. Wine and beer only. Reservations required. Patio. Visa, MC, AX. Parking lot. Casual.

---

## RANGOON RACQUET CLUB

9474 Little Santa Monica Boulevard
Beverly Hills   **Map 8**

Indian-British
★★
(213) 272-1494

Back in the glamour days before "Smoke Gets in Your Eyes" was a weather report, when movie stars drove Cords and Pierce Arrows, there were clubs like this one offering the best possible victuals with more than a dash of whimsy. Michael Romanoff's was the last of such exclusive watering holes... last, that is, until the Rangoon Racquet Club was started seven years ago by a group of investors who were lucky enough to find Manny Zwaaf.

Zwaaf, the amiable general manager of this enterprise, rose from the ranks of the legendary Restaurant Associates of New York where he nursed to life legends of the culinary art/business. He is an unrelenting perfectionist and a people charmer, not a bad combination to deal with the temperaments of the territory.

The decor consists of white ceiling fans, vertical brass railings and framed Victorian regimental photographs. Waiters are dressed in white colonial costumes, complete with golden epaulets.

When Rangoon first opened, critics said it would be a single season's success. They did not reckon, however, with Zwaaf's insistence on gorgeous food. Zwaaf has two separate chefs, one for lunch and one for dinner, so that neither is an echo of the other.

The dinner menu is eclectic if nothing else. There are 18 hors d'oeuvres in addition to the complimentary kosher pickles at each table. Rollmops in white wine with cracked green peppercorn and Dutch potato salad ($5.75), cracked Dungeness crab ($10), and Little Smorgas, a platter of smoked salmon and trout on toast with fresh horseradish and sour cream sauce ($10), are among the tasty beginnings.

The R.R.C. entrées—and there are two daily specials—include the Bengal Lancer (shrimp, chicken, beef, lamb, pork, scallops, sweet/sour and curry sauce, banana and seafood fritters, $18.50) as well as a splendid seafood curry, featuring shrimp, scallops, crab, squid, yellow rice and seafood fritters ($19.75). The curry dishes are served with the appropriate condiments and an array of chutney, ranging from hot to hotter to hottest. On the evening of my visit, the specials were a sautéed filet of white fish Provençal ($17.25) and a curry of lamb Rangoon ($16.75). There is also Woody's World Championship Chili ($13.25) for those who wish a more colonial taste.

. For luncheon there is a Center Court Salad with ham, cheese, chicken, shrimp, tomato and eggs ($6.75); tiny shrimp in an artichoke with cocktail Chantilly sauce ($8.25); as well as an assortment of sandwiches, burgers, eggs and specials.

One of the decorative desserts on both the luncheon and dinner menus is the bombe Pavlova (for two); ice cream, strawberries, triple sec, almonds, Chantilly—a delectable concoction.

**Expensive.** Open Monday through Saturday. Luncheon from 11:30 a.m. to 2 p.m. weekdays. Dinner from 6 to 11 p.m. Late night menu available 11 p.m. to 12:30 a.m. Full bar. Reservations required. All major credit cards. Valet parking evenings. Semi-dressy to dressy.

---

**RAPISARDI**                                           **Italian**
11919 West Pico Boulevard
Los Angeles          **Map 8**                    (213) 477-5043

Two knowledgeable, respected critics on the same restaurant: (Lois Dwan, Los Angeles *Times*): "It is a restaurant of honoroable intentions, housed in a stunningly beautiful building that is almost an art gallery... an extravagant, high-ceilinged room of marvelous space furnished with only a bar and a few tables... ignore the ruins. The restaurant is beautiful."

Bruce David Colen, *Los Angeles Magazine*: "This is how I imagine a very expensive, very clandestine pornographic book salon in Paris... must look. The amphitheatre-size bar area is deserted... rather lost looking bartender, a few lone patrons... equally lost... Captain leads us past... what appears to be the wall of a bombed farmhouse in Anzio."

The background: Dr. Carolyn Hays and her husband, Dr. Bernard Hall, both psychiatrists, met Franco Frachey, the maitre d' of the *S.S. Fairsea* on a voyage. The good doctors found they shared a love of Italian *alta cucina* and high art with Frachey—and if this were an old MGM flick, Mickey Rooney would be shouting: "Hey gang, we can put on our *own* show."

The project: to build the ultimate in Italian restaurants. Designer Leo Dardarian assembled the dazzling works of Alfio Rapisardi and his contemporaries and created what has become a *controversial* environment around them. "Controversial" may be an understatement. Cold, tomblike and pompous may be closer. The series of visual vignettes that appear in corners or at particular settings is not unlike a series of dramatic windows on the Via Veneto.

The food: ranges from Dwan's less-than-enthusiastic description to Colen's horror with a few adequate dishes (pastas, veal chop). It's almost like a put-on with Soupy Sales playing chef in the kitchen.

The prognosis: bleak at best. Not since the ill-fated La Roma di Notte on La Cienega Blvd. have we been promised so much and given so little. What makes it impossible is that the partners apparently *believe* this is the way a restaurant should be. The dishes are served with a flourish of pyrotechnical dimensions that only dramatizes their inadequacies. If (when?) this restaurant sinks slowly (quickly?) out of sight it would make a great wax museum.

**Expensive.** Open seven days. Luncheon 11:30 a.m. to 3

p.m. Monday through Friday. Dinner Tuesday through Sunday 5:30 to 11 p.m. Late supper to 2 a.m. Banquet facilities. Entertainment. Full bar. Reservations required. All major credit cards. Valet parking; self-parking. Dressy.

---

## THE RAYMOND RESTAURANT     Continental
1250 South Fair Oaks     ★★
Pasadena     **Map 7**     (213) 441-3136

One of the nicest trends in restauranting to emerge in recent years is the restoration of old homes. At least half of the restaurant is in Pasadena, the other half is in the incorporated community of South Pasadena. The restaurant was constructed within the framework of an old '30s bungalow. Walls are paneled in dark wood and floors are of varnished pine. There are old-fashioned stained booths and tables with gleaming white napery in the three small rooms. The wine bar is constructed with the wood workmanship that has all but disappeared, with the back bar doors fashioned from diagonal slats varnished and stained. The menu is no-fault. It's not intended to be pretentious but they manage to incorporate some innovative touches in appetizers like a crock of sautéed mushrooms in garlic butter or the artichoke hearts touched with anchovies. On our night the soup was cream of cabbage in a potato stock. Entrées include soup or salad and are reasonably priced from the chicken Dijon to the combination filet and scallops sautéed with veal in mustard sauce, or any of a half dozen other choices and specialties. The Raymond wisely eschews "homemade" desserts for delicacies like mousse pie from a splendid bakery. Luncheon is no less appealing with two outdoor patios in addition to the "house." The menu is somewhat abbreviated as you might expect with a selection of sandwiches, salads and specialties. The evening there was pure magic; it was rainy and cold and the little house's windows glowed with a hospitable welcome that bordered on the twilight zone. Once inside, the muted lighting, the photographs of how it used to be, and the fine fare with old-fashioned portions were contenting. If I was a cow I would have mooed. The wine list is Californian and intelligent. Beer is not neglected and is a fitting prelude to clear the palate of harried travelers. How nice it is to see such buildings and memories preserved instead of becoming obliterated at the first swipe of the wrecker's ball, and a cube erected in its place.

**Expensive.** Open Monday through Saturday. Luncheon from 11:30 a.m. to 2 p.m. Dinner Tuesday through Saturday from 6 to 10 p.m. Wine and beer only. Reservations advised. Patio. All major credit cards. Parking lot. Casual.

---

## RED BARN                                      American
8701 Van Nuys Boulevard
Panorama City          **Map 1**              (213) 894-5786

In searching for a restaurant that serves game—not freshly trapped game, of course; that's against the law in California—but dishes that still smack of having once—several generations—ago—lived in the wild, I went to the Red Barn imagining I'd find pheasant and boar and venison and quail, all commercially raised but still tasting of the hunt. All I could come up previously were a few restaurants with squab on the menu, a place in Tarzana that expected to have boar for Christmas and... at last the Red Barn.

The Red Barn is a good version of what dining is about, San Fernando Valley-style. In concept and at times in execution it's a pretty good place. But every time the meal is on the edge of kicking into a meaningful experience, it's spoiled by a plateful of some godawful horror, like the Red Barn's "cheese bread," which turns out to be a slice (one per person) of air bread with some salty cheese spread baked onto it. Not my idea of the sort of experience that expands your gustatory awareness.

But the point of the Red Barn is meat, and more particularly, game. The game dishes are "Royale Squab en

Casserole," roast mallard duck, Cornish game hen, quail, ringneck pheasant and buffalo steaks. Both the pheasants and the duck have to be ordered in advance. And, some day I'd like to take the time to order the duck and pheasant at the Red Barn, though I admit I'm more than a bit nervous about what they'd do to those innocent, yet gamey, birds. The quail, squab and game hens that I've tasted at the Red Barn seem to be cooked well enough, but the poor things are smothered in sauces that bury any vestige of their gamey flavor. I found the sauces can be cleaned off with some small difficulty, and that eating the birds dry with a mouthful of wild rice (the Red Barn is very into their wild rice) is a happy experience. I also found that eating anything with the Red Barn's cheese sauce, which is supplied on the side in a crock, is a very unhappy experience. The sauce, if I'm not mistaken, is made out of melted down rubber balls. It goes well only on the cheese bread, where it's best left abandoned. *M.S.*

**Moderate.** Open Monday through Thursday 11 a.m. to midnight; Friday and Saturday to 1 a.m.; Sunday 3 to 11 p.m. Closed Christmas. Full bar. Reservations accepted. All major credit cards. Parking lot. Casual.

---

## RED BARON STEAK HOUSE                    Steak
6951 Flight Road                                     ★
Riverside        **Map 5**                (714) 689-2003

A great idea that's spreading to airports all over; this is a World War I motif theme with the menu on a 105mm shell case. A T-33 jet canopy is used as the salad bar cover and the limited menu uses aviation nomenclature. The chain has spread to include Yucca Valley, Oxnard, San Jose, Livermore, Sacramento, Portland, and Seattle for folks who like good fly-ins for brunch, lunch, or dinner. The usual steaks and chops here, but it's fun and the rib bones are good.

**Moderate.** Open seven days. Luncheon from 11:30 a.m. to

2:30 p.m. Dinner from 5 to 10 p.m.; Friday, Saturday until 11 ap.m. Sunday brunch from 10:30 a.m. to 2:30 p.m. Limited banquet facilities. Closed Christmas. Live rock and roll band. Dancing. Full bar. No reservations. View of airport. Visa, MC, AX, DC. Parking lot. Casual.

## RED ONION                                          Mexican
(See phone book for listings)

Every guy remembers that voluptuous girl, that knockout who turned out to be a mental dud. Red Onions are like that, pretty on the outside, bland on the inside. Decor couldn't be lovelier, service is chain-cheerful. The bars are good at merchandising gimmick drinks, but the food on the massive menu isn't notable.

**Inexpensive to moderate.** Open seven days. Hours vary at each location. Open for lunch, dinner, Sunday brunch. Most locations have private party facilities. Children's menu. Full bar. Reservations recommended. Parking lot. All major credit cards. Casual.

## RED SAILS INN                                        Seafood
2614 Shelter Island Drive                                   ★
San Diego                                          (714)223-3030

Commercial fishermen make deliveries straight to the kitchen via the dock in this authentic on-the-waterfront atmosphere seasoned with local fishermen's tales — they eat here too. With that kind of "truck-stop" recommendation, it's no wonder Red Sails Inn has built up a stable winter crowd over the past 50 years. If you don't have time to linger, belly up to the oyster bar for a quick snack.

**Moderate.** Open seven days. Breakfast from 7 to 11:30 a.m. Luncheon 11:30 a.m. to 5. Dinner from 5 to midnight. Closed Thanksgiving, Christmas. Full bar. No reservations. Visa, MC, AX, DC. Parking across the street. Resort and casual.

## REGINA'S FOOD BOUTIQUE

371 North Western Avenue
Los Angeles      **Map 7**

**Argentinian-Italian**
★★
(213) 462-2525

Regina's stopped being El Gaucho Sarabia late last year, at which time it was transformed from an interesting asterisk of a restaurant into the kind of place I'm happy to bring visitors from out of town to show them the gastronomic wonders of Smogville. Regina's stopped being funky, and became something out of *Gentleman's Quarterly* or maybe *Architectural Digest*. The decor is magnificently clean, with tattersall walls off-setting a fine collection of *moderne* poster art. The colors are mostly blue and very cool; the service is witty; and the food is great.

Argentinian-Italian food seems to be firmly rooted in beef; there is a t-bone steak called *bife de costilla; churrasco a la pimienta* is a pepper steak; and *asado de tira* translates as rib tips. The steaks are large, though not thick, as is the Argentine style. The chef's hand at the grill is skillful, and best demonstrated on the house specialty (for two), the *parrillada crijolla Regina*, a dream of mixed grill combining flank ribs, skirt steak, sweetbreads (grilled! wonderful!), and Italian and German sausages. A magnificent platter that *really* separates the men from the vegetarians.

Aside from the beef dishes, Regina's is also at its best on the appetizer dishes—cold slices of breast of veal stuffed with eggs and pimentos, a bitingly astringent tongue in a vinaigrette sauce, one of the best *calamaretti fritti* I've ever come across, and *empanadas criollas* filled with meat and spice and the joy of Argentinian eating. With all this you can (and should) order Argentinian wine (which tastes Italian) with bottles of seltzer, blue bottles, like the type that used to be delivered to people's doors, back in a simpler day and time. *M.S.*

**Moderate.** Open Tuesday through Sunday. Luncheon 11:30 a.m. to 2:30 p.m. weekdays. Dinner from 5:30 to 11. Closed

Labor Day, Thanksgiving, Christmas, New Year's Eve. Beer and wine only. Reservations advised. V, MC. Street and lot parking. Casual.

---

## RENE'S                                              French
21418 Ventura Boulevard                                     ★
Woodland Hills      **Map 1**              (213) 887-9333

Woodland Hills abounds in good restaurants and Rene's is no exception. If it were any place else it would receive more attention, but it's another rose in the garden here. The veal is as well prepared as you'll find anywhere in the city, and the fact that it has become a favorite with such stiff competition means that the late Rene Duparc knew what he was doing, and Jean Marot continues the standard.

**Expensive.** Open Monday through Saturday. Luncheon from 11 a.m. to 2:30 p.m. weekdays. Dinner from 5:30 to 10:30 p.m. Wine and beer only. Reservations advised. Visa, MC, AX. Parking available. Casual.

---

## RENO'S                                             Mexican
1945 Eighth Street                                         ★★
Tijuana                                    (70-668) 385-9210

Gringos seem to feel that there is an underabundance of restaurants in the Tijuana area. This is not difficult to understand, given the often tacky appearance of bordertown nightlife (or day life, for that matter), and the don't-drink-the-water warnings given by well-meaning friends. But there are fine restaurants there, among the best in the Southland. One of these is Reno's, which has been around longer than anyone can remember. Small, intimate, and elegant with a magnificent chandelier, fine paintings, beautiful napery and fresh flowers, it excels at the art of serving. Good service is knowing precisely when — and when not — to serve. There is a thin line between attentive and obtrusive. Professional

545

waiters and captains seem born with that sense of timing that resembles choreography; the bad ones seem uncertain, overanxious, uninterested, or faltering, with their every comment an intrusion or a point killer. Reno's has all the good qualities and, seemingly, none of the bad. There appears to be two or more waiters in attendance at each table, and the dishes — lobster or shrimp ranchero or enchiladas or steak salsa — are pridefully presented in the manner of a magician producing a bouquet. The bar is precise in its formulae, although I like to drink the sangrita (not, for God's sake, the sangria) — a tall thin glass of good tequila, perhaps the Sauza golden variety, with a chaser of spicy hot tomato and lime juice. Be sure you pronounce the "t" in sangrita, or you'll be brought the sickly sweet abomination, the sangria of my nightmares.

**Inexpensive.** Open seven days. Monday through Thursday from 11 a.m. to 1 p.m., Friday through Sunday from 11 a.m. to 2 p.m. Closed Labor Day. Entertainment. Full bar. Reservations accepted. Visa, MC. Validated parking. Casual.

---

# RESTAURANT LA COSTA
Calle 7A #150
Tijuana

Mexican
★
(70-668) 385-8494

This is my favorite special occasion restaurant in Tijuana since it is moderately priced and always dependable. It's an unpretentious seafood restaurant with overtones of old San Francisco and helpful, genial waiters. Everything is fresh as you might expect in Mexico, and the white fish *à la Veracruzana* and the shrimp *Costa Azul* are specialties. They're open till midnight and you'll see private parties from the bullring taking late supper here. Casual, but the Hawaiian-style sportshirt is not welcomed.

**Inexpensive to moderate.** Open seven days from 10 a.m. to midnight. Full bar. Reservations accepted. Visa, MC. Parking lot. Casual.

## REUBEN E. LEE
American
★

151 East Coast Highway
Newport Beach          **Map 4**          (714) 675-5910 (Seafood Restaurant)
(714) 675-5811 (Sternwheeler)

There are two restaurants aboard this tastefully restored riverboat anchored in Newport Beach: the Seafood Restaurant and The Sternwheeler, which serves beef. The food in both is satisfactory, but better just for cocktails when the view can be fine. Entertainment is first cabin.

**Moderate.** Open seven days. Brunch Saturday, Sunday from 10 a.m. to 3 p.m. Luncheon from 11:30 a.m. to 4:30 p.m. Dinner 4:30 to 11 p.m. Entertainment. Full bar. Reservations advised. View. Visa, MC, AX. Parking lot. Casual.

---

## REUBEN'S
Steakhouse

(Approximately 50 locations throughout Southern California. Consult phone book for listings.)

A mass-produced quality steakhouse that somehow manages to endow each location with individuality, yet cannot completely avoid a certain plastic sameness. (Some locations are known as "Plankhouses".) The steaks — six different kinds — are good, well served by carefully trained waitresses of the "Hi there, my name is Millie" school. Appetizers include artichokes and mushrooms, both quite well prepared. Lobster and some seafoods are also available. The restaurants are architecturally superior, with more attractive interiors than most restaurants of any category. Each unit has cocktails and entertainment, usually on the order of an easy-listening guitarist.

**Moderate.** Hours differ at various locations. Entertainment. Full bar.

## REVERE HOUSE

**American**
★

900 West 1st Street
Tustin  **Map 6**

(714) 543-9319

The theme—early America—carries the load. The food is good, if not exotic, and the prime rib, fish, Cobb salad, and the "feast board" are moderately priced and worth seeking out. This honorable restaurant has been taking care of hunger pangs since 1955.

**Moderate.** Open seven days. Luncheon from 11 a.m. to 3:30 p.m. Dinner from 4:30 to 10 p.m. Sunday brunch 10:30. a.m. to 3 p.m. Banquet facilities. Child's menu. Reservations advised. All major credit cards. Parking available. Casual.

---

## REX'S FISHMARKET

**Seafood/Continental**
★

9229 Sunset Boulevard
West Hollywood  **Map 8**

(213) 550-1544

The fish come here from some of the best schools—in Hawaii. Everything is fresh that can be, including the Hawaiian Opakapaka, Maine lobsters, and abalone. There are special touches like the house salad dressing made with creamed spinach and topped with bay shrimp. There is more than a touch of class here.

**Expensive.** Open seven days. Luncheon served 11:30 a.m. to 3 p.m. weekdays. Dinner 6 to 11:30 p.m. Sunday through Thursday; to midnight Friday, Saturday. Closed Thanksgiving, Christmas, New Year's Day. Live piano entertainment. Full bar. Reservations recommended. All major credit cards. Valet parking. Semi-dressy; jackets not required.

## REX RISTORANTE

**Northern Italian**
★★★

617 South Olive
Los Angeles    **Map 7**    (213) 627-2300

Mauro Vincent had already created one of the Southland's finest Italian restaurants, Mauro's, in one of the poorest locations, amidst the used car lots of Glendale. When he was provided with the opportunity of creating a restaurant in a great old building with a seemingly unlimited budget, he took off on an architectural and gustatory mission, the results of which are eye-boggling to say the least.

Mauro induced interior designer Luciano Denardo, who has spent the greater part of his life restoring ancient buildings in Rome and Venice, to come to America. The building itself was a treasure of Lalique crystal, mirrors, windows, fixtures and doors that had been collected by Mr. Oviatt for his luxurious men's wear store on the premises. The towering oak columns with a mural showing angels from the New World meeting the Old World and some of the oak showcases have been retained, the latter converted into wine islands on the spacious first floor.

Entrance to Rex is through splendid ornamental iron gates under a *porte cochère* of black-and-white translucent glass tiles. The gorgeous front doors are made of heavy brass and Lalique. Inside, the first floor is a vast area of dark oak paneling, rose and lavender upholstered chairs and graceful tables topped with black Italian marble. The Lalique lighting fixtures set off an opulent Art Deco aura. Even the waiters wear the 1920s wing-collared shirts with their tuxedos. The room is sinfully spacious, accommodating 90 when it could easily handle twice as many. There are ornately carved, triangular tables for two, conceived by Vincenti who wanted tables *à deux* with elegance and privacy.

Dramatic stairways lead up to the mezzanne that surrounds and overlooks the first floor dining area. Upholstered chairs and sofas were designed especially for Rex by

549

Suzanne Geismar of Vermillion, Ltd. Upstairs is a sunken and elaborate lounge with a grand piano and a black marble dance floor and a long bar.

Table settings are from the fashionable houses of Murano and Riccia. There are heavy sextagonal glasses lined up before the silver place mats on black marble tables. The bread-baskets are of metal mesh. And simple arrangements of carnations and baby's breath in crystal bowls are centered on each table.

Mauro went after the greatest chef of Italy for his kitchens. Filippo Costas comes from the Gualtiero Marchesi. Assistant Vito Gnazzo is from the Antica Osteria del Ponte, a Michelin two-star establishment near Milan. The other assistant, Nicola Chatenay, is from another two-star restaurant, the Teatro di Piacenza, also in Milan. They work together, carefully and harmoniously, blending new and classic dishes.

The hors d'oeuvres I tasted included a ravioli *di pesce* (fish ravioli), *terrina di anitra ai pistacchi piccola insalata* (pâté of duck with pistachios and a small salad of cucumbers and duck hearts), *insalata fegato rose e olive nere* (pink chicken livers and black olives). The "pink" livers are cooked in clarified butter in a copper pan and stirred gently. I found the ravioli a bit too stiff for my taste, but the other appetizers, all under $8, were faultless.

Entrées included *pollo in lattuga* (chicken in lettuce) and a splendid dish that translates to medallion of veal in a vernaccia wine with sweetbreads and potatoes.

Mauro hopes to introduce a six-course, fixed-menu dinner, along with the regular menu offering. Antipasto, pasta, fish entrée, fruit and dessert will be priced somewhere in the $70 range. Presently, one can dine at Rex comfortably for $50, including wine; $30 for luncheon.

The lounge bar will lead a life of its own as a casually elegant place for the Dow Jones and the Dow Janes to meet. With the windows open above the muted traffic sounds, dancing is particularly romantic, although I couldn't find anyone who could do the Lambeth Walk or maxixe.

Rex should become a downtown tourist attraction given a little time.

**Expensive.** Open Monday through Saturday. Luncheon served 11:30 a.m. to 2:30 p.m. weekdays. Dinner Monday through Saturday 7 p.m. to midnight. Entertainment in lounge. Full bar. Reservations essential. Wheelchair access to restaurant; not to lounge and restrooms. All major credit cards. Valet parking in evening. Dressy.

---

## RHEINLANDER GERMAN RESTAURANT · German
2182 Avenida de la Playa ★
La Jolla (714)454-6770

An utterly charming fairy-tale house with a lovely garden and gazebos provides the background for fine German-Continental fare more sophisticated than the area has produced to date. The *bratwurst* is great, and all baking from dinner rolls to dessert is done in the small kitchen.

**Expensive.** Open seven days. Luncheon from 11:30 a.m. to 4 p.m. Dinner from 5 to 10 p.m. Sunday brunch 10 a.m. to 3 p.m. Accordion music. Full bar. Reservations advised. Patio. All major credit cards. Street parking. Casual to semi-dressy.

---

## RICABOB · American
5350 Katella ★
Los Alamitos **Map 6** (213) 598-9484

When the Los Alamitos racetrack opened in the middle of undeveloped farmland the local natives shook their heads at the apparent lunacy of it all. They watched vacant lots turn into shopping centers and rabbit hunting low brushland become major housing projects. It took a long time but there is finally a major league restaurant across from the track to accommodate the swarm of visitors during the extended season. As you might expect, the atmosphere is rustic elegance and the menu is simple but the eatin' is good. Fresh flowers and a dramatic interior might encourage more flights of fancy from the kitchen but there is little to complain about. The fresh fish and, of course, the steak—race track aficionados are meat eaters—is perfectly broiled and served with steamed vegetables. The salad bar is basic and good. All in all, this is an oasis of civilized dining across from the track so be sure to have your reservations confirmed in season. They don't throw their wait around — if you're there on time you'll usually get the table. If you're not, they'll not hold your table for long.

**Moderate.** Open seven days. Breakfast from 7 to 11 a.m. Monday through Saturday. Dinner 5 to 11 Monday through Saturday; 4 to 11 Sunday. Dancing; live music Tuesday through Saturday. Full bar. Reservations recommended on weekends. Visa, MC, AX, CB. Off street parking. Casual.

---

## RISTORANTE ERVINO
2431 North Tustin Avenue
Santa Ana      **Map 6**

**Continental**
★★
(714) 547-2575

Ervino is a perfectionist and a true restaurant professional, a hard-won achievement. His quietly elegant restaurant in Santa Ana is a step up from his former locations that produced the best submarine sandwiches in the world. Even then he had shown signs of his epicurean fantasies by holding special dinners when he could cook his heart out. His new place has devastating charm and may well become one of the temples of haute cuisine in Orange County. The continental menu is eclectic with a wide variety of dishes and Ervino has about the widest selection of cognac and cordials and specialty liqueurs in his neighborhood, if not the world. The wine list is lengthy with intelligent selections. The wines are there for a reason, not just to show off. If you talk to the Man himself, he may offer his advice on your dinner and accompaniments.

**Moderate.** Open Monday through Saturday. Luncheon from

11:30 a.m. to 2 p.m. weekdays. Dinner from 6 to 10 p.m.
Monday through Thursday; to 11 Friday, Saturday. Closed
all major holidays. Private party facilities. Reservations recommended. All major credit cards. Parking lot. Casual to
semi-dressy.

---

## THE RITZ
2106 West Ocean Front
Newport Beach          **Map 4**

**Continental**
★★
(714) 673-6363

Hans Prager was fascinated by the area. Beside the barnacle-
encrusted pilings of the old Newport Pier exists the last
dory fishing fleet on the Pacific Coast. Begun by Portuguese
fishermen in 1891. the small fleet still enacts the same
ritual of fishing from dawn to midmorning and then going
ashore to convert their boats into fish markets. These
rugged, suntanned fishermen are secure in their demanding
jobs since the state of California declared their beach an
offical landmark. And well they should, for the scene is like
Van Gogh suddenly come to life. The cluster of boats and
floral beach umbrellas, the working families that gaff the
fish, set up the scales and meticulously arrange the cleaning
knives, scrapers, sieves, and washing pans; the milling crowd
on the sidewalk speaking a variety of tongues—all seem
here to be painted or photographed. When Prager, a
respected restaurateur (he brought you Gulliver's and
opened Five Crowns), happened on to an old building in the
area, he decided he had to have it. So he quickly acquired
Hans Bucher as partner and made the landlord an offer he
couldn't refuse. Thus, The Ritz was born. A tongue-in-
cheek name for a restaurant that captures a touch of San
Francisco in the small, 48-seat room with waitresses in
tuxedos, comfortable booths and colorfully painted wood
panels and scones. Yet it is obvious that this is Prager's
dream and we dined there one evening to find him in a
chef's hat proudly ladling the best bouillabaisse I've come
across. Dinners include the "dorymen's catch of the day,"

New York Delmonico steaks, and a grand breast of duck Montmorency with wild rice. Prices include choice of a wide range of appetizers from quenelles of sole to spinach salad. (My favorite appetizer: hearts of romaine with Roquefort.) The wine list is limited but so intelligently put together and priced that you won't mind.

**Moderate.** Open Tuesday through Saturday. Luncheon from 11:30 a.m. to 3 p.m. weekdays. Dinner 5:30 to 11 p.m. Closed major holidays. Full bar. Reservations esential. Visa, MC. Public parking. Semi-dressy.

---

## RIVE GAUCHE
320 Tejon Place
Palos Verdes    **Map 2**

French
★
(213) 378-0267

Palos Verdes is fortunate to have this cafe in their opulent midst. It's hard to be more Gallic than the garlicky escargot or the *mousse de fois de canard* (duck liver). The onion soup is a warming touch on a cold night and the roasted quail with raspberries is unique in the area. Their long daily list of fresh fish usually includes a unique preparation or three. There's a dignified Grand Marnier soufflé (it must be ordered before dinner). The two Andre's (Moreau and Martin) are enjoying what Tommy Lasorda likes to call "the fruits of success" by intelligently limiting the number of tables each waiter must serve.

**Moderate to expensive.** Open seven days. Luncheon from 11:30 to 3 p.m. Tuesday through Sunday. Dinner from 5 to 10 p.m. daily. Sunday brunch 11:30 a.m. to 3 p.m. Banquet facilities. Wine and beer only. Reservations required. Patio. All major credit cards. Parking available. Semi-dressy.

---

*To obtain the best results from this Guide, consult*
*"How to Use this Guide" on page 27.*

# RIVE GAUCHE CAFE

**Continental**

★

14106 Ventura Boulevard

Sherman Oaks    **Map 1**

(213) 990-3573

Considering that it sits in a small mall across the street from an immense Ralph's, Rive Gauche Cafe is a strikingly attractive place to have lunch. While trucks stream up and down Ventura Boulevard, sunlight streams through the many windows and skylights of Rive Gauche. (A curious name by the way—the only interpretation is that Ventura Boulevard is a mighty river of commerce and that North of the Boulevard is the Right Bank while the rest of Los Angeles is the Left Bank, which is a ludicrous though charming idea).

Rive Gauche has a larger proportion of Ladies Who Lunch than your average French cafe. Perhaps this comes from the restaurant's convenient proximity to a supermarket, or from its central location in affluent Sherman Oaks. In any case, there are a lot of ladies lunching at Rive Gauche. They're lunching on a quiche lorraine or a slightly more interesting quiche Rive Gauche, a dish described on the menu as a concoction that "keeps our chef creative." You name it, and he'll create it... or you can leave yourself in the chef's hands, and take what you get.

The same is true of the crepe Rive Gauche (also described as "keeps our chef creative"), though the chicken and mushroom crepe, the *ratatouille,* the beef *bourguignone* and the seafood crepes are all light and lively in terms of their ingredients. But actually, my favorite lunchtime meal at Rive Gauche consists of an opening course of their terrific *coquilles* St. Jacques, followed by either the eggs Benedict or the eggs St. George (a Benedict variation, starring crab meat instead of Canadian bacon). Heavy on the sauces but hollandaise as good as Rive Gauche's should be cherished and enjoyed. And the Ladies Who Lunch, I've noticed, are very impressed by anyone who has the moxie to order anything as obviously urbane as a dish named St. Jacques *and* a dish named St. George.   *M.S.*

**Moderate.** Open seven days. Luncheon served Monday through Friday 11 a.m. to 5 p.m.; Saturday and Sunday from 10 a.m. Dinner Sunday through Thursday 5 to 10:30 p.m.; Friday and Saturday to 11:30. Full bar. Reservations accepted. Patio. All major credit cards. Parking lot. Casual.

---

## RIVIERA RESTAURANT — Continental
3333 South Bristol Street
Costa Mesa   **Map 4**            (714) 540-3840

There is one oddly discordant note in this otherwise fine restaurant improbably located in a covered shopping center: periodic lapses into incredible rudeness on the part of the management. I've had more than a few letters indicating that problem, and several friends of mine were treated unmercifully. Thus, the fact that this is a superior establishment with a sophisticated menu and an important wine cellar is negated to some degree by the kind of arrogance that presaged doom for many venerable New York establishments. If you can get through the evening without offending anyone, you will enjoy the wide variety of salads (spinach, Cobb, marinara, Caesar) prepared at your table, and large Mazatlan shrimp sautéed in garlic butter served with oregano and chopped onion. The house wine is a good one, Louis Martini, reflecting the integrity of the operation. Three favorite dishes are tartare steak, *gourmandise* of filet mignon (served in crêpes, with capped mushrooms glazed in cream sauce) and roast duck with orange sauce.

**Moderate.** Open Monday through Saturday. Luncheon from 11:30 a.m. to 3 p.m. Dinner from 5 to 11 p.m. Banquet facilities. Full bar. Reservations required. Visa, MC, DC. Parking available. Casual.

# R.J.'S THE RIB JOINT

252 North Beverly Drive
Beverly Hills      **Map 8**

**American**
★★
(213) 274-7427

First of all, the restaurant is beautiful. Under real antique ceiling fans operated by a series of conveyor belts there is a floor-to-ceiling bar along one side of the busy lobby area and the "Green Grocer," a new dimension in salad bars, finished in pine and decorated by stacks of open boxes filled with produce, on the other side. A wooden cage in the direct center acts as the check-in point, the nerve center from which reservations are taken and confirmed and obviously ravenous patrons, rendered helpless by the perfume of barbecue, are led to their tables. There is a mezzanine arrangement that's fun and great for watching celebrities, ordinary folk and the most beautiful waitresses extant. R.J.'s is brought to you by Bob Morris who brought you Gladstone's and Jetty's. Morris is a fanatic on the subject of fresh, and his menu proclaims: "There are too many frozen, prepared foods in restaurants and we are going to bring you meals the way they once were served." His meats are cooked over oak and hickory, baking is done on the premises (the chocolate and coconut cakes are two feet high and a slice covers the plate) and the bar uses fresh orange, grapefruit and pineapple juices in their mixed drinks or they serve it pure, if that's how you like it. The bar stocks 400 liquors and 50 beers from all over the world. The Green Grocer includes a variety of lettuces, spinach, avocado, sliced olives, fresh mushrooms, hearts of palm and far too many other items to list here. Dressings, all homemade, include a rich Roquefort, and salads are accompanied by fresh sourdough, rye, pumpernickel or egg bread. Following two visits for salad I ordered a bucket of clams, fat and steamed in their own broth. There were six in our party, and we all ordered different entrées, which nearly led to a mutiny in our ranks. There were platters of pork back ribs, slow cooked over hickory. There were mountains of brontosaurus-size beef ribs smoked over oak and served with a special sauce.

There was chicken (remember chicken?) and giant steaks and mammoth Maine lobsters. Side dishes included fresh steamed artichokes, big baked potatoes, sautéed Bermuda onions and mushrooms and fresh corn on the cob. The chili was all meat and the beverages — this is a family restaurant — included fresh lemonade and soft drinks. Prices are low and that includes unlimited visitation to the salad bar. Luncheon is mostly sandwiches.

**Moderate.** Open seven days. Luncheon from 11:30 a.m. to 4 p.m. Monday through Saturday. Dinner from 4 to 10 p.m. Sunday through Thursday; to 11 Friday, Saturday. Closed Christmas. Piano nightly; magicians Wednesday through Sunday. Full bar. Reservations recommended. Visa, MC. Valet parking. Casual.

---

## ROBAIRE'S FRENCH CUISINE
348 South La Brea Avenue
Los Angeles     **Map 7**

French Provincial
★
(213) 931-1246

At a time when the new and trendy restaurants are getting virtually all the attention we should not forget our old friends. Most of us have come to know certain restaurants on which we can rely. Unfortunately these kinds of establishments have been quietly competent for so long that we tend to take them for granted. Robaire's is just such a place. They opened when French restaurants were still new to us. The location is no longer chic, but M. Robaire and his wife have maintained the standards with Gallic determination and the rooms, now softened with age, are filled with a second and third generation clientele. It was, and is, a French restaurant designed to please Americans, and the extensive menu is reassuringly familiar. The *canapé* Robaire is a tradition: lobster and shrimp in a cream sauce *au gratin* on sour-dough toast. Other hors d'oeuvres include escargot, artichoke hearts vinaigrette and, for the hopelessly unadventurous, shrimp cocktail. Onion soup is excellent here, and a steaming bowl can provide a gustatory memory on a chill winter's night. The daily specials range from rabbit in burgundy sauce on Tuesday to Saturday's Cornish game hen stuffed with wild rice, and include salad, potatoes au gratin, miniature carrots and French rolls. The monthly special, couscous, reflects the touch of Tunis in the kitchen and has a serious following on the last Wednesday of every month. The French country specialties are a splendid introduction to cuisine Français. My favorite is a sort of French soul food that is overlooked by the more pretentious or splashy restaurants — *cassoulet*. This is a hearty dish of white beans, lamb, pork, sausage and cheese. Of course, the fish are fresh, and the meat, chicken and desserts predictable and good. The room is informal with soft lights and comfortable booths, and photo murals provide the decor. Many a fancy-French "Le Clippo" has come and gone while Robaire's continues to save our sanity on those occasions when we are hungry and need a reliable friend.

**Moderate.** Open seven days. Dinner from 5 to 10:30 p.m. Closed major holidays. Full bar. Reservations advised. Patio. All major credit cards. Valet parking. Semi-dressy.

---

**ROBBIE'S RIB**                                     **Barbecue**
2711 Olive Street                                             ★
Burbank          **Map 1**                     (213) 845-7897

**BRENDA'S RIB CRIB**
1926 North Lake Avenue                                       ★
Altadena         **Map 7**                     (213) 797-7978

This is essentially for take-out, but it's good enough to list for those with an urge for ribs barbecued over real hickory, sweet potato pies, beef and pork links, and chicken. Beans are baked to perfection, and there are certain times of my life when I'd rather eat there than anyplace else. The patio seats twenty-one. They have a slightly different menu at the Burbank location.

**Burbank: Inexpensive.** Open Tuesday through Sunday. Luncheon from 11:30 a.m. to 5 p.m. weekdays. Dinner 5 to

9 p.m. Tuesday through Thursday; 4 to 10 Friday, Saturday; 3 to 8 Sunday. Catering. Closed major holidays. Singing waiters and waitresses. Wine and beer only. No reservations. Visa, MC. Parking lot; street parking. Casual.

**Altadena: Inexpensive.** Open 11:30 a.m. to 8:30 p.m. Tuesday through Thursday; to 10 Friday, Saturday; 3 to 8 Sunday. Take-out service. No alcoholic beverages; but diners can bring their own. No reservations. Patio. No credit cards. Parking lot; street parking. Casual.

---

## ROBB'S ICE CREAM CO.

17621 Ventura Boulevard
Encino　　**Map 1**

Ice cream parlor
★★
(213) 784-0867

To the avid ice creamaholic, such niceties as the percentage of butterfat content, use (or lack of them) of preservatives, and other fine points assume great importance. Some of us spend hours arguing the merits of Baskin-Robbins vs. Swensen's or Haagen Dazs vs. Dreyer's. But I'll stack Robb's up against any of them for pure taste delight.

Robb's makes all of their own ice cream and uses absolutely no preservatives. Although Oreo (that's right, Oreo cookies mixed in ice cream) is the most popular, Robb's features about 35-40 flavors, on a rotating basis, many of which you'll find no place else: Cinaffee (a blend of cinnamon and coffee) and Banaffee (a mixture of fresh banana and coffee) among others. Two things set Robb's apart: the hot fudge and mix-ins. The hot fudge, made fresh from owner Roselle Cheren's own recipe, may be the best you've enjoyed. A small hot fudge sundae is $1.65, and a large one is $1.95—both are more than worth the price. My personal favorites are the mix-ins. Perhaps I remember, as a kid, mushing up two or three flavors into one soft, heavenly mound of flavor. Mix-ins are just that: choose your favorite ice cream from the board behind the counter, and have it softened and then enhanced by the available mix-ins. The most popular mix-ins are bits of Reese's candy and M&M's. Also available are fresh walnuts, mixed nuts, granola, crushed Heath Bars, butterscotch chips and pecans. A cup of ice cream (about eight ounces) with one mix-in is $1.45, for two mix-ins, it's $1.65. It's not cheap, but it sure is good. The chairs and tables offer a convenient view of the ice cream being made behind a large plate-glass window.

**Moderate.** Open seven days. Monday through Thursday from noon to 10:30 p.m.; To midnight Friday, Saturday; to 9:30 Sunday. Take-out. No reservations. No credit cards. No smoking. Casual.

---

## ROBERT'S RESTAURANT      Continental
1921 Ocean Front Walk          ★
Venice     **Map 2**         (213) 392-4891

In the burgeoning Venice area this quality operation has survived the trendy temporary operations that flourish briefly and subside. Robert's would be a good restaurant whatever the location and the fact that there is an ocean view and a patio for summer dining is only gilding this lily. The menu changes ever three weeks and always features fresh fish with a choice of duck and chicken. The fettuccine is especially noteworthy and the à la carte menu allows you to order half portions for an appetizer. John Goodman has his house in order.

**Moderate.** Open Tuesday through Sunday from 6 to 10:30 p.m. Banquet facilities. Full bar. Reservations advised. Patio. Ocean view. Visa, MC. Parking lot. Casual.

---

## RONARDO'S      Italian/Continental
553 Pine Knott Avenue        ★
Big Bear Lake        (714)866-7676

Ronardo's at Big Bear Lake was needed. It is an inexpensive, cozy, quasi-Italian, family-style restaurant with somewhat more emphasis on the quantity than on the quality of the food. All the empty dishes for the seven-course dinner are stacked in front of the individual diner to be filled from heaping platters; and seconds are available on the improbable chance that someone might still be hungry. Soup from the tureen is served with hot sourdough bread, a delicious way to conquer the winter chill and settle down to the serious business of eating. Lettuce salad in a light dressing, spaghetti, canned (but good) string beans flavored with pork and onions are followed by an entrée that is almost an after thought. Chicken livers, roast beef, prawns, and halibut steak are among the favorites; the steaks are not. Dessert of fruit and cheese with a huge pitcher of coffee tops off a leisurely feast that is priced reasonably. Beer and wine are available; and reservations are a good idea, particularly on Saturday.

**Inexpensive.** Open seven days. Dinner Sunday through Thursday from 5 to 9:30 p.m.; Friday, Saturday to 10 p.m. Sunday dinner 12:30 to 9 p.m. Banquet facilities. Wine and beer only. Reservations advised. Patio. Visa, MC. Parking available. Casual.

---

## ROSCOE'S HOUSE OF CHICKEN & WAFFLES

Soul food

1514 North Gower Street ★★
Hollywood     **Map 8**     (213) 466-7453

4907 West Washington Boulevard ★★
Los Angeles     **Map 8**     (213) 936-3730

Much like its nearby neighbor, South Town, Roscoe's is a soul food restaurant that's open 24 hours, and serves mostly breakfast, though other delights—like half a chicken smothered in gravy and onions, or a chicken burger—are also available. The breakfast served at Roscoe's is up there with the great breakfasts of my life, breakfasts that I will never forget, either as culinary achievements or as inches added onto my girth.

Consider, for instance, the breakfast referred to as

"Stymie's Choice." That translates as a huge portion of chicken livers, breaded in a coating redolent of herbs and spices that put Shake 'n' Bake to utter shame, sautéed and then smothered—I say, smothered!—with a gravy so rich that mere words do not offer ample assistance in describing the joy in these simple livers. The choice refers to the option of giblets over the livers, a possibility I certainly intend to look into before I shuffle off this mortal coil. Accompanying this feast, there are eggs fixed however, there are grits, and there are biscuits, hot and fresh from the oven and dripping butter.

Though I may never get over Roscoe's chicken livers, I do suspect that this is more than a one-dish eatery. The place is tremendously proud of its waffles ("Our own private mix") and they are very good. So is the chicken, served either as "¼ chix" or "½ chix," or in sundry other combinations like the "Jeanne Jones Omelette"—a clever combination of cheese and chicken pieces, or the "Oscar": three chicken wings with grits, an egg and biscuits.

Although I haven't tried Roscoe's during the wee hours, I was surprised to find the place not very busy at all one recent Sunday morning. Service was quick and witty. My only quarrel with the joint turned out to be over the orange juice. The large (at $1.60 wasn't much bigger than the small (at 90¢)... and neither were big enough to justify the price, a point that didn't diminish my enjoyment of Roscoe's one bit.   *M.S.*

**Moderate.** Open Monday 10 a.m. to 3 a.m.; Tuesday through Thursday 10 a.m. to 10 p.m. Friday and Saturday 10 a.m. to 3 a.m.; 2 a.m. at the Washington location; Sunday 10 a.m. to 10 p.m. Closed all major holidays. Full bar (Washington); beer and wine (Gower). No reservations. No credit cards: AX only at Washington location. Validated parking (Gower); free (Washington). Casual.

## ROUARD'S POLONAISE
225 South Beverly Drive
Beverly Hills **Map 8**

French/Basque
★★
(213) 274-7246

To most, "Basque" conjures up images of the unending feast, that hearty and abundant fare with two or three entrées served family style at communal tables. But Basque influence traces back to the Pyrenees and that takes in a lot of geographic and gastronomic territory. At the Polonaise the pâté *maison* of chopped chicken liver, the rich fish soup and the *petite langouste* "Rouard" bear little relation to the Basqueterias I've described. There is a splendid chef in command here and the kitchen is run under the exacting supervision of Jean Rouard. I've had a dish that could rival most any: a young boneless squab *en papilotte* with a raspberry sauce that was from the chef's own repertoire. The restaurant is small but very comfortable and well-appointed.

**Moderate to expensive.** Open Tuesday through Sunday. Dinner from 6 to 11 p.m. Monday through Saturday; 5 to 10 Sunday. Closed Christmas, New Year's. Full bar. Reservations essential. All major credit cards. Valet parking. Semi-dressy.

## ROY'S
8430 Sunset Boulevard
West Hollywood **Map 8**

Chinese

(213)656-1675

This is one example of how the dining public will allow itself to be importuned and hornswoggled if it's done in the guise of being that best of all things — "in." Could that be Bruce Springsteen or Linda Ronstadt across the room? Probably not. They are so awkward with celebrities that Buddy Hackett (at an adjoining table) was forced to give his ID to a waitress who, though nice and surfer-beautiful, apparently hadnn't yet achieved the intellectual level of a groupie. We were met at the front door by Mr. Charming Extrovert himself with a display of insolence and bad manners nearly unparalleled in my experience. (Later a friend told me about asking to be seated at the bar. "You made dinner reservations, didn't you?" the host demanded imperiously. "We're jammed at eight, and you'll have to eat so we can get your table." My friends, recognizing a hustle when they saw it, canceled their dinner and strolled to the bar, where they sat until long past eight, enjoying a fine view of the city — and of the nearly empty room.) Decor is disco-dazzling, with tiny lights along the back of the mirrored booths that made me feel like I was eating in a pinball machine. We were seated at a minuscule table for two (one-and-a-half?) by a waitress who was stewardess-sincere and kept asking, "Is everything all right?" Apparently she intended it as a rhetorical question, because when I answered in the negative, she smiled and nodded. The menu is presented on numbered, oversized cards, one item per card; I was dealt a losing hand. What's good about this place? The view is magnificent. The menu of special tequilas and vodkas is interesting. The Chinese beer was excellent. Our waitress was far more appealing than the food. But the dining experience was mediocre and expensive. The cuisine? Rock-Chinese.

**Expensive.** Open Monday through Saturday. Dinner from 6 p.m. to 2 a.m. Banquet facilities. Full bar. Reservations advised. Visa, MC, AX, DC. Valet parking. Casual.

---

## RUBY BEGONIA'S American/Continental
1500 South Raymond Avenue ★
Fullerton  **Map 6**  (714) 635-4211

This is one of those ersatz turn-of-the-century restaurants that springs up everywhere. You know, Tiffany stained glass, hanging plants, all the trimmings. But the food is good (try the steak Diane, the veal or shrimp Romero) and the tariff reasonable. There's live entertainment too. Not exactly elegant cuisine in the tradition of the great European chefs, but fun... and the food is a cut above average.

**Inexpensive to moderate.** Open seven days. Luncheon from 11:30 a.m. to 2:30 p.m. Dinner 5:30 to 10 p.m. Monday through Thursday; to 11 Friday, Saturday. Sunday brunch 9:30 a.m. to 2:30 p.m. Full bar. Entertainment Tuesday through Saturday; dancing. Reservations recommended. Visa, MC, AX. Parking lot. Semi-dressy.

---

## RUSSELL'S
**Hamburgers**
★

4306 Atlantic Avenue
Long Beach          **Map 3**          (213) 427-6869

If I had a dollar for every call or letter I've received nominating this place or that for "the best hamburger in Los Angeles," I could probably buy my own personal golden arches. But there is no such dispute about the best hamburger in Long Beach. A 45-minute wait is not unusual. And no wonder. Not only are the hamburgers thick and juicy — and the home fries even greasier than mother made them — but Russell's just may serve the best pies, not only in Long Beach, but in all of Southern California. Their Dutch apple is the best of its kind I've ever tasted. Their American apple is only a shade less scrumptious. Then there are the lemon meringue, pumpkin, and — when fresh fruits are in season — cherry, boysenberry, strawberry, rhubarb, peach — I could go on and on. Each is served with your choice of a huge mound of whipped cream or an even larger slab of vanilla ice cream. Among the fruit pies, I especially recommend the fresh strawberry and fresh peach; both are overflowing with fruit, and nary a trace of the gooey gelatin that so many restaurants use to cut costs.

**Inexpensive.** Open Monday through Saturday from 11 a.m. to 9 p.m. Closed Christmas. No alcoholic beverages. No reservations. No credit cards. Parking lot. Casual.

# THE RUSTY PELICAN
## American
2735 West Coast Highway     ★
Newport Beach    **Map 4**    (714) 642-3431

One of the most popular restaurants in the Newport area, the Pelican's inducements include a view of the bay, woodsy natural-texture interior, fine drinks, listenable entertainment, and good food. There's a neat upstairs bar and a shucked-to-order oyster bar to relieve the pain of waiting until your name is called (no reservations). The abalone and king salmon are particularly well-prepared.

**Moderate.** Open seven days. Luncheon from 11:30 a.m. to 3 p.m. Monday through Saturday; 10 to 3 Sunday. Dinner 4:30 to 11 p.m. Sunday through Thursday; to midnight Friday, Saturday. Closed Thanksgiving, Christmas. Entertainment. Full bar open 8:30 p.m. to 2 a.m. Limited reservations for dinner. Visa, MC, AX. Parking lot. Resort and casual.

# RUTH'S CATERING
## Jewish
7536 Clairemont Mesa Boulevard    ★
San Diego    (714) 565-7474

Tastes of New York in this strictly Kosher restaurant have attracted the homesick hungry who feast on chicken soup with matzo balls, chopped liver, gefilte fish, meat knishes, hot kugel, beef flanken and *tsimmes*, a carrot and prune dish. Everything is made from scratch and their business *is* catering but they enjoy serving the sit down customers. Not fancy but if you've heard of Zabar's you'll love it here.

**Inexpensive to moderate.** Open Sunday through Friday. Luncheon from 10 a.m. to 2 p.m. weekdays. Dinner 2 to 8 p.m. Monday through Thursday; from 4 Sunday. Closed major holidays. Wine and beer only. Reservations accepted. No credit cards. Parking lot. Casual.

# S

---

**SAGEBRUSH CANTINA**        **Mexican/Continental**
23527 Calabasas Road        ★★
Calabasas     **Map 1**       (213) 888-6062

9523 Culver Boulevard       ★
Culver City     **Map 3**       (213) 836-5321

Owner Bob McCord is a perfectionist who seems intent on ever expanding his outstanding restaurant. His Calabasas operation has grown from a small sandwich shop to a sprawling adventure that resembles a never-ending party. Apparently not satisfied with all that growth, McCord has taken over what was once Al Penni's eccentric restaurant in Culver City. Both restaurants offer good Mexican food, good atmosphere and fun at reasonable prices. The Calabasas location has become a steady favorite with many sports and entertainment stars, and even the customary wait seems less unpleasant while sipping a margarita on the gigantic patio area.

**Calabasas: Inexpensive to moderate.** Open Tuesday through Sunday. Luncheon from 11 a.m. to 4 p.m. Sunday, Tuesday through Thursday; to 5 Friday; 8 to 11 a.m. Saturday. Dinner to 10 p.m. Sunday, Tuesday through Thursday; to 11 Friday, Saturday. Closed Christmas. Entertainment. Full bar. Reservations recommended for parties of seven or more; no reservations for patio. Patio. Visa, MC. Parking lot. Casual.

**Culver City: Inexpensive to moderate.** Open Monday through Friday. Luncheon from 11 a.m. to 4 p.m. Dinner from 4 to 10 p.m. Monday through Thursday; to 11 Friday. Closed major holidays. Entertainment Friday. Full bar. No reservations. Visa, MC. Wheelchair access. Street parking. Casual.

---

## SAIGON FLAVOR
**Vietnamese**

1044 South Fairfax Avenue ★
Los Angeles  **Map 8**  (213) 935-1564

The menu may be strange, the dishes new to your palate, but this attractive restaurant and its cuisine are something very special. *Can Cua Chien* is crab claws with crabmeat inside surrounded by spiced shrimp and deep fried. *Ga Xao Hanh Nhon* is chicken sautéed with almonds. We could literally write a book about this French influenced Oriental cuisine that seems to blend the best of both worlds. You should rely on the fne staff for assistance or meet Duc Lehoang, the manager for inexpensive adventuring.

**Moderate.** Open Wednesday through Monday. Luncheon from 11:30 a.m. to 2:30 p.m. Dinner from 4:30 to 10 p.m. Wine and beer only. Reservations preferred. Visa, MC. Street parking. Casual.

---

*In order to obtain the best results from this Guide, please consult "Tips on Dining Out" on page 21.*

## ST. MORITZ

**Swiss**

★

11720 Ventura Boulevard

Studio City       **Map 1**                          (213) 980-1122

Purely Swiss, but like the nice indoor-outdoor cafes of Lucerne rather than the kitsch of Americanized Swiss taverns, with a garden full of greenery. The soups are from a stock pot. The *salad Neuchatel* is a zesty combination of bay shrimp, yogurt, and dill on bibb lettuce. *Poulet aux estragon* is the chicken's breast, lightly sautéed in a tarragon-flavored sauce. Schnitzels are crusty on the outside and topped lavishly with two fried eggs, anchovies, and capers. There is *cannelloni* that is sensational, made with spinach and cheese. There are daily specials—lamb dishes on Saturday, chicken on Sunday—and a good selection of wines.

**Moderate to expensive.** Open Tuesday through Sunday. Luncheon from 11 a.m. to 2 p.m. Dinner from 5 to 10 p.m. Full bar. Reservations required. Patio. Visa, MC. Valet parking. Casual.

---

## ST. TROPEZ

**French**

★

10323 Santa Monica Boulevard

West Los Angeles       **Map 8**                     (213) 277-6734

From the Provençale interior and the fragments of French that flit by as you enter, it is quite easy to expect a view of Saint Tropez through the window. It's not there, of course, but the feeling is, even though the St. Tropez is a part of the "New England Village," one of those plastic architectural transplants that seem to thrive in Southern California. Food at St. Tropaz is valid Gallic, verified one noon with a *pan bagna niçoise*, a huge sandwich-salad of marinated tuna, anchovies, and lettuce between enormous slices of French bread. There was also a beautifully mild cheese omelette served with crusty rounds from one of those long French loaves. Entrées include chicken Robert, shrimp Portofino, rack of lamb, and stuffed trout.

**Moderate.** Open Monday through Saturday. Luncheon from 11:30 a.m. to 2:30 p.m. Dinner from 6 to 10 p.m. Wine and beer only. Reservations essential. Patio. Visa, MC, AX, CB. Small parking lot; street parking. Casual.

---

## THE SALMON HOUSE
1970 Quivera Road
Mission Bay

**Seafood**
★
(714) 223-2234

A good idea, a salmon house done in the style of the Pacific Northwest Indian tribes (there are similar ones throughout the Northwest), but it hasn't spawned its way into our hearts yet. They use alder wood to barbecue fresh sockeye or Chinook salmon, and while I don't quarrel with their claim of "fresh," I would point out that much of the salmon in the far North is frozen. There's a fisherman stew, "catch of the day" and halibut prepared well and juicy. The place lacks something; perhaps it is too new and too mass production-oriented. The prognosis is favorable, however, and the location, facing the yacht harbor in Quivira Basin, is quite lovely. Children are welcome.

**Moderate.** Open seven days. Luncheon served Monday through Saturday 11:30 a.m. to 2:30 p.m. Dinner Monday through Thursday 5 to 10 p.m.; to 11 Friday, Saturday; 4:30 to 9:30 Sunday. Sunday brunch 10 a.m. to 3 p.m. at fixed price of under $10. Closed Christmas Day. Entertainment nightly. Full bar. Reservations recommended. View. Visa, MC, AX. Parking lot. Casual.

*In order to obtain the best results from this Guide, be sure to read the French, German, Italian and Oriental menu translators on page 705 to 710 of this Guide.*

# SALOMI
**5049 Lankershim Boulevard**
North Hollywood      **Map 1**

**Indian**
★★
(213) 506-0130

Salomi has an extremely broad selection of some of the best Indian dishes in town, served à la carte, in levels ranging from meek and mild to ferociously hot. Salomi serves not only Indian dishes but also journeys tentatively across the border into Bangladesh. There are Indian breads and pastries here, the equal of any I've found in Los Angeles. Puffy *poori*, like little doughboy balloons; matzoh-like *papadoms*; and *paratha* and *samosas*, diminutive Indian knishes, filled with spices and meats and vegetables. And, there are tiny condiment dishes, so filled with a complexity of flavors the senses reel—chutneys of mango and onion, pickles of mango and lime, and the eternally soothing *raitha*—a blessing in the form of cucumbers of yogurt, a dish to heal the palate.

As for the main courses at Salomi, there is a choice of 71 different curries, *biryanis, pilaos* and there's chicken from the tandoori oven, which is served red as a tomato, a redness that gets on your fingers and lips and doesn't come off for days. The dishes marked *madras* and *vindaloo* are the hottest, something the stoical waiters do not always warn you about. At Salomi, "You pays your money and you takes your choice." *M.S.*

**Moderate.** Open Monday through Thursday noon to 10 p.m.; Friday and Saturday to 11; Sunday 5 to 10. Beer and wine only. Reservations for four or more. Visa, MC. Parking lot. Casual.

*Please be sure to consult "Tipping Made Easy" on page 25 of this Guide.*

## THE SALOON

9390 Santa Monica Boulevard
Beverly Hills    **Map 8**

**Continental**
★★
(213)273-7155

At this writing, the restaurant is digging its way out of a fire, but it should be restored shortly.

When I first had occasion to write about The Saloon in Beverly Hills for a dining guide some years ago I noted, "If all the foxy chicks there at cocktail time were laid end to end, they'd reach from The Saloon to Dr. Scholl's foot pad store in Hollywood — and on a busy day, maybe back again." But times have changed. The foxy chicks have married their stockbrokers, lawyers and doctors and are more subdued, and The Saloon is taking itself more seriously these days now that Howard Rosov, the new owner, lowered prices and raised standards. Originally a restaurant version of an Andy Hardy movie plot line ("C'mon guys, we can do our own show"), it was opened by 40 celebrity partners headed by Grant Tinker, who used to share his wife Mary Tyler Moore with most of America on television. The theory was that 40 couples who dine out can successfully open their own restaurant. The theory doesn't work. People who dine out frequently enjoy variety. Also, they are eventually enraged by an errant busboy, a sloppy waiter, or any of the normal restaurant zits and end up stomping out in a rage and a Rolls. The Saloon is beautiful with its publike bar lounge and high ceiling. The main dining room is Hollywood-formal with plaid carpeting and banquettes, subdued lighting, etched glass, and mirror-lined walls, interspersed with lithographs and murals. In addition to fresh flowers, each table is adorned with a jumbo Ball jar of garlicky kosher dill pickles, a favorite with the expensively casual clientele, who nonchalantly peer around the room, seeking — mostly in vain — a familiar profile. The Saloon is still "in," beautiful, expensive, and — if you order carefully (fresh fish, broiled chicken, veal, T-bone steak) — it can be one of the most satisfying gustatory experiences in the area.

**Expensive.** Open Monday through Saturday. Luncheon

from 11:30 a.m. to 4 p.m. Dinner from 6 p.m. to midnight. Entertainment after 9 p.m. Full bar. Reservations advised. all major credit cards. Valet parking. Casual to semi-dressy.

---

## SALVATORE'S
8641 Garden Grove Boulevard
Garden Grove          **Map 6**

**Continental/Italian**
★
(714) 636-1011

Alka-Seltzer on the rocks would not be an unintelligent after-dinner drink in these European family-style budget emporiums. It's not that the food is indigestible. It isn't. While not *alta cucina*, it is generally well prepared, but far too abundant in both the number of courses and the sizes of the servings. The Jewish (or Italian or Chinese or Hungarian) mother syndrome — "Eat, eat, people are starving in India" — has made most of us guiltily stuff that last half-portion of lasagna through our protesting esophagus. As you enter the Woolworth-Italian plastic grape world of Salvatore's, you are immediately served a small glass of vermouth, with some urgency, by your waitress. You notice an entire stack of empty dishes at your place. A tureen of improbably good minestrone (or French vegetable on alternate nights) is unceremoniously set before the one most resembling the host of the party. He ladles at least two bowls to all, with maybe a third to himself. Conversation diminishes as chunks of fresh bread are buttered and dunked (if no one is looking) into the remaining dregs of soup before the tureen is replaced with a chilled bowl of simple salad, steeped in garlic and oil dressing. Then a platter of spaghetti about the size and shape of a football (not *al dente*, but who cares?). Then marvelous French fries, light and crisp with a hint of lemon to bring out the flavor. Then your choice of entrée, be it roast chicken, *cannelloni alla* Salvatore, homemade manicotti, Italian sausage, or scampi in creamed garlic sauce, or—well you get the idea. Steaming pitchers of coffee are provided, to be poured into stout green glasses in the manner of the bourgeois cafes. Naturally you will have ordered a liter of wine (thin but somehow appropriate), which may last through the dessert of fresh fruit and cheese. There is a different specialty every night as well as steaks, lobsters, and other dishes, but these are after-thoughts and are indifferently prepared.

**Inexpensive.** Open seven days. Luncheon from 11 a.m. to 2:30 p.m. weekdays. Dinner from 4:30 to 9:30 p.m. Monday through Thursday; to 11 Friday, Saturday; 4 to 9 Sunday. Closed Thanksgiving, Christmas. Full bar. Reservations recommended, especially on weekends. Visa, MC, AX. Parking lot. Casual.

---

### SAMBI OF TOKYO
8649 Firestone Boulevard
Downey        **Map 3**

**Japanese**
★
(213) 869-1171

A big, almost Disneylandish, Japanese restaurant with entertainment. Sambi is a logical development of the success of small Japanese restaurants. They've taken all the good points and literally enlarged upon them. It's a fine place to take the family or people who are relatively new to the art of Japanese cooking. The drinks are far better than at most Oriental restaurants where they seem to be served in small glasses without enough ice (or booze for that matter). This is not exactly restaurant row but Sambi's is worth a trip if you live anywhere in the vicinity.

**Moderate.** Open seven days. Luncheon from 11:30 a.m. to 2 p.m. weekdays. Dinner from 5:30 to 10 p.m. Monday through Thursday; Friday, Saturday from 5 to 11 p.m. Sunday from 5 to 10 p.m. Sunday brunch from 11 a.m. to 2 p.m. Banquet facilities. Entertainment. Dancing. Full bar. Reservations advised. All major credit cards. Parking available. Casual to semi-dressy.

## SAMURAI

731 South Highway 101
Solano Beach

**Japanese**
★★
(714) 481-0032

This celebration of Japanese food and arts features nice touches like free calligraphy with the birthday dinner and separate *tappan yaki* and *sushi* bars. The decor is enhanced by the owner's oil paintings and bonsai.

**Moderate.** Open seven days. Luncheon from noon to 3 p.m. weekdays. Dinner from 5 to 10 p.m. Full bar. Reservations requested. Visa, MC, AX. Valet parking. Casual.

## SAN CLEMENTE INN

125 Avenida Esplandian
San Clemente      **Map 4**

**American/Continental**
★
(714) 492-6103

The repelled invasion of the former White House press corps simply brought into focus what everyone in the area knew: the San Clemente Inn is one of the more graceful and relaxing places along the South Coast. There are beautifully landscaped grounds, an ocean view, and a terrace overlooking the pool. Hotel guests find it conveniently located near beaches, golf, and the charming small beach-towns in the area. Food is informal — steak, seafood, and some continental dishes prepared reasonably well and served with some care. Dancing and entertainment nightly at 8:30.

**Moderate.** Open seven days. Breakfast from 7 to 11:30 a.m. Luncheon from 11:30 a.m. to 5 p.m. Dinner from 5 to 9:30 p.m. Monday through Thursday; to 10:30 Friday, Saturday; to 9 Sunday. Sunday brunch 11 a.m. to 3 p.m. Entertainment. Dancing. Full bar. Reservations recommended. All major credit cards. Parking lot. Casual.

## SAND CASTLE
28128 Pacific Coast Highway
Malibu      **Map 2**

**Continental/Seafood**
★
(213) 457-9793

They've survived more perils — flood, fire, washouts — than Pauline, yet it's still a tranquilly rural getaway. The Continental menu selection ranges from a marvelous beef Wellington to an interesting entrée, scalone, a blend of scallops and abalone sauté amandine. Entrées include soup or salad, potato, vegetables and good bread. The service is devastatingly gracious. Our lady for the evening insisted that the pin spot light above our table was too glaring and she got a busboy to shift it. She was pleasant, outgoing, and helpful and the Sand Castle is fortunate to have the dedicated people that perform there. With the view, it's marvelous for luncheon and exciting for their brunch with dishes like our old friend eggs Benedict, crab Mornay or blintzes. A lovely, if long, drive from Los Angeles to north Malibu Center.

**Moderate to expensive.** Open seven days. Breakfast from 6 to 11 a.m. Luncheon from 11 a.m .to 4 p.m. Dinner from 5 to 11 p.m. Sunday brunch served all day. Banquet facilities. Children's menu. Entertainment. Dancing. Full bar. Reservations advised. Ocean view. All major credit cards. Parking available. Casual.

## SAN DIMAS MANSION
121 North San Dimas Avenue
San Dimas      **Map 6**

**Continental**
★
(714) 599-9391

Ring the doorbell and the butler will welcome you into an 1887 historic mansion—a graceful blend of genteel Edwardian grandeur in a contemporary restaurant. The menu is classic continental, there is a wide variety of wines, and pastry is prepared on the premises. Table settings of Bavarian china, silver, crystal and fresh flowers give this new place an old look of elegance.

**Expensive.** Open Wednesday through Sunday. Luncheon from 10 a.m. to 2 p.m. Dinner 6 to 10 p.m. Sunday brunch 10 a.m. to 2 p.m. Banquet facilities. Piano entertainment; fashion shows Wednesday and Friday; Harpist Sunday. Full bar. Reservations advised. Visa, MC. Parking lot; valet at night. Dressy.

---

## SAPPORO-YA

**Japanese**

Japanese Village Plaza ★★
Los Angeles    **Map 7**       (213) 680-3022

The "ya" in Sapporo-Ya means simply "a shop, place or house." In Japan, Sapporo-Ya would be referred to as *Soba-Ya*, or "noodle place." And that it is. Seated at tables at Sapporo-Ya, you are faced with a very serious selection of noodles. There are seven types of *ramen* noodle soups: salt, soy sauce, *miso*, butter, *cha su* (pork), *miso cha su*, and a big seafood-vegetable combination. Each of the *ramen* dishes is served in a bowl big enough to pretty easily make a meal for two persons. The ramen noodles are soft and slightly salty, and after you've picked out the pieces of vegetable and enjoyed some of the delicate pork broth, there's not much to do but discreetly slurp your noodles. But good as they are, the *ramen* dishes are not my favorite at Sapporo-Ya. That nod goes to the *yaki soba* dishes, which are noodles that are first boiled and then fried on a griddle with small pices of cabbage, carrots, bean sprouts, and either pieces of marinated pork or beef. The *yaki soba* is served topped with a small mound of red grated ginger and doused with a wonderful gingery sauce described by the restaurant as simply "homemade." There is also the Japanese equivalent of the Chinese pot sticker, which I ordered along with *Oshinko* pickles, which I figured were okay since pickles don't have too many calories. And my cup of green tea had no calories at all.   *M.S.*

**Inexpensive.** Open seven days from 11 a.m. to 10 p.m. Beer and sake only. Reservations for large parties only. Visa, MC. Validated parking. Casual.

---

## SARATOGA
7920 Sunset Boulevard
Los Angeles          **Map 8**

**Continental/Seafood**
★
(213) 874-3177

The blank concrete exterior of this restaurant suggests a cheerless neighborhood bar with no clue at all to the plush ambience, the wicker lamps, the curtained booths, and tasteful prints inside this surprisingly good, albeit unpretentious restaurant. The owner, Dave Higer, has been trying to overcome the image for several years. At luncheon, they're packed with the nearby advertising and recording executives, but dinner has been a lonely affair. That will probably be changed because Dave has introduced a fresh seafood menu along with his four veal scallopinis, steaks, and prime ribs. The scallops, flounder, and whitefish are flown in from the East every day, with live Maine lobster at the top of the list. The lobster is succulent, served either steamed or broiled as you choose, and in the most convenient manner I've ever encountered — even the claws are split and laid open for you. Dinners are modestly priced, but it's the food and atmosphere that add up to a pleasant occasion. The decor is by Audrey, Dave's wife, and she's accomplished a welcoming, colorful, cheerful look, unlike the mass-production vinyl resting places that proliferate throughout the area. The wine list is fair, a modest but adequate collection, and the cocktails are great. Be sure you see the blackboard specials before ordering from the extensive menu.

**Moderate.** Open Monday through Saturday. Luncheon served from 11:30 a.m. to 4 p.m. weekdays. Dinner from 4 to 11 p.m. Full bar. Reservations advised. All major credit cards. Parking available. Casual to dressy.

## SARNO'S CAFE DELL'OPERA         Opera Cabaret
1714 North Vermont                                    ★
Los Angeles         **Map 7**              (213) 662-3403

Since 1946 they've been singing their little hearts out in
this whimsical and happy place that caters to a show biz
crowd. The food is okay, but people really go there to have
a good time and listen to the performers introduced by the
singing host, Alberto. They're open until 2 a.m. and the
location is convenient to the Greek Theatre, Pantages or
even the Music Center a few miles away.

**Moderate.** Open Tuesday through Sunday. Luncheon from
11 a.m. to 5 p.m. daily. Dinner 5 p.m. to 1 a.m. Sunday,
Tuesday, Thursday; to 2 a.m. Friday, Saturday. After-
theatre dining. Entertainment. Wine and beer only. Enclosed
patio. Visa, MC. Parking lot. Casual.

## SAUSALITO SOUTH                        Continental
3280 North Sepulveda Boulevard                        ★
Manhattan Beach                         (213) 546-4507

On my second visit to Sausalito South, the new excitement
in Manhattan Beach, I was preceded by four middle-aged
mods. They were bored, jaded, and be-jeaned, staring inscru-
tably at the frenzy of wriggling bodies that seem attracted to
new places for at least a month or so. Just before their names
were called, they left, and I heard one of them mutter, "San
Francisco it ain't." I'm not sure what San Francisco they
remembered, but they were wrong. Here, for better or
worse—fortunately for better—is a clone of the restaurants
that have prolifereated throughout the Bay Area, certainly
more typical than an Ernie's or Doros or Blue Fox.

There is greenery and wood and beautiful people, fair to
excellent fresh fish in an atmosphere that may seem an
acoustical disaster to some, exciting to others. The *cioppino*

was good, certainly better than the red and dead concoctions of other piscatoriums. The seafood platter is hugemongous; the fresh Eastern scallops in mushrooms and puff pastry are tolerable; and the Alta Mira Ramos Fizz and Buena Vista Irish Coffee are worthy tributes to their namesakes. The cracked crab is handled as well here as in any wharf restaurant, and there is flair and imagination at the sauce pot. Desserts are unimpressive, but will, I expect, be better as they narrow the selection a bit.

Service is deft, impersonal and vulnerable, but there is such a pervading air of goodwill that little mishaps are tolerated.

I liked the oyster bar and the new/old kitchen chairs with that special atmosphere that is sometimes described as "California" and sometimes as "San Francisco." They have style.

**Moderate to expensive.** Open seven days. Dinner served Monday through Friday from 5:30 to 11 p.m.; Saturday from 5 to midnight; Sunday from 5:30 to 11:30 p.m. Closed Thanksgiving and Christmas. Full bar. Reservations advised. Patio. Visa, MC, AX. Wheelchair access. Parking lot. Casually elegant.

---

## SCANDIA

**Continental/Scandinavian**

9040 Sunset Boulevard

West Hollywood    **Map 8**

★★★

(213) 272-9521

Kenneth Hansen, one of the world's great and legendary restaurateurs, loved his Scandia on the Sunset Strip with a fierce and stubborn pride. When he selected Robert Petersen as the person to whom he would sell his landmark in July 1978, there were uneasy murmurings from three generations of Scandia-lovers. And when Hansen died in December 1980, there were many who felt that the restaurant would pass from the scene as well. But they despaired too soon and in vain. After a brief period of uncertainty the restaurant righted itself, and it became clear once again that Ken knew what he was doing.

Petersen, a publishing tycoon, and his actress wife, Margie, served a three-year apprenticeship under Hansen before they took the reins, and it wasn't always easy. Hansen, never the easiest of bosses, was as demanding of the Petersens as he had been of everyone. His training was extraordinarily effective, and Scandia alumni now operate restaurants throughout the world.

The present location opened on February 4, 1958, built to Hansen's specifications. Few changes, other than those imposed by aging, have taken place: the wine cellar was moved downstairs; the Belle Terrasse, a concrete patio with awnings, was fully enclosed and decorated in 1962 to bring over-all seating up to 250. The large main dining room with festive chandeliers, the cozy Danish Room, gleaming with copper pans, and the Skäl Room with its handsome, masculine bar, are busier than ever these days.

Dinner begins with a basket of bread including the wonderful salt bread, sweet limpa, and parmesan-encrusted slices of pumpernickel toast. Caroline Bates recalls a dinner in *Gourmet* magazine: "Our first courses were glorious: Viking platter, wispy little crêpes folded around Danish caviar, aquavit, scallions and a cloud of sour cream... a Danish version of oysters Rockefeller with a spinach puree... smoked whitefish."

Long before *nouvelle cuisine* became the buzz word, Scandia was serving dishes like scallops with slices of papaya, kiwi and orange in hazelnut butter, chicken prepared with lingonberries. At luncheon, there is a blackboard menu with the best of what's fresh and exquisite open-faced sandwiches. The dinner menu is more lavish and epicurean, and the supper menu, served until 1:30, is comprised of special dishes to accommodate the late of night: Welsh rarebit, eggs Benedict, chicken livers sautéed with onions and bacon, and the favorite dish, *Biff Lindstrom*, made with chopped sirloin, chopped beets, capers, and onions served with a fried egg on top.

The wine cellar, with over 30,000 bottles, was a collaborative effort between Ken Hansen and Nate Chroman, one of America's distinguished wine authorities. In the early days of Scandia, Chroman, who was not all that impressed with the wine list, used to bring in his own special favorites, albeit with much apprehension. Hansen observed his practice with a stony silence that endured until one memorable day when he approached Chroman's table: "He looked at the bottle and inquired bluntly if I was the blankety-blank diner who persisted in bringing his own bottles," Nate recalled in his *Times* column. "Before I could answer, he asked if he could sit down, nosed the wine from my glass and then requested another for himself."

Nate took over the administration of the wine cellar which grew in breadth and excitement, interrupted only when Hansen was enraged with then-President DeGaulle's attitude toward America and threw out all the French wines. That wine has been replaced.

There are many sentimental memories of the old Scandia and its proprietor. I remember courting a young lady who was serenaded by Hansen rendering "September Song" in a hoarse yet affecting voice. ("September Song" is a song that must never be sung well.)

Hansen would be the first to urge you to continue to enjoy his restaurant. He hand-picked his successor, and his greatness is so much a part of the splendid restaurant that it will assure and reassure those who come to Scandia. *Skol*.

**Expensive.** Open Tuesday through Sunday. Luncheon 11:30 a.m. to 2:30 p.m. Monday through Saturday. Dinner 6 p.m. to 1 a.m. Tuesday through Saturday; 5 to 12:30 a.m. Sunday. Sunday brunch 11 a.m. to 3 p.m. Closed Thanksgiving, Christmas. Full bar. Reservations required. Wheelchair access. All major credit cards. Valet parking. Semi-dressy for lunch; dressy for dinner.

## SCARANTINO'S ITALIAN INN    Italian

1524 East Colorado Street    ★
Glendale    **Map 7**    (213) 247-9777

A really good family restaurant. Social tact is making
people feel at home—when you wish they really were. I've
watched some snockered customers handled in fine style in
this thoroughly professional Italian restaurant with outstanding *manicotti* and a combination plate of scampi, veal
marsala, and *cannelloni*.

**Inexpensive.** Open Tuesday through Sunday. Dinner Tuesday through Saturday from 4:30 to 10 p.m.; Sunday 4 to
9:30 p.m. Wine and beer only. No reservations. Visa, MC.
Limited parking. Casual.

## SCHNITZELBANK    German

1037 Prospect Street    ★
La Jolla    (714) 454-5671

Hugh portions and homecooking is the code here. Lovely,
informal waitresses in jeans serve mostly informal clientele
on massive portions of *kasseler ripchen* (smoked pork chop)
and a savory sauerbraten with spaetzle and sweet and sour
cabbage. The beer tastes better here in huge (there's that
word again) mugs and the apple strudel is delectable. Best
of all, the restaurant is spared the kitsch—pastureland
paintings, bearded *bürgermeisters*—of most German restaurants.

**Inexpensive to moderate.** Open seven days 8 a.m. to 11
p.m. Children's menu. Wine and beer only. Reservations
advised for dinner. All major credit cards. Street parking.
Casual.

# SEAFOOD BAY                                      Seafood

3916 Sunset Boulevard                                      ★
Los Angeles        **Map 7**              (213) 664-3902

"Another seafood restaurant in Los Angeles?" you ask. Sure, when it is as good and honest and downright cheap as this one. Simon Buntich is a one man staff. He does all the produce selecting and goes directly to the fish market to save the money spent for delivery charges. He is geared to a fast turnover and doesn't serve alcoholic beverages or fancy coffees. Baklava is the only dessert. As a matter of fact it is a little like eating in a market amidst the refrigerator cases. A red snapper sandwich was priced at under $2. The blackboard specials are all almost always under $5, and you'll come across some species that may be new to you. "Spaghetti calamari" is a generous serving of pasta with squid, fresh tomatoes, peppers and cheese. *Calamari Italiano* is Buntich's hometown recipe of squid, sautéed with garlic and sauced with tomato, onion and green pepper.

**Inexpensive.** Open Monday through Saturday. Luncheon Monday through Friday 11:30 a.m. to 3 p.m. Dinner from 5 to 10:30 p.m.; Saturday to 11. Closed major holidays. No alcoholic beverages. No reservations. No credit cards; personal checks accepted. Street parking. Casual.

# SEAFOOD BROILER                                Seafood

(Locations in Brentwood, City of Industry, Glendale, Lakewood, Panorama City, Seal Beach, Studio City, Tarzana, Torrance. See phone book for listings.)

Newest and happiest trend in a long time is the proliferation of inexpensive seafood restaurants, a step above the fish market but not quite up there with the plush piscatoriums where your live lobster is introduced to you before being boiled or broiled. I could never enjoy eating something when they put a name on it. "This is Homer," a San Francisco waiter told me as Homer was struggling to get the hell out of there. When he was served up, with melted butter, I felt somewhat like a cannibal. (He was a little stringy anyway). Example of the trend is the Seafood Broiler, a seafood restaurant and market with locations in Lakewood, two in the valley, and one in Glendale. I had fresh, *fresh* succulent scallops on a skewer with cherry tomatoes and bacon, mashed potatoes with cheese, a cob — I hate the word "cobbette" — of corn, good cole slaw, and fresh rolls with butter. They use charcoal on the fish, shrimp, snapper, . . . and the combination of heat that sears in the juices plus the smokey flavor is wonderful. Service is a little too laid back. I mean it was embarrassing when my waitress came back and observed that I had devoured my 6 clams on the half shell "so quickly!" They don't take reservations here and everything is made of formica (except the waitresses and the fish) but the line moves along swiftly and it's worth a wait. You can have a shrimp or crab cocktail at the fish market counter while waiting for your name to be called. There's properly chilled beer and a house wine that's not too bad. I'd give them a near perfect rating if it weren't for the waitress who called attention to my gluttony. I did get even with her though. Next time we went the same girl aproached the table and I said, "Hello there, my name is Paul and I'm your customer for the evening." She looked just a touch like a halibut for a second, with her mouth open, but she recovered in time to sweetly argue in favor of a plastic bib for me. She argued quite unsuccessfully. This is a great place to introduce the tots to tuna or tortuava or whatever is fresh.

**Inexpensive.** Open seven days. Luncheon Monday through Saturday from 11 a.m. to 4 p.m. Dinner from 4 to 10 p.m. Wine and beer only. No reservations. Visa, MC. Parking lot. Casual.

# THE SEA LION

21150 Pacific Coast Highway
Malibu    **Map 2**

**Seafood**

★

(213) 456-2810

A quarter of a century ago sea lions cavorted in a special pond in front of the Sea Lion, a big unpretentious restaurant in the northernmost reaches of Malibu. Families would watch the whiskered mammals and reward their hoarse barks with hand-outs of bait, while waiting up to an hour or more for seats, hoping for one of the booths with picture windows, so close to the water they often glistened with ocean spray. The seals are no longer there, long ago giving way to the need for more and more parking, but this is still the inexpensive honest restaurant lovingly remembered by three generations. There are still no reservations. Your name goes down on the list, and you're called in turn, whether you're Kissinger or just plain Bill. Shortly after I was seated I overheard an elderly lady ask in a coy Shirley Temple voice, "Can you tell me where the little girls' room is, please?" "You mean the toilet, lady?" answered the hard-working waitress, scarcely missing a beat. That's the kind of place it is; everything is called by its proper name. Broiled sea bass, Northern ling filet, fried Columbia River smelt, salmon, scallops — all are described in the plainest possible terms, and all are prepared with that rare genius that foregoes sauces in favor of the natural textures and flavors of the seafood. Best of all is the Marine Salad, a gigantic bowl (enough for at least two) filled with generous chunks of crab meat, shrimp, lobster, and ripe avocado topped with homemade Roquefort that is a sensation. The wine list is very limited but choice, with California wines such as BV and Christian Brothers. (You'll pay twice as much in many places.) Cocktails are so-so at best, indifferently made and certainly not pushed.

**Inexpensive.** Open seven days from 10 a.m. to 10 p.m. Children's menu. Full bar. Reservations advised. View. No credit cards. Parking lot. Casual.

## SEA QUEST
**Seafood**
★

5835 East Los Angeles Avenue
Simi Valley      **Map 1**
(805) 522-5353

Simi Valley doesn't abound in restaurants and the fact that there is a good seafood place here is close to a miracle. The seafare is a touch European: Trout *amandine, sole au champagne, cioppino,* and it's well presented. Atmosphere is exotic aquariums, a salad bar, and the appropriate memorabilia.

**Moderate.** Open seven days. Dinner from 5 to 10 p.m. Limited banquet facilities. Wine and beer only. Reservations advised. Visa, MC, AX. Parking lot. Casual.

## SEASHELL
**Seafood**
★

19723 Ventura Boulevard
Woodland Hills      **Map 1**
(213) 884-6500

Fresh seafood in Woodland Hills is a luxury, and the Seashell has become quietly popular amongst the local gentry. Abalone, soft-shell crab, fresh mussels, and trout are masterfully prepared in this pleasant wood-paneled restaurant, where semi-formal French waiters are somehow not incongruous among their casually attired guests. This is fine dining, with chef-owner Dieter Wantig and his partner, Christian Desmet attending, supervising, tasting, and occasionally chatting with their customers. The bouillabaisse is rich in saffron, the salmon chowder well-herbed, and the salmon baked in sorrel sauce delightful. Here is the kind of moderately priced French seafood restaurant that is often sought; they've been doing their thing so well, I'm afraid some of us have taken them for granted. The wine list is exemplary, and we experienced a new wine — Sutter's Home white zinfandel. It's light, semi-dry, and has a delicate white-pink hue.

**Moderate.** Open 7 days. Luncheon weekdays from 11:30 a.m. to 2 p.m. Dinner from 5:30 to 10 p.m. Closed 4th of July, Labor Day, Christmas. Full bar. Reservations advised. All major credit cards. Parking lot. Casual to semi-dressy.

---

## THE SEA THIEF
5786 La Jolla Boulevard
La Jolla

**Seafood**
★
(714) 454-0703

Bouillabaisse is a precious, delicate dish, but I like the Americanized version as served here, with plenty of shellfish in a zesty saffron stock and good bread. It can only be ordered for two or more, which makes sense because it is too costly to prepare for a single portion. There is an oyster bar that's good, cocktails, and a better-than-average list of expected seafoods, in a pleasant atmosphere.

**Moderate.** Open seven days. Dinner from 4:30 to 11 p.m. Full bar. Reservations advised. All major credit cards. Parking lot. Casual.

---

## SENOR PICO AND MAMMA GRUBER'S
10131 Constellation Boulevard
Los Angeles          **Map 8**

**Mexican/Seafood**
★
(213) 277-4525

This restaurant is filled with Mexican antiques and works of art. The central atrium patio has two focal points—a hand carved terra cotta fountain banked in ferns and a canopied seafood bar with fresh seafood displayed on shaved ice. It is altogether an imaginative and highly professional operation that scores in all departments: decor is hacienda style, complete with courtyard and a fountain; and the food is good Mexican and "early Californian" with original touches and flair. *Langosta rancheros* is lobster pieces sautéed with chili spices and served in a shell; *caborca* lamb is stuffed with *chorizo*. Appetizers like *quesadillas* and *empanadas* are popular with

589

before-dinner drinks. Desserts include bananas in rum, fresh papaya, and feather-light *sopapillas* (sweetened bread served with a light syrup). The bartenders' margaritas are perfectly chilled, and there is sangria or *copa de vino* in pitchers.

**Moderate**. Open seven days from 11:30 a.m. to 11 p.m.; Sunday from 4 to 11 p.m. Closed Thanksgiving, Christmas, New Year's. Full bar. Reservations advised. All major credit cards. Valet parking. Semi-dressy.

---

## SGT. PEPPER'S
**American**
★
1408 Foothill Boulevard
La Verne  **Map 6**  (714) 596-3701

In El Adobe Village this restaurant just may be the closest to the American palate of any new restaurant in recent years. The food is light and not complicated. There are 17 omelettes that range from "Mandarin chicken" to "spinach mushroom," and the sandwiches show imagination and flair. The Italian sausage sandwich with onions, bell peppers and mushrooms is served on what tasted like a freshly baked French roll. The chicken cashew is our old friend chicken salad brought to the highest state of the art, served with roasted cashews and piled high on hunter's bread. Dinners include a meatloaf "Wellington," homemade beef stew, and fresh garden casserole.

The El Adobe Village is like a suburban Olvera Street with huge gates at the entrance and small shops around the plaza. Chef John Chauk was coaxed out of retirement to create a family restaurant for the location and he's obviously been given a free hand. While this is not a "serious" restaurant in the tradition of *haute cusine*, it is perhaps more relevant to the Southern California lifestyle. I found it interesting.

**Inexpensive.** Open Tuesday through Sunday. Luncheon from 11 a.m. to 4 p.m.; dinner from 4 to 9 p.m. Sunday 10 a.m. to midnight. Private party facilities. Closed major holidays. Wine and beer only. Reservations accepted. Visa, MC. Parking lot. Casual.

# SESAME AND LILIES

**French**
★★

7513 Sunset Boulevard
Los Angeles  **Map 8**

(213) 876-9044

How rare. How delightful. Sesame and Lilies is that sought-after combination that makes for a bona fide discovery; it's small (40 seats), plain (cheap wood paneling), unusual (a French restaurant operated by a Japanese lady) and inexpensive. In an unattractive storefront on the less appealing part of Sunset Boulevard, Sesame and Lilies (named for the owner's favorite selections from poet John Ruskin) flourishes amidst a clutter of shabby shops and photo studios. Yoshi Brelsford uses herbs and spices as an artist uses delicate tints. The escargot is steeped in garlic butter with just the right amount of zing. The salad of greens and fresh mushroom is lightly but sprightly dressed, and the *potage au citrouille* (cream of squash soup) is rich. Among the eight entrées are the best sweetbreads in Los Angeles, delicately breaded and topped with *sauce aurore*, cheese, and chopped parsley. The beef tongue is a revelation for those who think they don't like tongue; it's tender, smothered with a hearty red wine sauce and served with carrots touched with clove, and fresh spinach. The two English-style curries with homemade chutney, duckling *à l'orange*, and the tournedos continue the high standards of this creative kitchen. The *gnocchi* here are light potato dumplings baked in butter and cheese and just touched with garlic, a carryover from the days when Mrs. Brelsford operated an Italian restaurant in Paris. Desserts are unboring, an achievement more notable by the mediocre standards of dessert fare at many French restaurants in Southern California. The specialty on one occasion was a concoction of layers of Anjou pears baked with cream, rum, and macaroons.

**Moderate.** Open Tuesday through Sunday. Dinner Sunday through Thursday from 6 to 10 p.m., Friday and Saturday to 10:30 p.m. Wine and beer only. Reservations advised. Visa, MC, AX. Street parking and public parking across the street. Casual.

# SHANGHAI RED'S AND THE BACK ROOM

**Seafood/Continental**

13813 Fiji Way
Marina del Rey          **Map 2**

★

(213) 823-4522

Shanghai Red, the infamous madam of San Pedro, entertained a mixed bag. High class swells used her special back room. Hence, one divided restaurant, two menus. Gentility, elegance and fun are the key to the turn-of-the-century decor. It's cozy in the main room, divine in The Back Room. The antique photos alone could keep one interested endlessly. Fresh seafood is featured at Shanghai Red's. From Catalina and dabs, center cut swordfish steaks and *cioppino* to a cauldron of steamed clams... they have it all. Dinner includes a soup (a fine New England chowder) and salad (try the honey-mustard dressing), varied potatoes and a hot loaflet of sour dough bread. Atmosphere? I was with four teenagers, but watching the yachts and sailboats trailing home in after-glow of sunset beat *any* tranquilizer.

The posher folks in The Back Room enjoy the continental menu, slightly higher priced, and very elegant. Tableside service features flaming dishes from steaks (Diane, pepper, garlic) to desserts (banana flambé, oh, passion!!!). The pastry cart is a museum piece, an ogler's delight. The Back Room calls for fancy dress, but as General Manager Paul Childers says, "In the Marina, you cross your fingers."

The outside architecture is dockside corrugated metal. The entry is lush with waterfalls, ponds and tropical flora. One is welcome to gaze through the interior bordello setting. There is a bar area for non-diners. At last, a superior restaurant on Fisherman's Village.     *Jackie Joseph*

**Shanghai Red's: Moderate.** Open seven days. Luncheon 11 a.m. to 3 p.m. Monday through Saturday; 10 a.m. to 3 p.m. Sunday. Dinner 5 to 10 p.m. Monday through Thursday; to 11 p.m. Friday, Saturday; 4 to 10 p.m. Sunday. Closed Christmas. Full bar. No reservations. View. All major credit cards. Parking lot. Casual.

**The Back Room: Expensive.** Open seven days. Dinner 6 to 10 p.m. Monday through Thursday; to 11 p.m. Friday, Saturday; 5 to 10 p.m. Sunday. Closed Christmas. Entertainment. Full bar. Reservations suggested. View. All major credit cards. Valet parking; self-parking. Dressy.

---

## SHANGHAI RESTAURANT                    Chinese
4916 Hollywood Boulevard                               ★
Los Angeles        **Map 7**              (213) 666-7070

Emphasis is on Mandarin dishes in this unsurprising, prosaic Chinese restaurant with a cocktail lounge and entertainment. There is Peking duck and Mongolian beef, but best of all is the "whole fish."

**Moderate.** Open seven days. Luncheon from 11:30 a.m. to 3 p.m. Dinner 5 to 10:30 p.m.; Friday, Saturday 5 to 11:30 p.m. Banquet facilities. Entertainment nightly after 9. Dancing. Full bar. Reservations advised. All major credit cards. Valet parking. Casual to semi-dressy.

---

## SHANGHAI WINTER GARDEN                 Chinese
5651 Wilshire Boulevard                                ★
Los Angeles        **Map 7**              (213) 934-0505

The newest trend in Chinese food — too serious to be called a fad — is the cuisine that comes from China's province of Szechwan. The dishes are notably spicier than the more familiar Cantonese and Mandarin — so much so that unless the Westerner's eyes water throughout dinner, something's probably amiss in the kitchen. Not many restaurants prepare this food authentically, although it seems that every Chinese restaurant in the area is trying to cash in on its popularity. I recall a sign in front of a tiny storefront establishment in Hollywood that proclaimed, "Exquisite Japanese, Indian, Chinese, and Korean Food," with "Szechwan a Specialty" hand-lettered as an obvious afterthought. To achieve perfection in any of those schools of cuisine would be a major accomplishment for a huge kitchen

593

and master chef; to achieve even mediocrity in all of them would be a feat comparable to bicycling up the Washington Monument. The Shanghai Winter Garden, a lovely traditional-looking Chinese restaurant in the Los Angeles Miracle Mile district, is highly regarded for its Szechwan food, although it is served a bit milder than I expected, probably in deference to the yet uncalloused American palate. However, a tiny thimble-sized glass of red liquid pepper sauce is placed with deceptive innocence alongside the other condiments. It is wise to use only a drop or two. As in all Chinese restaurants, it is more fun and adventurous to explore the à la carte menu, although you would do well to discuss each dish with your waiter. I ordered more hot dishes than is usual, and enjoyed them all. The superb hot and sour soup and single orders of imperial shrimp with red sauce, sautéed shredded beef, and spicy diced chicken with peanuts (our favorite) were more than enough for a party of four.

**Moderate.** Open seven days. Luncheon from 11:30 a.m. to 3 p.m. weekdays. Dinner from 4 to 10:30 p.m. Closed Chinese New Year. Full bar. Reservations advised. All major credit cards. Valet parking. Casual.

---

## SHEP'S                                          American
10654 West Pico Boulevard
Los Angeles          **Map 8**              (213) 559-7900

One of the pages in Shep's menu is dedicated to "the dilemma of High Prices!!" which explains that the restaurant has been forced to raise its prices because of increased labor costs ("The minimum wage has increased 20 percent"), utility costs ("Have tripled"), insurance costs ("Practically doubled"), and so on. None of this explains the perfectly awful meals I've had at Shep's, lately. During one visit, I was kept waiting at the door for ten minutes even though there were empty tables visible; after another long wait, my order was taken by a young girl, woefully unfamiliar with the menu; and after an even longer wait, the food arrived. The stuffed *derma* had fallen apart and tasted old. It was served with a bowl of gooey gravy, which helped the *kishke* not one whit. The corned beef sandwich was served on a stale—not just dry, but genuinely stale—onion roll. The corned beef was dry; the Russian dressing I asked for was nowhere to be found. No pickle was served. I came away from my meal at Shep's wishing the place would invest a little more attention in the customer and keep its railing against the high cost of running a restaurant to itself. *M.S.*

**Inexpensive.** Open seven days from 7 a.m. to 1 a.m. Closed Yom Kippur. Beer and wine only. Reservations for large parties. Visa, MC. Parking lot. Casual.

---

## SHERMAN ROOM
16916 Sherman Way
Van Nuys    **Map 1**

**American**
★
(213) 881-9367

When Joyce and Bill Smith opened this restaurant a quarter of a century ago plain food was exalted and steaks were the main attraction. The fact that they built this place when the dollar had some sense to it means that you don't have to pay for expensive decor or costumes. Most steaks are served sizzling in 10-ounce portions although there are some mini portions for less. Salads are crisp, cold and good, and better dressed than some of the patrons. There are other entrées as well, mostly fish, but this is a steak-eaters heaven with prices that are about half that of most other beef emporiums. No nonsense waitresses, efficient service, and good cocktails are the tradition here. The wine list is not brilliant but it's adequate. Gary Ruiz has assumed the helm and has kept prices down.

**Moderate.** Open seven days. Luncheon from 11 a.m. to 3 p.m. Dinner from 5 to 10 p.m. Full bar. No reservations. No credit cards or checks. Parking lot. Casual.

## SHOGUN
Japanese
★

470 North Halstead Street
Pasadena     **Map 7**     (213) 351-8945

A Japanese restaurant located in the suburbs presents an
interesting phenomenon. The area hasn't been built up yet,
but it will. In the meantime, they are trying to please local
palates weaned on Bob's Big Boy and Denny's,—hence, the
teppan dinner with tossed green salad and French dressing.
But these folks know what they're doing. If their sushi isn't
the best right now it will be when everything clicks.
Meanwhile, it is good Japanese fare in a lovely interior.

**Moderate**. Open seven days. Luncheon 11:30 a.m. to 2 p.m.
(weekdays). Dinner from 5 to 10 p.m., Monday through
Thursday; 5 to 10:30 p.m. Friday, Saturday; Sunday, holidays
from 4:30 to 9:30 p.m. Banquet facilities. Full bar. Reservations advised. All major credit cards. Parking lot. Semi-dressy.

## SIAMESE PRINCESS
Thai
★★

718 North Highland
(at Melrose)
Los Angeles     **Map 7**     (213) 462-9707

I experienced a moment of *déjà vu* when we visited the Siamese Princess, a tiny storefront wedged between a pizza
parlor and a liquor store on Melrose in Hollywood. Each of
the 12 tables was adorned with a black tablecloth, a sterling
candelabra and a carefully arranged bouquet of fresh flowers.
In the center of the establishment was a full-size portrait of
the king and queen above a table with a clutter of small
framed photographs of the family, shown to us with pride
by Victor Sodsook, the proprietor. Improbably, there was
another wall covered with family photographs of Princess
Grace, Caroline and the Monaco royalty, displayed for the
guileless reason that Sodsook "loves them." There are moss
green walls, heavy gold Buddha stands, lovely table settings,

and classical music in the background. The dinner on this evening was everything a dining adventure should be, adhering to that Thai philosophy that one should feed the body and the soul. The dishes are skillful blending of Indonesian, Chinese and Indian, which together achieve a state of nirvana. We had *kaeng sum*, an orange-sour soup prepared with lemon and shrimp with vinegar and lime juice, and *pla nam* — an often used piquant fish sauce—topped with shredded omelette? There is an assortment of appetizers like "galloping horses" (ground pork, peanuts and spices served on pineapple and cilantro) and curries like "yellow chicken" (the color comes from the kakrut leaves, horapa and a wafting of fresh green chilis; the creamy quality is from coconut meat. Tell the waiter how spicy you want it), rice dishes and entrées, but my favorite is *wing kai* marinated stuffed chicken roll. My lady, who regards chicken wings with Olympian distaste, was enchanted by these; they were stuffed with a medley of chicken and other savories to be dunked in a marvelous sauce. Other entrées include "dear crab" (filled with crab meat, ground pork, yolk of egg and a zesty sauce), and fried pork with garlic. The massive menu includes a listing of noodles from which I recommend the *mee krob*, transparent Thai vermicelli, scallions, garlic, shrimp, and morsels of pork or chicken. Luncheon consists of smaller and less expensive portions of the dinner menu; all accompanied by fragrant jasmine tea. There's no wine or beer yet. I brought a great bottle of Chateau Jean Gewurtztraminer and opted to share it with the owner and the one waiter. When the bottle emptied I went next door to the liquor emporium only to find that their entire selection of whites consisted of Gallo Rhinegarten and Italian Swiss chablis. We had the Gallo; it was adequate, but you should bring whatever you like. There is no corkage, and white wine is placed into a beautiful silver bucket that materializes like magic when you are seated.

**Inexpensive to moderate.** Open seven days. Dinner from 6 to 10:30 p.m. No alcoholic beverages. Reservations advised. All major credit cards. Street parking. Casual to semi-dressy.

## SILVANA'S Italian
268 South La Cienega Boulevard ★
Beverly Hills **Map 8** (213) 659-8422

New into '81 is a stylish Italian restaurant, an early-on favorite with the restaurant critics and aficionados. Silvana's in Beverly Hills is an unlikely combination of an inexperienced restaurateur and a glamorous chef operating a restaurant that probably costs less then the foyer of most of the new biggies. Though it's too early to tell, Silvana's appears promising. Edward Colon used to be one of New York's finest when they were the finest. A retired detective from the mob-squad, he took a narrow storefront on La Cienega, covered the front windows and rolled panels of hand-painted duck canvas and covered the wall mirrors with lattice. However little he spent ("I'd be embarrassed to tell you") it seems to work. The carpet of deep green looks like a lawn and the room is surrounded by banquettes, a few booths and, on a busy night, a few tables in front of the center wine bar. Surprisingly there is no ornate cappuccino machine making strangling noises, although there is a caffe espresso.

Silvana is an accomplished chef and wherever she has worked, her dishes were the main attraction. My *mozzarella marinara* was OK but the deep-fried cheese lacked the touch of anchovy I like. The pasta *puttanesca* was served in a blander red sauce than I expected—I was accustomed to a white and very spicy sauce—but it is one of those dishes of vague ancestry and subject to interpretation. The lobster *diavolo* was excellent, served in a thermidor-style but chunked instead of diced, a generous whole lobster that was beautifully presented. There is a lobster thermidor flambéed in cognac with onions, cream and seasoning. Lobster is priced according to the daily market fluctuations and was $18 à la carte on my night. The pasta was offered "very *al dente*," "*al dente*," or "not *al dente*." The "very" was good. There's a full range of pastas, four soups and more than a few steaks. Emphasis is on veal dishes although Silvana has a nice touch with seafood and the scampi Tosca is admirable. While the *canoli*, one of my favorite desserts, had been highly touted it was disappointingly heavy and a bit oily. And, though this may seem picky, it may make for great decor to use wine bottles between the booths standing along the back separations but it is an improper way to store wine and could make a difference to the connoisseurs. In all this is a promising find and it is growing. The limited wine list is trying to match up with the menu and it will succeed.

**Moderate to expensive.** Open Monday through Saturday from 6 to 11 p.m.; until midnight on weekends. Closed major holidays. Beer and wine only. Reservations required. Most major credit cards. Wheelchair access. Parking lot. Casual to dressy.

---

## SIMON'S                                                    Yugoslavian
2836 Sunset Blvd.                                                    ★
Los Angeles          **Map 8**                          (213) 663-7422

They call themselves "the inflation fighter restaurant" and the high quality of food at low, low prices may be hard to beat anywhere. With entrées and daily specials from under $5, the dinners include soup, salad, fresh vegetables, sour-dough bread and even a home-baked dessert with Yuban coffee. The *sarma* is special and the chicken paprikash is even better.

The restaurant isn't fancy or pricy, but can come in very handy when you're hungry and want a quick and filling meal. It's one of those discovery places that you'd never find yourself (aren't you glad you bought this book?) because the outside is downright discouraging, if not depressing. Lunch-eon is even a greater value with prices you won't believe. The little vinyl wine list is one of those that most restaurants get free if they buy certain wines, but it is adequate and fairly priced. There is a wide variety of beers, so you can explore some that are new to this territory.

**Inexpensive**. Open Monday through Saturday. Luncheon from 11:30 a.m. to 2:30 p.m. weekdays. Dinner from 5 to 11 p.m. Wine and beer only. Reservations advised on weekends. Visa, MC. Street parking. Casual.

---

## SIMPLY BLUES
**American**
★

6290 Sunset Boulevard

Los Angeles      **Map 7**              (213) 466-5239

A Hollywood penthouse restaurant in the theatre district where the prices and food are good, is a rarity at any elevation. Simply Blues is a view restaurant but the booths are larger and more spacious than most rooftop operations and it overlooks the historic corner of Sunset and Vine. We are accustomed to *haute cuisine* à-la-Tower, high atop the Occidental building where the view, food, and prices are precious. It's either that or disasters; rooms that specialize in view but little else. This restaurant does everything well and the service is deft and competent. Dishes range from the seafood brochette with choice of mixed green or spinach salad, to Rock Cornish game hen with country stuffing. There are the customary assortments of steaks and standard menu items but their onion soup gratinée and their shellfish varieties deserve special recognition. Salads are a specialty and the wine list is full of surprises, rare boutique offerings at fair prices along with imported wines. The luncheon menu consists of lighter fare with a cutting board for hot and cold sandwiches, omelettes, crêpes, and fresh seafood. I like them best here, however, for their brunch. The champagne brunch included a fresh fruit plate and such delicacies as deviled crab on a toasted English muffin, eggs Benedict, crêpes Tetrazzini, hangtown fry (scrambled eggs with plump fresh oysters, spinach, potatoes and onions) and *huevos rancheros*. All are served with hometown potatoes, a freshly baked muffin and rolls.

**Moderate**. Open seven days. Luncheon from 11:30 a.m. to 3 p.m. weekdays. Dinner Sunday through Thursday from 5 p.m. to 1 a.m.; Friday, Saturday 4:30 to midnight. Sunday brunch 10 a.m. to 3 p.m. Closed major holidays. Entertainment nightly 9 p.m. to 1:30 a.m. Full bar. Reservations required. View. All major credit cards. Unvalidated subterranean parking lot; street parking. Casual to semi-dressy.

---

## SIZZLER FAMILY STEAK HOUSE
(See phone book for locations.)

No, these are not the same steaks you would get at Pacific Dining Car, but the prices are different as well. This is a good working concept that uses purchasing power to get more exotic foods within the family budget: crab, scampi and specialty dishes. These are immaculately clean, comfortable restaurants with salad bars. One of my favorite dishes in all the world is not quite on their menu. I order a baked potato and put it in my salad plate. Then I cover it with lettuce, sliced beets, croutons and garbanzo beans, slather the top with blue cheese cream dressing and mush around until it is thoroughly mixed. The texture and flavors of hot potato and cold salad are — to me —stupendous. I once had James Collins, President of the Sizzlers, on my radio show and told him about my potato orgy. Listeners subsequently have made this a popular dish. Try it.

**Inexpensive to moderate.** Open seven days. Children welcome. Self service. Wine and beer in most locations. No reservations. Parking lots. Casual.

---

## THE SLENDER SPOON
21008 Hawthorne Boulevard
Torrance          **Map 2**

Diet/Continental
★
(213) 542-2171

Bixby Knolls Shopping Center
4520 Atlantic Avenue
Long Beach        **Map 3**

(213) 423-1355

Studio Village Mall
11072 West Jefferson Boulevard
Culver City          **Map 3**                    (213) 397-7228

7132 Edinger Avenue
Huntington Beach          **Map 2**               (714) 842-4611

Perhaps the most balanced combination of entrée and desserts for serious dieters and those merely prudent may be found at The Slender Spoon. You can select complete dinners with different-sized entrée portions (four or six ounces) — entrées such as veal tostada, Bavarian stuffed cabbage, lasagna, knockwurst with sauerkraut, and tamale pizza (my favorite), all served with antipasto or salad. There are bakery specialties here, too, along with interesting dessert combinations (a banana split with three toppings). The real secret of The Slender Spoon and the other diet establishments is their recognition of the vast numbers of people who are determinedly diet-conscious but do not want to sacrifice their palates just to slip into smaller bathing suits. Speaking of figures, Southern Californians spend four billion dollars in restaurants each year. It makes dollars and sense that a plump proportion will quickly adopt this new and less clinical approach to dieting, a significant part of our lifestyle.

**Inexpensive.** Open Monday throgh Saturday. Luncheon and dinner Monday through Friday from 11 a.m. to 9:30 p.m. Saturday to 8 p.m. Closed major holidays. No alcohol. No reservations. No credit cards. Parking lot. Casual.

---

## SMITH BROTHERS FISH SHANTY          Seafood
8500 Burton Way
Los Angeles          **Map 8**                    (213) 272-4241

This is the kind of restaurant that reminds us of our obligation to tell you which restaurants we consider a dismal disappointment as well as those that are dining adventures. The Smith Brothers looks like it would be a great seafood restaurant with its nautical (but nice) exterior just off La Cienega and the fishnet-lantern look inside. It even seems like it would be a great seafood restaurant when you look at the menu. But this place has been resolutely serving some of the most dismal fare along what used to be "restaurant row," and there are no signs of improvement. They are about as interesting as a Republican convention and have ruined several evenings for me when I got that "they can't be as bad as I thought they were" itch.

**Moderate.** Open seven days. Luncheon served Monday through Friday from 11:30 to 4 p.m. Dinner served Monday through Friday 4 to 10 p.m., Saturday 3 to 11 p.m.; Sunday 3 to 9:30 p.m. Closed Thanksgiving, Christmas. Full bar. Reservations advised. All major credit cards. Valet parking. Casual.

---

## SMOKE HOUSE RESTAURANT

American
★★

4420 Lakeside Drive
Burbank　　**Map 1**　　　　　　(213) 845-3731

The Smoke House was one of the first serious restaurants in the Valley, and there was a time when you could spot more great stars enjoying broiled meats there than at any place in Hollywood or Beverly Hills. Everything is good; even the garlic bread is about the best you can find, but it's still a meat-eater's paradise, with dishes like center chops, calf's liver and the great steaks cut in their own butcher shops. The veal Oskar is a favorite in the area, but the most popular item here is the prime rib, served *au jus* with horseradish sauce. There is a special "early dinner menu" that offers some exceptional values. Desserts are homebaked; cocktails are man-sized; and there is entertainment.

**Moderate**. Open seven days. Luncheon from 11:30 a.m. to 4 p.m. Dinner from 4 to 11:30 p.m. Banquet facilities. Closed Christmas. Entertainment. Full bar. Reservations advised. All major credit cards. Valet and self-parking. Casual.

603

## SORRENTINO'S SEAFOOD HOUSE  Seafood/American

4100 Riverside Drive                                                ★
Burbank          **Map 1**                           (213) 849-5402

If it isn't "fresh" the waitresses will tell you so, and what more can you ask of a seafood restaurant except that the dishes are prepared well — and they are. Parenthetically, there is no law that says frozen foods must be awful. It depends upon how and when a catch like salmon is processed. Sometimes seafoods that are frozen at the peak of their freshness (to quote the Jolly Green Giant) are better than fresh mediocrity. More parentheses: the same holds true for some vegetables. There are chefs who can transform canned string beans into a dish far more flavorful that most "fresh" string bean concoctions. But they are the exceptions. Anyway, this is an honest, comfortable, pleasant, reasonable restaurant that's been around for more than twenty-five years. George Shub sees to it that live Maine lobsters are flown in daily (tourist class) and has an array of "gourmet" entrées, not the least of which is the fresh — or is it frozen? — abalone.

**Moderate to expensive.** Open seven days. Luncheon from 11:30 a.m. to 3:30 p.m. Dinner Sunday through Thursday from 4 to 11:30 p.m., Friday, Saturday to midnight. Closed Christmas. Entertainment. Full bar. Reservations advised. All major credit cards. Valet parking. Casual.

## SOURCE RESTAURANT                    Organic/Vegetarian

8301 Sunset Boulevard                                               ★
Los Angeles         **Map 8**                        (213)656-6388

One of the most highly respected of the restaurants that serve only the finest and freshest organically grown fruits and vegetables, the Source is also a celebrity mecca for the rockophiles. There are sandwiches of peanut butter and raisins, cream cheese and olives, or dates on wheat bread. The "Source Special" is melted cheese with avocado, mushrooms,

alfalfa sprouts, and sesame seeds, particularly satisfying with
a bowl of thick potato and leek soup. Fruit salads are technicolor productions with fresh pineapple, papaya, and bananas; there are freshly squeezed juices and freshly ground
coffee as well.

**Moderate.** Open seven days. Monday through Thursday
from 11 a.m. to midnight; Friday 11 a.m. to 1 a.m.;
Saturday 9 a.m. to 1 a.m. Sunday 9 a.m. to midnight.
Closed Christmas. No alcohol. No reservations. Patio. Visa,
MC, AX. Parking lot. Casual.

---

## SOUTH TOWN SOUL FOOD     Southern/Soul Food
1515 North Wilcox Avenue           ★
Hollywood     **Map 7**          (213)461-3245

"Soul food started out as a poor people's food, now it's
gourmet, and I wanted to create a restaurant for my friends
who might be timid about going to Watts." This, the answer
by Coco McVey when asked the inevitable question: "Can a
Bryn Mawr graduate find happiness as the proprietor of the
thirty-one-seat South Town Soul Food, located in the less
fashionable, even seedy, section of Hollywood?" The ebullient
Coco has not only found happiness, but unexpected riches,
as evidenced by the always-busy counter, the few tables, and
the thriving catering business she's developed. The small
restaurant looks exactly like a description out of a Faulkner
novel, and that's just how Coco intended it, hiring designer
Scott Fisher to gouge holes in the wallpaper, paint linoleum
patterns on the counter top, and hang garish and deliberately
faded signs on the walls. Even the wood grain has been
painted on, rough to the eye and smooth to the fingertips.
My dinner began with an appetizer of hot link slices in red
sauce, and included almost everything I've heard about and
always wanted to taste: black-eyed peas flavored with okra
and spices, piping hot cornbread muffins, crunchy pork
Louisiana, chitlins, oxtails, pigs' feet. Greens, red beans, corn
or yams (flavored with brown sugar and honey), rounded
out a feast that went well beyond the normal dinner —

because I went slightly insane, to the dismay of the waitress, in an unsuccessful effort to make up for all the years I've been deprived of this kind of down-home cooking. I didn't have room for neck bones, and only managed one dessert —sweet potato pie. Coco learned many of her recipes from the black cook who served her well-to-do Midwestern family, but there is nothing patronizing about the hospitality (authentic as the wallpaper), according to black people, white people, students, and those of every hue who are raptly attentive to the offerings. Most of the food is prepared by a cook, although Coco herself is no mean hand at the stove, and her "filé gumbo," made when the spirit moves her, is legendary. The gumbo consists of blue-shell crab (must still be crawling when the delivery from Louisiana arrives), turkey wings, jumbo shrimp, sausage, pork, ham, beef, green onions, and more, much more. But you get the idea and so do the gumbo addicts who call in daily to see if it's ready. Prices are very low, and the long menu states that "only organically grown vegetables and USDA choice or prime meats are served."

**Inexpensive.** Open seven days; never closes. Wine and beer only. Reservations advised in the evening. All major credit cards. Street parking. Casual to semi-dressy.

---

## SPORTSMEN'S LODGE
12833 Ventura Boulevard
Studio City          **Map 1**

**Continental**
★
(213) 984-0202

Time was when the Sportsmen's Lodge in Studio City had a catch-your-own-trout stream, rustic charm, and forty seats; it was considered far out, both geographically and gastronomically. The Valley has now engulfed the lodge, and it has become bigger and bigger until finally they can seat a thousand patrons in various degrees of splendor. They've even spawned a multi-story resort-style hotel. Huge glass walls overlook a landscaped pond, rustic bridges and a mountainlike stream with Disneyish charm. There are even swans. The food, I thought, as I maneuvered through the combined traffic of a bar mitzvah and an engagement party, would not be good. Bigness is rarely goodness, I thought. I was happily surprised. The wine list would be a credit to any of the expensive European bistros along Ventura Boulevard, with some rare California labels included among imported superstars. Dinner might begin with fresh cracked stone crab ("so fresh it's almost insulting," according to our waiter), served with a mustard mayonnaise, or shellfish served on rock salt, two of the numerous appetizers. The long seafood list is augmented by some epicurean dishes like boneless breast of chicken Valencia (with avocado), or boneless breast of chicken Oskar, served with asparagus tips, crab legs and a fine Bearnaise. The selection of steaks and beef includes deviled beef ribs, and the cakes and rolls are baked fresh each day in their own bakery. My personal favorite for dinner is the broiled Chinook salmon, served fresh. The Vegas-style cocktail lounge is electric after 9 p.m. and a great favorite in the area.

**Moderate.** Open seven days. Dinner served Monday through Thursday from 5:30 to 11 p.m.; Friday, Saturday to midnight; Sunday from 4:30 to 11 p.m. Early dinner Monday through Saturday from 5:30 to 6:15 and Sunday from 4:30 to 5:45 p.m. Sunday brunch 10:30 a.m. to 2:15 p.m. Closed major holidays. Entertainment. Dancing Tuesday through Saturday. Full bar. Reservations requird. Visa, MC, AX, CB. Valet parking. Semi-dressy.

---

## STEINBECK'S

**Continental**

217 Marine Avenue

★

Balboa Island

(714) 673-0570

Linda and Guy Colbert decided to call their tiny restaurant— nine tables, 22 seats Steinbeck's because it had known earlier success as Hemingway's. The Balboa Island location was successful from the beginning, the previous owners having moved to new and more prosperous quarters. By contrast

Linda and Guy are ecstatic with the restaurant and its clientele and will never, they say now, move up to a more commercial level. Their joy in cooking, along with chef Bill Schwenk and waiter Rick, the full staff, dictates, personal responsibility for every dish.

The printed menu ranges from *fettuccini*, a spinach pasta in cream with garlic and cheese, to a fine coquilles St. Jacques Mornay (poached scallops in a white wine cheese sauce) for openers. Entrées on the à la carte menu include *poulet moutard* (chicken with Dijon mustard, cream and shallots) to veal "normande," veal served with fresh sliced apples, apple brandy, cream and spices. There are lamb, steak and shrimp dishes as well. It is at fresh fish that they truly excel and the night of my visit the blackboard listed sole, sea bass and abalone. Sauces are made fresh to order and I had a Bordelaise with a New York steak that was well done. Desserts are made on the premises and I tasted all four: the Bavarian mint chocolate mousse cake, fresh strawberry trifle, praline cheesecake and a sinful satin pie.

The wine list is a joy. Though not extensive it is intelligently selected to accompany the bill of fare and represents some uncommon labels.

**Moderate.** Open seven nights for dinner 5:30 to 10 p.m. Closed major holidays. Beer and wine only. Reservations recommended. Visa, MC, AX. Wheelchair access. Casual to semi-dressy.

---

### STELLINI'S                                     Italian
9814 West Pico Blvd                                  ★★
Los Angeles          **Map 8**              (213) 274-7225

After a twelve year period as viceroy of The Luau, Joe Stellini worked up the courage to open his own restaurant in 1977. The emergence of a restaurant row of sorts on Pico Boulevard may be linked to the popularity of Stellini's. The restaurant, and its noisy but fun-crowded bar (which serves one of the best shots in town), is as idiosyncratic and attractive as its owner. The light wood paneling, hanging ferns, and wooden fans suggest a certain California mode, and yet the ambience is decidedly that of a well-run New York chop house which treats its clientele as though they were members of a club. Everyone who eats at Stellini's appears to know everyone else as well as the owner, who is always on hand. It is definitely one of the *in* places for celebrities ranging from Burt Reynolds to O. J. Simpson. You are also likely to see some of the loveliest women in town.

Aside from the informality and looseness of the enterprise, there is a more realistic reason for the crowds in such an intimate place—the high standard of the food. The menu is a delight, although oddly eclectic. Stellini's first chef was Chinese and after Joe's tenure at The Luau, it must have seemed perfectly logical to have such appetizers as baby back ribs, rumaki and *bali miki*, rather than the usual shrimp and crab cocktails one might expect. They are prepared expertly and the ribs (some of the best in L.A.) are served as an entrée, as well. The salads are large—to be shared—and feature a version of Chinese chicken salad, and my favorite, Joe's Italian salad, an antipasto of salami, mozzarella, garbanzos, pimentos.

The entrées have a more rational kinship. The New York steak, the pork chops, the double French lamb chops and the broiled veal chops are virtually impossible to beat in Los Angeles in terms of quality and preparation. Fresh fish is grilled to perfection, but don't expect any fancy sauces. Stellini despises them. However, lurking on the menu, is steak with green peppers (the Oriental influence again) and Pappa's Special, which might be lobster Cantonese, pork with Chinese peas, shrimp in lobster sauce, or whatever intrigues the chef.

The wine list is small and offers good values but is not exceptional.

What Stellini's presents is a kind of *recherché* embodiment of a New Yorker's dream steak house. For many of us, with its jumping bar, friendliness, and insouciance, it is the past recaptured.     *Norman Bogner*

**Expensive**. Open Tuesday through Sunday. Dinner served Tuesday through Saturday from 6 to 11:30 p.m.; Sunday from 5 to 11 p.m. Closed Christmas and one week for Rosh Hashona. Full bar. Reservations required. Visa, MC. Valet parking. Casual.

---

## STERN'S BARBECUE                          Barbecue
12658 West Washington Boulevard                    ★
Los Angeles        **Map 8**              (213) 390-3447

In one of the oldest continuously operating restaurants in Southern California the Stern family has been delighting up to 1,500 customers a day with hickory barbecue—whole briskets of beef suspended in a walk-in oven and roasted slowly for twelve hours. The biggest change since 1922 is, as you might guess, in the prices. Under the heading of "Would you believe?" here are a few examples extracted from their original menu: beef barbecue sandwich, 15 cents; special plate of barbecue served with baked beans and cole slaw, 35 cents; draught beer, 10 cents; cocktails, 20 cents (straight whiskies were a nickel less); and burgundy, 10 cents. Now Harold Stern is president and has expanded the operation to include a full-scale catering service. But the quality is still there.

**Inexpensive to moderate.** Open Monday through Thursday 11 a.m. to 10 p.m.; Friday and Saturday to 11 p.m.; Sunday 10 a.m. to 10 p.m. Closed Thanksgiving and Christmas. Full bar. No reservations. Visa, MC, AX. Wheelchair access. Parking lot. Casual.

*To obtain the best results from this Guide, consult
"How to Use this Guide" on page 27*

## STOTTLEMYER'S
712 East Colorado Boulevard
Pasadena     **Map 7**

**Delicatessen**
★
(213) 792-5351

569 South Lake
Pasadena     **Map 7**     (213) 449-5050

This unique operation was the brainchild of Paul Comi, an actor with over 400 credits, and writer Morton Goldberg. While collaborating on a TV screenplay, they got hungry, realized there was no good place to get sandwiches in the Pasadena area, and opened Stottlemyer's European Foods with 60 sandwiches for 60 cents on that first menu in 1968. Each sandwich has its own name, and they're all made from the best possible ingredients: imported cheese, sausage from the Old Country sausage makers, crusty fresh breads. Consider the Marquis de Sade: roast beef cooked in burgundy, with mushrooms, herbs and melted Swiss cheese. Or an Arnie Palmer: turkey with chopped liver and corned beef, Swiss cheese, and avocado on an onion roll. Or the Rudyard Kipling: roast beef, coconut, cashew, and chutney on an English muffin. Desserts include homemade baklava, along with French, German, and Armenian pastries at comparably low prices.

**Inexpensive**. Open seven days. Full menu available from 9:30 a.m. to 9 p.m. Sunday brunch from 11 a.m. to 6:30 p.m. Wine and beer only. No reservations. No credit cards. Parking lot. Casual.

---

## STOX II
5300 Beach Boulevard
Buena Park     **Map 6**

**American**
★
(714) 521-7903

Together again. Grif Griffin helped make Orange County restaurant history as the original executive chef of Mr. Stox in Anaheim, one of the first real major league restaurants out towards the Big A. Now, along with Al Allen, formerly the manager of the original Stox, his restaurant purveys the quality for which Griffin earned a reputation. The comfortable, spacious restaurant is wood panelled with touches of brick, antique kitchen utensils and memorabilia. The menu lists the basic American dishes like prime rib ($12.95 or $14.75, extra cut) steak ($10 to $14) and combinations...all sound deceptively mundane. From Grif's kitchen, they emerge trimphant.

**Moderate.** Open seven days. Luncheon served Monday through Friday 11 a.m. to 2 p.m. Dinner served Monday through Thursday 5 to 10 p.m.; Friday and Saturday 5 to 11 p.m.; Sunday 5 to 9:30 p.m. Closed Christmas and New Years. Entertainment. Full bar. Reservations accepted. Visa, MC, AX. Wheelchair access. Valet parking. Casual to semi-dressy.

---

## STRATTON'S
10886 Le Conte Avenue
Westwood    **Map 8**

**Continental**
★★
(213) 208-8880

Eugene Stratton may be the John Wooden of the restaurant bouquet in Westwood. His Strattons' is a continuous winner. It's located in the old Masonic Lodge, an award-winning building that has become an interesting shopping center. Through the iron gates and the patio is the square room with a high ceiling, a massive chandelier, and a woodsy look. There's a bartender-ess for libation to accompany the continental offerings. The iced cream of lemon soup is fine but the quiche Lorraine is legendary. The red snapper Niçoise is topped with fresh basil. This is a favorite with the brunch group and is better in all departments than most people realize.

**Expensive.** Open Tuesday through Sunday. Luncheon from 11:30 a.m. to 3 p.m. Dinner Tuesday through Thursday from 5:30 to 10 p.m., Friday and Saturday to midnight,

Sunday from 5 to 9 p.m. Sunday brunch from 11:30 a.m. to 3 p.m. Closed Christmas and New Year's. Full bar. Reservations required. Patio. Visa, MC, AX. Parking in adjacent building. Semi-dressy to dressy.

---

## STUDIO GRILL
7321 Santa Monica Blvd.
Los Angeles     **Map 7**

**Continental**
★★★
(213) 874-9202

In an era of restaurant interiors that look like a Napoleon blown apart, it is downright refreshing to have your own oasis — hidden from most people, but known by enough. Ardison Phillips has guided this restaurant to epicurean excellence following a zig zag course through virtually every known cuisine. There is shrimp in lime ginger sauce from Indonesia; seafood *diablo* from Spain, clams in *salsa verde* from the recipes of early California and the more European classics that are treated differently here with no regard to ancient ritual. Snails *en croute* baked in garlic and butter with parsley and a touch of Pernod, and capped with a puff pastry; fettucine served with fresh roasted red pepper sauce; and chicken poached in port with fresh orange and veal "birds" rolled and filled with mozzarella will give you a sampling of one day's selection. The two lamb dishes: "provençale" with an orange garlic sauce and leg of lamb with malt vinegar sauce are favorites. And the desserts are as they should be, a bouquet of delicacies from lemon cheese cake to Amaretto mousse pie to Gâteau Grand Marnier (chocolate cake laced with Grand Marnier and chocolate butter cream filling, and topped with chopped pecans). Ardison has stubbornly resisted any suggestions of adding gilt or removing the Pepsi-Cola sign—a remnant of a simpler, more innocent time. There are bunches of fresh flowers and the ancient walls are well hung . . . with paintings by the proprietor. The wine list is as it should be to accompany the sophisticated hand-written menu. Each label has been carefully selected to provide the correct wine for each price bracket.

**Moderate.** Open Monday through Saturday. Luncheon from noon to 2:15 p.m. weekdays. Dinner 6 to 10:15 p.m. Monday through Thursday: to 11:15 Friday, Saturday. Wine and beer only. Reservations necessary. All major credit cards. Street parking. Casual.

---

## STUFT NOODLE                                              Italian
215 Riverside Avenue                                              ★
Newport Beach          **Map 4**              (714) 548-7418

There's a savory minestrone soup and it's a real papa (Maurice) and mama (Alma) pasta paradise with a home touch. They serve eggplant parmigiana, lasagna, braciola, linguini with clam sauce, and fresh fish.

**Inexpensive**. Open seven days. Dinner Monday through Thursday from 5:30 to 10:30 p.m., Friday through Sunday from 5 to 11 p.m. Full bar. Reservations advised on weekends. Visa, MC, AX. Parking lot. Casual.

---

## SUB-STATION LTD.                                      Sandwiches
2212 South Figueroa                                              ★
Los Angeles          **Map 7**               (213) 749-0844

3429 West Sixth Street
Los Angeles          **Map 7**               (213) 381-7789

This is one of the more successful theme short-order restaurants, where sandwiches are given celebrity names (Ralph Nader: roast beef, ham, and Swiss; Howard Cosell: bologna and cheese), piled high and thick on good buns and washed down with pitchers of beer. The one downtown is sufficiently close to the Coliseum to make it a good idea for post-game activities (if you can get through the muggers).

**Inexpensive.** Open seven days. 6th Street location closed Sunday. Luncheon and dinner from 11 a.m. to midnight; 6th Street to 10 p.m. Wine and beer only. No reservations. Patio. No credit cards; MC at 6th Street. Parking lot. Casual.

---

## SU CASA
6738 La Jolla Boulevard
La Jolla

**Mexican**
★★
(714) 454-0369

Old world — inspired by a 16th century hacienda — and tasteful, this restaurant doesn't need to be as good as it is to attract crowds. There are fireplaces, handcrafted Mexican tile, and chairs made of wood and leather, with fresh flowers on every table. The Mexican cuisine is celebrated by critics around the world. Su Casa brings you the original cuisine that is representative of Sonora-style cooking. The Mexican pizza is marvelous and the chicken enchilada is unbelievable, but any of the combinations or dishes from the huge menu will be special. Try the omelette Mazatlan with ortega chile, green onions and topped with melted cheese and sour cream, avocado, and tomatoes!

**Inexpensive.** Open seven days. Luncheon served Monday through Saturday from 11 a.m. to 3 p.m. Dinner from 5 to 10 p.m. Banquet facilities. Entertainment. Full bar. Reservations accepted. All major credit cards. Parking lot. Casual.

---

## SUISHIN SUKIYAKI
511 State Street
Santa Barbara

**Japanese**
★★
(805) 962-1495

We suggest that you enter Suishin Sukiyaki from the parking lot at the rear of the building. There, a green-painted façade and Oriental rock garden warmly welcomes guests to Santa Barbara's oldest Japanese restaurant. Suishin Sukiyaki uses wood throughout its several rooms, creating a soothing and spacious atmosphere with the cool, earth tones. There's a *sushi* bar and a small display case of seafood. The two *tatami* rooms can provide a private and secluded feeling. There is a small selection of popular Japanese dishes on the dinner menu including beef, chicken, fish, and ginger beef *teriyaki, sukiyaki* and *shabu-shabu.* Dinners come with *suimono* (clear soup), *sunomono tsukemono,* rice, and a side order of *tempura.* For a less expensive meal, we recommend ordering à la carte. Beef *sukiyaki* comes in a metal pot with *shirataki* noodles, mushrooms, *tofu,* onions, scallions and bean sprouts. *Yosenabe* is served in an earthenware cooking pot with hearty portions of white fish, chicken, scallops, squid and vegetables. Both dishes make a substantial meal for one, and are served with clear soup, rice and *tsukemono.*

— *Shinobu Ishizuka*

**Moderate.** Open seven days. Dinner from 5 to 10:45 p.m. Closed October 1 to 7. Wine and beer only. Reservations advised for *tatami* room only. All major credit cards. Parking lot. Casual.

---

**SU LING**                                    **Northern Chinese**
170 North La Cienega                                          ★
Beverly Hills          **Map 8**              (213)652-4187

The effervescent hostess with a name like an unanswered telephone — Ning Ning Ning — was an unlikely introduction to Su Ling, one of the more impressive Mandarin-style restaurants in Southern California. Clad in a slinky, sequined black dress, Ning abruptly cut through that bit of aloofness and uncertainty that hovers over many Chinese establishments. "See that flower arrangement? I did it myself. Oh boy, I hope you like it." It was impossible not to like Ning, the beautiful restaurant and exquisite dinner that followed. Unlike the few successful Northern Chinese restaurants that have opened in recent years, Su Ling found its way here from the Orient instead of San Francisco (no good Chinese places ever seem to start in Los Angeles), where the Ling family is involved with the operation of restaurants in Taiwan, Taippei, Tokyo, and Hong Kong. Young Peter Ling, a tall handsome Chinaman, more Carnaby Street than Confucius, is intensely involved with the La Cienega restaurant; it reflects his elegant good taste from the 180 (somebody counted) hand-painted silk ceiling lanterns that provide a subtle glow and a strange feeling (the same silk is used above the booths) to the exceedingly pleasing classical Chinese music in the background. "Appetizers" in most Chinese restaurants means the platter of little feats. Here a tray of cold morsels — drunken chicken (marinated in Chinese sake), abalone, black mushrooms and celery — is served with two sauces, one a mixture of vinegar and ginger, the other hot oil. The waiter (what kind of Chinese name is "Herman"?) poured soy sauce into a small bowl, and we added the two sauces to taste. Crab and asparagus soup was a surprising blend of flavors brought more vividly alive when a teaspoon of the vinegar and ginger blend was added. I've never understood why important restaurants demand that you phone ahead 24 hours in advance for Peking Duck. Why can't they prepare a guesstimate of at least a few to serve as ordered? The seasoned skin is crisp, the meat sweet; skin, meat, and legs are beautifully arranged on a platter with slices of scallion and cucumber. Crêpe-like pancakes are expertly filled with a bit of all ingredients and topped with a special sweet sauce, then folded or rolled together to be eaten by hand. (A hot towel is provided following this dish.) The combination of flavors and textures will awaken your palate to the highly complex world of Chinese cooking. On other occasions, we ordered the chicken Hunan-style and shredded pork Szechwan-style and were delighted. A luncheon favorite is barbecued chicken salad. Service is on exquisite hand-painted plates, and there are Trader Vic-type rum drinks. Set dinners begin at $14.50, featuring such things as shrimp, sizzling rice soup, and including appetizers and entrées. You may want to consult with your waiter, whom you'll find most obliging. I'd recommend you try the hot Show Shin, a Chinese sake made from wheat instead of the more familiar rice sake.

**Moderate.** Open seven days. Luncheon from 11:30 a.m. to 4 p.m. Dinner from 4 to 11:30 p.m. Saturday and Sunday brunch from 11:30 a.m. to 3:30 p.m. Full bar. Happy Hour 4 to 6:30 p.m. Reservations advised. All major credit cards. Valet parking. Casual to semi-dressy.

---

## THE SUMMER HOUSE
21870 Victory Boulevard
Woodland Hills          **Map 1**

**Continental**
★
(213) 883-3030

Well named, The Summer House features the lush greenery for a gracious setting for a sophisticated menu selection. A favorite luncheon haunt for some of the celebrities who are really incognito here (even the restaurant didn't know who they were), enjoying the omelettes and imaginative sandwich combinations. Dinner is heavier and more conventional with prime rib, rack of lamb and bouillabaisse.

**Moderate**. Open seven days. Luncheon served Monday through Saturday from 11:30 a.m. to 4 p.m. Dinner Sunday through Thursday from 4 to 10 p.m., Friday and Saturday to 11 p.m. Sunday brunch from 10 a.m. to 2 p.m. Banquet facilities. Closed Christmas. Full bar. Reservations advised. Visa, MC, AX. Parking lot. Casual to semi-dressy.

---

## SUMMER PALACE
2121 Cloverfield
Santa Monica          **Map 2**

**Chinese**
★
(213) 829-0219

This restaurant opened originally as The Peking Pot but after a multitude of people tried to buy cookware there, they changed to the present name. Two of the most visual Chinese dishes are offered here — Mongolian Barbecue and the Peking Fire Pot. The Mongolian Barbecue lets you fill a bowl with thinly sliced pork, lamb, turkey, beef, vegetables and an assortment of sauces. Once your choice is made a chef cooks it before you on a raised grill. One thing that makes this restaurant unique among Chinese establishments is that they use no monosodium glutamate or animal fat in their cooking, relying on other natural spices for flavor. The portions are large and the à la carte menu is lengthy.

**Inexpensive to moderate.** Open seven days. Luncheon 11 a.m. to 2:30 p.m. weekdays. Dinner Sunday through Thursday from 5 to 10 p.m.; Friday and Saturday from 4 to 11 p.m. Wine and beer only. Reservations advised. Parking lot. Casual.

---

## SUNDANCE CAFE                    Mexican/American

350 North Robertson                              ★
West Hollywood        **Map 8**         (213) 659-1485

8478 Melrose Avenue                              ★
Los Angeles        **Map 8**            (213) 658-8292

This is a tiny, serve-yourself with Early Western funk, but it is a great example of what imagination and care can achieve on a limited budget. Outdoor seating in West Hollywood is a perfect setting for the selection of Mexican plates, all served with fresh fruit, fresh avocado, and fresh everything. The refried beans are addicting, and departures like avocado stuffed with bay shrimp or any of the sandwiches are slightly daffy but delicious. It's hard to spend more than $5 here, even with a tap beer or the house Inglenook. There's a takeout that's used by the *hoi polloi*, and the autographs and celebrity graffiti on the walls are more fun than Grauman's (or is it Mann's?) Chinese.

**Inexpensive.** Open seven days. Luncheon from 11 a.m. to 4:30 p.m. Dinner from 4:30 to 10 p.m. Sunday brunch from 11 a.m. to 3 p.m. Wine and beer only. No reservations. Patio. Visa, MC. Parking lot. Casual.

## SUSHI HOUSE  Sushi bar

21630 Ventura Boulevard  ★
Woodland Hills  **Map 1**  (213) 340-8690

The first good sushi bar to wander into the San Fernando Valley and it is located in restaurant-rich Woodland Hills. Actually the whole restaurant is one large sushi bar although there are a few well-prepared accompaniments. Sushi is at its highest state of the art with fish cut wafer thin. The chefs are friendly and enjoy their sometimes frenzied activity.

**Inexpensive to moderate.** Open Wednesday through Monday. Luncheon from 11:30 a.m. to 2 p.m. weekdays. Dinner from 5:30 to 10:30; to 10 p.m. Sunday. Closed Thanksgiving, Christmas. Beer and wine only. No reservations. Small patio. Visa, MC. Parking lot. Casual.

---

## SWISS ECHO  Swiss/Continental

10769 West Pico Boulevard  ★
West Los Angeles  **Map 8**  (213) 474-9340

If you see a line of people clutching brown bags in front of this fine little restaurant, they're just waiting their turn and bringing their wine. The German-Swiss dishes, like *bratwurst, sauerbraten* with potato pancakes and *schnitzels*, need a white fruity chilled chablis or riesling or liebfraumilch. There's a *coquille* St. Jacques that would do honor to a house of *haute cuisine*. The cheese and onion pie is delightful. Desserts are homemade. Fresh peach pie and chocolate pastry are especially good.

**Inexpensive to moderate.** Open Tuesday through Saturday. Luncheon from 11:30 a.m. to 4:30 p.m. Dinner from 4:30 to 10 p.m. Closed July 4, Christmas. Diners may bring their own wine; there is a very limited selection. Reservations required. No credit cards. Street parking. Casual.

# SYCAMORE INN

8318 Foothill Boulevard
Cucamonga **Map 5**

**Continental**
★
(714) 982-1104

In 1848, a little trailside inn was operated by Uncle Billy Rubottom and became widely known among travelers to the gold Rush territories. The Sycamore Inn is built around the historical monument dedicated to his hospitality and continues the tradition, with good food and friendly service in a splendid setting: a huge stone fireplace, Victorian fixtures, and red wingback chairs. Best dishes are the grenadine of beef Theodora, deviled crab in shell, and prime rib. Buffets are a specialty and reservations are accepted, but not on Saturday nights or major holidays. They have an outstanding wine list, one of the finest collectons in the area, with well over 100 labels.

**Moderate.** Open seven days. Luncheon Monday though Saturday from 11 a.m. to 3 p.m. Dinner Monday through Saturday from 5 to 11 p.m., Sunday noon to 10 p.m. Closed Christmas. Full bar. Reservations advise Sunday through Friday, not accepted Saturday or holidays. All major credit cards. Parking lot. Semi-dressy.

---

*To obtain the best results from this Guide, be sure to consult maps on the various Southern California areas in the front of the book.*

---

## TAD'S

**Mexican**
★

663 Rose Avenue
Venice    **Map 2**                        (213) 396-8819

Tad's is the only restaurant I've ever been to that kept
flashlights on the tables. Like too many restaurants, Tad's
is dark—obviously too dark. The small pencil flashlights are
probably there to help you read the menu but I used mine
to look at the food, too. The food is presented very well at
Tad's, and it's sort of a pity to lose the subtle arrangement
of the *ceviche* in the shadows, and to not be able to make out
the color of the sauce on the *papas huancaina.*

There's a certain Mel Brooks quality to dining at Tad's
that makes the place especially memorable. The piped-in
music leans heavily toward Gershwin. When you sit down,
a sweet elderly lady brings you a menu and takes your
drink order. Meanwhile, you can't help but notice this
fellow clad in black, high-topped basketball sneakers, running this way and that about the room, taking orders,
explaining dishes, schmoozing with the customers, deliver-

ing platters, and vanishing into the kitchen, where he cooks the food as well.

After awhile, Tad finally dashed up to my table, explained that the fish of the day was red snapper, that the *anticuchos* (beef heart) is marinated for exactly seven hours, and that the sea bass in the *seviche* is especially good that evening. Taking my order, he does a bit of a broken field run around some other tables, checking on the welfare of the diners, ultimately tumbling through the kitchen door. From the kitchen, I can hear the sound of oil burbling in a pan, and an occasional barbecued smell wafts across my table.

Finally, Tad emerges at a fast clip from the kitchen, holding a wonderful appetizer plate (a meal in itself, as we say in the trade) involving four exquisite chunks of charcoal broiled beef heart; a lettuce leaf covered with a whopping dollop of *seviche*, so piquant my eyes water at the first taste; a mound of nigh-on perfect rice, tasting of olive oil and garlic; three cold rounds of potato, topped with the mustard/mayonnaise taste of *huancaina* sauce; and an extraordinary *papa relleno*—a mashed potato omelette of sorts, stuffed with spiced chopped meat, onions and raisins. Everything looked very good, caught in the glow of my flashlight. But I always turned the light off after the food was in my mouth. I'm romantic like that.   *M.S.*

M.S.

**Moderate.** Open Tuesday through Saturday from 6 p.m. All dinners $8. Closed all major holidays. Beer and wine only. Most major credit cards. Reservations accepted. Small parking lot; street parking. Casual.

*In order to obtain the best results from this Guide, be sure to read the French, German, Italian and Oriental menu translators on page 705 to 710 of this Guide.*

## TAIL O' THE COCK                        American
477 South La Cienega Boulevard                    ★
Los Angeles        **Map 8**              (213)273-1200

12950 Ventura Boulevard
Sherman Oaks        **Map 1**             (213)784-6241

A tradition in Los Angeles for over forty years, this luxurious restaurant has all the good things that come with experience, reliability and integrity without showing any of the wear. The basically American food — steaks and salads, roast beef — will not thrill anyone, but it's always pleasant here. On Saturdays, there's a candlelight-and-wine dinner with soup or salad, entrées like roast duckling or sirloin of beef, and a homemade dessert like chocolate mocha pie, plus a carafe of wine that's especially low priced. Sunday brunch offers one of the widest varieties of dishes in town.

**Moderate.** Open seve days. Luncheon Monday through Saturday from 11 a.m. to 4 p.m. Dinner Sunday through Thursday 4 to 10 p.m.; Friday, Saturday to 11 p.m. Sunday brunch 10 a.m. to 3 p.m. Piano bar. Full bar. Reservations advised. Banquet facilities. All major credit cards. Valet parking. Casual to semi-dressy.

## TALIA'S                                    Italian
1148 Manhattan Avenue                            ★
Manhattan Beach        **Map 2**         (213) 545-6884

The "only Italian restaurant in Manhattan Beach" is on the first floor of a clapboard building that looks like it's weathered a few storms. Their white clam sauce and the veal are the best in this family-operated deli-trattoria.

**Inexpensive to moderate.** Open seven days. Breakfast served Saturday and Sunday from 8 a.m. to 2 p.m.; Luncheon served Tuesday through Sunday from 11 a.m. to 2 p.m.; Dinner served Sunday through Thursday from 5:30 to 10 p.m.; Friday and Saturday to 11 p.m. Closed Christmas and Easter. Wine and beer only. Reservations advised. Visa, MC. Street and validated parking. Casual.

---

## TALK OF THE TOWN

**Continental**
★★★

123 West Gutierrez
Santa Barbara

(805) 966-4910

This is one of the traditions that Santa Barbara clings to — a dressy restaurant that shows its experience in the kitchen and shows its age in the front of the house. The dress code is so rigid — coats and ties for men; dresses for women — that I have seen women in elegant pants suits ordered to leave the restaurant and escorted to the door by the maître d'. The weight and size of the menu can be intimidating, although I can't recall ever having had a bad dish. The bar and the bartender are full of character — a good way to begin, cozy and romantic. Dinner could start with smoked salmon with capers or shrimp *à la maison*, a sort of scampi. The vichysoisse is homemade and chilled properly. Entrées like chicken *ranato* (sautéed in olive oil with shallots and artichoke hearts) and trout with almond sauce and *cannelloni*, all served with fresh vegetables, share the menu with steaks, prime rib, and similar "safe" dishes. Desserts are an important part of the dinner. The wine list takes advantage of some of the better and lesser known California wines.

**Expensive.** Open seven days. Luncheon from noon to 2 p.m. weekdays. Dinner from 6 to 10 p.m., Sunday from 5 to 10 p.m. Full bar. Reservations required. All major credit cards. Parking lot. Dressy.

---

*In order to obtain the best results from this Guide, please consult "Tips on Dining Out" on page 21.*

## TALK OF THE TOWN

**American**

★

3730 East Foothill Boulevard
Pasadena    **Map 7**    (213) 793-6926

If I hadn't seen it, I wouldn't have believed it. While waiting near the front desk for some friends to join us for dinner, I watched the hostess greet each of the arriving guests by name, inquire about their horses and their relatives (in that order of importance in this horsy, woodsy place founded by super-jockey Ralph Neves), and take them to their favorite booths. The dining area, with red walls, dark wood paneling, stone fireplaces, and oil painting emanates relaxed cordiality and a sense of well-being. The food consists of generous portions of steaks, chops, prime rib, and scampi. Baked potatoes, like everything else in this clubby establishment, are oversized—and delicious. Among the appetizers is a *manicotti*, unexpected here. The salads are crisp, cold, and well-dressed, but you might like to try the Steak Eater's Delight—chopped Bermuda onions and tomato with croutons, cheese, and a special dressing. Entrées come with soup or salad, potato or sliced tomatoes, and good bread. A combination ticket that is favored here is the Big Winner—steak, lobster, and spareribs, with potatoes or *manicotti*. Waitresses are friendly and solicitious; the wine list is intelligent if unexciting. Desserts are homemade and good. During meets at nearby Santa Anita, they're jammed (they make a list of the next day's racing entries and hand them out to the diners), and you should make reservations as early as possible. The bar area, with its colorful displays of racing memorabilia—jockeys' silks, caps, photographs—really jumps at night.

**Moderate.** Open seven days a week. Lunch from 11 a.m. to 2 p.m. Dinner from 5 to 11 p.m. daily, midnight on Friday. Banquet facilities. Closed Thanksgiving, Christmas. Entertainment. Dancing. Full bar. Reservations advised. All major credit cards. Valet parking. Semi-dressy.

## TAMPICO TILLY'S                    Mexican
1025 Wilshire Boulevard                    ★
Santa Monica        **Map 2**        (213) 451-1769

Tilly's Terrace
Santa Monica Place
Santa Monica        **Map 2**        (213) 393-1404

A gorgeous implosion of colors, textures and Latin artifacts surround you in this lovely eccentric which has about as eclectic a menu as you'll find in a "Mexican" restaurant. The seafood is well prepared. The place abounds with private parties and there's dancing every night for public parties as well. Tilly's Terrace is brand new and modeled after Tampico Tilly's, which is a good barometer of its success. El neato.

**Moderate**. Open seven days. Luncheon served Monday through Saturday 11:30 a.m. to 4 p.m. Dinner Monday through Thursday from 4 to 9:30 p.m.; Friday, Saturday from 4 to 11:30 p.m.; Sunday 3 to 9:30 p.m. Sunday champagne brunch from 11:30 a.m. to 3 p.m. Limited banquet facilities. Entertainment. Dancing nightly. Full bar. Reservations accepted. Visa, MC, AX. Valet parking. Casual.

## TAORMINA RESTAURANT                Sicilian
10401 West Washington Boulevard            ★
Culver City         **Map 3**        (213) 559-7833

The fact that it takes its name from a famous resort and film festival village on the island of Sicily is some indication of what they'd *like* to do. What they do is a festive Italian look in the adaptation of an old bar and the establishment of their menu. Calf's brains are served here along with other regional rarities. The antipasto is outstanding and a far cry from the tired platters of little feats.

**Moderate**. Open Monday through Saturday. Luncheon 11:30 a.m. to 2:30 p.m. weekdays. Dinner from 5:30 to 10:30 p.m. Closed all holidays. Wine and beer only. Reservations advised. Visa, MC. Casual.

---

# TASTE OF SCANDINAVIA

**Smorgasbord**

21629 Devonshire
★

Chatsworth  **Map 1**
(213) 882-8200

21136 Ventura Boulevard
Woodland Hills  **Map 1**
(213) 348-1281

Also known as **King Swede Swedish Smorgasbord**
3001 Magnolia Blvd.
Burbank  **Map 1**
(213) 846-7239

These are the best of the cheapies where you can really fill up. The family—Pete Politis and Phil Boutakis—work around the clock to come up with buffet tables that groan with homemade macaroni salads, fruit salad, and many more.

The soup is homemade each day. There are always meat balls, usually chicken and ribs, and on Monday, Wednesday, and Friday they have rounds of beef sliced to order that tastes like good prime rib. At the least, there is a quartet of entrées and desserts. These are good, honest and comfortable places with no pretensions. Great if you're in a hurry or simply starving to death.

**Inexpensive**. Open Tuesday through Sunday. Luncheon served Tuesday through Saturday from 11:30 a.m. to 4 p.m. Dinner from 4 to 9 p.m. Open noon to 8:30 p.m. Sunday and holidays. Wine and beer only. No reservations. Visa, MC. Parking lot. Casual.

## TAYLOR'S PRIME STEAK HOUSE    Steakhouse

3361 West 8th Street    ★
Los Angeles    **Map 7**    (213) 382-8449

This is a clubby steakhouse preferred by the lawyers, politicians, and other suspicious characters in the midtown Wilshire district. Mr. Taylor likes people; that's why he opened his restaurant. Now people like him for the superior clam chowder, homemade soups, good fish, and daily specials, in addition to the steaks and prime beef. Food is cooked simply and well.

**Moderate**. Open seven days. Luncheon from 11:30 a.m. to 4 p.m. weekdays. Dinner daily from 4 to 11 p.m. Children's menu. Full bar. Reservations advised for dinner. All major credit cards. Valet parking. Casual to semi-dressy.

---

## TEA AND SYMPATHY    Tea Shop

369 17th Street    ★★
Costa Mesa    **Map 4**    (714) 645-4860

My last adventure in a British tea room was with Robert Morley, the rotund raconteur and epicure. He tucked in a napkin to cover his multitude of chins and held forth on this thoroughly British institution. "High tea, old boy, is not what you foreigners think it is—some kind of rapturous ritual." It was, Morley explained, whilst forking a scone, "a substantial meal." Meat pies, cold ham and beef, chunks of cheese and thick slices of freshly baked bread with fresh fruit are provided, along with a pot of very strong tea.

I have lamented the fact that there are no real tea rooms in Southern California with the possible exception of Agatha's in Santa Monica. Now, to my surprise and pleasure, an authentic replica has opened in Orange County of all unlikely places. Tea and Sympathy in Costa Mesa is the dream fulfilled of Toni Bruner, a native of London and a full-on restaurateur. If anything, Toni's shop is even cozier and more picturesque than those I remembered.

Every item in the shop comes from England, from the wallpaper with tiny flowers to the antique furnishings and silver tea service. Fine china, antique sideboards, clocks, chairs and English collectibles are all for sale.

Afternoon tea was first made fashionable by the Duchess of Bedford a century and a half ago. It was a time for delicious scandal to be discreetly exchanged across the silver service. Afternoon tea at Tea and Sympathy includes— as it did then—hot scones, tea cake, toasted English muffin, sherry trifle and cake from the cart. Two tea sandwiches, a hot scone served with raspberry jam and cream with a pot of stout English tea is a mere $3.95 per person.

British fare like toad-in-the-hole (sausage cooked in Yorkshire pudding) and steak and kidney pie are on the menu with daily specials for hungry, homesick Britons.

**Inexpensive.** Open Tuesday through Saturday 11 a.m. to 6 p.m. Light supper Friday to 9 p.m. Reservations accepted. Visa, MC. Casual.

---

# TEMPO                                     Israeli
16610 Ventura Boulevard
Encino          **Map 1**              (213) 981-7283

The first page of the menu at Tempo gives a brief introduction to the cuisine of Israel, which goes as follows: "Each of our dishes have their own country of origin such as *moussaka* and *baklava* which were introduced to Israel by the Greek Jews, or *shish kebab* and *shwarma* which the Jews from Turkey brought with them to Israel. We also have *felafel, humus* and many other kinds of salads which are originally Egyptian... With the combination of the food and atmosphere you will feel as if you are in Israel... " I certainly do appreciate Tempo's concern for recreasting the ambience of a street-corner cafe in Tel Aviv, which they do adroitly. But I do wonder whether the streets in Israeli really look anything like Ventura Boulevard in Encino. In Tel Aviv, maybe; certainly not in ancient Jerusalem.

There's a rear dining room and a counter at Tempo (a nice touch that counter, more restaurants should utilize counters, which are so convenient for single dinners, people in a hurry and those who like to watch the kitchen in action), and a covered patio facing onto Ventura. Diners discuss, argue, gossip while delving into orders of Tempo's elegant eggplant in vinegar, a scrumptious crazy quilt of eggplant, onions, red peppers and dill pickles. Or the eggplant salad, where the eggplant wrestles with spices both subtle and hostile. Or the fried eggplant. Or the eggplant and *tahina* (a sesame seed condiment, musky and a trifle overwhelming, but also very ubiquitous).

Obviously, the eggplant is served as an old friend at Tempo. This is not an oily, heavy eggplant, as in the culinary mythology of ancient Persia, but rather a light, refreshing eggplant. So revered is the eggplant at Tempo that the above four eggplant dishes are even served all together in the combination eggplant salad, which comes with three pieces of *felafel* (garbanzo bean fritters), and the order is one of the best food deals around.

But eggplant isn't all there is at Tempo. There are hot *pita* bread sandwiches filled with *shwarma* (a sort of spiced lamb and turkey roll, reminiscent of souvlaki, broasted on a vertical rotisserie), *shish kebab*, and skirt steak. There's *humus* (a ground garbanzo bean dip) and *tahina* and *burrekas* (deep-fried *filo* dough stuffed with cheese, spinach or beef). And, for truly serious eaters—or, perhaps, for a bar mitzvah—there are the complete dinners: the Ben-Yehuda (lamb chops, chicken *shish kebab*, ground beef *kebabs*), the Allenby or the Dizengof (chicken and beef *shish kebab*, lamb chops, ground beef *kebabs* and *shwarma*), and the top of the line Tel-Aviv (for four persons or more,—soup, combination salad, ground beef *kebabs*, chicken and lamb *shish kebab*, *shwarma*, lamb chops, grilled vegetables, rice, pickles and various amenities). *M.S.*

**Moderate.** Open seven days. Open 11 a.m. to 11 p.m. Sunday through Thursday: to midnight on Friday and Saturday. Wine and beer only. Visa, MC. Casual.

# TENMASA                                  Japanese
356 East First Street
Los Angeles          **Map 7**              (213) 680-4443

The Japanese Village Restaurant Plaza, of which Tenmasa is an integral part, is a fascinating concept in which counter dining and table dining meet and get along agreeably. Gathered about a central dining area, there are a half-dozen food bars, which variously serve noodles, *sushi*, steak, and of course, *tempura*. If you sit at one of the tables in the center, you get a menu that covers all the bars. If you sit at any of the bars, you've obviously opted for a more highly focused set of choices, and consequently that's what you get. The choices at Tenmasa are simpler than those at A Thousand Cranes... and the prices are, as a result, somewhat lower. There's a simple and very refreshing vegetable tempura; an assorted tempura which includes shrimp and some small whitefish, *tempuraed* in a school, as it were; and a lobster and vegetable *tempura*, which also includes shrimp. Because the chefs at Tenmasa are cooking not only for the people at the counter, but also for those who are seated out in the dining area, things can get pretty frenetic. Oil sizzles constantly, waiters come and go, and the feeling of personal service you get at A Thousand Cranes doesn't come across. But they do try their best, considering the obvious popularity of *tempura* in the Restaurant Plaza. The chefs always smile as they drop orders of *tempuraed* cauliflower, lotus roots, zucchini, pumpkin, eggplant, sweet potato, green beans, broccoli and whatever else might be in season on your plate. Unquestionably, the Tenmasa *tempura* bar is one of the best spots in town to station yourself should you be in need of a crash course in the logistics of mass-producing *tempura*, on the double.   *M.S.*

**Moderate.** Open Tuesday through Sunday. Luncheon from 11:30 a.m. to 2 p.m. Dinner from 5 to 10:30 p.m. Full bar. Visa, MC. Casual.

# TEPPAROD THAI NO. 1         Thai
4649 Melbourne Avenue
Los Angeles     **Map 7**          (213) 669-9117

# TEPPAROD THAI WEST
147 South Fairfax Avenue
Los Angeles     **Map 8**          (213) 932-9552

Your off-the-beaten-track kind of place may well turn out to be Tepparod Thai No. 1. Thai cuisine is spicy hot and requires some caution, but once beyond that barrier it is imaginative, intricate, and thoroughly enjoyable. Minced pork soup, Indian noodles, Siamese greens with chicken, fried beef sautéed in oyster oil, and chicken curry are just a few of the items from a long list that proved exciting. It's an inexpensive dining adventure.

**Melbourne Avenue: Inexpensive to moderate**. Open seven days. Luncheon Tuesday through Sunday from 11 a.m. to 3 p.m. Dinner Tuesday through Thursday from 5 to 10 p.m., Friday and Saturday to 11 p.m. Wine and beer only. Reservations advised. No credit cards. Street parking. Casual.

**Fairfax Avenue: Inexpensive to moderate.** Open seven days. Luncheon Monday through Saturday from 11:30 a.m. to 3 p.m. Dinner from 5 to 10 p.m. Wine and beer only. Reservations advised. Visa, MC. Parking lot. Casual.

---

# TERIYAKI SHIMON         Japanese
11943 Ventura Boulevard
Studio City     **Map 1**          (213) 769-7631

The workers at the CBS Studio Center in Studio City are among the luckiest lunchers in the world. Within a short jaunt from the sets are a super *sushi* bar (Terusushi), a great deli (Art's and the Polo Lounge of the Valley (Dupar's). In the midst of this largesse, Teriyaki Shimon opened recently, and it's become very popular thanks to its low prices, good-sized portions, and nicely-prepared Japanese fast food. If anything, the place has become too popular; during one recent visit, the kitchen was so backed up with orders-to-go that it took nearly half an hour to get around to my eat-in order.

Everything at Teriyaki Shimon is served in styrofoam, which is a standard at the Japanese fast food eateries around town. The salad (shredded lettuce, carrot in an unctuous orange dressing) sits quietly in one styrofoam compartment. The larger compartment houses some sticky rice and a variety of marinated and seasoned meats and *tempuras-teriyaki* chicken, *teriyaki* beef, *teriyaki* tuna, shrimp and vegetable *tempuras*. The teriyakied items all taste a bit too sweet, but I'll take a sweetened strip of beef anytime over those spots of grease on a bun that pass for burgers hereabouts.

*Won tons* (which are referred to on the front of Teriyaki Shimon as "wantangs"), greasy in the grand tradition of neighborhood Oriental food, are available as side orders, along with a soy-sauced fried chicken, and cups of egg flower soup. The whole experience is something less than a banquet at A Thousand Cranes, but then that's a little like comparing MacDonald's to L'Ermitage. As fast food goes, Teriyaki Shimon is good, clean, inexpensive fun.     M.S.

**Inexpensive.** Open Monday through Saturday. Luncheon 11 a.m. to 3 p.m. weekdays. Dinner from 5 to 9 p.m. through Saturday. Closed all major holidays. No alcoholic beverages. No reservations. Limited wheelchair access. Parking lot. Casual.

---

## TERU SUSHI
**Sushi bar**

11940 Ventura Boulevard                    ★★
Studio City        **Map 1**          (213) 763-6201

Teru Sushi is easily the busiest *sushi* bar in L.A., and also the one most filled with gringos. It's situated not far from the CBS Studio Center and draws its clientele not only from the studio but also from the significantly urbane neighborhood nearby. Teru is also the *sushi* bar most committed to being theatrically a *sushi* bar. The *sushi* chefs are always raising a great ruckus, hollering greetings to arriving and departing diners, making the whole place seem a bit like a Toshiro Mifune movie in the making. Aside from being theatrical, the bar at Teru is also utterly superb. The fish could hardly be fresher, the ingredients could not be combined with more finesse, and the choices could barely be broader. It's at Teru that I first encountered tiger's eye, and that I later encountered sea blossoms (sometimes called sea flowers), an *oshi*-style sushi made with sea bass. What I enjoy most about Teru (once I've managed to get in; half hour waits are not unusual) is the marvelous sense of life in the place. The customers seem truly happy (their joy fueled by *sake* and more *sake*). The staff appears to be having a good time, not just play-acting a good time. And the whole place is so darned infectious. How can you leave a restaurant unhappy when a half dozen men in *sushi samurai* garb are busy yelling, "Arigato Goziemashta" at you, even as they deftly slice away.　　*M.S.*

**Moderate**. Open seven days. Lunch from 11:30 a.m. to 2 p.m. Dinner from 6 to 11 p.m. Monday through Thursday; Friday, Saturday from 5 to 10 p.m. Full bar. No reservations. Visa, MC. Casual.

---

## TGI FRIDAYS　　　　　　　　　　　　American/Funk
(Locations in Costa Mesa, San Diego, Marina del Rey, Woodland Hills, others. See phone book for listings.)

A wowy-kazowy bawdy exchange in an atmosphere of unrelenting fun-fun-fun. The food is better than it needs to be with interesting variations of the baked potato skins and humorous entrées like Chinese "seafood tacos." There is a precious menu, cute waitresses and an air of palpable desperation. The fact that this is a successful chain—nearly 50 TGIFs exist—is a sociological commentary. If you are looking for the kind of mob scene depicted in "Looking for Mr. Goodbar" then TGIF is for you. Not me.

**Moderate.** Open seven days from 11:30 a.m. to 1 a.m. Sunday brunch menu $5.45 from 11:30 to 2:30. Full bar. No reservations. Visa, MC, AX, DC. Wheelchair access. Parking lot. Casual.

---

## THIN'S INN
2575 Pacific Coast Highway
Torrance      **Map 2**

Diet/Vegetarian
★
(213) 326-9673

2350 Workman Avenue
West Covina      **Map 6**

(213) 331-9173

Veal tostada, Hawaiian chicken, ginger beef and spaghetti with meat sauce don't sound like diet food—nor taste like it—but they are. This enlightened approach heralds the emergence of the new specialty restaurant that accommodates the thousands, millions (?) of people who are sick of being blanded to death, or worse. Their fish is broiled beautifully. All the meals are low in cholesterol and sodium but they're as appetizing as they sound and each item lists calories, carbohydrates, and diet equivalents. No longer do the diners have to be humiliated or treated as second-class citizens. This is a first class operation all the way and a tribute to John Gulugian and his staff.

**Inexpensive.** Open Monday through Saturday. Luncheon from 11 a.m. to 5 p.m. Dinner Monday through Friday from 5 to 10 p.m., Saturday to 8:30 p.m. Children's menu. Private party facilities in West Covina. Wine and beer only in West Covina; no alcoholic beverages in Torrance. No reservations. Visa, MC. Parking lot. Casual.

---

*Please be sure to consult "Tipping Made Easy" on page 25 of this Guide.*

# A THOUSAND CRANES

New Otani Hotel

Los Angeles    **Map 3**

**Japanese**

★

(213) 629-1200

It is frequently astonishing to observe the transformation of a blight area, through some miracle of enlightened enterprise, into luxury highrise apartments, condominiums and hotels. The guests at the New Otani in downtown Los Angeles so urbanely sipping tea and other potables would be deeply shocked to know the grisly history of that site in skid row. Perhaps that is why I was so taken with this graceful restaurant overlooking a tranquil carp pond (carpless because of the smog) and a massive rock setting with a dramatically nightlighted fountain. The owners of the New Otani, a Japanese group, were eager to understand the Western palate. Toward that end they wisely engaged Willie Miller. Mr. Miller began to work with a staff of mixed nationalities, many provided and subsidized by the Job Corps, and he has achieved high standards of cuisine for the American patrons of this Japanese hotel. It is ironic, therefore, that their best effort is the Japanese restaurant, a refreshingly simple room dominated by the glass wall and the view. There is a sushi bar, a tempura bar but no teppan service as at a Benihana. The hostess is Naomi Sakuda. The menu is classic Japanese with few surprises but the food is good and reasonably priced. After sampling a variety of sushi, a platter of no little feats, we had *shabu shabu*, a kind of Japanese fondue into which thinly sliced beef is dipped and cooked. Our waitress explained that the dish got its name from the sound made by the meat as it was swished through the broiling broth.

**Moderate to expensive.** Open seven days. Breakfast from 7 to 10 a.m. weekdays. Luncheon from 11:30 a.m. to 2 p.m. weekdays. Dinner from 6 to 10 p.m. Sunday brunch from 11:30 a.m. to 2 p.m. Banquet facilities. Full bar. Koto player. Reservations advised. Patio. All major credit cards. Validated parking. Semi-dressy.

## THREE DOLPHIN INN
156 South Topanga Canyon Boulevard
Topanga    **Map 1**

**Continental**
★
(213) 455-2138

Cottagey and fine, this old charmer ranges from ceviche, pheasant, quail or rabbit to freshly sautéed scallops and eggplant parmigiana. Desserts include chocolate or amaretto mousse pie and much more. Occasional Mexican dishes sneak on the menu and they're all homemade, of course.

**Moderate**. Open seven days. Dinner Monday through Thursday 6 to 9:30 p.m.; Friday through Sunday to 10 p.m. Saturday and Sunday brunch from 10 a.m. to 2 p.m. Mexican specialties Monday, Oriental specialties Tuesday nights. Closed Christmas Eve and Day, Thanksgiving, New Year's. Wine and beer only. Reservations advised. Visa, MC. Parking lot. Casual.

## THE THREE MERMAIDS
3539 Adams Avenue
San Diego

**Polish**
★★
(714) 281-3729

A Polish mermaid is not, as some of my former friends insisted in the hey day of Polish jokes, a fish from the waist up. Isabella Rutowaska and her daughters Zofia and Mariola created the oldest Polish restaurant in Southern California. The emphasis is on home cooking and it's like having your family prepare such delicacies as hunter's stew, stuffed cabbage rolls, Polish "rollettes" or crêpes filled with meat. Particularly interesting to Americans are the cold fruit soups or, my favorite, beer soup. Bread is baked fresh and there are combination plate samplings that give first-timers a taste of Poland. Desserts are especially good and not as rich as you'd imagine. There's a drink called *pola pola* that tastes a bit like flavored champagne and is made from raisins, lemon juice, honey, yeast and pumpernickel . . . then allowed to ferment as you will ferment if you have more than two. The creative food display more than makes up for what may be lacking in the atmosphere. The aroma of the *pirogi*, sausage, borscht and other good things is more than I can bear.

**Moderate.** Open Wednesday through Sunday. Dinner from 5 to 9 p.m. Wednesday, Thursday and Sunday; 5 to 10 p.m. Friday and Saturday. Limited banquet facilities. Wine and beer only. Reservations advised. No credit cards. Street parking. Casual.

---

## THE 301 CLUB
Mexican
301 West Santa Fe
★
Placentia **Map 6** (714) 528-9084

In the most unlikely section of the unlikely city of Placentia (near Anaheim) there exists a small restaurant that is constantly being "discovered" by new enthusiasts. The 301 Club looks no more distinguished than the pool halls and beer bars that flourish alongside, yet it is the home of what many believe to be the finest Mexican cooking in Southern California. The most expensive entrée is a combination plate including chile relleno, enchilada, taco, and tostada with rice and refried beans. Yet the modest prices are by no means the primary reason for its success. One has the inescapable feeling that the politicians, businessmen, and college community would continue to stand in line up to an hour even if that decimal point were moved over one notch. The immaculate premises look for all the world like a stage setting. At the 301 Club, you will observe patrons drinking tequila in the way the good saints intended, first downing the shot, then touching the tongue to salt held in the palm and biting a piece of fresh lime. This is not pretense, this is simply the way one drinks tequila at the 301. Our waitress, Pat, was a Chinese woman who giggled gratefully over the tip and who must have had difficulties beyond imagining not only in understanding the customer's English, but Mexican-English, as well. Cooking is by women. Visiting baseball stars, newspaper people, councilmen, mayors, and night club performers make up the colorful crowd. Luncheons are hectic, jam-packed to the rafters. For dinner you might try a Monday or Tuesday evening, when you will likely be admitted without waiting. No reservations accepted. The 301 has been in new hands for a while, but the spirit of Maggie, the former proprietor, lingers on.

**Inexpensive.** Open Monday through Saturday from 10 a.m. to 10 p.m. Monday through Thursday; to 11 p.m. Friday, Saturday. Entertainment weekends. Full bar. No reservations. Visa, MC. Street parking. Casual.

---

## TIA JUANA TILLY'S        Mexican/Continental

Avenida Revolución Septima 701            ★
Frontón Palacio            (70-668) 385-0624
Tijuana

This is the brainchild of the young management team that conceived Carlos 'N Charlie's and affiliated restaurants throughout Mexico, with three locations in California recently opened. All of them are based on a policy of fun and funk and the owners don't consider them "Mexican" restaurants. At Tilly's you'll find ribs barbecued over wood, icy creamed avocado soup, fresh fish and more, all served with fresh fruit and enthusiasm. There's a disco next door and you'll rarely find so many people having so much fun. Reservations are taken but I'd suggest you ask for Joe (Borbolla), he's the manager. It's not hard to find because everyone knows where the jai alai building, the Frontón Palacio, can be found.

**Inexpensive to moderate.** Open seven days from noon to midnight. Closed Christmas. Disco. Full bar. No reservations. Visa, MC. Pay parking. Casual.

---

*For best results, consult "How to Use This Guide" on page 27.*

## TICK TOCK HOLLYWOOD

**American**

★

1716 North Cahuenga Boulevard

Hollywood    **Map 7**    (213) 463-7576

It should be declared a landmark and this old familiar has acquired a wine license. The ancient tea room is dearly loved by people who sincerely believe the roasts, turkey, lamb, prime rib, steaks, chops, and fish to be the best in town. Homemade and home-baked are the standards here; and the cinnamon rolls (the good sticky kind), pies, and cakes are made fresh daily. Diners are surrounded by a large collection of antique clocks, and children (there's a child's menu) like to wait for them all to strike the hour. Lips that touch booze are not the lips here, but the tea is good; older people seem to enjoy the place most, probably because they have known it since 1930.

**Moderate**. Open Wednesday through Sunday. Luncheon from 11:30 a.m. to 2 p.m. Dinner from 4 to 8 p.m.; Sunday noon to 8 p.m. Banquet facilities. Children's menu. Wine and beer only. Reservations for large parties. All major credit cards. Valet parking. Casual.

## T & J RESTAURANT

**Greek/American**

★

8526 East Valley Boulevard

Rosemead    **Map 6**    (213) 288-8690

If a huge Denny's were to come to Greece, it would probably resemble this. That's not to put the place down but to illustrate the Americanization of food and atmosphere housed in this massive building that can seat 500 people. The menu veers from a few Greek dishes — *mosharaki à la Grecque, bracciolini di manzo* — to a much larger selection of safe fare like grenadine of beef, pepper steak, beef liver, fish and steaks. This is a family restaurant operated by the same fine folks since 1946 and children are welcome. It is the headquarters for a great deal of the private party business from small receptions to Greek weddings and there's a lot of pride exhibited in the service.

**Moderate.** Open Monday through Saturday. Luncheon Monday through Friday from 11 a.m. to 4 p.m. Dinner Monday through Thursday from 4 to 11 p.m.; Friday, Saturday to midnight. Closed Easter, Christmas. Banquet facilities. Organ bar; Monday, Wednesday Country-Western; dancing. Full bar. Reservations advised. All major credit cards accepted. Parking lots. Semi-dressy.

---

## TOKYO KAIKAN
225 South San Pedro Street
Los Angeles          **Map 7**

**Tempura bar**
★★
(213) 489-1333

As at many of L.A.'s *tempura* bars, there are several chefs who stand duty at different times. The bar at Tokyo Kaikan uses a shingle over the bar to announce the name of the chef at that moment, which is a touch I'm particularly fond of. Unlike the other *tempura* bars, there is no choice of what you get at Tokyo Kaikan. You simply sit down at the counter and patiently sip your *sake* while dishes of every ilk and persuasion begin to plop down in front of you. As a rule, the meal begins with *miso* soup, a small pickled cabbage salad, and on one recent visit, a small order of sea bass *sashimi*, a nifty change of pace from the usual plunge into *tempura*-land. Meanwhile, the chef on duty begins to vanish in clouds of *tempura* batter and sizzling oil. Out of the miasma appear massive fried shrimp, wondrous battered onions, lovely mushrooms, squid, oysters, cod, radish, sweet potato, green beans, eggplant and then, sonata-like the shrimp are reprised. At the end of the meal, when Tokyo Kaikan's *tempura* chef has left you breathless, floating on a crispy *tempura* cloud, the final fillip is delivered—a *tempura* of bananas and chrysanthemum blossoms. Absolutely devastating... and completely delicious.    *M.S.*

**Moderate.** Open Monday through Saturday. Luncheon served 11:30 a.m. to 2 p.m. weekdays. Dinner 6 to 10:30 p.m.; Saturday from 5. Closed all major holidays. Full bar. Reservations accepted. Most major credit cards. Validated parking All-Right lot days; free parking evenings. Casual.

---

## TOLEDO
11613 Santa Monica Boulevard
West Los Angeles          **Map 8**

Spanish
★★
(213) 477-2400

If the Toledo restaurant is not the first it is surely the only authentic Spanish restaurant in Southern California. And it's not a bleak store front operation with bullfight posters and canned sangria. Nor is "Spanish" a euphemism for "Mexican," a carry-over from more racist periods when lovely Mexican food was described as Spanish. You can still find remnants of that dim-witted era on signs of very old Mexican restaurants here. To fully understand the Toledo you must know about Pedro Calle. From the years of apprenticeship under his father in Madrid through his service with Perino's and Francois in Los Angeles, Pedro had a dream. He wanted to present the real Castilian foods in a setting that would be appropriate to the noble cuisine. Along with his partner Roberto Eng, formerly with Mr. Chow, he took over a bleak building haunted by past failures. Calle and Eng tastefully transformed the premises into two graceful rooms with rich art on the walls, a priceless silver chandelier, dark woods, fresh flowers, and a fireplace with wood stacked nearly to the ceiling. There is Russian service—food is prepared tableside to individual orders. The *paella* is inarguably the best saffron-kissed conconction of rice with seafood and shellfish and chicken in California. It should be ordered for two people or more to get the full effect of the preparation. In the Spanish tradition vegetables take on more importance as opposed to mere side dishes of other cuisines. There is spinach in double cream, artichokes sauteed with ham, mushrooms sauteed in garlic wine sauce, eggplant with cheese and tomato sauce and green beans in vinegar and oil. Seafoods range from a whole baked fresh fish to fresh fish in green sauce (salsa verde), shrimp in a marinade, clams steamed with wine and more. Poultry dishes include garlic chicken and a chicken with Rioja wine sauce. Most notable is the duckling, Seville-style, served with olives and onions. The duckling is welcome departure from the kind served in most continental restaurants slathered with jams and jellies or canned fruits to accommodate the Europeans' idea of the American palate. Among the other dishes I tried and recommend are the kidneys sauteed with sherry, tripe stew, sliced liver with wine, pepper, onion and mushrooms and an unusual presentation of brochette of beef with the meat skewered on an ornamental sword suspended six inches above the wooden platter. (Well, you had to be there.) Desserts include a cold chocolate souffle and a variety of custard, fruit and ice cream dishes. I have gone into more detail on the menu items because Spanish food is relatively new to this area. And while I do not want to create an impression that this is a posh restaurant, it's still a special ocasion place for dining adventures. The wine list, as you might expect, consists largely of Spanish varieties although there are some Californians as well.

**Moderate to expensive.** Open Tuesday through Sunday. Luncheon served Tuesday through Friday from 11:30 a.m. to 2:30 p.m.; Dinner Tuesday through Thursday from 5:30 to 11 p.m., Friday and Saturday to 11:30 p.m.; Sunday from 4 to 10 p.m. Closed major holidays. Wine and beer only. Reservations advised. Visa, MC, AX. Parking lot. Casual.

*To obtain the best results from this Guide, consult "How to Use this Guide" on page 27.*

## TOMMY'S HAMBURGERS

**Hamburgers**

2575 West Beverly Boulevard
Los Angeles　　**Map 8**　　　　　　　(213)389-9060

This is the original, the world famous, the landmark hamburger stand that always has a line, 24 hours a day. The last time I was there, the man in front of me was in a bathrobe and a hip cast from nearby St. Vincent's Hopital: "I just got so damned hungry thinking about these hamburgers that I sneaked out the ambulance entrance." The people behind me were old-style Abbie Hoffman speed freaks with the munchies; behind them was a nun. Hamburgers are thrown together in front of your smoke-filled eyes, and the pop — coke and all — is on the honor system; you help yourself. The only trouble with all this is that the hamburgers are not very good. They tend to be greasy, and the chili and onions overwhelm the flavors. Besides, until recently, they didn't give napkins; it was worse then, but it's still difficult for a man with a beard or mustache to eat here and still preserve his dignity. But it's a tradition, and there are not many of those left. Particularly at 3 in the morning.

**Inexpensive.** Open seven days a week, 24 hours a day. No alcoholic beverages. No credit cards. Parking lot. Casual.

---

## TONY ROMA'S

**American**
★

9404 Brighton Way
Beverly Hills　　**Map 8**　　　　　　(213) 278-1207

15760 Ventura Boulevard
Encino　　**Map 1**　　　　　　　　(213) 788-2470

319 Santa Monica Boulevard
Santa Monica　　**Map 2**　　　　　　(213) 393-0139

450 South Palm Canyon Drive
Palm Springs　　　　　　　　　　(714) 320-4297

2530 West Coast Highway
Newport Beach        **Map 4**                    (714) 642-9070

There are far better rib joints in town but few with the popularity and fanatic loyalty that these attract. This is a chain of restaurants that manages to make each restaurant look and feel like an original. The ribs are good—crisp and ungooped—and the atmosphere is almost Playboy casual with attractive waitresses and light entertainment. They are open until 1:30 a.m. for after theatre trade and if you don't mind waiting a bit (there are no reservations) you'll come away happy.

**Inexpensive**. Open seven days. Lunch from 11 a.m. to 4 p.m. Dinner from 4 p.m. to 1:30 a.m. Monday through Saturday; from 3 p.m. to 2 a.m. on Sunday. Entertainment. Full bar. No reservations. Visa, MC, AX. Parking. Casual.

---

## TONY'S ON THE PIER                          **Seafood**
210 Fisherman's Wharf
Redondo Beach        **Map 1**                    (213) 374-9246

Above a fish market on the Fisherman's Wharf, this view restaurant should be better than it is. While there are "dialy catches" that are accurate described, much of the menu lacks the kind of freshness you would expect at a seafood market. The service is a little awkward, too. Subtracting those negatives from tourism positives, here is a place worth visiting, but only because of its location.

**Moderate**. Open seven days. Luncheon served Tuesday through Sunday from 11:30 a.m. to 2 p.m. Dinner Sunday through Thursday from 2 to 11 p.m.; Friday, Saturday from 2 p.m. to 12:30 a.m. Closed Christmas, Thanksgiving. Full bar. No reservations. Entertainment nightly at 9 p.m. Visa, MC, AX. Underground parking. Casual.

# TONY'S SEA LANDING

**Seafood**

★

13612 Newport Avenue

Tustin      **Map 6**      (714) 731-2424

As someone born under the culinary sign of Aquarium, I have developed some strong preferences in American seafood restaurants. I like my fish to taste as close to the natural flavor as possible. This generally means the dishes should be unsullied by sauces in excess and that my shrimp must not be coated with that dreadful, breadful coating that tastes slightly of kerosene. At Tony's I encountered fresh seafood served in a pleasant, if unpretentious, atmosphere at reasonable prices. There is even an oyster bar, considered the second most important invention of the twentieth century by serious seafood lovers. The oyster stew is made from freshly shucked critters cooked in a creamery butter. There are clams on the half shell and a cold seafood platter with a bit of everything. But the menu has much more, from western snapper to mahi mahi to fresh Chinook salmon and your selection of either California or Maine lobster. (Actually, the California variety is every bit as good, but not as meaty as its eastern cousin.) There is a bountiful seafood counter where fresh fish look like brilliant still lifes on white crushed ice. The "Tony" is Tony Fistonich, interestingly, of Yugoslavian descent. Why interesting? Because it seems that all really good seafood operations like Sam's, Tadiches, and Chris' in San Francisco and Cigo's in San Pedro are operated by Yugoslavians with a natural talent for seafood restaurants. In Tustin, Tony runs the kitchen and his wife, Jean, runs the front of the house.

**Moderate.** Open seven days. Luncheon from 11 a.m. to 4 p.m. Dinner from 4 to 10 p.m. Closed major holidays. Children's menu. Wine and beer only. No reservations. Visa, MC, AX. Parking lot. Casual.

## TOP O'THE COVE

**Continental**
★

1216 Prospect Street
La Jolla

(714) 454-7779

La Jolla's "in" spot just happens to be a restaurant of such great character that it might flourish even if it didn't have a magnificent view high above the rocky coast, where Torrey pines reach out like surrealistic sculpture to the frothy shoreline. In the early 50's it was here that Pierre Galante proposed to Olivia de Havilland and the years have not dimmed its glitter as a star attraction. You can still chance upon Eva Gabor, Robert and Rosemarie Stack, or neighbor Dr. Salk rendezvousing here. To change the subject from rendezvous to menu, let me direct your attention to their specialty: sweetbreads, though absolutely anything you choose will do. And do nicely, too. Top o'the Cove is available for large private parties on Sunday evening or all day Monday.

**Expensive.** Open seven days. Luncheon from 11:30 a.m. to 2:15 p.m. Dinner from 6 to 10 p.m. Full bar. Reservations advised. Patio. View. Visa, MC, AX. Adjacent public parking. Semi-dressy to dressy.

## THE TOWER

**Continental**
★★

1150 South Olive Street
Los Angeles          **Map 7**

(213) 746-1554

The late Raymond Andrieux attained real height in formal French cuisine. His beautiful restaurant is on the top floor of one of the tallest buildings in downtown Los Angeles. There is a 360 degree unobstructed view that is a mosaic by day—I especially like to be there when it's raining—and spectacular at night with amber gold rivers marking the freeways. No *nouvelle cuisine* here, the emphasis is on elaborate Escoffier and the grand kitchen turns out memorable dishes that may include—at luncheon—Lyonaise sausage, baby cod and soft shell crab flown in from Boston and

Maryland from among the myriad selections. Dinner is majestic and dishes like Atlantic striped bass grilled with *beurre d'oseille* (butter and sorrel sauce) and braised Long Island duckling *aux navets* (with turnips) precede the desserts of which the *crepe souffle* is my favorite, a crepe filled with a Grand Marnier soufflé stuffed with candied fruits and served with *crème Anglaise* (a velvety custard cream) and decorated with sugared almonds. The man at the helm these days in the rightful heir apparent, Francis Canu, who served with the late, great Andrieux long enough to know every detail of the complex operation. When I think of Andrieux, I think of the time General De Gaulle paused for a moment before dedicating a statue of Napoleon in Montreal. "He was waiting," a French Canadian observed, "to see if the statue will take its hat off to him." Andrieux was confident, masterful and certain in matters of taste. He gave much of the gracious life to Southern California.

**Expensive.** Open Monday through Saturday. Luncheon served 11:30 a.m. to 2:30 p.m. Dinner from 6 to 10 p.m. Closed major holidays. Full bar. Reservations required. View. All major credit cards. Valet parking Olive Street entrance. Dressy.

---

## THE TOWERS
1555 South Coast Highway
Laguna Beach    **Map 4**

**Continental**
★
(714) 497-4477

The Towers is mystifyingly better than it should be. The location, in Laguna, and the fact that it is part of a high rise operation does not incline one to expect epicurean fare. Yet all of the traditional continental dishes are served well here and presented with style. Perhaps in the days of the Nixon White House down the coastline, sophisticated newsmen demanded better than hotel fare. Anyway, the quality has remained, enhanced by a spectacular view. My only gripe is that there are, on occasion, families with children, and while I love the sticky little things as much as anyone, they can interrupt a tranquil evening.

**Moderate.** Open seven days. Breakfast and luncheon from 7 a.m. to 3 p.m. Dinner Monday through Saturday from 5:30 to 10:30 p.m.; Sunday 4 to 10 p.m. Sunday brunch from 8 a.m. to 3 p.m. Full bar. Reservations advised. Private party facilities. Ocean view. All major credit cards. Valet parking. Casual.

---

# TRACTON'S RESTAURANT American
3560 South La Cienega ★
Los Angeles **Map 8** (213) 931-1581

16705 Ventura Boulevard
Encino **Map 1** (213) 783-1320

This club-like spot gives more for money spent than any other restaurant in Los Angeles. For example, the house specialty—prime rib of Eastern beef au jus—is almost two pounds. By exclusive arrangement with someone or something in Florida, Tracton's also has giant stone crabs at both luncheon and dinner as either an appetizer or a main course. The green goddess salad and baked potato are perfect. The bar is a favorite of the horse-and-baseball set, and there's a lot of action going on all the time. The address on La Cienega is no longer as fashionable as it was over twenty years ago when Red Tracton built his place, but the food and festivity will bring 'em in.

**Expensive**. Open seven days. Luncheon from 11 a.m. to 3:30 p.m. weekdays. Dinner from 4 to 11 p.m.; to midnight Friday, Saturday. Banquet facilities . Entertainment. Dancing. Full bar. No reservations. All major credit cards. Valet parking. Casual to semi-dressy.

---

*To obtain the best results from this Guide, be sure to consult maps on the various Southern California areas in the front of the book.*

# TRADER VIC'S
**Continental/Polynesian**
★★★

9876 Wilshire Boulevard

Beverly Hills **Map 8** (213) 274-7777

"When I started in the restaurant business, I did everything to keep customers. I sang — and I even let them stick an ice pick in my wooden leg," quoth Trader Vic Bergeron, entrepreneur, artist, adventurer, and active head of a Polynesian empire that stretches from America to Japan to Europe and above (for United Air Lines). Perhaps his greatest achievement, virtually unprecedented in my experience, was to establish quality control that works ("I never bought a cheap chicken") for a large chain of first-rate restaurants. "Consistency is the name of the game," according to Michael T. Tsao former general manager of the Beverly Hilton-owned location. "Everything you see and taste here is exactly the same in every Trader Vic's whether it's in the Bay area, where he started forty years ago, or our newest in Tokyo." How come? "We have a commissary in Emeryville that makes every important mix and sauce—we even grow a lot of our own ingredients, leaving nothing to (mis)chance." It's not just the food on the gigantic menu that you can depend on; the rum drinks (three basic rums, fresh juices when possible) are quite probably the best and most carefully made anywhere. Characteristically, there are about two dozen different kinds of glasses, a different shape for every wildly named libation—Suffering Bastard, Missionary's Downfall, and Dr. Funk's Son, which is served embedded in a block of ice. As I settled in the tropical opulence of the dining room, I was told that the "he-man" drink popular with the more virrile cognoscenti was the Tiki Puka Puka (151-proof Jamaican rum, lemon, and orange base). While I enjoyed the drink enormously, the "he-man" part didn't square. I somehow couldn't visualize Burt Reynolds walking up the bar and drawling, "Gimme a Tiki Puka Puka—neat." Besides, it's the kind of drink you can only have one of, because if you drink it all you can't order it again because you can't pronounce it again. But the rum drinks were an ideal way to soothe my psyche—I felt like plantation gentry in the wicker peacock chair—for the feast that followed. While you may feel a little silly ordering Bongo Bongo soup, do. It's made with purée of oysters, purée of spinach and cream with herbs and spices, and it's sensational. I next tried lobster mousse, made with Worcestershire, brandy, wine and egg, finished with hollandaise and cream—as good as I remembered it in the Oakland Trader Vic's. The Mediterranean prawns are mammoth shrimp in a heavy garlic sauce. I watched my Indonesian rack of lamb taken from the round Chinese clay ovens in a glassed-in room that adds to the atmosphere. Peanut sauce for the lamb and Chinese vegetables with noodles were part of the main course that was followed by banana fritters and peach flambé. I could go on, but you get the idea, and so do the thousands who flock regularly to this citadel of idealized Polynesia, where every detail is meticulously handled by a long-time competent staff. They're big on parties, too, particularly feasts of suckling pig (for twenty or more).

**Moderate to expensive.** Open seven days from 4:30 p.m. to 1:30 a.m. Limited banquet facilities. Full bar. Reservations required. All major credit cards. Validated parking. Semi-dressy.

---

## TRAPPERS INN
115 North Harbor
La Habra      **Map 6**

**American**
★
(213) 691-7784

This is one of my favorite off-the-beaten path restaurants in an area that is a gustatory desert. The motif is a blend of modern and rustic to achieve a Hudson Bay or trappers look. The food is honest and served well. There's a chef's daily special, about a dozen middle of the road entrées and a few—chicken Kiev, veal à la Canadian, frog legs—that are exotic for the area. Arlene Bullard continues the quality operation taking the reins after the loss of Bill, a local favorite who is sorely missed. There's a downstairs private room that's comfortable for medium-sized parties. Cocktails are a good value.

**Moderate.** Open seven days a week. Lunch served weekdays from 11:30 a.m. to 3 p.m. Dinner from 5 p.m. to midnight; 4 to 10 p.m. Sunday. Entertainment. Dancing. Full bar. All major credit cards. Parking lot. Casual to semi-dressy.

---

## TRULY YOURS                                   Seafood
9725 Reseda Boulevard
Northridge          **Map 1**          (213) 993-4714

Chef Robert Gindroz, a fine professional, is trying to do too much here. There is no necessity for nearly a hundred selections on the menu no matter how starved the North Valley may be. To their credit, most everything is O.K. but I'd rather have a menu that displays the talents of the chef instead of the printer.

**Inexpensive.** Open Sunday through Thursday from 11 a.m. to 10 p.m., Friday and Saturday to midnight. Sunday brunch 11:30 a.m. to 3:30 p.m. Closed Christmas Eve. Beer and wine only. Reservations for six or more advised. Patio. Visa, MC. Wheelchair access. Parking lot. Casual.

---

## TRUMPS                                        Nouvelle
8764 Melrose Avenue                                ★★★
West Hollywood          **Map 8**          (213) 855-1480

From the bright and contemporary decor to the simple menu of exotic dishes this restaurant is the boldest personal statement in recent memory. It was a gamble to see if Southern California was ready for a step up in class, but, happily, the gamble has paid off. Already a favorite with the classical musicians in the area—good eaters all—I get the feeling that the Trumps people have new surprises in store, on a continuing basis.

The food defies any description except *nouvelle*. It zig zags wildly through a half dozen cuisines and settles where it wants. The soup may be yellow split pea with sauerkraut served up in a pitcher, the salad a concoction of sashimi dressed with lemon juice, olive oil and green peppercorns on Japanese mushrooms topped with slices of avocado and papaya; the entree, a perfect fish stew, and the dessert a splendid and original production.

Trumps serves weekday tea, a civilized ritual invented for the purpose of exchanging gossip. Now it's deal-making whilst downing a sherry and selecting from an array of finger sandwiches (goat cheese and herbs, smoked chicken), glazed scones with fresh guava jam, triple thick cream and honey. A dessert platter of bite-sized everything accompanies the Darjeeling tea.

**Expensive.** Open for lunch Monday through Saturday 11:45 a.m. to 3 p.m. Tea served 3:30 to 5:45 p.m. Dinner Monday through Thursday 6:30 to midnight; Friday and Saturday 6:30 to 12:30 a.m. Closed major holidays. Cocktails. Reservations required. Patio. Visa, MC, AX. Wheelchair access. Valet parking. Semi-dressy

---

## THE TWIN DRAGON RESTAURANT            Chinese

8597 West Pico Boulevard                                        ★
Los Angeles        **Map 8**                      (213) 655-9805

1550 South Harbor Boulevard
Anaheim         **Map 6**                         (714) 772-4400

20461 Ventura Boulevard
Woodland Hills         **Map 1**                   (213) 887-4505

The cuisine of Shanghai—with a bow to Szechwan—is served in the Los Angeles location better than in Anaheim, but both are among the finest exponents of the art of coastal

Chinese cookery (more emphasis on seafoods, soups, and spices). The menus are confusing, with Chinese characters, and the waiters have difficulty with the language. In self-defense, there is a tendency to order the "set dinners," good but not the best dishes in the house. I'd recommend an appetizer of shrimp toast (pieces of shrimp with smooth egg-white, deep fried) or pork with lucerne and egg (the main ingredients are pork, egg, bean sprouts, and soy jam, rolled at the table in flour crêpes and eaten like a taco). You should try the three-flavor sizzling rice soup and, among the entrée dishes, Szechwan chicken, beef broccoli, or Szechwan shredded pork.

**Moderate.** Open seven days. Luncheon Monday through Saturday from 11:30 a.m. to 2:30 p.m. Dinner Sunday through Thursday from 5 to 10:15 p.m.; to 11:15 p.m. Friday, Saturday. Sunday brunch from 11:30 a.m. to 2 p.m. Full bar. Reservations advised for six or more. All major credit cards. Parking lot; street parking. Casual to semi-dressv.

---

## TWO GUYS FROM ITALY
**Italian**

1644 North Cahuenga Boulevard ★
Hollywood    **Map 7**    (213) 462-6747

I wandered into Two Guys from Italy in Hollywood with mixed feelings. It had been an important restaurant—D' Amore's—frequented by the Italian celebrity set, assorted swingers, and a cast of girls with sunny dispositions and shady pasts. The walls were covered with celebrity photographs (does Frank Sinatra have his autographed picture in every Italian restaurant?), and the tables were lit by candles flickering in old Chianti bottles. You know the type of place I mean. Thus, I was pleased to find that although Two Guys is a chain operation (some 30 in the Southwest), they do a fine job—significantly better than the pizzeria the name implies. Complete dinners include minestrone or salad, a relish tray, savory garlic bread, and dessert. And the lengthy menu ranges upward through pastas, boneless breast of chicken *cacciatore*, sausage and peppers to *cioppino*. There's a family dinner with too many courses to list. Robert Whenen is extremely proud of this operation, perhaps the bet place in the Hollywood area for those asttending the Huntington Harford Theatre. His selection of wines and liqueurs and the flair with which they are presented are unique in an inexpensive place of this kind. Luncheon is less expensive ad offers a more limited selection. And, of course, there is pizza in a wide variety.

**Moderate**. Open seven days. Luncheon served from 11:30 a.m. to 4 p.m. weekdays. Dinner from 4 to 11:30 p.m., Friday and Saturday until 12:30 p.m. Closed Labor Day, Thanksgiving. Children's menu. Full bar. Reservations preferred. Visa, MC, AX. Validated parking. Casual.

*In order to obtain the best results from this Guide, be sure to read the French, German, Italian and Oriental menu translators on page 705 to 710 of this Guide.*

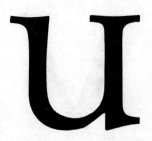

## UNICORN CAFE           French

31727 Coast Highway
South Laguna          (714) 499-5359

South Laguna is a restaurant graveyard although Maurice Brerot, formerly the operator of La Chaumiere in Beverly Hills could have the exception here. The total charm of this converted cottage is devastating. The foyer opens into the main dining room with a large antique hutch that has been converted into a wine rack. The view from the windows overlooks the rooftops of homes that staircase down the cliff to the sea beyond. The stairway leads down to a brick patio shaded by a giant pine.

Specialties include all fresh fish, rabbit, duck with peppercorn sauce and lamb. All are well and cheerfully served. However, this restaurant must survive through the bleak Laguna winters when the tourists have gone home and there is a general air of desolation. I wish them well.

**Moderate**. Open Tuesday through Saturday. Dinner at 5:30 p.m. Wine and beer only. Reservations advised. Ocean view. Visa, MC. Street parking. Semi-dressy.

V

---

**VALENTINO**                                    **Italian**
3115 Pico Boulevard                                ★★
Santa Monica          **Map 2**          (213) 829-4313

Hosts can be intimidating, especially maître d's of French or
Italian restaurants. With the American trait of seeking
approval from the Man in Charge—ships' captains, railway
conductors, airplane pilots—we have a conditioned reflex to
dissemble in the presence of a man carrying a clipboard or
standing behind a podium. It is in restaurants where this
quirk in our otherwise aggressive personalities becomes
troublesome. We order and accept dishes in a language we do
not understand and, because they think us stupid, we're
reluctant to ask questions. This is a rather long preamble to
Valentino and the firm suggestion that you ask about the
dishes unfamiliar to you. The young owners seem to enjoy
discussing their efforts. (Most owners and waiters do, except
in New York, where courtesy is an offense against the
union.) The *calamareti*, they'll tell you, is the more tender
baby squid, fried in the style of Sicily. The rabbit is roasted

with rosemary, and the *fettuccine* and *gnocchi* (potato dumplings) are homemade "by my mother." *Crema fritta* is fried cream served flaming here, more for the flavor it imparts than—as is customary these days—for the show. The wine list is extensive and represents obvious care; you might get helpful suggestions on some of the lesser known labels. I would recommend any of the dozen different wines from Beaulieu Vineyards, one of California's best wine producers.

**Expensive**. Open Monday through Saturday. Luncheon Friday only from 11:30 a.m. to 2:30 p.m. Dinner Monday through Saturday from 5 to 11:30 p.m. Full bar. Reservations required on weekends. Banquet facilities. All major credit cards. Valet parking. Semi-dressy.

---

## VALEE ROSE

Flower Hill Shopping Center
Del Mar

**Natural Foods**
★
(714) 481-8861

Grazing is a popular pastime in Del Mar with horses and now with people at the Gatekeeper. If organic tostadas turn you on, made with lettuce, tomatoes, alfalfa sprouts, and pinto beans, then this is the place. Lotsa lettuce things, good soup, fine whole grain bread and a "happenburger" will give you an idea of what to expect. (If vegetarians are so all fired on that subject, why do they name many of the dishes after meat? Like vegeburger, parsnip cutlets, etc.?)

**Inexpensive.** Open seven days. Luncheon from 11 a.m. to 2:30 p.m. weekdays. Saturday, Sunday brunch 9 a.m. to 5 p.m. Dinner Sunday through Thursday 5 to 9:30 p.m.; to 11 Friday, Saturday. Reservations recommended. Full bar. Parking lot. All major credit cards. Parking lot. Casual.

---

*For best results, consult "How to Use This Guide" on page 27.*

## VELVET HORN                    American/Polynesian
5970 Orangethorpe
Buena Park        **Map 6**                    (714) 523-5262

This place is trying with some success to be all things to all people. The reliable steak, the zest of Polynesian dishes, eggroll appetizers and spareribs, prime ribs, and seafood are all there. For that big sporting event you go in the lounge where you see the headliner of the week on a big 4 by 4 television screen. Other entertainment is a succession of trios, both vocal and instrumental.

**Moderate**. Open Monday through Saturday. Luncheon from 11 a.m. to 5 p.m. weekdays. Dinner Monday through Saturday from 5 to 11 p.m. Closed Thanksgiving, Christmas. Entertainment. Full bar. Reservations advised. Banquet facilities. All major credit cards. Parking lot. Casual to semi-dressy.

---

## VELVET TURTLE                         American
(See phone book for listings.)                    ★

We've written so despairingly about the monotonous, inept steak-and-lobster restaurants that seem to be relentlessly pro-liferating in Southern California that it seems only fair to pay tribute to a group that almost gets it all together. The Velvet Turtle is massive, but it avoids the cavernous look by tasteful decor and separated areas. The menu is limited, but there are touches of imagination and flair — a gazpacho that doesn't taste like chilled V-8 juice, barbecued beef bones, prepared-to-order rack of lamb, and salmon poached in chablis, along with the more familiar entrées.

They studied the formula restaurant and decided to upgrade each component—service, food, drinks, and entertainment — to the high standards usually identified with a single restaurant under the taut control of a single owner. Owners may be absent, but management isn't. We watched the manager of the Fullerton operation do a complete circle of the room every quarter hour, observing, talking with the patrons, setting the pace. The fresh shrimp cocktail was — happily —really fresh, the shrimp firm and not overcooked, the sauce well prepared. The half avocado stuffed with king crab was near perfect. And the beef, as you might expect, is expertly handled and presented. There is not a more generous or flavorful prime rib anywhere, and that includes those restaurants that specialize in prime rib. My steak was charred and rare, exactly as I had ordered it; and the abalone sauté amandine retained its flavor and texture. Dinners are accompanied with a choice of soup du jour, gazpacho, or a fresh green salad. Potatoes are roasted and quartered instead of baked, and the crisp brown sections are a welcome change. The Velvet Turtles (sounds like a rock group) are popular with businessmen at luncheon, and the menu offers an array of imaginative sandwiches, salads, and omelettes. Sunday bruncheon includes fruit in champagne with a bountiful spread of entrées. All locations offer pretty much the same quality throughout.

**Moderate.** Hours and prices vary. Full bar. Reservations advised, especially for large parties and on weekends. All major credit cards. Valet parking. Casual to semi-dressy.

---

# VERACRUZ
2306 South Union Street
Los Angeles **Map 7**

Mexican/Seafood
★
(213) 746-9156

Too many Mexican restaurants serve what I describe as starch on starch with a side order of starch and starch. And if the sauce this starch is served with has no moxie, you're left with starch served multiple ways. But this is a restaurant where the salsa tastes fresh and hot, with enough cilantro and chopped onion to cause mild tachycardia. But no one (at least not according to the *Journal of the American Medical Association*) has ever died directly from an overdose of fresh salsa. What the good sauce does at

Veracruz is get the blood flowing fast enough to prepare you for the restaurant's choice of more than two dozen seafood dishes, ranging from a superb *ceviche* ($2.95), in which a variety of sea creatures (octopus, shrimp, red snapper at least) have been "cooked" by acidic marination in lemon juice and cilantro. There are seafood cocktails ("cocteles") of octopus, shrimp, abalone, crab and various mixtures thereof, ranging in price up to $5.95; and there are good chowders, including one called *siete mares* which gives you a stewpot of seven types of fish for $5.75. The cocktails are temptations; the chowders are meals in themselves. And both are preludes to the *camarones* and the *huachinango*.

*Huachinango* is Mayan for red snapper, and it's surely one of the noblest food fishes to swim the seas. And the things they do to their snapper! Imagine a large snapper sliced open, filled with a mixture of shrimp and crab, then closed covered with hot sauce and cheese, and baked. The result is *huachinango relleno con mariscos ($6.75)*, a fish-within-a-fish of a dish, served with a hard-boiled egg on a stick rising from its midsection and impaled green olives at either end. The darn thing looks like the Beatles' Yellow Submarine... but it tastes like fish heaven.

All dishes at Veracruz—from the *camarones gigantes al ajillo* (prawns awash in garlic, $6.25) to the grilled lobster ($7.75) are served with a peppery, slightly murky fish soup, and rice flavored with onions fried in port fat. There are also dishes like tongue *tanchera* and the usual range of starches, all of which are beside the point. The big game at Veracruz is the fish    *M.S.*

**Moderate.** Open Tuesday through Sunday. Luncheon and dinner from 11 a.m. to 9 p.m. weekdays; from 10 a.m. to 10 p.m. weekends. Closed Christmas, New Year's. Beer and wine only. Reservations suggested on weekends. Visa, MC. Street parking. Semi-dressy.

## VERITA'S CANTINA

10323 Santa Monica Boulevard

West Los Angeles   **Map 8**

Mexican
★★
(213) 277-3362

This is the high art of Mexican cuisine because Verita Thompson was desperate to prove that tamales and tacos do not a Mexican restaurant make. And her tiny, intimate, two-story cantina in New England Village on Santa Monica in the West Side proves her point well, and profitably. (Ms. Thompson purchased the entire shopping complex.) The recipes have been handed down through her family, with dishes from Yucatan (liver sautéed in tequila with onions, mushrooms, and carrots) and an intriguing rack of lamb in a "drunken sauce" made with the unlikely combination of crème de menthe and tequila, among other things. The lamb is $10 with soup or salad and dessert. There are crêpes stuffed with chicken and cheese sauce, and chicken breast stuffed with corn dressing and served with a zesty green mole sauce, too. Verita (pronounced "Var-eé-ta") is a gracious hostess, who manages to greet every guest as though he had stepped into her living room, while still keeping an eye on the hundreds of significant movements that only restaurateurs understand. A favorite of the celebrity set, her avocado-zucchini soup and lemon cake with lemon sauce were particular turn-ons for the people from the "Mary Tyler Moore Show." If you ever thought that all Mexican food was accompanied by re-fried beans served in a decor of serapes and costumed señoritas, then be prepared for a refreshing, if not inexpensive, surprise. Also be sure to get there early enough to browse through the whimsical Enchantment World Gallery as you enter the village. Run by artists who love and paint children and who're not afraid to experiment (the enamel paintings are fascinating), it's a kind of visual aperitif.

**Expensive.** Open Monday through Saturday. Lunch from 11 a.m. to 3 p.m. Dinner from 5 to 11 p.m. Limited banquet facilities. Children's menu. Entertainment. Full bar. Reservations required. Patio. All major credit cards. Valet parking. Semi-dressy.

## VERONIKA                                    Hungarian
8164 West 3rd Street
Los Angeles        **Map 7**                  (213) 656-9330

A gorgeous little restaurant that promises more than it delivers. The chef-person, Veronika Lampel, has great intentions, but something is lost in this Hungarian-European flowery restaurant twixt kitchen and table. There are some unusual (for Los Angeles) dishes: nine pork variations, *torten* and *le goulasche de boeuf*, a rather Frenchified name for good goulash. As a matter of fact the restaurant, apparently believing that Hungarian places are associated with tackiness, seems to be masquerading as a French one and that seems sad. I'm sure that the lovely chef could cook up a storm of less familiar dishes and we need another French restaurant about as much as (you finish the sentence).

**Moderate to expensive.** Open Tuesday through Sunday from 6 to 11 p.m. Wine and beer only. Reservations required. patio. Visa, MC, AX, DC. Valet parking. Semi-dressy to dressy.

---

## VERONIQUE                                       French
8536 Rosemead Boulevard                              ★★
Pico Rivera        **Map 6**                  (213) 949-7711

A charming and surprising restaurant with a country French atmosphere. The blackboard menu changes frequently and is far from unsophisticated. *Quenelles* (fish dumplings poached in white wine), filet of lamb *perigeaux* (lamb in Madeira wine), *coquille Parisienne,* or *veau marengo* might be on the menu along with soup or salad. If you found this restaurant in Paris, you'd feel elated. Pico Rivera is closer.

**Moderate to expensive**. Luncheon from 11:30 a.m. to 2 p.m. weekdays. Dinner from 5:30 to 9 p.m. Tuesday through Friday; to 9:30 p.m. Saturday. Wine and beer only. Reservations advised. All major credit cards. Parking lot. Semi-dressy.

# VIA FETTUCCINI    Italian

14670 Ventura Boulevard    ★
Sherman Oaks    **Map 1**    (213) 990-6290

7111 Melrose Avenue    ★
Los Angeles    **Map 7**    (213) 936-5924

I find that most good Italian meals have a manic edge to them, a certain sense that the kitchen is about to collapse in a heap of noodles and sauce. Via Fettuccini plunges straight into that infectious madness, decking itself out like a culinary version of Fellini's 8½, with three rings worth of entertainment whirling about you. What other Italian restaurant that you know of serves an appetizer of chopped liver, not as good as the standard at Nate & Al's, but not bad either for an Italian restaurant not well known for keeping kosher? Where else can you sit on seats made out of old wine cases covered with red leatherette? And in what other Italian restaurant could you find Clint Eastwood sitting at a rear table with Sondra Locke with absolutely no one paying them the slightest bit of attention? Like I said, there's a certain funhouse elegance to Via Fettuccini, which follows through in every element of the place, right down to the menu with its Rube Goldberg pasta machine illustration, drawn by co-owner Laura Regini.

The food at Via Fettuccini is a bit erratic, but fluctuates more to the good than the awful. The appetizer of *mozzarella marinara* ($3.25), for instance, is a perennial favorite, crisp and saucy. The *braciole e patate* ($4.35), slices of rolled flank steak stuffed with a variety of pickled vegetables is a real crowd pleaser, as is the spicy potato salad served on the side. And I've always found the pastas (there's a choice of 46 different pasta dishes among the *spaghetti, fettuccine, linguini, taglierini, ravioli, manicotti, cannelloni, panzotti, lasagne, gnocchi, agnolotti* and *cappelletti* to be fresh and good though sometimes the sauces don't quite live up to the pastas. But what the heck, there's no pretension at Via Fettuccini. Via Fettuccini sets out to make good pasta. For the most part, that's just what it does.   *M.S.*

**Los Angeles: Moderate.** Open seven days. Luncheon from 11:30 a.m. to 3:30 p.m. Dinner from 3:30 to 11; Sunday from 5. Closed July 4, Thanksgiving, Christmas, New Year's. Beer and wine only. Reservations accepted. Patio. No credit cards. Parking lot. Casual.

**Sherman Oaks: Moderate.** Open seven days from 5 to 10 p.m.; to 11 weekends. Closed Christmas. Entertainment. Wine and beer only. Reservations suggested. All major credit cards. Parking lot. Casual.

---

# VICKMAN'S                                       American
1228 East Eighth Street                               DA★★
Los Angeles        **Map 7**              (213) 622-3852

What Los Angeles restaurant opens at 3 a.m.? It's downtown at the produce mart, where truck drivers, delivery men, and farmers gather in Vickman's—as they have for 50 years—for great baked goods (the strawberry pie in season may be the best around) and plain but abundant fare like roast beef or stuffed pork chops. Vegetables are fresh, of course, and soups—particularly on a cold morning—are ambrosial. Beer is sold by the can, and the place is staffed by fast-moving, determined waitresses.

**Inexpensive**. Open Monday through Saturday from 3 a.m. to 3 p.m. Closed Sunday, major holidays. Beer only. No reservations. No credit cards. Parking lot. Casual.

---

# VICTORIA STATION                      Prime Rib/American
(See phone book for listings)

Victoria Station, another new concept, is impressive to the eye, much less so to the taste. Four real boxcars that open off the reception area display artifacts and signs that would delight any railroad hobbyist. Implementation of the theme includes handing you a ticket with your table number, period costumes, salt and pepper in Watney beer bottles, and very hard, very uncomfortable wooden booths. The discomfort may be somewhat calculated, as the waiter pointed out, because the name of the game is "turnover," and people can't sit around uncomfortably for much more than half an hour. Getting to the salad bar is a traffic hazard, and you may find yourself doing the Alphonse and Gaston minuet with the cross-traffic. That's the only place where bread is available, so if you want more, back you go. There are three basic items on the dinner menu: steak, prime rib, and the shrimp Victoria, described as "giant shrimp in wine and garlic sauce." The shrimp are the Mexican or South American variety, and only two of my six had any flavoring — and those two, too much. Sautéed mushrooms were an embarrassment, overcooked, with no flavor at all. Stationmaster dessert turns out to be rather ordinary cheesecake.

**Moderate.** Hours and prices vary. Luncheon from 11:30 a.m. to 2:30 p.m. Dinner Monday through Thursday from 5 to 10 p.m., Friday and Saturday to 11 p.m. Closed Christmas. Full bar. Reservations advised. Visa, MC, AX, DC. Parking lots in all locations. Casual to semi-dressy.

---

## VIETNAM PEARL
Vietnamese
1461 South La Cienega Boulevard ★
Los Angeles **Map 8** (213) 652-3279

Vietnam Pearl is one of the more authentic restaurants that serves this French-influenced Oriental fare. A modest operation—it began as kind of a take-out restaurant—there are rather plain tables but good, attentive service with a willingness to explain each dish. I began with a barbecued pork appetizer on a skewer (good), graduated to a crab and asparagus soup (excellent) and then to an entrée of "salt and sweet crab" (marvelous). There is a full range of beers although I find the Kirin from Japan perfect accompaniment to the semi-spicy. Vietnam Pearl is no-nonsense restaurant, no prettier than it needs to be, but well worth visiting.

**Inexpensive**. Open Monday through Saturday. Luncheon from 11:30 a.m. to 3 p.m. weekdays. Dinner from 5 to 10 p.m. Wine and beer only. Reservations advised. Visa, MC. Parking lot. Casual.

---

## VILLA CAPRI                                    Italian
6735 Yucca Street                                   ★★
Hollywood        **Map 7**                  (213) 465-4148

Back in 1949 before autographed pictures of Frank Sinatra were considered standard equipment for Italian restaurants— sort of like the portrait of the queen in English pubs—Patsy D'Amore had a photograph of an improbably lean, impossibly young Sinatra. The fact that it was merely one of the hundreds of intimately inscribed celebrity photographs may give you an idea of the role Patsy's place played in the history of Hollywood.

Everyone who ever even knew an Italian ate there, courted there, got engaged and disengaged there. Patsy was the first personality restaurant host, the West Coast edition of Toots Shor, and he presided over his first restaurant on Cahuenga— it's since moved to Yucca—with class and a no-nonsense disregard for the phonies. You didn't have to be a celebrity to feel good at Patsy's. It helped, of course, but he had the ability to make everyone feel important.

And so I had mixed feelings about revisiting Villa Capri after two decades. Would the spaghetti Caruso, prepared with the plump chicken livers, still taste as good? Would the veal *piccanti* still have the fresh lemony tang and would the *fettuccine Alfredo* still be high drama? It was all there, as good as I remembered.

There's a reason. Rose D'Amore met Patsy in his first restaurant and lived the violent opera of Italian restaurants. She's now the boss. Daughter Filomena (a 9-1/2) remembers the strict standards and serves now as luncheon hostess. Son Joey, who is off building more grandiose projects, still comes back to help momma.

Although the Villa is a block away from Hollywood Blvd., the crazies, more interested in punk than pasta, don't come near the place. The celebrities still do. It's among the few good restaurants near the Hollywood Bowl, the Pantages or any of the other non-X-rated attractions left.

The menu is like a primer to basic Neopolitan cuisine. Aside from the familiar pastas there is an assortment of dishes that are honest and very good. Nine veal dishes, six chicken variations and special favorites like sausage and peppers, liver Veneziana and pork chops *pizzaiola* are available. The complete dinner includes a splendid antipasto, soup, spaghetti, ice cream, rum cake or cheese and cake with coffee.

The *calamari fritto* was the most luscious and most tender I've tasted. There's also a full range of pizzas (there are some who claim that Villa Capri introduced the pizza to the West Coast and vice versa).

The maitre d', Nicola, supervises crisp service and the room looks like a set for *Godfather III*. I particularly like to sit near the wood burning—even in summertime—fireplace and enjoy the average two-to-three-hour dinner.

Luncheon menu is abbreviated with a *plat du jour* that includes soup or salad with coffee. Among the à la carte entrees, one of the luncheon favorites is the Capri special, beef ground with onions, spinach and eggs. There are diet plates as well but if you're on a diet what the hell are you doing in a place like this?

The Jimmy Durante room can handle private parties from 20 to 100 people and may be a welcome relief from hotel banquet fare. Great wine list.

**Moderate**. Open Monday through Saturday. Luncheon served from 11 a.m. to 3 p.m. weekdays. Dinner weekdays from 3 p.m. to 1 a.m., Saturday from 6 p.m. to 1 a.m. Closed Labor day. Full bar. Reservations advised. Private party facilities. Visa, MC, AX. Valet parking. Casual to semi-dressy.

## VILLA FONTANA
**Continental**
★

21 Town and Country
Orange    **Map 6**    (714) 547-0911

This is one of the beautiful restaurants of Orange County, with Spanish tiles, fine leather wall hangings, and the ambience of a fourteenth-century palace. The menu is continental, and the flaming spinach salad is one of the highlights. Steak Diane and rack of lamb are favorites in this house of character operated by Henry Grum, formerly of the Los Angeles Country Club. The cocktail lounge is masculine and understated, with comfortable full-backed swivel chairs.

**Moderate to expensive.** Open Monday through Saturday. Luncheon served from 11:30 a.m. to 2:30 p.m. weekdays. Dinner from 6 to 10 p.m. Banquet facilities. Closed Labor Day, Thanksgiving, Christmas. Entertainment. Full bar. Reservations advised. Visa, MC. Parking lot. Semi-dressy.

## VILLA NOVA RESTAURANT
**Italian**
★

3131 West Coast Highway
Newport Beach    **Map 4**    (714) 642-7880

When the late Allen Dale founded the glamorous Villa Nova on the Sunset Strip, he established noble standards of cuisine presented within the atmosphere of a friendly Italian castle. It is comforting to know that Mrs. Dale has continued that dedication to excellence, even though the location has changed. From the colorful, outrageous mural-bedecked exterior and the friendly staff, to the individually prepared dishes by executive chef Walter Gentile (over thirty years with the Dales), the Villa Nova in Newport offers a tantalizing excursion into the foods of Central and Northern Italy. I like their own mozzarella appetizer, a square of cheese deep-fried in bread crumbs and lovingly covered with marinara sauce and the ubiquitous anchovy.

Also *piatto Villa Nova* (thin-sliced filet mignon baked with eggplant, parmesan cheese, mushrooms, and tomato sauce) and the *vitello Castellana*, an entrée with alternating layers of veal, prosciutto, parmesan cheese, and special sauce. The dishes range from expected pastas to a wide assortment of exotic creations. Don't expect snack-shop service. Each dish is prepared to order, but you can enjoy an excellent antipasto in anticipation. Do expect informal service and an excellent wine assortment (our favorite chianti, Brolio Riserva), and the feeling that you have had the Italian experience.

**Moderate.** Open seven days. Dinner from 5 p.m. to 1 a.m., Monday through Saturday, and 4 p.m. to 1 a.m., Sunday. Closed Christmas. Children's menu. Piano bar. Full bar. Reservations advised. Bay view. All major credit cards. Valet parking. Casual.

---

**VILLA SOMBRERO**                           **Mexican**
6101 York Boulevard                                ★★
Los Angeles     **Map 8**              (213) 256-9784

Joe Wambaugh, the ex-cop is not only a talented author, but he is, in his way, a gourmet. For several years he's been touting me on this Mexican restaurant near the police station in Highland Park. I came as a cynic, how could any Mexican restaurant be that much different from any other good Mexican restaurant? I left as a convert.

While the ambience is a bit shocking, kind of like the interior of pink Cadillac I saw in Ensenada that had flowers growing in it—somehow it works. There is Frederick's of Hollywood plush, a large mural of a virgin (?) being sacrificed on the alter of some long forgotten gods, pink roses and artfully folded napkins. The margarita was good; the authentic Mexican music, well—authentic; and the tuxedoe'd waiters are gracious beyond belief. The menu provides some surprising selections: a whole lobster split in half and cooked in the grill with spices and butter was less than $15. Scallops "ranchero," a special of the day, were giant scallops cooked to a perfect degree of firm tenderness and sauced with bell pepper, onions and tomatoes. Best of all was another special, the barbecued pork, lean, tender and savory.

The *carne asada* is made with large filet mignon and the chicken dishes are a specialty of the kitchen along with the basic Mexican fare served up in an unbasic manner.

Be sure to have a tequila with Felipe, the owner, who tends the small bar and ask for his recommendations. At the conclusion of the dinner the kitchen ladies will be thrilled if you ask them to come out to thank them. Really.

**Medium.** Open seven days. Luncheon served Monday through Thursday 10 a.m. to 3 p.m. Dinner from 5 to 11 p.m.; Friday, Saturday and Sunday from 10 a.m. to 11 p.m. Closed major holidays. Cocktails. Reservations required, especially on weekends. All major credit cards. Wheelchair access. Parking lot. Casual.

---

## VINCE AND PAUL'S STEAK HOUSE

American/Steakhouse

★

1521 West 7th Street
Los Angeles          **Map 7**                    (213) 483-2543

Many of the employees are stockholders in this fifty-year-old open-grill steak house, and that's one of the best guarantees of good food and service there is. Here is restaurant nostalgia: a good bar with man-sized drinks, generous portions of simple fare like steaks and prime rib, with some near-forgotten favorites like fried chicken country style, or pork chops with applesauce. The atmosphere is pleasant, comfortable, and subdued.

**Moderate.** Open seven days. Luncheon served from 11 a.m. to 2:30 p.m. weekdays. Dinner Monday through Saturday from 4:30 to 11 p.m.; Sunday from 1 to 9 p.m. Closed major holidays. Full bar. Reservations accepted. All major credit cards. Parking lot; street parking. Casual.

672

## THE VINTAGE PRESS

Continental
★

216 North Willis Street
Visalia

(209) 733-3033

The Shakespeare Festival faltered last year but is rumored to return in '82, and if you're going to the festival I can't think of a finer midsummer night's scene. Imagine the Beverly Hill's Bistro transplanted improbably in Visalia and you'll get a glimmering of what John Varanian's place is like. It's highly respected by the wine-making crowd, but the food is king here and they have one dish, mousseline chicken (chicken stuffed with chicken mousse, avocado and leeks) that is beautiful. The menu lists fresh provolone veal in a variety of dishes including a delicate lemony veal piccata. The sole Florentine, chicken with peppercorn and the cutomary and obligatory beef dishes are certainly the best in this hamlet and would compare with San Francisco's best. Even King Richard would have gone back for seconds, for it's food prepared as you like it. All's well that ends well, andt he desserts are a happy ending. Luncheon weekdays is a luxurious experience that would tame any shrew. Lest you think I make Much Ado About Nothing, let me go on to say that this is the complete compleat experience.

**Moderate.** Open Monday through Saturday. Luncheon from 11:30 a.m. to 2 p.m. weekdays. Dinner from 6 to 11 p.m. Banquet facilities. Full bar. Reservations advised. Visa, MC, AX. Parking lot. Casual to semi-dressy.

---

## VIRGILIO'S

Italian
★★

2611 South La Cienega Boulevard
Los Angeles          **Map 7**

(213) 559-8532

"I don' drink I don' smoke. All I want my whole life is to please the customer." Virgilio fans his fingers around his head—to speak sucn sentiment involves intricate Latin gestures—and he leans back and watches and remembers.

Virgilio Del Mare was a captain at Valentino's when he made his commitment to open his own restaurant, Virgilio's. He must have seemed like Don Quixote to his family, for Virgilio picked a dilapidated bungalow on a hopelessly industrial block of La Cienega, closer to skid than Restaurant Row. He moved in and lived among the rubble of his neighbors who still threw their industrial waste in his front yard, scrounged for equipment and worked 15-hour days for seven years to create his restaurant. As the improbable emerged as the possible, he redoubled his efforts to gather a staff and to afford the $200 a month for rent.

The tiny, yellow stucco entrance is misleading: the bungalow rambles through a series of rooms seats well over 150. Decor is New York Italian with wine walls, wrought iron, oil paintings and soft lights.

Since October 1979, when the restaurant opened, it has become a great favorite of many who have tried to keep it their secret. Dustin Hoffman, Paul Anka, Robert Vaughn and Elizabeth Montgomery dine there, as do the captains and lieutenants of industry.

Dishes were deftly prepared tableside without undue flourishes or high drama. Some pastas are homemade among the 20 on the menu; all are very good.

The cost of most of the dishes—few are over $10—is about half the tariff of high-rent districts, and all entrées include a fine salad or soup, vegetable and good bread.

Dishes we tried included *calamari fritti* (fresh squid marinated in milk and quick fried) for $7.50; shrimp *scamp di la casa* in a rather bland garlic sauce; *mozzarella marinara*, a not-exciting version of fried cheese. The most popular entrée by far is the *costata di vitello* (a veal chop sautéed with mushrooms and Madeira), although our highest rating went to the sweetbreads Capri ($7.50) that were lightly sautéed with shallots, mushrooms and olives. The veal and chicken dishes, while Northern Italian in style, are nonetheless imaginatively prepared.

The luncheon menu is an abbreviated version with even

lower prices than the dinner offerings, and a long luncheon on the patio is serendipity.

His dessert cart is as much an expression of his aspirations as the full menu. *Cannoli* are homemade and stuffed with creamy fruit and chocolate-studded filling. There are fresh raspberries, strawberries and dishes like fried cream and, my favorite, orange curacao. After-dinner drinks include the special cappuccino, Venetian coffee, espresso and Cesar's Connection prepared by the maitre d'.

The wine list is not yet as complete as it will be as it takes years to develop a great cellar, but it does include some interesting imports and a good selection of California wines.

**Moderate.** Open seven days. Luncheon from 11 a.m. to 3 p.m. weekdays. Dinner 5 to 11 p.m. Entertainment. Full bar. Reservations suggested. Patio. All major credit cards. No wheelchair access. Valet parking. Casual to semi-dressy.

---

### VITO'S                                                    Italian
2807 Ocean Park Boulevard                                       ★
Santa Monica        **Map 2**                        (213) 450-4999

Vita Somma's credentials are impeccable. He was a captain at Valentino and Marquis West, and he supervises his personal restaurant with the attention to detail familiar at such fine houses. It is a family restaurant in a unique use of the word. One brother, Roberto, serves as the only captain; another brother—Maximilian—is the waiter.

Vito's celebrates the good cooking of Southern Italy with *puttanesca* (fresh tomatoes, olives, anchovies, garlic, capers) and *marinara mozzarella* prepared well. The *zuppa di pesce* is a savory soup of shellfish, and the pastas taste homemade. Desserts are more spectacular than necessary but it is an intelligent menu, altogether, and the restaurant has quickly become a favorite of the celebrity set.

**Moderate to expensive.** Open for lunch Monday through Friday 11:30 a.m. to 2:30 p.m. Dinner Monday through Saturday 5:30 to 10:30 p.m. Closed major holidays. Cocktails. Reservations accepted. Visa, MC, AX. Wheelchair access. Valet parking. Semi-dressy.

---

*To obtain the best results from this Guide, be sure to consult maps on the various Southern California areas in the front of the book.*

# WAN-Q RESTAURANT
American/Cantonese

8751 West Pico Boulevard
★

Los Angeles **Map 8**
(213) 272-1880

Thirty-one years ago Benny Eng opened a modest but good
Cantonese restaurant here. Then he was swept up in the
technicolor tide of Polynesia. Now Mr. Mu continues a
proud but good establishment that serves lavish fare and
super tropical drinks at relatively modest prices. This is also
the home of one of the great dinner values in Southern
California: an eleven-course Mauna Loa dinner—a Chinese
orgy. This is a successful and inexpensive luncheon spot as
well. Finally, there is a thriving take-out business; it has
become a tradition for many of the studio workers to stop
off for some of the special dinners, particularly Wan-Q's
special Cantonese chow mein, on their way home.

**Inexpensive to moderate.** Open seven days. Luncheon Sunday through Thursday 11:30 a.m. to 3 p.m. Dinner Monday through Thursday 3 to 10 p.m.; Friday through Sunday to 11 p.m. Closed Thanksgiving. Full bar. Reservations advised. Take-out. Visa, MC, AX, DC. Parking lot. Casual.

# THE WAREHOUSE RESTAURANT

**International/Polynesian**

4499 Admiralty Way      ★★
Marina del Rey    **Map 2**      (213) 823-5451

3540 Via Oporto      ★★
Newport Beach    **Map 4**      (714) 673-4700

This is a unique restaurant in Southern California, and in this case "unique" is not a euphemism for poor food. Created by international photographer Burt Hixson, The Warehouse combines the moods and themes of many nations into a mélange that would have provided a great backdrop for an early Warner Brothers movie. You sit on crates and huge peacock-tail chairs amidst bags of Mexican spices and bales of South American coffee. The Marina del Rey restaurant has a marvelous view from the veranda, and a great old antique cage elevator takes you up to the second floor. There are picturesque alcoholic concoctions in addition to the simpler booze, and there's even an international beer list. The food is good, particularly the gigantic Malaysian shrimp and Tahitian chicken, but the atmosphere is the stand-out. It's a must for out-of-towners. It's popular among the locals for luncheon (weekdays) and the dinners are reasonable. Entertainment is usually the more soothing variety; last time I was there, it was a harpist.

**Moderate.** Open seven days. Luncheon from 11:30 a.m. to 2:30 p.m. weekdays. Dinner from 5 to 10 p.m. Monday through Thursday; to 11 p.m. Friday and Saturday; 4:30 to 10 p.m. on Sunday. Sunday brunch from 9:30 a.m. to 2:30 p.m. Closed Thanksgiving, Christmas. Entertainment. Full bar. No reservations. Patio. Marina view. Visa, MC, AX. Parking lot. Casual to semi-dressy.

# WARSZAWA

**Polish**
★★

1414 Lincoln Boulevard
Santa Monica          **Map 2**                    (213) 393-8831

I've never understood why there was not a good Polish restaurant in Southern California, or for that matter, in most
American cities. Lord knows we have ethnicity of every
imaginable variety from Thai to Taiwanese to Chinois to
West African. But no Polish — until now. The Warszawa
(pronounced veer-cha-vuh, honest) is an authentic Polish
restaurant in Santa Monica. Elina Lejman presides over the
cozy enterprise — four small rooms — and the menu is
limited to those dishes that Elina herself prepares. With
recognition she will afford a full kitchen staff to create some
of the great soups native to Poland made at times with fresh
fruit and at other times with beer. Presently there is borscht
served hot or cold (depending on the season) that is always
rich and savory. Another soup, the *grochowka*, which is made
with peas and smoked ham, is thick and hearty. An appetizer
called *zimne nozki* is as delectable as it is difficult to pronounce, a kind of meat and vegetable aspic. The Warszawa
salad is typical of Polish cuisine, completely independent of
outside influence. It's a spicy, sweet and sour mingling of
sauerkraut, apples and carrots. Of the eight entrées you
should try either the *pierogi* (pasta shells stuffed with meat,
cheese and mushrooms and lightly fried) or the roast duckling
Polish style with apple stuffing and dumplings. There's a
hunters' stew on the dinner as well, a traditional dish made
with beef, pork, sausage and bacon, and served with dumplings. Desserts are home-made and marvelous. We tried
'em all from the crêpe with strawberry sour cream to the
home-made rum walnut torte, and even tucked in the iced
coffee with ice cream, whipped cream and nuts. Beverages
include a good strong French coffee, several varieties of tea,
a spicy fruit drink and two Polish beers. The wine list (no
cocktails) is limited if worldly and the *egri bicaver* is a favorite

with men because it translates into the macho sounding "bull's blood." They're situated in what is said to be the oldest building in the area — I wouldn't argue — and it's intelligently decorated with Polish graphics and posters. If Warszawa sounds familiar, it used to be in Berkeley.

**Moderate.** Open Wednesday through Monday. Dinner from 5:30 to 10 p.m. Wine and beer only. Reservations advised. All major credit cards. Street parking. Casual.

---

## THE WEINSTUBE

German
★

17739 Sherman Way
Reseda          **Map 1**
(213)345-1994

Some years ago, when my first restaurant guidebook was fresh off the press, I wrote about the Weinstube in Reseda, that rarity of rarities, a good German restaurant. Both the goose and I were hanging high that evening, helped along by massive quantities of Becker's, liebfraumilch, gemutlichkeit, and dumplings. My memory of that evening was, in a word, fuzzy. On my next visit I re-entered with some trepidation, wondering if my glowing memories were merely a lapse of my critical senses. The first glance at the menu was reassuring. A German restaurant is more than sauerbraten or schnitzel. Here was *seezungenrollchen* (filet of sole), poached in white wine with baby shrimps, lobster meat, mushrooms, and green onion, and finished with cream. There was a saddle of venison and pheasant and young goose (in season), along with the "Butcher's Feast,"(a plate of bratwurst, knockwurst, broiled smoked pork chop with hot German potato salad, red cabbage and wine sauerkraut). And more, much more. It's an unpretentious place — like an inn of the Black Forest might be imagined — with red-checked tablecloths and the obligatory antlers and clocks in a warm atmosphere.

**Moderate.** Open Tuesday through Sunday. Luncheon from 11:30 a.m. to 2 p.m. weekdays. Dinner from 5 to 10 p.m. Wine and beer only. Reservations advised. Visa, MC, AX, CB. Parking lot. Semi-dressy.

---

## WEST END GARDEN
11835 Wilshire Boulevard
West Los Angeles    **Map 8**

**Continental**
★
(213) 477-2947

Proprietors Cabrera and Denerone were restless, even with their successful Land's End in Venice, and so they came up with this not quite-so-haute bistro. Hamburgers and omelettes and light dishes are the offerings here with touchs of class in the kitchen that show up in more ambitious veal dishes. There's a good touch with seafood as well and you'll know it's fresh and choice. My favorite dish is the chicken breast *papicion* ($7.95) that's rolled in sesame seeds and served with mushrooms in cream sauce.

The restaurant appears to be a successful compromise sort of Tishman-French.

**Moderate.** Open seven days from 11 a.m. to midnight. Sunday brunch 11 a.m. to 3 p.m. Full bar. Reservations accepted. Visa, MC. Valet parking. Casual.

---

## WESTSIDE CAFE
11909 Santa Monica Boulevard
West Los Angeles    **Map 8**

**French Continental**
★
(213) 473-0124

The celebrity leaned back between takes of a TV interview I was conducting on wine and food, and I took advantage of the respite to ask him which was his favorite restaurant. His eyes crinkled in thought for a moment and he mused, "I'll bet you think I'll name one of the superstars, right?" He was right; I *was* surprised to hear him exult about this small, informal restaurant with a blackboard menu. Seafood is the art here although vegetables are fresh and soup is

681

homemade. When available, the chicken "Westside" is something-else. It's marinated in mustard. Luncheon features good crêpes, omelettes and salads.

**Moderate.** Open Tuesday through Sunday. Luncheon served Tuesday through Friday from 11:30 a.m. to 2 p.m. Dinner Tuesday through Saturday from 5:30 to 10 p.m.; Sunday from 5 to 9 p.m. Closed Christmas. Full bar. Visa, MC, AX. Parking lot. Casual.

---

## THE WHALE'S TAIL          Seafood and Prime Rib
3950 Blue Fin Circle
Oxnard                            (805)985-2511

This Channel Island restaurant was completed after two years of construction, and the architecture is a perfect setting for the seafood inside. It has one of the area's first shellfish bars, a cocktail lounge with live entertainment and a nautical theme inside. A 24-foot aquarium runs behind the length of the upstairs bar. A fine family restaurant in the area and the touches—salad bar is in a boat—make this a superior theme restaurant. There's an unobstructed view of the harbor and an early dining menu.

**Inexpensive.** Open seven days 11:15 a.m. to 3 p.m. weekdays. Dinner Monday through Thursday from 5 to 10:30 p.m., Friday and Saturday to midnight, Sunday from 4 to 10:30 p.m. Champagne Sunday brunch from 10:30 a.m. to 2:30 p.m. Live groups nightly. Full bar. Reservations advised. All major credit cards. Parking lot. Casual to semi-dressy.

---

*To obtain the best results from this Guide, consult
"How to Use this Guide" on page 27.*

## THE WHITE HOUSE
340 South Coast Highway
Laguna Beach        **Map 4**

**American**
★
(714) 494-8088

Still standing in its original location after almost 50 years, the White House has become a tradition. The stars of Hollywood patronized it: Bing Crosby, Mary Miles Minter (but we're all too young to remember her, aren't we?) and Cecil B. DeMille. Perhaps they're responsible for the comprehensive menu, which jumps from lox and bagels to tacos. Recently, a salad bar has been added. The three menus—breakfast, luncheon and dinner—should satisfy even the most temperamental star. Jazz performers entertain nightly from 9:30 p.m. to 1:30 a.m.

**Moderate.** Open seven days. Luncheon 10 a.m. to 5 p.m. Dinner from 5 p.m to midnight. Entertainment till 1:30 a.m. Full bar. Reservations advised on weekends. Visa, MC, AX. Parking lot. Casual.

---

## THE WHITE OAK
**Newporter Inn**
**1107 Jamboree Road**
**Newport Beach**        **Map 4**

**Continental**

(714) 640-4182

The mediocrity of this slick commercial restaurant is particularly deplorable to me because I remember how hard the Newporter Inn tried to be a special place for special people. It appears now to be more a convention center than hotel, and though the menus are modern miracles of graphic arts, the thrill is gone. Their concept is to enable you to choose from among nine entree selections and 20 sauces.

**Moderate.** Open seven days. Luncheon served Monday through Friday 11 a.m. to 2:30 p.m. Dinner Monday through Thursday 5:30 to 10:30 p.m.; Friday and Saturday to 11 p.m.; Sunday 5 to 10 p.m. Sunday brunch 10 a.m. to 2 p.m. Full bar. View. All major credit cards. Parking lot; valet parking. Semi-dressy.

---

## WIENER FACTORY
14917 Ventura Boulevard
Sherman Oaks          **Map 1**

**Hot Dogs**
★★
(213)789-2676

Every once in a while I visit a restaurant in which the ambience contributes as much as the food to a memorable dining experience. Sparkling chandeliers, soft lighting, warm attentive service — all can be as important to me as having my steak blood-red, my hollandaise the perfect consistency, and my mousse feather-light. But ambience, for all the continental implications of the term, need not always signify polished silver and gleaming crystal; it can also apply to paper plates and plastic cups. Ambience is as vital to the funky as it is to the fashionable. All of which brings me — often — to the Wiener Factory in Sherman Oaks. The Wiener Factory serves what is arguably the best hot dog in Los Angeles — if you'll permit me to stretch slightly the traditional definition of "hot dog." The *pièce de résistance* is a spicy Polish sausage (and I do mean spicy), topped with sauerkraut, brown mustard, and a pickle spear on a warm hot dog bun. There are almost a dozen other sausages, knackwurst, and more traditional frankfurters, including all-beef knackwurst with red cabbage that engendered squeals of delight in a lady friend so elegant and refined that she looks down her nose at all other hot dogs with the same disdain she has for the football games at which they are so often consumed. But as good as the hot dogs are at the Wiener Factory they must share billing with . . . the walls. That's right, the walls. For there, scribbled at the forbearance of owners Kevin Lentz and Scott Matis, is some of the best graffiti West of the New York subway system. The visual onslaught actually begins outside with the sign proclaiming: "We Sold Over 4 Hot Dogs This Year." Then, inside are such observations as:

"Will Rogers Never Met Cal Worthington." "Vincent's Van Goes." "Lester Maddox Has Sickle Cell Anemia." "For Sale: Spacious Cemetery Plot. See to Appreciate. Must Sell Due to Illness." "Maximum Occupancy of This Room Not to Exceed 8000 Persons." The graffiti used to include a few contemporary political observations as well, but they got tired of repainting the entire wall every time someone died or went to jail. They also used to have some pretty raunchy aphorisms on the rest room walls, but they decided things were getting out of hand so they retreated to the risible but not risqué. One of the best entries on the wall, however, is the price list, although the hot German potato salad may be the best I've tasted. Have a small cup of that while biting into the spicy Polish sausage—its casing fairly crackling, oozing flavor—and you're in funk heaven.

**Inexpensive.** Open seven days. Luncheon from 11 a.m. to 5 p.m. Dinner from 5 to 10 p.m. Closed Easter, Christmas, New Year's. Wine and beer only. No reservations. No credit cards. Parking lot. Casual.

---

## WIND AND SEA RESTAURANT          American
25152 Del Prado                                         ★
Dana Point          **Map 4**                (714) 496-6500

The restaurant is surrounded by water on three sides, providing a great view of the Marina goings-on; it is, naturally, in a strategic position to provide weekend sailors with their daily dram (or two or five) of libation. The menu features lobster, steak, king crab legs, prime rib, and stuffed grapeleaves. There is outdoor dining in the patio and there are docking privileges.

**Moderate.** Open seven days. Dinner from 5 to 10:30 p.m. Clsoed Christmas, New Year's. Entertainment. Full bar. Reservations advised. Patio. Visa, MC, AX. Parking lot. Casual.

## THE WINDSOR
### 3198½ West 7th Street
Los Angeles    **Map 7**

**Continental**
★★
(213) 382-1261

This grand restaurant is a tribute to Ben Dimsdale, whose relentless drive for perfection has resulted in an internationally recognized restaurant of the highest quality. All these accolades are bestowed even though the Windsor is located in an improbable neighborhood — midtown Los Angeles — and the room is virtually dominated by an enormous circular bar, certainly an unlikely layout for fine cuisine. The staff, both in the kitchen and the front of the house, are the best that money can buy. The cuisine, under the umbrella term "continental," has dishes rarely found on the continent: homemade head cheese, breast of turkey *à l'Indienne* (or diablo, with brandied peaches), along with the more familiar menu items. I've never known a person of good palate who didn't respect this operation. The wine list is what you would expect here. Perfection is not inexpensive; you will pay dearly for your evening.

**Expensive.** Open Monday through Saturday. Luncheon from 11:30 a.m. to 3:30 p.m. Dinner from 3:30 p.m. to midnight. Banquet facilities. Full bar. Reservations advised. All major credit cards accepted. Valet parking. Semi-dressy to dressy.

## WINE BISTRO
### 11915 Ventura Boulevard
Studio City    **Map 1**

**French**
★★
(213) 766-6233

When it comes to bellying up to the bar and bending an elbow, wine drinkers have always been treated as second-class citizens. While bourbon drinkers are often confronted with a choice of half-a-dozen brands to choose from, wine drinkers who want to order by the glass have to settle for whatever swill the bar is serving; and judging from experience, swill *dignifies* the stuff that many bars serve to their wine-drinking patrons.

As a wine bar, the Wine Bistro is not quite what I've been looking for. The wine selection is small, and just a bit on the precious side. But as a bistro, the place is a real gem. Woody and warm, with those slightly faded mirrors that give a room a sense of conspiracy. The food, as at Cafe Monet, is very basic French: *croque monsieur*, filet of sole Veronique, calf liver Bercy, shrimp scampi. The food is also quite delicious. An order of salmon with mustard sauce was so good I had to be restrained from eating the dishware. A cream of celery soup was the very essence of celery, clean, crisp and honest. The filet of sole danced a happy tarantella with the white grapes that made it Veronique. And behind the bar, one of those wonderful brass espresso makers with an eagle on the top made a myriad of jolly sounds, churning out cup after cup of espresso and very fine capuccino, just like a good bistro coffee maker should.   *M.S.*

**Expensive.** Open Monday through Saturday. Open 11 a.m. to 11 p.m. weekdays. Saturday from 5:30 to 11. Closed all major holidays. Beer and wine only. Reservations required. All major credit cards. Valet parking. Casual.

---

**THE WINE CELLAR**                    **Continental**
1107 Jamboree Road                              ★
Newport Beach        **Map 4**        (714) 644-1700

In the Newporter Inn that Del Webb built is one of the lesser known, but most successful, dinner operations. The Wine Cellar is actually that—a working wine cellar with antiques and artifacts that create an illusion of another, more gracious age. The menu here is a variation of the style of dinner offered at Robaire's and is changed four times a month. You can call or write for a calendar menu. The fixed cost plus tip (everything is plus tip) is very inexpensive for this elegant hideaway. It is frequently used by the State Department to entertain major politicos and by big businessmen from the neighborhood. Like most of these places, you "own" your table for the evening.

**Expensive.** Open Tuesday through Saturday. Dinner seatings at 7 and 8:30 p.m. Entertainment. Full bar. Reservations required. All major credit cards. Valet or self-parking. Semi-dressy to dressy.

---

## WHOMPHOPPER'S WAGON WORKS   Western
100 Universal City Plaza
Universal City  **Map 1**   (213) 508-3939

The latest in the theme restaurant that has the effect of making diners feel like they are actors in an old Western, not a bad idea come to think of it, for the Universal Studios complex.

Waiters are dressed like cowpokes, the building resembles a giant barn and raucous noises emanate from everywhere. Surprisingly, the food is pretty good, particularly "Major Drake's Buffalo Chili" served with a green salad. Mexican appetizers, barbecued chicken and ribs and steaks are reasonably priced. The kids and Aunt Agatha from Alberta will love it.

**Moderate.** Open seven days for lunch and dinner from 11 a.m. to 2 a.m. Closed Christmas. Live band. Cocktails. Reservations accepted weekdays only. View. Major credit cards. Wheelchair access. Parking lot. Casual.

---

## WOODY'S WHARF   Seafood/American
2318 Newport Boulevard       ★
Newport Beach  **Map 4**   (714) 675-0474

Not the Newport-funky spot the name indicates, this is a bayside restaurant with a limited selection of good dishes—they do only what they know they can do well—and the atmosphere is cordial, even clublike, around the bar. The abalone approaches greatness, the generous pounded portion nearly too big for the plate. The proprietor often catches his own fish, and there are also good steaks, sandwiches and salads.

**Moderate.** Open seven days. Luncheon from 11 a.m. to 5:30 p.m. weekdays. Dinner Sunday through Thursday from 5:30 to 11 p.m., Friday, Saturday to midnight. Saturday, Sunday brunch from 10 a.m. to 5:30 p.m. Closed Thanksgiving, Christmas. Full bar. Reservations advised. All major credit cards. Parking lot. Casual.

---

## WORLD FAMOUS                                      Seafood
701 Thomas Street                                         ★
San Diego                                    (714) 488-0634

Located on the boardwalk, this place bears a resemblance more to a greasy spoon than to the fine seafood restaurant it is. There aren't many dishes on the menu, but they're done well. Halibut, shrimp, and especially the huge portions of abalone, are tender and fresh and lightly breaded. "Catch of the night" could be red snapper, swordfish, or halibut; it really is freshly caught and tastes like it. Entrées are served with salads and warm squaw bread, and fresh corn is served in season.

**Moderate.** Open seven days. Breakfast and luncheon weekdays from 8 a.m. to 3 p.m. Dinner from 5 to 11 p.m. Saturday and Sunday brunch from 8 a.m. to 2:30 p.m. Closed Thanksgiving and Christmas. Full bar. No reservations. Visa, MC, AX, DC. Street parking. Casual.

*In order to obtain the best results from this Guide, please consult "Tips on Dining Out" on page 21.*

y

---

**YAGURA ICHIBAN**  **Japanese**
101 Japanese Village Plaza  ★★
Los Angeles  **Map 7**  (213) 623-4141

While Japanese restaurants continue to grow in an alarming manner — soon there will be more Japanese restaurants than French if the trend continues — only a few really offer a distinctive menu. At this lovely restaurant the robatayaki is a good example of the country-style cooking of Japan. The name "Yagura" means "fire tower" and refers to the restaurant's location next to the free standing blue-tiled tower which is the landmark of the Japanese Village Plaza. Owner Seiichi Nakada added "Ichiban" to connect his new establishment with the 15 year old Ichiban (No. 1) restaurant around the corner that is still operated by his family.

This newest restaurant is a five part operation. There is a small sushi bar, a traditional tatami room seating about 16, a regular dining room, a cocktail lounge with a piano bar, Japanese entertainment, and a robata counter. Chefs in traditional blue coats with bandannas rolled around their foreheads, grill the food to order at the counter. They also have

690

kushi-age, similar to tempura but with a flavored crumb breaking instead of the typical tempura batters. A first time visitor might want to try the "Ezo course" which combines grilled filet of salmon, grilled bacon, rolled scallops, skewered pork, and skewered quail eggs.

The restaurants in the Plaza draw around 80% Japanese clientele and reservations are definitely required.

**Moderate.** Open seven days. Luncheon weekdays from 11 a.m. to 2:30 p.m. Dinner weekdays from 5 to 10:30 p.m., Saturday and Sunday from 11 a.m. to 10:30 p.m. Piano bar. Full bar. Reservations required on weekend. Patio. Visa, MC, AX. Public parking lot. Casual.

---

# YAKITORI II
3740 Sports Arena Boulevard
San Diego

**Japanese**
★★
(714) 223-2641

Yakitori II is a spacious, busy restaurant featuring a unique menu with full-color photographs of all the dishes (including *sushi*). The decor is tasteful, with a 12th century Samurai battle scene mural in the cocktail lounge, painted by the owner Victor Murashige. Yakitori II had its origin in Guam, where its parent restaurant, Yakitori I, was founded in 1973. There is a *sushi* bar and a large cocktail lounge. Waitresses are dressed in *happi* coats. The menu includes several authentic Japanese appetizers, including *kani sui*—thinly sliced cucumber, steamed crab legs and kelp with rice vinegar and a dash of salt; and *nuta*—raw tuna rolled in soybean paste and vinegar, sprinkled with dried kelp and green onions. Combination plates, such as the shrimp, *yakitori* and chicken *tatsuta*, allow you to sample a variety of tastes. The dinner menu includes many popular Japanese dishes, including a vegetable *tempura, sukiyaki* and *yakitori*. Dinners include your choice of white steamed rice or *yaki meshi*—stir-fried rice with carrots, green onions, and finely chopped pork. For dessert we recommend the *awa yuki*—a meringue stuffed with strawberries. *Shinobu Ishizuka*

**Inexpensive.** Open seven days. Luncheon from 11:30 to 3 p.m. weekdays; Saturday and Sunday from noon to 5 p.m. Dinner Sunday through Thursday from 5 to 10 p.m.; Friday, Saturday to 11 p.m. Banquet facilities. Children's menu. Closed Christmas, Thanksgiving. Wine and beer only. No reservations. All major credit cards. Parking lot. Casual.

---

## YAMASHIRO

**Japanese**

1999 North Sycamore Avenue
Hollywood    **Map 7**    (213) 466-5125

As a native of Southern California I've always taken pride in unusual, off-the-beaten-track restaurants that reflect the glory and history of our area. Certainly the Yamashiro restaurant, located up a steep incline above the Magic Castle in Hollywood, has the glamour, excitement and spectacular view to make it a must on my personal tour. Now, happily, it has the food. It wasn't always so, but the determination of Thomas Glover, third generation owner of this massive property, and new manager Andy Saito from Inagaku in New York, have worked wonders.

As you drive west along Franklin Avenue, a very narrow road leads you up a steep hill to an Oriental palace with 12 acres of terraced gardens. This great structure has had a colorful and sometimes gamey history. Once the head-quarters of the 400 Club, comprised of Hollywood's legends and financiers, it went through various transitions until, in 1960, it was opened to te public.

There are Japanese feasts served on artfully arranged platters for $13.95, a price I'd pay for the view from the glassed-in terrace. Tempura is light and well prepared. There is a vegetable tempura dinner at $8.95. Yakitori, chicken and vegetables on a skewer, is $9.95.

Best of all, they now serve sushi, prepared by a sushi chef familiar with the art. It would be a wonderful dish to order at cocktail time to accompany your choice of libation.

Mr. Baylin has wisely provided a basic American and continental menu for visitors who may come and marvel but who may not have the palate for Japanese fare. The steaks are steak-house quality, and there are seafood and veal dishes as well.

Luncheon is lighter fare with omelettes, sandwiches and salads. To me, however, there are few places so grand and filled with intrigue as this great and beautiful old structure that must now take its place as a culinary, as well as tourist, landmark. The private rooms are interesting for large parties.

**Moderate.** Open seven days. Luncheon from 11:30 a.m. to 3:30 p.m. everyday. Dinner 3:30 to 11 p.m. Sunday through Thursday; to midnight Friday, Saturday. Saturday and Sunday brunch from 10:30 a.m. Full bar. View. Reservations suggested. V, MC, AX. Valet parking. Casual.

---

## YAMATO
Japanese

Century Plaza Hotel ★
Century City  **Map 8**  (213) 277-1840

60 Fashion Island ★
Newport Beach  **Map 4**  (714) 644-4811

Japanese fare is light, delicate, cultured cuisine artfully arranged and ceremoniously served to entice the senses with color, smell, texture — even sound. At Yamato, first in San Francisco, random words from the menu ripple as musically as water in a pebbly brook—*suimono, misoshiru, sunomono, shashimi*; how much more caressing to the ear than the English translation —broth, bean soup, salad, fillet of raw fish. The menu is constructed around four basic dishes — shrimp tempura, sukiyaki, salmon, and chicken teriyaki — accompanied by a variety of beef, chicken, and lobster dishes. The Imperial Dinner begins with *suimono* (clear broth), crisp *sunomono* (fresh vegetable salad with sweet vinegar), followed by shrimp tempura and seasonal vegetables, dipped in batter and deep-fried. Skewered chicken teriyaki is next; then sukiyaki made with sliced tender beef, *tofu* (soy bean curd), young bamboo shoots, spinach, fresh mushrooms, celery, green and sweet onion, and *shirataki* (yam noodle), prepared at the table by the kimonoed waitress. American potables are available, though sake and Japanese beer make the experience more tranquil. Yamato's distinctions are architectural as well as gastronomical. The interior of forty native woods and fifteen varieties of bamboo was fabricated in Japan and assembled in San Francisco. Shoji-screened private rooms, tatami-matted floors, peeled and polished posts and — spanning the pond — the *nari bashi* or "sound" bridge (with a built-in squeak that announces a patron's passage) create a timeless environment exquisitely appropriate to the cuisine and service. The Yamato in the Century Plaza Hotel is designed like an ancient Japanese inn, with off white walls and dark beams, a theme shared by the Yamato in Newport Beach. All purvey the same quality of food and service, although I am more familiar with the San Francisco ancestor than with the progeny. You can sit Japanese style—shoes off, squatting on the floor, a backrest behind you—at all Yamatos. I'm partial to tables and chairs, which are available.

**Moderate to expensive.** Open seven days. Luncheon from 11:30 a.m. to 3 p.m. weekdays. Dinner from 5 to 10 p.m. daily. Closed major holidays. Full bar. Reservations advised. All major credit cards. Valet and self-parking. Semi-dressy.

---

## YANG CHOW RESTAURANT     Chinese
819 North Broadway     ★★
Los Angeles    **Map 7**    (213) 625-0811

During the several years Yang Chow has been open it has established itself as one of the better Chinese restaurants in the Los Angeles area. The menu offers over 150 selections from all the regions of Chinese cooking including many of the more unusual dishes such as braised sea cucumber, sautéed kidney, and hot and spicy squid. A family operated Chinatown restaurant having none of the garish interior design found in some of its larger neighbors, it offers high quality Mandarin food served promptly by waiters who are always helpful in recommending the day's best selections. Some of the outstanding dishes sampled include: sautéed live crab (live dungeness crab cooked to order), hot and sour soup, *mu shu* pork with Peking pancakes, *kung pao* shrimp, braised tender bean curd, and shredded beef with hot garlic sauce.  *Hugh Carpenter*

**Moderate.** Open seven days. Luncheons from 11:30 a.m. to 2:30 p.m. Dinner Sunday through Thursday 2:30 to 9:30 p.m.; Friday, Saturday to 10:30. Wine and beer only. Reservations advised. Visa, MC. Parking lot. Casual.

---

## YE OLDE KING'S HEAD
116 Santa Monica Boulevard
Santa Monica          **Map 2**

**British/Pub**
★
(213) 394-9458

A British pub is a proud monument to the Anglo-Saxon beer drinkers who required the first "convenience" food in recorded history. So busy were they with their darts and gossiping that finger food—Cornish pastries, Scotch eggs, fish and chips and some unidentified frying objects became *de rigueur*. The old Mucky Duck in Santa Monica used to be the hub of the pubs but the Mucky no longer exists. Dart teams from this pub take on those from the pubs in other areas; there is even a $50,000 dart classic held each year. Food prices are skid-row low and the juke box is always lit up with Beatles tunes. Beers on draught include Watney's, Bass, John Courage, and Guinness, and there are bottles of Newcastle Brown, Fosters, Harp, and more of the same. Equal parts English, Welsh, Irish, Scotch, Australian and New Zealander clientele help everyone feel at home, and their hospitality and sense of fun often turn a cold winter's night into a cozy remembrance.

**Inexpensive.** Open seven days. Monday through Saturday from 11 a.m. to 11 p.m. Sunday from noon to 2 a.m. Closed Thanksgiving, Christmas. Wine and beer only. No reservations. No credit cards. Public parking lot across the street. Casual.

---

## YOUNG SING
643 North Spring Street
Chinatown          **Map 7**

**Chinese**
★
(213) 623-1724

Young Sing tends not to be quite as much like a Marx Brothers movie as Mon Kee, up the street, but foodwise, it does give Mon Kee a run for its money. As at Mon Kee, the choice of seafood dishes at Young Sing is nothing short of staggering. There are a dozen shark's fin dishes, which include a two degrees of shark's fin—superior shark's fin (as in braised superior shark's fin in brown sauce) and premier shark's fin (as in braised premier shark's fin with brown crab meat sauce). There are four bird's nest dishes, and six abalone dishes to choose from, among them a fine sliced abalone and duck web feet served in oyster sauce dish. Duck's feet are actually very good, if a bit fatty, as long as yu don't conjure up the sad image of a legless Donald Duck.

There are 55 other seafood dishes at Young Sing to choose from which should be enough to satisfy the needs of even the most provincial diner. There's a sliced conch with mixed vegetables dish that a friend who's suspicious of even tuna fish ate with relish and gusto. The whole crispy fish with garlic sauce hung off its platter at both the head and tail end, though the head and tail were all that remained after my table of locusts descended on this exquisitely-prepared, seductively-spiced red snapper. (We also had a choice of rock cod, black trout, catfish, flounder and sea bass.) I passed, however, on a dish called "lobster with mixed fruit salad." I was afraid that might turn out to be exactly what the dish would be.   *M.S.*

**Moderate.** Open seven days 11:30 a.m. to 12:30 p.m. Closed Chinese New Year. No alcoholic beverages. Reservations required. Visa, MC. Parking lot. Casual.

---

## YUGOSLAVIAN VILLAGE

3365 Barham Boulevard
Los Angeles     **Map 7**

Yugoslavian
★
(213) 876-2063

There are many who felt that the Yugoslavian Village would not survive its shabby exterior. Happily, a coat of chocolate-brown paint, some natural wood shingles, and a new outdoor dining area have pumped new business into this deserving exponent of Yugoslavian and Serbian cuisine. There are many variations on veal and lamb grilled over charcoal, along with *cevapcici* (homemade beef sausage) and meat or feta cheese *bureks*; stuffed cabbage or *sarma*, *moussaka*, and other entrées from the region. Soup or salad is included with dinner and the rolls are homemade.

**Inexpensive.** Open Tuesday through Sunday. Dinner Tuesday through Thursday from 5 to 11 p.m., Friday through Sunday to midnight. Entertainment. Full bar. Reservations advised. Patio. Visa, MC. Parking lot. Casual.

---

*Please be sure to consult "Tipping Made Easy" on page 25 of this Guide.*

# Las Vegas Listings

General rule: Don't eat in your hotel. Service is usually awful, help is arrogant, and the food pitiful. Take a little time away from the neon and enjoy a fine dinner as a breather from the frenetic pace of the desert. Following are some guidelines.

## ALPINE VILLAGE                                     German
Paradise Road near Hilton                                  ★
                                              (702) 734-6888

Many's the faint heart I've wooed (since 1950) at this venerable German establishment, rich in *gemutlich*, song and really good Bavarian food. Super nice.

## THE BACCHANAL                                       Roman
3570 Las Vegas Boulevard
                                              (702) 731-7110

Overdecorated, overpriced and more than a little silly this pretentious Roman romp is O.K. for a kicky experience—a nice place to visit but I wouldn't want to eat there.

## BATTISTA'S                                         Italian
Next to MGM Hotel                                          ★
                                              (702) 732-1424

Reasonable, fun.

## BACKSTAGE
In Union Plaza

**American**
★
(702) 382-2100

Go here for their sherry-laced black bean soup and more than just fine dining. Theme of Broadway backstage area. Pian bar and singer.

## BINION'S SOMBRERO
Downtown

**Mexican**
★★
(702) 382-1600

Best Mexican with ribs, too.

## CHATEAU VEGAS
Desert Inn Road (near Convention Center)

**Continental**
★★
(702) 735-7990

"Juliano's" Room a favorite. (Suckling pig serves six. Advance notice required.) Other rooms less expensive. Reservations. Open 24 hours.

## CHICAGO JOE'S
820 South 4th Street

**Italian**
★
(702) 382-5246

This tiny red house turned restaurant also serves seafood (Chicago Hot Shrimp their specialty). Hang loose here. Opens 11 a.m. to 11 p.m.

## CHIN CHIN'S
2300 Desert Inn Road

**Chinese**
★
(702) 733-7764

The chef cooks your food to order. Honors special dish requests. High on quality. Authentic Take-out available. Closed Sunday. Open 5 to 11 p.m.

## THE FLAME
1 Desert Inn Road

**American**
★

(702) 735-4431

The Flame planned a perfect menu a dozen years ago and stuck with it. You see what you get whether you choose a sirloin, New York porterhouse, or brochette on a board. Open 24 hours.

## GOLDEN STEER
308 West Sahara

**Steaks**
★★

(702) 384-4470

This is where the locals go for steaks. Bar lounge, nice old fashioned atmosphere. Reservations required.

## HILDA'S RESTAURANT AND LIVINGROOM LOUNGE
2618 East Lake Mead Boulevard

**American/Spanish**
★

(702) 649-1094

Homemade soup, bread, rolls, pie and pastries. Meals are home-style. Servings are generous. Famous for Spanish delicacies. Reasonable. Full bar. Dancing to live music. Open seven days from 7 a.m. to 11 p.m.; Sunday 7 a.m. to 3 p.m.

## HOUSE OF LORDS
Sahara Hotel

**American/Continental**
★★

(702) 737-2111

A cut above the usual hotel dining room fare. I have actually had a good dinner here and it was served well. I wish the same for you. Full bar. Open seven days from 6 to midnight for dinner.

## JOLLY TROLLEY  Steaks
Across from Sahara Hotel  ★
(702) 385-3168

Steaks sized and price to order. Dinner price includes salad bar, dessert and coffee. Open seven days from 11 a.m. to 2 a.m.

## MAMCHEN'S DELI TAVERN  Deli
Las Vegas Hilton  ★
(702) 732-5111

In a hurry? Step up to the food bar. Or sit a spell. Either way, it's kosher here. Memories of Old Vienna.

## PALACE COURT  French
3570 Las Vegas Boulevard South  (702) 731-7110

Nearly as bad as most of the so called "gourmet rooms" in Las Vegas. My waiter thought I was a nuisance when I complained about the inch of water at the bottom of my wine glass. He then—believe it—reached in with a napking to sop it out. If this were the last restaurant in the world I'd go.

## PAMPLEMOUSSE/THE MORNING AFTER  French
44400 East Sahara Avenue  ★
(diagonally across from the Sahara Hotel)  (702) 733-2066

Chef Pete Dawson brings solid experience and a lilting sense of humor from the Sydney, Australia area. Famous from their beginning for quiche, omelettes, crêpes, and salads, their dinners have expanded to entrées such as pepper steak, trout, snapper, and sea bass prepared a couple of ways, scallops with cream sauce and cheese topping, and roasted Cornish hen with a wine sauce on the side. There's a cream caramel dessert much like a flan and chocolate mousse among other difficult choices. Breakfast here can be a satisfying experience. Owner George La Forge has already spruced up the place splendidly and has further plans in mind.

## PEPPERMILL
2985 Las Vegas Boulevard South
(across from Stardust)

**American**
★★
(702) 735-4177

Prbably the best coffee shop in the whole world. Best stew I ever ate, served inside a loaf of sourdough bread. Salads and sundaes are spectaculars. There's a cozy bar lounge with a fireplace while you wait (no reservations) and the service is friendly—a rarity—the food splendid! You m ay pay much more, but you won't dine better. Good atmosphere. Interesting view. Open 24 hours.

## SAMARIE'S ITALIAN RESTAURANT
2734 East Lake Mead
North Las Vegas

**Italian**
★
(702) 649-7748

A favorite with the natives. Reasonable. Open from 11:30 a.m. to 6 p.m.

## SANDS COFFEE SHOP
Sands Hotel

**Cantonese**
★
(702) 733-5000

There's a secret. At midnight they serve great Cantonese— try the won ton—for the hotel execs and performers. Open to the public.

## SHOWBOAT
2800 East Fremont

**American**
★
(702) 385-9161

Mark Twain may have inspired this friendly Mississippi steamboat setting. Family-style. Easy on the purse. Open 24 hours.

## STAGE ONE
### Deli
★
3655 South Maryland Parkway
Opposite Boulevard Mall
(702) 733-7005

A good deli with more than 330 sandwiches. Take-out or sit down. Daytime only.

## STARBOARD TACK
### Seafood
★
2601 Atalantic
(702) 457-8794

Best lobster, king crab. Salad bar. Nice atmosphere. Moderate prices. No reservations.

## VILLA D'ESTE
### Italian/Continental
★
365 Convention Center Drive
(702) 735-3653

Fresh seafood. LUnch 11:30 a.m. to 3:30 p.m. Dinner 5 p.m. to midnight. Reservations recommended.

## VILLAGE PUB
### American
★
4178 Koval Lane
(702) 734-8560

Long Island steamed clams are rushed in by the thousand each day. Or, you can opt for breast of chicken or tail of lobster. Open 24 hours.

## THE VINEYARD
### Italian
★★
Boulevard Mall
(702) 731-1606

An appetizer freak? Like fresh-baked bread? This is your kind of place. They even have a balcony. Large servings, small prices. 11:30 a.m. to midnight.

# BRUNCH

Caesars Palace is still the best.
Frontier is good too.
Landmark serves both Saturday and Sunday.

# Menu Translator

## Guide to German Menus

| | | | |
|---|---|---|---|
| **Abendessen** | Dinner | **Kaffee** | Coffee |
| **Apfel** | Apple | **Kaffeekuchen** | Coffee cake |
| **Apfelmus** | Applesauce | **Kalbfleisch** | Veal |
| **Auflauf** | Souffle | **Kalbskotellett** | Veal cutlet |
| **Austern** | Oysters | **Karotten** | Carrots |
| **Backhuhn** | Breaded, fried chicken | **Kartoffeln** | Potatoes |
| **Backwerk** | Cakes | **Käse** | Cheese |
| **Belegte Brote** | Open sandwiches | **Käseplatte** | Cheese platter |
| **Bier** | Beer | **Knoblauch** | Garlic |
| **Birnen** | Pears | **Lammscripp-** | Lamb chop |
| **Blumenkohl** | Cauliflower | **chen** | |
| **Bockwurst** | A rather heavy type of | **Milch** | Milk |
| | frankfurter | **Mittagessen** | Lunch |
| **Brathuhn** | Roast chicken | **Muschein** | Mussels |
| **Bratwurst** | A pork sausage | **Nachspeisen** | Desserts |
| **Brot** | Bread | **Obst** | Fruit |
| **Brüehe** | Consommé | **Omelette** | Omelette |
| **Eiskaffee** | Iced coffee | **Pfannkuchen** | Pancakes |
| **Ente** | Duck | **Pfirsich** | Peach |
| **Erbsen** | Peas | **Pfaumen** | Plums |
| **Erdbeeren** | Strawberries | **Quark** | Cottage cheese |
| **Fisch** | Fish | **Rindsbraten** | Roast beef |
| **Forelle** | Trout | **Roggenbrot** | Rye bread |
| **Fruchtsalat** | Fruit salad | **Rosenkohl** | Brussel sprouts |
| **Frühstück** | Breakfast | **Rosinen** | Raisins |
| **Garneien** | Shrimps | **Rühreier** | Scrambled eggs |
| **Gebratene** | Roast legs of lamb | **Salz** | Salt |
| **Lammkeule** | | **Schweinsripp-** | Pork chop |
| **Gekochte Eier** | Boiled eggs | **chen** | |
| **Gemischter** | Mixed salad | **Schweizerkäse** | Swiss cheese |
| **Salat** | | **Senf** | Mustard |
| **Gemüse** | Vegetables | **Speck** | Bacon |
| **Grüne Bohnen** | Green beans | **Spiegeleier** | Fried eggs |
| **Grüner Salat** | Lettuce | **Tee** | Tea |
| **Gurke** | Cucumber | **Tomaten** | Tomatoes |
| **Gurken** | Cucumbers | **Weissbrot** | White bread |
| **Gut durchge-** | Well-done | **Würstchen** | Sausages |
| **braten** | | **Zitrone** | Lemon |
| **Halb roh** | Rare | **Zucker** | Sugar |
| **Huhn** | Chicken | **Zwieback** | A type of dry-toast |
| **Hummer** | Lobster | | |

# Guide to French Menus

| | |
|---|---|
| Abricôt | Apricot |
| Agneau | Lamb |
| Ail | Garlic |
| Airelles | Berries |
| Alose | Shad |
| Aloyau | Sirloin of beef |
| Ananas | Pineapple |
| Apértif | Any appetizer drink taken before a meal |
| Artichaut | Artichoke |
| Asperges | Asparagus |
| Assiette | Platter; a plate |
| Babeurre | Buttermilk |
| Béchamel | A thick white sauce |
| Beurre | Butter |
| Bifteck | Beefsteak |
| Bisque | A soup made from shellfish |
| Blanquette d'agneau | A stew of lamb made with mushrooms and onions |
| Blinis | Thin, unsweetened pancakes |
| Bombe | Dessert of ices, whipped cream, and various fruits |
| Bordeaux | Claret (wine) |
| Bouillabaisse | A fish stew made with saffron, wine, and herbs |
| Bouillon | Broth |
| Bourgogne | Burgundy (wine) |
| Brocoli | Broccoli |
| Brouillé | Scrambled |
| Brut | Dry (as applied to wines); unsweetened |
| Cacao | Cocoa |
| Café au lait | Coffee with hot milk |
| Canard | Duck |
| Caneton | Duckling |
| Carotte | Carrot |
| Carré de porc | Filet of pork |
| Cerises | Cherries |

| | |
|---|---|
| Cervelles | Brains |
| Champignons | Small mushrooms |
| Chantilly | Served with whipped cream |
| Chapon | Capon |
| Châteaubriand | Filet of steak |
| Chaud | Hot |
| Choix | Choice |
| Chou | Cabbage |
| Choucroute | Sauerkraut |
| Chou-fleur | Cauliflower |
| Citron | Lemon |
| Coq au vin | Chicken cooked in a wine sauce containing onions, ham, mushrooms, etc. |
| Côquille St. Jacques | Scallops in sauce |
| Côte de boeuf | Ribs of beef |
| Crème | Cream |
| Crevettes | Shrimps |
| Croissant | A typical breakfast or teatime pastry made in the shape of a crescent (roll) |
| Cuiller | Spoon |
| Déjeuner | Lunch: also used occasionally to mean breakfast (*petit déjeuner*) |
| Digestif | Any after-dinner liqueur |
| Dindon | Turkey |
| Douce | Sweet |
| Eau | Water |
| Entrecôte | Rib steak |
| Entrecôte chateau | Large, thick steak |
| Epinards | Spinach |
| Escalopes de veau | thin slices of veal; veal scallops |
| Escargots | Snails |
| Faisan | Pheasant |

|  |  |
|---|---|
| **Filet de boeuf** | Filet of beef |
| **Foie** | Liver |
| **Fourchette** | Fork |
| **Froid** | Cold |
| **Fromage** | Cheese |
| **Gâteau** | Cake |
| **Gigot d'agneau** | Leg of lamb |
| **Glace** | Ice; ice cream |
| **Hareng mariné** | Pickled or marinated herring |
| **Haricots verts** | Green beans |
| **Homard** | Lobster |
| **Hûitres** | Oysters |
| **Jambon** | Ham |
| **Jus de fruit** | Fruit juice |
| **Lait** | Milk |
| **Laitue** | Lettuce |
| **Langouste** | European lobster; crawfish |
| **Lapin** | Rabbit |
| **Légumes** | Vegetables |
| **Lyonnaise** | Served with onions |
| **Mignons de boeuf** | Very small cuts of beef |
| **Moules** | Mussels |
| **Moutarde** | Mustard |
| **Noisettes d'agneau** | Boneless lamb chops |
| **Oeufs** | Eggs |
| **Oeufs pochés** | Poached eggs |
| **Oeufs sur la plat** | Fried eggs |
| **Oignon** | Onion |
| **Omelette** | Omelette |
| **Pain** | Bread |
| **Pain grillé** | Toast |
| **Pâté de foie gras** | Fine goose liver paste with truffles |
| **Pâtisserie** | Pastry |
| **Pêche** | Peach |
| **Petite marmite** | A classic French beef soup containing vegetables, toasted bread, etc. |
| **Petits pois** | Small green peas |
| **Poire** | Pear |
| **Poisson** | Fish |
| **Poitrine de veau** | Breast of veal |
| **Pomme** | Apple |
| **Pomme de terre** | Potato |
| **Porc** | Pork |
| **Potage** | Soup |
| **Poulet** | Chicken |
| **Prix fixe** | At a fixed price |
| **Ragoût** | Stew |
| **Riz** | Rice |
| **Rosbif** | Roast beef |
| **Rôti de veau** | Roast veal |
| **Salade** | Salad |
| **Sauce Allemande** | A cream sauce made with egg yolks and lemon juice |
| **Sauce Barcey** | Sauce made from fish concentrate, white wine, and shallots |
| **Sauce Béarnaise** | A sauce made with eggs, butter, shallots, etc.; a classic sauce with steak |
| **Sauce Bigarade** | Orange sauce for duck |
| **Saucisson** | Sausage |
| **Sec** | Dry |
| **Sel** | Salt |
| **Service compri** | Service (charge) included |
| **Service non compri** | Service (charge) not included |
| **Sucre** | Sugar |
| **Tasse** | Cup |
| **Thé** | Tea |
| **Truite** | Trout |
| **Veau** | Veal |
| **Verre** | Glass |

# Guide to Italian Menus

| | | | |
|---|---|---|---|
| Acqua | Water | Filetto alla mignon | Filet of beef |
| Aglio | Garlic | | |
| Agnellino | Baby Lamb | Filetto di tacchino alla crema | Creamed breast of turkey |
| Agnello arrosto | Roast Lamb | | |
| Al burro | With butter | Forchetta | Fork |
| Al forno | Baked | Formaggio | Cheese |
| Alla griglia | Broiled | Fragole | Strawberries |
| Anitra | Duck | Frittata | Omelette |
| Arancia | Orange | Frutta | Fruit |
| Arista | Roast loin of pork | Funghi | Mushrooms |
| Birra | Beer | Gamberi | Shrimp |
| Biscotti | Cookies | Gelati di frutta | Fruit ices |
| Bistecca | Steak | Gelato | Ice cream |
| Brodo | Broth | Gelato di crema | Ice cream |
| Bue | Beef | | |
| Burro | Butter | Granatina | Hamburger patty |
| Caffé | Coffee | Granchio | Crab |
| Caldo | Hot; warm | Insalata | Salad |
| Cannelloni | Rolled noodles, stuffed with meat, baked in sauce | Insalata mista | Mixed salad |
| | | Istingolo | Stew; _ragout_ |
| | | Lardo | Bacon; lard |
| Cappone | Capon | Lasagne imbottite | Broad noodles baked in layers with sauce and cheese |
| Carciofi | Artichokes | | |
| Carne | Meat | | |
| Carne tritata | Chopped meat | Latte | Milk |
| Castrato | Mutton | Lattuga | Lettuce |
| Cioccolata | Chocolate | Legumi | Vegetables |
| Cipolle | Onions | Limone | Lemon |
| Colazione | Lunch | Linguini | Narrow noodles |
| Coltello | Knife | Lumache | Snails |
| Costolame di bue | Ribs of beef | Maiale | Pork |
| | | Manzo | Beef |
| Costolette di agnello | Lamb chops | Mela | Apple |
| | | Merenda | Snack, small in-between meal |
| Costolette di maiale | Pork chops | | |
| | | Meringa di cioccolata | Chocolate meringue |
| Cozze | Mussels | | |
| Crostacei | Shellfish | Minestra | Entree; either pasta or soup |
| Dolci | Sweets, desserts | | |
| Fagiano | Pheasant | Montone | Mutton |
| Fegatini di pollo | Chicken livers | Mostarda | Mustard |
| | | Muscoli | Mussels |

| | | | |
|---|---|---|---|
| Noci | Nuts | mugnaia | |
| Olio | Oil | Sorbetto | Sherbet |
| Ostriche | Oysters | Spezzatino di | Veal stew |
| Pane | Bread | vitello | |
| Pane tostato | Toast | Spinaci | Spinach |
| Panna | Cream | Spumoni | A rich ice cream usually filled with fruit and nuts |
| Pasta | Noodles, macaroni, spaghetti | | |
| Patate | Potatoes | S.Q. | An abbreviation indicating that the item is charged according to the size |
| Pepe | Pepper | | |
| Pera | Pear | | |
| Pesca | Peach | | |
| Pesce | Fish | Stracciatella | Bouillon containing beaten eggs and cheese |
| Pesto | Green garlic sauce | | |
| Piatti del giorno | The daily specials | Stufatino | Veal stew |
| | | Succo di arancia | Orange juice |
| Piselli | Peas | | |
| Pollame | Poultry | Succo di frutta | Fruit juice |
| Pollo | Chicken | Tacchino | Turkey |
| Polpette | Meat balls | Tavola fredda | Cold buffet (literally cold table) |
| Pomidoro | Tomato | | |
| Pranzo | Dinner | Tè | Tea |
| Prima colazione | Breakfast | Tordi allo spiedo | Small birds roasted on a spit |
| Prosciutto | Smoked ham, served paper thin | Torta | Cake; pie, tart |
| | | Trota | Trout |
| Riccio | Sea urchins a Mediterranean shellfish | Turnedo | Filet of beef |
| | | Umido | A stew |
| Riso | Rice | Uova | Eggs |
| Risotto | Rice dish | Uva | Grapes |
| Rosbif | Roast beef | Valdostana di vitello | Veal with ham and cheese |
| Sale | Salt | | |
| Salsa | Sauce | Vermicelli | Very fine variety of spaghetti |
| Salsicci | Sausage | | |
| Saltimbocca alla romana | Veal and ham cooked in wine | Vitello | Veal |
| | | Vongole | Clams |
| Scallopine di vitello alla bolognese | Veal slices, with ham and cheese | Zabaglione | A foamy egg dessert, made with wine |
| | | Zucca | Squash |
| Scungilli | Conch, a shellfish | Zucchero | Sugar |
| Sogliola alla belia | Filet of sole with sauce | Zuppa | Soup |

# Guide to Oriental Menus

**Bulkogi**     Korean barbecued beef, usually cooked at table on a *hwaro*

**Cha su**     barbecued pork

**Gyoza**     pan fried pork dumplings

**Huo Kuo**     Chinese hot pot, in which various ingredients (fish, vegetables, meat) are cooked at table

**Hwaro**     Korean gas brazier used for booking *bulkogi*

**Kim chee**     (Hot! hot!) Any number of Korean pickles, all of which are very hot

**Koo jul pan**     a Korean appetizers plate, in which sundry cold ingredients are served on a lazy susan for wrapping in pancakes

**Mee krob**     the classic Thai dish of crisp rice noodles, egg, pork and shrimp

**Miso**     fermented soy bean paste

**Miso cha su**     fermented soy bean paste and barbecued pork, in this case used as a flavoring for noodles

**Onigiri**     Japanese rice balls, wrapped in seafood, usually containing pickled plum bits or salted salmon

**Oshinko**     pickled vegetables

**Oshi-style**     a variety of sushi in which the rice is formed within a box press rather than being wrapped in seaweed

**Pud Thai**     thin Thai noodles flavored with peanuts, chili, bean sprouts and shrimp

**Ramen**     Chinese noodles served in pork broth in Japanese restaurants

**Sake**     Japanese rice wine, usually served warm, anad consumed from porcelain thimbles

**Sashimi**     slivers of raw fish or other seafood, served as a rule in a simple yet elegant fashion

**Shinsulla**     a Korean hot pot, in which various ingredients are stewed at table

**Sushi**     Japanese canapes of vinegared rice topped with seafood (but not always) and eaten by hand

**Tanmen**     A noodle dish containing Chinese cabbage, mushrooms, bamboo shoots, carrots, and spinach in a pork broth

**Tempura**     A school of Japanese cooking involved deep-frying just about anything in batter

**Teriyaki**     beef, chicken or fish grilled with a sweet sauce

**Udon**     thick, wheat flour noodles

**Wonton**     meat and shrimp filled dumplings in thin egg noodle wrappers

**Yakatabune**     combination dish of two types of cold noodles served with a side of tempura in a small wooden boat-like container

**Yaki soba**     Chinese noodles cooked on a grill with a variety of vegetables and meats and served in Japanese restaurants

# Regional Styles of Chinese Cooking

## by Hugh Carpenter

Chinese cooking can be divided into four regional styles located around the major areas of Canton, Szechwan, Peking and Shanghai. As for the term "Mandarin" rather than denoting a style, this term is used by Chinese restaurants to indicate that they offer some of the best known dishes from all the various regions of China.

**Cantonese food**: Cantonese cooking emphasizes color and textural contrasts, strives to accent the natural flavor of ingredients, and excels in quick stir-fry dishes. This region is famous for steamed dumplings (*dim sum*), shark's fin soup, frogs' legs, pigeon recipes, and snake. Among their favorite seasonings, they prefer light soy sauce over heavy soy, and cook with ginger, garlic, salted, fermented black beans, oyster sauce, sweet and sour concoctions, and curry.

**Szechwanese food**: The Szechwanese use more seasonings and in greater variety than other provinces. Authentically prepared their food tastes fiery hot and spicy. Besides relying heavily on fresh and dried chiles, their cooks use hot chili oil, chili paste, hot bean sauce, ginger, lots of garlic, heavy soy rather than light soy, the highly aromatic Szechwanese pepper, sesame oil, sesame seed paste, star anise, and cinnamon.

**Peking food**: A wheat (not rice) growing area, the northern Chinese eat a great deal of noodles, steamed breads and stuffed dumplings, and season their food with lots of garlic, scallions, leeks, as well as using brown bean sauce, heavy soy sauce, wines and vinegars. The province of Shantung is known for its

711

fruits, apples and pears, as well as for its great chefs. Many refer to Peking as the culinary center of north China, but it has no native cooking style, borrowing instead on styles of the surrounding provinces and from chefs who journey to the capital from all over China.

**Shanghai food**: Shanghai and the cooks of eastern China excel in cooking fresh and salt water fish and shellfish to bring forth the natural flavor. But many dishes have more sauce and are more robust tasting than the foods found elsewhere in China. Meats cook longer, often seasoned with generous amounts of soy sauce and rock sugar, or her cooks braise meat in a "master sauce" kept "alive" by reserving a small amount of the sauce to add to the next braised dish. Even when stir-frying, the cooking process is lengthened by reducing the heat and simmering the food until tender.

# WINE RECOMMENDATIONS
## ALL WINES ARE RETAIL-PRICED
### OUTSTANDING EUROPEAN WINE VALUES

| | |
|---|---|
| Beaumes de Venise — Red Côtes du Rhone | $3.99 |
| Canteval — Red and White Burgundy | $2.99 |
| Chantefleur — Red and White Burgundy | $3.49 |
| Entre-Deux-Mers, Barton White Bordeaux | $3.39 |
| Green Label Moselle, Deinhard | |
| White German Moselle Riesling | $4.99 |
| St. Macaire, Barton, White Bordeaux | $3.39 |
| Vouvray, Henri Leger, White Loire Chenin Blanc | $3.29 |

### CALIFORNIA

**Barbera**
Pedrizetti '73 $3.00; Papagni $3.43; Louis Martini $3.70; Heitz $4.25; Sebastiani $4.35

**Black Muscat**
Novitiate $5.50

**Burgundy**
Gallo Hearty Burgundy $1.70; Inglenook Navalle $2.46; Taylor California Cellars $2.60; San Martin '77 $2.74; Heitz $2.75; Franciscan (Cask 318) $2.99; Souverain $3.49; Beaulieu '76 $3.90.

**Carignane**
Fetzer Mendocino $3.50

**White Burgundy**
Foppiano $3.75; Mill Creek (Burgundy Blanc) '79 $3.95; Mirassou $4.39.

**Cabernet Sauvignon**
Colony $1.99; Stone Creek '77 $2.99; Sebastiani Mountain

$2.95; Los Hermanos '77 $3.00; Louis Martini '76 $4.45; Caymus Liberty School '76 $4.75; Fetzer Mendocino '77 $5.00; Beaulieu Beautour '77 $4.95; Spring Mountain Dehlinger '78 $7.00; Diamond Creek '75 $7.25; Jordan '76 or '77 $11.99; Caymus '76.

### Chablis
Gallo (Chablis Blanc) $1.89; Stone Creek '78 or '79 $2.09; Los Hermanos $2.39; Almaden Mountain $2.50; Taylor California Cellars $2.60; CK Mondavi $2.19; Geyser Peak (Summit) $2.40; Paul Masson $2.70; Beaulieu $3.50

### Charbono
Parducci '75 $5.00; Inglenook $5.09; Souverain $5.75.

### Chardonnay (Pinot Chardonnay)
Stone Creek '78 $4.64; Sebastiani $4.95; Louis Martini $5.15; San Martin $5.49; Wente $5.80; Sonoma $5.89; Parducci '78 $6.00; Mirassou $6.39; Beringer '78 $7.00; Dehlinger '78 $7.50; Fetzer '78 $7.50; Estrella River '78 $8.50; Burgess Cellars (Bell Canyon) '78 $5.75; Clos du Val '77 $6.00; Lambert Bridge $9.50; Chateau St. Jean (Robert Young) $14.49; Chateau Montelena $10.95; Grgich Hill $11.50; David Bruce $13.35; Mt. Veeder $12.00

### Chenin Blanc
Stone Creek '78 $2.59; Inglenook Navalle $2.57; Los Hermanos $2.49; San Martin $3.99; Charles Krug '78 $4.50; Mirassou '78 or '79 $4.69; Dry Creek '79 (dry) $4.75; Callaway Sweet Nancy (sweet) '78 $30.00.

### Chianti
Gallo $1.95

### French Colombard
Gallo $2.29; Foppiano $3.10; Sonoma $3.59; Parducci '78 $3.75.

### Fumé Blanc
Christian Bros. Napa Fume $4.76; Beringer $5.50; Dry Creek '79 $6.95; Robert Mondavi '78 $7.50

### Gamay
Christian Bros. Gamay Noir NV $4.25; Charles F. Shaw (Napa) '79 $5.49.

714

**Gamay Beaujolais**
Louis Martini '78 $3.69; Inglenook '78; Sebastiani '78 $4.15;
Stag's Leap $4.69.

**Gewurztraminer**
Almaden $4.50; Louis Martini (dry) $4.48; Geyser Peak $5.29;
Firestone '78 $5.25; Preston '77 (Washington) $5.50.

**Green Hungarian**
Weibel $3.59

**Grignolino**
Heitz $4.25

**Johannisberg Riesling**
Monterey Vineyard '78 or '79 $4.69; Paul Masson (Pinnacles)
'77 or '78 $5.00; Firestone NV $5.25; Saint Michelle '78
(Washington) $5.50; Jekel '79 $6.00; Llords & Elwood '78 $6.50;
Chateau Montelena $6.75; Chateau St. Jean $5.79; Joseph
Phelps $10.95.

**Merlot**
Louis Martini $4.25; Davis Bynum '77 $4.99; Firestone (Aroyo)
'77 $6.00.

**Malvasia**
Beringer Malvasia Bianca $3.59

**Moscato Amabile**
Sutter Home $4.25; Angelo Papagni $4.25.

**Muscat Blanc (Canelli or Frontignan)**
Christian Bros. Chateau La Salle (sweet) $3.25; Concannon '79
(semi-dry) $5.00.

**Petite Sirah**
Cresta Blanca $3.66; Almaden NV $4.24; San Martin $4.50;
Wente $3.85; Mirassou $4.69; Concannon '76 $4.75; Fetzer
NV $5.00; Caymus '75 $5.50; Callaway '77 $7.50.

**Pinot Blanc**
Paul Masson $3.95; Almaden $4.25; Wente $4.30; Novitiate
$4.49; J. Lohr '78 $6.00; Fetzer NV $6.50.

## Pinot Noir

Pedroncelli '75 $3.75; Louis Martini $4.25; Foppiano $4.30; Landmark '77 $5.00; Mill Creek '78 $5.45; Souverain '75 $5.49; Beaulieu (Beaumont) '77 $5.50; Monterey Peninsula (Estancia) $6.00; Stonegate '76 $6.00; Clos du Val '78 $6.50; Pope Valley (Napa) $6.50; Robert Mondavi '77 $7.00; Firestone '76 $7.50; Gundlach-Bundschu '77 $7.85; Beaulieu (Carneros) '76 $8.00; Sebastiani (Proprietor Reserve) '69 $10.75.

## Pinot Noir Blanc

River Oaks $3.75; Sebastiani $4.35; Caymus $4.50; Gemello '78 $6.75.

## Port

Novitiate $3.49; Almaden Ruby $4.59; Ficklin $5.59; Llords & Elwood Proveab Port $4.25.

## Rosé

Christian Bros La Salle $3.00; Mirassou Petite Rosé $3.65; Llords & Elwood Rosé of Cabernet '78 $4.75; Heitz Grignolino Rosé $4.25.

## Ruby Cabernet

Colony $1.99; Almaden NV $3.00; Barengo (Estate) $4.50.

## Sauvignon Blanc

Wente $5.00; Monterey Vineyard (Botrytis, sweet) '75 $5.50; Santa Ynez Valley (dry) '79 $6.50; J. Lohr (dry) '78 $6.00.

## Sherries

Llords & Elwood Dry Wit Sherry $4.25; Gallo Livingston Cream Sherry $1.65; Cresta Blanca Triple Cream Sherry $3.75.

## Sparkling Wines

Le Domaine Champagne $3.59; Hanns Kornell Champagne $8.50; Angelo Papagni Spumante d'Angelo $6.29; Almaden Blanc de Blancs $8.39; Domaine Chandon Napa Valley Brut $9.75; Mirassou Au Natural Champagne $9.25; Korbel Natural $9.69.

## Spanish Sparkling Wines

Codornieu Brut $6.99; Freixenet Carta Nevada $4.99.

## Zinfandel
River Oaks Soft Zinfandel $3.05; Almaden NV $3.61; Barengo NV $3.89; Stone Creek '78 $3.99; Sutter Home (El Dorado) '79 $4.25; Souverain '76 $4.50; Monterey Peninsula (Templeton) '77 $4.95; Dehlinger '78 $5.50.

## White Zinfandel
Sutter Home $4.25

# Restaurant Writing
## The State of the Art

Some years ago I wrote an article entitled "The Waitergate Affair" for a journalism publication that was later reprinted in *Coast* magazine. Along with other factors, the article decried the parasites: columnists and publications who publish *quid pro quo* editorial approval in return for the advertising space purchased. Although there have been notable improvements, restaurant writing is still a long way from being respectable.

Surprisingly, it is the suburban newspapers that have proved the more progressive. Larry Lipson, restaurant editor for the *Valley News*, writes a daily column on restaurants and his views are respected within the industry as fair and objective. Herb Baus writes two major columns each week for the *Santa Ana Register*, giving detailed accounts of the restaurants both in and out of his area. He, too, is a good, dependable writer.

On the other hand, the major Los Angeles newspapers have responded feebly, if at all, to the tremendous interest in dining out. When you want to go to a movie or a play you can read reviews beforehand in the local media. But when you want to eat in a restaurant you are largely on your own.

Until recently the Los Angeles *Herald Examiner* featured the New York shrill of Carole Lalli. My, but she was intolerant of us. "Some people," she once wrote, "do not even know the difference between West African and Moroccan cuisine!" On another occasion she complained stridently about the owner of a small restaurant who had the nerve, the *nerve*, to sit, however briefly, at her table. Mrs. Lalli went to great pains to point out that she *was* after all with an important food writer from New York. In a September, 1980, column she was critical of the friendly service at the L'Escoffier Room; it was not in keeping with their image, she felt. It is difficult to imagine what the many blue-collar readers of the *Examiner* make of Mrs. Lalli's microscopic analyses, frequent affront with the construction of a sauce, and the inevitable comparison to New York. To its credit, the *Herald Examiner* has beefed up restaurant reporting with fine writers like Sharon Boorstein and Merrill Shindler.

Lois Dwan of the Los Angeles *Times* is probably one of the most knowledgeable restaurant writers in the nation. Unfortunately, her column appears only on Sundays, buried in the back pages of the thick *Calendar* section.

Mrs. Dwan does not like me. As a matter of fact she "resents" me. In "The Waitergate Affair" I wanted to demonstrate the fact that the *Times* did not carefully edit nor apprently understand her column. She was, I wrote, "one of the true innocents of the *Times*." I told the story of the time she was tricked by some mischievous colleagues into writing about a restaurant that did not exist. Even worse, the name of that apocryphal eatery was the phonetic spelling of some X-rated words that are easily recognizable in the Rams' locker room—if a bit shocking. I described her role as "den mother" to a restaurant "writers" association that annually gives questionable awards. (The group's founder and first president resigned and charged the association with fraud, pay-offs, influence peddling and worse.) Mrs. Dwan finally resigned, but not until she had given her friends the respectability of years of *Times* coverage. Her protracted dissociation would be comparable to Dr. Frankenstein's disavowal of the monster.

Indeed, she struck back in what was, for her, a daring manner. Invited to a media event and arriving alone, Mrs. Dwan was seated at a table with the Ralph Storys and with me and my lady (of that evening). She subsequently wrote of that event that she was the "asterisk" at a table of a "minor celebrity" who, it seemed to her, chattered away about bathroom curtains the whole night long. Her parting shot, the knockout blow, was a fortune cooky puzzler: "—rudeness without wit is a mud pie." The *Calendar* folks, an elitist if talented pocket of the *Times*, have continued to protect their readers from me. When their radio columnist turned in an article about my talk radio program, it was killed, certainly a curious if not unprecedented act.

The Los Angeles *Times* is a fine newspaper that has earned international respect and local envy. They should recognize that their readers spend more time in eating places than they do at the movies or at sporting events combined. The readers' need for information should call for a column with more frequency than, say, a column on stamp collecting or chess.

On the magazine scene, things get better. *Los Angeles'* Bruce David Colen is an honest and accurate reporter. He, like all reviewers, does not expect everyone to agree with him (he hated the Marrakesh; I loved it) but simply to respect and to be guided by his opinion.

Ruth Reichl has been given the impossible task of covering both Northern and Southern California for *California* (formerly *New West*). She is a knowledgeable, entertaining and instructive writer. But *Texas* (the magazine, not the state)—who took over *New West*—should realize that there are more restaurants in Southern California alone than in Texas (the state, not the magazine).

Elmer Dills does an excellent job on both radio and television (KABC) exploring the restaurants of Southern California. He is fair, rarely seen at free-loading functions and his experience as a diplomat abroad gives him rich background from which to draw.

The dismal state of the art is due in part to the sloppy and sometimes shoddy public relations agencies that feed on restaurant owners' egos by getting their pictures and items into "soft" media publications that sell their credibility along with the ad. Not long ago I was on a deadline and I called a PR person who represented a certain ethnic restaurant. I was doing a story about the cuisine. When the answers to my questions proved improbable and inaccurate I asked to speak directly to the owner. "You will speak to me, or not at all," was the reply. I subsequently wrote the owner of the restaurant explaining that I required direct access to him and that while his public relations people were undoubtedly competent, I needed direct answers. The outraged press agent later wrote a letter sending a copy to the various "restaurant writer" association members headed (their caps): "WHAT A WALLACH THING TO DO!!!!"

Angry press agents and ad selling "writers" have frequently written letters to my publishers and my producers urging that I be fired. Most were threatening letters of one sort or another. One of my editors used to complain if he didn't get at least one such misguided missile a month.

And some criticism can be justifiably directed at me. My radio program is supported by advertising, a great deal of it from restaurants. However, I do not read the commercials and I have been careful to place frequent disclaimers to the effect that advertising on the program does not constitute endorsement. In some cases, after hearing a commercial on my show, I've commented that I personally did not care for that particular restaurant or advertiser.

While these annual reports on restaurant writing tend not to make me popular with some PR people and a few alleged writers, it is interesting that the restaurants themselves have rarely complained about criticism. Indeed, many of my more lasting friendships have developed after I wrote unfavorable reviews. And your letters indicate that you too have come to distrust the media on the subject of restaurants. Too often Ma's Pizza joint becomes "the yummiest restaurant this side of Frank Sinatra," and too often there's the expected ad just inches away. Credibility should be the stock in trade of any restaurant reviewer, yet there's an unfortunate dearth of it in Southern California.

## Southern California Area Map

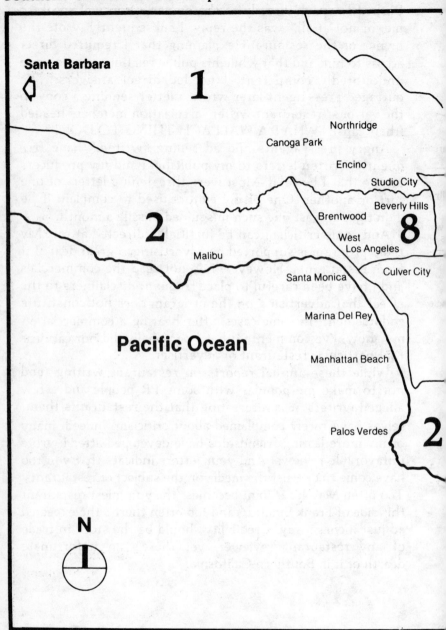

See detailed maps on pages 30 to 39 of this Guide.

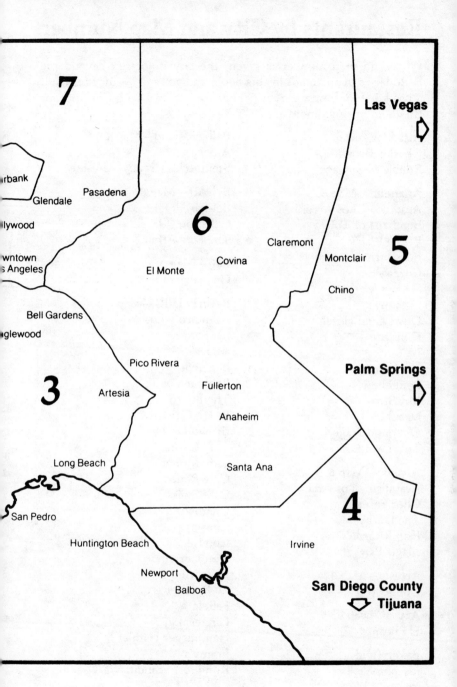

7

rbank

Glendale

Pasadena

llywood

wntown
s Angeles

6

El Monte

Covina

Las Vegas ⬦

Claremont

Montclair

Chino

5

Bell Gardens

glewood

3

Pico Rivera

Artesia

Fullerton

Anaheim

Palm Springs ⬦

Long Beach

San Pedro

Santa Ana

4

Huntington Beach

Irvine

Newport

Balboa

San Diego County
⬦ Tijuana

# Restaurants by City and Map Number

Where no map number is given, the city is located beyond the boundaries of the maps in this book, and you may want to consult a road map of Santa Barbara, Ventura or San Diego Counties, or the Palm Springs/Indio area.

**Altadena—Map 7**
Charley Brown's
Robbie's Rib Cage

**Anaheim—Map 6**
Acapulco y Los Arcos
Benihana of Tokyo
Bessie Wall's
Bob Burns
Cozza's
Daisy's Market
Delaney's
Disneyland Hotel
Don Jose
JW's
Las Lomas
Longellow's
Mr. Stox
Mizuho
Overland Stage
The Twin Dragon

**Arcadia—Map 6**
Acapulco y Los Arcos
Chez Sateau
The Derby
Don Ricardo's
Magic Pan

**Artesia—Map 3**
Don Jose

**Azusa—Map 6**
El Encanto

**Bakersfield**
Josephina's

**Balboa Island—Map 4**
Amelia's
Steinbeck's Creative Cuisine

**Bel-Air—Map 8**
Bel-Air Hotel
Cafe Four Oaks
The Fine Affair

**Bell—Map 3**
Guadalajara Inn

**Beverly Hills—Map 8**
Acapulco y Los Arcos
Ah Fong's
Andre's
Bagatelle
Benihana of Tokyo
The Bistro
Bistro Garden
Brown Derby
Cafe Casino
Cafe Monet
Cafe Rodeo
Cafe Swiss
Chambord
Chasen's
Coterie
Don Hernando's
El Padrino
En Brochette
Felfela
Gingerman
Hamburger Hamlet
Jimmy's
Konditori Scandinavia

La Bella Fontana
La Dolce Vita
La Famiglia
La Polonaise
La Scala
Lawry's Prime Rib
Lawry's Westside Broiler
L'Escoffier
Magic Pan
Maison Gerard
The Mandarin
Marco Polo
Michelangelo's
Michel Richard
Mr. Chow
Mr. H
Moghul

Nate 'n Al's
Old World
Orlando Orsini
Polo Lounge
Rangoon Racquet Club
R.J.'s The Rib Joint
Rouard's Polonaise
Saloon
Silvana's
Su Ling
Tony Roma's
Trader Vic's

**Big Bear**
Ronardo's

**Big Sur**
Nepenthe

**Brea—Map 6**
Big Yellow House
Bobby McGee's
Magic Pan

**Brentwood**
Bicycle Shop
Caribbean Terrace
Gatsby's
Hamburger Hamlet
La Terrazza Italian
Lettuce Patch
Peppone
Seafood Broiler

**Buena Park—Map 6**
Amagi
Arnold's Farmhouse
The Buttery
Hungry Tiger
Knott's Berry Farm
Stox II
Velvet Horn

**Burbank—Map 1**
Acapulco y Los Arcos
Butcher's Arms
Chadney's
Genio's
Glacier Gourmet
Hampton's
Paul's French Cuisine
Piero's
Pinocchio
Robbie's Rib Cage
Smoke House
Sorrentino's
Taste of Scandinavia

**Calabasas—Map 1**
Agostino's Ristorante
Calabasas Inn
Sagebrush Cantina

**Canoga Park—Map 1**
Castagnola's
Chicken Naturel
Epicure Inn

725

Kandel's
Michael's Canoga Inn

**Carlsbad—Map 4**
Pisces

**Carpinteria**
Eggception

**Century City—Map 8**
Bruno's Chartreuse
Clifton's Cafeteria
Garden Room
Hamburger Hamlet
Jade West
Josephina's
The Playboy Club
Plaza Four
Senor Pico
Yamato

**Cerritos—Map 3**
Big Yellow House

**Chatsworth—Map 1**
Catch of the Sea
Taste of Scandinavia

**Chinatown—Map 7**
Diamond Sea Food
Golden Pagoda
Grand Star
Hunan
Young Sing

**City of Industry—Map 6**
Seafood Broiler

**Claremont—Map 6**
Griswold's Indian Hill

**Corona Del Mar—Map 4**
Charthouse
Five Crowns
Hemingway's

Maison Alexis
Matteo's
Quiet Woman

**Coronado**
Chez Loma
Chu Dynasty
Prince of Wales

**Costa Mesa—Map 4**
Alfredo's
Big Yellow House
Bordeaux
Hamburger Hamlet
La Cave
La Cuisine of Newport
Magic Pan
Mandarin Gourmet
Pronto
Riviera
Tea and Sympathy
TGI Fridays

**Covina—Map 6**
Monique
Pizza Time Theatre

**Cucamonga—Map 5**
Sycamore Inn

**Culver City—Map 3**
Breakers Seafood Company
China Palace
Hot Licks Cafe
Ponderosa
Sagebrush Cantina
Slender Spoon
Stern's BBQ
Taormina

**Dana Point—Map 4**
Captain's Anchorage
Charthouse
La Cuisine of Dana Point
Wind and Sea

**Del Mar**
The Albatross
El Pescador
Fourno's Oven West
Jake's Del Mar
Valée Rose

**Downey—Map 3**
Kings
Sambi of Tokyo

**Eagle Rock—Map 7**
Pat and Lorraine's

**Encino—Map 1**
Acapulco y Los Arcos
Adam's
Ah Fong's
Amber's
Benihana of Tokyo
Bouillabaisse
Castagnola's
D'jit Pochana
Du Par's
Golden Bowl
Hamburger Hamlet
Houlihan's Old Place
Le Hot Club
Lettuce Patch
Mon Grenier
Monteleone's
Monty's
Robb's Ice Cream
Tempo
Tony Roma's
Tracton's

**Escondido**
Acapulco y Los Arcos
Chez Orleans
Chuck's Steak House
The Forum Ristorante

**Fallbrook**
Caldron

**Fountain Valley—Map 4**
Crossroads

**Fullerton—Map 6**
The Cellar
Dal Rae
Don Jose
Elmer's Place
Giovanni's
Pizza Time Theatre
Ruby Begonia's
Velvet Turtle

**Garden Grove—Map 6**
Acapulco y Los Arcos
Belisle's
Big Yellow House
La Fayette
Pizza Time Theatre
Salvatore's

**Glendale—Map 7**
Acapulco y Los Arcos
Aoba
Cafe Le Monde
Churchill's
Du Par's
Great Scot
La Strada
Magic Pan
Mauro's
Pike's Verdugo Oaks
Puerta Del Sol
Scarantino's
Seafood Broiler

**Glendora—Map 6**
Jacques

**Granada Hills—Map 1**
Futami

**La Habra—Map 6**
El Cholo
Pizza Time Theatre
Trapper's Inn

**La Jolla**
Carlos 'n Charlie's
Charthouse
Chuck's Steak House
El Chalan
L'Auberge
La Valencia
Marine Room
Oak Tree
Ocean Fresh Cafe
Rheinlander
Schnitzelbank
The Sea Thief
Su Casa
Top o' the Cove

**Lakewood—Map 3**
Clifton's Cafeteria
Seafood Broiler

**La Mesa**
Christian's Danish Inn

**La Verne—Map 6**
Sgt. Pepper's

**Lomita—Map 2**
Longfellow's

**Long Beach—Map 3**
Acapulco y Los Arcos
A Tout Va Bien
Bobby McGee's
Bogart's
Castagnola's
Charley Brown's
Charthouse
Crab Shell

Delius
Hamburger Henry's
Houlihan's Old Place
Jungry Jose
Kalmegdan
Kings
Le Bistro
Pizza Time Theatre
Russell's
Slender Spoon
Velvet Turtle

**Los Alamitos—Map 6**
Ricabob

**Los Angeles—Map 7**
Adagio
Ahihei
Alberto's
Anna Maria Ristorante
Art's Chili Dogs
Bayanihan
Beaudry's
Bergin's Tavern
Bernard's
The Birchtree
Budapest Hungarian
Bull 'n Bush
Bullock's Wilshire Tea Room
Carl's
Casa Carnitas
Casey's Bar
Cassell's Hamburgers
Chaos
Chinese Friends
City Cafe
Clifton's Cafeteria
Cook's Steak 'n Chop House
The Cove
Dario's
Dragon Pearl
Dresden Room

Du Par's  
The Egg and the Eye  
El Cholo  
El Cid  
El Coyote  
El Dorado  
El Paseo Inn  
Firenze Kitchens  
Francois  
General Lee's  
Grand Avenue Bar  
Green Jade  
Green Leaves  
Hamoyoshi  
Hamburger Hamlet  
Hanabishi  
Hanil  
Harry's Deli  
H.M.S. Bounty  
Horikawa  
Hyang Mi  
Ignazio's  
Inagiku  
Itchey Foot  
Kings  
Kin Jo  
Korea Gardens  
La Fonda  
La Salsa  
La Strega  
La Villa  
Lawry's California Center  
Les Freres Taix  
Little J's  
Little Joe's  
Los Burritos  
Los Feliz Inn  
Lowenbrau Keller  
Lucky Restaurant  
Madrid  
Man Fook Low  

Marcus Steak House  
Maurice's Snack 'N Chat  
Medallion  
Mifune  
Miriwa  
Mon Kee  
Murray's Cafe  
New Moon  
Nikola's  
Nipa Hut  
Orient Express  
Original Pantry  
O'Shaughnessy's  
Pacific Dining Car  
Papa Choux  
Pavilion  
Perino's  
Philippe the Original  
Pink's  
Plum Tree Inn  
Police Academy  
Regina's  
Rex Ristorante  
Robaire's French Cuisine  
Sapporo-Ya  
Sarno's  
Seafood Bay  
Shanghai Winter Gardens  
Siamese Princess  
Substation Ltd.  
Taylor's  
Tenmasa  
Tepparod Thai  
A Thousand Cranes  
Tokyo Kaikan  
The Tower  
The Twin Dragon  
Velvet Turtle  
Veracruz  
Veronika  
Via Fettuccini

Vickman's
Vince and Paul's
Virgilio's
The Windsor
Yagura Ichiban
Yang Chow
Yugoslavian Village

**Los Angeles (West) Map 8**
Adriano's
Anna's
Apple Pan
At Marty's
Belmont Pier
Bergin's West
Bit O' Scotland
Bouchon
Canard de Bombay
Canter's
Captain's Table
Carmine's
Casa Cugat
Chicago Pizza Works
Chicken Naturel
Chuck's Steak House
Chung King
Dem Bones
Du Par's
Entourage
Farmer's Market
Fortune Fountain
Giuseppe!
Golden Temple of
    Conscious Cookery
Greenhouse
Hamburger Hamlet
Harry's Bar and Grill
Homer and Edy's Bistro
Junior's
Kin Jo
La Creperie Bretonne

La Grange
La Masia
La Place
La Salsa
Le Restaurant
L'Orangerie
Ma Maison
Mangia
Mouling
Rapisardi
Roscoe's House of Chicken
    and Waffles
Saigon Flavor
St. Tropez
Shep's
Simon's
Stellini's
Sundance Cafe
Swiss Echo
Tail O' The Cock
Tepparod Thai
Toledo
Tommy's Hamburgers
Tracton's
Velvet Turtle
Verita's Cantina
Vietnam Pearl
Villa Sombrero
Wan-Q
West End Garden
Westside Cafe

**Malibu—Map 2**
Baja Cantina
Charthouse
Don the Beachcomber
Holiday House
H.M.S. Sandcastle
La Scala Malibu

Moonshadows
Nantucket Light
Sand Castle
The Sea Lion

## Manhattan Beach—Map 2
Cafe Pierre
Courtney's
Courtney's Bistro
Lettuce Patch
Olde Manhattan Spaghetti Faire
Orville and Wilbur's
The Pelican
Talia's

## Marina Del Rey—Map 2
Akbar Indian Restaurant
Baja Cantina
Benihana of Tokyo
Cafe Parisien
Castagnola's
Charley Brown's
Charthouse
Chuck's Steak House
Crab Shell
Don the Beachcomber
Fiasco
Gulliver's
Hungry Tiger
Shanghai Red's
TGI Fridays
The Warehouse

## Mission Bay
Salmon House

## Mission Valley
Chu Dynasty
Lettuce Patch
Presidente

## Mission Viejo—Map 4
Big Yellow House

Bobby McGee's
Lettuce Patch
Pizza Time Theatre

## Monrovia
Big Yellow House
La Parisienne

## Montclair
Big Yellow House

## Montecito
Cafe del Sol
Olive Mill Bistro

## Monterey Park
China Palace

## National City
Big Yellow House

## Newport—Map 4
Ambrosia
Ancient Mariner
Anthony's Pier 2
Arches
Benihana of Tokyo
Blackbeard's Galley
Bob Burns
Bobby McGee's
Cannery
Charthouse
Crab Cooker
Delaney's
Houlihan's Old Place
The Lakeside
Le St. Tropez
Little Joe's
Marrakesh
Old Spaghetti Factory
Reuben E. Lee
The Ritz
Rusty Pelican
Stuft Noodle

Tony Roma's
Velvet Turtle
Via Fontana
Villa Nova
The Warehouse
The Wine Cellar
The White Oak
Woody's Wharf
Yamato

## North Hollywood—Map 1
Alexander's
Bob Burns
Chicken Naturel
Erawan
Far East Terrace
Le Petit Chateau
Little Vienna
Maison Gerard
Marv's Deli
Puerta Del Sol
Salomi
Sportsmen's Lodge

## Northridge—Map 1
Don Ricardo's
Fujiya
Josephina's
Truly Yours

## Oceanside
Cafe Europa
Charthouse

## Ojai
The Ranch House

## Orange
Casablanca
Chez Cary
D'Amico's
Don Jose
El Cholo
Feastboard

Hobbit
La Brasserie
Miyako
No-No's
Opaso 2
Orange Hill
Villa Fontana

## Oxnard
Castagnola's
Lobster Trap
The Whale's Tail

## Pacific Beach
Casina Valadier

## Pacific Palisades—Map 2
Dante
Gladstone's 4 Fish

## Palm Desert
Dunbar's
Iron Gate

## Palm Springs
Cattails
Di Amico's
Don the Beachcomber
Hamburger Hamlet
Hungry Tiger
Las Casuelas Terraza
Lord Fletcher Inn
Louise's Pantry
Lyon's English Grille
Melvyn's
Nate's Deli
Old World
One Thousand East
Pal Joey's
Tony Roma's

## Palos Verdes—Map 2
Hungry Tiger
Le Monaco
Rive Gauche

**Panorama City—Map 1**
Little Shanghai
Red Barn
Seafood Broiler

**Pasadena—Map 7**
Acapulco y Los Arcos
Beadle's Cafeteria
Beckham Place
Brotherton's Farmhouse
Castagnola's
The Chronicle
Dino's
Hamburger Hamlet
Josephina's
Kabakian's
Kabuki
Maldonado's
Marianne
Michael's Italian Cuisine
Miyako
Monty's
Panda Inn
The Raymond
Shogun
Stottlemyer's
Talk of the Town
Velvet Turtle

**Pico Rivera—Map 6**
Clearman's Steak 'N Stein
Dal Rae
Veronique

**Placentia—Map 6**
301 Club

**Playa Del Rey—Map 2**
The Cliff House
Lemon Tree by the Sea

**Rancho Bernardo**
Monterey Jack's

**Rancho Mirage**
Charthouse
Mario's
Medium Rare

**Redlands**
Edward's
Griswold's Smorgasbord

**Redondo Beach—Map 2**
Beachbum Burt's
Castagnola's
Charthouse
Millie Riera's
Tony's on the Pier
Velvet Turtle

**Reseda—Map 1**
The Weinstube

**Riverside—Map 5**
Gerard's French Restaurant
Mission Inn
Pitruzello's
Red Baron Steakhouse

**Rolling Hills—Map 2**
Borrelli's

**Rosemead—Map 6**
Charley Brown's
T & J Restaurant

**Running Springs**
Lloyd's

**San Bernardino—Map 5**
Bobby McGee's
Little Kitchen

**San Clemente—Map 4**
San Clemente Inn

**San Diego**
Anthony's Harborside
Anthony's Star of the Sea

Antoine's Sheik
Atlantis
Aztec Dining Room
Bali Hai
Casa De Pico
Fontainebleau Room
Frenchy Marseilles
Giulio's
Hamburguesa
Hob Nob Hill
Houlihan's Old Place
Imperial House
Kiyo's
La Chaumine
Lubach's
Magic Pan
Mandarin China
Mikisan
Mister A's
Nino's
Old Spaghetti Factory
Old Town Mexican Cafe
Old Trieste
The Prophet
Red Sails Inn
Red Sails Inn
Ruth's Catering
TGI Fridays
World Famous
Yakitori II

**San Dimas—Map 6**
San Dimas Mansion

**San Gabriel—Map 6**
Panchito's

**San Jacinto**
Janthina's

**San Juan Capistrano**
El Adobe de Capistrano

**San Pedro—Map 3**
Cigo's
Papadakis Taverna
The Paragon Inn
Ports O' Call
Princess Louise

**Santa Ana—Map 6**
Acapulco y Los Arcos
Antonello
Benjie's
Gin Ling
Harlequin Dinner Playhouse
Horikawa
Hungry Tiger
Nieuport 17
Ristorante Ervino

**Santa Barbara**
Big Yellow House
Casa de Sevilla
Castagnola's
Charthouse
Chuck's Steak House
Eggception
Encina
The Good Earth
La Chaumiere
La Marina
Penelope's
Suishin Sukiyaki
Talk of the Town

**Santa Maria**
Frederick's

**Santa Monica—Map 2**
Anna Maria's La Trattoria
Au Chambertin
Bagel Nosh
Belle-Vue French Restaurant
Ben's Place
Bob Burns

Cafe California
Cafe Casino
Charmer's Market
Chez Jay
The Chronicle
Donkin's Inn
Famous Enterprise Fish Co.
The Galley Steak House
Great American Food and
   Beverage Co.
Gypsy's
Hamburger Henry's
Hiro Sushi
Jack's at the Beach
Knoll's Black Forest Inn
La Brochette
Le Cellier
Les Anges
Le St. Michel
Les Pyrenees
Lettuce Patch
The Lobster
Madame Wu's Garden
Ma Façon
Marquis West
Michael's
Moby's Dock
Old Venice Noodle Company
Pelican Restaurants
Pinocchio West
Pioneer Boulangerie
Pontevecchio
Summer Palace
Tampico Tilly's
Tony Roma's
Valentino
Vito's
Warszawa
Ye Olde King's Head

## Seal Beach—Map 6
Noel's
Seafood Broiler

## Seaport Village
Su Casa

## Sepulveda—Map 1
Mel's Landing

## Sherman Oaks—Map 1
Albion's
Aux Delices
Camille's
Chef Gregoire
Chuck's Steak House
Fiore d'Italia
Hamburger Hamlet
Ho Toy's
Hungry Tiger
Josephina's
La Fondue Bourguignonne
La Frite
La Grange Aux Crepes
Lannathai
La Pizza
Le Cafe
L'Express
Tail O' the Cock
Via Fettuccini
Wiener Factory

## Simi Valley—Map 1
Sea Quest

## Solano Beach
Samurai

## Solvang
Danish Inn
Mollerkroen

**Studio City—Map 1**
Art's
Chez Naturel
Coriander
Domo
Du Par's
Harry's Open Pit BBQ
Jailhouse Chili Co.
Jerry's Famous Deli
La Serre
La Ve Lee
Le Pavillon
Maneeya Thai
Marrakesh
Mulberry Street
St. Moritz
Seafood Broiler
Teriyaki Shimon
Teru Sushi
The Wine Bistro

**Sun Valley—Map 1**
Acapulco y Los Arcos
Don Ricardo's
Pizza Time Theatre

**Tarzana—Map 1**
Ameci Italian Restaurant
Le Sanglier
Monteleone's
Mort's Deli
Seafood Broiler

**Thousand Oaks—Map 1**
Charley Brown's
Hungry Tiger
Magic Pan
Velvet Turtle

**Tijuana**
El Abajeno de Guadalajara
Giuseppi's
La Costa

La Especial
Reno's
Restaurant La Costa
Tiajuana Tilly's

**Toluca Lake—Map 2**
China Trader

**Topanga—Map 2**
Inn of the Seventh Ray
Three Dolphin Inn

**Torrance—Map 2**
Alpine Village Inn
Benihana of Tokyo
Chalet de France
Golden Goose Pub
Houlihan's Old Place
Ichabod Crane's
Lettuce Patch
Magic Pan
Marengo
Miyako
Seafood Broiler
Slender Spoon
Thin's Inn
Velvet Turtle

**Tustin—Map 6**
Don Jose
Revere House
Tony's Sea Landing

**Universal City—Map 1**
Fung Lum
Whomphopper's

**Upland—Map 5**
Magnolia's Peach

**Van Nuys—Map 1**
Du Par's
El Gato
Hoppe's Old Heidelberg
Longfellow's

Our Contribution
Pelican's Roost
Sherman Room
Otto's Pink Pig

**Venice—Map 2**
Chez Helene
La Cabana
La Grange Aux Crepes
Land's End
Pelican's Catch
Robert's Restaurant
Tad's

**Ventura**
Charley Brown's
Lemon Turtle

**Victorville**
Ferrarese Family Deli

**Visalia**
Vintage Press

**Westchester—Map 3**
Hungry Tiger

**West Covina—Map 6**
Charley Brown's
Clifton's Cafeteria
Thin's Inn

**West Hollywood—Map 8**
Ah Fong's
Alouette
Antonio's
Carlos 'N Charlie's
Chianti
Cock 'N Bull
Cyrano
Dan Tana's
Gitanjali
Great American Food and
  Beverage Co.

Hugo's
La Petite Maison
La Toque
L'Etoile
Moun of Tunis
Moustache Cafe
Nucleus Nuance
The Palm
The Patio
The Pear Garden
Rex's Fishmarket
Roy's
Saratoga
Scandia
Sundance Cafe
Trumps

**Westlake—Map 1**
Boccaccio's
Lettuce Patch

**Westwood—Map 8**
Acapulco y Los Arcos
Ah Fong's
Alice's Restaurant
Asuka
Bratskellar
Carl Andersen's Chatham
Charthouse
Chuck's Steak House
The Good Earth
Hamburger Hamlet
Harry's Open Pit BBQ
Hungry Tiger
Koutoubia
La Fondue Bourguignonne
Lamonica's
La Salsa
Mario's Italian
Matteo's
Monty's Steak House

Moustache Cafe
Old World
Paul Bhalla's
Pinocchio
Stratton's

**Woodland Hills—Map 1**
Bob Burns
Casa de Carlos
Chang's
Charley Brown's
The Good Earth
Hamburger Hamlet
La Frite
Le Huyen

Le Papillon
Magic Pan
Mort's Deli
Nut Shell
Rene's
The Seashell
Summer House
Sushi House
Taste of Scandinavia
TGI Fridays
The Twin Dragon
Velvet Turtle

# TYPES OF CUISINE

## ALBANIAN
Ajeti's

## AMERICAN
Adam's
Albatross
Alice's
Amber's
Ancient Mariner
Anna's
Anthony's Harborside
Apple Pan
Arnold's
Art's Chili Dogs
Atlantis
Bali Hai
Beadle's Cafeteria
Belisle's
Ben Brown's
Ben's Place
Bergin's West
Bessie Wall's
Big Yellow House
Bit O'Scotland
Blackbeard's Galley
Bob Burns
Bobby McGee's
Bratskellar
Brotherton's Farmhouse
Brown Derby
Bull 'n Bush Steakhouse
Bullock's Wilshire Tea Room
The Buttery
Cafe California
Cafe Courtney
Cafe Rodeo
Calabasas Inn
Caldron

Cannery Restaurant
Captain's Anchorage
Carl's Jr.
Casey's Bar
Cassell's Hamburgers
Cattleman's Wharf
Chadney's
Charley Brown's
Charmer's Market
The Charthouse
Chez Jay
Chicken Naturel
China Trader
Chuck's Steak House
Clearman's Steak 'n Stein
The Cliff House
Clifton's Cafeteria
Cook's
Courtney's Bistro
Crossroads
Daisy's Market
Delius
The Derby
Di Amico's
Disneyland Hotel
Donkin's Inn
The Dresden Room
Dunbar's
Du-Par's
Edward's Mansion
The Egg and the Eye
The Eggception
El Encanto
Elmer's Place
En Brochette
Farmer's Market
Feastboard

740

Fiasco
The Galley Steakhouse
The Garden Room
Genio's
Gingerman
Great American Food
and Beverage Co.
Griswold's Indian Hill
Gulliver's
Hamburger Hamlet
Hamburguesa
Hamburger Henry's
Hampton's
Harlequin Playhouse
Harry's Open Pit BBQ
Hob Nob Hill
Houlihan's
Hungry Tiger
Ichabod Crane's
International House of
Pancakes
The Iron Gate
Itchey Foot
Jacques
Jailhouse Chili Company
Jake's Del Mar
Jolly Roger
Kings
Knott's Berry Farm
La Cave
Lawry's California Center
Lawry's Prime Rib
Lawry's Westside Broiler
Le Hot Club
Lemon Tree by the Sea
Lillian's
Little J's
Little Joe's
The Little Kitchen
The Lobster Trap
Longfellow's

Louise's Pantry
Magnolia's Peach
Marcus Steak House
Marie Callendar
Marine Room
Medium Rare
Mr. H
Mr. Stox
Monterey Jack's
Monty's Steak House
Moonraker
Moonshadows
Mort's Deli
Nepenthe
Nieuport 17
Oak Tree
The Old World
Original Pantry
Orville and Wilbur's
O'Shaughnessy's
Otto's Pink Pig
Overland Stage
Pacific Dining Car
Pal Joey's
The Palm
Pat and Lorraine's
Patio Restaurant
Penelope's
Peking
Philippe the Original
Pike's Verdugo Oaks
Pink's
The Playboy Club
Police Academy
Polo Lounge
The Ponderosa
Red Barn
Red Baron
Reuben E. Lee
Reuben's
Revere House

Ricabob
R.J.'s
Ruby Begonia's
Russell's
The Rusty Pelican
San Clemente Inn
Sgt. Pepper's
Shep's
Sherman Room
Simply Blues
Sizzler
Smoke House
Sorrentino's
Stox II
Sundance Cafe
Tail O' The Cock
Talk of the Town (Pasadena)
Taylor's Prime Steak House
TGI Fridays
Tick Tock Hollywood
T & J Restaurant
Tommy's
Tony Roma's
Tracton's
Trappers Inn
Velvet Horn
Velvet Turtle
Vickman's
Victoria Station
Vince and Paul's
Wan-Q
The Whale's Tail
White House
Wiener Factory
Wind and Sea
Woody's Wharf
Whomphopper's

## ARGENTINIAN
Regina's Food Boutique

## ARMENIAN
Kabakian's

## BARBECUE
Carl's
Dem Bones
Harry's Open Pit BBQ
Love's Wood Pit BBQ
Malik Carter's
Robbie's Rib Cage
Stern's

## BELGIAN
L'Auberge
Le Papillon

## CAFETERIA
Beadle's
Clifton's

## CHINESE
Ah Fong's
Bali Hai
Cathay de Grande
Chaos
China Palace
China Trader
Chinese Friends
Chu Dynasty
Chung King
Colonel Lee's
Diamond Sea Food
The Dragon Pearl
Far East Terrace
Fortune Fountain
Fung Lum
General Lee's
Gin Ling
Golden Bowl
Golden Pagoda
Grand Star
Green Jade
Green Leaves

Ho Toy's
Hunan
Imperial Dynasty
Jade West
La Chinoise
Little Shanghai
Lucky
Madame Wu's
The Mandarin
Mandarin China
Mandarin Gourmet
Man Fook Low
Miriwa
Mr. Chow
Mon Kee
Mouling
New Moon
Orient Express
Panda Inn
Penguin Palace
Plum Tree Inn
Roy's
Shanghai
Shanghai Winter Garden
Su Ling
Summer Palace
The Twin Dragon
Wan-Q
Yang Chow
Young Sing

## COLUMBIAN
El Dorado

## CONTINENTAL
Adagio
Albatross
Alexander's
Ambrosia
Andre's
Arches
At Marty's

Beachbum Burt's
Beaudry's
Bel-Air Hotel
Ben Brown's
The Birchtree
The Bistro
Bistro Garden
Bob Burns
Boccaccio's
Bogart's
Brown Derby
Bruno's Chartreuse
Cafe del Sol
Cafe Europa
Cafe Four Oaks
Cafe Le Monde
Cafe Rodeo
Caldron
Caribbean Terrace
Carl Andersen's Chatham
Casablanca
Casa de Sevilla
Cattails
Cattleman's Wharf
The Cellar
Chasen's
Chez Cary
Chez Jay
Chez Loma
Chez Sateau
The Chronicle
Churchill's
City Cafe
Coriander
The Coterie
Courtney's
Courtney's Bistro
The Cove
Cyrano
Dal Rae
Dan Tana's

Dante  
Disneyland Hotel  
Don Hernando's  
The Dresden Room  
El Abajeno de Guadalajara  
El Adobe de Capistrano  
El Encanto  
El Padrino  
Emilio's  
Encina  
Epicure Inn  
Farmer's Market  
Fiasco  
The Fine Affair  
François (Huntington Beach)  
Frederick's  
The Garden Room  
Gatsby's  
Gingerman  
Gio's  
Giuseppi's  
Grand Avenue Bar  
Greenhouse  
Griswold's Indian Hill  
Harlequin Dinner Playhouse  
Heart of Europe  
Hemingway's  
H.M.S. Bounty  
The Hobbit  
Holiday House  
Hugo's  
Imperial Dynasty  
Imperial House  
Inn of the Seventh Ray  
Jacques  
La Bella Fontana  
La Famiglia  
La Grange  
The Lakeside  
La Marina  
La Petite Maison  

La Place  
La Scala Malibu  
La Strada  
La Toque  
La Valencia  
L'Etoile  
Lloyd's  
Los Feliz Inn  
Lubach's  
Maldonado's  
Mamma Fesada's  
Marco Polo  
Marengo  
Marine Room  
Medallion  
Mediterranean Room  
Melvyn's  
Michael's  
Michael's Canoga Inn  
Mischa's  
Mission Inn  
Mister A's  
Mr. H  
Mr. Stox  
Musso and Frank's  
Nieuport 17  
Nikola's  
Nucleus Nuance  
Olive Mill Bistro  
One Thousand East  
Orange Hill  
O'Shaughnessy's  
Otto's Pink Pig  
Papa Choux  
Paul's French Cuisine  
Pavilion  
Peking  
Perino's  
Pike's Verdugo Oaks  
Plaza Four  
Polo Lounge

Prince of Wales
Princess Louise
The Quiet Woman
The Ranch House
The Raymond
Rex's Fishmarket
Ristorante Ervino
The Ritz
Rive Gauche
Riviera Restaurant
Robert's
Ronardo's
Ruby Begonia's
Sagebrush Cantina
The Saloon
Salvatore's
San Clemente Inn
Sand Castle
San Dimas Mansion
Saratoga
Sarno's
Sausalito South
Scandia
Shanghai Red's
Slender Spoon
Sportsmen's Lodge
Steinbeck's
Stratton's
Studio Grill
The Summer House
Swiss Echo
Sycamore Inn
Talk of the Town (Santa Barbara)
Three Dolphin Inn
Tiajuana Tilly's
Top O' The Cove
The Tower
The Towers
Trader Vic's
Villa Fontana
The Vintage Press

The Warehouse
West End Garden
Westside Cafe
The Windsor
The Wine Cellar
The White Oak

## CREPES AND WAFFLES
International House of Pancakes
La Grange Aux Crepes
Magic Pan
Michel Richard

## CUBAN
Chaos

## DELICATESSEN
Art's
Bagel Nosh
Benjie's
Canter's
Dario's
Ferrarese Family Deli
Greenblatt's
Harry's
Jerry's Famous Deli
Junior's
Kandel's
Marv's
Mort's
Nate 'n Al's
Nate's
Philippe the Original
Pinocchio's
Ruth's Catering
Stottlemyer's
Substation Ltd.

## DESSERT
Glacier Gourmet
Robb's Ice Cream

## DIET
The Lettuce Patch
Slender Spoon
Thin's Inn

## EGYPTIAN
Felfela

## ENGLISH
Beckham Place
The Butcher's Arms
Cock 'N Bull
Five Crowns
Great Scot
Gulliver's
Lord Fletchers Inn
Lyon's English Grille
Rangoon Racquet Club
Tea and Sympathy
Ye Olde King's Head

## FAST FOOD/TAKE OUT
Apple Pan
Art's Chili Dogs
Carl's Jr.
Chicken Naturel
Hot Licks Cafe
La Salsa
Philippe the Original
Pink's
Russell's
Substation Ltd.
Tommy's
Wiener Factory

## FILIPINO
Bayanihan
Nipa Hut

## FRENCH
Albion's
Alouette
Ambrosia

A Tout Va Bien
Au Chambertin
Au Petit Cafe
Aux Delices
Bagatelle
Belle-Vue
Bernard's
Bicycle Shop Cafe
Bordeaux
Bouchon
Cafe Casino
Cafe Courtney
Cafe Monet
Cafe Parisien
Cafe Pierre
Camille's
Carmine's
Casina Valadier
Cattails
Chalet de France
Chambord
Chef Gregoire
Chez Claude
Chez Helene
Chez Orleans
Chez Sateau
Cordon Bleu
Entourage
The Fine Affair
Fontainebleu Room
François (Los Angeles)
Frenchy Marseilles
Gerard's
Greenhouse
Hot Licks Cafe
Jimmy's
JW's
La Bella Fontana
La Brasserie
La Brochette
La Chaumiere

La Chaumine  
La Creperie Bretonne  
La Cuisine  
La Fayette  
La Fondue Bourguignonne  
La Frite  
La Grange  
La Parisienne  
La Petite Maison  
La Place  
La Polonaise  
La Serre  
L'Auberge  
Le Bistro  
Le Cafe  
Le Cellier  
Le Dome  
Le Monaco  
Lemon Turtle  
Le Papillon  
Le Pavilion  
Le Petit Chateau  
Le Restaurant  
L'Ermitage  
Les Anges  
Le St. Germain  
Le Saint Michel  
Le Saint Tropez  
Le Sanglier  
L'Escoffier  
Les Freres Taix  
Les Pyrenees  
L'Etoile  
L'Express  
L'Orangerie  
Ma Facon  
Maison Alexis  
Maison Gerard  
Ma Maison  
Marengo  
Marianne  

Mon Grenier  
Monique  
Moustache Cafe  
The Nutshell  
Olive Mill Bistro  
Paul's French Cuisine  
Penelope's  
Pioneer Boulangerie  
Prince of Wales  
Rene's  
Rive Gauche  
Robaire's  
Rouard's Polonaise  
St. Tropez  
Sesame and Lilies  
The Tower  
Trumps  
Unicorn Cafe  
Veronique  
Westside Cafe  
Wine Bistro  

## GERMAN
Alpine Village Inn  
Hoppe's Old Heidelberg  
Knoll's Black Forest  
Lowenbrau Keller  
Rheinlander  
Schnitzelbank  
The Weinstube  

## GREEK
Fourno's Oven West  
Papadakis Taverna  
T & J Restaurant  

## HUNGARIAN
Budapest  
Little Vienna  
Monique  
Veronika

## INDIAN

Akbar
Canard de Bombay
Gitanjali
Gypsy's
Moghul
Paru's
Paul Bhalla's
Rangoon Racquet Club
Salomi

## INDONESIAN

J.B.'s Little Bali

## ISRAELI

Tempo

## ITALIAN

Adriano's
Agostino's
Alberto's
Alfredo's
Ameci
Amelia's
Andre's
Anna Maria Ristorante
Anna's
Antonello
Borrelli's
Carmine's
Casina Valadier
Chianti
Chicago Pizza Works
Cozza's
D'Amico's
Dan Tana's
Dante
Dario's
Dino's
Emilio's
Fellini's
Ferrarese Family Deli

Fiore d'Italia
Firenze Kitchens
The Forum
Frederick's
Genio's
Giovanni's
Guilio's
Giuseppe!
Giuseppi's
Harry's Bar
Ignazio's
Itchey Foot
Josephina's
La Dolce Vita
La Famiglia
La Monica's
La Pizza
La Scala
La Strada
La Strega
La Terrazza
Little Joe's
Mamma Fesada's
Mangia
Marco Polo
Mario's
Mario's Italian
Marquis West
Martoni's
Matteo's
Mauro's
Michael's Italian Cuisine
Michelangelo's
Millie Riera's
Monteleone's
Mulberry Street
Nino's
No-No's
Olde Manhattan Spagheti Faire
Old Spaghetti Factory
Old Trieste

Old Venice Noodle Co.
Orlando-Orsini
Peppone
Piero's
Pinocchio's
Pitruzello's
Pontevecchio
Pronto
Rapisardi
Regina's
Rex Ristorante
Ronardo's
Salvatore's
Scarantino's
Silvana's
Stellini's
Stuft Noodle
Talia's
Taormina
Two Guys From Italy
Valentino
Via Fettuccini
Villa Capri
Villa Nova
Virgilio's
Vito's

## JAPANESE
Ahihei
Amagi
Aoba
Asuka
Benihana of Tokyo
Domo
Fujiya
Hamayoshi
Hanabishi
Hiro Sushi
Horikawa
Imperial Gardens
Inagiku

Kabuki
Kin Jo
Kiyo's
Mifune
Mikisan
Miyako
Mizuho
Pear Garden
Sambi of Tokyo
Samurai
Sapporo-Ya
Shogun
Suishin Sukiyaki
Sushi House
Tenmasa
Teriyaki Shimon
Teru Sushi
A Thousand Cranes
Tokyo Kaikan
Yagura Ichiban
Yakitori II
Yamashiro
Yamato

## JEWISH
Benjie's
Canter's
Harry's Deli
Kandel's
Mort's
Nate 'n Al's
Nate's
Ruth's Catering

## KOREAN
Hanil
Hyang Mi
Korea Gardens
Pear Garden

## LEBANESE
Antoine's Sheik

Kabakian's

## MEDITRRANEAN
Belmont Pier
Golden Goose

## MEXICAN
Acapulco y Los Arcos
Antonio's
Aztec Dining Room
Baja Cantina
Carlos 'n Charlie's
Casa Carnitas
Casa Cugat
Casa de Carlos
Casa de Pico
Casa de Sevilla
Don Jose
Don Hernando's
Don Ricardo's
El Abajeno de Guadalajara
El Adobe de Capistrano
El Cholo
El Cid
El Coyote
El Gato
El Paseo
El Torito
Gardens of Taxco
Giuseppi's
Guadalajara Inn
Jailhouse Chili Co.
Jungry Jose
La Cabana
La Costa
La Especial
La Fonda
La Salsa
Las Casuelas Nuevas
Las Casuelas Terraza
Las Lomas
Los Burritos

Mario's Restaurant
Old Town Mexican Cafe
Panchito's
Presidente Restaurant
Puerta del Sol
Red Onion
Reno's
Restaurant La Costa
Sagebrush Cantina
Senor Pico
Su Casa
Sundance Cafe
Tad's
Tampico Tilly's
301 Club
Tiajuana Tilly's
Vera Cruz
Verita's Cantina
Villa Sombrero

## MIDDLE EASTERN
Antoine's Sheik
La Ve Lee
Lemon Turtle

## MOROCCAN
Dar Maghreb
Koutoubia
Marrakesh
Moun of Tunis

## ORGANIC/VEGETARIAN
Chez Naturel
Golden Temple of Conscious
  Cookery
The Good Earth
Inn of the Seventh Ray
Lettuce Patch
Nucleus Nuance
Our Contribution
The Prophet
The Source

Thin's Inn
Vallée Rose

## PERUVIAN
El Chalan

## POLISH
Three Mermaids
Warszawa

## POLYNESIAN
Bali Hai
Beachbum Burt's
Don the Beachcomber
Ports O' Call
Trader Vic's
Velvet Horn
The Warehouse

## RUSSIAN
Mischa's

## SCANDINAVIAN
Ben's Place
Christian's Danish Inn
Danish Inn
Griswold's Smorgasbord
Konditori
Mollerkroen
Scandia
Taste of Scandinavia

## SEAFOOD
Amelia's
Anthony's Harborside
Anthony's Pier 2
Anthony's Star of the Sea
Atlantis
Belmont Pier
Bit O' Scotland
Bobby McGee's
Bouillabaisse
Breakers Seafood Co.
Captain's Anchorage

Captain's Table
Castagnola's Lobster House
Catch of the Sea
The Crab Cooker
The Crab Shell
Delaney's
Diamond Seafood
El Pescador
Famous Enterprise Fish Co.
Gladstone's 4 Fish
Golden Goose
H.M.S. Sandcastle
Holiday House
Hungry Tiger
Jack's at the Beach
Janthina's
JW's
La Costa
Land's End
The Lobster
The Lobster Trap
Maxwell's
Mel's Landing
Millie Riera's
Moby's Dock
Mon Kee
Monterey Jack's
Nantucket Light
Noel's
Ocean Fresh Cafe
Orville and Wilbur's
The Palm
Pelican's Restaurants
Piero's
Pisces
Red Sails Inn
Rex's Fishmarket
The Salmon House
Sand Castle
Saratoga
Seafood Bay

Seafood Broiler
Sea Lion
Sea Quest
Seashell
Sea Thief
Senor Pico
Shanghai Red's
Smith Brother's Fish Shanty
Sorrentino's
Tony's on the Pier
Tony's Sea Landing
Truly Yours
Vera Cruz
The Whale's Tail
Woody's Wharf
World Famous

## SOUL FOOD/CREOLE
Homer and Edy's Bistro
Malik Carter's
Maurice's Snack 'n Chat
Murray's Cafe
Roscoe's House of Chicken
  and Waffles
South Town Soul Food

## SOUTH AMERICAN
Gio's
La Villa

## SPANISH
Cafe del Sol
Casa de Sevilla
La Masia
Madrid
Mission Inn
Toledo

## SWISS
Cafe Swiss
St. Moritz
Swiss Echo

## THAI
D'jit Pochana
Erawan
Green Leaves
Lannathai
Maneeya Thai
Opaso 2
Siamese Princess
Tepparod Thai

## VIETNAMESE
Le Huyen
Saigon Flavor
Vietnam Pearl

## YUGOSLAVIAN
Cigo's
Kalmegdan
Nikola's
The Paragon Inn
Simon's
Yugoslavian Village

# BANQUET FACILITIES

Adam's
Agostino's
Alberto's
Alpine Village Inn
Amagi
Anthony's Harborside
Antonello
Atlantis
Bali Hai
Bayanihan
Beachbum Burt's
Belle-Vue
Ben Brown's
Bullock's Wilshire Tea Room
Butcher's Arms
Cafe Courtney
Cafe Parisien
Caldron
Captain's Anchorage
Casa de Carlos
Castagnola's Lobster House
Cattleman's Wharf
Chadney's
Chang's
Chez Cary
China Trader
Chu Dynasty
Cock 'n Bull
The Coterie
The Cove
Cozza's
Crossroads
Dal Rae
D'Amico's
Danish Inn
The Derby
Dino's
Donkin's Inn

Don Ricardo's
The Dragon Pearl
Edward's Mansion
El Abajeno de Guadalajara
El Adobe de Capistrano
El Cholo
El Cid
El Coyote Cafe
El Encanto
El Gato Gardenside
El Paseo
Emilio's
Entourage
Ferrarese Family Deli
The Fine Affair
Fiore D'Italia
Five Crowns
Fountainebleau Room
Fung Lum
The Garden Room
Gatsby's
General Lee's
Genio's
Gin Ling
Gio's
Golden Temple
Grand Star
Griswold's Indian Hill
Griswold's Smorgasbord
Harry's Deli
Hemingway's
Holiday House
Hoppe's Old Heidelberg
Hunan
Ichabod Crane's
Imperial House
Inagiku
Inn of the Seventh Ray

Jack's at the Beach
Jacques
Jade West
Janthina's
Jungry Jose
Kabuki
Kandel's
La Brasserie
La Brochette
La Chaumine
La Cuisine of Newport
La Fayette
La Grange Aux Crepes
Lakeside
La Marina
La Place
Las Casuelas Terraza
Las Lomas
Le Cellier
Le Hot Club
Le Monaco
Le Petit Chateau
Les Freres Taix
L'Express
The Lobster Trap
Longfellow's
Lubach's
Madame Wu's
Mandarin
Mandarin Gourmet
Marcus Steak House
Restaurant Marengo
Mario's Italian
Marquis West
Marrakesh
Maxwell's
Medallion
Medium Rare
Melvyn's
Michelangelo's
Mikisan

Mischa's
Mission Inn
Mr. Stox
Monty's
Mouling
New Moon
Nipa Hut
No-No's Italian
Old Spaghetti Factory
Old Venice Noodle Company
Old World
Orient Express
Panchito's
Paul Bhalla's
Penguin Palace
Perino's
Pike's Verdugo Oaks
Police Academy
Polo Lounge
Ports O' Call
Pronto
Rapisardi
Red Baron Steakhouse
Reuben E. Lee
Revere House
Rive Gauche
Robaire's French Cuisine
Robert's
Ronardo's
Roy's
Ruby Begonia's
Salvatore's
Sambi of Tokyo
Sand Castle
San Dimas Mansion
Seafood Broiler
Senor Pico
Shanghai Restaurant
Shogun
Smoke House
Sportsmen's Lodge

Stern's Barbecue
Su Casa
Tail O' the Cock
Talk of the Town (Pasadena)
Tampico Tilly's
Tepparod Thai West
A Thousand Cranes
Three Mermaids
Tick Tock Hollywood
T & J Restaurant
The Tower
The Towers
Tracton's

Valentino's
Velvet Horn
Verita's Cantina
Vietnam Pearl
Villa Fontana
Villa Nova
Vintage Press
The Windsor
Whomphopper's Wagon Works
Yakitori II
Yamashiro
Yamato

# BRUNCH

Adriano's
Agostino's Ristorante
Alfredo's
Alice's Restaurant
Ancient Mariner
Anthony's Harborside
Aztec Dining Room
Baja Cantina
Bali Hai
Bayanihan
Beachbum Burt's
Bel-Air Hotel
Ben Brown's
Bessie Wall's
Big Yellow House
Blackbeard's Galley and Grog
Bob Burns
Bogart's
Brown Derby
Cafe California
Cafe Courtney
Cafe Del Sol
Cafe Four Oaks
Cafe Pierre
Calabasas Inn

Caldron
Cannery Restaurant
Caribbean Terrace
Catch of the Sea
Cattleman's Wharf
Charley Brown's
Charthouse (some locations)
Chef Gregoire
Chez Naturel
Chez Orleans
Chez Sateau
China Trader
The Cliff House
Cock 'N Bull
Crossroads
Daisy's Market
D'Amico's
Delaney's
The Derby
Disneyland Hotel: Chef's Kitchen
Don Jose
Donkin's Inn
Don the Beachcomber
Dunbar's at the Beach

Edward's Mansion
El Adobe de Capistrano
El Cholo
El Gato Gardenside
El Padrino
Elmer's Place
El Torito
En Brochette
Encina
Fellini's
Fiasco
Fine Affair
Five Crowns
Frederick's
The Gatekeeper
Gingerman
Good Earth
Great Scot
Hamburguesa
Hampton's (Hollywood)
Harlequin Dinner Playhouse
Hemingway's
Holiday House
Houlihan's Old Place
Ichabod Crane's
Inn of the Seventh Ray
Jake's Del Mar
Janthina's
Jerry's Famous Deli
Jungry Jose
La Creperie Bretonne
La Cuisine of Dana Point
La Grange Aux Crepes
La Marina
La Masia
Land's End
Las Casuelas Nuevas
Las Lomas
La Villa
Le Monaco
The Lobster Trap
Marine Room

Maxwell's
Mediterranean Room
Melvyn's
Mission Inn
Mister H
Monterey Jack's
Mouling
Ocean Fresh Cafe
Pacific Dining Car
The Patio
Pelican Restaurants
Pike's Verdugo Oaks
Pitruzello's
Polo Lounge
Ports O' Call
Princess Louise Restaurant
Pronto
The Quiet Woman
Red Baron Steakhouse
Red Onion
Revere House
Rheinlander German Restaurant
Rive Gauche
Ruby Begonia's
Salmon House
Sambi of Tokyo
San Clemente Inn
Sand Castle
San Dimas Mansion
Scandia
Simply Blues
Sportsmen's Lodge
Stottlemyer's
Stratton's
The Summer House
Sundance Cafe
Tail O' The Cock
Tampico Tilly's
TGI Fridays
A Thousand Cranes
Three Dolphin Inn

The Towers
Truly Yours
Twin Dragon
The Warehouse
West End Garden

The Whale's Tail
The White Oak
Woody's Wharf
World Famous
Yamashiro

# CHILDREN S WELCOME

Acapulco y los Arcos
Agostino's
Alpine Village Inn
Amber's
Ameci
Amelia's
Ancient Mariner
Andre's Town & Country
Anna's
Anthony's Harborside
Apple Pan
Arnold's Farmhouse
Art's Chili Dogs
Atlantis
Au Petit Cafe
Aztec
Bagel Nosh
Beadle's
Belisle's
Benjie's
Bessie Wall's
Big Yellow House
Bob Burns
Bobby McGee's
Borrelli's
Brown Derby
Budapest Hungarian
    Restaurant
Bullock's Wilshire Tea Room
Buttery
Cafe del Sol
Carl's Jr. Hamburgers
Casa Cugat
Casa de Carlos

Castagnola's Lobster House
Catch of the Sea
Chalet de France
Chang's
Charlie Brown's
Cigo's
Clifton's Cafeteria
Cozza's
Crossroads
Dal Rae
Daisy's Market
D'Amico's
The Derby
Dino's
Disneyland Hotel
Don Ricardo's
Edward's Mansion
El Abajeno de Guadalajara
El Adobe de Capistrano
El Cid
El Coyote Cafe
El Encanto
El Gato Gardenside
El Paseo
Famous Enterprise Fish Co.
Feastboard
Ferrarese Family Deli
Frederick's
Gardens of Taxco
Genio's
Gin Ling
Giovanni's
Giuseppi's
Golden Goose

Golden Pagoda
Great American Food and Beverage Co.
Griswold's Smorgasbord
Guadalajara Inn
Hamburger Henry's
Hoppe's Old Heidelberg
Hunan
Hungry Tiger
International House of Pancakes
Itchey Foot
Jacques Restaurant
Jailhouse Chili Company
J.B.'s Little Bali
Jolly Roger
Josephina's
Jungry Jose
Kabuki
Kalemegdan
Kings
Knott's Berry Farm
La Cave
La Fondue Bourguignonne
Lakeside
La Place
Las Casuelas Terraza
Las Lomas
Lawry's Prime Rib
Les Freres Taix
Little Joe's
Little Vienna
Lloyd's
Los Burritos
Love's Wood Pit BBQ
Magic Pan
Mamma Fesada's
Mario's Restaurant
Maxwell's
Medium Rare
Michael's Italian Cuisine
Mission Inn
Mr. Stox

Miyako
Mizuho
Moby's Dock
Mollerkroen
Moun of Tunis
Nieuport 17
Nikola's
No-No's Italian
Old Spaghetti Factory
Old Venice Noodle Company
Old World
Our Contribution
Panchito's
Pike's Verdugo Oaks
Pink's
Pioneer Boulangerie
Pitruzello's
Ponderosa
Presidente Restaurant
Princess Louise
Puerta del Sol
Red Onion
Reno's
Reuben E. Lee
Revere House
Robert's
Ronardo's
Sand Castle
San Dimas Mansion
Schnitzelbank
Scarantino's
Seafood Broiler
Sea Lion
Sea Thief
Sgt. Pepper's
Shanghai Restaurant
Sizzler Family Steakhouse
Smoke House
South Town Soul Food
Sportsmen's Lodge
Stern's Barbecue
Stuft Noodle
Su Casa

Taste of Scandinavia
Taylor's Prime Steak House
Thin's Inn
Three Mermaids
Tick Tock Hollywood
T & J Restaurant
Tony's Sea Landing
The Towers
Trappers Inn
Two Guys From Italy

Verita's Cantina
Victoria Station
Villa Nova
Vintage Press
The Weinstube
The Whale's Tail
Wiener Factory
Whomphopper's Wagon Works
Yagura Ichiban
Yakitori II

# DANCING

Anthony's Harborside
Bobby McGee's
Cattleman's Wharf
Chez Orleans
The Derby
Don Hernando's Hideaway
The Dragon Pearl
Garden Room
Ichabod Crane's
Iron Gate
Jade West
Lakeside
Le Hot Club
L'Escoffier
Little J's
Marine Room
Medallion Restaurant
Melvyn's

Mischa's
Mr. Stox
Pal Joey's
Paragon Inn
Plaza Four
Red Baron Steakhouse
Reno's
Ricabob
Sambi of Tokyo
San Clemente Inn
Sand Castle
Shanghai Restaurant
Sportsmen's Lodge
Talk of the Town (Pasadena)
Tampico Tilly's
Tia Juana Tilly's
T & J Restaurant
Tracton's Restaurant
Trappers Inn

# DINING ADVENTURES

Alpine Village Inn
Ajeti's
Bel-Air Hotel
Bessie Wall's
Bobby McGee's
Brotherton's Farmhouse

Brown Derby (Hollywood)
Bullock's Wilshire Tea Room
El Paseo Inn
Farmer's Market
Fung Lum
Griswold's Smorgasbord

The Hobbit
Imperial Dynasty
La Fonda
La Marina
La Masia
Mister A's
Mulberry Street
Papadakis Tavern

Philippe the Original
Police Academy
Polo Lounge
Reuben E. Lee
301 Club
Toledo
Vickman's

# ENTERTAINMENT

Adagio
Adam's
Agostino's Ristorante
The Albatross
Alfredo's
Alpine Village Inn
Ambrosia
Ancient Mariner
Anthony's Harborside
Atlantis
At Marty's
Bali Hai
Bayanihan
Beachbum Burt's
Beaudry's
Bel-Air Hotel
Belisle's Restaurant
Bergin's West
Bernard's
Bessie Wall's
Bob Burns
Bogart's
Bouillabaisse
Brown Derby (Hollywood)
Bullock's Wilshire Tea Room
Butcher's Arms
The Buttery
Cafe California
Cafe Four Oaks
Cafe Le Monde
Cafe Swiss
Camille's

Cannery Restaurant
Caribbean Terrace
Casablanca
Casa Cugat
Casey's Bar
Cattleman's Wharf
Chadney's
Chang's
Chez Cary
Chez Orleans
China Trader
Chuck's Steak House
    (Westwood)
Churchill's Restaurant
Cigo's
Courtney's
The Cove
Cozza's
Dal Rae
D'Amico's
The Derby
Di Amico's
Dino's
Disneyland Hotel: Coffee
    House
Don Jose
Donkin's Inn
Don the Beachcomber (Marina)
Don Hernando's Hideaway
The Dragon Pearl
Dresden Room

El Abajeno de Guadalajara
El Adobe de Capistrano
El Cid
El Encanto
El Gato Gardenside
El Padrino
El Paseo Inn
Elmer's Place
En Brochette
Far East Terrace
Five Crowns
Fontainebleau Room
Fourno's Oven West
Francois (Arco Plaza)
Francois (Huntington Beach)
Garden Room
Gardens of Taxco
Gatsby's
General Lee's
Gingerman
Gio's
Golden Pagoda
Golden Temple of Conscious
  Cookery
Grand Ave. Bar
Grand Star
Great American Food and
  Beverage Company
Hampton's (Hollywood)
Harlequin Dinner Playhouse
Heart of Europe
Homer and Edy's Bistro
Hoppe's Old Heidelberg
Ichabod Crane's
Imperial Gardens
Imperial House
Iron Gate
Itchey Foot
Jade West
Janthina's
Jerry's Famous Deli
Jungry Jose
JW's

La Bella Fontana
La Fonda
The Lakeside
La Masia
Las Casuelas Nuevas
Las Casuelas Terraza
Las Lomas
La Strada
La Villa
Lawry's California Center
Lawry's Westside Broiler
Le Cafe
Le Hot Club
Les Anges
The Lobster Trap
Maldonado's
Marco Polo Ristorante
Mario's
Marquis West
Mauro's
Maxwell's
Mediterranean Room
Melvyn's
Michaelangelo's
Mikisan
Mischa's
Mister A's
Mizuho
Moby's Dock
Mollerkroen
Monteleone's
Monterey Jack's
Moun of Tunis
Mulberry Street
Nieuport 17
Olive Mill Bistro
One Thousand East
Orville and Wilbur's
Papa Choux
Paragon Inn
Paul Bhalla's Cuisine of India
Pavillion
Penelope's

Perino's
Pike's Verdugo Oaks
Pitruzello's
Pizza Time Theatre
Playboy Club
Plaza Four
Polo Lounge
Presidente Restaurant
Princess Louise
The Prophet
Puerta Del Sol
The Quiet Woman
The Ranch House
Rapisardi
Red Baron Steakhouse
Reno's
Reuben E. Lee
Reuben's
Rex's Fishmarket
Rex Ristorante
Rheinlander German
  Restaurant
Ricabob
R.J.'s the Rib Joint
Ruby Begonia's
The Rusty Pelican
Sagebrush Cantina
Sambi of Tokyo
San Clemente Inn
Sand Castle
San Dimas Mansion
Sarno's

Shanghai Red's The
  Back Room
Shanghai Restaurant
Simply Blues
Smoke House Restaurant
Soorentino's
Sportsmen's Lodge
Stox II
Su Casa
Tail o' the Cock
Talk of the Town (Pasadena)
Tampico Tilly's
301 Club
T & J Restaurant
Tony's on the Pier
Tony Roma's
Tracton's Restaurant
Trappers Inn
Velvet Horn
Verita's Cantina
Villa Fontana
Villa Nova
Virgilio's
The Warehouse
The Whale's Tail
The White House
Wind and Sea
The Wine Cellar
Whomphopper's Wagon Works
Woody's Wharf
Yagura Ichiban
Yugoslavian Village

# INEXPENSIVE

Acapulco y Los Arcos
Ahihei
Amber's
Anna Maria Ristorante
The Apple Pan
Arnold's Farmhouse
Art's Chili Dogs

Aztec Dining Room
Bagel Nosh
Beadle's Cafeteria
Ben's Place
Big Yellow House
Bob Burns
Brotherton's Farmhouse

Butcher's Arms
Cafe Casino
Cafe Courtney
Carl's
Carl's Jr. Hamburgers
Casa de Carlos
Casa de Pico
Cassell's Hamburgers
Chicken Naturel
Chinese Friends
Chung King Restaurant
City Cafe
Cliff House
Clifton's Cafeteria
Courtney's Bistro
Crab Cooker
Don Jose
Don Ricardo's
Dragon Pearl
Du Par's
The Eggception
El Abajeno de Guadalajara
El Coyote Spanish Cafe
El Gato Gardenside
El Pescador
El Torito
Feastboard
Ferrarese Family Deli
Gardens of Taxco
The Gatekeeper
Genio's
Giuseppi's
Greenblatt's
Griswold's Smorgasbord
Guadalajara Inn
Hamburguesa
Hampton's
Hanabishi
Harry's Open Pit BBQ
Hob Nob Hill
Hot Licks Cafe
International House of Pancakes

Jailhouse Chili Company
Jerry's Famous Deli
Kings
Kiyo's
La Cabana
La Salsa
Las Casuelas Nuevas
The Lettuce Patch
Lillian's
Little J's
Little Joe's
Little Kitchen
Little Shanghai
Longfellow's
Los Burritos
Louise's Pantry
Lowenbrau Keller
Lucky Restaurant
Magic Pan
Malik Carter's
Mandarin Gourmet
Mario's Restaurant
Marv's Deli
Michael's Italian Cuisine
Mon Kee
Mort's Deli
Mouling
Mulberry Street
Murray's Cafe
Nikola's
Nipa Hut
Olde Manhattan Spaghetti Faire
Old Spaghetti Factory
Old Venice Noodle Company
Original Pantry
Our Contribution
Pat and Lorraine's Coffee Shop
Penguin Palace
Phillippe the Original
Pink's Famous Chili Dogs
Pioneer Boulangerie
Police Academy

Presidente Restaurant
The Prophet
Puerta Del Sol
Robbie's Rib Cage
Robb's Ice Cream Co.
Ronardo's
Russell's
Salvatore's
Sapporo-Ya
Scarantino's
Seafood Bay
Seafood Broiler
Sea Lion
Shep's
Simon's
Slender Spoon
South Town Soul Food
Stottlemyer's
Stuft Noodle
Substation Ltd.

Su Casa
Sundance Cafe
Taste of Scandinavia
Tea and Sympathy
Teriyaki Shimon
Thin's Inn
301 Club
Tia Juana Tilly's
Tommy's Hamburgers
Tony Roma's
Truly Yours
Vietnam Pearl
Vickman's
The Whale's Tail
Wiener Factory
Wine Bistro
Yakitori II
Ye Olde King's Head
Yugoslavian Village

# LATE DINING

Ahihei
Alberto's
The Apple Pan
The Arches
At Marty's
Belisle's
Bergin's West
Bicycle Shop Cafe
Cafe Monet
Canter's Delicatessen
Carlos 'n Charlie's
Carl's
Casa Carnitas
Charmer's Market
Chasen's
China Trader
Cozza's
Cyrano
Dal Rae

Dan Tana's
Diamond Sea Food
Dino's
Du Par's
El Abajeno de Guadelajara
El Cid
El Gato Gardenside
El Padrino
El Torito
Emilio's Ristorante
Fellini's
Gingerman
Gio's
Gladstone's 4 Fish
Grand Avenue Bar
Greenblatt's
Hamayoshi
Hamburger Henry's
Hanil

Harry's Open Pit (Hollywood)
Hot Licks Cafe
Junior's
La Fonda
Lakeside
La Pizza
La Salsa
Le Dome
Le Hot Club
L'Express
Lloyd's
Magic Pan
Martoni
Monteleone's
Moustache Cafe
Old World
Original Pantry
Orville and Wilbur's
Pacific Dining Car
Pink's Famous Chili Dogs
Polo Lounge

Rangoon Racquet Club
Rapisardi
Reno's
Roscoe's House
Roy's
Sarno's Caffe Dell' Opera
Scandia
Shep's
Simply Blues
The Source
South Town Soul Food
TGI Fridays
Tony Roma's
Trader Vic's
Trumps
Two Guys From Italy
Villa Capri
Villa Nova
Whomphopper's Wagon Works
Ye Olde King's Head

# PATIO

Adriano's
Agostino's
Andre's Town & Country
Anna Maria
Anthony's Pier 2
Art's Chili Dogs
Baja Cantina
Bali Hai
Bayanihan
Beachbum Burt's
Bel-Air Hotel
Ben Brown's
Bistro Garden
Boccaccio's
Bouchon
Bruno's Chartreuse
Cafe Casino
Cafe del Sol

Cafe Four Oaks
Cafe Pierre
Cafe Rodeo
Cafe Swiss
Cannery Restaurant
Caribbean Terrace
Casa Cugat
Casina Valadier
Cassell's
Charmer's Market
Chez Helene
Chez Loma
Chez Naturel
Cliff House Restaurant
Cyrano
Disneyland Hotel
Donkin's Inn
Don Ricardo's (Sun Valley)

Dunbar's at the Beach
El Cholo
El Cid
El Paseo Inn
El Pescador
En Brochette
Encina
Farmer's Market
Fellini's
Fiasco
Fine Affair
Fiore d'Italia
Five Crowns
Fourno's Oven West
Gio's
Gladstone's 4 Fish
Golden Temple of Conscious
   Cookery
Green Leaves
Griswold's Indian Hill
Griswold's Smorgasbord
Hamburger Henry's
Hampton's
Hemingway's
Holiday House
Homer and Edy's Bistro
Inn of the Seventh Ray
Jake's Del Mar
Jerry's Famous Deli
La Brasserie
La Grange Aux Crepes
   (Venice)
La Marina
Land's End
La Place
La Scala Malibu
Las Casuelas Nuevas
Las Casuelas Terraza
La Terrazza Italian
La Toque
L'Auberge
La Ve Lee

Lawry's California Center
Le Bistro
Le Cafe
The Lemon Turtle
L'Ermitage
Le St. Germain
Le St. Michel
L'Express
Ma Maison
Mangia
Mario's Italian
Maxwell's
Mediterranean Room
Melvyn's
Michael's
Mission Inn
Moonshadows
Mouling
Nepenthe
Nucleus Nuance
Oak Tree
Ocean Fresh Cafe
Old World
Orlando-Orsini Ristorante
Our Contribution
Panchito's
The Paragon Inn
Paru's
Patio Restaurant
Pelican Restaurants
Piero's Seafood House
Pink's
Pioneer Boulangerie
Pitruzello's
Polo Lounge
Ports O'Call
Presidente
Quet Woman
Ranch House
The Raymond
Rheinlander German
   Restaurant

Rive Gauche
Rive Gauche Cafe
Robaire's French Cuisine
Robbie's Rib Cage (Altadena)
Robert's
Ronardo's
Sagebrush Cantina
St. Moritz
St. Tropez
Sarno's
Sausalito South
The Source
Stratton's
Substation Ltd.

Sundance Cafe
Sushi House
A Thousand Cranes
Top O' the Cove
Truly Yours
Trumps
Verita's Cantina
Veronika
Virgilio's
The Warehouse
Wind and Sea
Yagura Ichiban
Yugoslavian Village

# THREE STARS

Ambrosia
Anthony's Star of the Sea Room
Art's
Bernard's
Cassell's Hamburgers
The Cellar
Chez Cary
Chianti
Courtney's
Francois (Los Angeles)
Imperial Dynasty
Knott's Berry Farm
La Cuisine of Dana Point
La Scala

L'Escoffier
L'Orangerie
Marrakesh
Michael's
Pacific Dining Car
Pisces
Rex Ristorante
Studio Grill
Talk of the Town (Santa Barbara)
Trader Vic's
Trumps

# VIEW

Atlantis
Baja Cantina (Malibu)
Beachbum Burt's
Beaudry's
Ben Brown's
Cafe Courtney
Calabasas Inn
Cannery Restaurant
Caribbean Terrace
Courtney's
Crab Shell (Marina)
Delaney's
Disneyland Hotel
Donkin's Inn
Dunbar's
El Encanto
Fiasco
Fung Lum
Garden Room
Gladstone's 4 Fish
Holiday House
Jake's Del Mar
La Marina
Land's End
Las Casuelas Nuevas
Las Casuelas Terraza

Le Monaco
Marine Room
Maxwell's
Millie Riera's Seafood
Moby's Dock
Moonshadows
Nepenthe
Olde Manhattan Spaghetti Faire
Pavilion
Ports O' Call
Red Baron Steak House
Reuben E. Lee
Robert's
Salmon House
Sand Castle
Shanghai Red's
Simply Blues
Top O' The Cove
The Tower
The Towers
Unicorn Cafe
Villa Nova Restaurant
The Warehouse
The Whale's Tail
The White Oak
Whomphopper's Wagon Works
Yamashiro Room